OLD LANDS

Old Lands takes readers on an epic journey through the legion spaces and times of the Eastern Peloponnese, trailing in the footsteps of a Roman *periegete*, an Ottoman traveler, antiquarians, and anonymous agrarians.

Following waters in search of rest through the lens of Lucretian poetics, Christopher Witmore reconstitutes an untimely mode of ambulatory writing, chorography, mindful of the challenges we all face in these precarious times. Turning on pressing concerns that arise out of object-oriented encounters, *Old Lands* ponders the disappearance of an agrarian world rooted in the Neolithic, the transition to urban styles of living, and changes in communication, movement, and metabolism, while opening fresh perspectives on long-term inhabitation, changing mobilities, and appropriation through pollution. Carefully composed with those objects encountered along its varied paths, this book offers an original and wonderous account of a region in twenty-seven segments, and fulfills a longstanding ambition within archaeology to generate a polychronic narrative that stands as a complement and alternative to diachronic history.

Old Lands will be of interest to historians, archaeologists, anthropologists, and scholars of the Eastern Peloponnese. Those interested in the long-term changes in society, technology, and culture in this region will find this book captivating.

Christopher Witmore is professor of archaeology and classics at Texas Tech University. He is co-author of *Archaeology: The Discipline of Things* (2012, with B. Olsen, M. Shanks, and T. Webmoor). Routledge published his co-edited *Archaeology in the Making* in 2013 (paperback 2017, with W. Rathje and M. Shanks). He is also co-editor of the Routledge series *Archaeological Orientations* (with G. Lucas).

OLD LANDS

A Chorography of the Eastern Peloponnese

Christopher Witmore

Routledge
Taylor & Francis Group
LONDON AND NEW YORK

First published 2020
by Routledge
2 Park Square, Milton Park, Abingdon, Oxon OX14 4RN

and by Routledge
52 Vanderbilt Avenue, New York, NY 10017

Routledge is an imprint of the Taylor & Francis Group, an informa business

British Library Cataloguing-in-Publication Data
A catalogue record for this book is available from the British Library

Library of Congress Cataloging-in-Publication Data
A catalog record has been requested for this book

ISBN: 978-0-8153-6343-9 (hbk)
ISBN: 978-0-8153-6344-6 (pbk)
ISBN: 978-1-351-10943-7 (ebk)

Typeset in Perpetua
by Swales & Willis, Exeter, Devon, UK

For Liz, Eli, and Liam

CONTENTS

ACKNOWLEDGEMENTS

In the fifteen-year course of researching and writing this book I have accumulated a lifetime of debts. My gratitude has not abated. I am deeply beholden to those whom kindly set aside precious time to accompany me on various paths, many now less taken. To John Cherry, Elissa Faro, Alex Knodell, Thomas Leppard, and Bradley Sekedat, archaeologists, friends, and knowledgeable companions, whom I joined in the course of regional work between Nemea and Nafplion. To Lena Zgouleta and Zoe Zgouleta, my friends and guides to many sites and places throughout the Peloponnese. To Georgia Ivou, for her unabated generosity with a wealth of archaeological detail related to Asine, Epidaurus, and everything in between. To Yorgos Agathos, Sigi Ebeling Agathos, Iosif Ganossis, and the late Yiannis Gogonas, for their friendship and kindness in Nafplion, Ermioni, and Tolo. To Evangelia Pappi and other personnel from the Ephorate of Antiquities of the Argolis, for their hospitality and care. To Mpampis Antoniadis, who openly contributed a great deal of information on Nafplion, and the Argive plain, more generally.

I am indebted to the many students who have contributed to this project over the years. To Krista Brown, Ryan Hall, Will Hannon, Jenny Lewis, Billy Pierce, Ann Sunbury, Jordin Ward, and Nathan Wolcott, the eight who ventured into the Bedheni Valley in 2010, my gratitude runs deep. I thank Brandon Baker, Edgar Garcia, Evan Levine, Caleb Lightfoot, Kristine Mallinson, Justin Miller, and Jackson Vaughn for enduring various paths with excitement and enthusiasm. Lively and inspirational engagements with students—Brandon Baker, Kelsey Brunson, Edgar Garcia, Ryan Glidewell, Evan Levine, Ron Orr, Karen Taylor, and Nathan Wolcott—in a graduate seminar in fall of 2013 provided occasion to bring further shape to the study. I also want to thank Danielle Bercier, Caleb Lightfoot, and Justin Miller for their comments and feedback on various segments of this chorography; Catherine Zagar for the energy and dedication she brought to working through many hours of video from along numerous paths; Alex Claman for all his hard work with footnotes, references, and indexing; and the undergraduate researchers in the Program in Inquiry and

Investigation at Texas Tech University for sharing their thoughts around the concerns raised in some of the segments.

We are shaped by our conversations. I have learned from those whom I hold in a place of profound admiration: Ben Alberti, Sue Alcock, Doug Bailey, Curtis Bauer, Levi Bryant, Sheila Bonde, Peter Carne, Kurt Caswell, John Cherry, Bruce Clarke, Ewa Domanska, Matt Edgeworth, Sylvan Fachard, Stein Farstad-voll, Hamish Forbes, Jen Gates-Foster, Alfredo González-Ruibal, Scott Gremillion, Donald Haggis, Graham Harman, Callum Hetherington, Richard Hingley, Ian Hodder, Idoia Elola, Georgia Ivou, Michael Jameson, Corby Kelly, Alex Knodell, David Larmour, Don Lavigne, Tom Leppard, Jeff Love, Gavin Lucas, Robert Macfarlane, Richard Martin, Ian Morris, Laurent Olivier, Bjørnar Olsen, Þóra Pétursdóttir, Josh Piburn, Bill Rathje, Joe Rife, Darrell Rohl, Sydnor Roy, Haun Saussy, Michel Serres, Michael Shanks, Chris Taylor, Christina Unwin, Timothy Webmoor, Lena Zgouleta, and Zoe Zgouleta.

Support has come from a number of institutions over the years, beginning with the Department of Classics and Archaeology Center at Stanford University, the Andrew W. Mellon Foundation, and the Joukowsky Institute for Archaeology and the Ancient World at Brown University. This project was sustained by grants from the Competitive Arts, Humanities, and Social Sciences fund; the Scholarship Catalyst Program; the College of Arts and Sciences; the Humanities Center; the office of the Vice President for Research; and the Department of Classical & Modern Languages & Literatures at Texas Tech University. Numerous segments were written at the National Humanities Center (NHC), where I held the Donnelly Family Fellowship in 2014–15. Nurtured within the center's superb intellectual environment, this book took on new direction and shape. I want to thank Brooke Andrade and Sarah Harris for working miracles in library services, Karen Carroll for copyediting several segments of the book, and Marie Brubaker and Don Solomon for their unwavering scholarly support. I am grateful to a number of fellows from the NHC for their encouragement and intellectual companionship—Mary Elizabeth Berry, Corrine Gartner, Ann Gold, Mark Hansen, Cecily Hilsdale, Noah Heringman, Colin Jones, Jeff Love, Josephine McDonagh, Jonathan Sachs, Lizzie Schechter, Anna Sun, Gordon Teskey, and Bonna Wescoat. A fellowship at the Center for Advanced Studies (CAS) in Oslo opened more space and time for me to write in conjunction with the *After Discourse* project headed by Bjørnar Olsen. The exceptional group of scholars at CAS, Bjørnar Olsen, Hein Bjerck, Doug Bailey, Mats Burström, Alfredo González-Ruibal, Timothy LeCain, Saphinaz-Amal Naguib, and Þóra Pétursdóttir, proved to be not only supportive, but also inspirational.

I recognize the privilege that comes with gaining access to unpublished archives, beginning with those of the Argolid Exploration Project thanks to the late Michael Jameson. I thank John Cherry and Chris Cloke for opening the archives of the Nemea Valley Archaeological Project; I am grateful to the late Pierre MacKay for sharing translations of Evilya Çelebi's *Seyahatname* for both the Argolid and the Corinthia; to Malcolm Wagstaff for details concerning Leake and the Second Ottoman Period more generally. The notebooks of William Martin Leake are held by the Faculty of Classics, University of Cambridge, in their branch of Cambridge University Library. I am indebted to the American School of Classical Studies in Athens in facilitating various permissions over the years. To Hamish Forbes for his generosity with the wealth of detail that can only come with a lifetime of working with communities on the Methana Peninsula. To Heleni Palaiologou for information concerning her work in the area of Mycenae.

Several friends and colleagues took time to provide comments on earlier drafts of the segments—Doug Bailey, Mary Elizabeth Berry, John Cherry, Hamish Forbes, Georgia Ivou, Colin Jones, Evan Levine, Jeff Love, Justin Miller, Laurent Olivier, Jonathan Sachs, Guy Sanders, Lizzie Schechter, Michael Shanks, Anna Sun, Gordon Teskey, Bonna Wescoat, Lena Zgouleta, Zoe Zgouleta, and Pamela Zinn. I am particularly indebted to Alfredo González-Ruibal, David Larmour, Don Lavigne, and Bjørnar Olsen, who provided excellent advice on most segments. I thank Peter N. Miller for the kind invitation to present on chorography, and for a series of lively discussions, at the Bard Graduate Center. Caleb Lightfoot has proved to be an extraordinarily creative and energetic collaborator; he has put his mark on the design of this book and the associated maps—I owe him a special thanks. Working with Matthew Gibbons and Katie Wakelin of Routledge has been tremendously rewarding. I also wish to express my gratitude to Colin Morgan for managing the last stages of production and Andrew Melvin for copy-editing the final manuscript.

Finally, it may seem a strange norm to leave one's most heartfelt gratitude to the end, but not for those who undertake the journey. Day in and day out, the co-bearers of the challenges and beneficiaries of the privileges associated with this book have been my family: Eli, Liam, and, especially, Liz. When other reasons languished, you three never did.

AUTHOR'S NOTE

Topics are listed at the beginning of each segment in order to give the reader a sense of what lies ahead. Otherwise, you, dear reader, are asked to join in the journey.

Place names vary throughout the book and this variance is an artifact of fidelity. Spellings such as Anapli, Nauplia, and Nafplion are used in different segments true to historical specificity. This variety holds for units of measurement, whether in feet or meters, timed stops or stadia. This book seeks to maintain diversity as part of the story of these old lands. It is also a matter of conformity to both the mode of engagement and the identities of those in whose paths we follow. These differences of nomenclature and metrology are critical to understanding the ichnography of contemporary standards, which are always an achievement. While it is no ancillary concern to map out the diversity which lies behind the accomplishment that is consistency, it is anachronistic to disavow it. Some segments are historical; some are taken from notebooks, video diaries, and photography, and worked out through further research. This is not always made explicit in the writing as, as a matter of purpose, it depends on the aims and objectives of the segment. Lastly, a word should be said with regard to maps. These come at the end. Designed by Caleb Lightfoot, flat projections are properly situated as achievements, among others, rather than starting points.

Portions of the following segments have appeared in altered form elsewhere. Segment 11 formed part of "The End of the 'Neolithic'? At the Emergence of the Anthropocene," in S. Pilaar Birch (ed.), 2018, *Multispecies Archaeology*, Abingdon: Routledge, 26–46. Fragments of Segment 12 were incorporated into "Complexities and Emergence: The Case of Argos," in A.R. Knodell and T.P. Leppard (eds.), 2017, *Regional Approaches to Society and Complexity Studies in Honor of John F. Cherry*, London: Equinox, 268–87. Some material from Segment 14 is found in "Echoes Across the Past: Chorography and Topography in Antiquarian Engagements with Place" (with M. Shanks), 2010, *Performance Research* 15(4), 97–106.

PREFACE

In those ages before Greece became explicit as an optimal picture of lands seen from above, not all spaces were accorded equal value. Some things, some places, were more potent than others. Some groves were more favored by the gods; some ravines were more haunted by ghosts, some springs had their stories not to linger after dark, their magical spells that befell the wayward, or their nymphs and satyrs to lead one astray in tangled thickets. For so many of the ancients, the world emanated out from the common hearth under a home-centered sky. The Roman *periegete* who directed his readers around Greece in the second century CE did not describe a measured space spreading out in every direction. Rather, we read of walled enclosures offering themselves as protective containers. We read of agoras that lend themselves to the territorial form, where roads, named for the places they connected, issued, and converged. Radiating outwardly from the shared ground of the center the polis acquired its form as a series of encompassing spheres.

Apart from those repeatedly articulated histories where tattered fragments suggestive of the Greek past are cobbled together into the discrete contours of linear succession, not all times are externalized into a passage temporality or reducible to a homogeneous continuum. Some objects, though held to be separate by measured spans of history, are in reality co-extensive. Some surfaces, some walls, some foundations, folded into the polychronic ensemble of land, are suggestive of a time more weather-like than linear. Even though the hallowed halls of Mycenae fell to destruction after 1200 BCE, Bronze Age walls endured as part of the composition of Hellenistic communities. Even though Roman road pavements had been buried for over a millennium, the form of the *cardo maximus* continued to orient buildings, property boundaries, and streets in the late seventeenth century. A different species of contact occurs between persisting quanta of Jurassic limestone slabs laid upon Neolithic surfaces and the throngs of tourists who traipse across them to stand before the Bema of Ancient Corinth.

The entities that comprise these old lands compose legion spaces. The objects entangled into its composition give rise to unruly times. If other spaces, other times open in the shadows of what has been disclosed then, as this book wagers, it is because space and time arise from vigors within, and frictions between, actual things. In search of rest, waters stream through deep strata, dissoluting a karstic course through a chthonic domain twelve hundred millennia in duration. Megaron (the great hall of Mycenaean palaces), temple, and the exhibition space of the museum stage authority, separate observers, and structure groups, and through the recurrence of form, something of the Bronze Age, Hellenistic period, and modern Greece swerve into proximity. Through the tone of their bells, a ruminant orchestra on the browse broadcasts the positions of individual sheep to shepherds under dense juniper canopies. Waiting out the germination of plants, agrarians live in accordance with the rhythms of season, weather, rye, scarcity, and surplus. With smart devices, whose actions were anticipated in magic, augury becomes pervasive by holding knowledge of distant events instantly. Each situation evokes distinctive spaces and times. Understanding each situation also demands something of a metaphysical overhaul, where time and space are not specified in advance, but are composed differently over idiosyncratic paths alongside things. To illuminate these situations, an alternate account of Greek lands is requisite.

Though the objects of this book are legion, they compose the old lands today known by the names they were so well known in antiquity, the Corinthia and the Argolid. The heartlands of Greece, here surfaces and folds were ancient in their radical, agrarian modification before the strong walls of Mycenae were raised. For millennia these aged and storied lands have exerted a profound influence upon the human imagination. The allure is, yes, that of antiquity and history, of myth and change, of wonderous ruin, relinquished burden, and departed worth. What weight has not been given to its renowned citadels, cities, or sanctuaries: Isthmia, Corinth, or Nemea, Mycenae, Tiryns, or Argos, Asine, Epidaurus, or Troizen? But there is also the draw of the land itself, the agrarian countryside, the high mountains, wide valleys, forested slopes, broken shores, the wine dark seas. There is the appeal of its people, their vitality, and their struggles—all foreigners who are beguiled to venture among them do so with their leave.

This book takes the form of a chorography. This term, "chorography," is rooted in the Greek word *chorographia*, a combination of *chôra* ("place", "land", "country") or *chôros* ("a definite space or place") and *graphia* ("writing"). Thus, the term accommodates an alternative between two nouns, *chôra* or *chôros*, and the mode of engagement, *graphia*. Ancient chorographies described, delineated, and documented a country, land, or region.[1] In the seventeenth and eighteenth

---

1 See Strabo 10.3.5 for a discussion of the proper function of chorography (Ephorus gave the best account of the founding of cities, kinships, migrations, and original founders, "but I," Plutarch says, "shall show the facts as they now are, as regards both the position of places and the distances between them; for this is the most appropriate function of Chorography"); see also 8.3.17.

centuries, antiquarians embraced chorography in their studies of community and history, memory and ruins, places both vanished and extant.[2] In learning from these traditions, this book ventures farther by finding more in chorography's etymological vagueness, for this ambiguity between *chôra* or *chôros* suggests a dual commitment to land, to its legion objects, and to how we dwell, or to space and how it is constituted.

Chorography: the very word suggests a different fidelity. A literary genre crafted in a world prior to comprehensive abstractions, it holds the potential for different understandings of the lands and spaces of the Eastern Peloponnese. By its very nature a chorography cannot *begin* with the refined map, with the purified representation, with the flat abstraction to the exclusion of other spaces. It must set out along the path, over the ridge, through the pass, behind the wall *in medias res* (in the midst of things) with an open disposition. In this, one submits to a naive trust that at the telos of this endeavor an account of these lands will emerge, numerous spaces will unfold, hopefully less forced or coerced and more encouraged, more coaxed, into coming forth. This also holds for regions, which are dominated by the sense of an encompassing area. Indeed, even the cherished notion of landscape is tethered to the mode of viewing terrain as picture, not to the land itself.[3] What comprises a region has to be made and, yet again, this should not be settled in advance.

Latin etymology reminds us of the polyvalence of the term *regio*: line, direction, boundary, part of a larger area or space, district, administrative subdivision, division or parcel (of land), part or division (of the sky or universe), part (of the body), sphere (of thought, activity). With so many meanings, let us linger briefly with the first—*lines* are fundamental to regions.[4] A line measured from Tiryns to Aria laid the baseline for the first map of the Peloponnese produced by geodesic triangulation. A line blasted from the Saronic Gulf to the Gulf of Corinth unsealed a monstrous conduit between the Aegean and Adriatic closed since the Pleistocene. A line laid from Corinth to Argos opened the land to routine crossings in two directions at guaranteed times. For the majority of those who lived and died in this region, lines were not so much drawn *around* flatlands, as manifest in an engagement across water, along roads, over high

---

2 Consider the work of William Gell (1810), Walter Scott (1814), or John Wallis (1769). On chorography and archaeology, see Gillings (2011), Rohl (2011, 2012), Shanks (2012, 79–82), Shanks and Witmore (2010).

3 Debunking land in favor of landscape is not without precedent. In bolstering his definition landscape, Tim Ingold, for example, reduces "land" to that which is homogeneous and quantifiable, to something that weighs and forms a kind of lowest common denominator (1993, 153–54). I do not share this assessment. Were we to play at dialectical one-upmanship, one might contend that the "scape" gets in the way of land, but this would get us nowhere. Indeed, the etymology of "landscape" in "land" and "schap" proves to be somewhat more nuanced; see, for example, Andrews (1999, 28–9), Cosgrove (2004); also Cosgrove and Daniels (1988), McInerney and Sluiter (2016).

4 Ingold (2007a).

passes, through uplands, low valleys, or towns, under olive or carob, by walls, through doors, along corridors, or by referencing other times and places at a distance.[5] To draw a line on a map is a beginning, but it is not our starting point.

This chorography takes shape over twenty-seven segments. These segments cross the length and breadth of the Eastern Peloponnese, from the isthmus of Corinth to Mycenae, from Argos to Asine, from Ermioni into the Saronic Gulf. One of the simplest forms of geometric space, "segment" is taken in its etymological sense of "seg-," from *secare*, to cut, and "-ment," as with the Latin suffix -*men*, -*mentum*, the product of this action. One must acknowledge that by writing land through a series of segments they give the impression of holding a preference for lines spatial over lines temporal, and that these spatialized lines are wholly arbitrary in their points of entry and division. What distinguishes this chorography from such a sleight-of-hand replacement of lines temporal with lines spatial, besides, as noted above, the specification of spaces and times as composed through contact and engagement, is that each segment is a portion of an actual thing. A neglected path taken over Malavria forms a very different sense of distance from a rail car moving through aged defiles south of Nemea. Open areas for Argive assembly in 272 BCE do not spatialize crowds in the same manner as squares in modern Nafplion. If these segments form lines, then it is because linearity is a quality of the object described and its rapports, whether within and along streets in Ancient Corinth, the Hadrianic aqueduct, vineyard trellises, or the transects of survey archaeologists. This, of course, is not to deny lines their dignity as objects; it is to emphasize that one is not reducible to the other.

As an archaeologist, I know what I am expected to say concerning my self-location and rationale for writing a chorography. This book, and the labors that contributed to it, fit into a very long tradition of scholarship concerned with landscape, place, and region in Greece; the ancients, Strabo the geographer, and Pausanias the *periegete*; the travelers and antiquarians, nearly all Northern Europeans; the Classical topographers; the travel writers; the archaeologists.[6] As the latter, I realize that I am obliged to locate myself with respect to my predecessors and their traditions; my debt to them is tremendous. I am obligated to specify the ways I participate in these cultures by weighing previous scholarship, situating myself among the intelligentsia; this endeavor helps to demonstrate one's credentials and establish trust in what is written. Archaeology is not without its expectations for how one structures a book; for how problems are to be

---

5 On the notion of region, see Oliver (2001).
6 A litany would include Jacob Spon and George Wheler, Sir William Gell and Edward Dodwell, François Pouqueville and William Martin Leake, among many others; Ernst Curtius and Herbert Lehmann, Eugene Vanderpool and William Kendrick Pritchett; the chorographer Antonios Miliarakis; the archaeologists Michael Jameson and James Wiseman; the travel writer Patrick Leigh Fermor.

posed. Theoretical frameworks should be set out in advance and everything follows from there—description and analysis through application. In this way we demonstrate how one's expertise shapes what lies before you; we also predetermine, we contain our objects of concern. But this is not that book.

An important disciplinary context for this chorography is that of regional archaeological survey. Over the last fifty years these old lands have been trudged by archaeologists, geographers, anthropologists, and others who have focused on the articulation of discrete regions over the last twenty millennia and more.[7] Methodological approaches, disciplinary commitments, and areas of expertise supply predetermined frames for what has become of past lands, packaging its objects for other past-oriented fields, history and philology. The resulting descriptive geographies, site reports, or regional histories circumscribe objects, held to be archaeological, in a space and time regarded as primal and external, homogeneous and stable. Despite the emphasis on *diachronic* perspectives, lending emphasis to that which passes *through* time, researchers nonetheless order their findings into periods arranged into a linear sequence.[8] Each object, whether site, landscape, or region, is locked into a horizon of expectation defined by a chain of succession and replacement—Neolithic then Bronze Age then Iron Age, Archaic then Classical—where they are relegated to the confines of their own eras—the Hellenistic, the Roman, the Ottoman—or a more nuanced continuum nonetheless gauged in such terms. This chorography could lend further nuance to these longstanding traditions. It could give shape to the undocumented recesses formed between their lines from the angle of historical trajectory. It could write out its routes across the succession of various eras. But this is not that book.

For what it is worth, archaeology is a conflictant field. It has yet to shed fully the empirical notion that it is, with respect to its objects, a cumulative tradition—advancing with ever more detail to generate comprehensive knowledge of the past. Drawing on continually refined methods, consistent, repeatable, compatible, with an even greater fidelity to what remains, a fuller picture of the continuity and discontinuity of human experience over the long term may be achieved.[9] From the angle of discursive competence, each endeavor may attend to lacunae, lend emphasis to the neglected, refine the achievements of

7 Among them are the Eastern Korinthia Archaeological Survey, the Nemea Valley Archaeological Survey, the Berbati-Limnes Archaeological Survey, the Argolid Exploration Project, and the Methana Survey Project. One could also add the Mycenae Survey and the Argolid Survey, but these were temporally circumscribed.

8 Here, we should acknowledge a renewed interest in the road, route, and track among archaeologists as objects worthy of engagement and study See, for example, Alcock, Bodel, and Talbert (2012), Marchand (2009); also Snead, Erickson, and Darling (2009). Much of this work, of course, can be situated as part of a longstanding tradition within archaeology and classical topography: Hope Simpson and Hagel (2006), Lavery (1990), Wiseman (1978).

9 See Witmore and Shanks (2013).

others, and fill in the remaining gaps, which continue to open under the weight of relevance that comes with research. Beginning with the text, everyone cultivates an awareness of the ignored zones, the vague portions where they might add definition, perhaps zoom in to a little more detail, on the path towards a more intricate understanding of "landscape," its changes and metamorphoses, whether within a particular era or across the millennia. The expanding encyclopedia of knowledge burdens every researcher with an impossible task. Yet, how does one reconcile this expectation of taking up the heritage of one's object in its entirety with that of the critical gesture, which consigns previous ways of understanding, older paths to knowing, to the scrap pile of obsolescence? Self-contained bits and pieces continue to amass, involuntary memories of a land's own past refuse to succumb to the expectations that seek to link them in search of a more comprehensive picture.[10] This endeavor, while necessary, will bring us no closer to our objects, which will always exceed our attempts to come to terms with them.[11]

Some 150 years ago, archaeology parted ways with chorography. Description came to privilege the analysis that divided. Land was carved up by specialization; chthonic underlands for archaeology; prediluvian strata for geology; exceptional monuments for architectural history; Classical sculpture for art history; ancient literature for philology; flora and fauna for biology; contemporary Greece for anthropology and geography. Archaeology, like other fields of knowledge, invested in a cumulative picture of science wherein its objects were made to revolve around a discipline, rather than the discipline revolving around its objects. What might seem untimely from one angle is, from the other, timely, if not long overdue. Given our precarious times we must find a perspective that both grounds and reaches, that struggles for depth, for roots, that is inclusive of the full diversity of land objects and their rapports, while aspiring to be as subtle as the situation at hand. This is a vast endeavor. I am fully aware that too much weight may be placed on a word to the point of over-determination. I have found chorography to permit me the freedom of movement, which academic specialization prohibits and these old lands demand.

As for the things themselves, which only reveal so much of their being in any given situation, research can never take form as full disclosure. These lands, comprised as they are of trillions of things, can never be fully exhausted. Given the repeated mention of *thing* and *object*, these terms should be clarified at the start. A thing is taken in its etymological sense of gathering; that is, as an entity whose composite reality draws upon a variety of situations, but is not reduceable to any or all of them. An object is taken in the sense of the Latin

10 Compare Alcock and Cherry (2004), Barker and Mattingly (1999–2000) with Olivier (2011), Shanks (1992).
11 Here, I find much common ground with the object-oriented approaches of Levi Bryant (2011, 2014) and Graham Harman (2011, 2013, 2016a).

objectum; that is, an obstruction, that which is exposed, thrown, or cast before anything else. Both terms serve to evoke any autonomous entity that cannot be broken down into its parts or reduced to its effects.[12] As naively given things are made explicit and objects of the past come into being in the course of field-work, old perspectives fall to that which emerges. Across the centuries of arch-aeological work, given the diversity of approaches to site, land, and region there is less continuity than one would hope. With such massive bodies of scholarship, it seems daunting to return to the land with an altered perspective. Yet, we are in need of another way to apprehend what has become of the past, not as a "total record,"[13] but as a diverse series of chorographic engagements informed by archaeology. In learning from the wall, the path, the condition of the field, the trash on the surface; by surrendering oneself to being nudged along by the things encountered is to embrace the risk that comes with trusting that a possibility will reveal itself.

Archaeology does not have a regional synthesis unique to itself, which is to say that it persists in borrowing from history, it endures in regarding the past as history (of course, by so doing such an account is no less archaeological).[14] In writing this book I have aspired to that longstanding disciplinary ambition among archaeologists to generate a synthesis that can stand as a complement and alternative to a linear and ordered history. Consequently, such a synthesis might avoid historical expectations that shape how we conceive of these old lands by beginning not with what was, but what has become of it.[15] To claim, however, that this chorography stands as a complete synthesis—that is, as an assemblage of disjoined fragments forged into a cogent whole—would be disin-genuous. From the perspective permitted by the maps published at the end of this book, the image of connected segments is but paper-thin. The path, broken by encounters, digressions, excurses, is anything but linear. The nodes, whether held by pleats or torn by rents between different moments, interlocutors, experiences, are anything but homothetic; that is, understood as fixed and simi-lar points of correspondence. Nor does this chorography ignore history. Perhaps it aspires to a synthetic treatment aware of its own impossibility. It could even be claimed that this chorography constitutes an anti-synthesis, for any commit-ment to things is oblique, disjointed, and utterly specific. Uncertainties aside, although this chorography cannot hope to paper over fragmentation or disjunc-ture, it does have the virtue of aspiring to archaeology as literature.

It is indeed the archaeological that we must now single out for the consider-able nuance it brings to chorography. A longstanding tradition of the antiquarian on the road, the phenomenological tradition of landscape through experience,

---

12 After Harman (2013, 6–7); also see Witmore (2014a, 206, 2020).
13 Lucas (2012, 18–73).
14 See Olivier (2011), Olsen (2010); also Souvatzi, Baysal, and Baysal (2019).
15 Olsen, Shanks, Webmoor, and Witmore (2012).

the attention paid to subtle differences in surface, shape, substance is built into the field's history and conditions one to simply observe the things around them.[16] The archaeologist—if one might be permitted to indulge such a composite character—is attuned to look for grimy bits of pottery by the trail. The archaeologist notices where what is buried extrudes from the soil or how surface form suggests what lies below; they recognize how disparities in the orientation of rubble or the material in a wall recalls different hands at work or how a few gnarled olives hold the line of an old terrace freed from its girdle of sundry stone. The archaeologist cultivates a deep appreciation for human and nonhuman being over the long term; they are habituated to care for that which is crumbling, for what lies abandoned, and how it fits with what is near. The archaeologist raises questions of change, of ruination, of what other times are co-extensive with the encounter.

Of course, the archaeologist is not without certain impediments to perception. Often their art of noticing relegates the scatter of broken ceramics to the status of intermediary, a means to something else.[17] In looking for evidence for what was, they often overlook what is, which may be ultimately incompatible with the will to historical truth that frames what guides them. The archaeologist has not always taken into account the erstwhile that is part of a reality that is here and now. Yet, through accumulated experience, an archaeologist might develop the requisite patience to hesitate in the face of the tumulary mound; by virtue of its thingly propensities, they may yet strike out towards the unanticipated. By being open to the surprise of things, by being attuned to their suggestions, an archaeologist is conditioned to redefine their goals and orientations. It is here that I may submit two last motives for writing this book: to take a land so studied as to be familiar and conjure forth a new strangeness where the smack of wonder, the shiver of astonishment, may yet resound; and to offer an audacious defense of these old lands as uncompressible, of the countryside, an assemblage of legion things in themselves, as inexhaustible.

This is not the first book to pose such problems or to advance such propositions for how to proceed. Phenomenology invites its adherents to return to things, foremost understood as *phenomena*, and this term signals a concern for that which appears and make itself apparent to a human observer.[18] Elevating firsthand observation and experience over caricatures of measured reportage and distilled representation it advocates thick, rich description of land, centered on the medium of the walking, sensing body.[19] Rather than revolving exclusively around things inscribed on paper, it asks us to venture into the lived world, to be engaged on the ground, where other angles, connections, relationships might

16 Olivier (2011, 53).
17 Olsen, Shanks, Webmoor, and Witmore (2012).
18 Tilley (1994, 2010); also Brück (2005).
19 Tilley (2010, 25–6); compare Hamilakis (2013), Olsen (2010), Shanks (1992).

arise through the effective disposition of *being there*. There is much to commend about this perspective. What makes the following chorography different lies in how it neither abandons the natural sciences nor the affairs between actual objects which exist apart from that privileged rapport between the human and world. To this we may add a more frugal point. Walking returns some sense of gravity to the paths and distances once trudged without other recourse. Yet, human engagement with land shifts with the experience of being in a car or on a train, riding on a horse or within a boat, as does walking in the company of others.[20] Likewise, some crossings are wholly nonhuman, whether one follows waters in search of rest or goats on the browse; and thus, they arise through the effective disposition, I would contend, of *being-alongside-others there*.[21]

At variance with a flattened image of bounded lands, another sense of space is also highlighted by those who champion connectivities and networks.[22] The notion of network, behind theories of connectivity, embraces this twentieth-century spatial grammar and deploys it as an operative principle in a world where point-to-point movement was the exception rather than the rule. It is not simply the case that networks hold greater meaning from distant offices with bright monitors where the intervening expanses are annulled to nothing, for the equipotency of points tethered by thin, electronic connections is grounded in a homogeneous space. Because the constitutive ingredient is the dot, the point of intersecting lines, which are deprived of volume, the *network*, no less than flat scenographies, subsumes inhabitable, three-dimensional spaces to two-dimensional with its assumed symmetries.[23] While learning from these perspectives, this book sets out on a different path. So why should anyone read it?

First, *Old Lands* returns to the lived ground of the trail, the terroir, the soil, the objects that compose the lands (*chôrai*) of the Eastern Peloponnese in order to articulate something of their asymmetrical, incompressible, surplus realities outside of maps, apart from the two-dimensional. Such an endeavor demands a sustained philosophical exploration of heterogeneous spaces (*chôroi*). Second, this book offers an ancient, untimely, form of ambulatory writing as a timely mode for addressing present challenges. Rather than remain within the comfortable confines of our idiosyncratic fields of knowledge, it refuses to break up that which resists being broken by venturing in directions suggested by actual things confronted on the ground. Third, this book splits with an academic apartheid that sorts times into their own delineated boxes and offers what might well be described as an archaeological account of a polychronic, mixed

---

20 Also see Thrift (2008, 75–88); compare Tilley (2010, 27–8).
21 Elden and Mendieta (2009), Latimer (2013).
22 Compare Horden and Purcell (2000), Malkin (2003), Vlassopoulos (2007). Ian Morris (2003) is one of the few to treat this development with suspicion; still, network theory in archaeology is not without its utility (see Knappett 2013).
23 The problem with the notion of network, as Peter Sloterdijk (2009, 6) has pointed out, is that it tends to neutralize existential space; also see (2013, 249–57).

ensemble that remains true to the objects encountered, which are themselves participants in its co-articulation, its co-realization.

How else might other spaces arise from the surface of the page? How might the articulation of heterogeneous spaces inform us in our pressing need to return to ground? Will the juxtaposition of different spaces and times open new insights into how to live well with these old lands? These are among some of the questions that give rise to this book. In these precarious times we, all of us, are in desperate need of an integrated method that tarries on the ground, pauses in the field, observes the soil, the trees, the vines, the weeds, that emerges with things, that forms out of land.[24] Archaeologists have yet to develop a style of writing whose twists and turns are receptive to provocations roused by the things encountered.[25] This account is embedded with thick description, an intense, even obsessive, fidelity to locality, to utter specificity. Attuned to the ruined wall, the terraced contours, the vineyard soil, the unwholesome vapors above marshes, the life-giving waters of ancient springs, this account follows their hints, their suggestions to larger lessons or to that which is less obvious. Strabo and Pausanias, the antiquarians, teach us another way to write without imposing arbitrary boundaries indicative of disciplines.[26] It would be disingenuous to deny how, for me, this book fits into a larger puzzle, what has been described elsewhere as a symmetrical archaeology.[27] Still, in writing a chorography a different set of loyalties arise to the telos of this endeavor; that is, to *chôra*, land, country, or to *chôros*, place and space. Situating these as the outcomes reminds us of the struggle to see apart from what maps manifest from the angle of ninety degrees. Thus, after an engagement with the initial flattening of the Peloponnese with the *Expédition scientifique de Morée* (1829–32) the ensuing narrative grasps at the lands over which it moves, by which its course is counselled.

Segments 1 through 9 move from the isthmus of Corinth to the citadel of Mycenae. Along the road that crosses the isthmus to Ancient Corinth, the book begins with several objects suggestive of the proportionality of the Peloponnese: the canal that severs thousands of years of terrestrial crossings to create an island were a peninsula existed; the wall that prevents and permits movement; the marine terraces raised upon what becomes of trillions of fossilized corpses. It walks through the differences between the diachronic and polychronic, history and archaeology, in Ancient Corinth. It juxtaposes Northern European and Ottoman perspectives on the walled enclosures of Acrocorinth in the late seventeenth century. It drives in isolation along a concrete highway that reduces and

24 Latour (2018); Serres (2015a).
25 See discussion in Pétursdóttir and Olsen (2017).
26 Here we may note other fine examples in the work of Robert Byron (1937), Bruce Chatwin (1987), Barry Lopez (1986), Robert Macfarlane (2012, 2019), Rebecca Solnit (2010).
27 Olsen (2012), Olsen, Shanks, Webmoor, and Witmore (2012), Olsen and Witmore (2015), Shanks (2007), Webmoor (2012), Witmore (2007a, 2019a).

compresses old geographical barriers and distances, and radically redefines the nature of locality and human consciousness in the region. It slows to a walk through *chôra*, investigating soils and terroir, and tasting of wines. With survey archaeologists, it explores how space comes to be understood in regional archaeological projects and discusses landscape practices along a field transect in Nemea. With the poetics of Lucretius, it courses with waters through a channel that, in mimicry of karstic forms, reoriented a *chreode* hundreds of thousands of years in the making, and into ruin. It joins Gertrude Bell on an 1899 journey by train through the Tretos Pass and works through the radical changes in speed, distance, time, volume, and power that accompany the railroad. In light of Walter Benjamin's theses on the concept of history, it moves through Mycenae by learning how archaeology, beginning with Schliemann, was led astray here by a genuine historical image.

Segments 10 through 18 attend to the old ways between Mycenae and ancient Asine. Progressing from the grave of archaeologist Humfry Payne to the Argive sanctuary of Hera, the book retraces a Bronze Age route by terraces of relinquished labor, over tombs of ancestors, inherited and adopted. It moves with the monocultural inversion that flips the entire Argive plain from a locus of calculated scarcity to that of reckless abundance. It undertakes a comparison (*synkrisis*) of patient forms of government with independent poleis and impatient governance with risk-taking kings. From a seat in the Hellenistic theatre of Argos, against the backdrop of a Northern European desire for a lost Greece, it works through the creation of a mono-linguistic territory and the nationalistic definition of the soil. Using clues from his unpublished logbooks it accompanies William Martin Leake from Argos to Anapli in 1806, in the course of creating of a map based on timed distances with Ottoman post horses, and writing his descriptive geography, *Travels in the Morea*. In the company of those who make a living in Nafplion it takes to its streets, exploring the transformation of a town defined since the eleventh century by its enveloping form in cosmopolitan insularity. Accompanying James George Frazer to Epidaurus it explores how a polytheistic geography was emptied of meaning with the coming of Christianity and demonstrates how his fieldwork in Greece and commentary on Pausanias are fundamental to the shaping of *The Golden Bough*. Raising themes of display and alienation, it details how an archaeological museum arranges artifacts into an itinerary through time and region. With archaeologist Georgia Ivou it journeys to Asine and ruminates over legal objects and archaeology, heritage and law.

Segments 19 through 27 journey to Ermioni then traipse over the Adheres Mountains and into the Saronic Gulf. In the company of a local fisherman turned watersports guide, this portion of the book begins at sea between Tolo and Vivari and touches upon matters of concern related to tourism, the end of traditional boat making, near-shore fish, and a precarious and uncertain future for traditional fishers, commercial long-line trawlers, and corporate aquaculturalists. Upon returning to dry land it traces differences in the definition of land and belonging between

Mesolithic foragers and tenant farmers under Ottoman overlords with eight students. It crosses a forgotten pass among herds into the Southern Argolid, over upland plains, and through a marginal gorge, highlighting estranged relations to an altered countryside persistent in its capacity to hold and engender. It conjures the forgotten spaces that emanated out from hearth under a home-centered sky. It contends with the olfactory burden of living with one's own ordure in a polis without sewers or cesspits. It follows braided paths over a mountain range in the footsteps of antiquarians, Classical topographers, and others who have traced Pausanias's path to Troizen. Exploring an old antagonism between agriculture and archaeology and a positive understanding of ruination, it strolls through the garden world of Ancient Troizen and situates the afterlife of a polis in light of Heidegger's notions of *Gelassenheit* (releasement towards things) and *Seinlassen* (letting what is inexplicable stand as such). Trailing an Englishman, an Italian artist, and a janissary to Methana, it raises questions of truth and falsity with respect to reason, science, and history. Casting off by ferry into the Saronic Gulf, it churns through escalations of human pollution in sea and air while grasping for ground.

This book turns on matters of longstanding archaeological concern. Many segments transpire at watershed moments in how we understand space, reflecting on the disappearance of an agrarian world rooted in the Neolithic; the transition to urban styles of living; changes in communication, movement, and metabolism that follow internal combustion engines. Some segments, grounded by encounters with lithic scatters and springs, fields and groves, enclosures and truck roads, turn around issues of dwelling and belonging among hunter-gatherers, herders, agrarians, and urbanites. Others develop around key concerns that arise out of the encounter: object memory, agrarian patriotism, and estranged belonging; changing mobilities; archaeology versus history; pollution and the appropriation of ground, sea, and air; truth and the construction of knowledge; the nature of things and ontology; enclosure and exhibition; topology and duration; ever-changing relations between humans, their fellow creatures, and the wider environmental milieu; the need for thick description; and coming to ground in a new climate regime. Although some segments are dated, which serves as an indication that they transpired through a single crossing, all are, in fact, iterative.

Each segment results from spending time in a place, walking paths, visiting and revisiting the same grounds, again and again. Repetition of interaction serves to build familiarity, even a habitual competence, what de Certeau discusses as *metis*, a Greek word that among other things speaks to an experience born out of years of repeated crossings.[28] Such repetition, without flat abstractions, helps to shed presuppositions that come with returning to ground with an estranged perspective. Where pastoral imagery no longer makes sense in the wake of the radical modification of Greek lands, by repeating a path

---

28 1988, 81–83; also see Macfarlane (2012, 264), Olsen (2010, 116–17) on habit memory.

through experiential learning, by coming to see things from a different angle, by remaining open to letting go in a flash of insight, we may come to grasp different understandings of these lands.[29] Just as the ambulatory mode is a way of engaging things encountered along the path, automobile, train, boat, or mount provide necessary contrasts. In walking, one moves slowly, engaging smells, being attentive to the textures of the path, to tracks in the soil, to geoponics, to weeds.[30] In a car, one races along in mutual isolation, trading a closeness to land objects for comfortable interiors at speed.

As one must find the humility to trust in the thing encountered to open thought in its direction, the confidence in one's own ability to connect, and the audacity to remain open to other possibilities, an excursus on the nature of chorography comes at the end. Likewise, to begin with the map is to reinforce the power of projected, two-dimensional space over others. The object-oriented disposition offered here requires a writer, whether archaeologist or other, to place aside the map that conditions what is to be observed and how to observe it. This is not to abandon maps completely. Maps are among other achievements that come at the telos of this endeavor and readers are cautioned not to treat this imagery as the only path to accessing the spaces opened by this chorography. Such a book asks for a lot of patience on the part of its reader who may find reward with the argument by staying true to the path. To help the reader prepare for the journey a litany of concerns raised along the way are placed at the front of each segment.

This book draws on a decade and more of traveling, interviewing, observing, photographing, collecting, noting, videoing, reasoning, and arranging the wealth and character of this region. It draws upon many more decades in revisiting sites discussed by others and connecting features on the ground with the achievements of predecessors. Upon setting out I was not sure where the path would lead me; I was not sure where the writing would go. While I have ceded much of what I brought to the path in order to learn new ones, this text, to be sure, is fraught by my limitations. I continue to grapple with how to locate myself vis-à-vis such a work. Whereas more on the issue of authorship will be said by way of an epilogue, for what it is worth, as an archaeologist and inheritor of agrarian obligations, as a former stonemason and student of the Classics, as a walker raised among herds, and a father mindful of the challenges my sons will face, I have been shaped by both the page and the pagus. Over twenty-five years of breaking its earth, heeding the call of its recesses, these Greek lands merge with the person. I recognize a need to return to the soil, to land, to understand the actual things both in themselves and for others, who struggle for ground, as now we all must do. Just as these old lands offer a rare opportunity to explore that struggle at a depth over its diverse surfaces, this journey

29 Also see Bradley (2003).
30 Also González-Ruibal (2019, 162).

opens an occasion to learn how to struggle in our precarious times. Many of the segments that follow expand beyond the archaeologist to imagine the engagement of others or to take the path with them. Thus, the reader should be aware that these segments shift in and out of different perspectives—some at variance with my own—I, we, or the third person, through what we might term avatars, such as the Ottoman traveler Evliya Çelebi, archaeologist Gertrude Bell, or Plutarch's Pyrrhus of Epirus.

One might see such a project, which draws together so many previously separate concerns, as the culmination of a career. Had I waited, this book might not have been written. A certain rashness and naivety was necessary to its character and scope. For what one lacks in carrying the burdens of knowledge, one may gain in an alacrity and audacity of imagination, which counts for a great deal, arguably more, with respect to these old lands; I can only hope to have honored it.

Bibliography

Alcock, S.E., J. Bodel, and R.J.A. Talbert 2012. *Highways, byways, and road systems in the pre-modern world*. Chichester: Wiley-Blackwell.

Alcock, S.E., and J.F. Cherry (eds.). 2004. *Side-by-side survey: Comparative regional studies in the Mediterranean World*. Oxford: Oxbow Books.

Andrews, M. 1999. *Landscape and Western art*. Oxford: Oxford University Press.

Barker, G., and D. Mattingly (eds.). 1999–2000. *The archaeology of Mediterranean landscapes*. Vols. 1–5. Oxford: Oxbow.

Bradley, R. 2003. Seeing things: Perception, experience and the constraints of excavation. *Journal of Social Archaeology* 3(2), 151–68.

Brück, J. 2005. Experiencing the past? The development of a phenomenological archaeology in British prehistory. *Archaeological Dialogues* 12(1), 45–72.

Bryant, L. 2011. *The democracy of objects*. Ann Arbor, MI: Open Humanities Press.

Bryant, L. 2014. *Onto-Cartography: An ontology of machines and media*. Edinburgh: Edinburgh University Press.

Byron, R. 1937. *The road to Oxiana*. London: Macmillan & Co.

Chatwin, B. 1987. *The songlines*. New York, NY: Viking.

Cosgrove, D. 2004. Landscape and landschaft. *German Historical Institute Bulletin* 35(Fall), 57–71.

Cosgrove, D., and S. Daniels (eds.). 1988. *The iconography of landscape: Essays on the symbolic representation, design and use of past environments*. Vol. 9. Cambridge: Cambridge University Press.

De Certeau, M. 1988. *The practice of everyday life*. Berkeley, CA: University of California.

Elden, S., and E. Mendieta 2009. Being-with as making worlds: The "second coming" of Peter Sloterdijk. *Environment and Planning D: Society and Space* 27, 1–11.

Gell, W. 1810. *The itinerary of Greece*. London: Payne.

Gillings, M. 2011. Chorography, phenomenology and the antiquarian tradition. *Cambridge Archaeological Journal* 21(1), 53–64.

González-Ruibal, A. 2019. *An archaeology of the contemporary era*. London: Routledge.

Hamilakis, Y. 2013. *Archaeology and the senses: Human experience, memory, and affect*. Cambridge: Cambridge University Press.

Harman, G. 2011. *The quadruple object*. Winchester: Zero Books.

Harman, G. 2013. *Bells and whistles: More speculative realism*. Washington, DC: Zero Books.

Harman, G. 2016a. *Immaterialism: Objects and social theory*. Cambridge: Polity Press.

Hope Simpson, R., and D.K. Hagel 2006. *Mycenaean fortifications, highways, dams, and canals*. Sävedalen: Paul Åströms Förlag.

Horden, P., and N. Purcell 2000. *The corrupting sea: A study of Mediterranean history*. Oxford: Wiley-Blackwell.

Ingold, T. 1993. The temporality of landscape. *World Archaeology* 25(2), 152–74.

Ingold, T. 2007a. *Lines*. London: Routledge.

Knappett, C. (ed.). 2013. *Network analysis in archaeology*. Oxford: Oxford University Press.

Latimer, J. 2013. Being alongside: Rethinking relations amongst different kinds. *Theory, Culture & Society* 30(7–8), 77–104.

Latour, B. 2018. *Down to earth: Politics in the new climate regime*. Cambridge: Polity Press.

Lavery, J. 1990. Some aspects of Mycenaean topography. *Bulletin of the Institute of Classical Studies* 37, 165–71.

Lopez, B. 1986. *Arctic dreams*. New York, NY: Scribner.

Lucas, G. 2012. *Understanding the archaeological record*. Cambridge: Cambridge University Press.

Macfarlane, R. 2012. *The old ways*. New York, NY: Viking.

Macfarlane, R. 2019. *Underland: A deep time journey*. New York, NY: W.W. Norton & Company.

Malkin, I. 2003. Networks and the emergence of Greek identity. *Mediterranean Historical Review* 18(2), 56–74.

Marchand, J. 2009. Kleonai, the Corinth–Argos Road, and the "axis of history." *Hesperia* 78, 107–63.

McInerney, J., and I. Sluiter 2016. General introduction. In J. McInerney, I. Sluiter, and B. Corthals (eds.), *Valuing landscape in Classical antiquity: Natural environment and cultural imagination*. Leiden: Brill. 1–21.

Morris, I. 2003. Mediterraneanization. *Mediterranean Historical Review* 18(2), 30–55.

Oliver, G.L. 2001. Regions and micro-regions: Grain for Rhamnous. In Z. Archibald, J. Davies, V. Gabrielsen, and G.J. Olivier (eds.), *Hellenistic economies*. London: Routledge. 137–73.

Olivier, L. 2011. *The dark abyss of time: Archaeology and memory* (trans. A. Greenspan). Lanham, MD: AltaMira Press.

Olsen, B. 2010. *In defense of things: Archaeology and the ontology of objects*. Lanham, MD: AltaMira Press.

Olsen, B. 2012. Symmetrical archaeology. In I. Hodder (ed.), *Archaeological theory today*. Cambridge: Polity. 208–28.

Olsen, B., and Þ. Petursdottir (eds.). 2015. *Ruin memories: Materiality, aesthetics and the archaeology of the recent past*. New York, NY: Routledge.

Olsen, B., M. Shanks, T. Webmoor, and C. Witmore 2012. *Archaeology: The discipline of things*. Berkeley, CA: University of California Press.

Pétursdóttir, Þ., and B. Olsen 2017. Theory adrift: The matter of archaeological theorizing. *Journal of Social Archaeology* 18(1), 97–117.

Rohl, D. 2011. The chorographic tradition and seventeenth-and eighteenth-century Scottish antiquaries. *Journal of Art Historiography* (5), 1–18.

Rohl, D. 2012. Chorography: History, theory and potential for archaeological research. In M. Duggan, F. McIntosh, and D.J. Rohl (eds.), *TRAC 2011: Proceedings of the twenty-first theoretical Roman archaeology conference*. Oxford: Oxbow Books. 19–32.

Scott, W. 1814. *Border antiquities of England and Scotland*. London: Longman, Hurst, Rees, Orme, and Brown, Paternoster-row; J. Murray, Albermarle-street; John Greig, Upper-street, Islington; and Constable and Co. Edinburgh.

Serres, M. 2015a. *Biogea*. Minneapolis, MN: University of Minnesota Press.

Shanks, M. 1992. *Experiencing the past: On the character of archaeology*. London: Routledge.

Shanks, M. 2007. Symmetrical archaeology. *World Archaeology* 39(4), 589–96.

Shanks, M. 2012. *The archaeological imagination*. Walnut Creek, CA: Left Coast Press.

Shanks, M., and C. Witmore 2010. Echoes across the past: Chorography and topography in antiquarian engagements with place. *Performance Research* 15(4), 97–106.

Sloterdijk, P. 2009. Spheres theory: Talking to myself about the poetics of space. *Harvard Design Magazine* 30, 1–8.

Sloterdijk, P. 2013. *In the world interior of capital: For a philosophical theory of globalization*. Cambridge: Polity Press.

Snead, J.E., C.L. Erickson, and J.A. Darling 2009. *Landscapes of movement: Trails, paths, and roads in anthropological perspective*. Philadelphia, PA: University of Pennsylvania Press.

Solnit, R., B. Pease, and S. Siegel 2010. *Infinite city: A San Francisco atlas*. Berkeley, CA: University of California Press.

Souvatzi, S.G., A. Baysal, and E.L. Baysal 2019. *Time and history in prehistory*. London: Routledge.

Thrift, N. 2008. *Non-representational theory: Space, politics, affect*. London: Routledge.

Tilley, C. 1994. *A phenomenology of landscape: Places, paths, and monuments*. Oxford: Berg.

Tilley, C. 2010. *Interpreting landscapes: Geologies, topographies, identities*. Walnut Creek, CA: Left Coast Press.

Vlassopoulos, K. 2007. Beyond and below the polis: Networks, associations, and the writing of Greek history. *Mediterranean Historical Review* 22(1), 11–22.

Wallis, J. 1769. *The natural history and antiquities of Northumberland*. London: W. and W. Strahan.

Webmoor, T. 2012. STS, symmetry, archaeology. In P. Graves-Brown, R. Harrison, and A. Piccini (eds.), *The Oxford handbook of the archaeology of the contemporary world*. Oxford: Oxford University Press. 105–20.

Wiseman, J. 1978. *The land of the ancient Corinthians*. SIMA 50. Göteborg: Åström.

Witmore, C. 2007a. Symmetrical archaeology: Excerpts of a manifesto. *World Archaeology* 39(4), 546–62.

Witmore, C. 2014a. Archaeology and the new materialisms. *Journal of Contemporary Archaeology* 1(2), 203–24.

Witmore, C. 2019a. Symmetrical archaeology. In C. Smith (ed.), *The encyclopedia of global archaeology*. New York, NY: Springer.

Witmore, C. 2020. Objecthood. In L. Wilkie & J. Chenoweth (eds.), *A cultural history of objects: Modern period, 1900 to present*. London: Bloomsbury.

Witmore, C., and M. Shanks. 2013. Archaeology: An ecology of practices. In W.L. Rathje, M. Shanks, and C. Witmore (eds.), *Archaeology in the making: Conversations through a discipline*. Abingdon: Routledge.

PROLOGUE

The measure of the Morea?

A cairn, a chain, and a triangle, the Carte de la Morée, *the* Expédition scientifique de Morée, *a frontispiece, Arachneo, archaeological encounters, other measures, other spaces*

When French surveyors raised a truncated cairn of dry stacked stones on St Elie de Khéli, the highest point of Mt Arachneo, there was nowhere in the Morea from which to view the region in its entirety.[1] For those consumed by this endeavor, erecting a two-meter monument of stone in 1829 served to signal how this visual deficiency would soon change.

Beginning from a simple point in Nafplion, French surveyors calculated with a repeating theodolite—an 8-inch Gambey—an angle off a known base, a 3,500-meter line staked out over unencumbered plain between Tiryns and Aria.[2] From a point to the ends of a segment with known length, they determined the interior angle and, with this, the precise measure of two other lines to form a triangle. With this primary shape, the surveyors then established a second triangle from a survey station on the Larissa of Argos. Between Argos and Nafplion another side, another measured line, now extended across the plain. From this length, soon gauged from the summit of St Elie de Khéli, a third triangle was ascertained; one with the proportion requisite for measuring though triangulation the whole of the Morea, a region increasingly called by its ancient name, the Peloponnese.

What begins in the flat plain, where divisions between plots had long been maintained by agrarians, moves to the tops of mountains. From a primary triangle, the simplest of forms after the point, segment, and angle, a latticework

---

1 Peytier, Puillon de Boblaye, and Servier describe the stations as *des cônes tronqués offrant un très bon pointé* (1833, 90); for the dimensions of the signal cairns, see Bory de Saint-Vincent (1834, 20).

2 These measurements were undertaken with a chain calibrated against a copper meter at various temperatures (Peytier, Puillon de Boblaye, and Servier 1833). On the 3,500-meter baseline, see Segment 14.

of these simple forms was built. Through geometry the highest peak in the Eastern Morea is flattened.[3]

In order to see the whole of this region from anywhere, its mountainous contours, its gentle slopes, its deep valleys must be translated onto a uniform, precisely measured plane; and this flat surface is given new relevance with latitude and longitude tethered to the globe for the first time. In this way, that which is heterogeneous and variable is translated into that which is homogeneous and stable. Set to a scale of 1:200,000, the resulting map—the *Carte de la Morée*—was published in six sheets, only three years after the raising of the cairn on Arachneo.[4] After 1832, a young King Otto can spread out the map on any table in any room of his little palace in Nafplion. He can examine a scaled-down, yet faithful, image of the peninsula, and thereby dominate the region at the center of a fledgling nation.[5]

There had been other maps of the Morea. Prior to 1800, the most reliable maps were derived from Admiralty surveys. Though the shape of the coastline, the location of ports, and streams were detailed, features in the regional interior remained in question. Prior to 1832, those intrepid few who ventured inland with cartographic ambitions derived their distances from estimations based on timed movements and paces counted between points.[6] No features had been obtained through geodesic measurement.[7] So when the director of the *Expédition scientifique de Morée* (1829–1832), Colonel Jean Baptiste Geneviève Marcellin Bory de Saint-Vincent, argued that the advantage held by the geographer Émile Le Puillon de Boblaye over all his predecessors in clarifying ancient geography was that he knew "*l'état des lieux tels qu'ils sont réellement*" (the state of the places as they really are), the colonel had in mind a *géographie actuelle* derived through geodesic triangulation.[8] This was a cartographic enterprise whose precision could be measured in deviations of a meter or less between Argos and Arachneo, a distance exceeding 22 kilometers.

In vaunting the topographical endeavors of the *Expédition*, the feats of ancient heroes may not have been far from Bory de Saint-Vincent's thoughts. (Indeed,

---

3 Through zenith distances from the sea by Nafplion, the surveyors also calculated the precise height of Mt Arachneo for the very first time: 1,199 meters (that is, 1,198.7 meters).

4 Drawn and engraved by the director of the *Dépôt de la guerre* and the *Ecole d'état-major*, Jean Jacques Germain Pelet, the Carte was published in 1832 (Pelet 1832).

5 The literature on maps and state power is immense; see, for example, Driver (2001), Elden (2013, 324–27), Harley (2002, 51–108).

6 See Segment 14.

7 Examples of these maps include that of François Pouqueville published with *Voyage de la Grèce* (1826–27) and William Martin Leake with *Travels in the Morea* (1830); also see Livieratos (2009), Witmore (2004, 2013a, 137–45); Witmore and Buttrey (2008); on the problem of the interiors, also see Bory de Saint-Vincent (1834, 18).

8 Bory de Saint-Vincent (1834, 54).

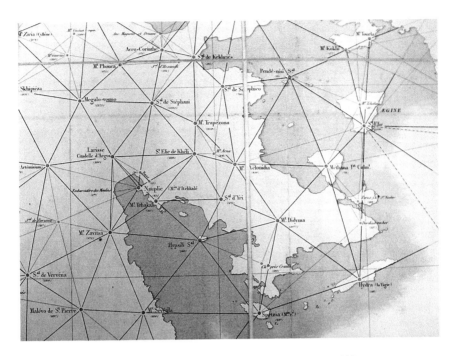

Detail of triangulation with baseline from *Carte trigonomètrique de la Morée* (1832).

the last signal to have been erected on Arachneo, the French had conjectured, announced the fall of Troy, as stated by Aeschylus's Clytaemestra.[9]) Plagued by fever and hardship, officers within the topographical brigade endeavored with their activities to the bitter end; one devoted *capitaine* purportedly met his death with pencil in hand.[10] Why such an endeavor came to gain so radical an importance requires a demonstration of how this map proved fundamental to securing those sites and objects documented by the *Expédition* for all future forms of knowledge and its production.

Erecting signals, stretching chain, measuring lengths and angles, noting these tabulations in lists, such tasks were only part of the mission. Modeled upon the collaborative body behind the *Description de l'Egypte*, the *Expédition* involved the

9 *Agamemnon* 309; Puillon de Boblaye (1836, 53); also see Frazer (1898 Vol. III, 233).
10 Bory de Saint-Vincent (1834, 19, 50–51).

intense scrutiny of the Morea from numerous scholarly angles.[11] While surveyors eyed yonder heights in establishing their triangles, topographers and geographers, artists and architects descended on other areas of the Morea to undertake their various pursuits. That the whole of this state-sponsored mission was overseen by the *Dépôt de la Guerre* should not go unnoticed.[12] Having aided in issuing the final eviction notices to the Ottomans, the French embrace the mantle of liberators as a sufficient justification for carrying out these endeavors. To the liberators goes the license. To the protectors goes the privilege. To the discoverers goes the distinction.

It is no coincidence that the frontispiece to the first volume published by the *Expédition* in 1831—dedicated to architecture, sculptures, and inscriptions —was comprised of the most celebrated vestiges of the Classical past to be encountered by the Architectural Division in the course of their labors. At the center of the page stands an aedicule crowned by an acroteria-fringed marble found at Epidaurus, held aloft by caryatids of Roman Loucos near Astros. Sundry sculptural pieces litter the foreground: by the plinths of the two caryatids recline Athena (in the Roman guise of Minerva) and Herakles (Hercules), fragments of metopes uncovered by the architect, Abel Blouet, and company at the temple of Zeus in Olympia; at the center sits a sphinx drafted from Delos, a composite capital found in Coron, and small funerary vases found in tombs of Aegina.[13] Among these superlative stones lies an inscription upon which are indicated the main cities explored in the course of the French exploits. In the background on the right rises the Acropolis of Athens; on the left looms Acrocorinth. Below the latter, in the middle ground, are three figures: a French soldier shows to a Greek a French frigate *"qui débarque les troupes par lesquelles la liberté et la paix sont rendues à la Grèce"* (which landed the troops by which freedom and peace were restored to Greece).[14] At their feet kneels *"un Turc rendant ses armes"* (a Turk returning his weapons).[15] Here, France stands between Greece and the Ottoman Empire.[16] In the midst of all, set within the immutable marble of the central monument is an inscription to the *Expédition* itself— the title of the first volume, ordered by the government of France, with its date and author.

---

11 See Bourguet (1998), Bracken (1975), Lepetit (1998), Wagstaff (2004a).

12 On the political, economic, and social consequences of state-sponsored mapping projects in the nineteenth century, see (Driver 2001; Scott 1998); in the context of France, see Godlewska (1999).

13 Blouet (1831, 3).

14 Ibid.

15 Ibid.

16 While Abel Blouet and Bory de Saint-Vincent regarded their work as a contribution to science and the arts, they nonetheless reassert a Northern European prerogative formerly laid open through conquest and occupation.

Frontispiece from Blouet 1831, Gennadius Library, ASCSA (photo by Don Lavigne).

The next image to follow the frontispiece will come at the end, as the first of the plates: a map of the Peloponnese. Upon its flat surface ancient sites are indicated as points; ancient names are supplied in brackets. Dashed lines connect one site to others indicating the paths taken by Blouet's group. With this map one gets the impression that the achievements of the French would more than just connect the dots; these liberators would lift the veil of time and expose a Classical past in the sense of making it known (this is precise meaning of "discover," to "lift the covering").[17] And yet, for Ernst Curtius, famed "father" of Classical archaeology, future excavator of Olympia, the scientific gains of the three volumes eventually published by the Architectural Division were not in proportion to the lavishness of their expenditure.[18] Because of the delay caused by climate and sickness in the execution of the triangulation survey, Blouet was forced to base his map on one published by Pierre Lapie in 1826.[19] Lapie's map lacked the first-rate precision of what was to come. Its delimitation of the Morea coastline rested on partial certainty. Its depiction of the interior of the region was wholly arbitrary. Had Blouet waited, Curtius's assessment might have been different, if only because of the French architect's cartographic base.

Without the work of the topographical brigade, vestiges of the Classical past could not be made fully known, much less kept, safeguarded, and archived for all time. This aspiration could only be fulfilled after 1832. With the addition of the descriptive geographies published by Puillon de Boblaye, which included illustrations, the *Carte de la Morée* becomes a primary visual mode for fixing objects and observations to the whole of the Morea; it also becomes a basis for manipulating such information at a distance.[20] After the *Expédition* "what it is to see and what there is to see" in the Morea is redefined.[21] The French endeavors were now tethered to the map which will guide all ensuing endeavors of similar purpose.

In the first historical geography of the peninsula published in German, the *Peloponnesos* (1851–1852), Curtius placed the *Carte* out front. Opposite the title

17 Martin Heidegger recognized the importance of such a truth-event in terms of *alêthéia*, the Greek word for truth, which he translated as "unconcealment" (2008a). For Heidegger, science and technology open a methodical assault on that which is hidden or naively given. As a systematic invasion of being, this process is ongoing; its character is that of a self-fulfilling prophesy that results in the impoverishment of being. For more concerning the semantic importance of "discover" in the context of maps and exploration, see Sloterdijk (2013, 99).

18 "Im Allgemeinen kann man sich des Eindrucks nicht erwehren, dass der wissenschaftliche Gewinn nicht im Verhältnisse zu der Pracht der Ausstattung steht" (Curtius 1851–1852, 135).

19 For a comparison of the two maps, see Curtius (1851–1852, 133–34), Ploutoglou et al. (2011).

20 Witmore (2013a, 137–45).

21 Latour (1986, 9).

page a version of the French map is situated as the frontispiece to Volume 1 (its presence is all the more notable over the course of two volumes sparsely supplied with illustrations, all either planimetric views of sites or topographic profiles). With this map, as Curtius noted, Peloponnesian chorography for the first time obtained a secure and firm foundation.[22] It was a firm foundation, indeed. The *Carte* formed the basis for all subsequent maps of the Peloponnese produced throughout the nineteenth century.[23] Yet by the century's end the inconsistencies in maps based upon the French survey had become too numerous to be corrected by wrestling with its constraints in the resulting projections. Need also arose for maps at different scales.[24] At 1:25,000, 1:10,000, and 1:5,000, maps can be used for land registers, planning of public and private works, securing names to any and all locations, or backcountry trekking. With a variety of scales, one confronts the combination of the expansion of the map to capture the most minute of details and the pervasiveness of the two-dimensional extended into every domain. What had been the most powerful articulation of power possible in the early nineteenth century now infiltrates all aspects of life.[25] The map now shapes how space is understood.

No one can deny the gains. Future anthropologists, archaeologists, classicists, botanists, geographers, and topographers would no longer have to count their paces, time their distances, or write out their trails to the base of mountains. With key points now firmly positioned in the region on paper, there is little need to repeat the act of tethering each point to its encompassing milieu. As with Curtius, they too would place the map at the beginning. For this was a map that

22 In noting *"durch diese Karten hat die peloponnesische Chorographie zuerst eine feste und sichere Grundlage erhalten,"* Curtius (Curtius 1851–1852, 134) underlined the importance of such a map for the progress of knowledge.

23 Throughout the later nineteenth century it would form a basis for subsequent maps—*Carte de la Grèce* (1852) (in twenty sheets at a scale of 1:200,000) was followed by the Austrian Staff Map (1880) (1:200,000), Greek Ordnance Map (1885) (eleven sheets at a scale of 1:300,000), *General-Karte des Knigreiches Griechenland* (1885) (1:300,000), *Topographische und Hyposmetrische Karte des Peloponnes* (1892) (in four sheets at a scale of 1:300,000).

24 A new Geodesic Mission (*Geodaitikí Apostolí*) was initiated in 1889. What begins as an Austrian Military Mission under the direction of Lieutenant Colonel Heinrich Hartl would become a Greek military endeavor in 1895—renamed in 1926 as the Hellenic Military Geographical Service (HMGS)—thus ending the history of Northern European control over the mapping, demarcating, and naming of Greek localities. Over the course of many decades, a new infrastructural base would be established on the basis of a new cycle of survey, geodesy, and triangulation. Whereas the *Carte de la Morée* was based upon 183 principle points over the Morea and the surrounding islands, the HMGS would establish 26,739 (first and second order) trigonometric control points over the whole of Greece (see Naval Intelligence Division (1944, 397–403), Peytier, Puillon de Boblaye, and Servier (1833, 102–06); also see the HMGS website: http://web.gys.gr/portal/page?_pageid=33,36335&_dad=portal&_schema=PORTAL).

25 Latour (1986); on maps and nineteenth-century military power, see Driver (2001).

maintained an optical fidelity to the physical proportions and visual properties of the entire Morea as seen from above, and such a map will precondition nearly all modes of regional engagement and geographical disclosure under the guise of scientific research. One need not, of course, reduce maps to those inscriptions that seek to transport something of the physical world without distortion at a distance.[26] There are other maps and modes of mapping.[27] It is, however, with a base map whose accuracy served the purpose of visually transporting measurable qualities of the land that anyone from anywhere could go directly to their object of concern and continue with it along the cumulative path of scientific research, the profitable path of economic development, the efficient path of technological progress, or the formalistic path of legislative authority. Between the Argive plain or Arachneo and the scientific interlocutor comes such a map. Because of a trust that locales were secure vis-à-vis other geographical features, information about a region can now be gathered bit by bit. A *homogeneous space* becomes the base line of description, scientific and otherwise, a ground against which these old lands would come to divulge their secrets.

⌒

When the archaeologist David Rupp, in the company of colleagues, climbed the slopes of Arachneo nearly 150 years after the topographical brigade raised their cairn these researchers began on a secure footing.[28] Upon Arachneo, the Roman traveler Pausanias had situated the altars to Zeus and Hera.[29] Charles de Vaudrimey, the staff officer in charge of the Argolid section of the French topographical brigade, associated a large enclosure in the saddle between its two peaks, Profitis Elias (St Elie de Khéli) and Arna, with the two altars.[30] Curtius, following in Vaudrimey's footsteps, further affirmed the location of the altar within the enclosure at the saddle.[31] In the wake of these associations, the labors undertaken by subsequent researchers rested upon a known information base that could be questioned, revisited, and refined.

Rupp and his colleagues proceed into observation with a certainty of what and how that could only arise from the page. First, they embrace the

---

26 This is not to reassert that phenomenological distrust of maps (see Aldred and Lucas 2019, 30–1), only to situate maps that follow in the line of the *Carte* as manifesting one space among others without allowing them to assert one space above others.

27 See Tuan (1977), Turnbull (1994, 2000); also Gillings, Hacıgüzeller, and Lock (2019).

28 Rupp made two visits to the peak—in 1973 and 1975. Among other colleagues to accompany him were Eugene Vanderpool, Merle Langdon, and John Camp (Rupp 1976, note 10).

29 On Pausanias, see Segments 17 and 22.

30 Bory de Saint-Vincent (1834, 51).

31 Curtius (1851–52, 418).

proposition that Pausanias placed the altars on the summit, not in a depression below. Serving as a directive to that which has yet to be articulated, this proposition pointed them to the enclosure in the saddle. There they proceed to undermine the site as the location for these altars. Using diagnostic sherds of pottery—identifiable on the grounds of material, shape, and/or decoration—found on the surface within its walls they establish temporal coordinates: "Bronze Age (ca. 3200–1100 BCE) onward."[32] After situating the large enclosure within an earlier timeframe, they demonstrate through lack the error of previous identifications. Because no objects (erstwhile blocks or sacrificial debris) are revealed here to support the associations of Curtius and Vaudrimey, the location of the altars is detached from the saddle enclosure. Through the labors of Rupp and his colleagues these textual objects will be (re)connected with objects on the summit of Profitis Elias, around the very point where French topographers raised their cairn. At the peak, Rupp and his colleagues photograph objects rendered as features of what Pausanias mentioned. They pace out an area covered in broken ceramics. They stretch out measuring tapes over remnants of walls. They produce a plan of the site. Concentrations of pottery—dated Late Geometric to early Archaic (mid-eighth to mid-seventh century) and Archaic to Classical (700–323 BCE)—are manifest as shaded areas against white ground. Undefined lines of stone acquire definition as either foundations or forms between outcrops. For fields like archaeology it is a given that photographs, maps, and plans constitute a priori modes of engaging its objects. These media underwrite consistent, repeatable, and standardized practices for how to deal with the unruly things suggestive of antiquity.[33] Thus, their ongoing enrollment ensures that those who seek out such objects encounter them within the radius of routinized activity which they themselves open.[34]

Over thirty years after Rupp's survey, archaeologists will return to the summit of Arachneo. Olga Psychoyos and Yannis Karatzikos investigate the peak in the wake of its devastation.[35] They note how ground east of the outcrop where the French raised their cairn had been leveled by bulldozer. They find how objects documented by Rupp had been obliterated in the course of building a new chapel.[36] They detail how walls and surfaces buried in the 1970s now lay exposed before them. To the east of the outcrop, they mention how an

---

32 Rupp (1976, 264).

33 Witmore (2006, 2009).

34 Cf. note 17 on Heidegger and *alêtheia*; also see Sloterdijk (2016, 204–05).

35 In the context of developer-funded investigations, excavations were undertaken by the 4th Ephorate of Prehistoric and Classical Antiquities from February 2009 and October 2010 (Psychoyos and Karatzikos 2015, 2016).

36 Construction of the chapel was abandoned afterwards, but a few courses of stone were raised.

Arachneo Summit looking east, 2017.

antenna had been erected by the Hellenic Telecommunications Organization (OTE). While changes and coming interventions on the peak call to them, once again, the page directs archaeologists in what to seek and find, what to observe, and how to observe it.

Around a concrete geodesic column erected by the Hellenic Military Geographical Service to replace the French signal cairn, these new archaeologists lay out the Cartesian grid over an area of 60 x 40 meters. By stretching tapes across the peak, squares and rectangles on the ground take on the properties of squares and rectangles on the page. The flat surface orients and directs practitioners in the process of making visible what is revealed to remain. In a formidable surge of imitation, they too take photos of rocky surfaces. They too put dates to previously undisclosed objects upon this summit. Objects formerly buried are framed as of late Bronze Age; their forms are secured to the page. Once again, researchers proceed by filling in white space, thus adding to the explicit ground of the articulated past.

In publication Rupp situates his plan, photographs, and descriptions subsequent to a map of the "Argeia and Epidauria."[37] A dot marked "1199" tethers both map and plan together. An established benchmark, a concrete column raised upon the loftiest outcrop, now, in turn, ties image to the highest point of the peak. On paper this measured point is marked within the contours of Arachneo, which is set within the outline of the coastline, with respect to other points, Nafplion, Argos, and Mycenae. Psychoyos and Karatzikos also begin with the map. Similarly, all other images are situated as subsequent to an initial figure of

37 Rupp (1976, 262).

Google Earth.[38] In both maps, named points and lines are situated within a frame, and what on the page comes to represent a node floating within a constellation of other nodes encapsulated by white space, on the ground translates into a continuous surface connected to other continuous surfaces round an imperfect sphere. What is left of ancient altars, a prehistoric sanctuary, a ruined chapel, and a chapel foundation abandoned in the midst of construction are defined from above in uninterrupted relation to other lands on a globe. Through the map, space spreads out in every direction, and the observer knows where to stand. Across these continuous, unbroken surfaces might not all points come to be treated with equal interest?[39]

Look again upon the caryatids which hold aloft the roof of immutable posterity. There is an allure to long hidden things now disclosed, and by extension that which is hidden, those things yet to be revealed, call to those who seek to make them explicit. What had become of the Classical past was, for Blouet, as with the antiquarians before him, literally *terra incognita*, albeit defined within a land now documented with ever-increasing detail.[40] Beginning with points, lines, and areas, other zones await definition with ever-higher degrees of articulation. After the initial flattening, every researcher is directed towards the vaguely defined portions where they might lend definition. Making an area explicit is tied to filling in whitespace, whether around points, along lines, or across areas of the countryside. Increasingly refined articulations obscured that excess within objects, what things might have shown of their own accord had they not been burdened with systematized observations that begin with the page.

Do we need maps to give form to regions? Is the path through the measured, optimal image shown from the angle of 90 degrees the only way to an awareness of the lands it conveys? Does the flat projection betray spaces at variance with those of the mapmaker? Archaeology is a non-zero-sum game and such documents are its necessary returns. The fate of those objects archaeologically disclosed speaks to the importance of such modes of engagement and manifestation. For without the publication of their labors, what had become of these altars and those chthonic objects below them prior to their destruction

---

38 Psychoyos and Karatzikos (2015, 261).

39 Sloterdijk (2013, 255).

40 William Gell, the English antiquarian, had already compared the lack of knowledge concerning Greece to the uncharted African interiors (1810, i). The rationale of filling in white space for the charted land of the Greek past remains implicit within all forms of research, whether it be with archaeological surveys casting ever-finer meshed nets over "landscapes," or with Classicists who legitimate overturning rocks because no one else has bothered to do so. For example, Forbes and Mee, in their introduction to the Methana Archaeological Project, are explicit in their rationale of contributing knowledge to what was "largely a blank spot on the map" (1997, 1).

would have been fully bulldozed into oblivion. Still, if the mode of revealing is the map, the plan, the photograph, then one grasps those qualities that can be manifest in two dimensions. If the past is conceived within the confines of a laminar history, then what has become of the past is relegated to episodes within or through compartments specified along the timeline. It is not what the flat projection fails to translate, or how it sieves away the world, but that we should always embrace the map, the plan, the planimetric perspective, as the mode of revealing the world that is so peculiar.

When Heidegger stated that "the being of beings is sought and found in the representedness of beings," he drove home the point that the world picture (*Weltbild*) was *the world grasped as picture*.[41] Archaeologists, architects, geographers, developers, whosoever is concerned with making these old lands explicit are obliged to the picture in advance. It not only grounds everything that we do, but conditions how we conceive of our objects and ourselves. As Heidegger pointed out, "such a projection maps out in advance the way in which the procedure of knowing is to bind itself to the region that is opened up."[42] Geometric forms now undergird recognizable forms of the things-themselves and secure the ground-plan for those consistencies extracted from a naively given continuum of inconsistencies. Objects named and dated call forth the measured image of that which exists in excess of the name and image. All acquisitions of terrace walls, field plots, roads, ceramic scatters, etc., begin with the optimal image. The picture is the mode of revealing; it mediates what and how something is made explicit for the observer who is lured into seeing themselves as standing apart from that which is shown.[43] In this sense, and others, surveyors, cartographers, geographers, and archaeologists belong together.

⟨ornament⟩

When in times of drought ancient farmers made the long trek to the top of Arachneo to give sacrifice to Zeus and Hera, any comprehensive view of the island of Pelops was an artifact of divine privilege; that is, assuming an ancient conception of the divine that imagined gods as refusing to content themselves with oblique angles and embracing a direct, sky-centered view to the world below. The closest these ancient agrarians could come to such superhuman

41 2002, 68.
42 Ibid., 59.
43 Sloterdijk (2013, 94–97). Here, it is worth mentioning the new horizon of technologies that operate towards the production of the optimal image, which opens other avenues of production —drones, satellite imagery, and other forms of remote sensing.

vision was to look upon distant lands from these heights, known in even more ancient times as Sapyselaton.[44] Plowing fields, awaiting the germination of rye, grinding grain, finding love, and seeking fortune, human acts occurred firmly on the ground, which, without the reproduced and projected image, was the seat of knowing for these ordinary mortals.[45] This is not to assume that ancient farmers lacked the capacity to understand the shape of the land or the imagination to render that shape on a flat surface; rather, it is to acknowledge that their eyes grasped the land with other views that one could only regard as partial after the trigonometric flattening of Arachneo with the aid of signal cairns and theodolites, stakes and an engineer chain.

The French map, archaeological maps, photographs, illustrations, all translate actual objects onto a surface while maintaining something of their qualities without distortion. In making land explicit from right angles, maps subsume objects suggestive of diverse spaces to what can be rendered as a flat surface, which is internalized by the observer as the grounds for knowing. Always beginning here, we have forgotten how the projected space conditions our understanding of space by absorbing other spaces. In this, the encompassing definition of a region comes to dominate all other meanings. Yet, any assessment of a region defined in such a way is premature for most of the inhabitants of these old lands. In order to think of spaces that precede the map it is at least partly necessary to exhume other conceptions of these lands from history. It is also a question of thinking of space differently. For space externalized, projected, and homogeneous cannot be primordial in the way maps, and later satellite imagery, suggest. Beginning with the actual labors, locales, and instruments that lead to the *Carte*, the *outcome* of French cartographic endeavors, serves us this lesson.

Prior to the arrival of the French surveyors, subsequent archaeologists, bulldozers, and telecommunications, everyone drawn to this peak approached it without the ideal formalities that situated this post-*Carte* perception. If ancient peoples bothered to take the measure of these heights, then they did so in other ways: perhaps in the number of shaded stops along the path; perhaps with the amount of water or *kykeon* swilled from a waterskin; perhaps in the intensity and texture of mastic gum, which passes over the tongue from bitter to pine. If they attempted to overcome distance, then they did so by looking up, or down: sacrifices were perhaps recognized by trails of smoke that could be seen from below; those who sacrifice upon these high altars only need look to gain a fleeting appreciation of something suggestive of the view enjoyed by gods. Yet, the ancients did not see as one does through the map. And to

---

44 A name which suggests the prevalence of the silver fir.
45 Serres (2017, 132).

continue with this line of thinking reinforces an understanding of knowledge centered exclusively upon humans as observers, rather than something that sparkles among objects outside of us.

No one really knows why this peak was called *Arachneo*. The Greek *arachne*, the spider's web, radiates out in thin, gossamer lines. *Arachne* specifies a particular type of sundial, one ascribed to Eudoxus.[46] Later, the spider designates the ecliptic, the twelve-point circle, perhaps derived from the horizon system, on the astrolabe.[47] The relation between these things and the peak has meaning. From the point of axis at the peak, where signals flare, where clouds rise, where fires to Zeus and Hera burn, and knowledge shimmers, the web extends like falling shadows into the surrounding lands and onto the page. An object of reference from distant lands, this lofty summit served to mark those storied locales about its base. A point of observation above all other points is where the calculated and repeatable observation that absorbs these lands begins. Yet, the name proved tenacious, for, it is said, *Arachnaea* was still in use among agrarians at the turn of the nineteenth century.[48] Cairns, altars, slotted crag, and detritus left by those drawn here, at the point of the peak one encounters something approaching the gnomon-like self-showing of knowledge,[49] which is all too easily stifled. *Arachneo*: the name suggests an axis of knowing before the page and outside of us.

These lands are patient of interpretation in terms of the modes of manifestation we happen to deploy,[50] but *we*, our *media*, are not the only objects that enable observation, or otherwise.[51] Chorography, that ancient genre deployed by the likes of Pausanias and Strabo, offers another way to suggest a diversity of spaces, apart from the a priori container or continuous surface or homogeneous background. This is not about recouping some sense of the naivety that came with living in a world without pervasive two-dimensional images of the region. Rather, in rounding this mountain, this axis of knowledge, through the old lands of the Eastern Peloponnese, this book seeks to understand how interactions with and between peaks, routes, roads, crests, valleys, walled cities, paths and plots, houses and hearths, mounts and engines gave rise to radically different spaces.

To submit everything to the law of leveling is an error empirically, aesthetically, and speculatively. We err empirically by amplifying our sense of sight, for we have heavily circumscribed our ability to see by failing to be attuned to that

---

46 Vitruvius 9.8.1; Schaldach (2004).
47 Neugebauer (1949).
48 Frazer (1898 III, 233–34).
49 Serres (2017, 130–35).
50 Echoing Whitehead (2010, 136).
51 Also see Bryant (2014).

surplus reality which defies the page. We err aesthetically by allowing the necessary repetition that underlines our practices to shape our narratives, for we neglect to the detriment of the page the artistry of the achievement in writing these old lands. We err speculatively by failing to appreciate those other spaces ill served by the leveling, spaces that pervaded past lives, and spaces that might make a difference in how we might ourselves learn to live with the land.

Bibliography

Aldred, O., and G. Lucas. 2019. The map as assemblage: Landscape archaeology and mapwork. In M. Gillings, P. Hacıgüzeller, and G. Lock (eds.), *Re-mapping archaeology: Critical perspectives, alternative mappings.* London: Routledge. 29–46.

Blouet, G.A. 1831–38. *Expédition scientifique de Morée, Ordonnée par le Gouvernement français: Architecture, Sculptures, Inscriptions et Vues du Péloponèse, des Cyclades et de l'Attique, mesurées, dessinées, recueillies et publiées par Abel Blouet.* Volumes I–VI. Paris: Firmin Didot.

Bory de Saint-Vincent, M. 1834. *Expédition scientifique de Morée: Section des sciences physiques. Tome II – Partie 1. Géographie.* Paris: F.G. Levrault.

Bourguet, M.N. (ed.). 1998. *L'invention scientifique de la Méditerranée. Égypte, Morée, Algérie.* Paris: École des Hautes Études en Sciences Sociales.

Bracken, C.P. 1975. *Antiquities acquired: The spoliation of Greece.* Newton Abbot: David & Charles.

Bryant, L. 2014. *Onto-cartography: An ontology of machines and media.* Edinburgh: Edinburgh University Press.

Curtius, E. 1851–52. *Peloponnesos eine historisch-geographiche Bechreibung der Halbinsel.* Gotha: J. Perthes.

Driver, F. 2001. *Geography militant: Cultures of exploration and empire.* Oxford: Wiley-Blackwell.

Elden, S. 2013. *The birth of territory.* Chicago, IL: University of Chicago Press.

Forbes, H., and C. Mee. 1997. Introduction. In C. Mee and H. Forbes (eds.), *A rough and rocky place: The landscape and settlement history of the Methana Peninsula.* Liverpool: Liverpool University Press. 1–4.

Frazer, J.G. 1898. *Pausanias's Description of Greece.* Six volumes. London: Macmillan & Co.

Gell, W. 1810. *The itinerary of Greece.* London: Payne.

Gillings, M., P. Hacıgüzeller, and G.R. Lock. 2019. *Re-mapping archaeology: Critical perspectives, alternative mappings.* New York, NY: Routledge.

Godlewska, A.M.C. 1999. *Geography unbound. French geographical science from Cassini to Humboldt.* Chicago, IL: Chicago University Press.

Harley, J.B. 2002. *The new nature of maps: Essays in the history of cartography.* Baltimore, MD: Johns Hopkins University Press.

Heidegger, M. 2002. The age of the world picture. In J. Young and K. Hayne (eds.), *Off the beaten track.* Cambridge: Cambridge University Press. 57–72.

Heidegger, M. 2008a. On the essence of truth. In D.F. Krell (ed.), *Basic writings.* London: Harper Perennial. 111–38.

Latour, B. 1986. Visualization and cognition: Thinking with eyes and hands. *Knowledge and Society* 6(6), 1–40.

Leake, W.M. 1830. *Travels in the Morea.* 3 vols. London: John Murray.

Lepetit, B. 1998. Missions scientifques et expeditions militaries. Remarques sur leurs modalités d'articulation. In M.N. Bourguet (ed.) *L'invention scientifique de la Méditerranée. Égypt, Morée, Algérie*. Paris: Éd. de l'École des Hautes Études en Sciences Sociales. 97–116.

Livieratos, E. 2009. *Chartografikés peripéteies tis Elládas, 1821–1919*. Athens: MIET-ELIA. (Cartographic adventures of Greece, 1821–1919).

Naval Intelligence Division. 1944. *Greece, Volume I: Physical geography, history, administration and peoples*. Norwich: Jarrold and Sons.

Neugebauer, O. 1949. The early history of the astrolabe. *Studies in Ancient Astronomy IX. Isis.* 40(3): 240–56.

Pelet, J.J.G. 1832. *Carte de la Morée, rédigée et gravée au Dépôt général de la guerre*. Paris: Dépôt général de la guerre.

Peytier, Puillion-Boblaye, and Servier. 1833. Notice sur les opérations géodésiques exécutées en Morée, en 1829 et 1830, par MM. Peytier, Puillon de Boblaye et Servier; suivie d'un catalogue des positions géographiques des principaux points déterminés par ces opérations. *Bulletin de la Société de géographie* 19, 89–106.

Ploutoglou N., M. Pazarli, C. Boutoura, M. Daniil, and E. Livieratos. 2011. Two emblematic French maps of Peloponnese (Morée): Lapie's 1826 vs the 1832 map (Expédition Scientifique). A digital comparison with respect to map geometry and toponymy. *Proceedings, 25th International Cartographic Association Conference*, 3–8 July 2011, Paris. Available at: https://icaci.org/files/documents/ICC_proceedings/ICC2011/.

Pouqueville, F.C.H.L. 1827. *Voyage de la Grèce*, Vol. 5. Paris: Firmin Didot.

Psychoyos, O., and Y. Karatzikos. 2015. Mycenaean cult on Mount Arachnaion in the Argolid. In I. Tournavitou and A.L. Schallin (eds.), *Mycenaeans up to date: The archaeology of the north-eastern Peloponnese, current concepts and new directions*. Stockholm: Svenska Institutet i Athen. 261–76.

Psychoyos, O., and Y. Karatzikos. 2016. The Mycenaean sanctuary at Prophitis Ilias on Mount Arahnaio within the religious context of the 2nd Millennium BC. In E. Alram-Stern, F. Blakolmer, S. Deger-Jalkotzy, R. Laffineur, and J. Weilhartner (eds.), *Metaphysis: Ritual, myth and symbolism in the Aegean Bronze Age*. Leuven: Peeters. 311–19.

Puillon de Boblaye, M.E. 1836. *Expédition scientifique de Morée: Recherches géographiques sur les ruines de la Morée*. Paris: F.G. Levrault.

Rupp, D.W. 1976. The altars of Zeus and Hera on Mt Arachnaion in the Argeia, Greece. *Journal of Field Archaeology* 3(3), 261–68.

Schaldach, K. 2004. The Arachne of the Amphiareion and the origin of Gnomonics in Greece. *Journal for the History of Astronomy* 35(4), 435–45.

Scott, J.C. 1998. *Seeing Like a State: How certain schemes to improve the human condition have failed*. New Haven: Yale University Press

Serres, M. 2017. *Geometry: The third book of foundations*. London: Bloomsbury Academic.

Sloterdijk, P. 2013. *In the world interior of capital: For a philosophical theory of globalization*. Cambridge: Polity Press.

Sloterdijk, P. 2016. *Foams: Spheres III*. South Pasadena, CA: Semiotext(e).

Tuan, Y.-F. 1977. *Space and place: The perspective of experience*. London: Arnold.

Turnbull, D. 1994. *Maps are territories: Science is an atlas*. Chicago, IL: University of Chicago Press.

Turnbull, D. 2000. *Masons, tricksters and cartographers: Comparative studies in the sociology of scientific and indigenous knowledge*. Amsterdam: Harwood Academic Publishers.

Wagstaff, J.M. 2004a. Surveying the Morea: The French expedition, 1828–1832. In C. Foster (ed.), *Travellers in the Near East*. London: Stacey International. 167–82.

Whitehead, A.N. 2010. *Adventures of ideas*. New York, NY: Free Press.

Witmore, C. 2004. On multiple fields: Between the material world and media – Two cases from the Peloponnesus, Greece. *Archaeological Dialogues* 11(2), 133–64.

Witmore, C. 2006. Vision, media, noise and the percolation of time: Symmetrical approaches to the mediation of the material world. *Journal of Material Culture* 11(3), 267–92.

Witmore, C. 2009. Prolegomena to open pasts: On archaeological memory practices. *Archaeologies* 5(3), 511–45.

Witmore, C. 2013a. The world on a flat surface: Maps from the archaeology of Greece and beyond. In S. Bonde and S. Houston (eds.), *Representing the past: Archaeology through text and image*. Oxford: Oxbow Books. 127–52.

Witmore, C., and T.V. Buttrey, 2008. William Martin Leake: A contemporary of P.O. Brøndsted, in Greece and in London. In B.B. Rasmussen, J.S. Jenson, J. Lund, and M. Märcher (eds.), *P.O. Brøndsted (1780–1842) – A Danish Classicist in his European Context*. Copenhagen: Royal Danish Academy. 15–34.

1

LINES IN STONE

Roads, canals, walls, faults, and marine terraces

Diolkos, circumnavigating the Peloponnese, maritime or terrestrial crossing, aversion of risk, the canal and the monstrous, the Hexamilion, of lines and things, of objects and change, crossroads and quarries, life and death as a geological force, Diogenes, burial

Of the myriad lines that mark the Corinthian isthmus, a few offer concrete suggestions as to the proportionality of the Peloponnese, which we may render in spatial and temporal terms—the ancient portage road; canals, failed and achieved; the Hexamilion; the road to Corinth; the walls of sundry monuments; geological faults; and marine terraces.

Looking down from the summit of Acrocorinth Strabo referred to the narrowest strip of the isthmus, where two bays press against either side, as the *diolkos*.[1] This word comes from *dielko*, "to draw" or "drag across." It suggests that in antiquity this slender portion of the isthmus was recognized as a slipway

---

1 Strabo 8.2.1; 8.6.4; 8.6.22.

for ships.[2] With the ancient construction of the portage road, which is often called by the same name—*diolkos*—the maritime is held to here cross dry land, perhaps under the Corinthian tyrant Periander at the beginning of the sixth century BCE.[3]

To use the isthmus as a slipway it had to be deemed a profitable trade-off to circumnavigating the whole of the Peloponnese, especially its treacherous southern passages.[4] As one sails south then west from the southern bay of the isthmus, they will pass in the distance of 110 nautical miles upwards of a dozen headlands, near-shore islands, and convenient anchorages before turning the cape. Particularly perilous, the Island of Pelops plunges precipitously into the sea at Cape Malea.[5] For those who "forget their home" to brave this passage, across a wide gulf they set their sights on the gateway to Hades—Cape Matapan. After rounding this promontory, another wide gulf and the third cape, Akritas, awaits. There, amidst sea cliffs and islands on either side of the cape one finds sheltered harbors, which the Venetians knew by the names Coron and Modon.[6] From the western harbor, ancient Methone, to Patras is another 120 nautical miles along sandy and storied shores.

In 1881 it was reckoned that nearly 3,000 steamers passed round Cape Matapan.[7] The *London Standard* contended that a canal through the isthmus would save vessels heading from the Adriatic twenty-four hours; sixteen hours would be gained by Italian vessels, and eight for those from Gibraltar.[8] The difference in distance from Lefkas to Athens via the cape and through the canal is 117 nautical miles: 295 and 178 respectively. Under sail the full distance round the Peloponnese required as much as a week or more, depending on winds, weather, and shifting currents.[9] In the summer the prevailing winds are from

2 Comparative examples exist in the context of Viking Norway. Along the west coast, it is not uncommon for low-lying isthmuses to have toponyms with the root "drag," suggesting points where ships were dragged in order to advert risk of treacherous seas.

3 The excavator of the road, Nikolaos Verdelis, attempted to link its construction to the Corinthian tyrant, who was later said to have planned a canal through the isthmus (Diogenes Laertius 1.99). Archaeologically, the date of the *diolkos* is far from clear: Pettegrew (2011, 559; 2016, 59–68).

4 Strabo 8.6.20; also see Morton (2001, 81–85).

5 The waters of this cape have laid claim to untold treasures of the Ancient World, including one of Sulla's ships laden with the plunders of war; Lucian, *Zeuxis* 3; also Pettegrew (2016, 145–46).

6 In Modon, more than a millennium before the Venetians, the traveler Pausanias spoke of a temple raised to Athena with the epithet *Anemotis*, "she who calms the winds." For an archaeological history of these ports and this peninsula, see Davis (2008).

7 This number was comprised of 1,300 postal steamers, 1,300 ordinary commercial steamers and some 300 military vessels; *Vienna Dispatch to the London Standard*, in the *New York Times*, June 27, 1881.

8 Ibid.

9 *The Periplous* of Pseudo-Scylax gives a distance of seven and a half days (49–55), which is based on equating 500 stades to a day (69; Shipley 2011, 118–31).

the northwest and so, depending on the direction of your journey, they were either a help or hindrance. In spring and autumn, depressions passing south over Cape Malea give rise to strong southerlies or northerlies, which reach gale force in winter.[10] It was not uncommon to pass anxious nights in the gulfs awaiting more favorable winds.[11] For those who ventured under sail, the avoidance of the capes, especially in the winter, was not incidental to speed and distance.

Against their wine-dark agonies—weather and winds, reefs and waves, gods and monsters—ancient seafarers cared less for shaving off hours or the measured calculation of distances.[12] When you are hanging horizontal from the clewline with the yardarm buried in the surge you tend not to think of expanses measured in stadia.[13] The sea disquiets metrology. When other options exist, maritime risks whether genuine or exaggerated are accorded different weight. Both the *diolkos*, with its causeway, and the canal may be viewed as alternative lines to those which run over restless waters. A rare luxury for a sailor—to pay for another path. Ancient Corinth, some assume, got rich from its slipway.[14] Modern Greece, some jest, is still paying for the canal.[15]

The modern canal is seen as marking the end of a long history where a maritime thoroughfare across the *diolkos* was anticipated somewhat homothetically by the portage road.[16] Yet, should this ancient line be understood in terms of the modern canal? One errs by rendering these trans-isthmian objects as commensurate in their meaning.

Doubt has been expressed as to whether the paved, portage road was ever used as a drag way for ships.[17] Into question has been called the frequency with which vessels were conveyed across the *diolkos* in antiquity. In brief, the distance across the *diolkos* is far—6 kilometers. Its crest is high—70 or 80 meters above

---

10 Naval Intelligence Division (1944, 82–88); also see Heikell (2010, 25).

11 Such were the circumstances of the *Mentor* the day before the vessel sank with the Parthenon Marbles off Kythera in September of 1802; see Leontsinis (2010).

12 It has long been assumed that the sailing seasons did not include winter—new research asserts otherwise; see Arnaud (2005), Beresford (2013). Still, the sea was always a place of danger and loss in the Ancient Greek imagination; see Lindenlauf (2003); also Beaulieu (2016).

13 Serres (1989, 27).

14 Only portions of the portage road, excavated by Nikolaos Verdelis in the late 1950s, have been unearthed (Verdelis 1958, 1962). The terminus of the portage road on the Saronic Gulf is a matter of conjecture. It was cut and covered by debris from the excavation of Nero's canal (Pettegrew 2016, 186).

15 Large commercial vessels do not use the canal. Several companies went bankrupt in the course of its construction, and it demands continual upkeep and maintenance, which is not covered by the tolls.

16 See, for example, Fowler (1932, 55–56), Salmon (1984, 202), Wiseman (1978, 48); also see Pettegrew (2016, 167).

17 Pettegrew (2011, 2016); also Koutsoumba and Nakas (2013), Lohmann (2013).

sea level. Its grade is steep—2.3 per cent to or from the apex.[18] To move ships over such a formidable obstacle—and consider, most merchant ships were not large,[19] 15 meters, more or less—is a tremendous venture.[20] To transport goods from the Saronic Gulf to the Sea of Corinth, or vice versa, would have required two ships and docking facilities on each side. This is improbable.[21] Yet, an erstwhile trans-isthmian road exists and demands explanation. That this road is paved with large limestone slabs suggests a significant investment of labor and resources. That deep grooves are present in its stone surface suggests repeated use. For all these suggestions, fragments of a paved road say nothing as to what over them was conveyed—bulk goods or ships. Indeed, it was more practical, when compared to a stone railway, to drag heavy vessels over greased logs.[22] To account for its presence, the paved road has been reinterpreted as a supply way flagged in the Classical period for provisioning the Isthmian district, with its sanctuary.[23] The paved road no more foresees the canal than the term *diolkos* indicates frequent maritime portages.

The timeless image of a commercial Corinth, where economic advantage was gained through exploitation of its strategic position at the crossroads of the Mediterranean and the habitus of regular trans-isthmian crossings, according to David Pettegrew, mirrors modern maritime sensibilities shaped by sea lanes, canal construction, and amplified shipping traffic.[24] This assertion serves to highlight a fundamental shift in orientation, efficacy, and value. For Pettegrew, the trivialization of maritime traffic by modern societies obscured ancient understandings of the isthmus by generating a picture of the *diolkos* as a "great maritime highway functioning throughout antiquity."[25] In breaking with the

18 Lohmann (2013, 215), Pettegrew (2016, 117).

19 The Kyrenia ship, a fourth-century BCE Greek merchant ship, was 14 m in length; see Katzef (1972, 50–52), Sanders (2005, 3–4). Roman merchant ships were much larger; Pomey and Tchernia (1978).

20 Pettegrew (2011).

21 Long presumed to be a quay or landing platform associated with the portage road, the stone platform on the Sea of Corinth may have been associated with the Roman effort to cut an ancient canal (see Pettegrew 2016, 61–64).

22 Koutsoumba and Nakas (2013), Lohmann (2013).

23 Pettegrew (2016, 65–68).

24 This shift in orientation is ideological and ontological. Peter Sloterdijk (2013, 40–41) has underlined the modern revision of the earth predominated by landmasses to one predominately aquatic. The modern revelation of the earth as a waterworld inflated the importance of the aquatic as the central medium of movement and gave rise to an inversion of perspective centered upon the nautical.

25 Pettegrew (2016, 241). In this, moreover, isthmian images accessed at a distance exerted their influence. "A glance at the map of the Mediterranean shows how important such a canal would be for the trade of all the ports of France, Italy and Austria with Smyrna, Constantinople and the Black Sea." Thus speaks the Athens Correspondent of the *London Times* in April of 1869.

homothetic conception of these lines—portage road and canal—Pettegrew not only reasserts the importance of the isthmus as a bridge for connecting two bodies of land—Central Greece and the Peloponnese—he also champions an image of historical contingency: a gate and crossroads from the seventh to third centuries BCE, a fetter till the destruction of Corinth in 146 BCE, a portage under extraordinary circumstances between the fifth and first centuries BCE, a center created through later imperial investment, a district affected by the changing conditions of late antiquity.

Let us note: whether the maritime crossing of the isthmus was routine or exceptional is at root also a question of dimensionality.[26] Was the ancient *diolkos* a Mediterranean object or an Isthmian one?[27] When left with two possibilities in a closed circle of options each is subject to overturn in a perpetual reversal. Was the *diolkos* an object of trade and a trade-off for circumnavigation of the Morea or a bridge connecting regional districts through the transshipment of bulk goods?[28] When sufficient ambiguity remains it is a logical error to deny one of two options. If in the stone road one encounters an object that has been subject to disproportion, in the *diolkos* one encounters an object that offers itself to both maritime and terrestrial crossings. In this, however, the relations between sailors, merchants, Corinthians, colonists, and lines across the *diolkos* are not temporally invariant.

At the isthmus, Nero, the Roman Emperor, encountered a Mediterranean object, an obstacle to connecting east and west. Between his long shadow and his imagined canal rested the volume equivalent of the earth and stone used to raise the pyramids at Giza, Dahshur, and Saqqara.[29] Before Nero's death in 68 CE, over 2,500 meters of canal were cut at his whim by a throng of ten thousand—engineers with instruments, prisoners with picks, soldiers with shovels, conscripted laborers with baskets. That such a hubristic endeavor was grossly out of proportion with

26 Archaeologists often conceive of dimensionality in terms of scale, which is more about size and zoom in two dimensions than the qualities of an actual object like the isthmus or the Peloponnese.

27 The extent to which the isthmus manifests itself to one direction or the other is partially an artifact of scope. Pettegrew (2016) draws heavily upon data from the Isthmian hinterlands generated by the Eastern Korinthia Archaeological Survey (Tartaron et al. 2006). Longstanding evidence for Corinth's Mediterranean significance comes from farther afield—consider the overwhelming presence of Phoenician dedications at Perachora (Kilian-Dirlmeier 1985, 225–30) or the extraordinary numbers of Corinthian vases found in the Western Mediterranean (see, for example, Vallet and Villard 1964). Such evidence plays less of a role in Pettegrew's study.

28 Of course, this is a matter also of the historical imagination, for which image of traffic, terrestrial or maritime, is appropriate? The angle of historical contingency provides a more sober argument than that which was championed by Pettegrew in (2011); compare Pettegrew (2016, 65–66).

29 11,000,000 cubic meters of earth and stone: see Tsakos, Pipera-Marsellou, and Tsoukala-Kondidari (2003, 24). Pettegrew suggests that construction of the ancient canal would have required the extraction of 10,000,000 cubic meters of material (2016, 174).

ancient sensibilities among all but the megalomaniacal finds expression in Cassius Dio, who speaks of bleeding earth, of groaning ground, and of apparitions that caused men to shrink from the endeavor before it even began.[30] But an emperor stepped forward with a golden pickaxe to mattock through these ghastly portents. In Nero's wake his monstrous intervention retroactively redefined the *diolkos* as a site of hubristic failure; for Apollonius, Pliny, Quintilian, Statius, Suetonius, all speak of it. And here, at the scene of the crime, huge lacerations beset by giant mounds and deep pits in the underworld lingered as memories.[31] A broken line pressed ahead of itself into the future and anticipated what was to come. Indeed, such manifest devastation served as a vainglorious invitation to affluent others who wished to take up the titan challenge.

At last attempt, the canal emerges as a national achievement. Where others had failed, the modern Greeks, following on the bankruptcy of the French firm that oversaw the construction of the Suez, will succeed. But this ancient failure and the modern achievement are not commensurate. In the wake of Suez, dynamite and a metabolic regime of fossil fuels would give different meaning to what is humanly possible. Foremen directed crews to remove fill from the ancient cuts; engineers lit fuses to blow apart compacted marls; bucket-conveyor operators manipulated levers to shift broken sandstone into dump cars conveyed over rails; dredge pilots worked toggles to activate bucket chains in raising alluvium from the channel outlets; barge-men drove away loads under steam-power—it is through an amplified human–mechanical effort that a monstrous conduit is cut through calcified kilometers to connect seas.[32] From now on, it will increasingly be the case that fewer will wonder in quite the same way at "how difficult it is for human beings to force what the gods determine."[33] Under the excess energy conditions of the age of fossil fuels, what had been an artifact of authoritarian will is generalized among everyone as a routinized project, one that fabricated a linear monstrosity out of proportion with all ancient sensibilities short of the tyrannical.[34] Through the straight line that violently severed the *diolkos*, a different regime of metabolism and risk descends upon the isthmus and with it follows a change of scale, an acceleration of pace, and a sublime mobility; these, as will be demonstrated, will come to define these old lands retroactively. The Peloponnese is now true to its ancient name—Island of Pelops.

---

30 63.16.1; also see Fowler (1932, 57), Pettegrew (2016, 166).
31 Pettegrew (2016, 185–86).
32 What would have demanded more than a generation of unceasing labor and a mountain of cadavers unfolds in just over a decade with the help of motorized technologies of a neo-titanic age.
33 Pausanias 2.1.5.
34 See Heidegger (2003, 109); also Sloterdijk (2012a).

Works to expand the Corinth Canal around 1947–48 (Getty Image # 105219606).

Beginning near the southern outlet of the canal, Eleftherios Venizelos runs with the isthmus to Hexamilia and continues on to Ancient Corinth. Not far from its intersection with the road to Epidaurus, this macadam line bisects the remains of the Hexamilion, the ancient wall constructed between 408 CE and 450 CE, in the reign of Theodosius II to shield the Peloponnese against incursions from the north. From this breach, the wall weaves its way along the edge of a ravine, around a former Roman arch turned protected gateway, and continues along the periphery of the church grounds of Ágios Ioánnis, its modern cemetery, and under a pine forest to the north.[35] Its name speaks of its length: 6 miles from wave-washed bastion to wave-washed bastion. To safeguard and defend, to prevent entry, or to permit it; this was the three-fold task of the Hexamilion.

An ancient crossroads, it was through the gateway that major terrestrial routes from central Greece joined those of the Peloponnese.[36] The erstwhile arch once marked the threshold to the Island of Pelops before the great sanctuary to Poseidon. It was here that maritime routes from the Aegean and Asia met the isthmian shore. It was from the sea that the dead body of Melikertes was returned by a dolphin and buried here by Sisyphus, legendary founder of Corinth, purported originator of burial ritual.[37] Around the grave of the dead boy, known henceforth as Palaemon, the sea god and protector of sailors, ancient festivals were founded to his chthonic grandeur and to the glory of Poseidon athletes competed for the spruce-crown.[38]

After Nero, this place, circumscribed by a sacred precinct, centered upon a temple of Poseidon and the subterranean abode of Palaemon, bristled with new construction and was reemphasized as a common center of the Greek world.

The Hexamilion cut by Eleftherios Venizelos.

35 See Gregory (1993).
36 Pettegrew (2016, 48–59), Wiseman (1978, 45–79); also see Sanders and Whitbread (1990).
37 Burkert (1983, 197).
38 Gebhard (2005).

Pilgrims, Roman elite, and priests with their sacrificial animals; merchants, trades-men, and peasants with their laden carts; wrestlers, *pankratiasts*, and charioteers seeking fame with their well-bred horses, all were drawn here.[39] Lines of transport and transit along and across the isthmus, lines of communication and travel on the sea, all converged here. With the construction of the Hexamilion three centuries later, this area will persist as both crossroads and threshold. Here, two lines would now intersect: one to facilitate movement, the ancient road to Corinth; one to dis-rupt and control it, the six-mile wall.

When Tim Ingold asserted that "people inhabit a world that consists, in the first place, not of things but of lines" he not only invited readers to regard places like Isthmia as knots tied together by lines of human engagement beyond legion, but also chose to embrace the proposition that a thing's qualities are deeper than its being.[40] For Ingold, a woven "meshwork" of lines forms along paths over the isthmus, intermingling in the sanctuary, and interrupted by the wall. Lines of movement are synonymous with lines of constant becoming. Thus, along roads and over sea, lines of human inhabitation have for centuries converged at the ancient sanctuary of Poseidon, binding together with lines of building in what Ingold regards as an ongoing process of formation. Later, the lines of terra-firma-bound Visigoth invaders over the bridge from the north reinscribed the isthmus as a border between east and west.[41] While such an emphasis on lines celebrates the liveness of human inhabitation, experience, and movement,[42] it nonetheless reduces roads, walls, and sanctuaries to their appearances or effects for interlocu-tors of the featherless, bipedal, and flat-nailed variety,[43] ultimately denying other things their fair share.[44] That lines belong to objects, and objects give rise to their lines, is less a matter of imagined liveness, and more a confrontation with the reality of their present being. Although the Hexamilion once imposed its line across the entire isthmus, here, by the sanctuary, the location and orientation of the wall was planned by Roman engineers, and dictated by a series of ravines, and the ridgeline upon which it rose. Here the placement of a garrison fortress

---

39 Gebhard (1993), Pettegrew (2016, 194–98).
40 Ingold (2007a, 5).
41 Pettegrew (2016, 209); also see pages 68–74 for a discussion of earlier fortification walls.
42 Also see essays in Ingold (2011).
43 A reference to the pantomimic materialism of Diogenes, who with a plucked rooster forced Plato to augment his definition of the human as a "featherless biped" with an addendum: "with flattened nails" (Diogenes Laertius 6.40). I will return to Diogenes at the end of the road taken to Corinth in this segment.
44 A thing is an assemblage that cannot be broken down into its parts or reduced to its effects (Olsen and Witmore 2015, 191, Witmore 2014a, 206; after Harman 2013, 6–7). This definition of *thing*, therefore, eschews any opposition to people. Likewise, "object," a term sometimes used in place of thing, is not defined in contradistinction to a subject (see Witmore 2020).

was conditioned also by what had become of an ancient sanctuary. From there, columns, cornices, ashlar blocks, pedestals, and sundry wall stones were stripped from the erstwhile temples, the formerly sacred buildings, the old shrines, theatre, and whatever had been built within the sanctuary of the evicted sea god.[45] This quarried stone, termed "spolia," offered its qualities to new construction, and was recut to smooth on the outer surface of the fortress wall.[46] Elsewhere, the northern facade of the Roman bath and an existing archway provided ready-made foundations, incorporated by its line. Through a motley ensemble of different features, the Hexamilion traces the form of other things which are suggestive of other times. Here a linear object emerged to once again redefine the isthmus, by altering movement and agrarian economy across its expanse. Still, once released to its own trajectories, it is not so much the line that persists, but the wall, which extends into its futures.[47]

From the breach, Eleftherios Venizelos skirts the site of the ancient sanctuary to Poseidon, continues past the archaeological museum, and through the town of Kyrás Vrýsi where sidewalks backed by fences crowd either side of the asphalt surface. Behind them, the concrete hulks of houses pass in a steady stream of repeating forms. Beyond the village, the road passes into open fields and olive groves broken by workshops, villas, and facilities, agricultural and industrial. The line of this road, named for a Prime Minister linked indelibly with the shape of Modern Greece, follows that of the ancient road from the Sanctuary of Poseidon to ancient Kromna, Hexamilia, and through the Kenchrean Gate into Corinth.[48] Along its extent, this road offers a line different to that of history.

To the right, within a twenty-minute walk of Isthmia, the line of Eleftherios Venizelos trails past Hellenistic tumulary ground among olives less than two generations old and the scattered detritus suggestive of late Roman settlement in fields surveyed by archaeologists some two decades ago.[49] To the left, within another ten minutes, twentieth-century tarmac holds the forms of earlier roadways two and

45 For more on the coming of Christianity and the expulsion of false gods, see Segment 17.
46 Frey (2016, 128–75); also see Kardulias (1995, 2005).
47 Just as the erstwhile Hexamilion persists in disrupting other lines of movement, it continues to offer its qualities to other situations, having emerged as a number of different objects. Whereas numerous modern roads cut through the old wall line, the new National Road and railway to Patras were raised on overpasses built to avoid it. Now, just south of where these four bridges cross an excavated and conserved section of the wall, a natural-gas pipeline built to supply industries between Corinth and Megalopolis was buried beneath it.
48 Pettegrew (2016, 84–85), Tartaron et al. (2006, 495, Figure 16); Wiseman (1978, 64–69).
49 Excavated in 1961 and 1962, archaeologists dubbed the Hellenistic tumulary monument the West Foundation (Broneer 1962, 16–18); for a discussion of late Roman artifact scatters interpreted in terms of settlement, see Pettegrew (2015).

a half millennia in duration near where Roman dead once found repose in tombs cut within Pleistocene strata.[50] Ahead, directly above the trodden roadway, towers Acrocorinth, whose primordial stone holds memories of the Jurassic. Around the ancient tumulus turned open excavation, olives may be seen to grow, year by year, generation after generation. With tenacious pottery churned to the surface by plow, archaeologists and agrarians may recognize a different past for what are now cereal fields. Against a rock two hundred million years in the making, those changes that have occurred on either side of this road may also stand out. And yet, our ways of thinking change tend to oscillate between that which is fixed, timeless, and unchanging, and that which is fluid, dynamic, and mobile. Why must we continue to turn between these two extremes? If the choice is that the isthmus is stable and persistent or, as Pettegrew asserts, contingent; if the choice is that this land endures as a fixed object or is subject to perpetual perishing and unceasing novelty, then neither option is sufficient when it comes to understanding change. Amidst pervasive and constant metamorphosis, how can any differences in objects appear? Against the eternal, how can changes be anything other than accidental? One cannot gain a sense of variable dynamism without that which persists and endures.

Let us go back along ten minutes of tarmac to the Hellenistic tumulary ground. In an open cereal field, located some 100 meters north of the road, archaeologists exhumed objects, which offered hints of the following sequence: an pit was cut into the ground then filled with ash, weapons, pins, and strigils, among other things, then covered by a circular tumulus; above and around the tumulus, a larger, oblong mound, fronted by polygonal masonry, emerged; around this second mound a three-sided enclosure of ashlar, again oriented towards the road, was added; centuries later, into what had become a tangled heap of earth, fallen stone, and buried foundations, a cist was cut and lined with tile to receive the corpse of an older woman; later, again, this site was robbed of stone blocks and left to persist as a low mound, shaped by roots, plow, and wind.[51] In thinking with Ingold we may consider this mound as a bundle of lines "that flow, mix and mutate, sometimes congealing into more or less ephemeral forms that can nevertheless dissolve or re-form without breach of continuity."[52] Yet, in so doing we fail to recognize two important points: that at every turn objects change because they exist rather than exist because they change; and that these changes were more sporadic than gradual.[53] Indeed, the isthmus as a whole testifies to such

---

50 Let us note in passing how such polychronic juxtapositions suggest a time which is less linear and more topological, like a folded and tattered fabric; see Segment 2.

51 On the date of West Foundation and its imagined relation to history, see Jackson (2015); on the Roman inhumation, see Rife (2012, 88–91).

52 2011, 86.

53 Harman (2016a, 7, 44–46), Witmore (2020).

saltational changes: the construction of roads across the *diolkos*, the ancient lacer-
ation from Nero's failure, the modern canal, the walls across the isthmus, this
road to Corinth.[54] In each case, objects have fused with this land to retroactively
define it, and yet the land nonetheless provides the enduring backdrop against
which these mergers stand out. Here, we begin to struggle for the meaning of
chôra, a word to which we will return.

Farther along Eleftherios Venizelos, just beyond a jog to the south, the road
crosses the path of an earlier trans-isthmus wall,[55] and soon comes to a crossroads.
Ancient in its form, here the road to ancient Corinth meets the road between Kenchreai, the eastern port of ancient Corinth, and the coastal area of Lechaion, the
northern port.[56] Around this intersection, a town called "Kromna" by James Wiseman persisted from the Archaic into the early-Hellenistic.[57] Beyond this crossroads,
Eleftherios Venizelos assumes its path along the base of a low ridge. Into this ridge,
which stretches for over a kilometer to the left of the road, ancient stonecutters
opened numerous quarries. Within the two largest, the faces recede to the north
and south to form a large open hollow. Archaeologists regard the stone faces as the
last line of extraction for building stone, sources for blocks hauled to Delphi and
Epidaurus,[58] Isthmia and Corinth.[59] Held in the cuts are the memories of past
quarry practices, of marks made by those who toiled here, as if these, important
though they are, were the only story to be pulled from the stone. Along these lines,
memories of human labor meet memories of the terrestrial. The former, the concern of archaeologists; the latter, the concern of geologists.

The stones of the Peloponnese do not recount a time without living things.
Here, this ridge arose as a compilation of tectonics and sea, sand and aquatic life;
this far exceeds human history. Below the surface of primeval seas, an unrelenting
submarine shower of dead microorganisms deposited millions of tons of calcium
carbonate as shells and skeletons onto a sea floor of silts and sands. Generation
after generation of corpses by the trillions rained to rest upon earlier graves.[60]
This underworld, comprised largely of the buried dead, pressed upwards through

---

54 For Ingold, this road can only be "disclosed processionally," unfolding as a series of turns, vistas,
    crossroads, and stops (2011, 146). Such a proposition fails to account for how the road offers
    more than a trajectory for my movement; as an object, the road exceeds my engagement with it.
55 Here much of the fabric of the wall has been rubbed out. A kilometer or more to the north, the
    line of the wall disappears; see Wiseman (1963); also Pettegrew (2016, 70–74).
56 On these crossroads, see Pettegrew (2006, 248–327; 2016, 71–74, 85–86); also see Caraher
    et al. (2006, 14–21), Wiseman (1978, 66); also Tartaron et al. (2006, 495, Figure 16).
57 Wiseman (1978, 66); also see Caraher et al. (2006, 14–21), Pettegrew (2016, 83).
58 Wiseman (1978, 68).
59 See Hayward (2003).
60 Among the fossils of marine organisms are *Strombus bubonius* found at New Corinth and *Patella
    safiana* found at Ancient Corinth. Their presence provides clocks for geologists to construct the
    terrestrial past; Keraudren and Sorel (1987, 103).

Hexamila quarries with Acrocorinth in the background.

the subduction of the African plate. Two hundred, perhaps two hundred and fifty, thousand years ago this was open sea and a wide channel linked the Saronic Gulf with the Gulf of Corinth. Broken terraces continued to creep skyward between faults. Here, a dune formed and sands mixed grain by grain with calcium carbonates. Oolite formed over the slow stretch of the Middle Pleistocene. Through uplift these edges were raised and further shaped by receding shores as marine terraces.[61] A sea-dividing isthmus formed slowly and sporadically over ten thousand human generations.[62] Dry land only exists here because of marine life, and what becomes of it; this forgotten underworld exposed along faults and quarry faces in marine terraces dominates the reality of this isthmus, and the whole of the Peloponnese, from below.[63]

Over this chthonic domain, the road weaves a path through Hexamilia, a village of some one hundred and fifty to two hundred houses, most of which are concrete, some of which are stone, partially recycled from ancient monuments quarried from the primordial tombs of aquatic dead, and whitewashed. Somewhere, near here, the American Philhellene, Samuel Gridley Howe established Washingtonia, a short-lived refugee colony in the wake of the Greek War of Independence.[64] Beyond Hexamilia, the road again passes through agrarian fields mixed with ruined funerary monuments, and crosses the old train line, which passes round the Peloponnese.[65] Beyond, the road terminates at the old national road to Argos (EO-7). Here a series of lines, the EO-7, the A7 motorway (Moréas),[66] the road to Lechaeon,

---

61 Keraudren and Sorel (1987), Collier (1990).
62 Standard introductions to the geology of the region often ignore the role of microorganisms; see, for example, Bintliff (2012, 11–20).
63 Here, as Paul Westbroek (1991) has argued, life actively intervenes in geological transformation in death.
64 Gregory (2007, 180), Sanders (2014, 111).
65 See Segment 8.
66 See Segment 4.

interrupt the old road from Hexamilia, which turns across the stream, the Leuka, as a dirt track to eventually return to pavement, cross the road to Lechaeon, and meet a break in the city walls of ancient Corinth. It is here, by the so-called Kenchrean Gate, that Pausanias placed the tomb of Diogenes.[67]

In life, the Cynic philosopher walked the line of the ancient road. At least twice a year he crossed the *diolkos* with its paved roadway. Diogenes passed by the sanctuary of Poseidon and, perhaps, even gazed upon the great tumulus, bearing witness to its moments of metamorphosis. Through the crossroads of so-called Kromna, he ambled over the chthonic realm of the dead and through the city walls of Corinth. Like a Persian king, it is said that he moved with the seasons, between his winter domain in Athens and summer abode, here in the Cranium of Corinth.[68] With but a cloak, Diogenes chose to live destitute, like a dog in the open air of the gymnasium, located somewhere near this gate. Unburdened by estate or social status, he relinquished the yoke of obligation and struggle. Living without property, hearth, or marriage, without money, stores, or utensils, Diogenes abandoned what others held to be necessary conditions for living in a polis. What fourth-century lovers of truth called *theoria*—the detached philosophical contemplation of a spectacle, often outside the polis—the dog philosopher lived from within and below.[69] In living without things, their being becomes all the more manifest; this perspective born of lack, out of love for wisdom, fuels his legendary acumen in the moment.[70]

Contemplate Diogenes' example and one may observe the blind hubris of the canal as a constructed artifact, the vainglory that follows the monstrous manipulation of geology. Do not neglect that which is low and one may contemplate microorganisms and their skeletal vestiges, which have played a far greater role than collective humanity in shaping this isthmus. Eschew the comforts of historical convention, and one may find new wonder with what becomes of the past. Find courage to take the risk of working towards the lesson of true humility in the face of things, and one may come to ground, and follow a different path. Seek out an engagement with the objects that comprise these lands without cloaking them with abstractions. Struggle for a line with and through things at ground level.

From the gate, the road forks right to pass a fenced hollow containing the exposed foundations of a large, early-Christian basilica. What had been seen as a long and low swelling, too lengthy, too wide, to be anything other than an accident of the terrain held what was dubbed the Kraneion Basilica.[71] A meter

---

67 2.2.4; also see Fowler (1932, 77–78), Wiseman (1978, 85–86).
68 Dio Chrysostom 6.1–6.
69 On philosophical *theoria*, see Nightingale (2004).
70 Also see, Serres (1989, 64–97).
71 Carpenter (1929, 346).

below a field of wheat and vetch lay the foundations of a nave, 50 meters long, 10 meters wide, framed by two aisles, fronted with narthex, backed by a large apse, and an attached triconch above a hypogeum.[72] The ruins of the basilica, as the Cynic philosopher's gymnasium, were claimed by the earth, which continued to shelter the buried dead.[73] Yet, here the earth, which has also claimed Sisyphus's town, may be held as the proper originator of burial.

From the exposed ruins of the basilica, it is but a short distance into Ancient Corinth and its *plateia* (square), which caps a wonderous chthonic underworld.

---

[72] Excavations conducted by the Greek Archaeological Service unearthed what had been left covered by earlier excavations (Pallas 1970).

[73] The ruins of the basilica, which as a cemetery church were riddled with subsequent burials. Rhys Carpenter reported that nearly sixty tombs were exhumed in the course of the initial excavations (1929, 357).

Bibliography

Arnaud, P. 2005. *Les routes de la navigation antique: Itinéraires en Méditerranée*. Paris: Editions Errance.

Beaulieu, M. 2016. *The sea in the Greek imagination*. Philadelphia, PA: University of Pennsylvania Press.

Beresford, J. 2013. *The ancient sailing season*. Leiden: Brill.

Bintliff, J.L. 2012. *The complete archaeology of Greece: From hunter-gatherers to the 20th century AD*. Chichester: Wiley-Blackwell.

Broneer, O. 1962. Excavations at Isthmia 1959–1961. *Hesperia* 31(1), 1–25.

Burkert, W. 1983. *Homo Necans: The anthropology of ancient Greek sacrificial ritual and myth*. Berkeley, CA: University of California Press.

Caraher, W., D. Nakassis, and D.K. Pettegrew. 2006. Siteless survey and intensive data collection in an artifact-rich environment: Case studies from the Eastern Corinthia, Greece. *Journal of Mediterranean Archaeology* 19(1), 7–43.

Carpenter, R. 1929. Researches in the topography of ancient Corinth. *American Journal of Archaeology* 33(3), 345–60.

Collier, R.E.L. 1990. Eustatic and tectonic controls upon quaternary coastal sedimentation in the Corinth Basin, Greece. *Journal of the Geological Society, London* 147, 301–14.

Davis, J.L. (ed.). 2008. *Sandy Pylos: An archaeological history from Nestor to Navarino*. 2nd ed. Princeton, NJ: American School of Classical Studies at Athens.

Fowler, H.N. 1932. Corinth and the Corinthia. In H.N. Fowler and R. Stillwell (eds.), *Corinth I.i: Introduction, topography, architecture*. Cambridge, MA: Harvard University Press.

Frey, J.M. 2016. *"Spolia" in fortifications and the role of the common builder in late antiquity*. Leiden: Brill.

Gebhard, E.R. 1993. The Isthmian games and the sanctuary of Poseidon in the early empire. In T.E. Gregory (ed.), *The Corinthia in the Roman period*. Ann Arbor, MI: University of Michigan. 78–94.

Gebhard, E.R. 2005. Rites for Melikertes-Palaimon in the early Roman Corinthia. In D.N. Schowalter and S.J. Friesen (eds.), *Urban religion in Roman Corinth: Interdisciplinary approaches*. Cambridge, MA: Harvard University Press. 165–203.

Gregory, T.E. 1993. *Isthmia: Volume V. The Hexamilion and the Fortress*. Princeton, NJ: American School of Classical Studies at Athens.

Gregory, T.E. 2007. Contrasting impressions of land use in early Modern Greece: The Eastern Corinthia and Kythera. In S. Davies and J.L. Davis (eds.), *Between Venice and Istanbul: Colonial landscapes in early modern Greece*. Princeton, NJ: American School of Classical Studies at Athens. 173–98.

Harman, G. 2013. *Bells and whistles: More speculative realism*. Washington, DC: Zero Books.

Harman, G. 2016a. *Immaterialism: Objects and social theory*. Cambridge: Polity Press.

Hayward, C. 2003. The geology of Corinth: The study of a basic resource. In C.K. Williams and N. Bookidis (eds.), *Corinth, the centenary: 1896–1996*. Princeton, NJ: American School of Classical Studies at Athens. 15–42.

Heidegger, M. 2003. Overcoming metaphysics. In J. Stambaugh (ed.), *The end of philosophy* (trans. J. Stambaugh). Chicago, IL: University of Chicago Press. 84–110.

Heikell, R. 2010. *West Aegean: The Attic Coast, Eastern Peloponnese and Western Cyclades*. 2nd ed. St Ives: Imray Laurie Norie & Wilson.

Ingold, T. 2007a. *Lines*. London: Routledge.

Ingold, T. 2011. *Being alive: Essays on movement, knowledge and description*. London: Routledge.

Jackson, A.H. 2015. Arms from the age of Philip and Alexander at Broneer's West Foundation near Isthmia. In E. Gebhard and T.E. Gregory (eds.), *Bridge of the untiring sea: The Corinthian isthmus from prehistory to Late Antiquity*. Princeton, NJ: American School of Classical Studies at Athens. 133–57.

Kardulias, P.N. 1995. Architecture, energy, and social evolution at Isthmia, Greece: Some thoughts about Late Antiquity in the Korinthia. *Journal of Mediterranean Archaeology* 8(2), 33–59.

Kardulias, P.N. 2005. *From classical to Byzantine: Social evolution in Late Antiquity and the Fortress at Isthmia, Greece*. Oxford: British Archaeological Reports.

Katzef, M.L. 1972. The Kyrenia ship. In G.F. Bass (ed.), *A history of seafaring*. London: Thames & Hudson. 50–2.

Keraudren, D., and D. Sorel. 1987. The terraces of Corinth (Greece): A detailed record of eustatic sea-level variations during the last 500,000 years. *Marine Geology* 77, 99–107.

Kilian-Dirlmeier, I. 1985. Fremde Weihungen in Griechischen Heiligtumern vom. 8. Bis zum Beginn des 7. Jahrhunderts v. Chr. *JRGZM* 32, 215–54.

Koutsoumba, D., and Y. Nakas. 2013. Díolkos. ena simantikó techniko ergo Tis archaiotitas. In K. Kissas and W.D. Niemeier (eds.), *The Corinthia and the Northeast Peloponnese: Topography and history from prehistoric times until the end of antiquity*. München: Hirmer. 191–206.

Leontsinis, G. 2010. The wreck of the *Mentor* on the coast of the island of Kythera and the operation to retrieve, salvage, and transport the Parthenon sculptures to London (1802–1805). In A.M. Tamis, C. Mackie, and S. Byrne (eds.), *Philathenaios: Studies in honour of Michael J Osborne, Greek Epigraphic Society*. Athens: Arts Books. 249–73.

Lindenlauf, A. 2003. The sea as a place of no return in ancient Greece. *World Archaeology* 35(3), 416–33.

Lohmann, H. 2013. Der Diolkos von Korinth–eine antike Schiffsschleppe? In K. Kissas and W.D. Niemeier (eds.), *The Corinthia and the Northeast Peloponnese: Topography and history from prehistoric times until the end of antiquity*. München: Hirmer. 207–30.

Morton, J. 2001. *The role of the physical environment in Ancient Greek seafaring*. Leiden: Brill.

Naval Intelligence Division. 1944. *Greece, Volume I: Physical geography, history, administration and peoples*. Norwich: Jarrold and Sons.

Nightingale, A.W. 2004. *Spectacles of truth in classical Greek philosophy: Theoria in its cultural context*. Cambridge: Cambridge University Press.

Olsen, B., and C. Witmore. 2015. Archaeology, symmetry and the ontology of things: A response to critics. *Archaeological Dialogues* 22(2), 187–97.

Pallas, D.I. 1970. Anaskafikí erevna eis tin Vasilikín tou Kraneiou en Koríntho. *Praktika*, 98–117.

Pettegrew, D.K. 2006. *Corinth on the Isthmus: Studies of the end of an ancient landscape*. Doctoral dissertation, Ohio State University.

Pettegrew, D.K. 2011. The Diolkos of Corinth. *American Journal of Archaeology* 115(4), 549–74.

Pettegrew, D.K. 2015. Corinthian suburbia: Patterns of Roman settlement on the Isthmus. In E. Gebhard and T.E. Gregory (eds.), *Bridge of the untiring sea: The Corinthian Isthmus from prehistory to Late Antiquity*. Princeton, NJ: American School of Classical Studies at Athens. 289–310.

Pettegrew, D.K. 2016. *The isthmus of Corinth: Crossroads of the Mediterranean world*. Ann Arbor, MI: University of Michigan Press.

Pomey, P., and A. Tchernia. 1978. Le Tonnage maximum des navires de commerce Romains. *Archaeonautica* 2, 233–51.

Rife, J.L. 2012. *Isthmia IX: The Roman and Byzantine graves and human remains*. Princeton, NJ: American School of Classical Studies at Athens.

Salmon, J.B. 1984. *Wealthy Corinth: A history of the city to 338 BC*. Oxford: Oxford University Press.

Sanders, G.D.R. 2005. Urban Corinth: An introduction. In D.N. Schowalter (ed.), *Urban religion in Roman Corinth: Interdisciplinary approaches*. Cambridge, MA: Harvard University Press. 11–24.

Sanders, G.D.R. 2014. Landlords and tenants: Sharecroppers and subsistence farming in Corinthian historical context. In S.J. Friesen, S.A. James, and D.N. Schowalter (eds.) *Corinth in contrast: Studies in inequality*. Leiden: Brill. 101–25.

Sanders, G.D.R., and I.K. Whitbread. 1990. Central places and major roads in the Peloponnese. *Annual of the British School at Athens* 85, 333–61.

Serres, M. 1989. *Detachment* (trans. G. James and R. Federman). Athens: Ohio University Press.

Shipley, G. 2011. *Pseudo-Skylax's Periplous: The circumnavigation of the inhabited world text, translation and commentary*. Exeter: Bristol Phoenix Press.

Sloterdijk, P. 2012a. The time of the crime of the Monstrous: On the philosophical justification of the artificial. In S. Elden (ed.), *Sloterdijk Now*. Cambridge: Polity Press. 165–81.

Sloterdijk, P. 2013. *In the world interior of capital: For a philosophical theory of globalization*. Cambridge: Polity Press.

Tartaron, T.F., T.E. Gregory, D.J. Pullen, J.S. Noller, R.M. Rothaus, J.L. Rife, L. Tzortzopoulou-Gregory, R. Schon, W.R. Caraher, D.K. Pettegrew, and D. Nakassis. 2006. The Eastern Korinthia Archaeological Survey: integrated methods for a dynamic landscape. *Hesperia* 75(4), 453–523.

Tsakos, K., E. Pipera-Marsellou, and D. Tsoukala-Kondidari. 2003. *Corinth Canal: Ancient Corinth, Lechaion, Kenchreai, Isthmia, Loutraki, Heraion: Historical and archaeological guide*. Athens: Hesperos.

Vallet, G., and F. Villard. 1964. *Megara Hyblaea 2: La céramique Archaïque*. Paris: Boccard.

Verdelis, N.M. 1958. Die Ausgrabung Des Diolkos Wahrend Der Jahre 1957–1959. *AM* 73, 140–45.

Verdelis, N.M. 1962. Anaskafí tou Díolkou. *Prakt*, 48–50.

Westbroek, P. 1991. *Life as a geological force: Dynamics of the earth*. New York, NY: W.W. Norton & Company.

Wiseman, J. 1963. A Trans-Isthmian fortification wall. *Hesperia* 32(3), 248–75.

Wiseman, J. 1978. *The land of the ancient Corinthians*. SIMA50. Göteborg: Åström.

Witmore, C. 2014a. Archaeology and the new materialisms. *Journal of Contemporary Archaeology* 1(2), 203–24.

Witmore, C. 2020. Objecthood. In L. Wilkie and J. Chenoweth (eds.), *A cultural history of objects: Modern period, 1900 to present*. London: Bloomsbury.

2

ANCIENT CORINTH

Descent into memory, ascent into oblivion

A plateia, eidolia, *the Glaukê and exclusion, what has become of a temple,*
a photograph, vestiges, historicism, the forum and duration, names to foundations,
Paul and the Bema, the Peirene, Sispyhus and his stone

August 11, 2007. I finish my coffee, place the black notebook into my rucksack,
and reach for my camera as we step from under the canopy and into the sunlit
plateia of Ancient Corinth.[1] Formed at the confluence of five streets, the tri-
angular square is anything but rational. The rectangular-stone pattern stamped
into its concrete surface cannot conceal its unruliness. Tables and chairs, awnings and umbrellas, spill out into public space, which is fringed by cafes and
tavernas. Shaded canopies lay claim to common ground and mask façades of
concrete and glass. To the south, there is an open gate for one-way foot traffic
exiting the archaeological site, which impinges upon the heart of the village.

---

1 My companions on this visit were Brad Sekedat and Zoe Zgouleta.

Beyond, the street transitions into a stairway that descends 4 meters into a massive excavated hollow to meet the Lechaion Road. Off to the right of the gate sits a *periptero*, a kiosk which sells sunglasses, postcards, cigarettes, ice cream, and drinks. Its proprietor hovers by a display rack containing plastic-wrapped guidebooks in a dozen different languages.

Despite its differences, the *plateia* of the village of Ancient Corinth seems to lay, more or less, in the same location as the Ottoman bazaar.[2] Even in the wake of the earthquake of 1858, which occasioned the construction of New Corinth on the coast to the northeast, the form of the bazaar has persisted.[3] With but slight deviations, the orientation of façades and roads hold an image of Turkish Corinth, although the Ottoman era surfaces lie beneath the cafes and *periptero*, the tables and chairs, the concrete pavement over which tourists pass. Common infrastructure persists here in ways individual buildings rarely do. The direction of streets, the delimitation of property boundaries, the demarcation of the fields, or the line of terraces beyond, this mingled ensemble exists as *eidolia* of buried roads, ruined structures, and erstwhile land systems, Ottoman and Roman among others.[4] *Eidolia*, images, forms on the surface suggest what is unseen deep below.[5]

As we walk west, towards the entrance to the archaeological site, we pass the old museum. From behind the fence sundry blocks of cut stone call my attention. Surplus objects lie about the courtyard of the old museum, now an *apothêkê*, a storehouse for the Archaeological Service and the American School of Classical Studies at Athens (ASCSA). Ahead, the street is flanked by shops on the right and the excavated area on the left. A precise delineation of present and what has become of the past, the iron fence surrounding the archaeological site would seem to give form to the barrier between what is and what was. Of course, this is not the case.

Ancient Corinth seems oblivious of the present. Everywhere age-old forms, emanating from objects hidden below, press upward. Everywhere, the wreckage of

---

2 Superimposed maps of from 1831–33 and 1963 suggest as much; see Kaplan (2001); also see Kaplan (2010).

3 Archaeology tends foremost to situate the object as material, which, as an open area of stamped concrete, would make for an oversimplification of this *plateia* (Meskell 2005, Ingold 2007b; also see Harman 2016b).

4 Beyond this area, rural lands were transformed under the weight of Roman Centuriation. Indeed, the form of the Flavian plan for the region gives form to field boundaries just east of the amphitheatre (Romano 2003, 293). On roads, field partitions, and crop marks bearing the form of Roman roads, see Doukellis (1994), Romano (2003, 2005), Walbank (2002); also Palinkas and Herbst (2011).

5 The study of such morphologies is what undergirds the subfield of *archéogéographie* (see Chouquer 2007, 2008; Watteaux 2017).

Street through Ancient Corinth.

the past, whether on the surface or freed from the soil, weighs discordantly upon the living. Everyone who dwells in the modern village takes direction from ancient forms or old things surrounded by fences. Everything here teeters on the edge of a gaping abyss, the product of archaeological excavations undertaken by the ASCSA since 1896; this chasm threatens to swallow the whole *plateia*, shaded awnings, stamped pavements, *periptero*, and all.

Few tourists are drawn to Ancient Corinth for the living village. Nonetheless, souvenir shops cater to vacationers, with postcards of stone temples and bronze satyrs with penises rendered in exaggerated proportion. Ceramic reproduction studios offer pots of every shape, of every era, with every conceivable decoration. Within the line of shops along the west road to the site entrance, shelves are laden with miniature bronzes, and gleaming white figurines of Classical gods and goddesses. The Aphrodite of Knidos and Cycladic figurines, bald philosophers and bearded emperors, Ionic columns and Geometric horses, casts of white marble dust and polyester resin occupy every available centimeter on the tables in between. Ancient Corinth is a community that survives off tourism by selling skeuomorphs.[6]

We pause to peer into the window of the last shop and eye through a recurrence of ancient forms—*anamorphoses*. The Archaic temple can be seen as a reflection in the glass. Backed by the wave-washed slopes of Acrocorinth, seven columns tower above what remains of the extractive endeavors of archaeologists.[7] Along here, just beyond the fence, lies what they refer to as the north market.[8] A series of open-fronted

6 Copies of objects made from another material.
7 *Períklyston*, wave-washed or "washed on all sides by the sea" as with an island, is a term used by Euripides (Fr. 1084 (Nauck)) to describe Acrocorinth as emphasized by Strabo (8.6.21), who means it in a different sense: as washed in the depths of the mountain by subterranean waters.
8 Forming a market square, the northern half lies buried below the road (Scranton 1951, 180–88, De Waele 1930).

stalls, each flanked by two projecting partitions and backed by a common wall of cut stone, mirror the repetition of tourist shops across the street.

We continue on by the shaded park and across a Tarmac pavement lined with makeshift market stalls and tour buses. In absolute contrast to its surroundings the parking lot rises above hollows formed to expose the Greek theatre and the Roman Odeon. To the south of the parking lot a metal gate and a ticket booth marks the entrance to Ancient Corinth. Beyond, a gravel path, shaded under pine and framed by low shrubs, leads to the museum, which sits within the line of a precinct surrounding the remains of a temple to a god, or gods, yet to be (re)named.[9]

—

June 22, 2014. I turn off the gravel path and pause on a platform before a sign. Ahead, a perforated cube of bedrock known as the Glaukê fountain emerges behind the serrated profiles of quarried walls from the depths of an eroded cavity. Into this erstwhile fountain, the young wife of Jason, the daughter of Creon, threw herself in an effort to wash away the burning poison of Medea, or so the Ancient Corinthians held when the Roman *periegete* Pausanias visited Corinth in the second century CE.[10] The story of the Glaukê may be read by anyone who stands here before the sign. Upon this elevated surface, a photograph shows a later season of excavation from 1908; illustrations present reconstructions of its Hellenistic façade; plans situate it within two phases, that of the Hellenistic and Roman. By means of this installation (the sign, the platform, and the position of the monument with respect to an observer), the object is framed as the Glaukê, and one is induced to sustain this interpretation.

I take the path around the massive block of native limestone to the east. From the area encompassing this quarried cube, archaeologists removed field plots, debris, soil, and stones; with local laborers they displaced ruined walls once built to incorporate the carved block of limestone into an erstwhile house, of which no component remains.[11] In the shadows of antiquity these subterranean recesses formerly called to those who regarded them as useful for animals, shade, or other purposes. Now two quarried reservoirs retain their full forms beneath an oppressively thick roof of bedrock; two other basins lie exposed, without covering. "The Fountain of Glaukê"—a small marble plaque set into north corner of the monument also bears this label. Where carved stone reservoirs have proved obstinate enough to persist amid diverse situations, they have confirmed themselves incapable of holding a name without the

---

9 Scholars nonetheless seek to put a name to the temple—see Walbank (1989); on the taxonomic impulse, see Segment 24.

10 On Pausanias, see Segments 17 and 22.

11 Elderkin (1910) mentions the former existence of the Glaukê as a house, a use which he regarded as a "degradation of the fountain to alien purposes."

The Glaukê fountain.

addition of the sign. Nowhere along this path do I see an old Turkish appellation for the monument, "Boudroumi" (prison).[12] Here, due to its exclusion, what had been just prior to 1899 is now more distant than what had been nearly seventeen centuries earlier when Pausanias passed by here.[13]

Respecting old walls and ancient forms, the paths ahead bend as if affected by the gravitational pull of the erstwhile temple, the high center of the excavated core of Ancient Corinth. Seven standing columns and a portion of architrave constitute what has become of the Archaic temple. I walk along a paved surface and once again pause on a platform before a sign. The narrative frames these remains as the "Temple of Apollo," as mentioned solely by Pausanias.[14] Constructed around 540 BCE, the temple originally had thirty-eight columns, six by fifteen in the peristyle, plus four more; two set *in antis* at either entrance. A photograph labeled "view of the temple from the southwest, 1909" dominates the sign.[15] An arrested moment

12 Richardson (1900, 458).
13 On the paradox of how one past is elevated and advances, while another, in this case the Ottoman, is neglected or destroyed, see Voutsaki (2003); also Hamilakis (2007).
14 On the identification of the temple, see Bookidis (2003, 248–50), Bookidis and Stroud (2004).
15 The year 1909 is a mistake. Portions of the architrave and columns were consolidated in 1906. Arrested in the course of construction by the 1858 earthquake, the roofless schoolhouse was removed in the same year (Stillwell 1932, 130, note 1, and 132).

The Archaic temple.

captured over a century ago (indeed, the date on the sign is incorrect: the photograph was actually taken in 1901) reveals slight differences to what now stands before the observer. Formerly broken in the photo, the western-most block of the southern architrave is here restored. Formerly worn and wrecked, the bases of the columns are now square and solid; where there were clefts and cavities, the stone surfaces are now sealed smooth. In the photograph, a roofless building stands at the eastern end of the temple. Little of the Capodistrian School remains.[16] While the photo assures me that the ruin was once here in the background to that which stands before me still, it reveals yet another object that was demolished in favor of this monument, one unencumbered by everything subsequent to its supposed time.[17] In its present appearance it stands purified.

The same photograph accompanies a series of images in an article I carry in my rucksack.[18] Its author, Benjamin Powell, a fellow of the ASCSA, marveled at the still-standing columns of the temple. Like many "Grecian temples in a more or less ruined condition," it has, as he put it, "survived the changes and

16 A portion of the foundations now forms a viewing platform on the eastern end of temple hill. On the Capodistrian School, see Robinson (1976, 238–39).
17 Cf. Barthes (1981, 115); also see Pétursdóttir and Olsen (2014), Shanks (1997).
18 Powell (1905).

chances of time unto our own day."[19] Powell gleaned something of these changes and chances from a cascade of descriptions and illustrations compiled by visitors who read and wrote books over the last three centuries. In 1751, James Stuart drew twelve standing columns, of which nine were set below a nearly unbroken stretch of architrave, partially incorporated into the boundary wall of an estate.[20] Around 1785, a drawing executed by an artist under the British ambassador showed that the single column, formerly enduring *in antis* before the *opisthodomos* (rear vestibule), had fallen or been removed.[21] By 1795, four more columns had disappeared along with the beams they once supported.[22] In 1801, Edward Dodwell portrayed the seven columns along with the remaining portion of the architrave as partially incorporated into the high enclosure walls of this house compound. By 1829, the house and its walls had been reduced to piles of rubble amid the base of the seven standing columns.[23] For Powell, such descriptions gave us a sense of a "temple" as an enduring witness to changes that occurred in its midst. By situating description after description, these mutations are linked in a causal sequence, which gives structure to a linear time. Granted form in Powell's narrative, this sequence culminates with the archaeological intervention itself.

From around the base of seven standing columns archaeologists cleared overgrowth, debris, and soil in 1886.[24] After having been called by many names, the naming of Apollo as the god once housed here occurred in 1897.[25] By situating the excavation of the area, along with the renaming of the temple, after the sequence of antiquarian accounts Powell reinforces an arbitrary separation between past and present.[26] The photograph caps his historiographical sequence by showing the "present condition (1901) of the west end of the temple." Powell, who died tragically a few days before he was to receive his PhD from Cornell in 1905, merely hints at the fact that he is one of the three figures standing upon the architrave.[27] One can only wonder, as I do now, which of the

---

19 Ibid. 44.
20 Three generations earlier Jacob Spon reported seeing twelve columns, his travelling companion, George Wheler, eleven, with another standing apart from these (Powell 1905, 48; Spon 1678, 296; Wheler 1682, 440). According to Spon the columns stood "*à la maison du Vayvode*" (at the house of the *voyvoda*), the Ottoman official appointed to collect taxes for the district (Spon 1678, 296).
21 Leake (1830 III, 246); also see Stillwell (1932, 130).
22 Leake states that a British traveler, Mr. Hawkins, found it in its present state. According to one account, they were blasted with gunpowder to make room and material for a large addition to the house complex of the governor (Clarke 1818, 552–53).
23 Blouet (1831–1838, Plate 80).
24 The initial excavations were conducted under W. Dörpfeld; see Richardson (1897, 455).
25 Ibid. 464.
26 Olivier (2011, 109).
27 Powell (1905).

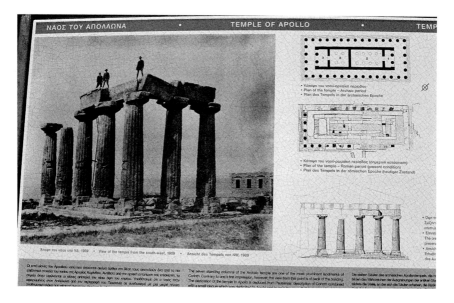

View of the temple from the southwest, 1901.

darkened silhouettes belonged to him. Phantoms all; having lost the power of speech, they look back at us from the air that we take to be the past, the thin air into which we too will dissolve.

Twenty years after Powell's death, what was once again returned to history as the "Temple of Apollo" was completely cleared down to foundation blocks and bedrock. According to the sign, "although most of this mid-sixth century B. C.E. building has been destroyed, the bedrock preserves cuttings made to receive the foundation blocks and thus allows a reconstruction of the temple's plan." Within the bedrock below the temple, the form of the overall building is held in cuttings, in vestiges of its original configuration. "Vestige": the cut, the mark, the trace revealed in the supporting bedrock provides an indication of the footprint of the Archaic temple.[28] As with the vestigial figures in the photograph, it suggests that which is not here.[29]

28 Architectural fragments provide hints of the earlier seventh-century temple that stood here (Rhodes 2003). With respect to the concept of "vestige," also see Lucas (2012, 33).

29 Indeed, it is said that the whole temple was originally coated in hard white stucco, for vestiges were found on protected portions of the capitals and covered portions of fallen shafts (Stillwell 1932, 122–23).

What lies behind the vestige? The ancients who labored to cut stone, to set blocks, and to plaster the surfaces of what stands here before the sign? The devout who revered the bronze statue of the god in the shade of his house of solemn stone? The archaeological predecessors whose labors aimed to bring about the return of the sun god's temple? Such questions situate what stands before me as an effect of such causes, which are themselves conceived as lived history. Yet, it is a particular form of historicism that situates a completed past, separated off from the present, as what stands behind what is here—seven consolidated columns adjacent to bedrock cuttings behind a cordon. Strictly speaking, it is the object that brings something of *its* past to the fore as vestiges, as material memories.[30]

Apollo: this name only was ascertained after roads, landmarks, and other objects of orientation were freed from their chthonic sojourn in 1896. The return of these things is what allowed archaeologists to connect what is here to what is mentioned in the description of Corinth by Pausanias.[31] Glaukê: this name followed only after what had become of the fountain had been cleared of overburden. That names were not held by stones left to themselves demonstrates how we have imposed here a past that is quite foreign to them. For the naming is about locating the object in history, and a very specific history at that, for what stands here is not labeled "quarry," "garden wall," or "estate partition in the house of the *voyvoda*."[32] That these columns, blocks, and cuttings have endured beyond the desires of those who were swept up by "change and chance" is sidelined by semantic substitutions and attempts to maintain them in what is held to have been their past.[33] What stands here is less a witness to a lost past than the very medium that makes pasts possible.

⌒

June 30, 2010. From the burdened columns, the concrete path follows the line of the Roman road downhill past remnants of structures at the west end of a giant open area, what has become of the forum, what was once the social and religious center of the Roman city. A third of the way down this path another sign calls out to us.[34] It presents an aerial photograph of the archaeological site

---

30 Olivier (2011, 6), Olsen (2010, 126–28).
31 Bookidis and Stroud (2004) have recently brought new evidence to bear upon this attribution.
32 These too form other past identities for the object standing before the sign; on the chronopolitics of such monuments, see Witmore (2013b); also see Segment 9.
33 The preserved monument may be thought of as a *synechoche*, as Graham Harman argues, a new compound object (Harman 2016a, 43).
34 This visit was in the company of my family, colleagues, and students.

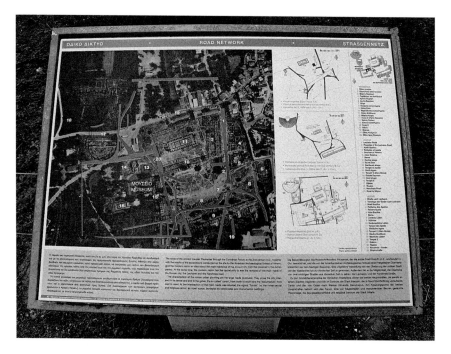

Road network sign.

with the road network of Ancient Corinth. Colored lines frame each network within periods bearing their own temporal specificity—Classical, Hellenistic, Roman. To the right, three smaller maps, ordered sequentially from top to bottom, illustrate the objects of each phase. Across these frames, the development of the urban center plays out.

For five generations, archaeologists have removed stone, soil, and debris from the areas around the temple hill.[35] Organizing walls and classifying artifacts, archaeologists sorted out what was retained from the accumulation. Into successive periods they placed objects, generating a chronicle that begins with the earliest traces of human presence down to the most recent, stopping just short of the supposed non-archaeological territory of the present. Gaps were filled to create an unbroken continuum and events gave cadence to a sequence of episodes. Here, those episodes appear to begin in the dark shadows of Prehistory with distributed habitations originating in the Neolithic, eight and a half millennia ago; they continue with the dispersed hearths of Helladic communities whose individual

35 Fowler (1932, 3).

46

names are long forgotten; these are followed by Early Iron Age successors who claimed this ground with their buried dead. After what is believed to have been a synoecism in the eighth century BCE, the familiar cadence of the Archaic, Classical, and Hellenistic ensues down through the Roman destruction of 146 BCE, which is trailed by the founding of a Roman Corinth in 44 BCE. Late Antiquity, Byzantine, Frankish, and Ottoman are bookended by devastation in the Greek War of Independence (1821–32) and the 1858 earthquake.[36] With their laminar and historically defined distances, these episodes are regarded as successive and enclosed as links within a chain of terminations and replacements.

In the forum below, a broad, open area encircled by a stone girdle of miscellaneous ruin, concrete and rubble foundations lie stripped of their revetments. Framed by architectures without their completions, large portions of the forum accommodate crowds of columns, bits of architrave, and stone blocks, many carved from the sandy limestone terrace upon which the Archaic temple rises. Set out in ordered rows and clusters, these sundry stones linger, as if waiting to be returned to what they suggest themselves to have been. To what era, the question must be asked, do they belong?

In the forum, another sign states that the remains at its west end belong to buildings that date to the first and second century CE. The question seeks temporal coordinates for the object and this answer leaves them there. This answer suggests these things are only knowable in historical terms; that their true identity belongs to an arbitrary sliver cut from the continuum of history. Once again, by virtue of what it neglects, the sign implies that what lies here is derivative of a particular moment; that it owes its existence solely to the efforts of those who lived at that time. Thus sealed within its own time capsule, it appears to be strung with others along a line like beads of a rosary.[37] Each bead impacts the subsequent one by virtue of its position. Looking back from the vantage point of the present, reverberations will pass from one to the next. Every now and then vibrations travel farther. Rarer still, a tremor will radiate all the way down the string to its end; the present. Over the course of history, then, the close proximity of eras in their line of succession is what allows the events they contain to act upon each other. Yet how can

---

36 This narrative structure provides the entry point for nearly every publication generated by the American Excavations, including the new edition of the *Ancient Corinth Site Guide* that will be published seven years after this visit (Sanders et al. 2017). Still, an artefact of practice, the Corinth Volumes preserve the non-linear, non-sequential engagement with the polychronic memories of Corinth in their dates of publication, despite striving to fill in the narrative sequence of history.

37 A connection to Walter Benjamin's metaphor for historicism (Benjamin, Eiland and Jennings 2006, 397).

proximities and separations along a simple line account for the proximities and separations of the legion things which lie before us, which support and direct everyone who passes here?

I look back at the sign. Not far from where we stand, the forms of past road networks, overlap and, by virtue of their persistence, intermingle under this concrete path, which itself merges with the Hellenistic and Roman road to Sicyon. To the north, three young students stand upon a marine terrace before Doric columns set against a blue sky. To the east, a large tour group trails behind a guide as they cross the forum hollow towards the Lechaion Road and the Peirene fountain. For how long have these things endured?

Surely the question of duration is more fundamental to the objects that are here.[38] The hill and hollow, shaped by callous waves and dancing torrents, are more than two hundred thousand years in the making.[39] The springs, located at the outlet of this low valley, have gushed forth along the line between impervious marls and porous stone for tens of millennia. The forum, paved in slabs of Jurassic limestone more than one hundred and fifty million years older than what lies below, derives its form, orientation, and dimensions from erstwhile stoas and structures approximately 2,300 years in their extension.[40] Here objects linger. With what do they come into contact? Surely this specifies a different species of contiguity than what is suggested by a string of beads. Roman touches Classical. Ottoman rises upon the Archaic. Archaic soars high upon the Pleistocene.[41] Out of this mixed, polychronic ensemble arises another time.[42]

⸻

July 24, 2018. The concrete path terminates in a gravel surface framed by cicada-enlivened pines. I veer into the open forum. Thirsty areas of dry grass curb a dirt and gravel path worn down by throngs of visitors. To the left lies the west terrace. Upon it sits a collection of foundations and stone walls, including a square core of concrete and broken rubble and assorted blocks of shattered marble returned to the light in the early half of the twentieth century. Reposed

38 Olivier (2008), Olsen (2010).
39 Hayward (2003, 2004).
40 For more on what lies below the forum and the surrounding monuments, see: Lavezzi (1978), Williams (1978, 1981); more recently, see: James (2019); also Sanders et al. (2017, 51–103).
41 Here, we should take caution not to homogenize and, as Shanks and Tilley (1992, 53–4) argued, politicize time in terms of periodicity (also see Witmore 2019c). Again, objects exceed any sense of periodicity.
42 Serres and Latour (1995, 57–62), Witmore (2006, 2015b).

in silent obstinacy, the form of these objects suggests a past as temples. Having fallen to obscurity, scholars have not failed in their attempts to recall their names.[43] For within the envelope of the forum Pausanias placed a temple of Tyche, a shrine to the Pantheon, a fountain to Poseidon, and statues to Apollo, Aphrodite, and Hermes, with their illustrious houses, and other god-pleasing statues placed in the open air.[44] A curved block from an architrave bears the name *Cnaeus Babbius Philinus*, municipal officer (*aedile*), high priest (*pontifex*).[45] Thus inscribed, the stone speaks of the benefactor who commissioned the circular building that once stood upon the square core. Adjacent to this monument, a concrete podium rises upon the remains of basins, an indication that an erstwhile fountain thrusts up from below. Only one such structure was mentioned by the traveler. Did this temple retain Neptune's name? How can one be certain? This ruined house, and the remainder, are simply labeled by letter—F, G, H, J, D, K—their designations having yet to rise beyond suppositions.

I walk over lines of smooth paving stones and hardened earth and eventually take a seat on a slab of marble in the shade of a chinaberry tree. Dozens of tourists are gathered around the Roman Rostra, what according to the archaeologist Oscar Broneer may have been the Bema mentioned in the Book of Acts.[46] It was to the Bema that the Apostle Paul was led by his accusers, the elders of the Synagogue, to be judged by Gallio, the proconsul. I hear Paul's words: "For the perishable must clothe itself with the imperishable, and the mortal with immortality."[47] Someone reads from the First Letter to the Corinthians. They follow in the footsteps of Paul. Did Paul stand upon this spot? The crowd speaks of the man, the *reus*, the accused who is led because of the case, the *res*, the same term as the thing, the foundation upon which rises our term, *reality*.[48] What of the stone itself? The Bema, the step from which to speak, is held to be the Corinthian version of the Rostrum, the platform from which to speak. A concrete core, faced with well-cut blocks of limestone, 15 meters in length, over 2 meters in height. The crowd stands before this monument, where Broneer suggests Paul once stood. At its center, upon stones silent to history, a small marble plaque upholds the name, Bema. Again, how tenuous it is to return names to mute stones? And, how powerful?

What is presented as a past pealed back from obscurity appropriates the *res* over to the *logos*, which casts the thing itself into obscurity. Once again, this act nullifies the stone that makes that past possible; the stone which continues to bear that

---

43 See Scranton (1951), Williams (1989).
44 2.2.8; also see Hutton (2005, 149–55).
45 Scranton (1951, 17–32).
46 Broneer (1937).
47 1 Corinthians 15:53.
48 This association is made by Michel Serres (1987, 307; English translation 2015b, 176).

which rises in its midst. Upon the remains of water basins issues a concrete podium to a temple that some take to honor the same god.[49] Upon the premises of these earlier temples, an ancient monastery was erected.[50] Upon the square core of concrete which lost its name as the Babbius monument rose the narthex of the Church of St John.[51] Upon the Bema, another church found stability and orientation. Below its floor, its walls and core provide a hard edifice for recept-acles for the dead.[52] Here the sign suggests that the location of this church likely owed itself to the association of the Bema with Paul.[53] Again, the name, soft, is elevated above the stone edifice, hard. Yet, the interpretation appropri-ates the stubborn propensities of stones, which offer themselves to subsequent constructions, over to an association, one that rests upon comparatively flimsy foundations. How would the crowd react if they knew Broneer was wrong? If we are to be faithful to history, then would such a judgement have been passed at the center of the open forum? Would not a basilica have been the most likely venue for a bema, an assembly, and the tribunal?[54] The remains of three basil-icas, likely venues for law courts, flank this forum; one to the north, another at the east end, and one to the south.[55]

What upholds the Bema as the site of Paul's judgement? Signs and an inscription. Nearby, 2 Corinthians 4.14 is chiseled in stone. The text inter-venes to benefit one meaningful past above so many others. To what end? One hundred and fifty thousand visitors come to Corinth each year. Most, no doubt, to trace the footsteps of Paul; to stand where he, as we must suppose, stood. When it comes to large crowds, there is no more accommo-dating space than an open forum.

June 22, 2014. We walk across a square pavement of limestone in the direc-tion of the Peirene fountain.[56] Without acknowledging other ruins at this end of the forum, we soon reach poros blocks freed from the weight of their

---

49 Scranton (1951, 32–39).
50 Ibid. 73.
51 Ibid. 17.
52 Morgan (1936, 473).
53 Also see Scranton (1951, 132).
54 This suggestion was first voiced by Guy Sanders (2015a).
55 The basilica to the north is known as the Lechaion Road Basilica (Stillwell 1932, 193–211). The one to the east is known as the Julian Basilica (Scotton 1997). The last is the South Basilica and latest to be constructed, perhaps during, or just after, Paul's trial (Weinberg 1960, 58–77).
56 On this pavement, see Scranton (1951, 111). During the latter half of this journey I was joined by Brandon Baker and Evan Levine.

fallen burdens. Cordons guide us along a gravel path between decapitated pylons, the unhampered supports for massive arch that marked the transition to the Lechaion Road.[57] We step right onto an elevated platform and lean against the balustrade before a rabble of walls. From below, a cavity beckons to us. Three semi-circular niches frame a rectilinear basin at the head of a façade containing six arched chambers. The Pierene fountain marks the source around which the city spread out. For tens of millennia, this spring drew humans and other animals here. For eight and a half millennia it provided water for those who dwelt in its vicinity. Savored by all who ventured to this source, it continued to supply waters to the modern village until upstream wells lowered the water table and surface pollution insured no one could safely consume its primordial gift.

What now opens here within a ruined triconch court emerged from chthonic darkness as an object of archaeology, the logos that works its way towards the old, the ancient. Guided by stubborn stone experienced from the angle of what was lost to history, archaeologists made choices as to what should remain and what should go.[58] Here a saturated underworld laid buried below sporadic accumulation, beneath the walled garden of Giorgios Tsellios.[59] Here conduits tapped ancient channels cut deep into the porous rock to deliver waters to numerous wells, three fountains, and the fields beyond.[60] Here ancient stones unrelentingly upheld chambers in subterranean obscurity iteratively experienced solely by those who built wells and maintained conduits underground. In order to exhume this subsurface world, gardens and beanfields, enclosure walls and wells were dislodged. Overburden was removed. Byzantine graves were exhumed. From against the ancient façade, a Byzantine chapel was dismantled.[61] It was not simply the case that some pasts advanced at the expense of others, for the reality of the mixed, polychronic ensemble with its intermingled durations was effaced in favor of a sequentially phased monument. Peering into this underworld while pushing back considerations of the Peirene as yet another witness to a past world now forever gone conjures thoughts of myth.

Sisyphus, the first king of Corinth, known in his time as Ephyra, rolls his stone uphill, only to repeat this act once the stone plunges to rest at the base of

---

57 Edwards (1994).
58 That these early excavations, subsumed as they were to historical expectations, destroyed what had become of the past is well attested (see Robinson, B.A. 2011, 74–80).
59 Ibid. 68.
60 Two of these fountains were located in the *plateia* (ibid., 68–70).
61 Ibid., 77.

The Lechaion Road.

the slope.[62] This myth suggests an eternal return, which plays out here between death and life, stone and *logos*, archaeology and history, memory and oblivion. No, the descent is not into darkness. To the contrary, the journey down is to memory. Left to itself the stone announces its being in the flash of its fall. Sisyphus faces the object. Here, alien things struck those who descended into wells and later exhumed them from the soil with surprise and wonderment;[63] and we may empathize, for in that instant when we stand vulnerable before that which refuses to bow to our preconceptions, archaeologists also face the object, if only for the briefest of moments. From this hollow the ascent, insofar as the object is concerned, is into oblivion. Just as Sisyphus forgets his stone through a habitual engagement with *his* burden, that which is framed as *of a detached past* can no longer elude definition. The material past rises in explication, and through substitution and habituation, the object itself passes in obscurity under the shadow of what it is supposed to have been.

We walk down stairs and pass over the ancient limestone slabs of the Roman road that once led to the port of Lechaion. Returned to "the drudgery of being useful," this road, a portion of the erstwhile *cardo maximus* of the Roman city, has never ceased to exist.[64] Once laid, this road condensed and hardened to be directed ahead of itself into futures unwritten.[65] For a thousand years these stones offered support to unforeseen pedestrians and unexpected orientations. And, just as now a former Classical roadway presses upwards from below, this Roman pavement also withdrew under the weight of episodic accumulation, only for something of it to cling on in form and orientation as

---

62 Here I am building upon an argument made by Michel Serres in *Statues* that situates the eternal return in terms of swings between *logos* and the thing itself (1987, 301–11; English translation 2015b, 172–78).
63 See Robinson, B.A. (2011, 68).
64 Benjamin and Jennings (2002, 39); also see Olsen (2010, 119–21).
65 Bergson (1998, 4).

a more restricted avenue lined by Medieval buildings. It is said that the road to the coast was not fully abandoned until 1858. And yet, for all "the whirlwind's wrath and the earthquake's shock" this roadway has, in its stubborn permanence, endured in itself. As an artery to the *plateia* it now upholds the unlikely foot traffic of a half-a-dozen vacationers, including a sunscreen-coated family whom in idle curiosity we overtake.[66] In exhuming these stones from Lethe, we could scarcely imagine a more definitive break with the past. And yet the story of Sisyphus and his stone cautions all to beware of how transcendence is but a myth.[67] This hollow speaks to the perpetual return. A gapless cycle that turns in marine terraces shaped by discontinuous uplift and submergence; in quarries carved into blocks for an Archaic city, which twist under foundations of buildings burned and broken; in a Roman forum raised on the inextricably tangled ground of Classical, Helladic, and even Neolithic detritus; and in archaeological monuments suggestive of a persistent past.

We reach the end of the pavement, ascend stairs to the *plateia* and, encumbered with our own burdens, continue to pass over present ground.

---

66 Byron's words, from *The Siege of Corinth*, 1.5.
67 Latour (1993, 67–76).

Bibliography

Barthes, R. 1981. *Camera lucida: Reflections on photography* (trans. R. Howard). New York, NY: Hill and Wang.

Benjamin, W., H. Eiland, and M.W. Jennings. 2006. *Selected writings, Volume 4: 1938–1940.* Cambridge, MA: Belknap Press.

Benjamin, W., and M.W. Jennings. 2002. *Selected writings, Volume 3: 1935–1938.* Cambridge, MA: Belknap Press.

Bergson, H. 1859. *Extraits de Lucrèce, avec un commentaire, des notes et une étude sur la poésie, la philosophie, la physique, le texte et la langue de Lucrèce.* Paris: C. Delagrave.

Blouet, G.A. 1831–38. *Expédition scientifique de Morée, Ordonnée par le Gouvernement français: Architecture, Sculptures, Inscriptions et Vues du Péloponèse, des Cyclades et de l'Attique, mesurées, dessinées, recueillies et publiées par Abel Blouet.* Vols. I–VI. Paris: Firmin Didot.

Bookidis, N., and R.S. Stroud. 2004. Apollo and the Archaic temple at Corinth. *Hesperia* 73(3), 401–26.

Bookidis, N. 2003. The sanctuaries of Corinth. In C.K. Williams and N. Bookidis (eds.), *Corinth, the Centenary: 1896–1996.* Princeton, NJ: American School of Classical Studies at Athens. 247–59.

Broneer, O. 1937. Studies in the topography of Corinth in the time of St Paul. *Archaiologikí efimerís* 76, 125–33.

Chouquer, G. 2007. Les centuriations: topographie et morphologie, reconstitution et mémoire des formes. *Archeologia Aerea. Studi di aerotopografia archeologia* II, 65–82.

Chouquer, G. 2008. *Traité d'archéogéographie: La crise des récits géohistoriques.* Paris: Errance.

Clarke, E.D. 1818. *Travels in various countries of Europe, Asia and Africa Section 2,* Vol. 6. London: T. Cadell and W. Davies.

De Waele, F.D. 1930. The Roman market north of the temple at Corinth. *American Journal of Archaeology* 34(4), 432–54.

Doukellis, P.N. 1994. Le territoire de la colonie romaine de Corinthe. In P.N. Doukellis and L.G. Mendoni (eds.), *Structures rurales et sociétés antiques: actes du colloque de Corfou, 14–16 mai 1992.* Paris: Les belles lettres. 359–90.

Edwards, C.M. 1994. The arch over the Lechaion Road at Corinth and its sculpture. *Hesperia* 63(3), 263–308.

Elderkin, G.W. 1910. The fountain of Glauce at Corinth. *American Journal of Archaeology* 14(1), 19–50.

Fowler, H.N. 1932. Corinth and the Corinthia. In H.N. Fowler and R. Stillwell (eds.), *Corinth I. i: Introduction, topography, Architecture.* Cambridge, MA: Harvard University Press. 18–114.

Hamilakis, Y. 2007. *The nation and its ruins: Antiquity, archaeology, and national imagination in Greece.* Oxford: Oxford University Press.

Harman, G. 2016a. *Immaterialism: Objects and social theory.* Cambridge: Polity Press.

Harman, G. 2016b. On behalf of form. In M. Bille and T.F. Sørensen (eds.). *Elements of architecture: Assembling archaeology, atmosphere and the performance of building spaces.* New York, NY: Routledge. 30–46.

Hayward, C. 2003. The geology of Corinth: The study of a basic resource. In C.K. Williams and N. Bookidis (eds.), *Corinth, the centenary: 1896–1996.* Princeton, NJ: American School of Classical Studies at Athens. 15–42.

Hayward, C. 2004. A reconstruction of the pre-8th century BC palaeotopography of central Corinth, Greece. *Geoarchaeology* 19(5), 383–405.

Hutton, W. 2005. *Describing Greece: Landscape and literature in the Periegesis of Pausanias.* Cambridge: Cambridge University Press.

Ingold, T. 2007b. Materials against materiality. *Archaeological Dialogues* 14(1), 1–16.

James, S. 2019. The South Stoa at Corinth: New evidence and interpretations. *Hesperia* 88(1), 155–214.

Kaplan, L.G. 2001. Modern Corinth, 1676–1923. Corinth Computer Project. Available at: http://corinth.sas.upenn.edu/moderncorinth.html.

Kaplan, L.G. 2010. "Writing down the country": Travelers and the emergence of the archaeological gaze. In A. Stroulia and S.B. Sutton (eds.), *Archaeology in situ: Sites, archaeology, and communities in Greece.* Lanham, MD: Lexington Books. 75–108.

Latour, B. 1993. *We have never been modern* (trans. C. Porter). Cambridge, MA: Harvard University Press.

Lavezzi, J.C. 1978. Prehistoric investigations at Corinth. *Hesperia* 47(4), 402–51.

Leake, W.M. 1830. *Travels in the Morea.* 3 vols. London: John Murray.

Lucas, G. 2012. *Understanding the archaeological record.* Cambridge: Cambridge University Press.

Meskell, L. (ed.). 2005. *Archaeologies of materiality.* Oxford: Blackwell.

Morgan, D.H. 1936. Excavations at Corinth, 1935–1936. *AJA* 40(6), 466–84.

Olivier, L. 2008. *Le Sombre abîme du temps: Mémoire et archéologie.* Seuil: Paris.

Olivier, L. 2011. *The dark abyss of time: Archaeology and memory* (trans. A. Greenspan). Lanham, MD: AltaMira Press.

Olsen, B. 2010. *In defense of things: Archaeology and the ontology of objects.* Lanham, MD: AltaMira Press.

Palinkas, J., and J.A. Herbst. 2011. A Roman road southeast of the forum at Corinth: Technology and urban development. *Hesperia* 80(2), 287–336.

Pétursdóttir, Þ., and B. Olsen, 2014. Imaging modern decay: The aesthetics of ruin photography. *Journal of Contemporary Archaeology* 1(1), 7–56.

Powell, B. 1905. The Temple of Apollo at Corinth. *American Journal of Archaeology* 9(1), 44–63.

Rhodes, R.F. 2003. The earliest Greek architecture in Corinth and the 7th-century temple on Temple Hill. In C.K. Williams and N. Bookidis (eds.), *Corinth: Results of excavations conducted by the American School of Classical Studies at Athens.* Vol. 20. Princeton, NJ: American School of Classical Studies at Athens. 85–94.

Richardson, R.B. 1897. The excavations at Corinth in 1896. *American Journal of Archaeology* 1(6), 455–80.

Richardson, R.B. 1900. The fountain of Glauce at Corinth. *American Journal of Archaeology.* 4(4), 458–75.

Robinson, B.A. 2011a. *Histories of Peirene: A Corinthian fountain in three millennia.* Princeton, NJ: American School of Classical Studies at Athens.

Robinson, H. 1976. Excavations at Corinth: Temple Hill, 1968–1972. *Hesperia* 45(3), 203–39.

Romano, D.G. 2003. City planning, centuriation, and land division in Roman Corinth: Colonia Laus Iulia Corinthiensis & Colonia Iulia Flavia Augusta Corinthiensis. *Corinth: Results of excavations conducted by the American School of Classical Studies at Athens.* 279–301.

Romano, D.G. 2005. Urban and rural planning in Roman Corinth. In D.N. Schowalter (ed.), *Urban religion in Roman Corinth: Interdisciplinary approaches.* Cambridge, MA: Harvard University Press. 25–59.

Sanders, G.D.R. 2015a. Telling the whole story at multi-period sites: Corinth. Paper delivered at Telling the Whole Story at Multi-Period Sites, April 15, 2015, American School of Classical Studies at Athens.

Sanders, G.D., J. Palinkas, I. Tzonou-Herbst, and J. Herbst. 2017. *Ancient Corinth: Site guide.* American School of Classical Studies at Athens.

Scotton, P.D. 1997. *The Julian Basilica at Corinth: An architectural investigation.* Doctoral dissertation, University of Pennsylvania.

Scranton, R.L. 1951. *Corinth, 1.iii: Monuments in the lower Agora and north of the Archaic temple.* Princeton, NJ: American School of Classical Studies at Athens.

Serres, M. 1987. *Statues. Le second livre des fondations.* Paris: Éditions François Bourin.

Serres, M. 2015b. *Statues: The second book of foundations.* London: Bloomsbury.

Serres, M., and B. Latour. 1995. *Conversations on science, culture, and time.* Ann Arbor, MI: University of Michigan Press.

Shanks, M., 1997. Photography and archaeology. In B.L. Molyneaux (ed.), *The cultural life of images: Visual representation in archaeology.* Routledge: London. 73–107.

Shanks, M., and C. Tilley. 1992. *Reconstructing archaeology.* London: Routledge.

Spon, J. 1678. *Voyage d'Italie, de Dalmatie, de Grèce et du Levant.* 3 vols. Lyon: Cellier.

Stillwell, R. 1932. The Temple of Apollo. In H.N. Fowler and R. Stillwell (eds.), *Corinth I.i: Introduction, topography, architecture.* Cambridge, MA: Harvard University Press. 115–134.

Voutsaki, S. 2003. Archaeology and the construction of the past in nineteenth-century Greece. In H. Hokwerda (ed.), *Constructions of Greek past: Identity and historical consciousness from antiquity to the present.* Groningen: Egbert Forsten. 231–255.

Walbank, M.E.H. 1989. Pausanias, Octavia and Temple E at Corinth. *Annual of the British School at Athens* 84, 361–94.

Walbank, M.E.H. 2002. What's in a name? Corinth under the Flavians. *Zeitschrift für Papyrologie und Epigraphik* 139, 251–64.

Watteaux, M. 2017. What do the forms of the landscapes tell us? Methodological and epistemological aspects of an archeogeographic approach. In J.-M. Blaising, J. Driessen, J.-P. Legendre, and L. Olivier (eds.), *Clashes of time: The contemporary past as a challenge for archaeology.* Louvain: Presses Universitaries de Louvain. 195–220.

Weinberg, S.S. 1960. *Corinth I.v The Southeast Building, the Twin Basilicas, the Mosaic House.* Princeton, NJ: American School of Classical Studies at Athens.

Wheler, G. 1682. *A journey into Greece.* London: Printed for William Cademan, Robert Kettlewell, and Awnsham Churchill.

Williams, C.K. 1978. Corinth 1977, Forum Southwest. *Hesperia* 47(1), 1–39.

Williams, C.K. 1981. The city of Corinth and its domestic religion. *Hesperia* 50(4), 408–21.

Williams, C.K. 1989. A re-evaluation of Temple E and the west end of the Forum of Corinth. In S. Walker and A. Cameron (eds.), *The Greek renaissance in the Roman Empire.* London: University of London, Institute of Classical Studies. 156–62.

Witmore, C. 2006. Vision, media, noise and the percolation of time: Symmetrical approaches to the mediation of the material world. *Journal of Material Culture* 11(3), 267–92.

Witmore, C. 2013b. Which archaeology? A question of chronopolitics. In A. González-Ruibal (ed.), *Reclaiming archaeology: Beyond the tropes of modernity.* London: Routledge. 130–44.

Witmore, C. 2015b. No past but within things: A cave and archaeology in the form of a dialogue. In M. Mircan and V.W.J. van Gerven Oei (eds.), *The allegory of the cave painting reader.* New York, NY: Mousse Publishing. 375–94.

Witmore, C. 2019c. Chronopolitics and archaeology. In C. Smith (ed.), *The encyclopedia of global archaeology.* New York, NY: Springer.

3

ACROCORINTH

From gate to summit

Movement through gates, Evliya Çelebi, Jacob Spon and George Wheler, storage vessels, segregation and resentment, a dream, what to observe, the Seyahatname, *the travelogue, spiritual insurances,* la science de l'Antiquité, *conspicuous walls, lofty views and low exclusions*

After upwards of an hour riding by horseback from the lower town of Corinth along the *kalderim*, a paved Turkish road, Evliya Çelebi, a self-described "wandering dervish and world traveler," reaches the lowest gate of the castle of Corinth.[1] What he describes as the first of three mighty, iron-clad castle gates is set at the base of the steep and imposing western cliffs. Before the arched gateway Evliya takes pause to mention the fine view. Here his optic is not that of aesthetic appreciation, but of a sweeping sight that is characteristic of strength. An unimpeded panorama was advantageous to those ever-prepared "sentries, lookouts, and armed gate-guards" who kept watch with unbroken attentiveness, whether by night or day. The year is 1668, and it is mid-summer.

---

1 On Evliya's self-description as a "dervish or Sufi type—a man without worldly ties, not dependent on the employment or favours of others," see Dankoff and Kim (2010, xiii).

After having measured a dozen Doric columns standing at the house of the *voyvode*,[2] Jacob Spon, a medical doctor and antiquary, and George Wheler, a Protestant and English royalist with something more than a penchant for botany, take the path from Corinth. They ride for a mile over sloping ground to the foot of the hill and then along avenues very steep and paths very narrow, full of many twists and turns. After not less than an hour they arrive at what they designate as the one entrance with two gates to the citadel of Acrocorinth.[3] Spon and Wheler had gained leave to go wherever they pleased due to the protection of the English Consul in Athens, a license obtained from the sultan granting free passage, and the "mediation of a couple of Dollars" with the castle commandant.[4] It is February, 1676.

Son of the chief goldsmith to the Ottoman sultan, Evliya Çelebi is wealthy, highly educated, and well connected within the elite circles of the Ottoman court. His title, Çelebi, signals his status as a gentleman of refinement. His obsession, travel, was a life-long vocation blessed by the Prophet Mohammed, who appeared to him in a dream thirty-eight years earlier.[5] His ambition, to journey "through the seven climes and the four quarters of the world," had led him from Istanbul to Bursa, the Caucasus, and Crimea, to Damascus, Baghdad, and Tabriz, to Dubrovnik, Hungary, and Vienna.[6] The hardships of the road were not suffered alone, for Evliya traveled in the company of friends, slaves, horses, and soldiers.[7] Though here unmentioned, some portion of this entourage now passes through the arched gateway with its iron-plated door. Though here unacknowledged, this group continues past a little loggia occupied by the guard. Silent on the tongue of talkative history, they nonetheless ascend with their companion, their patron, their master, along a steep, raised roadway braced between limestone precipice

2 Whereas Spon reported twelve columns associated with what will be identified as the Temple of Apollo, Wheler reported eleven, with another pillar standing apart from these (Spon 1678 II, 296; Wheler 1682, 440; also see Stillwell 1932, 128).

3 Spon (1678 II, 299), Wheler (1682, 440). Unaware of Evliya's account, Antoine Bon (1936, 148–49) ponders whether the first of the three gates had been destroyed in the siege of 1458. Perhaps the first gate had fallen into disrepair when Wheler and Spon entered eight years after Evliya. Whatever the situation, they do not mention it.

4 Compare Spon (1678, 298–99) to Wheler (1682, 440).

5 "It was the night of Ashura in the month of Muharram, the year 1040 (August 10, 1630)" (Volume 1, Folio 6b–8a; also see Dankoff and Kim 2010, 4).

6 Dankoff and Kim (2010, xvii–xxv).

7 Evliya always travels in the company of others. Upon leaving Anapoli (Nafplion) for Crete, Evliya enumerates his entourage, which, in addition to travelling companions, consisted of six slaves, seven horses, two loads of heavy baggage, and a trunk of clothing (Volume 8, Folio 283a; also see Dankoff and Kim 2010, xix).

and mortared-stone parapet. After about 200 paces, by Evliya's reckoning, the party arrives at the second gate.[8]

Spon and Wheler met in Rome in the midst of their Grand Tours. When Wheler eventually proposed to continue to Greece, he offered to cover Spon's expenses. It was a calculated risk. In the late seventeenth century few Northern Europeans were so intrepid as to venture into Roumeli and the Morea. A war with Venice continued to smolder. Pirates and corsairs constantly threatened shipping and to be a Frenchman in Greece after 1669 was to invite the ire of those loyal to the Ottoman Empire.[9] Spon pretended to be an Englishman and together they traveled from Venice to Spalato, Corfu, Zante, Delos, Constantinople, Smyrna, Ephesus, Delphi, and Athens.[10] Now, before the first of Acrocorinth's two gates, Spon and Wheler are obliged to dismount from their horses. A necessary spectacle replete with connotations of respect and vulnerability, the Northern Europeans must enter the castle by foot. Whether the dragoman of the English Consul in Athens, Mourati,[11] or their guide, Yani, accompany them, they do not mention.

It is through the arched passage of the second gate that the first enclosure of the castle is revealed. Evliya describes this area as "a small subdivision" consisting of "200 Greek houses, some churches and 10 shops" stretching about 500 paces up a steep, rocky slope. Here one finds not a single Muslim house. Neither gardens nor orchards are to be seen. Before him stand only the "ill-fated houses" of "infidel Greeks." The fact that Greeks are even allowed to reside within castle is an artifact of "having been granted pardon and peace when they gave over the keys of the castle to the Sultan Mehmed."[12] Does his choice of words reflect something of the distain with which Evliya, a member of the Ottoman elite, beholds the non-Muslim population? Whatever the answer, Evliya notes these details in his journal, on one of a myriad of pages that he will later compile into the *Seyahatname*, the *Book of Travels*, the longest

---

8 We should note that Evliya, as Pierre MacKay puts it, is not reliable with numbers higher than ten. MacKay suggests that "he seems to pluck them from his imagination for their sound alone" (1968, 387).

9 A French contingent was sent to aid the besieged Venetians in Candia—Evliya happened to be part of the Ottoman campaign in Crete at the time.

10 In order to gain entry to Acrocorinth Spon passed himself off as an Englishman. This nationality was affirmed by the dragoman of the English Consul, Mourati (Spon 1678 II, 298; Wheler 1682, 440).

11 Given Mourati's obligations as a dragoman (see Segment 8), and "armed with his Barrat or License" (Wheler 1682, 425), there is little reason believe that he is absent from this outing. Given that they had to take leave of their horses, which were furnished by Yani, a service rendered "at a cost of ten *Timins* a day, that is, about three Shillings, Six-pence" a day, (ibid.), it is likely that their guide waited by the gate.

12 See *Seyahatname* Volume 8, 258a12–14; Mackay translation, n.d. Also see MacKay (1968, 389).

first-person narrative in Ottoman literature—perhaps the longest "travel account by any writer in any language."[13]

On this area between the first and second gate, Spon is silent. Wheler, however, does not omit a description. "This side of the Rock is well covered with houses."[14] Some are the primary residences of both "Turks" and Christians (non-Muslim Greeks); others are the secondary abodes of those who maintain two houses: one in the lower town for business or pleasure and one in the castle where these families kept the best part of their movable property. For the castle provided refuge from corsairs who, on occasion, raided the lower town. Both Spon and Wheler keep journals, which upon their return to France and England they will publish as travelogues of their journeys throughout the Mediterranean: *Voyage d'Italie, de Dalmatie, de Grèce et du Levant* (1678) and *A Journey into Greece* (1682), respectively. *A Journey* will be a partial translation of Spon's account, augmented by Wheler's own, as he later puts it, "divine reflections on the various events of things, and phænomena of nature."[15]

After climbing over steep, cobbled surfaces Evliya approaches the third gate, which is flanked on either side by two great, square towers. One tower "is filled to the brim with millet, barley, wheat and bearded rice"; the other "is filled with clean firewood." There are also "horse-driven mills, and wheel mills driven by man-power and thousands of hand-mills." Here, the fact that Evliya knows the location of necessary provisions should the castle come under siege speaks to his ability to access whatever he wishes. No matter how exaggerated their quantity, the fact that Evliya mentions the contents before passing through the gate also suggests that he is oblivious to a distinction between beholding walls from the outside and contemplating them from within.

Before coming to the strongly built second gate, with its two towers, Wheler makes reference to the "Catholicon," which is kept in repair, in contrast to some other small churches, which are in ruin.[16] Inside, Wheler and Spon take note of old manuscripts including two liturgies of St Basil—what Spon described as *une Liturgie de Saint Chrysostome*—on parchment scrolls. Comparable to a Latin *volumen*, they take these documents to be of some antiquity. Although Spon passes lightly over details described by Wheler, he embraced every opportunity to find and, if possible, copy ancient texts,

---

13 Dankoff and Kim (2010, xi and xxii).
14 Wheler (1682, 441).
15 Wheler (1682, Preface, unnumbered).
16 Pierre Mackay suggests that the Catholicon may have been located where the ruins of the later Venetian church now sit (1968, 393; see Bon 1936, 260–61).

especially inscriptions.[17] For Spon, "the study of antiquities is [foremost] a textual matter," for "our antiques are nothing if not books, whose pages of stone and marble were written with iron and chisel."[18] Once published, and multiplied, the books of Spon and Wheler would themselves offer their pages as storage vessels of human achievement; repositories for objects gathered and safeguarded, with utmost care and devotion, against the depredations of time.[19]

To cross freely through gates is the prerogative of the privileged. Now Evliya and his entourage pass through high walls, which were "in ancient times built strong from top to bottom of cut stone," as Evliya notes elsewhere in his description of the castle. Something in the careful execution of the precise joints between well-hewn blocks of limestone and poros in the southern tower hints at pride and intramural identity; something in what lies above and behind these ancient portions suggests utility and expedience.[20] Do differences of form hint at different orientations to walls?[21] Walls inclusive of many are those largely experienced as integral of community and innate. Walls that enclose the domain of the privileged few are those that are largely experienced as alien, as exclusive, as abhorrent.[22]

Through this third gate, according to Evliya, lies the Muslim area of the castle. Within this inner circle of protection, two hundred multi-storied houses, raised of masonry and roofed over with tiles, cluster together.[23] There are four mosques, those of Sultan Mehmed the Conqueror and Ahmed Paşa, the Beyzade, and the Fethiye ("mosque of the conquest"), which had been converted

---

17 Upon arriving in Corinth Spon and Wheler immediately set to making inquiries regarding inscriptions. In the cellar of the Athenian merchant Panagioti Cavallari, they were shown an inscription that honored Faustina, wife of Antoninus Pius (Spon 1678 II, 296; Wheler 1682, 440). Wall and soil would hold the inscription of Faustina till 1914, when in the course of excavations in Corinth (West 1931). Though neither Spon nor Wheler published the inscription, Wheler's notebook contained a copy of the inscription including the lowest line, which had broken away at some point after their visit (Meritt 1947, 181–82).

18 Schnapp (1997, 182); with Schnapp's translation from Spon (1673); also see Etienne and Etienne (1992, 38).

19 Much has been made of European attitudes towards the Classical past under the proverbial Ottoman yoke; see Constantine (2011, 8), Morris (1994, 20–3), Shanks (1996, 55–6). My deliberations here are aimed somewhat more at how these travelers translate something of the object encountered into two dimensions and visually retain it in their notebooks (see Witmore 2006, 2013a). Arranged by location, Volume III of Spon's *Voyage* contains copies of many of the inscriptions he encountered in the course of his journeys.

20 For more on this tower, see Carpenter (1936, 10–15); Andrews (2006[1953], 138–40), Athanasoulis (2009, 59–61).

21 For pride-infused walls, see Segment 12.

22 Here I am building on an argument made by Sloterdijk (2014, 213–14).

23 Volume 8, 258a20.

from a Christian church. There are also two "neighborhood mosques," a coffee house, and a small shop. Evliya suggests that no Christians would be permitted to enter this quarter, were it not for the fact that some Muslims had "infidel" wives.[24] At home in this environment, Evliya experiences the castle as an insider, and those who experience walls from within are permitted a perspective of inclusiveness amid exclusivity. Those who only behold high walls from the outside are left to develop an estranged sense of belonging.

Spon says nothing of the second gate, save that one must pass through it to be completely in. Within this inner sphere he notes three mosques with their minarets, in addition to five or six small churches.[25] Of the houses, Wheler notes how more are in ruin than inhabited. Permitted to pass, both Northern Europeans are oblivious to any differences of accommodation behind high walls. Only eight years earlier, a Christian population was contained within the outer protective shell between the second and third gates. Only eight years earlier, this inner circle of security seems to have been partially closed to this non-Muslim majority. Between these separate districts, do walls continue to uphold a sense of mutual isolation among Muslims and non-Muslim Greeks who dwell apart? Spon and Wheler do not say. For these well-connected travelers of means such spaces could be weighed with respect to curiosity rather than estrangement.[26]

Evliya will preface the *Seyahatname* with a detailed description of his dream. In the Ahi Çelebi mosque, in the presence of the Prophet, his Companions, and the Saints, he receives instruction to satisfy his desire "to be a world traveler and unique among men." True to the Islamic "path of truth," he is urged to go forth and perform the *gaza* (to fight on behalf of the faith); to visit the tombs of those present in the dream's congregation (*ziyaret*); to undertake the *Hajj* by visiting the holy cities.[27] He is told what to observe and record: "the well-protected kingdoms through which [he passes] the strange and wonderful monuments, and each land's praiseworthy qualities and products, its food and drink, its latitude and longitude."[28] "Compose a marvelous work," he is instructed.[29]

---

24 It should be noted that archaeologists have documented examples of mixed Christian and Muslim burial practices in late-seventeenth-century Corinth; see Zervos et al. (2009).

25 Spon (1678 II, 299); Spon actually mentions the parchment rolls after noting the second gate. However, this ordering seems to be an artifact of grouping everything within the container of the castle as a whole.

26 Subsequent travelers and antiquarians in the second Ottoman period, from Chateaubriand (1814, 164) to Leake (1830 III, 257), would be barred from following in the footsteps of Spon and Wheler, and had to contend themselves with their descriptions.

27 Dankoff and Kim (2010, xvi and 7).

28 Ibid., 7.

29 Ibid.

Approaching something of a descriptive geography, the *Seyahatname* will mix itinerary with sketches of local history, administrative organization, surveys of towns, food, agriculture, parochial manners, dialects, and names. It will include reportage, whether news, rumor, gossip, anything worth telling that has entertainment value, whether for him or his readership, the Ottoman elite. That his observations are heavily conditioned by his faith and the intricacies of the Koran is unmistakable. Having memorized the whole of the Book, Evliya carried the Koran around *within himself*, and could recite it in eight hours should opportunity permit.[30] That he sets out under such sanctified auspices, carrying the blessings of the Prophet, his Companions, and the Saints, adds a level of divine security, for no matter where Evliya should venture God offers an ever-present shield of spiritual protection.[31]

Spon's strongest inclination was towards the "knowledge of ancient monuments."[32] That "Greek travelers had merely brushed the surface of this curiosity" only intensified his desire.[33] What remained on yonder heights of Aphrodite's temple? What of the celebrated Peirene, the spring where, according to Strabo,[34] Pegasus was caught by Bellerophon while drinking? While nothing is said of the former, both Spon and Wheler will mention the latter, for the optic of the Northern Europeans was refracted through classical texts. For Spon, the texts of Pausanias, Pliny, and Strabo held answers to the question of what to observe—indeed, through their words, he will be the first to reconnect numerous ancient sites with their former names.[35] If the genre of the travelogue was well suited to a variety of purposes—a day-by-day register of paths taken, of things done, a narrative of personalities, conversations, hardships, and dangers, both experienced and averted—combined with a record of what was deemed most worthy of observation and study, then it is because the books of Spon and, by association, Wheler would establish the model.[36] It is in pointing out such matters "of more than ordinary curiosity" that the Acrocorinth is made intelligible for those Northern Europeans who will read their books and who will follow in their footsteps.[37]

A man of taste, Evliya remains true to the moment in his writing. He savors the flavor of oranges in Corinth when he later takes pause to delight in the

---

30 *Seyahatname* Volume 6, 47a–b; Dankoff and Kim (2010, xii).

31 Evliya is the plural of *veli*, which means "friend of Allah" in Arabic.

32 Spon (1678 I, Preface, unnumbered). For an English translation of Spon's Preface, see Schnapp (1997, 351–52).

33 Spon (1678 I, Preface, unnumbered).

34 8.6.21.

35 Also Stoneman (1987, 80).

36 See Schnapp (1997, 353).

37 Wheler (1682, 419).

marmalade lemons, pomegranate, and fig trees of the gardens and orchards. Here, within this inner, higher sector of the castle, he quenches his thirst with "delicious life-giving water, cold as ice even in the month of July," which is held within two vaulted cisterns under the mosque of Sultan Mehmed. Within his description, the immediacy of sapidity is juxtaposed with extensiveness of an encompassing sight:

> There are, by will of God, 366 sources of water on top of this steep, high rock which touches the very sky, of which the western sources all yield bitter water, but those of the east yield water as sweet as the water of life itself.[38]

Differences of taste follow an orientation to the east and to the highest levels. Evliya transcribes the dedicatory inscriptions of two fountains at higher elevation with abundant flow and no others. The bitter waters that issue from fountains to the west are good as a digestive or for watering animals.[39] For Evliya it is beyond human wit to comprehend how the castle of Corinth is so well supplied with waters—it is a miracle of God the Creator, the greatest guarantor of utmost security.

A "Christian Traveller and Philosopher," Wheler embraces an opportunity to comment on how the Christians here, lacking an adequate shepherd, are wayward in their conversion to Islam.[40] Upon his return to England, he will take the vows to become a priest in the Church of England, thus fulfilling an oath to God made in Dover, at the outset of his travels, in return for the highest level of protection and prosperity.[41] Under this encompassing carapace of spiritual security Wheler undertakes his eclectic pursuits as a connoisseur of weeds and a cartographic surveyor. Writing as a naturalist, he takes note of plants that call to his curiosity, and even provides sketches of key specimens: *Aristolochia clematitis* and *Scorzanera Radice rotunda* from Hymettus, Astragalus from north of Megara, and Arbutus on Pentelicus.[42] Examples of flora are rendered by being shown, and thus he is able to return to England with something more of these specimens, rare or unknown. In a similar vein, Wheler includes pictorial maps to accompany descriptions: Athens, Megara, and Corinth. By giving spatial expression to objects encountered as select illustrations, Wheler provides what words alone cannot convey.[43]

---

38 *Seyahatname* Volume 8, 258a25; Mackay translation (n.d.).

39 Fascinating are matters of hydrology, for on these limestone heights lower fountains and wells would not have been immune to the effects of gravity and permeability, which is indifferent to waste and waters alike.

40 Wheler caustically refers to Islam as "Turkish superstition" (1682, 441).

41 Ramsey (1942, 7).

42 Wheler only published a select minority of his drawings. Woodcuts of his illustrations proved to be a burden to the publisher; Wheler (1682, Preface).

43 Witmore (2006).

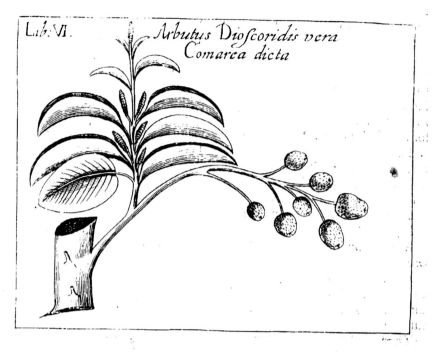

Lib: VI.   *Arbutus Dioscoridis vera*
              Comarca dicta

Illustration of *Arbutus* from *A Journey into Greece* (1682).

Conditioned by his medical knowledge and training, the question of how to observe ancient monuments takes on a new level of intensity in Spon's anti-quarian pursuits—though, for him, the term "antiquarian," *d'antiquariat*, fell short of his ambitions.[44] In defending the work he undertakes in the course of his travels, Spon will later champion *la science de l'Antiquité*, which focuses on the careful study of monuments through which the "Ancients transmitted their religion, history, politics and other arts and aspired to pass them down to posterity."[45] Comprised of eight subdivisions, the *science of antiquity* encap-sulates: (1) numismatics; (2) epigraphy; (3) architecture; (4) iconography, which included the study of statuary and miniatures; (5) glyptography, the study of engraved stones set in rings, talismans, and ornaments; (6) toreumatography, the study of reliefs (from *toreutikos*, of work in relief); (7) angeiography, "a vast and thorny field that explains weights, vases, instruments," and other things; and (8)

44 Spon (1679, 63).
45 Spon (1679, 63).

bibliography.[46] It is fitting that Spon will bookend his litany of subdivisions with objects that can be read. Although Spon's archaeological perspective was conditioned by objects unique or unfamiliar, by things out of place or of precious composition, by what could be seen above ground and, thus, by monuments implicit within the old lands within which they themselves are situated, his pursuits insured that these things would be framed by the written word. By conditioning the return visits of subsequent antiquarians, by undergirding all archaeological routines in the coming centuries,[47] *la science de l'Antiquité* will also underwrite the loss of the naively given character of objects old. What had existed in the open, without the bookish casings of familiarity, would be drawn increasingly into a circle of ever-refined awareness as if it had always been there.

Evliya notes that the castle was founded in the time of John the Baptist.[48] It is not that Evliya fails to contemplate the world of ancient ruins around him;[49] rather, he seems to affirm current powers by selectively refusing to point too far beyond them. Thus, if the well of the past was capped within Evliya's description then it was because one could not draw from it too deeply in the context of Ottoman aggrandizement.[50] In structuring his narrative of the castle as a series of enclosures comprising five subdivisions, Evliya's description is esteem-driven. It begins with the external appearance of the outer circuit of this lofty platform.[51] Crowned by 7,777 merlons, this outer wall is "mighty as Alexander's dyke" and "fourteen thousand paces in circuit."[52] Thus, with adulation and reverence, Evliya describes the outward manifestation of Ottoman

46 Spon (1679, 63–72). In 1685, he will later coin the term *archaeographia* to cover this science of antiquity (Miller 2017, 216).
47 See Stoneman (1987, 70–83), Miller (2017); also see Shanks (1996, 52–90).
48 A contemporary of Jesus Christ, John the Baptist lived through the early quarter of the first century CE.
49 It would be a mistake to ignore Evliya's engagement with a deeper past, which is evident elsewhere in his Greek travels (i.e. Volume 8, 282b4). That this engagement is ancillary to his interests in Acrocorinth serves to reinforce the argument made here. Also see Anderson (2015).
50 Something of a contrast is revealed in how the limitless supremacy of the Ottomans saturates future time, which Evliya invokes through prayer: "may it [the Morea] remain in the possession of the Ottomans till the end of time, o God our helper" (Volume 8, 259b7).
51 Thus, if walls were strained under the burden of their own weight then we would not know it from Evliya's account. When the Venetians take possession of Acrocorinth nearly two decades later (August 9, 1687) records suggest that it was in a deplorable state of deterioration (Bon 1936, 149–50).
52 "Alexander's dyke" probably refers to the great iron wall of Dhu'l Qarnayn. This name is translated from Arabic as "he of the two horns," and is taken to be Alexander the Great. In the Koran (Sura 18) Dhu'l Qarnayn built an iron wall, unscalable and unbreachable, to keep out the inhabitants of Gog and Magog (Stoneman 2008, 156, 161–62, 178–79). I am grateful to Justin Miller for this association.

security.[53] In noting how comparable battlements are not to be found in any other worldly fortress, for this is "a castle without equal," he glorifies the most conspicuous attribute of Ottoman supremacy. For to lavish praise upon mighty walls is to lavish praise upon those who maintain them. Such is the positive semantics of high walls and strong enclosures, for Evliya's description lends itself to the celebration of incomparable strength and unremitting force. It also speaks to a castle of Corinth whose center of gravity is in the present.

Wheler describes how the two principal peaks of the rock are enclosed by a wall about 2 miles in length. In the course of ascending to the highest point, upon which sits "a little mosque," he takes note of the castle tower upon the southwestern rise. At the summit, their efforts are rewarded with what in the world was "one of the most beautiful views," for Spon, and "one of the most agreeable prospects," for Wheler. Upon these very water-washed heights Strabo once stood and gave archetypical expression to the view by enumerating the lofty, snow-clad crests of Parnassus and Helicon, the Corinthian Gulf, the lands of Phocis, Boeotia, Megaris, the countryside of Corinthia and Sicyonia.[54] With an elevated perspective on ground that they had themselves traversed in the course of their travels, Spon continues with the isles of the Saronic Gulf, across to Athens and Cape Colonne (Cape Sounion).[55] Wheler, however, notes how the promontory of Sicyon bears northwest by north, the Phocian promontory of Cyrrha, north-northwest, the snow-covered summit of Parnassus, north.[56] Wheler enumerates his points of reference as they show upon a compass. Using the summit of Acrocorinth as a station, he will later compile these angles into a map of Attica, the Saronic Gulf, and the Isthmus. Renowned features, fortresses, ancient sites are situated in two dimensions with latitudinal supports.[57]

From within the inner redoubt with its tall keep, "a soaring rampart, crowned by a platform that touches the very sky," Evliya is permitted an encompassing view of the castle of Santa Maura on the threshold of the

---

53 Volume 8, Folio 257a—Mackay translation (n.d.). The first paragraph of Evliya's description, for Pierre MacKay, "is pure bombast, and is best omitted entirely from consideration" (1968, 391). Yet, here, Mackay, who is concerned with the empirical truth value of the *Seyahatname*, fails to appreciate the psychopolitical importance Evliya's description. Mackay also states that for Evliya "numbers have no meaning" (1968, 387), yet here numbers serve an important ornamental purpose within the overall narrative.

54 8.6.21; also see Wallace (1969a).

55 1678, 300; in Wheler's map of Corinth (1682, 439), the walls of Acrocorinth crown a promontory above the Isthmus and the distant peaks are labeled. Such maps provide checklists of what is seen. As a pictorial statement this map also entered into an exchange with other maps (and illustrations, as with the map of Athens) published in his book.

56 1682, 442–43.

57 Wheler was one of the earliest travelers to enroll a mariner's needle to observe relative positions of places for the purposes of triangulation; Wheler (1682, Preface).

Adriatic, the city of Árta, the mountains over Yánina, the twenty-three islands of the Aegean Sea.[58] This is a path open to but a miniscule minority. For the agrarian majority, the semantics of this redoubt and its tower was hardly a matter of proximity. Removed by virtue of high crags, walls, and guards, and, thus, always perceived at a distance, this tower nonetheless intensified the explicit awareness of lords on high for those down low. Perhaps constructed some four centuries earlier under the Frankish overlord Villehardouin, the keep (in 1668) is the residence for the commandant and the castle attendant. For these favored few, an elevated tower broadcasts their standing as overseers and protectors. For the excluded multitudes, how could the keep appear as anything other than an object of resentment? Such bitter feelings call back to another time when the verticality of enclosures within enclosures gave concrete expression to the old hierarchy, the *scala naturae*, to which such overlords subscribed in the protection of their vassals.[59] In such times, it had hardly mattered whether the lord of the keep was present or not, for the tower was ever ready to signal their power to look down from above.[60]

At the summit, Spon and Wheler are fixed upon the distant points of reference amid storied lands. Spon says nothing of the ground held in tenure by agrarians below. Wheler relishes in the prospect of the plain of Corinth with its well-watered, well-tilled, yards well planted with olive and vine. At the sight of the town with orchard and garden, spires of cypress, mixed with fields of corn Wheler takes delight. For him, it is an image of plenty. From this distant summit (a word derived from the Latin *summus*, the highest (part of), the superlative form of *superus*, above, as in *superior*) all they can do is look upon a harlequin patchwork of deep antiquity whose pathways, roads, and lines of tenure trace the ancient form of Roman land division.[61] The exception to the rule, they survey a landscape with an elevated perspective. Before them extends a pervasive albeit distant background, and yet here noble masters, Northern European and Ottoman, stand uplifted above the shared condition of the peasant base. Like the lords of the keep, do these travelers embrace the precisely opposite view of what the farmer holds to be lofty and low? Does not the invisibility of this agrarian world come from a lack of belonging? Whatever the

---

58 *Seyahatname* Volume 8, 258b1–5.

59 See Bloch (1962, 1967); for an in-depth archaeological and historical exploration of the Morea in the wake of 1204, see Gerstel (2013).

60 The Ottoman rotation of responsibility supposedly put a check on the notion of an absentee overlord, for the Haga in command of the castle is one of four in rotation throughout the year. On the ontology of walls and towers, see Sloterdijk (2014, 237–306).

61 I do not only mean this in terms of the antiquity of agrarian form, but also the antiquity of agrarian *being* (see Witmore 2018a).

answer, antiquarianism excludes this world and classical archaeology is born of this exclusion.[62]

Evliya and party eventually make their way to the summit of the castle, a deserted region of "foxes, jackals and hares" to pay respects at the tomb of Gazi Ibrahim Baba. On this summit, the name Gazi Ibrahim Baba will pass into oblivion. His name, and the memory of his tomb as a place of pilgrimage, will be safeguarded in the pages of the *Seyahatname*.

Heirs of Spon's *la science de l'Antiquité* will seek out what remains of Aphrodite's temple. They will come to identify what becomes of the tomb's poros walls, "square in plan, measuring about six metres on a side," surrounded by a walled court and "a cloister-like series of rooms along its northern border" as a "small Turkish mosque" (a mistake inherited from Wheler).[63] They will situate this structure upon the foundations of an "earlier mosque," adjacent to the foundations of a mediaeval tower, upon and adjacent to the foundations of an early Christian church, upon the foundations of the foam-born goddess's temple.[64] Held to be derivative of Aphrodite's temple, future archaeologists will remove large portions of what are revealed to be successive structures, constructed of reused material, including what had become of the tomb of Gazi Ibrahim Baba—a battery platform, and "a small hut of miserable construction."[65] Unknown to his excavators, Gazi Ibrahim Baba's remains will be found in 1926 among many other simple, unmarked graves "about the Turkish Mosque."[66]

With his movement through the castle unimpeded, Evliya and party exit by the North Gate. By way of a steep path of 5,000 paces, they return to Corinth. Eight years later, this gate is unmentioned by Spon and Wheler, who retrace their steps to the west gate where they had taken leave of their horses. They reach their lodgings by evening.

---

62 Subsequent inheritors of the antiquarian perspective, archaeologists will continue to look to the overt monuments, ruins, vestiges, and objects of art (see, for example, Bianchi Bandinelli 1976), until the agrarian base comes to be experienced as tenuous and losable at its point of cessation in the latter half of the twentieth century (see Snodgrass 1987).

63 Blegen (1930, 25); on Wheler's identification of the tomb as a "little mosque" see Wheler (1682, 442); also see discussion in MacKay (1968, 395).

64 Blegen suggests that two "Turkish mosques" seem to have succeeded the Christian church. "The first was very small, and only a portion of its foundations have survived" (1930, 25). The second almost directly overlaid the first. Concerning the Medieval tower, see Rife (2008).

65 Blegen (1930, 3); for a history of this archaeological intervention, see Kourelis (2017, 738–46).

66 Ibid., 25.

Bibliography

Anderson, B. 2015. "An alternative discourse:" Local interpreters of antiquities in the Ottoman Empire. *Journal of Field Archaeology* 40(4), 450–60.

Andrews, K. 2006[1953]. *Castles of the Morea*. Princeton, NJ: American School of Classical Studies at Athens.

Athanasoulis, D. 2009. *The castle of Acrocorinth and its enhancement project (2006–2009)*. Ancient Corinth: 25th Ephorate of Byzantine Antiquities.

Bandinelli, R.B. 1976. *Introduzione all'archeologia classica come storia dell'arte antica* (Vol. 334). Roma: Laterza.

Blegen, C.W. 1930. Excavations at the summit. In C.W. Blegen, O.T. Broneer, R. Stillwell, and A.R. Bellinger (eds.), *Acrocorinth: Excavations in 1926*. Cambridge, MA: Harvard University Press. 3–28.

Bloch, M. 1962. *Feudal society*. Chicago, IL: University of Chicago Press.

Bon, A. 1936. The Medieval fortifications of Acrocorinth and vicinity. In R. Carpenter and A. Bon (eds.), *Corinth III ii: The defenses of Acrocorinth and the lower town*. Cambridge, MA: Harvard University Press. 128–281.

Carpenter, R. 1936. The Classical fortifications of Acrocorinth. In R. Carpenter and A. Bon (eds.), *Corinth III.ii: The defenses of Acrocorinth and the lower town*. Cambridge, MA: Harvard University Press. 1–43.

Chateaubriand, F.-R. 1814. *Travels in Greece, Palestine, Egypt, and Barbary, during the years 1806 and 1807*. New York, NY: Van Winkle and Wiley.

Constantine, D. 2011. *In the footsteps of the gods: Travellers to Greece and the quest for the Hellenic ideal*. London: I.B. Tauris.

Dankoff, R., and S. Kim. (eds.). 2010. *An Ottoman traveller: Selections from the book of travels of Evilya Çelebi*. London: Eland.

Etienne, R., and F. Etienne. 1992. *The search for Ancient Greece*. London: Thames & Hudson.

Gerstel, S.E.J. (ed.). 2013. *Viewing the Morea: Land and people in the Late Medieval Peloponnese*. Washington, DC: Dumbarton Oaks.

Kourelis, K. 2017. Flights of archaeology: Peschke's Acrocorinth. *Hesperia* 86(4), 723–82.

Leake, W.M. 1830. *Travels in the Morea*. 3 vols. London: John Murray.

MacKay, P. 1968. Acrocorinth in 1668, a Turkish account. *Hesperia* 37(4), 386–97.

Meritt, B.D. 1947. Honors to Faustina at Corinth. *Classical Philology* 42(3), 181–82.

Miller, P.N. 2017. Coda: Not for lumpers only. In B. Anderson and F. Rojas (eds.), *Antiquarianisms: Contact, conflict, comparison*. Oxford: Oxbow. 210–19.

Morris, I. 1994. Archaeologies of Greece. In I. Morris (ed.), *Classical Greece: Ancient histories and modern archaeologies*. Cambridge: Cambridge University Press. 8–48.

Ramsey, R.W. 1942. Sir George Wheler and his travels in Greece, 1650–1724. *Essays by Divers Hands, being the Transactions of the Royal Society of Literature of the United Kingdom*. New Series 19, 1–38.

Rife, J. 2008. Leo's Peloponnesian fire-tower and the Byzantine watch-tower on Acrocorinth. In W.R. Caraher, L.J. Hall, and R.S. Moore (eds.), *Archaeology and history in Roman, Medieval and post-Medieval Greece: Studies on method and meaning in honor of Timothy E. Gregory*. Aldershot: Ashgate. 281–306.

Schnapp, A. 1997. *The discovery of the past*. New York, NY: Harry N. Abrams.

Shanks, M. 1996. *Classical archaeology of Greece: Experiences of the discipline*. London: Routledge.

Sloterdijk, P. 2014. *Globes: Spheres II*. South Pasadena, CA: Semiotext(e).

Snodgrass, A.M. 1987. *An archaeology of Greece*. Berkeley, CA: University of California Press.

Spon, J. 1673. *Recherche des Antiquités et Curiosités de la ville de Lyon*. Lyon: Imprimerie de Jacques Faeton.

Spon, J. 1678. *Voyage d'Italie, de Dalmatie, de Grèce et du Levant*. 3 vols. Lyon: Cellier.

Spon, J. 1679. *Réponse à la critique publiée par M. Guillet sur le Voyage de Grèce de Jacob Spon*. Lyon: Amanlei.

Stillwell, R. 1932. The temple of Apollo. In H.N. Fowler and R. Stillwell (eds.), *Corinth I.i: Introduction, topography, architecture*. Cambridge, MA: Harvard University Press.

Stoneman, R. 1987. *Land of lost gods: The search for classical Greece*. Norman, OK: University of Oklahoma Press.

Stoneman, R. 2008. *Alexander the Great: A life in legend*. New Haven, CT: Yale University.

Wallace, P.W. 1969a. Strabo on Acrocorinth. *Hesperia* 38(4), 495–99.

West, A.B. 1931. *Corinth VIII.ii Latin inscriptions 1896–1926*. Cambridge, MA: Harvard University Press.

Wheler, G. 1682. *A journey into Greece*. London: Printed for William Cademan, Robert Kettlewell, and Awnsham Churchill.

Witmore, C. 2006. Vision, media, noise and the percolation of time: Symmetrical approaches to the mediation of the material world. *Journal of Material Culture* 11(3), 267–92.

Witmore, C. 2013a. The world on a flat surface: Maps from the archaeology of Greece and beyond. In S. Bonde and S. Houston (eds.), *Representing the past: Archaeology through text and image*. Oxford: Oxbow Books. 127–52.

Witmore, C. 2018a. The end of the Neolithic? At the emergence of the Anthropocene. In S.E. Pilaar Birch (ed.), *Multispecies archaeology*. London: Routledge. 26–46.

Zervos, O.H., Rohn, A.H., Sanders, G.D.R., and Barnes, E. 2009. An early Ottoman cemetery at ancient Corinth. *Hesperia* 78(4), 501–615.

4

ALONG THE A7 (MORÉAS), BY CAR

Measured line, acceleration, non-lieux, *a list of signs, adverts (soft pollution),
automobility, on speed, on detachment, on appropriation, on "anthropological place"*

2012, spring. I turn left, cross the lane for oncoming traffic on the EO-7 (Ethnikí
Odós 7) and enter the A7 motorway, otherwise known as the Moréas (Aftokinitó-
dromos Moréas). Deduct a delay of a minute or two for the toll and it now takes
seven minutes to get from here, the entrance ramp at Ancient Corinth, to the exit
for Ancient Kleones. From the top of the ramp to the bottom, my speed increases,
from 40 to 120 kilometers an hour.

K89.2: along the shoulder, just above the level of the guardrail, rectilinear green
signs with white lettering broadcast increments to the tenth of the kilometer.
K89.3: "K" refers to Kalamata and gauges the distance from Athens heading south.
Heading north, the signs are prefaced by "A" for Athens—A89.4—in both directions the numbers mark the distance to the capital city. Less frequently, large green
signs specify my distance to Kalamata—149 kilometers—or, indeed, Nafplion,
Tripoli, or Sparta. Athens connects with these other cities and together each form
two points of reference, two nodes for a measured line. Along the Moréas, all

specified destinations are rendered as equivalent; all distances are equally known, or, dare I say, equally dominated.

K90.1: framed by concrete barriers, backed by cypress trees, underscored by a continuous flat surface, the peak of Profitis Elias lies straight ahead. Bypassing towns and villages, constructing a line as straight as possible between two points is an ancient, Roman strategy. However, apart from the domain of nautical movement, it was the railroad that prepared this region for the fundamental changes associated with automobility, the transportation of people and goods along a continuous surface of smooth roads.[1] Passing through Solomos, following the valley bottom around the southern flanks of Profitis Elias through Chiliomodi, by Agios Vasileios, through Dervenakia and the Tretos Pass, the old national road, the EO-7 both deviates from earlier routes and falls in with others, those long familiar to inhabitants of the region.[2] The A7 breaks with this old geography.

K91.0: I pass a small truck loaded with white tables and chairs. Speed increases, and time intervals are known, along the straight line. With the Moréas, the maximum speed rose from 50, the limit on the old national road, to 120 kilometers an hour. With the Moréas, the commute from Athens to Kalamata decreased from six, even seven, hours to two (sometimes it takes half as long and more to get from Chalandri to the city center in Athens). With such speed—already anticipated in myths of heroes on winged horses and gods upon flying chariots veiled in mist—follows an extreme reduction of distance, initiating profound transformations in the shape and character of this region, and the consciousness of those who traverse it.

K92.1: Cypress, Aleppo pine, and an unbroken line of mesh fencing frame the views out. Oleander is planted down the median of the highway. The picturesque and the poison fringe a linear swath of asphalt and concrete over 20 meters wide. This highway lays claim to the space it now occupies. An area formerly open to myriad forms of movement and interaction now belongs exclusively to automobiles and other motor vehicles. Between Corinth and Kalamata, all secondary movement perpendicular to this wide, flat, enclosed, unbroken surface is now confined to select crossroads, which pass above or below, like one just now at K93.1.

K93.2: a few tenacious weeds and grasses force tenuous abodes in cracks along the shoulder and at the base of the guardrail. A heap of fir mangled into red muscle

---

1 See Segment 8.

2 The old national road broke with the earlier route from ancient Corinth, which passed north of Acrocorinth to eventually meet up with the ancient Tretus Pass; on the history of its construction, see Elias and Elias (2003, 529–33); for the ancient routes see Marchand (2009, 120–29; also 2002, 444). The A7 replaced the old national road incrementally. The Corinth/Tripoli segment was constructed between 1984 and 1990.

and black entrails lies nearby—too big to have been a beech marten; too small to have been a medium-sized dog; it was likely a large cat. Over 2.9 million square meters of tarmacked Peloponnese is now inhospitable to all forms of life, peripatetic and plant.[3] Even so, the managers of the Moréas cite an increase in safety and a decrease in time spent on the roads, quick to point out the environmental consequences of the latter.[4]

K93.9: below the heights of Pendeskouphi on the right and the Agios Nikolaos Monastery on the left—neither location made known to motorists with words—a sign broadcasts the rest area for Spathovouni with its Eco gas station and a fast food venue, Goody's: 1,000 meters. For Marshal McLuhan highways were fundamental in reversing the ancient pattern of work with agrarian societies—the city ceased to be the center of leisure and the country ceased to be a center of all work.[5] An oversimplification, admittedly; nonetheless, McLuhan's hyperbole suggests an inversion of foreground and background that is evidenced everywhere.

K95.4: I pass the entrance to the Spathovouni rest area, which sits at the top of the rise. Behind the concrete and steel silhouette of this "area"—seemingly neutral ground—views open intermittently onto the agricultural fields, portions of the plain of Kleonai, to Mt Phoukas, and the diffuse grey heights of distant Arcadia. The old proportions that separate this rise from the plain or mountains beyond no longer make sense at 120. With acceleration, as it is

Swath of the Moréas near the Spathovouni rest area.

---

3 This figure, which pertains only to the paved surface area of the Moréas, a 20 by 147,000 meter highway stretching from Corinth to Kalamata, easily detracts from the radical upheaval in our moral and emotional relations with the animal dead (see Lopez 1998).
4 Between 2009 and 2014 the number of road fatalities fell by 46 per cent in Greece. There were 988 fatalities on Greek roads in 2012 and less than 10 per cent of these occurred on motorways. See https://www.nrso.ntua.gr/data/; also see: http://www.benefit4transport.eu/wiki/index.php?title=Case_Studies:_Moreas_Motorway,_Greece.
5 McLuhan (1994[1964], 38 and 94).

often noted, follows spatial contraction.[6] The A7 allows for rapid traversals in relative comfort and is thus an extension of the city. Corinth, New and Old, Argos, and Nafplion become suburbs of Athens through the reduction and compression of old geographical barriers and distances.[7] With an objective point of departure and destination, the interstitial spaces become no more than undefined ground between these nodes of definition; a transit zone, which seems to bear no relation to specific persons or the places they inhabit beyond the barrier fence.[8]

K96.6: I speed by the blasted flank of Profitis Elias. The straight, level, measured surface has no hard deviations for slope or precipice. Wide radii for horizontal curves are demanded as much by Trans-European Highway standards as by the idiosyncrasies of valley or ridgeline or the need for averting villages or towns. Insofar as the highway goes it is even space devoid of terrace lines, property boundaries, ravines, villages, people, animals—those old specificities, those old things, which once conditioned movement here. Laid open for anyone with an automobile, the Moréas has robbed these locales, which have flipped into the interstitial, and those distances which formerly impacted local economies, of their dignity.[9]

K97.3: a cut through the slope to the left marks the beginning of a kilometer-plus section of completed-then-abandoned motorway, because it failed to meet Trans-European standards—two curves fell under the minimum radius. This is precisely delineated, measured, and uniform space—excessive resistances, no matter the cost, cannot be tolerated. Casting aside the idiosyncrasy of the foreground, a smooth even surface of uninterrupted asphalt or concrete is homogeneous space. Prescribed by consistent guidelines, the Moréas seems to be the same as any other European motorway. This is a *non-lieu*.

K97.9: *non-lieux* are, as defined by Marc Augé, non-relational—that is, rapports are not established or maintained with farmers, crossroads, stream crossings, or carob trees. *Non-lieux* are non-historical—one does not confront the buildings, monuments, or locales that embody history. *Non-lieux* are devoid of any concern for identity—"complicities of language, local references, the

---

6 For Paul Virilio, like Marshall McLuhan and Heidegger before him, with reduced distance, old time intervals recede, and space is nullified with the acceleration of movement and communications. On speed, consider Virilio's "dromology" (2006), the theory of speed and the society it defines, and "picnolepsy" (2009a), an epileptic state of consciousness generated by speed.

7 See Segment 8; also Serres (1993). This is, of course, Heidegger's point concerning the reduction of distances.

8 With super-highways, as McLuhan (1994[1964], 94) put it, "roads became a wall" separating humans and the country.

9 For other archaeological examples of the spatial, ecological, and temporal consequences of such reduction, see González-Ruibal (2019, 141–45). Also see González-Ruibal (2008).

unformulated rules of living know-how" are not part of this terrain.[10] (Anyone can always get the same pickle sauce on a Goody's cheeseburger, whether in Spathovouni or Sparta.)

K98.6: a large green sign cautions that there is a speed camera ahead. K98.7: a white sign within a red circle indicates a toll post, 800 meters. K98.8: another sign indicates a reduced speed of 100. Prescriptive, informative, and prohibitive signs, as underlined by Augé, saturate non-places. Pervaded by text, pervaded by instructions, pervaded by consistency, standards, and regularity these signs indiscriminately fashion a consistent user.

K99.0: I move over to the left to pass a motorist changing a tire. To assert that this is anything but a non-place for those who have broken down or those who work on the road, for those who have lost someone along its way or those who have tagged concrete dividers or bridges with graffiti is insubstantial—humans possess the ability to electrify every centimeter of this concrete surface with meaning.[11] No, to repeat, the key issue is that the Moréas has redefined the nature of locality and human consciousness.

K99.5: I slow to 20 for the Spathovouni toll station. A green sign gives the toll rates: 2.50 Euros for a car, 8.90 Euros for large lorries. With the economic downturn these tolls insure the old paths will not be forgotten. Rather than pay the toll, many would prefer to drive the old national road, incurring the cost of the delay.

K99.7: I lower the window in anticipation of passing a toll to the collector. A blast of hot air tinged with diesel exhaust mixes with the air-conditioned atmosphere of the automobile. John Coltrane now competes with the repetitive sound of passing tires on expansion cracks, the reverberating engine noise of idle cars in the queue, and squeal of breaks as the lorry inches forward. Automobiles, lorries, busses, all lay claim to their surroundings with their excretions. Local air conditions are not without their inevitable risks, which are increasingly made explicit: diesel exhaust is carcinogenic,[12] proximity to motorways has been linked to the development of childhood asthma,[13] heavy metals have contaminated roadside soils.[14] The cacophony of these passing vehicles permeates

---

10 Augé (1995, 101).

11 For examples, see Dalakoglou (2010), Dalakoglou and Harvey (2012).

12 The World Health Organization classified diesel engine exhaust as carcinogenic in June of 2012 —see press release No 213 (www.iarc.fr/en/media-centre/pr/2012/pdfs/pr213_E.pdf).

13 Gauderman et al. (2005).

14 Lead, expunged with the exhaust of automobiles burning leaded gasoline prior to the 2000 European Union ban, accumulated in soils up to 50 meters from the shoulder (see Chow 1970). Greece was permitted a one-year reprieve from the 2000 European Lead Gasoline ban (Reitze 2001, 329). Automotive catalytic converters lose platinum, rhodium, and palladium, which accumulates in roadside soils (see Jarvis, Parry, and Piper 2001; also Christoforidis and Stamatis 2009).

the surrounding fields, even drowning out the cicadas. With its passing traffic, the Moréas spreads beyond the fence, appropriating even more land.[15]

K99.7: I pass 2.50 Euros with a smile and in a smooth motion receive a receipt. I place this verification of payment in the center console and accelerate from the tollbooth.K99.8: six minutes, seventeen seconds on the Moréas—barring accidents or breakdowns, my arrival in a few minutes at the acropolis of ancient Kleonai is assured. But time guarantees are inconsequential compared to acceleration, to speed, which is held to change everything. For Paul Virilio, as with McLuhan, space is annulled in routine crossings at 120-plus kilometers per hour, which is tied to other forms of distance compression—quasi-instantaneous exchanges across the electronic ether, the supersonic movement of planes. This spatial annulment, corresponding to the end of space as the main factor of social engagements, makes it possible for Virilio to assert the polluting effects of speed—spatial, atmospheric, and psychological—and the primacy of time.[16] Can we even maintain the focus of our attention or thought for more than a few seconds? The pollution is related not only to distances or to the air we breathe, not only to the faculty of awareness, but also to substances, which are now taken for granted.[17]

K101.0: a cut through a low rise bars any views beyond the foreground. From my seat within the enclosed, air-conditioned atmosphere of the automobile it is easy to forget the world. It is easy to withdrawal even further from the great outside in such designed comfort. But it is not space so much as a sense of space that is lost. Virilio's thesis on speed fails to appreciate the mobile rooms which speed along with us, or house the screens and pages that cancel the distance between you, dear reader, and here. Within the space of this car, better known as a brand, I continue to listen to jazz at the same tempo.[18] I take a sip of my water without haste. Within the confines of the mobile interior—a personalized capsule—I have individuated personal space, my music, my things, an enclosed chamber all my own, mutually isolated from other personalized capsules, along the shared expanse of the highway.[19] Does alienation and loss follow on the creation of these human-specific bubbles for rapid traversal of the Moréas?

K102.4: Agios Vasileios, 1,000 meters. I reduce my speed. A guardrail and a mesh fence along the edge neither fully obscure the low hill nor blot out the

15 See Serres (2011).
16 Virilio (2006).
17 Virilio (2009b, 27).
18 Rental car agencies rent by class. In place of a Ford Escort, I received a BMW 1 series (116i)—a benefit for anyone who rents a car for several weeks in the midst of the economic downturn.
19 See Sloterdijk (2013, 249–57) on the "uncompressible."

olive grove, the cypresses, or the parallel agricultural track on its flanks (there are surprisingly few billboards along this stretch). Yes, here is where former localities are regulated to passing distance, and of these the transitory motorist has become ignorant. Yet, what is less often appreciated is how with this new object follow new idiosyncrasies and freedoms. The erstwhile outside is taken for granted, to be sure, but it is always possible to brake at any point along the median. It is always possible to turn off at the next exit. It is always possible to explore an area of the middle ground or to set off to the most distant horizons of Arcadia. This freedom of controlled movement is a part of the psychology of automobility; as is guilt, for a driver can no longer get away with a naivety as to what is spewed out the tailpipe; as is fantasy-cum-delusion, for not all locales are equally accessible to the motorist.[20]

K103.0: a larger sign announces Ancient Kleones, 500 meters. I slow more. Automobility has as much to do with the realization of freedoms along the road as with transport. Over the last thirty years alone, car ownership in Greece, despite leveling off in the current economic situation, has climbed from roughly 1 in 7 to 1 in 2.[21] The pervasiveness of cars, and roads, has brought a degree of mobility once known only to a select few in the distant past—Roman emperors, overlords at Acrocorinth, sailors, and merchants—to nearly everyone capable of driving within Greece. Still, with the awareness that follows on the pervasive rise of CO_2, one should not stop at considering this exponential growth short of globally. In the time it took to add one billion new humans, one billion new internal combustion engines have also been produced.[22]

K103.4: merging into the exit lane for Ancient Kleones, I pass under the bridge and slow to enter the hard turn. At the top of the exit, I look out the window at a so-called inert background. Often the only association to the lands beyond the shoulder relates to a desire to pass them by at high speed on the way to somewhere else. Yet driving a car does not annul space so much as cancel rapports with specific things—old roads between villages, elder tracks over neglected passes, erstwhile paths down to dead cats, watering holes or animal troughs hewn in stone, brush shelters for agricultural workers who once remained in the field for a nap but now drive back to the comforts of an air-conditioned home, or the

---

20 Sloterdijk connects this freedom of movement to the figure of the centaur (2011b). The image of the mythical hybrid of human and steed encapsulates how this freedom of movement has as much to do with attitude and addiction as travel and transport.

21 In 2012 there were 5,167,557 cars in circulation (Hellenic Statistical Authority 2013, 31), up from 1,259,335 in 1985. Car numbers from 1985 are available through the statistics database of the Hellenic Statistics Authority (see www.statistics.gr/portal/page/portal/ESYE).

22 Witmore (2019b, 144).

old church of Agios Nikolaos, which lies across the road.[23] These things, these rapports gain new meaning from inside a car traveling on the Moréas, but that does exhaust them of their reality.

I turn left toward Ancient Kleones. Formerly known as Kondostavlo, the town now takes its name from the ancient polis of Kleonai. Across the vineyards to the north, the outline of the acropolis is partially traced by cypresses around two low, olive-covered hills. This was a major crossroads of movement through the region in the Classical period, and at other times. Located on the ancient interstate route that ran from Corinth to Argos to Tegea, Kleonai was a key piece in a game of political alliances among the ancients.[24] From the perspective of an outside orientation, Kleonai was a key node along a line, or what is more, a place situated along a route—what has been dubbed as "an axis of history."

A rectilinear brown sign announces the "Temple to Hercules" with an arrow pointing right. I turn onto the paved surface of a single-lane road. Framed by vineyards the road heads off in the direction of the acropolis of Kleonai, for which there is no sign. Nonetheless, both temple and acropolis hold memories of a time when distance

Remains of the temple of Herakles.

23 This area is known as Kourtesa. A khan once stood here, which provided shelter to travelers (Marchand 2009, 145–50; also see Wiseman 1978, 109 and 111). On roads and the devastation of specific rapports, also see González-Ruibal (2019, 141–45).

24 This argument has been voiced by Jeanette Marchand (2009).

was regulated by physiology and was given meaning in those terms, but not from without; rather, from within. This was also an "anthropological place" in Augé's terminology.[25] Here, the notion of *demos* once encompassed both the land and the people who worked and inhabited it—a community of the living behind shared walls in close proximity to their dead, buried in the earth. For those who lived here, meaning emanated less from along a route than from the shared hearth, the *oikos* (both in terms of house and household), the terrain of shared existence, invested with a common history and memory held aloft by monuments and participation, charged with ancestral and divine presence, and by bounded fields with their furrows, and delimited groves with their trees, both sustained by familial and communal labor. As a polis within a geography of other territorial poleis, Kleonai braced itself against the outside, by entering into alliances—political, divine, geographical, material, etc.— favorable to its self-perpetuation.

A pothole jars the undercarriage of the vehicle. The A7, a new axis, forms a rift with this history and the geography that once sustained it. City-oriented life, speed, communications technologies, all structure a sense of space and time, which radically breaks with both erstwhile movement and territorial engagements, thousands of years in the making. With the complete reorientation of experience along the Moréas, the material past, the history of the area has been relegated to the margins. Augé was right to point out the difference in making explicit history as heritage, as sites of importance on signs from the road—only the most iconic of archaeological sites are marked along the Moréas (at K107.2 a brown sign announces the exit for Mycenae). To the motorist these old locales come as options, rather than obligations.[26] When we return to these places many enter an estranged land of holidays and tourism.

I drive up and park the car next to the exposed remains of a temple associated with Herakles, the wandering *hērōs theos* successful amid the ever-present dangers of the great outside—an appropriate figure of the divine with which to build solidarity.[27] I weave a path through tall thistles and along the top of architectural blocks arranged in rows. From the *crepidoma*, I look back across vineyards of Agiorgitiko and Moschofilero to the hill and its olive groves, which shade the remains of the acropolis of Kleonai.

---

25 Augé (1995, 42–74).

26 By "obligation," which is derived from the Latin root *ligare*, to bind, I am referring to how we were formerly bound to points of reference, to specific places in that lifeworld associated with the old mobility.

27 The association of the temple remains with that of Herakles is based on a reference in Book 4 of Diodorus Siculus, section 33. According to Diodorus, Herakles killed Eurytus, son of Augeas, near Cleonae, "where a temple of Herakles still stands." For the excavation of the temple, see Karo (1913); for photos and reconstruction, see Mattern (2012). *Hērōs theos* is used by Pindar (*Nemean*, 3.22) as a description of Herakles, both hero and god.

Bibliography

Augé, M. 1995. *Non-places: Introduction to an anthropology of supermodernity*. London: Verso.

Chow, T.J. 1970. Lead accumulation in roadside soil and grass. *Nature* 225(5229), 295–96.

Christoforidis, A., and N. Stamatis. 2009. Heavy metal contamination in street dust and roadside soil along the major national road in Kavala's region, Greece. *Geoderma* 151, 257–63.

Dalakoglou, D. 2010. The road: An ethnography of the Albanian–Greek cross-border motorway. *American Ethnologist* 37(1), 132–49.

Dalakoglou, D., and P. Harvey. 2012. Roads and anthropology: Ethnographic perspectives on space, time and (im)mobility. *Mobilities* 7(4), 459–65.

Elias, X., and Z. Elias. 2003. *O Teos Demos Kleonon 19os – 20ós Aiónas* (The former municipality of Kleonon 19th – 20th century). Vol. 1. Athens: Dim. Kleidas & Co.

Gauderman, W.J., E. Avol, F. Lurmann, N. Kuenzli, F. Gilliland, J. Peters, and R. McConnell. 2005. Childhood asthma and exposure to traffic and nitrogen dioxide. *Epidemiology* 16(6), 737–43.

González-Ruibal, A. 2008. Time to destroy: An archaeology of supermodernity. *Current Anthropology* 49(2), 247–79.

González-Ruibal, A. 2019. *An archaeology of the contemporary era*. London: Routledge.

Hellenic Statistical Authority. 2013. *Greece in Numbers*. Athens: Author.

Jarvis, K.E., S.J. Parry, and J.M. Piper. 2001. Temporal and spatial studies of autocatalyst-derived platinum, rhodium, and palladium and selected vehicle-derived trace elements in the environment. *Environmental Science & Technology* 35, 1031–36.

Karo, G. 1913. Archäologische Funde in Yahre 1912. *Archäologischer Anzeiger* 28, 95–121.

Lopez, B. 1998. *Apologia*. Athens, GA: University of Georgia Press.

Marchand, J. 2009. Kleonai, the Corinth–Argos road, and the "axis of history". *Hesperia* 78, 107–63.

Marchand, J.C. 2002. *Well-built Kleonai: a history of the Peloponnesian city based on a survey of the visible remains and a study of the literary and epigraphic sources*. Doctoral dissertation, University of California, Berkeley.

Mattern, T., 2012. Das «wohlgebaute Kleonai» Neue Ausgrabungen in einer Stadt des «Dritten Griechenlands». *Antike Welt*, 46–54.

McLuhan, M. 1994[1964]. *Understanding media: The extensions of man*. Cambridge, MA: MIT Press.

Reitze, A.W. 2001. *Air pollution control law: Compliance and enforcement*. Washington, DC: Environmental Law Institute.

Serres, M. 1993. *La Légende des anges*. Paris: Flammarion.

Serres, M. 2011. *Malfeasance: Appropriation through pollution?* Stanford, CA: Stanford University Press.

Sloterdijk, P. 2011b. Society of centaurs: Philosophical remarks on automobility (trans. K. Ritson). *Transfers* 1(1), 14–24.

Sloterdijk, P. 2013. *In the world interior of capital: For a philosophical theory of globalization*. Cambridge: Polity Press.

Virilio, P. 2006. *Speed and politics: An essay on dromology*. Los Angeles, CA: Semiotext(e).

Virilio, P. 2009a. *The aesthetics of disappearance*. Los Angeles, CA: Semiotext(e).

Virilio, P. 2009b. *Grey ecology*. New York, NY: Atropos Press.

Wiseman, J. 1978. *The land of the ancient Corinthians*. SIMA50. Göteborg: Åström.

Witmore, C. 2019b. Hypanthropos: On apprehending and approaching that which is in excess of monstrosity, with special consideration given to the photography of Edward Burtynsky. *Journal of Contemporary Archaeology* 6(1), 136–53.

5

KLEONAI TO NEMEA

*A world engaged through walking, agrarian memories, a weed pharmacopoeia,
grains, vineyards and viticulture, terroir, soil-marks, chôra, Kondostavlo,
a winery and wine, Agiorgitiko, a second mouth, crossing over, the Nemea Valley*

Two hundred years ago, Gell marked the acropolis by triangulation.[1] On the
compass, Phoukas (Mt Apesas) bears N. 30 W. Acrocorinth, N. 65 E. Known
locally as Tourla, this round elevated crown rests in the midst of well-kept
groves and vineyards. Yet, from here, on the summit, every direction holds
impediments to the walker. Having remained un-plowed, the top of the knoll is
now overgrown in a thicket. Gnarled and twisted Aleppo pines have laid claim
to the intermediate spaces between formerly tended olive trees. Maquis has
acquired what ground remains, maintaining its dominion with impenetrable

1 1810, 21.

barriers. I look in vain for a path into the heart of ancient Kleonai's upper acropolis, probable shelter to earlier Bronze Age remains.[2] Even to skirt the upper edge of the knoll is not without its unique hazards. Open voids are cut deep into earth and bedrock. Archaeologists have yet to dig in this ground, so these are indications of illicit excavation.[3] In any case, the upper acropolis is not my final destination, but rather my starting point. I begin here in order to avoid more expedient paths to the Nemea Valley.

Stepping down the steep escarpment turns into a scramble, which ends by a cut bearing tooth marks from the digging bucket of a backhoe—signs of more clandestine prospection. My way, no more than a double track incised with the iterative crossings of a truck, twists its course through an olive grove along the northeastern flank of the upper acropolis. Passing underneath fragrant canopies, I have to push away limbs weighed with blossoms in late May. This time of year, clouds mix with blue sky in the mid-morning. To the west, dense, grey plumes build over Phoukas, but the weather will hold, at least for an hour or two.

The path soon passes under high-power lines and across another thicket. At its edge is a haphazard cairn of rubble and ashlar dredged from earth. Afterwards, overgrowth crowds the track. In the moment, I see this thicket not so much a break between different landholdings as a space of neglect; I search for its reason. Why would someone relinquish these olives to overgrowth? Perhaps it is I who fail to see the wisdom in sparing areas untilled. Such thickets may have once produced a few bundles of firewood in a year, a purpose less uncommon in the midst of the current economic crisis. Remnants of a burn pile in the path disrupt such thoughts. They suggest the open area around a few olives was recently cleared of undergrowth. Beyond, the track passes over a surface strewn thick with stones. Here, bits of amphora, coarse pottery, roof tiles, and slag are pervasive. And there, poppies vie for apian attention.

At the edge of the grove, the track intersects with a truck road. Better worn, this way traces the top of the circuit wall of ancient Kleonai, the line of which is demarcated, here and there, by Italian cypresses. Now obscured below the dense cover of cypress and an understorey of loppings, little of the wall is visible along the embankment that falls off to the right. Ahead, the road descends the slope. Decomposing poros blocks are prominent here—perhaps they are remnants of a former tower?[4] As the grade steepens, the gravel road

---

2 See Marchand (2002, 348–49).

3 Marchand (2002, 391) discusses reports by local residents of illicit excavations in the area. Mattern (2013, 329) mentions a robber trench cut in 2008. For recent archaeological work at Kleonai, see Mattern (2012, 2013).

4 See Marchand (2002, 364).

disappears below a sweep of concrete pavement roughened for friction with a length of plank. This stretch of hard surface jogs west at the bottom. A lone European pear tree signals the concrete's terminus.

Stone and concrete mark this place with their hardness, and endure. But the pear tree offers a living memory situated at a confluence of paths. Off to the left, an apricot orchard is planted amid a few older olives. Thick irrigation lines are draped through the boughs of trees otherwise burdened under masses of green fruit. A sputtering tractor, somewhere to the north, is the only indication of a farmer's presence in otherwise silent groves. It is too late in the morning for most.

Among those who work this land, this area enclosed by the erstwhile city walls is known as Volimoti. The meaning of the word is lost.[5] All the same, words fail to convey what here remains unsaid. The orchard of fruit trees, the lane of cypress, or the grove of olive, a wide terrace or a thin footpath ground to bare, fresh-tilled soil, worked surfaces, pruned branches, discarded trimmings, black cinders from a brush fire, buried irrigation pipes, all these things express without words what has become of agrarian toil, for such is "the harlequin costume of Mother Work."[6]

Atop the embankment, at the terminus of the line of Italian cypress, a ribbon of maquis takes over. After 50 meters, I pass along a section of the embankment recently cleared of this overgrowth. To the right, my elevated path affords a view over the adjacent stand of olives to the north. A patchwork of green and brown plots—groves and vineyards—throngs the stream of Kakorema, which feeds into the Longopotamos River. This gives over to fallow plots and maquis at elevation, in the direction of the pass, which assumes the river's name.[7] My path sticks to the uncultivable strip atop the erstwhile wall. For how long have these old stones provided foundation to this track? I cannot say. But it is not implausible that these root-worked walls have held a path ever since agriculture took hold of the acropolis, in the wake of a partial abandonment in the Late Roman period (ca. 400 CE), at some point in the course of living with the aftermath of ancient Kleonai.[8]

For a distance of 60 to 70 meters, I continue to follow the right furrow of the road atop of the raised embankment. Along the bank to the left, Jerusalem sage takes over as the dominant ground cover. I recall, in the moment, how the English traveler Edward Dodwell mistook this sage-like plant (*Phlomis fruticosa*),

---

5 Ibid., 350.
6 Serres (2008a, 238).
7 From Kleonai to Corinth, Jeannette Marchand recently traced the ancient route through the Longopotamos Pass (2009).
8 Marchand (2002, 443).

Road lined with Jerusalem sage.

with its "bunches of yellow flowers, and a green berry about the size of a small cherry," for wild sage (*salvia pomifera*).[9] Still, like Dodwell, I too look here with eyes guided by the text.

The road slopes down, slicing across the line of the ancient city wall.[10] At its end are the remnants of stonewalling. From here and to the west cypresses have been cut down and overgrowth has been cleared from the line of the former wall. A newly graded road continues to run parallel to what would have been its exterior face. The space between road and remnant wall is planted in olives; these are arranged in lines perpendicular to the road varying between two and four trees deep. On the right, verdant vines cling to trellises in equidistant rows, supplied by drip irrigation.

I come to a crossroads. Here, weeds are trampled down under a tangle of footprints at a water supply—a main valve, spray-painted *16*, with an irrigation

9 Dodwell goes on to remark how "the underpart of the leaves is covered in with a white woolly substance, easily detached by the wind, and which, on coming in contact with the eyes, causes a violent smarting pain, that lasts for about a quarter of an hour" (1819 II, 228). Also see Segment 26.
10 On this section of the city wall, see Marchand (2002, 368).

manifold. Fresh shoots and clusters lay discarded along the rows in the adjacent stretch of vineyard. It was thinned only this morning. I take the left lane, which follows a route more or less parallel to the erstwhile city wall of Kleonai. Along here, tight borders are inscribed between plots. As one moves away from Volimoti, there are fewer rocky margins and thickets left to their own. Fewer also are those trees and bushes that formerly crowded the path—Aleppo pine, Italian cypress, kermes oak, lentisc, and bean trefoil. The lack of niches spared for these seemingly extraneous plants says little concerning their former utility. From the Aleppo pine came the resin favored for local wine, among other things. Spires of Italian cypresses serve to signal the location of specific holdings and offer unbroken shade to those who wait out the hotter portions of the day at the plot. From the gall of the kermes oak, a scarlet dye was once extracted.[11] From lentisc, a sticky resin, a gum mastic, was derived and even chewed for oral hygiene.[12] Bean trefoil was known as a cathartic and emetic.[13]

Fresh shoots and clusters in a trimmed vineyard.

11 Forbes (1964, 102–6).
12 According to Pereira it was used "to sweeten the breath, and preserve the teeth and gums" (1842 Vol II, 1624).
13 Sfikas (2001, 94–95).

Along this lane, a white ribbon framed by flowering banks of rockrose or cistus and various knapweeds, springs forth a pharmacopoeia. In the neglected margins, I see milk thistle (*Silybum marianum* or *Carduus marianus*), a remedy for snakebites in Dioscorides. The choleretic properties of this plant were pointed out by Pliny the Elder, and silymarin, extracted from its seeds, was used in liver treatment.[14] There, underneath a volunteer blackberry, I see mallow (*Malva sylvestris*), a folk remedy for throat and stomach ailments whose very name holds on to its use as an emollient.[15] Nearby grows chamomile (*Matricaria chamomilla*), which possesses antiseptic and soothing qualities recognized by Dioscorides. I see common red or corn poppy (*Papaver rhoeas*), which has slight narcotic properties, below Queen Anne's lace (*Daucus carota*). The latter's broad white umbel is the *staphylinos* of Hippocrates and Dioscorides.[16] Before me, I note various knotgrasses (*Polygomum* spp.) and a leafy plant that resembles chicory (*Cichorium intybus*), widely considered to be good for health.[17] Nearby there is a creeping yellow flower that is reminiscent of black mustard (*Brassica nigra*), which is normally cultivated and forms a staple of the *materia medica*.

On the right, fresh tillage among maiden olives has left the ground free of weeds. In an agrarian world, the weed pharmacopoeia has perhaps always been relegated to those embankments too steep, those ravines too deep for cultivation, or to those rocky areas, like that of the ruined city wall. Left to fallow land, untilled, these ruderal plants are consigned to the liminal zones. It is tempting to look for agrarian wisdom inscribed into these neglected margins, to read the presence of these plants as a persistent holdover of a time when tradition preserved their utility, but such thoughts easily edge into romantic hyperbole. To the extent that agrarian logic simply seeks to make the best use of a plot, the orientation is to that of profit, and, hence, productivity.[18] Otherwise, the presence of these seemingly extraneous plants is a testament to their own germinating tenacity.[19]

On the left, cypress spires once again mark the line of the former wall, which makes an abrupt turn to the southeast. Along here the road slots through the rise of the hill to form a holloway. Over scented banks mottled bursts of efflorescence drown out humble grasses that linger in the shadows on either

---

14 Kuntz and Kuntz (2008, 896).
15 Nikitidis and Papiomitoglou (2011, 97).
16 Pereira (1842 Vol II, 1474–76); also see André (1958, 56).
17 Baumann 1993, 131; also considered famine food, chicory was widely consumed in Europe during times of war; see Vorstenbosch et al. (2017).
18 See Segment 11.
19 The literature on seed dormancy and volunteer cereals is tremendous; see Bewley (1997) and Pickett (1993) for references.

side. Among them are stands of volunteer oats (*Avena sativa*).[20] It seems a strange irony that those guided flora that were developed and maintained across hundreds of generations now join weeds in the unguided margins.[21] Within but a few generations, and in the wake of a massive decline in agriculturalists,[22] the introduction of new cultivars, the abandonment of individual stores, a new mobility less resistant to rapid crossings, and an exclusive investment in cash crops, a precipitous and pervasive genetic erosion has occurred in local varieties of cultivated cereals—barley and wheat, oats and rye.[23] Among those agrarians that remain arises a situation where local cereal varieties account for an estimated 1 per cent of the cultivated acreage in Greece today.[24]

Above the roadside, to the south, sits a disused field shack and beyond the managed contours contain olives and vines, but fewer and fewer cereals. Whether along this lane, or among the rich bottomlands of the Kleonai Valley to the south and east of Volimoti, one encounters a scene of both productivity and forfeiture, where the arduous duty that came with safeguarding the Mediterranean triad as a mixed regime has been relinquished.[25] The loss of cultivars has not been without its countermeasures, such as gene banking. Involving archival procedures managed elsewhere, this solution does not involve the farmer, who has passed from the helm of deciding how best to manage loss.

After passing numerous olive groves, I come to one of several vineyards on the right. Along these rows I see indications of viticultural practices common in Napa Valley, New South Wales, or Bordeaux. Young vines, no more than a couple of decades in age, are arranged in close proximity. The main stems are tall, around a meter in height. The trellising or *palissage* present here shows careful training of the cordon along wires stretched between metal posts. The method of pruning, done in winter, is known as a single Royat, named after the Auvergnat town from which the practice derived. Trellis works, though not uncommon among past viticulturalists, were once superfluous to the growing of vines in the wider region. With what is now regarded as the old method, vine stocks were trained low to the ground, scarcely more than 30 centimeters in height, without additional supports. Each vine formed, in the words of Chateaubriand, a cup "of isolated

---

20 Oats, like other cereal crops, do not survive in the ground for more than a couple of years. Thus, they must be self-sown, growing from their own seed bank, year after year.

21 On plants as objects of archaeology within the afterlife of a garden landscape, see Farstadvoll (2019a and b).

22 See Segment 11; also see Witmore (2018a).

23 With the loss of local cereal varieties also follows the loss of their long-term microbial symbionts in the soil (see Finkel et al. (2017) for review and discussion of relevant research).

24 MEECC (2014, 31), Stavropoulos (1996, 13–14).

25 Refer to Renfrew (1972) for an understanding of the longevity of olive-vine-cereal polyculture.

verdure, round which the grapes hang in autumn like crystal droplets."[26] About these verdant cups a low depression was excavated in order "to retain humidity at one season," and "prevent the grapes from touching the [hot] soil" at another.[27] Still, there were always subtle variations between vineyards, just as there are now. Along here, these differences are less a consequence of dissimilar varieties than competing philosophies between growers.

In the Kleonai Valley, as elsewhere, contracts with local wineries encourage the cultivation of select grapes. An after-effect of satisfying international demand is that local cultivars are often uprooted, which contributes to a substantial reduction in the number of varieties grown at scale. Nemea is celebrated for its red-black grape, Agiorgitiko. The name is derived from the village of Agios Georgios, now New Nemea. Local viticulturists hold the vine to be ancient, adapted to the Phliasian plain millennia ago.[28] Diverse soils, steep valleys, differences of taste, cultivation practices, all have conspired in the long-term development of Greek grape varieties.[29] The description and classification of cultivated grape varieties is known as ampelography, from the Greek for "vine," *ampelos*, and "writing," *graphos*. Ampelographic collections account for seven hundred cultivars of Greek vines, of which around three hundred are still cultivated.[30]

The road jogs slightly to the west, and a gentle slope falls away on both sides. Across from a pear tree ringed by self-sown oats and volunteer vines I pause at a vineyard draped with bird netting. The earth between the rows is fresh-tilled—there are no extraneous plants to compete with the vines or impart flavors to the grapes. I kneel to clutch a handful of soil. Cultivars unique to specific localities are often referred to as autochthonous, from the Greek *auto-chthon*, from the earth, born of the soil. Buff-grey in color, friable, dry, yet clayey, these limestone soils are neutral, perhaps tending slightly towards alkaline, and rich in carbonates, which are typical characteristics for marls. These are young soils; geologists refer to them as Inceptisols.[31] This is good soil for Moschofilero, or even more common varieties such as Chardonnay and Syrah. Viniculturists say that poor soils make for better grapes, as the vines are forced to root out extensively into the subsurface, propagating a ramiform labyrinth of subterranean veins. To the extent that vines form lines in the earth, it would seem appropriate to grant a different meaning to ampelography, if only

---

26 1814, 118.
27 Redding (1833, 259–60).
28 Bakasietas (2011, 185).
29 Banilas et al. (2009).
30 Kotínis (1985); also Lazarakis (2006, 50).
31 See Bakasietas (2011).

metaphorically. Of course, vines do not write: they root, and through a dense arterial rootwork soils impart flavor, and, thus, add to the character of the fruit.[32]

Rising from the ground, I grab an irrigation line. These are draped along every row, in every vineyard that I have passed. It would be a mistake to see them as an indication of homogeneous consistency, free of the variabilities in quality and yield that come with weather.[33] Drip irrigation allows vine-growers to maintain a balance between fertility of the soil and water in the wake of the rains, most of which fall before March. But it would be anathema to contemporary modes of production if the grape were immune to the effects of this locality. The wine industry speaks of *terroir*, another French word, which suggests how terrain and microclimate influence the character of grapes.[34] At an elevation of 240 meters, this weed-free ground, in this northwest-sloping plot, in the midst of these olive groves, with this climate, and these soils, and none other, make these vines different from those grown elsewhere. *Terroir* evokes a notion of locality that can never be mistaken as a point among others in a global grid or regarded as a plastic backdrop to viniculture. *Terroir* reminds us that there are aspects of variety that cannot be entered on the ledger (the "terrier") or classified through the nomenclature of Linnaeus. From here the road angles slightly uphill and olives dominate. *Terroir* is not only spatial. Its connection to microclimate insures that the vintage, *millésime* in French or *sodeiá* in Greek, is never precisely the same from year to year. The year 2000 produced an excellent vintage of Agiorgitiko. The following year generated a bumper crop, while unseasonably heavy rains in late August of 2002 wiped out the entire harvest. Thus, the character of these grapes suggests a different notion of time, not unlike the weather—*le temps, o kairos*: both French and Greek preserve this deep bond between time and the weather.[35]

After more than a kilometer since setting out, my path forks right at a crossroads. From here, Ancient Kleones must be less than a kilometer away. The road arcs slightly left and passes through a series of groves up to the top of a rise. The packed surface holds the imprint of a dozen and more crossings—trucks, a moped, and, most recently, a tractor. This different regime of labor's companion adds little nourishment to the soil beyond heavy metals and compaction. As I walk by a procession of trimmed cypress boles, a magpie darts low across the path.

---

32 These insights are ancient, Vitruvius 8.3.12; Theophrastus *Enquiry into Plants* 2.5.7.
33 See Segment 11.
34 The Modern Greek term *oinopedion*, "wine fields" or "land suitable for wine," is sometimes used instead of *terroir*, but it does not conjure the same range of meaning.
35 Serres (2008a, 159), Serres and Latour (1995, 60); in archaeology see Witmore (2006).

Over the rise, small vineyard plots are carved out of the olive groves. Here and there, the road surface is so hard that I leave no track, no imprint, no trace. Only in the plowed margins does one sink into the soil. Soon, I come to another vineyard. This one is immaculately tended. In its tilled earth is written the ichnography of a recent thinning.[36] From their tracks, it appears that two viticulturists began at the road from the lowest row and moved uphill along each side. Step, step, pause. Shift, step. The ground registers the progression of their labors. Indeed, a multitude of agrarian marks are held in the humus along this path. Furrowed parcels, deep tillage, cairn piles, berms, cant-marks, road cuts, boot-scuffed paths, hoof-trodden corners exemplify inscribed ground. Subsurface features within the walls of Volimoti are manifest as soil-marks. Just as opened voids on Tourla record interventions into the earth, slotted ground, here in this vineyard, will reveal itself as cuts, pits or ditches, and fills.[37]

The road to Ancient Kleones.

36 For a definition of this term, see Segment 14.
37 In preparing the bed for a vineyard, it was common among viticulturists to cut pits knee-deep into the earth and invert the soil by rolling (*kílisma*) the organic topsoil to the bottom in a repeated sequence of slots; see Halstead (2014, 271); on the antiquity of similar techniques, see Pikoulas (2011).

The adjacent vineyard has been left to ruin. Stripped of their wires, metal trellises stand bent. Amid weeds, collapsed vines struggle. Those who worked this ground are also buried in it—graves and tombs are borne within earth.[38] Still, the soil shows no favoritism. Olives and cypresses, weeds and vines carve out root-formed veins in the earth and the subsurface holds these webbed trails long after their passing as microbial fodder. The humus is sustained by the decomposition of rootstocks and weeds. It shelters seeds, which can burst forth in the spring or lie dormant for years, decades, or, under the right conditions, centuries. Such is the saving power of the soil.[39] It is also a lesson of the margins, the place where something of these mixed pasts burst forth into view.

Plato speaks of the *chôra* as a malleable, enduring substrate akin to the odorless base that receives the fragrance of jasmine, cinnamon, or henna; not unlike the soft wax held in a tablet that holds the impressions of the stylus.[40] The *Timaeus's* excursus on the receptacle went to lengths not to confuse the repository of traces with the actual ground encountered here, with the tracks, roads, plots, furrows, deep beds, soil, the dust-fringed prints, discarded shoots and clusters, and abandoned vineyards that have integrities in themselves.[41] Elsewhere the *Timaeus* hits upon another nuance of the term, *chôra*, as the wetnurse of becoming, the womb that both receives and shares in that which has emerged.[42] While the Platonic *chôra* is elusive, it is underlying and generative. Yet, there is another way to understand the *chôra*, a more realist conception, as a space that arises through contacts, exchanges, and rapports between actual entities encountered along the way, which is long.

At the bottom of the hill, the road crosses a channel of the Kakorema. Here the soil changes to Entisols.[43] Ahead, the terrain forms a low basin, just east of the village. This would have made the best land for cereals and pulses. Now most plots are under vines, some are under young olives.[44] Apart from the presence of other cash crops, a similar situation is to be found throughout the bottomlands of the Kleonai Valley. Who among the anonymous agrarian citizens of ancient Kleonai could have possibly envisioned an age of Athena and Dionysus without Demeter?

---

38 See Segment 10.

39 The ecology of soil seed banks has been recognized for decades; see Leck, Parker, and Simpson (1989). Gavin Lucas (2012) has also made a case for the auto-archive, with respect to the archaeological record. On the importance of the chthonic as the object of archaeology, see Nativ (2018).

40 *Timaeus* 50e.

41 *Timaeus* 51a.

42 *Timaeus* 52e.

43 Orange in color, the soil here developed through weathering and erosion.

44 Many of the plots in this area are also fenced in.

Before the edge of the village, the road transitions into a paved surface. Elevated, most of the village sits above an agrarian composition. It is here, on the edge of the plain, that people once waited out the maturation of plants, just as others before them did from within the shared walls of ancient Kleonai. It is not that particular agrarian practices are or are not guarded, that skills are or are not preserved, that tracts are or are not spared in the way that they were. None of this compares to a situation where the entire *modus vivendi* of agrarian life in the way it was formerly lived has passed to oblivion.[45] Lived relations with the humus below my feet have shifted. But all is not lost. Much is held within the soil.

To the west, clouds now spill over Phoukas, now obscured behind thick veils of rain on its eastern slopes. I pass a compound comprised of a walled enclosure including a house, several outbuildings—stores and animal shelters—all mud-brick, all made of this same earth. Renamed Ancient Kleones in 1963, the town was known as Kondostavlo, "short stables."[46] Though locals still use the latter term, there are no oxen, mules, or donkeys to be found among these erstwhile stalls. The absence of these former labors' companions has been given meaning through statistics as grim as those of local cereal varieties. Since 1950, in Greece, three of the five native breeds of cattle have ceased to exist and the remaining two only account for 0.64 per cent of the cattle population; all six indigenous horse breeds are threatened with extinction, as is the one breed of buffalo.[47]

Leaving the agricultural land, I take to the main road, which weaves a circuitous path uphill, through town, then southwest over the Mantzoraïka plateau. Mudbrick houses with tile roofs change over to concrete houses with flat roofs—to step across the intersection is to move between two pasts simultaneously present. At last, people enter the scene. An old man bids me good day; a woman waters the plants on her veranda; a dog barks; two lorries, one laden with produce and one empty, pass on the street; a child screams from inside a house; a moped whines by. Oriented towards the main street, buildings are arranged side by side as adjacent cells. On the left, there is a market, a cultural assembly building, and a *kapheneion* (coffeehouse) where men sit at shaded tables flanking the door. Directly across the street is another *kapheneion* where a few youths converse in the sun. Next is a building housing the offices of the agricultural corporative of ancient Kleonai and the municipality of Nemea; a fluted column sits out front as a stamp of governmental

---

45 See Witmore (2018a).

46 Though it was not recognized as a town till 1912, the earliest reference to Kondostavlo dates to the fifteenth century; see Marchand (2002, 14).

47 MEECC (2014, 31).

authority. Soon, I pass a pharmacy, a café, and a gas station. Parked trucks and cars line the street, which begins to give off smells—roasted meat, baked moussaka, laundry, diesel exhaust, and antifreeze. A church is followed by a square. On its far side, plain trees shade the spring, once the source of an aqueduct for ancient Kleonai.[48]

A large drop of rain smacks the asphalt. More follow. With dark clouds looming over the ridge I hasten my pace uphill towards the winery at the edge of Ancient Kleones where I might wait out the passing rains. The course of the village along the main road to Nemea amounts to two straightways and four turns, two hard, two slight. Houses are stacked up the hill. Their presence here suggests a change in the former tendency towards closeness between house and plot. Now the orientation is to a view over the Agios Vasilios Valley, and proximity between here and yonder seems less of a consideration.

It begins to pour as I reach gates flanked by walls emblazoned with the mask of Dionysus. I rush past the winery's production facility, the largest building in the village, on the way to the tasting room, which is set on a high terrace overlooking the plain. As I open the door, Joanna greets me immediately. She stands behind the bar, waiting on a number of visitors. Even though the dust turned mud still clings to my boots and trousers, she warmly offers me a glass.

Joanna pours a young, dry, white wine—last year's Moschofilero. The liquid has a delicate golden hue. Chilled to 11°C, the temperature draws out an aroma of green apples, citrus, and cistus. The flavors are acidic and crisp. It takes decades to develop a sensitive palate. If only I could discern the subtleties of the *terroir* ... Is that a hint of olive? And pear? Yes, these grapes were harvested from Kleonai vineyards.

Joanna follows with a blend of Moschofilero and Chardonnay, also last year's vintage. It smells of peach and melon. We discuss Georg Riedel. The renowned glassmaker has built a reputation on how differently shaped glasses can better express the aromas of different wines. Emanating from the nose, his claims in their reception were not without some skepticism. Analytical studies will subsequently make Riedel's philosophy explicit through visualization. Imaging technology will reveal how the wine glass concentrates ethanol vapor at the rim, leaving an area of comparably lower alcohol concentration, and, thus, enhanced aromas, in the center of the glass.[49] It will be left to science to fully validate what discerning palates already knew; for clear analytical knowledge seems to come, not from smell or taste, but from vision.

---

48 Charitos (1968, 8); also see Marchand (2002, 79).
49 Arakawa et al. (2015); just as Vitruvius was among those Romans who, despite their silver-laden tables, preferred earthenware for the purity of the wine's taste (8.6.11), glass also makes a material difference.

Joanna shifts into red, with a Nemean Agiorgitiko, aged five years in oak barrels. It tastes of cherry, and is subtly spicy (the piquancy of the grape is said to increase with altitude). Veritable chorographies can be written through wine, with its varieties, vintages, and *terroirs*. Ancient mouths knew differences specific to land, not only in terms of varieties, but also the modes of production. From Athenaeus we read of Coan, Cnidian, Chian, and other wines mixed with seawater.[50] Gathered into his text, *The Deipnosophists*, are myriad perspectives of ancient authors whose works have been otherwise lost. Alcman speaks of fragrant wines "free from fire," unboiled, from Carystus on the border of Laconia and Arcadia and from the Five Hills located seven furlongs from Sparta. Galen speaks of sweet and dry Falernian wine; the former, darker in color, was made when the south wind blew through the vineyard, and the latter came from the same grapes, no doubt, at an earlier stage of ripening. Such variable practices insured that the ancient world had its share of bad wine and acquired tastes. Still, Athenaeus only speaks of wine and of others speaking of wine.

Joanna pours an Agiorgitiko blend from both old and young vines of different *terroirs* from the higher elevations of Koutsi. Aged four years in French oak, it is deep red, sanguine in color. Locals refer to this wine as the "blood of Herakles." What might be taken as a subtle suggestion of both the area's association with the wandering demigod, slayer of the Nemean Lion, or a belief in the grape's deep antiquity, speaks to the enduring survival of a grape in its valley, through generations of labor, through iterative, repeated rapports with agrarians. Beyond the trail of blood, the longevity of the grape is understood obliquely. First comes the text: Ottoman tax registers point to the importance of viticulture in the region, which is echoed in earlier fourteenth-century records;[51] and one mention of Phliasian wine, from an excerpt of Middle Comedy by Antiphanes, contained within Athenaeus.[52] Second follows geography: the relative isolation of the area and the difficulty that comes with moving wine overland hints at a protected niche. Third, archaeology: perhaps the most oblique of all, for while it may reveal suggestions of past viticulture, it cannot fully connect the specific grape to this soil, even with the rare gift of pips or organic residue.[53]

---

50 *The Deipnosophists* 1.59, a text often translated as *The Learned Banqueters* or *Doctors at Dinner*.
51 Kourakou-Dragona (2011, 165).
52 1.27d.
53 For an archaeobotanical study of grape pips from the third century BCE, see Megaloudi (2005); on the contribution of organic residue analysis see McGovern and Hall (2016); for comparative DNA studies, see Pagnoux et al. (2015), Bakasietas (2011, 185) mentions DNA studies conducted on this Agiorgitiko grape variety.

The last glass poured by Joanna is a mix, Syrah and Agiorgitiko, aged five years. The aroma is that of wild cherry, bitter chocolate, and eucalyptus. After tasting Joanna's wine, one recognizes how the page fails the pagus. Words are odorless and tasteless, yet the reception of the ancient world has remained focused here. It has ignored our other mouth, what Michel Serres describes as a second tongue.[54] Just as the texts of Plato and Athenaeus have been prolonged through the care of a manuscript tradition, could Agiorgitiko have passed along through an anonymous agrarian tradition of undisclosed longevity?

This wine gives me my taste by giving me its taste—Serres, like others before and after him, urges us to shake loose the delirium of language only, and embrace the thing itself also.[55] His plea is not a re-manifestation of that ancient antagonism between the lived and the read (or rather, archived, stored in a standing reserve of gene banks in case it ever needs to be read); rather, it appeals to the difference wine makes. Through this glass one tastes something of this *terroir*, something of the soil. Across the tongue passes something of the mixed pasts of Nemea;[56] among them perhaps is a deep antiquity.[57]

The rains have passed. I thank Joanna for the hospitality and leave with a couple of bottles. As I walk across the facilities, I glance at the numerous pallets—empty, green-glass wine bottles wait to be filled. Though opaque in its undefined duration, there is a saving power to wine, in the existence of the Agiorgitiko grapes themselves. Still, it is difficult to account for the changes in aromas and flavor that follow with contemporary modes of production: stainless steel vats, oak barrels for aging, sulphur dioxide and sorbic acid to prevent oxidation and bacterial spoilage, storage in glass bottles, drinking from appropriately shaped glasses. Innovation has not been without its casualties—the

---

54 2008a.

55 2008a, 155. Wary of what he labels as a "pragmato-centrism," Yannis Hamilakis has recently suggested a turn from specific entities to sensorial flows. The suggestion, however, is built upon a false opposition between things and flows. It turns a blind eye to sensation as an attribute of rapports between specific kinds of entities. Indeed, with this purported move, this glass of wine is reduced to its affects and ultimately lost in a dramatic stream bristling with the touch, taste, odor, sound, and look of memories and ideas in an incessant, nonspecific dynamism; see Hamilakis (2013, 191–203).

56 On taste and nostalgia, see Serematakis (1994),.

57 Arguments for the antiquity of the grape are not without their inevitable cultural and economic benefits. They are also hardly immune to dialectical impulses. One could equally argue in favor of the agrarian spirit of experimentation with a long-term and perpetual reworking through cross-grafting and mixing varieties for different circumstances. Any arguments for deep antiquity remain speculative possibilities and here it would be more appropriate to situate the variety as a polychronic achievement. In any case, one must assume within both the manuscript and agrarian traditions an adherence to a certain level of fidelity and care, which is given greater perspective when comparative examples are present.

infusion of resin,[58] the use of raisined grapes,[59] or added flavors—other fruits, spices, or herbs. Did the wine retain the sweetness of plums grown nearby? How did the ancient practice of twisting the stems of grape clusters to starve them of sap affect taste? Whatever flavors are or are not among us, the point is an old yet contentious one that there is a different way to encounter antiquity—first taste, then voice.[60]

I return to the road. The rains have drawn out the scent of earth and thyme. Sunlight is beginning to stream through breaking clouds. After a few hundred meters, olive groves cede to maquis. Crossing over the heights of the Mantzoraïka plateau, one encounters a different plant world of low shrubs. Spiny broom (*Calycotome villosa*), spiny spurge (*euphorbia acanthothamnos*), and thorny burnet (*poterium spinosum*)[61] thrive on this goat-worked ground, and present grazing animals and wayward walkers with a formidable, barbed ambush. Prickly oaks (stunted kermes), which give the ridge to the south its name, Drymoni (from the Greek *drys*, for "oak"), grow here and there among these shrubs.

Along this way, the ground holds ruts, ceramic scatters, and forms that hint at the course of an ancient route from Kleonai to Nemea.[62] At the saddle, a large estate is planted in maiden olives and fenced off from the surrounding maquis, which again takes over for a few hundred meters before surrendering to apricot orchards, olive groves, and vineyards. After a little more than a half a kilometer, the road meets with the Nemea Road and the turn-off to Archaia Nemea. Ahead, a winery sits amid large vineyards off the flank of a hill known as Evangelistria or Tebe.

For 600 meters the road climbs in curves and arcs to crest within a stand of cypresses. Soon, in the descent to the plain of Nemea, the old road breaks off to the south and continues to a terminus just before the lower end of the Hellenistic stadium. This abandoned stretch bisected the stadium until May 1989, when the road was moved to allow archaeologists to continue with the expansion of this ancient object by removing centuries of accumulation.

---

58 Extracted from the Aleppo pine among other trees (see Segment 21). It is best if the resin is matched to vines grown in the same soil, thus Tourla or the south side of the Kakorema for those grapes grown between Volimoti and Kondostavlo.

59 This was to the benefit of both taste and longevity.

60 Thus goes the old empiricist motto: *nihil in intellectu quod non prius in sensu*—"there is nothing in the mind that was not first in the senses" (Aquinas [1256–59] 1972, Question 2, Article 3, Response 19).

61 Thorny burnet was often cut and used as fuel or as packing for wine bottles.

62 Ruts in the limestone were documented by Pikoulas (1995, 47–48); also see Marchand (2002, 73–77); sherd scatters found by the Nemea Valley Archaeological Project (NVAP) led Chris Cloke (2016, 119–22) to suggest this as the most likely route between Kleonai and Nemea.

Beyond a slight sweep, the temple and the valley come into view, and soon the road passes Konstantinos Peppas Square, on the right. Built in memory of the president of the township of ancient Nemea during the first revived Nemean games in 1996, the plateia surrounds an Ottoman-era fountain[63] and is shaded under plain trees and enclosed by a low stonewall. Beyond, in the vicinity of the spring, Oscar Broneer excavated a deposit of hundreds of votive miniatures, primarily Archaic in date (late seventh and sixth century BCE) in 1925.[64] A reminder of the divine regard with which waters were held, what remains of this collection is now kept in the Nemea Museum.[65]

Below the plateia are two vineyards and a third tucked farther in. All, I suspect, Agiorgitiko. Here, the hills open to afford a fine view of the valley, an intricate palette of green, with the sanctuary at center. Nemea: the name comes from the verb *nemomai*—"divide, allocate or distribute, pasture or graze."[66] On the surface, the agrarian contours of this valley would seem to have required a millennium of agrarian tenacity, thus lending support to the former meaning. Indeed, with the pervasiveness of the vineyards, it would be easy to assume that the variegated partitions of the valley are now morphing into monotony. Yet, within this valley any wayward beliefs that this divided patchwork is of deep antiquity have been overturned.[67]

From here, two hundred years ago, observers beheld a different scene. Plots of wheat, olive, and vines were located across the valley on the western hillside closer to the old village, Koutsoumadi. This village was oriented towards Agios Georgios and the larger Phliasian plain to the west, rather than to what lies here. The floor of this valley was peripheral land, used for grazing, due to its marshy nature.[68] It was in the wake of the Greek War of Independence that the valley bottom became National Lands. Opened to purchase at low rates,

---

63 This fountain is marked on the French *Carte de la Morée* (1832).

64 Broneer's notes and material were stored in the Nemea Museum, but remained unpublished until a master's thesis by Signe Barfoed (2009). The area of the spring was subsequently situated within a large Middle to Late Byzantine site labeled 600, Diaselo Irakliou, by the NVAP (see Segment 6); Cherry, Davis and Mantzourani (1986, 21); also see Cloke (2016, 354–55).

65 What the soil kept for over two millennia is currently lost—six to seven hundred unpublished pieces are now missing from the collection (Barfoed 2009, 17).

66 Compare Kritzas (2003–04, 54) to Marchand (2002, 19); also see Curtius (1879, 313). Frazer, who saw the valley in 1880, suggested that "Nemea" came from the Greek *nemos*, a wooded pasture or a glade (1898 III, 90).

67 Wright et al. (1990).

68 Frazer tried to explain that the valley bottom, on account of its marshy nature, was better adapted to pasturage than tillage (1898 III, 90). In any case, my approach follows a route taken by nineteenth-century antiquarians who ignored precisely this view in favor of the ruined temple of Zeus; see Sutton (1995).

Road by a cemetery, with vines and temple in the distance.

Koutsoumadiotes acquired plots and began to plant currants in the valley bottom. Grazing lands were slowly developed for viticulture.[69]

An enclosed cemetery sits off the north side of the main road. Raised plat-forms are arranged in rows. Few date to before World War II. With the old way of living, graves were left to the memory of soil and earth and, thus, were incapable of providing deep roots for historical referentiality.[70] Now elevated marble boxes seem to hover above the humus, which is largely paved over, save for the fringes where weeds stubbornly take root. Accompanied by enclosed glass cases, not unlike museum displays, outfitted with incense burners and what Hamish Forbes aptly refers to as "icon-like" images of the deceased,[71] the design of recent grave markers attempts to forestall, at least for an untold number of subsequent generations, the inevitability of quietly fading away into oblivion.

Vineyards frame both cemetery and road. Most of the graves belong to mem-bers of two prominent houses (*oikoi*)—Papaioannou and Palivou—names

69 McGrew (1985), Sutton (1997, 28 & 30), Wright et al. (1990, 596–603); also see Segment 11.
70 On the transformation of burial and the memorialization of the deceased, see Forbes (2007, 259–61); also Danforth and Tsiaras (1982).
71 Forbes (2007, 260–61).

associated with Nemean viniculture. The Papaioannou estate crest bears the date, 1876, the year an earthquake leveled the old village of Koutsoumadi. Those villagers who had holdings in the valley moved to family compounds near their land, around which formed two villages, Linoi and Irakleion. In 1883 French engineers opened the blockage in the Nemea River, draining the marshes.[72] Three years later, Antonios Miliarakis described the valley as being cultivated everywhere in vines and olive groves.[73]

Soon the road turns abruptly to the south on a line between sanctuary and stadium. I continue west, returning to a dirt truck road lined with vineyards. Different varieties once grew here. Currants were destroyed by *Phylloxera* in the 1950s, and the families transitioned into other types of wine grapes.[74] Now, older varieties, such as the Bakouri, have become less viable and are virtually extinct.[75] The soil here is not unlike that near Volimoti—Inceptisols. Here, the rule is one of variation, of fluctuation, and the soil holds memories of change and metamorphosis.[76] But to go deeper, one need not always enter the soil, for the long term may lie on the surface, waiting to be revealed through an archaeological and forensic mode of *poiesis*.

My path ends at the fence, in the midst of a vineyard, flanked by overgrown margins, and a rare oat field, freshly reaped; an iron gate prevents me from going any further. New columns have risen on the temple of Zeus, which was once known as *Treis Colonnais* (three columns).[77]

---

72 Miller (1990, 12).

73 1886, 162.

74 See Wright et al. (1990, 596–97).

75 See Bakasietas (2011, 185, footnote 3).

76 Soil samples taken not far from here, in 2015, revealed significantly high levels of copper in the earth around the older vineyards of Nemea, resulting from the use of copper-based fungicides (Kelepertzis et al. 2016).

77 On Treis Colonnais see Laurent (1821, 158); On the Temple Reconstruction Project, see: http://nemeacenter.berkeley.edu/projects/temple-zeus-reconstruction-project.

Bibliography

André, J. 1958. *Notes de Lexicographie Botanique Grecque*. Paris: H. Champion.

Aquinas, T. 1972 [1256–59]. *Quaestiones disputatae de veritate*. Roma: Editori di San Tommaso.

Arakawa, T., K. Iitani, X. Wang, T. Kajiro, K. Toma, K. Yano, and K. Mitsubayashi. 2015. A sniffer-camera for imaging of ethanol vaporization from wine: The effect of wine glass shape. *The Analyst* 140(8), 2881–86.

Bakasietas, K. 2011. The Agiorgitiko Vine variety. In S. Kourakou-Dragona (ed.), *Nemea: Beloved land of Zeus and Dionysos*. Athens: Foinikas Publications. 185–90.

Banilas, G., E. Korkas, P. Kaldis, and P. Hatzopoulos. 2009. Olive and grapevine biodiversity in Greece and Cyprus: A review. In *Climate change, intercropping, pest control and beneficial microorganisms*. Dordrecht: Springer. 401–28.

Barfoed, S. 2009. *An archaic votive deposit from Nemea: Ritual behavior in a sacred landscape*. MA thesis, University of Cincinnati.

Baumann, H. 1993. *The Greek plant world in myth, art, and literature* (trans. W.T. Stearn and E.R. Stearn). Portland, OR: Timber Press.

Bewley, J.D. 1997. Seed germination and dormancy. *Plant Cell* 9, 1055–66.

Charitos, K.B. 1968. *Kleonai*. Athens.

Chateaubriand, F.-R. 1814. *Travels in Greece, Palestine, Egypt, and Barbary, during the years 1806 and 1807*. New York, NY: Van Winkle and Wiley.

Cherry, J.F., J.L. Davis, and E. Mantzourani. 1986. *A report to the Ephoreia of antiquities, Nauplion, on sites within the survey which require protection*. Unpublished.

Cloke, C.F. 2016. *The landscape of the lion: Economies of religion and politics in the Nemean countryside (800 B.C. to A.D. 700)*. Doctoral dissertation, University of Cincinnati.

Curtius, G. 1879. *Grundzüge der griechischen Etymologie*. Leipzig: Teubner.

Danforth, L.M., and A. Tsiaras. 1982. *The death rituals of rural Greece*. Princeton, NJ: Princeton University Press.

Dodwell, E. 1819. *A classical and topographical tour through Greece*. 2 vols. London: Rodwell and Martin.

Farstadvoll, S. 2019a. *A speculative archaeology of excess: Exploring the afterlife of a derelict landscape garden*. Doctoral dissertation, UiT The Arctic University of Norway.

Farstadvoll, S. 2019b. Growing concerns: Plants and their roots in the past. *Journal of Contemporary Archaeology* 5(2), 174–93.

Finkel, O.M., G. Castrillo, S.H. Paredes, I.S. González, and J.L. Dangl. 2017. Understanding and exploiting plant beneficial microbes. *Current Opinion in Plant Biology* 38, 155–63.

Forbes, H. 2007. *Meaning and identity in a Greek landscape: An archaeological ethnography*. Cambridge: Cambridge University Press.

Forbes, R.J. 1964. *Studies in ancient technology*. Vol. 4. Leiden: E.J. Brill.

Frazer, J.G. 1898. *Pausanias's Description of Greece*. 6 vols. London: Macmillan & Co.

Gell, W. 1810. *The itinerary of Greece*. London: Payne.

Halstead, P. 2014. *Two oxen ahead: Pre-mechanized farming in the Mediterranean*. Chichester: Wiley-Blackwell.

Hamilakis, Y. 2013. *Archaeology and the senses: Human experience, memory, and affect*. Cambridge: Cambridge University Press.

Kalivas, D., and K. Bakasietas. 2011. Soil and climate conditions of the vine-growing district of Nemea. In S. Kourakou-Dragona (ed.), *Nemea: Beloved land of Zeus and Dionysos*. Athens: Foinikas Publications. 191–99.

Kelepertzis, E., I. Massas, G. Fligos, M. Panagiotou, and A. Argyraki. 2016. Copper accumulation in vineyard soils from Nemea, Greece. *Bulletin of the Geological Society of Greece* 50(4), 2192–99.

Kotínis, C. 1985. *Ellinikós Aμpelografikós Átlas*. Athens.

Kourakou-Dragona, S. 2011. From Agiogitiko wine to Nemea's appellation of origin wines. In S. Kourakou-Dragona (ed.), *Nemea: Beloved land of Zeus and Dionysos*. Athens: Foinikas Publications.

Kritzas, C. 2003–04. Literacy and society: The case of Argos. *Kodai* 13/14, 53–60.

Kuntz, E., and H.D. Kuntz. 2008. *Hepatology: Textbook and atlas*. 3rd ed. Berlin: Springer.

Laurent, P.E. 1821. *Recollections of a Classical tour*. London: G. and W.B. Whittaker.

Lazarakis, K. 2006. *The wines of Greece*. London: Mitchell Beazley.

Leck, M.A., V.T. Parker, and R.L. Simpson. 1989. *Ecology of soil seed banks*. New York, NY: Academic Press.

Lucas, G. 2012. *Understanding the archaeological record*. Cambridge: Cambridge University Press.

Marchand, J.C. 2002. *Well-built Kleonai: a history of the Peloponnesian city based on a survey of the visible remains and a study of the literary and epigraphic sources*. Doctoral dissertation, University of California, Berkeley, CA.

Marchand, J. 2009. Kleonai, the Corinth–Argos Road, and the "Axis of History." *Hesperia* 78, 107–63.

Mattern, T. 2012. Das «wohlgebaute Kleonai» Neue Ausgrabungen in einer Stadt des «Dritten Griechenlands». *Antike Welt*, 46–54.

Mattern, T. 2013. Kleonai. Neue Forschungen in einer Stadt des «Dritten Griechenlands». In K. Kissas and W.D. Niemeier (eds.), *The Corinthia and the Northeast Peloponnesus. Topography and history from prehistory until end of the antiquity*. München: Hirmer. 323–32.

McGovern, P.E., and G.R. Hall. 2016. Charting a future course for organic residue analysis in archaeology. *Journal of Archaeological Method and Theory* 23(2), 592–622.

McGrew, W.W. 1985. *Land and revolution in modern Greece, 1800–1881: The transition in the tenure and exploitation of land from Ottoman rule to independence*. Kent, OH: Kent State University Press.

Megaloudi, F. 2005. Burnt sacrificial plant offerings in Hellenistic times: An archaeological case study from Messene, Peloponnese, Greece. *Vegetation History and Archaeobotany* 14, 329–40.

Miliarakis, A. 1886. *Geographia Politiki, Nea kai Archaia tou Nomou Argolidos kai Korinthos*. Athens.

Miller, S. 1990. *Nemea: A guide to the site and the museum*. Berkeley, CA: University of California Press.

Ministry of Environment, Energy & Climate Change. 2014. *National biodiversity strategy & action plan*. Athens: MEECC. Available at: www.cbd.int/doc/world/gr/gr-nbsap-01-en.pdf (accessed: 17 March 2016).

Nativ, A. 2018. On the object of archaeology. *Archaeological Dialogues* 25(1), 1–47.

Nikitidis, N., and V. Papiomitoglou 2011. *Green plants and herbs of Greece* (trans. J. Pittinger). Rethymno: Mediterraneo Editions.

Pagnoux, C., L. Bouby, S. Ivorra, C. Petit, S.M. Valamoti, T. Pastor, S. Picq, and J. F. Terral. 2015. Inferring the agrobiodiversity of *Vitis vinifera* L. (grapevine) in ancient Greece by comparative shape analysis of archaeological and modern seeds. *Vegetation History and Archaeobotany* 24(1), 75–84.

Pereira, J. 1842. *The elements of materia medica and therapeutics.* Vol. II. London: Longman, Brown, Green, and Longmans.

Pickett, A.A. 1993. Cereals: Seed shedding, dormancy and longevity. *Aspects of Applied Biology* 35, 17–28.

Pikoulas, Y.A. 1995. *Odikó Díktyo kai Amuna. Apó tin Kórintho sto Argos kai tin Arkadía.* Athens: Horos.

Pikoulas, Y.A. 2011. Ancient vineyards at the Temple of Zeus at Nemea. In S. Kourakou-Dragona (ed.), *Nemea: Beloved land of Zeus and Dionysos.* Athens: Foinikas Publications. 73–78.

Redding, C. 1833. *A history and description of modern wines.* London: Whittaker, Treacher, & Arnot.

Renfrew, C. 1972. *The emergence of civilization: The Cyclades and the Aegean in the third millennium B.C.* London: Methuen & Co.

Serematakis, C.N. 1994. *The senses still: Perception and memory as material culture in modernity.* Chicago, IL: University of Chicago Press.

Serres, M. 2008a. *The five senses: A philosophy of mingled bodies.* London: Continuum.

Serres, M., and B. Latour. 1995. *Conversations on science, culture, and time.* Ann Arbor, MI: University of Michigan Press.

Sfikas, G. 2001. *Trees and shrubs of Greece.* Athens: Efstathiadis Group S.A.

Stavropoulos, N. 1996. *Greece: Country report to the FAO International Technical Conference on Plant Genetic Resources.* Leipzig. Available at: www.fao.org/fileadmin/templates/agphome/documents/PGR/SoW1/Europe/GREECE.PDF (accessed: 17 March 2016).

Sutton, S.B. 1995. The making of an ancient site: Travellers, farmers, and archaeologists in nineteenth century Nemea. *Simeion Anaforas (Point of Reference)* 3, 14–21.

Sutton, S.B. 1997. Disconnected landscapes: Ancient sites, travel guides, and local identity in modern Greece. *Anthropology of Eastern Europe Review* 15, 27–34.

Vorstenbosch, T., I. de Zwarte, L. Duistermaat, and T. van Andel. 2017. Famine food of vegetal origin consumed in the Netherlands during World War II. *Journal of Ethnobiology and Ethnomedicine.* 13(1), 63.

Witmore, C. 2006. Vision, media, noise and the percolation of time: Symmetrical approaches to the mediation of the material world. *Journal of Material Culture* 11(3), 267–92.

Witmore, C. 2018a. The end of the Neolithic? At the emergence of the Anthropocene. In S.E. Pilaar Birch (ed.), *Multispecies Archaeology.* London: Routledge. 26–46.

Wright, J.C., J.F. Cherry, J.L. Davis, E. Mantzourani, S.B. Sutton, and R.F. Sutton, Jr. 1990. The Nemea Valley Archaeological Project: A preliminary report. *Hesperia* 59, 579–659.

6

NEMEA

A transect

Through the valley, John Cherry, sites, survey archaeology, Site 7 (Tourkomne-
mata), tracts and transects, maps, extensive and intensive, Annaliste *affinities,*
time, space and synthesis

July 27th, 2008. Between columns of grey brown and swaths of cypress green, the
sanctuary of Nemea passes in flashes out of the car windows to the right. To the left,
vines splayed on trellises in row after row blend together in rhythmic succession. The
road is still covered in shade, save intermittent slivers and widening gashes touched by
the late-morning light. Ahead the grey asphalt swings east around the boundary of the
sanctuary. Linear cracks and undulations in the macadam are registered by the car's
suspension as we enter the turn. It is just before 10 am.

Soon, the Vrachati Road bends back to the north and the broad, flat top of
Mt Phoukas looms directly ahead. Ensnared by the striking table-mountain,
John Cherry recalls his Pausanias, "there 'Perseus was the first to sacrifice to Zeus
Apesantios'" (Zeus of Mount Apesas).[1] An archaeologist with specialties in

1 Pausanias 2.15.3; also see Sutton (2001).

Mt Phoukas from the Vrachati Road.

Aegean prehistory and landscape, among other things, John has been at the fore-front of intensive survey archaeology, forging regional perspectives from the sur-face, for over three decades.[2] John, along with Jack Davis and a team of fieldwalkers, surveyed and collected ceramics and bone from the summit of Phou-kas in 1985 (labeled Site 306), as part of the Nemea Valley Archaeological Project (NVAP).[3] Co-director of the landscape survey (with Davis and Eleni Mantzour-ani) from 1984–1990, John's regional perspective is one grounded in fieldwork, a direct engagement with the encompassing milieus, the agrarian bottomlands, the intermediate zones, the undefined interstices, and the upland margins.

Though he has not been down this road in years, John remembers it well. He calls our attention to a low rise ahead, just off to the right. "That is Site 402, Magoula."[4] Vineyards spread over the slopes of a gentle knoll, topped by a fallow field; apart from the rise, this series of parcels appears to be no different from any other fields on the valley bottom. Still, beneath the vines and stubble, objects visible in the plow soil hint at a multi-period presence, Roman

2 Alcock and Cherry (2013), Cherry (2011); also see contributions to Knodell and Leppard (2017).
3 On the NVAP, see Alcock, Cherry and Davis (1994), Athanassopoulos (2016), Cherry et al. (1988), Cloke (2016), Wright et al. (1990).
4 *Magoula* is a Greek term often applied to a height, especially a broad mound, with ruins.

or Late Roman to Byzantine.[5] Though a Prehistorian by training, survey archaeologists like John tend to be equally area specialists, obliged to understand the deep history of all human activity in this valley.[6] Thus, to be effective, collaborative projects like NVAP demand a wide range of expertise spanning numerous specialties and subfields within archaeology and beyond.

From the back seat, the third member of our party, Alex Knodell, asks about colluviation within the valley.[7] Broken by periods of stability and soil formation, there have been three phases of sediment deposition across this basin since the Neolithic. It was within the second phase that much of the Classical landscape and Byzantine remains of Site 402 were buried. According to John, the Nemea Valley is now in the midst of the third phase, with bulldozing fields, and the movement of soil through plowing and drainage.

The road enters a series of curves, which seem out of place on the flat valley bottom. John motions for me to slow down and points to a small dirt road on the left. We turn. Crossing the dry bed of the Nemea River, we veer north on an unpaved farm road. John mentions that "there is another scatter of Byzantine objects, Site 6, just across the river to the east, in an area known as Kolonitsa (the 'little hill')." Sites are elusive entities. With colleagues, John had characterized them as "anomalously dense concentrations of artifacts with definable spatial limits."[8] To situate sites as "anomalous" yet "definable" underscores their unruly yet disclosable qualities. Revealed in the course of archaeological practice, sites, for John, are achievements; that is, they emerge across a series of steps, in working with specific objects—discarded sherds of pottery, broken roof tiles, flakes of chipped stone, shattered millstones, chunks of mortar and masonry, pieces of bone, etc. Indeed, as John and his colleagues argued, these things constituted the most basic units of study.[9]

Bracketed by vineyards, the road meets with another then forks back towards the river. These fields were among the first to be surveyed in 1984. As a new methodology, pedestrian survey brought a range of formerly inconspicuous materials into

5 Excavations were carried out here under Papachristodoulou in 1977 and 1978; see Cloke (2016, 756–63).
6 For John, a core aspiration for any archaeologist is to find "the full range of surviving evidence for past human activity or habitation within a given area, and to do so in an efficient and accurate manner" (2005, 248–49).
7 In 2008, Alex, now Associate Professor at Carleton College, was a graduate student at Brown University.
8 Wright et al. (1990, 606).
9 Wright et al. (1990, 603). It should be noted that by characterizing sites as "achievements," I am not suggesting that "sites" lack reality as an entities-in-themselves. Scatters, spolia-laden churches, and ruderal areas encompassing cairn piles exceed any articulation or co-creation on the part of archaeologists and the things found.

the register of archaeological relevance. What hitherto had been regarded as "back-ground noise" became signal, what had been considered worthless—"the junk you find on the surface"[10]—came to hold value, what had been merely latent became amply explicit.[11] By according enduring rubbish its dignity as "individual artifacts," archaeologists began to search for what had become of various pasts in places they would not have looked otherwise.[12] Naively given for some, ignored by others, the result amounted to more than the fact that surface scatters advanced to become objects of concern; pedestrian survey showed how not all far-reaching, archaeo-logical research into the long term required removal of a concealing matrix of soil (no small feat in a field dominated by site-centered approaches defined through excavation; that is, circumscribed holes cut into the earth at places like the sanctu-ary, stadium, and basilica). John developed and justified these practices and later defended them against assailants.

We park off the dirt road near a ruin. A field house when John last visited the area, this husk of a former building is now without a roof. Half mudbrick superstruc-ture, half stone base, the outer surface reads as two different clocks. We can see, in the mudbrick fabric of the upper storey, a checkerboard exterior of strifes and deep-ening rills; these hint at seasonal change, inflicted by rains tracing out seams, from year to year. The lower storey, by contrast, is far more stubborn. Apart from a few stress cracks in the mortar, it shows little change; thus, its stone walls linger on, withstanding weather, and here they will remain long after dissolved mudbrick has ceased to wash over them.

Before they grab their packs, John and Alex scan the ground near the car. Alex points out a red-ware sherd, which John immediately recognizes as Early Roman. From here and to the west, in an area known as Tourkomnemata (Turkish graves), fieldwalkers detected abundant and diverse objects on the sur-face of numerous agricultural plots. NVAP would eventually name this "Site 7."

We gather around a clipboard holding a map of Site 7. Marked with letters corres-ponding to ground cover—vines, olive, weeds, stubble, and maquis—individual agri-cultural plots are delimited as "collection units" and artifact find spots are indicated with various symbols. Referencing the map, John mentions how the plots have

---

10 Flannery (1976, 51).

11 From both inside and outside Greece this history has been recounted many times; compare Jameson, Runnels and Van Andel (1994, 3–7) to Schon (2004) on the shift in relevance to knowledge; see Witmore (2007b); also Cherry, Davis and Mantzourani (1991, 47–52).

12 Redman (1974); Given gaps in coverage—areas under maquis, foliage, or the thin ribbon of unexamined ground between the surveyors along transects—all variants of intensive survey amount to what has been termed "probabilistic." With probabilistic survey, a subset of a larger region was sampled to gain some impression about the whole. Recent research under the banner of full-coverage survey, so hubristic as to fall into hyperbole, purports to have explored every potential dark corner and shaded niche of a given block of land (Fish and Kowalewski 1990).

transformed since he last visited the site in the 1980s. New vineyards have appeared. New areas are under scrub. Some property lines have shifted. The extent to which cartography accompanied surveys is profound. Level surface features lend something of themselves to visualization on flat canvases from the vertical angle of 90 degrees and maps are the primary mode for securing the artifacts and sites disclosed through survey. The map is the mode of manifesting and revealing. The map mediates what is made explicit and how something is engaged. As a visualization of particular qualities as seen from above, the map also conditions any return.[13] With field methods oriented towards the acquisition of knowledge on the flat surface, through NVAP, nearly one hundred sites eventually burst forward to mark out formerly blank space at a scale of 1:5,000 and above.

Avoiding the tight alleys between the vines, we walk west, intuitively spreading out over an open field to scrutinize the level surface of recently tilled, red-clay soils. Alex points out several pieces of Roman amphora. John notes the presence of a chert scraper. For surface scatters to step forward into consideration a unique mode of engagement with land had to be devised: fieldwalking or pedestrian survey. In these fields, team members, spaced at intervals of 15 meters, walked straight lines, foot transects, scanning the ground for contrived forms. Tile fragments, pottery sherds, and lithics otherwise missed by any other method were counted along each transect's line. Chipped stone, glass, metal, and ceramics deemed to have diagnostic properties were collected. Vegetation, visibility, and artifact quantities were noted. At odds with obstacles of the countryside, fieldwalking had to be delimited within "tracts." "Natural or arbitrary areas of relatively uniform vegetation, land use, and visibility," the tracts for Site 7 and the surrounding valley corresponded to

Mudbrick and stone structure near Site 7.

13 See Prologue.

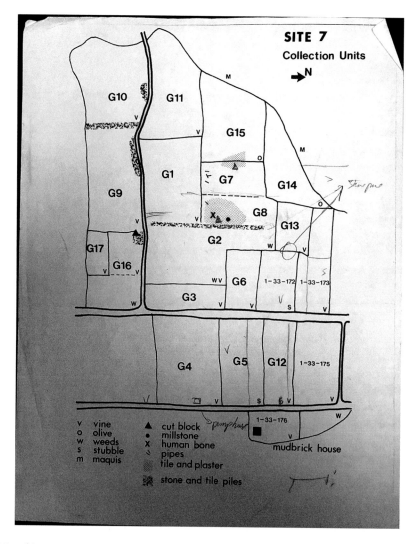

Map of Site 7.

the variable frames of the agrarian pagus—field plots enclosed by berms, changes in cultivation, broad terraces, olive groves buffered by roads, maquis-covered slopes, and cliff-rimmed heights.[14]

At the edge of the plot, we reconvene with the map on a field road. Referencing a concentration of tile, plaster, and terracotta pipes, John points west over another

---

14 Cherry et al. (1988, 162); Wright et al. (1990, 604); Practitioners noted how tracts were less than two hectares in size.

vineyard to an area disturbed by deep plowing and subsequent kiwi cultivation. Pedestrian survey is a method that knows from where it has come and to where it must go.[15] I am not referring to the path of disciplinary history—we will soon come to that—rather, I am speaking of the procedure of knowing, which begins here with the map. Set out in advance, the total survey area of NVAP was divided into five different topographical zones (I–V). Over these zones, a grid of 1 square kilometer sectors was laid, and within these sectors tracts were sequentially numbered (we currently stand between I-33-175 and I-33-173). Zone after zone, sector after sector, track after track, areas awaiting illumination were identified, investigated, and marked off. Consistent, orderly, repetitive, intensive survey followed synthetic routines and set out procedures for replication; it is a method that seeks exactitude with economy.

From the field road, we walk west through high stubble in I-33-173. Artifact density, calculated with counts tabulated against transect length, determined whether an anomalous concentration was an area to be revisited, first for verification, then for collection. It was only after the work of verification, carried out by John and Jack Davis, that Tourkomnemata was defined as Site 7. An emergent entity, Site 7 retroactively defined all individual artifacts as objects to be studied as parts of a whole. These objects were then gathered along transects spaced every 10 meters within collection units (marked as G1–G17) corresponding to discrete tracts. John calls this "transect and grab."[16]

We weave our respective paths by a new rubble cairn and along a terrace towards an area overgrown in maquis and scrub. Intensive survey follows in a long line of pilgrimage, travel, and exploration within Greece—from Pausanias to Wheler and Spon to Leake and Pouqueville to Vanderpool and Pritchett—all were either oriented towards elucidating potent places, specifying objects of Classical concern, or identifying historically relevant topographic features. However, unlike all these earlier ventures, regional survey raised the bar to new encompassing levels, which John has specified in terms of intensity, diachronic orientation, interdisciplinarity, and a conceptual basis oriented towards a circumscribed patch of territory.[17]

According to John, the material was most abundant and well preserved in the series of plots to the west and east of this overgrown area. We pause to take a few photographs and scribble some notes. Phoukas looms above us to the east. Unlike Site 7, the association of the table-mountain with the worship of Zeus Apesantios was a known quantity. Earlier regional work in Greece was lured in by similarly obvious places, because one knew that a site was likely to be found there. John had himself pointed out the problems with these "extensive" approaches. Left to their

15 See Wright et al. 604–08; also Cloke (2016, 52–56).
16 An alternative method, employed on Mt Phoukas (Site 306), involved creating a grid of 10 by 10 meter squares and collecting artifacts from within.
17 Alcock and Cherry (2004, 3); Cherry (2003, 140–41).

own, extensive surveys tended to follow preconceptions, stick to the obvious places, and stay within historically circumscribed timeframes.[18]

Alex points out a glazed-ware fragment; associated with the Medieval era, such objects once fell outside of preferred domains of temporal interest. With the advent of "intensive" survey, no temporal coordinate would take precedence over any other. It was not only that new work on hitherto neglected temporal compartments occurred (Late Antiquity, Byzantine, Frankish, Ottoman, Venetian, Modern), but also their diachronic or cross-temporal interrelation was regarded as an explicit matter of concern. Intensive survey has not been without its critics and there are those who claim exceptions to its rules—that by bestowing privilege to a particular place and period, details might arise in ways that they would not have otherwise.[19] In truth, such complementarity was not lost on projects such as NVAP, which never withheld on extensive survey—after all, Phoukas was eventually explored. Ultimately, whether a survey is extensive or intensive, temporally circumscribed or diachronic, was the wrong question to ask, for, as John has pointed out, all forms of survey can only be understood in light of the purposes they serve.[20]

According to John, among the artifacts collected here were the following: a base of a black-glazed vessel, fragments of amphora, kraters, cooking pots, plates, and lamps, rims and handles, chunks of roof tile and lengths of terracotta water pipe. Subsequent study of these objects suggested a wide range of domestic activities indicative of habitation. Multi-temporal in character, Site 7 may have been a cluster of farmsteads or, at times, a sizable hamlet.[21] When situated within the region as a whole subtle shifts in scatters datable to different eras suggest metamorphoses in settlement and population, ecology, and land use over several millennia. Given such scope, one can see why landscape studies quickly allied themselves with *Annaliste* history.[22] Braudel's perspective on historical durations unfolding as those "slow but perceptible rhythms," those noiseless

---

18 For example, archaeologists, such as Richard Hope Simpson, have investigated regions on more extensive scales through a combination of questioning local informants, aerial photography, and surface reconnaissance focused on the more obvious archaeological features of a given area (cf. Cherry 2003; also see 1983). With the University of Minnesota Messenia Expedition (McDonald and Rapp 1972), to take another example, systematic surface reconnaissance amounted to the use of military-derived aerial photography as a guide to extensive coverage. Areas deemed fruitful for surface search were then visited on the ground (see Witmore 2005, 22–32).

19 These exceptions relate to the work of Curtis Runnels and colleagues on Mesolithic sites between Nafplion and Kandia in the Argolid (Runnels 2009; see Segment 20) and on the south coast of Crete (Strasser 2010; also see Bintliff 2012, 37–39).

20 Cherry 2011.

21 Objects characterized as of Prehistoric, Classical, Hellenistic, Early Roman, Late Roman, Byzantine, or Modern periods were present; see Cloke (2016, 540–73). On the suggestion that the site was a hamlet, see Cloke (2016, 278).

22 Cherry, Davis, and Mantzourani (1991), Jameson, Runnels, and Van Andel (1994).

"underlying currents," accommodated the ebbs and flows that survey archaeologists would formulate over the long term.[23]

Alex and John discuss plans for the publication of NVAP. The final publications will be broken along a timeline—the first survey volume will deal with the Medieval landscape and Site 7 will be divided into different volumes between the Early to Late Roman and the Medieval.[24] While patterns of ebb and flow, of fluctuation in the intensity of land use and density of population were emphasized in survey rationales, the outcomes often fall back into compartmentalized blocks of homogeneous time. This is how archaeologists often proceed. By situating the recovered artifacts by date, ordering them into a sequence, practitioners use this linkage as a narrative thread, one delimited within temporal compartments corresponding to areas of expertise. Though the succession of distinct eras in linear time provides convenient frames for a synthesis, this historicity has never fully encapsulated archaeological practice, nor imparted to our objects of concern their fair share.[25]

We walk precariously among dozens of concrete columns, some broken, most whole and attached to ample concrete footings. Many are stacked neatly, side by side. Others are thrown haphazardly here and there, mixed in with rubble and worked stone in cairn piles. John tells us how, in the 1980s, the European Common Market (European Economic Community, or EEC) subsidized the cultivation of kiwi, a fruit native to China. Large columns, sunk deep into the soil, were used as trellis supports for kiwi canopies. Now the aftermath of this agrarian experiment is here as a wreckage stretching over the whole of a parcel as far as the edges of the surrounding vineyards. Part of the remit of NVAP, in disclosing as-of-yet-undisclosed objects, was to advance them as that which is in need of protection. John and his colleagues went to extra lengths to specify sites at risk from deep plowing, looting, and development.[26] They also witnessed the devastation firsthand.[27] With the bulldozed path for the Moréas (A7), Classical towers, large sections of the Hadrianic Aqueduct,

---

23 Braudel (1972, 20–21), Cherry (1983, 376), Cherry, Davis, and Mantzourani (1991, 10); also see Barker (1995), Bintliff (1991, 6–9).

24 Athanassopoulos (2016); other volumes deal with the excavations of the Early Bronze Age, the Middle and Late Helladic periods associated with the excavations on Tsoungiza Hill in detail; see Pullen (2011), Wright and Dabney (2019).

25 Olsen et al. (2012).

26 Cherry, Davis, and Mantzourani (1986); efforts by NVAP led to the declaration of Site 402 as an "archaeological site," which accords it protections under the Byzantine Ephoreia (also see Segment 18).

27 In 1985, field crews encountered survey stakes for the Moréas set along a wide, straight path without heed for the variegated patchwork of old pathways, plots, or places in the Xerokampos Valley. Crews returned the following summer to encounter a bulldozed swath raised on an even grade through the countryside. Such projects can be framed in broader terms as the desolation of a multi-temporal ensemble that is the rural world. By projecting itself into the future this mega-project ensures a complete reorientation of experience (see Segment 4).

Composite view of Site 7.

and Neolithic sites, revealed prior to their destruction, were relegated to oblivion.[28] These concerns lie behind the choice of our destination.

We walk over soils full of tile and plaster in an adjacent vineyard. Though the present was not outside the remit of NVAP as a whole, it was situated as a domain of anthropology and, thus, was delimited as nonarchaeological territory.[29] Here, the past was, in effect, sealed, and regarded as completed.[30] What John and his colleagues had understood from the angle of its consequences to the archaeological record was bracketed off as "modern." And yet, here we are revisiting Site 7 in order to investigate what has become of European Union subsidies, to document agrarian interactions with what has become of other pasts, to understand how Tourkomnemata lingers on amid transformation.

28 Cherry (2003, 155); also see Lolos (1997, 278, 279, 280, and 283) (see Segment 7).
29 Olivier (2013); also see Stroulia and Sutton (2009).
30 Olivier (2011).

On the map, we note the presence of cut blocks and stone piles; we mark in changes in land distribution and use. By identifying scatters as sites, NVAP encountered these pasts not as objects of another era, but as spatially coextensive things.[31] By calling attention to the ways that things indicative of what has become of the past are gathered here in the present, which is the ground for all archaeological possibility, the achievement of intensive surveys was as much spatial as temporal. Still, by aiming for a historical synthesis that unfolds across several volumes, we distance ourselves from the simultaneous presence of things associated with multiple pasts, and the polychronic ensemble itself falls away. Just as other understandings of space and time are possible, so too are other syntheses that hold on to this side of land, not from the angle of critique, but complementarity.

Alex calls us over to look at a few fragments of terracotta pipe. In just a few years, Alex will co-direct his own regional survey on the Mazi plain in northwest Attica.[32] Just as all time periods, short of the present, were to be touched to the same degree, with the proliferation of subsequent survey projects, every space was to be treated with equal interest. By filling in white space at the regional level, each survey would implicitly point out new areas of concern. There are always blank zones waiting to be explored.

Ultimately, John has recognized the far-reaching possibilities presented by comparative survey data in disclosing changes in settlement, land use, and demography across the whole of the Mediterranean. No, these aspirations are not grounded in that old empiricism where a deeper, more faithful understanding of the past will emerge through the sum of regional studies—where the full diversity of remains would bring the past fully into comprehension. No, this region was not envisioned as a portion of a homogeneous space, as a portion of a regular grid. For John, every site is absolutely unique. Nonetheless, such work requires a system of classification to establish the rules of the game and set the boundaries in which fieldwork is carried out. Such work is both necessary and dangerous.[33]

We walk back to the car, and return to the road by which we came. Making our way south, John plans to show us a ruined portion of the Hadrianic Aqueduct, after we stop off at Agia Sotira, where archaeologists are excavating Late Bronze Age chamber tombs.[34]

---

31 Also see Lucas (2015).

32 On the Mazi Archaeological Project, see Fachard, Knodell, and Banou (2015), Knodell, Fachard, and Papangeli (2016, 2017).

33 The dangers, as I see them, relate to the very system of classification deployed by archaeological projects, which circumscribe the conditions of possibility for all such research, grounding the acquisition of things, structuring how they are made known and retained (Witmore 2009).

34 Excavations were undertaken here between 2006 and 2008 under R. Angus K. Smith, James C. Wright, and Mary K. Dabney; see Smith et al. (2017).

Bibliography

Alcock, S.E., and J.F. Cherry (eds.). 2004. *Side-by-side survey: Comparative regional studies in the Mediterranean world.* Oxford: Oxbow Books.

Alcock, S.E., and J.F. Cherry, with M. Shanks and C. Witmore. 2013. Susan E. Alcock and John F. Cherry. In Rathje, Shanks, & Witmore (eds.), *Archaeology in the making: Conversations through a discipline.* London: Routledge.

Alcock, S.E., J.F. Cherry, and J. Davis. 1994. Intensive survey, agricultural practice and the classical landscape of Greece. In I. Morris (ed.), *Classical Greece.* Cambridge: Cambridge University Press. 137–70.

Athanassopoulos, E.F. 2016. *Nemea Valley Archaeological Project, Volume II: Landscape archaeology and the Medieval countryside.* Princeton, NJ: American School of Classical Studies.

Barker, G. 1995. *A Mediterranean valley: Landscape archaeology and Annales history in the Biferno Valley.* London: Leicester University Press.

Bintliff, J.L. 1991. *The Annales school and archaeology.* Leicester: Leicester University Press.

Bintliff, J.L. 2012. *The complete archaeology of Greece: From hunter-gatherers to the 20th century AD.* Chichester: Wiley-Blackwell.

Braudel, F. 1972. *The Mediterranean and the Mediterranean world in the age of Philip II.* New York, NY: Harper and Row.

Cherry, J.F. 1983. Frogs around the pond: Perspectives on current archaeological survey projects in the Mediterranean region. In R. Keller and D.W. Rupp (eds.), *Archaeological survey in the Mediterranean area,* BAR 155. Oxford: British Archaeological Reports (BAR). 375–416.

Cherry, J.F. 2003. Regional survey and its future. In J.K. Papadopoulos and R.M. Leventhal (eds.), *Theory and practice in Mediterranean archaeology: Old World and New World perspectives.* Los Angeles, CA: Cotsen Institute of Archaeology, University of California. 137–59.

Cherry, J.F. 2005. Survey. In C. Renfrew and P. Bahn (eds.), *Archaeology: The key concepts.* London: Routledge.

Cherry, J.F. 2011. Still not digging, much. *Archaeological Dialogues* 18, 10–17.

Cherry, J.F., J.L. Davis, and E. Mantzourani. 1986. *A report to the Ephoreia of Antiquities, Nauplion, on sites within the survey area which require protection.* Unpublished.

Cherry, J.F., J.L. Davis, A. Demitrack, E. Mantzourani, T.F. Strasser, and L.E. Talalay. 1988. Archaeological survey in an artifact-rich landscape: A Middle Neolithic example from Nemea, Greece. *American Journal of Archaeology* 92, 159–76.

Cherry, J.F., J.L. Davis, and E. Mantzourani. 1991. *Landscape archaeology as long-term history: Northern Keos in the Cycladic Islands.* Los Angeles, CA: Institute of Archaeology, University of California.

Cloke, C.F. 2016. *The landscape of the lion: Economies of religion and politics in the Nemean countryside (800 B.C. to A.D. 700).* Doctoral dissertation, University of Cincinnati.

Fachard, S., A.R. Knodell, and E. Banou. 2015. The 2014 Mazi Archaeological Project (Attica). *Antike Kunst* 58, 178–86.

Fish, S.K., and S.A. Kowalewski. 1990. *The archaeology of regions: A case for full-coverage survey.* Washington, DC: Smithsonian Institution Press.

Flannery, D.V. (ed.). 1976. *The early Mesoamerican village.* London: Academic Press.

Jameson, M.H., C.N. Runnels, and T. Van Andel. 1994. *A Greek countryside: The Southern Argolid from prehistory to the present day.* Stanford, CA: Stanford University Press.

Knodell, A.R., and T. Leppard (eds.). 2017. *Regional approaches to society and complexity studies in Honor of John F. Cherry*. London: Equinox.

Knodell, A.R., S. Fachard, and K. Papangeli. 2016. The 2015 Mazi Archaeological Project: Regional survey in Northwest Attica (Greece). *Antike Kunst* 59, 132–52.

Knodell, A.R., S. Fachard, and K. Papangeli. 2017. The 2016 Mazi Archaeological Project: Survey and settlement investigations in Northwest Attica (Greece). *Antike Kunst* 60, 146–63.

Lolos, Y.A. 1997. The Hadrianic Aqueduct of Corinth (with an appendix on the Roman aqueducts in Greece). *Hesperia: The Journal of the American School of Classical Studies at Athens* 66(2), 271–314.

Lucas, G. 2015. Archaeology and contemporaneity. *Archaeological Dialogues* 22(1), 1–15.

McDonald, W.A., and G.R. Rapp. (eds.). 1972. *The Minnesota Messenia Expedition: Reconstructing a Bronze Age regional environment*. Minneapolis, MA: University of Minnesota Press.

Olivier, L. 2011. *The dark abyss of time: Archaeology and memory* (trans. A. Greenspan). Lanham, MD: AltaMira Press.

Olivier, L. 2013. The business of archaeology is the present. In A. González-Ruibal (ed.), *Reclaiming archaeology: Beyond the tropes of modernity*. Abingdon: Routledge. 117–29.

Olsen, B., M. Shanks, T. Webmoor, and C. Witmore 2012. *Archaeology: The discipline of things*. Berkeley, CA: University of California Press.

Pullen, D.L. 2011. *Nemea Valley Archaeological Project, Volume I: The Early Bronze Age village on Tsoungiza Hill*. Princeton, NJ: American School of Classical Studies.

Redman, C. 1974. *Archaeological sampling strategies*. Reading, MA: Addison-Wesley.

Runnels, C.N. 2009. Mesolithic sites and surveys in Greece: A case study from the Southern Argolid. *Journal of Mediterranean Archaeology* 22(1), 57–73.

Schon, R. 2004. *Seeding the landscape: Experimental contributions to regional survey methodology*. Doctoral dissertation, Bryn Mawr College.

Smith, R.A.K., M.K. Dabney, E. Pappi, S. Triantaphyllou, J.C. Wright, P. Karkanas, G. Kotzamani, A. Livarda, C. MacKay, M. Ntinou, M. Roumpou, A.M. Stahl, and G. Tsartsidou. 2017. *Ayia Sotira: A Mycenaean chamber tomb cemetery in the Nemea Valley, Greece*. Philadelphia, PA: INSTAP Academic Press.

Strasser, T.F. 2010. Stone Age seafaring in the Mediterranean: Evidence from the Plakas region for Lower Palaeolithic and Mesolithic habitation of Crete. *Hesperia* 79, 145–90.

Stroulia, A., and S.B. Sutton. 2009. Archaeological sites and local places: Connecting the dots. *Public Archaeology: Archaeological Ethnographies* 8(2–3), 124–40.

Sutton, S.B. 2001. A temple worth seeing: Pausanias, travelers, and the narrative landscape at Nemea. In S.E. Alcock, J. Cherry, and J. Elsner (eds.), *Pausanias: Travel and memory in Roman Greece*. Oxford: Oxford University Press. 175–89.

Witmore, C. 2005. *Multiple field approaches in the Mediterranean: Revisiting the Argolid Exploration Project*. Doctoral dissertation, Stanford University.

Witmore, C. 2007b. Landscape, time, topology: An archaeological account of the Southern Argolid, Greece. In D. Hicks, G. Fairclough, and L. McAtackney (eds.), *Envisioning landscape*. One World Archaeology. Walnut Creek, CA: Left Coast Press. 194–225.

Witmore, C. 2009. Prolegomena to open pasts: On archaeological memory practices. *Archaeologies* 5(3), 511–45.

Wright, J.C., and M.K. Dabney. 2019. *The Mycenaean settlement on Tsoungiza Hill*. Princeton, NJ: American School of Classical Studies at Athens.

Wright, J.C., J.F. Cherry, J.L. Davis, E. Mantzourani, S.B. Sutton, and R.F. Sutton, Jr. 1990. The Nemea Valley Archaeological Project: A preliminary report. *Hesperia* 59, 579–659.

7

AN ERSTWHILE AQUEDUCT

Lucretian flow

The chreode, *the Hadrianic Aqueduct, Lucretius, wonder, on liquidity, equations and problems, atoms, the* clinamen, *metamorphosis, hydrodynamics and the flow of time*

Rains fall in laminar showers and collide with barren slope; waters soak through soil-laden cracks and descend along liquid-smoothed veins into limestone formed under deep Cretaceous seas; from the heights of Mt Ziria, the ancient Kyllini, down through subterranean passages, waters follow forced-fluid paths into the depths of a karstic underworld; eventually they diffuse and mix in an aquifer underlain by an impermeable layer of flysch and phyllites; under pressure waters effuse in springs at the foot of the mountain, and with weather and season the intensity of the outflow varies; along a channel into the basin of Stymphalos these waters stream and, at times, pool into a languid lake of Heraclean renown; agitation all but ceases; water in large volumes exists in a state just shy of rest, relative stability: whirling winds lash at the lake surface, the touch of hastening gusts takes on visible form as playful fingers of perturbation;

within the polje of Stymphalos, waters eventually plunge, resuming their path through unseen karstic conduits; carrying sediments, laden with logs, broken branches, and organic detritus, working loose silt and settled matter, the ponor is, occasionally, clogged. Under the ever-increasing weight of waters, the blockage weakens, liquid volumes coerce aqueous avenues through the debris and muck, the plug blasts open, a vortex forms, turbulent flow returns, the chaotic surge scours, stubborn limestone succumbs, under pressure waters shape passages and pools, in the darkness calcium carbonate enters into an atomic dance with hydrogen ions; turbulence increases and dissipates with seasons; eventually, new blockages develop. Old blockages diminish. For hundreds of millennia waters worked away at this *chreode*, waters conformed to its path, and forms were made, unmade, and remade.

Through secret subterranean streams, the Argives believed these Stymphalian waters fed the Erasinus.[1] It seems that they were not far off. Karstic conduits weave a course under several intervening ridges and thalwegs[2] to connect the Stymphalos polje with the springs south of Argos.[3] The ancients marveled at hydrology; they were awestruck by the porous and permeable underworld where waters flowed. The divine progeny of Okeanos, mastered by Poseidon, rivers and springs gave birth to the lineages of kings, judged contests between jealous gods, and dried up with divine whim in the persistent persecution of humans. Specific to locality, from these waters life sprang forth. Born of the river Inachos, Phoroneus was the first inhabitant of Argive lands. Subaqueous conduits were also envisioned as connecting lands under the seas—such stories served to link people to a patch of porous ground.[4] For all such reasons, and more, rivers and springs received offerings. At the grotto of the Erasinus, the Argives sacrificed to Dionysus and Pan. In honor of the former, Argos held a festival named the *turbe*, the root of turbulence; this term both refers to the throng and connotes disorder, confusion, tumult.[5]

---

1 Strabo 8.6.8; Pausanias 8.22.3; see Clendenon (2009); on the observation of subterranean rivers by the Ancient Greeks, see Baleriaux (2016, 104–07).

2 *Thal-weg*, from the German term for the valley's (*thal*) way (*weg*).

3 Tracer studies conducted in 1984 identified a connection between the Stymphalos polje and the springs at Lerna and Kiveri, which are, astonishingly, south of the Kefalari, though Morfis and Zojer admit this association is not without its problems (1986, 277–78). These studies concluded that the source of the Kefalari at Argos, the ancient Erasinus, is associated with the Scotini polje, while there is also minor flow from the Alea polje, just over 10 kilometers south of Stymphalos (Morfis and Zojer 1986, 287; also see Crouch 2004, 113–14; Higgins and Higgins 1996, 70).

4 See Segment 20.

5 See Pausanias 2.24.6; Dionysus was connected to liberation from social and sexual controls. Here, though it was little used in antiquity, it is worth noting what Jameson calls the "potentially powerful image of Dionysus as a force corresponding to Aphrodite" (Jameson, Stallsmith, and Cartledge 2014, 70–71).

In tapping Arcadian waters and delivering them to the foot of Aphrodite's rock, the Second Corinthians, through the patronage of Hadrian, eventually prevail. With a reproduction of imagined karstic forms in contrived liquid-paths of stone and mortar, Corinth appropriated waters from the valley of Stymphalos, robbing fluvial portions from both the thirsty Argive plain and gulf, to grace the probable provincial capital,[6] to eventually replenish the Sea of Corinth. Did anyone see the irony of this situation in light of the age-old rivalry with Argos? Perhaps. But, what is more, note the subtle annulment of distance through the reconfiguration of flow. Yes, this reconfiguration was only possible under Rome, for in crossing polis boundaries this conduit would have been impossible to secure in earlier times.[7] Still, drainage formerly dictated by karstic forms without human intervention was redistributed into new receptacles by new masters. In overcoming slopes, valleys, and an underworld of pools and conduits, a new *chreode*, a new path of necessity, was formed.[8]

Channeling cold and wholesome waters to Roman cities, aqueducts ranked supreme among the manifestations of the Empire's greatness.[9] Though Dionysius of Halicarnassus would qualify this oft-cited assessment as a matter of opinion, waters aplenty were not without their pride-infusing effects for city-dwellers. Indeed, in a world where waters were lacking, cities like Corinth were spaces of comparable comfort. From the safe shores of the city, there were fewer worries with regard to those liquid shortages lurking just beyond the city gates with their supplicant-worn statues. Where excess was exhibited in superfluous displays at ornamental fountains, a deep appreciation for differences of taste can be easily written off as part of a habitus of abundance.[10] At the fountain is ultimately where engineers usurp philosophers, for he who can channel water holds power.[11] Yet, for the urban masters of water, "pride looms with its poisons."[12] Tranquility follows for those whom in

---

6 Cold and wholesome waters aplenty come from the base of mountains as Vitruvius recognized (8.1.2).

7 Here, I am reiterating an argument made by Susan Alcock (1993, 124–25). Before reaching Corinth, as she points out, the aqueduct passed through what had become the territories of Pheneos, Phlius, Kleonai, and Argos. Under these poleis such a structure would have existed beneath the dangling sword of perpetual jeopardy.

8 Roman aqueducts were considered, as emphasized by Frontinus (*De Aqueductu* 1.16), indispensable (*necessariis*) and, thus, it is not inappropriate to think of them in terms of the *chreode*. For a contrast with the Anavalos canal system, see Segment 11.

9 *Antiquitates Romanae* 3.67.5.

10 Through Hadrian's aqueduct a new flavor streamed into Corinth, for waters acquire their taste from the properties of the soil (Vitruvius 8.3.12), and these waters were quite unlike those of the celebrated Preirene, which coursed through conglomerates, sandstones, and limestone, to gush forth over lime-rich marls (see Robinson, B.A. 2011, 4–5).

11 Serres (2000, 84).

12 Taken from David Slavitt's translation of Lucretius, which takes liberties with 5.47–48: *quidve superbia spurcitia ac petulantia? quantas efficiunt clades!* "Pride looms with its poisons, and petulance gnaws from within, ready to devastate the moment's equipoise" (trans. Slavitt 2008, 191).

observing and learning from "nature," from the greater order of things, come to understand Roman Corinth as but a precarious waypoint for waters in their rush towards rest. Following in the line of Epicurus, Lucretius spoke of such a path.

With an appeal to the foam-born goddess of love, Lucretius begins his remarkable poem *De rerum natura* (*On the Nature of Things*). Writing around 55 BCE, Lucretius is concerned with the nature of the real without recourse to proud gods, without those flights of imagination that mask power through deception, under the ruse of divine domination, which leaves all truth behind.[13] Nature is autonomous. Gods are indifferent. Nature is a self-governing entity that exists due to its own reasons. Gods have nothing to do with how it behaves.[14] For Lucretius, "it is knowing the way things are that awakens the deepest wonder."[15] Wonderment was also tied to the fact that humans are made of the same stuff as water, limestone, and the stars above. We do not occupy a place of privilege; our nature, rare and improbable, is that of nature, which brims with myriad rare and improbable creatures. This surprise was not perplexing; for Lucretius, it was invigorating, as it prompted a deep, even jovial, desire to know. Observe the stream closely. Do not look beyond its nature for its explanation. A different understanding of reality, and time, may, in following Lucretius, emerge from the close evaluation of things themselves— here, water and an aqueduct, flow and its path. We must turn back up this *chreode* and begin again.

From the source springs on the southeast slope of Ziria, waters were directed into a conduit—the *specus*—a solid, covered channel of rubble masonry bonded with clay mortar, held aloft on arched supports; protected from the sun with its heat, liquid volumes flowing across the northern portion of the Stymphalos basin entered a slight curve in the channel, a deviation from the straight path directed by an older dam, perhaps Mycenaean in date, and passed into a tunnel cut through the solid rock of Mt Apelauros; from here, these waters will eventually drop more than 400 meters over the full length of the aqueduct, a distance of 85 kilometers. A land survey determined course and grade for this conduit. Inclination and declination were referenced against that which was

---

13 ... *quorum omnia causa constituisse deos cum fingunt, omnibu' rebus magno opere a vera lapsi ratione videntur* (Lucretius 2.174–76). "... when they imagine that the gods have ordered all things for men's sake, in every way they have fallen far from truth" (trans. Melville 1997, 41). Concerning the date of composition, see Volk (2010).

14 2.167–81.

15 Greenblatt (2011, 199).

without slope.[16] Here, one may assume the use of the chorobates. With this 20 foot wooden plane, leveled against plumb lines, Eucleadian space was first established. Water can also reveal the level—a linear trough gouged out of the center of the planar surface existed for this purpose.[17] Against the reference of the plane, a controlled space necessary for establishing control, an optimal path was calculated and an optimal declination was gauged.[18] Recall geometry, from *geo-metria*, is rooted here, in land survey, in the measurement of fields and slopes. The angle arose out the deviation from a neutral, uniform space; this cleared the ground for the labor crews and masons to begin. No, this work was not indifferent to constraints. Locality asserted itself along the full course of the aqueduct. Working with the affordances of geological forms, with bedrock and outcrop, slope and soil, the overall declination was established in steps.

From the eastern outlet of the rock-cut tunnel, waters reunited with the built *specus* and followed the contours of the northern Skoteini Valley; soon waters passed along the Psari River in an underground conduit, a *rivus subterraneus*; this *specus* was shaped for flow. First, declination: the overall gradient, 5.2 meters/kilometer, was substantially more than the minimum possible angle.[19] Thus, steeper slopes and perhaps even cascades were built into the line. Second, the channel: capped by quarter-round moldings, the bottom corners of the lining projected as waterproof portions of circles into the flow. Third, surface and friction: composed of *opus signinum*—cement rammed with crushed ceramics—the outermost surface of the lining was carefully smoothed.[20] In a straight channel with consistent declination, micro-eddies formed at the channel interface—any surface textures increased resistance to flow—yet, smoother currents rush down the middle of the channel. Both stable and unstable, homeorrhesis (a consistency of flow) occurred locally, only to shift again, with changes in curvature and declination, into turbulent flow. Both curvature and declination of the channel were dictated by locality; thus, they vary. With an increase in curvature and slope followed an increase in the degree of turbulence.

Turning across the river over arched supports, waters enter another subterranean aqueduct along the bank of the Psari before issuing through a second rock-cut tunnel; on the slope of Tsoukana, at Katebises, the *specus* narrows, the

---

16 Here, I am following the path of Michel Serres, who followed that of Lucretius (2000, 43–44; French original; 1977; also see Webb 2006).

17 Vitruvius 8.5.2.

18 Vitruvius 8.5.1; Serres (2000, 45).

19 While Vitruvius provides a recommendation, *ne minus in centenos pedes sicilico*, "not less than a quarter of an inch for every hundred feet" (8.6.1), in terms of ancient Greek mathematics this angle had far more significance (Serres 2000, 10–12).

20 Lolos (1997, 282).

vault lowers, waters are forced into a constrained passage;[21] here there is another change in flow. Laminar flow is the ideal. Organized, orderly, each thin layer of water moves in parallel without mixing with the lamina above or below. Deviation from laminar flow occurs with declination, curves, boundaries, or constraints within the channel. Turbulent flow is pervasive throughout the aqueduct. It is characterized by rotations and swirls where waters mix and churn. What physicists now model with equations, Lucretius formed with words. This churning of the contemporary and ancient is not absurd; ample justification has been provided elsewhere.[22] Lucretian atomism is expressed as poetics and is modeled in the manner of liquids.

Along the base of Tsoukana, waters surged into a turn south along the slope of Tsepournia, rounding the southern end of the Platani Valley, then the northern margin of Kaka Tsiroupia, eventually to course across a bridge over the stream of Drampala, and rush round the northeastern slopes of Xerobouni; in the curve, force increased; with the rate of flow, pressure varied. This, the volume and velocity of the flow, may be calculated within a wide margin of possibility. Here, the flow rate may have been as low as 0.45 cubic meters/second, or as high as 0.96 cubic meters/second; through this channel, anywhere from 39,000 cubic meters to 83,000 cubic meters passed daily.[23] Requisite to this calculation are the hydraulic radius, derived from the size of the vessel and the amount of water it can hold, the grade of declination, and the roughness of the surface.[24] The calculation of open channel flow treats each of these objects as a factor within an equation ($V = R_h^{2/3} S^{1/2}/n$). Hence, the average velocity of the cross-section is V, the hydraulic radius is R_h, the hydraulic slope is S, and the surface-friction coefficient is n. As symbols within a particular mathematical form, the quantitative units abstract away from the specific objects. Because the calculation presupposes the quantifiable across varied situations, the problem is idealized. Herein lies the power of the algebraic—the calculation is shaped into a generalized form applicable to a diversity of objects and scenarios. Yet, herein

---

21 Ibid., 283.
22 See Serres (2000).
23 This wide variability of flow rate, calculated using the Manning formula (Manning 1891), relates to the coefficient used for surface friction. While the upper estimate requires a low Gauckler–Manning coefficient corresponding to a slick surface, 0.015, the lower estimate uses 0.032, which denotes a rougher, high-friction surface. The hydraulic radius = .25 square meters (this measurement is based upon the height of lime plaster within the *specus* and its width) and declination = 5.2 meters/kilometer. Using the Manning formula, Yiannis Lolos calculates the volume of water to Corinth as 80,000 cubic meters/day (Lolos does not reveal the surface-friction coefficient). One also has to account for the variable flow rate from the source (see Lolos 1997, 295–96).
24 The hydraulic radius is the ratio of the channel's cross-sectional area of flow to the wetted perimeter (see Manning 1891).

also lies a distinction with ancient Greek mathematics where specific problems remained true to objects, which were situated in local configurations.[25] There were no equations, which, in demanding a single formulation of a problem, could give rise to solutions with wider utility.[26] The particular was stated in terms of the particular. Largely expository, the mathematical analyses of Archimedes, for example, were simply creative and elegant ways to state problems in a world where there were other creative and elegant ways.[27]

Turning south, around what is now the village of Gymno, on the eastern flanks of Xerobouni, waters flowed in a wide arc curving back to the east, towards a rock outcrop; presented with a choice between cutting deep into the outcrop or setting the channel on arches to draw out the curve, Roman engineers chose the latter; here, on the northeastern slope of Ntourmiza, the path and the flow modify each other; the tight curve induces turbulence, shear stress eats away the smooth lining of the outer channel, a breech forms; an immense population of comingled atoms escapes, washing over the arches, depositing heavier particles, encasing a portion of this section in calcium carbonate. In the beginning, atoms rain down through the limitless void in laminar showers. A chance deviation, which is the minimal angle of contingency, the primordial *clinamen*, occurs.[28] Never coming to rest, atoms swerve. They begin to move in all directions, bouncing off each other, and comingling. Atoms enter into the ceaseless generation, destruction, and regeneration of things. Michel Serres has argued that the shadow of the Syracusan, Archimedes, looms large within the poetics of Lucretius. Without the indefinite divisibility of the circle or the related notion of the minimal angle, the atom would not have been born.[29] With Lucretius, Serres contends that we witness the transposition of ancient Greek mathematics and the physics of turbulence into poetic form. Whereas Archimedes turned his science towards Ares (Mars), Lucretius struggled to reorient his poetry in the direction of Venus (Aphrodite).

From the northeastern slope of Ntourmiza, waters rushed southeast into a wide arc around the southern edge of Megalovouni, turning northeast amid a series of limestone crags and depressions where the path alternated between long troughs cut through bedrock and raised channels set upon supporting walls; here, again, the channel was porous; here, again, a rind of calcium

25 Netz (2004, 11–63); also 2016.
26 Netz (2004, 56).
27 Ibid., 57. On the expository, rather than heuristic, nature of ancient Greek mathematics, see Netz (2000).
28 Serres (2000); also see Lucas (2005, 74), Webb (2006).
29 Serres (2000, 11).

carbonate covers the arch supports, suggesting protracted leakage through a rupture in the *specus*.[30] This limestone crust holds the stone and mortar arches in place, it keeps the masonry from toppling down the slope, it preserves their form. Whether this chance occurrence was the result of illicit tappings by agrarians or of unmitigated turbulence working its way through the cement lining, mortar, and stone is ambiguous—that a leakage occurred is unequivocal. Here, we encounter an involuntary memory, an accident, which reminds us that the passage is also porous. To force waters in a particular direction is to work against flow. To counter the ceaseless wearing-down within the channel, one enters into a perpetual struggle. Maintenance is required; along here and there repairs are manifest as supporting buttresses, which were added subsequent to construction.[31] Maintenance also becomes visible when it is lacking, for here Sisyphus has abandoned his burden, turbulent waters and an *opus signinum*-lined *specus* were eventually left to themselves, and the stone is left to itself and the plain at the bottom of the hill.

This breach in the curve is the *clinamen*, the swerve of Lucretius, which "appears as freedom, because it is precisely this turbulence that refuses forced flow."[32]

From Belanidia waters once coursed away from the slopes of Megalovouni, through buried conduits across a valley, and round the conical northern flank of Stroggylo, the waters previously turned south, then east, across the Xerias River over the back of a solid bridge of monumental proportion;[33] under the

Portion of the Hadrianic Aqueduct on the slopes of Megalovouni.

---

30 Lolos (1997, 284). One should not rule out the possibility that these deposits also resulted from a local return to flow, where waters washing down limestone slopes pour into an abandoned channel and seep over arches.
31 Ibid., 291.
32 Serres (2000, 84).
33 See Biers (1978).

onslaught of riparian rills fine masonry and ponderous stone eventually toppled down. Vaults fell. Arches crumbled. Relentlessly scouring waters were returned to their primordial path, the original *chreode* that coursed into the insatiable sea south of Argos. Where waters once flowed, number-less boots and hooves ground to dust a collapsed *specus*. Rising as a haze of motes, what remains of the conduit is dispersed by winds unseen. Everything eventually disintegrates into the minute particles from which it was born, particles too miniscule for crude eyes to discern. Everything returns to the swirl of those constituent atoms, and it is these constitutive elements that are eternal within the void, empty space, which is also eter-nal, and out of these other conjunctions will form.[34]

Only fragments remain to suggest the overall course of the erstwhile aque-duct. Between these fragments are gaps. Beyond the bridge over the Xerias, the *river subterraneus* turned north. Beyond Tourkobrysi, the stretch between Alepotrypes and Rachi Mantzorou is now largely destroyed, displaced in the construction of the Moréas motorway. Along this stretch a few ruins persist, including the partially buried remains of the only known settling basin. Fur-ther on, in the area of Dervenakia, portions of the underground water channel are visible on either side of the road.[35] For Lucretius, *adsidue quoniam fluere omnia constat*, it is certain that all things are in a perpetual flow, although differently.[36] Channels, arched supports, mortars, and rubble are slow-moving fluids.[37] Thick and heavy, their viscous flows move at a rate measured in mil-lennia. "We perceive the outer, picturesque side of phenomena," as a young Bergson put it,[38] for everything in the world is made up of a deeper reality of primary particles, the "seeds of things" (*primordial rerum*), which are permanent.[39] Atoms are of different shapes, imparting their character to the things they comprise. Liquids are composed of smoother and rounder atoms, not unlike poppy seeds. Harder objects, bronze and iron, stone and diamonds, have tightly knitted atoms; their warp and weft are drawn together with hooked particles containing branch-like protrusions.[40] Atoms swerve and

34 Lucretius 1.215–270 and 5.306–23.

35 Lolos (1997, 278).

36 5.280; also Serres (2000, 46).

37 For an archaeological example where the material world is conceived in terms of the character of flow, see Edgeworth (2011)

38 Bergson and Baskin (1959, 50); French original, 1884.

39 One could argue that from an atomist perspective, the former aqueduct is derivative, existing at the surface of enduring particles. This would amount to a species of what Graham Harman (2011, 8–10) refers to as "undermining." My purpose, however, is not to critique this ancient line of thought on metaphysical grounds.

40 Lucretius 2.440–55.

collide. Atoms meet and separate, generating all manner of conjunctions in the ceaseless mutation of forms.[41]

We were wrong to look for the coherence in the progressive movement, a locus of quenchless thirst. Lucretius is right: look closely and keenly; do not neglect the details, and from what you observe induce what occurs in all matter.[42] Just as the downward flow steals away atoms of limestone from Ziria, it redeposits them elsewhere.[43] The principle is one of *isonomia*—"the degradation of one thing there corresponds to the birth somewhere of another."[44] Here, the wearing away, the scouring out; there, the build-up of carbonate deposits encasing the lining of the *specus*, coating stones in a limestone crust. But this is a proximate time, beyond that of several human generations, stretching across human societies and their machinations. This is not the deep time beyond the evolution of species, in the formation of limestone, or deeper still, atomic time.[45] Though things diminish in their own times, the sum of matter remains constant.[46]

Constant change and incessant renewal, perpetual perishing and endless novelty, these are the bedfellows of time. Against the plumb line of linear history, temporal flow is homogenous and invariant. Yet, more profoundly, the aqueduct, with the help of Lucretius, gives form to a chaotic theory of time. Serres is also right: "the best model is the thing itself, or the object as it exists."[47] This aqueduct returns to the rubble, lime, and crushed ceramics out of which it was composed, and out of these new things are formed.[48] Waters scour away the lining of the channel; mortars exposed to rain wash away; villagers take apart a brick structure, perhaps a settling basin at the base of a cascade;[49] the turbulent stream beats around the piers of the solid bridge. Elsewhere, portions are held fast by earth, the vaulted channel persists as a subterranean conduit; the Ephoreia of Antiquities in Nafplion consolidates the washed-out foundations of the piers, the solid bridge over the Xerias bides the shock of streams a little longer with concrete foundations.[50] The remains of the channel beyond the

41 Serres (2000, 85).

42 *Dumtaxat rerum magnarum parva potest res exemplare dare et vestigia notitiai* (Lucretius 2.123–24). "To some extent a small thing may afford an image of great things, a footprint of a concept" (trans. Melville 1997, 39).

43 Lolos (1997, 296). On carbonate build-up in aqueducts, see Sürmelihindi et al. (2013).

44 Serres (2000, 128).

45 There is an ongoing debate within Lucretian scholarship as to whether Epicureans regarded time as atomic; compare Morel (2002) and Sorabji (1983, 371–77) to Warren (2006) and Zinn (2016).

46 Lucretius 2.62–79.

47 2000, 164.

48 Lucretius 2.62–79.

49 Lolos (1997, 290).

50 This operation occurred in 1974, see ibid., 286, note 30.

arch-raised turn on Ntourmiza is used as a path by shepherds; portions of an aqueduct form agrarian bridges across deep ravines used for carrying an irrigation line between olive groves; the old, rock-cut conduit through Mt Apelauros is expanded for a new aqueduct, the Bochaikos Chandakas,[51] and waters are restored to the path of the Roman aqueduct. Observe the flow closely: accelerations, slow creeps, pools, eddies, surge, countercurrents. A temporal turbulence runs through the fabric of an aqueduct, just as it runs through the text of Lucretius. It is entirely local and original.

51 Lolos (1997, 277).

Bibliography

Alcock, S.E. 1993. *Graecia Capta: The landscapes of Roman Greece*. Cambridge: Cambridge University Press.

Baleriaux, J. 2016. Diving underground: Giving meaning to subterranean rivers. In J. McInerney, I. Sluiter, and B. Corthals. (eds.), *Valuing landscape in Classical antiquity: Natural environment and cultural imagination*. Leiden: Brill. 103–21.

Bergson, H. 1884. *Extraits de Lucrèce, avec un commentaire, des notes et une étude sur la poésie, la philosophie, la physique, le texte et la langue de Lucrèce*. Paris: C. Delagrave.

Bergson, H., and W. Baskin. 1959. *The philosophy of poetry: The genius of Lucretius*. New York, NY: Philosophical Library.

Biers, W.R. 1978. Water from Stymphalos? *Hesperia* 2, 171–84.

Clendenon, C. 2009. Karst hydrology in ancient myths from Arcadia and Argolis. *Greece. Acta Carsologica* 38(1), 145–54.

Crouch, D.P. 2004. *Geology and settlement: Greco-Roman patterns*. Oxford: Oxford University Press.

Edgeworth, M. 2011. *Fluid pasts: Archaeology of flow*. London: Bloomsbury.

Greenblatt, S. 2011. *The swerve: How the world became modern*. New York, NY: W.W. Norton.

Harman, G. 2011. *The quadruple object*. Winchester: Zero Books.

Higgins, M.D., and R.A. Higgins. 1996. *A geological companion to Greece and the Aegean*. London: Duckworth.

Jameson, M.H., A.B. Stallsmith, and P. Cartledge. 2014. *Cults and rites in ancient Greece: Essays on religion and society*. Cambridge: Cambridge University Press.

Lolos, Y.A. 1997. The Hadrianic Aqueduct of Corinth (with an appendix on the Roman aqueducts in Greece). *Hesperia: The Journal of the American School of Classical Studies at Athens* 66(2), 271–314.

Lucas, S.C. 2005. Liquid history: Serres and Lucretius. In N.B. Abbas (ed.), *Mapping Michel Serres*. Ann Arbor, MI: University of Michigan Press. 72–83.

Manning, R. 1891. On the flow of water in open channels and pipes. *Transactions of the Institution of Civil Engineers of Ireland* 20, 161–207.

Melville, R. 1997. *Lucretius on the nature of the universe*. Oxford: Clarendon Press.

Morel, P.-M. 2002. Les ambiguïtés de la conception épicurienne du temps. *Revue philosophique de la France et de l'étranger* 127(2), 195–211.

Morfis, A., and H. Zojer. 1986. *Karst hydrogeology of the Central and Eastern Peloponnesus*. Venice: Springer Verlag.

Netz, R. 2000. Why did Greek mathematicians publish their analyses? In P. Suppes, J.M. E. Moravcsik, H. Mendell, and W.R. Knorr (eds.), *Ancient and medieval traditions in the exact sciences: Essays in memory of Wilbur Knorr*. Stanford, CA: CSLI Publications, Center for the Study of Language and Information. 139–57.

Netz, R. 2004. *The transformation of mathematics in the early Mediterranean world: From problems to equations*. Cambridge: Cambridge University Press.

Netz, R. 2016. Mathematics. In Irby, G.L. (ed.), *A companion to science, technology, and medicine in ancient Greece and Rome*. Vol. 1. Chichester: John Wiley & Sons. 77–95.

Robinson, B.A. 2011. *Histories of Peirene: A Corinthian fountain in three millennia*. Princeton, NJ: American School of Classical Studies at Athens.

Serres, M. 1977. *La naissance de la physique dans le texte de Lucrèce*. Paris: Les Editions de Minuit.

Serres, M. 2000. *The birth of physics*. Manchester: Clinamen Press.

Slavitt, D.R. 2008. *De rerum natura: The nature of things – A poetic translation*. Berkeley, CA: University of California Press.

Sorabji, R. 1983. *Time, creation and the continuum*. London: Duckworth.

Sürmelihindi, G., C.W. Passchier, C. Sptl, P. Kessener, M. Bestmann, D.E. Jacob, and O. N. Baykan. 2013. Laminated carbonate deposits in Roman aqueducts: Origin, processes and implications. *Sedimentology* 60(4), 961–82.

Volk, K. 2010. Lucretius' prayer for peace and the date of "De Rerum Natura". *Classical Quarterly* 60(1), 127–31.

Warren, J. 2006. Epicureans and the present past. *Phronesis* 51(4), 362–87.

Webb, D. 2006. Michel Serres on Lucretius: Atomism, science, and ethics. *Angelaki* 2(3), 125–36.

Zinn, P. 2016. Lucretius on time and its perception. *Kriterion* 30(2), 125–51.

8

TO MYKENES STATION, BY TRAIN

Gertrude Bell, a new mobility, transformations in speed, distance, time, volume
and power, Khani Anesti, the world from a window, land into landscape,
a dragoman, an alternate route to Mykenes by foot, the telegraph

Wednesday April 12, 1899, 11:40 a.m. The Nemea railway station sits in an elevated saddle, pinched between the low flanks of Rachi Mantzorou and Pana-gorrachi, at the head of the Tretos Valley. Gertrude Bell, the intrepid traveler and aspiring archaeologist, feels a jolt, followed by a momentary shudder, as the train grinds away from the stone and mortar platform.[1] Ahead, the railway

---

1   The Gertrude Bell diaries are available online through the University of Newcastle. Bell does not mention details of her journey beyond noting the presence of snow on Helicon and the Arcadian mountains, and the departure and arrival times at Mykenes Station. Between the diary entries and the letters to her mother, she gives two different times for her departure. *Baedeker's Greece* puts the times from Athens to Corinth by train at three to 3.5 hours and from Corinth to Argos and Nauplion at three hours. Bell's arrival at noon suggests that she took the through train. The time of twenty minutes between Nemea and Phichta Station (Mycenae) is published under "Notes from Athens" by Sryridon Lambros in *The Athenaeum* No

descends slowly and evenly to the west where it will make a tight arc around the khan of Dervenakia and enter the pass by the same name to the south. Accompanied by her father, Hugh Bell, her uncle Thomas Marshall, a classical scholar and translator of Aristotle, and a dragoman named Constantine Icomenides, she takes the through train from Athens to Argos. It is a clear sunny day. The best views, according to *Baedeker's Greece*, are to the left of the coach.

The train picks up speed. The tracks ahead are just over a decade old. To be precise, Bell's journey is only three days shy of thirteen years since the completion of the Athens–Argos–Corinth interchange. Yet later that evening, from her room in the Hôtel des Etrangers in Nauplion, Bell would write little in her diary concerning her travels by train from Athens to Mycenae. A new kind of traveler in Greece, the translator of Khwaja Shams-ud-Din Mohammad Hafez-e Shirazi's *Divan* (1897), and the future founder of the Iraq Museum, she was already well sensitized to this new mobility.

Historians of technology have long understood how railways signaled changes in speed, distance, time, volume, and power;[2] the speed of movement, the distance traversed, the guarantee of time synchrony, the volume transported, and the mode of power. Up to the introduction of the railroad, travel and transport had well-defined limits, which, notwithstanding the introduction of the horse, subtle differences in quadruped physiology, transformations in wheeled transport and roads, the development of post stations, or the design of ships and the use of sail, had remained remarkably consistent over the long term.[3] This new mobility radically changes human rapports with these old lands.

The train evens out at twenty-three miles an hour.[4] A billowing plume of black smoke hangs just above the cars as they slip one after the other into a series of slight turns of decreasing insignificance. The valley is bracketed to the left by the three-humped mass of Panagorrachi, a slope speckled in grey rock, red earth, and phrygana, and to the right by slopes covered in a patchwork of maquis, phrygana, and agricultural plots, some under cultivation, some left fallow and clothed in scarlet anemones (a favorite of Gertrude's). The Arcadian mountains, now looming in the distance directly over the path of the train, are covered in snow. The experience of moving through this valley on the

---

June 26, 3061, 1886, 853 (also see Organ 2006). Timetables from 1899 are also available in Bradshaw's *Continental Timetable*.

2 See William Chronon's excellent book *Nature's Metropolis* (1991).

3 Bell would herself be party to radically different modes of conveyance over the course her journey in the Peloponnesus. In a few days, she would write to her mother from an inn in Kalamata about the nine difficult hours she had spent on the roads, mostly bridle paths, over the Langada Pass from Sparta to the port town on the south coast.

4 Timetables from the late nineteenth century provided measured distances in English miles. I maintain these measures here.

very same morning as that of having left Athens was unknown to any traveler before 1886. Seen off from the Peloponnesian station in Athens by Mr Bell, an associate of the British School, at 7 a.m., Gertrude and company will arrive at Mycenae in time for lunch, at noon. These 84.5 miles, which once required a few days on foot, or a couple of long days on the hoof,[5] could now be traversed in five hours.

Over the course of the nineteenth century, travelogues would give way to travel guides, and it is hardly surprising that something of these differences can be gleaned in how they direct the attention of the traveling reader. Sir William Gell intended his logbook, *The Itinerary of the Morea*, to be of use to those travelers who, as he put it, journeyed with the purpose of observation.[6] After falling into the direct road from Corinth to Argos, Gell would enumerate noteworthy features of the pass and situate them with respect to timed distances.

The train now enters the wide curve around the khan of Dervenakia (Khani Anesti), an inn, adjacent to a spring and watermill, within a glade shaded by towering poplars, cypresses, and mulberry trees.[7] Near here, from his mount, Gell noted a guardhouse on the left. After fifteen minutes through the narrow defile of the Tretos, he recorded a fountain on the left, the opening of the "glen," and, on the right across the brook, an ancient ruin, known as Ellenon Lithari. Beyond, the village of Zacchari sat on a hill at a distance of a mile. After another eight minutes, a tumulus to the right. From here, in a span of forty-six minutes, Gell passed another *derveni*,[8] a point of inundation in the road, tracks from ancient wheels, remnants of walls, two more tumuli, a chapel, the river crossing, and yet another tumulus at the entrance to the plain of Argos. Beyond, Gell noted the village of Phiti (Phichtia) to the right, but marked thirty minutes on the path directly to the village of Kharváti, by ancient Mycenae.[9]

A deep cut, drilled and blasted out of the flank of Agrilovouni, shields from passengers who choose to look out open windows in the last carriage the fact that the engine has crossed into the mouth of the ravine known to the ancients as the Tretos. A decade after Bell's trip, *Baedeker's Greece* (1909) would add a new section entitled "route From Corinth to Argos and Nauplia by Railway."

---

5 For travel times on foot, see Sanders and Whitbread (1990).

6 1817, x.

7 See Frazer 1898, 86.

8 From the Turkish word *derbent*, *derveni* refers to both mountain pass and guard.

9 1817, 160–61. Falling within that genre of traveler hints and continuing the geographical tradition of filling in white space with objects of antiquarian interest, Gell's engagement with the Tretos anticipates some of the transformations to come. Quite unlike Pausanias, who was not so much ambivalent to these kinds of detail as they were naively given in a mode of what Heidegger deemed ready-to-handiness, for Gell these things would come to be regarded as present-at-hand and these old lands would all be viewed with equal interest (see Segment 24).

Of the pass of Dervenaki, which lies just beyond the station at Nemea, which lies 20 miles from Corinth, itself 57 miles from Athens, the guide would note that the ancient road from Corinth to Nauplia led across this route. And that "on August 6, 1822, the Turkish troops under Dramali, marching from Corinth to Nauplia, were met at this point by the Greeks under Kolokotonis and Nikitas, but succeeded in forcing their passage, though with heavy loss."[10] From here, the discussion turns to the plain of Argolis. The station at Mykenes lies 27.5 miles from Corinth.

Out the coach windows, the steep lower slope of Agrilovouni rises to the right; the stream at the bottom of the pass slices deep to the left. William Gell felt his route book would be of more service to the interested traveler in mountainous country where measures of distance bear no proportion to the realities on the ground. With the railway, however, miles have meaning. Bell and party are privy to a radical reduction of distance. The 7.5 miles that they will traverse in twenty minutes is a significant reduction of the ninety-nine minutes it took Gell to move leisurely as an observant rider on a mount. The train also works to amplify: the time it once took to move just over 15 miles by foot at a slow pace is now more or less equivalent to 84.5 miles by narrow-gauge (1 meter) rail. Corinth, Nemea, Mycenae, Tiryns, and Argos are not only drawn nearer to Athens, but, as Spyridon Lambros would point out in his column for *The Athenaeum* only a month after the opening of the Corinth–Argos line, they are also drawn closer to one another.[11] Formerly requiring upward of four days, the so-called "little tour" of the Peloponnese now could be accomplished with greater convenience in fewer than two.[12] Greek geography acquires a very new definition.

Ahead, an opening in the pass comes into view. Hugh Bell checks his pocket watch: 11:45. With the railroad, a uniform time, set with respect to Athens, replaces local times.[13] This small change loosens yet another obligation to one's immediate position. Prior to a uniform railroad time, the position of a place with respect to its line of longitude determined its time within Greece. Reckoned by the position of the sun, 11:45 in Athens occurs three minutes and fifteen seconds before 11:45 in Corinth and three minutes and forty-five seconds before 11:45 in Argos. In the ancient world, locality and sun mediated time

---

10 Baedeker (1909, 332); for other discussions of the pass and its archaeological remains, see Frazer (1898, 85–87), Wiseman (1978, 113), Alcock, Cherry, and Davis (1994), Pikoulas (1995, 56–59, 273–76), Marchand (2009, 151–57).
11 Lambros (1886, 853).
12 Bell would forego Corinth and Nemea and opt for Epidaurus by horse from Nauplion, in the same amount of time.
13 Smith (1901 [1893]); also Bartky (1989).

reckoning. With the railroads, time breaks with both locality and sun, in all but one locality, Athens.[14] For the first time in history one can stand in Argos at noon, reckoned by the hand on a clock, and assume that it is the same time in Athens. Uniform time shores up the foundation of railroad timetables, which translates into a regular schedule—a small step in what seems to be an increasing evaporation of geographical space.[15] Spatial idiosyncrasies now succumb to new routines.

The train completes its round of a sharp turn, what amounts to little more than a half circle in the line, and veers south into another tight portion of the pass. Travel by rail is not affected by rain, wind, cold, or heat in the same way as previous trade and travel, whether by land or sea. Even summer was not without its perils. William Martin Leake commented on the heat of the Tretos in August.[16] Not long after Leake himself had passed near the area in 1806, a Tartar was found dead on his mount at Kharváti (Mycenae) after traveling through the pass from Corinth, where he had thoroughly prepared himself with plenty of wine and rakí (Leake muses that there seemed "no reason why a dead Tartar might not travel a whole stage as well as a sleeping one, which often happens").[17]

The enclosing environment of the train carriage, now heading south, shields travelers from exposed vulnerability within the pass. An important step in what can be characterized as a kind of general immunology,[18] such artificial interiors allowed Bell and her entourage to indulge in the selective refusal of participation in the way the Tartar could not, whether through daydreaming, dozing, or death. Not even those select few who had rare recourse to the litter or sedan chair, to the chariot *tethrippon* or *synoris*, or to the carriage or covered mule cart could completely annul the idiosyncrasies of location. Their occupants still felt the ruts, rocky stream crossings, and muddy ways; oiled canvases and wooden roofs could keep neither heat nor humidity nor cold completely at bay; and bushes would routinely subject the occupants to "serious inconvenience."[19]

The train swings left into another turn, one forced by the slope. A steep descent by Greek railroad standards, between Nemea and Mycenae the trans-Peloponnese line achieves its maximum gradient, 1 in 40.[20] Even though the line will descend over 200 meters in this short distance, a smooth gradient and

---

14 At least, until Greece adopts European standard time.
15 See Segment 4.
16 Leake (1830 III, 337–38).
17 Leake (1830 III, 338).
18 After Peter Sloterdijk's thesis in the Spheres trilogy (2011a, 2014, 2016).
19 Gell (1810, vii).
20 See Naval Intelligence Division (1944 II, 358–59).

wide curve provided a contrived and even surface that dulled the exterior world enough to allow the locomotive to live up to its namesake: "locationally mobile units."[21] Bell's journey from Athens to Mycenae in the comfort of a mobile waiting room constitutes a day-out from the pass and all its former hardships. Through traffic will no longer involve a requisite stop at the khan of Dervenakia, or either of the *derveni*; here, under the Ottomans, one was forced to pay a fee of a piastre or two—that is, whenever the guards happened to be present.[22] Exempt from both the constraints of topography and the whims of local guards, travelers now pay at the station, or, as with the Bells' journey, have their dragoman see to it.

The train completes another curve to the right and soon crosses the elevated heights of a bridge. Set on a monumental platform over a single stone archway, clasped tightly about a pebble-strewn streambed, its battered faces of smoothed masonry are roughened by rocky stubble consisting of hundreds of projecting grey, limestone blocks. Out the window to the left, slopes, still benefiting from recent rains, slide in deep, verdant hues toward valley bottom. Thickets of oleander, myrtle, and arbutus embrace the stream. Beyond, the majestic peaks of Profitis Ilias and Sarra tower in the distance.

Actual entities that had been part of travel through this pass for thousands of years—the myrtle which offers shade, the wheel ruts in limestone which guide the cart, the rocky crossing in the clear and shallow stream, the taste and sound of water moving in the channel along which the Nemean lion once lurked, the numerous tortoises that now remain—recede from the immediate, peripatetic, experiential interactions of passers by train. These things either gain a new status as elements of contemplation within a scene now viewed from the comfort of one's seat, or they withdraw from association altogether, awash in a kinetic Greek countryside framed by a series of windows in a room. The smell of thyme is masked by pipe smoke in the cabin. Land becomes landscape, and a pass, which had been a factor in transport for thousands of years, is transformed into a smooth descent from the Nemea station, the slight jolts of a few turns and a curiosity in the background. Bell and her party are no longer privy to the haunted recesses of a lion; they will not happen upon the abject memories of Dramali's defeat held in the rough stone walls thrown up by the Greek defenders, the bones of horses and their riders scattered throughout the pass and along the flanks of the hills. Such things are less likely to be historical referents observed from a window than imagined objects of conversation. Save for the shifts in bodyweight that result from turns dictated by landform, the

21 Sloterdijk (2013, 35).
22 Gell (1810, 26).

pass itself recedes as one draws back the window shade. From the comfortable angle of the interior, the railroad ensured that the Tretos Pass was hardly different from any other smooth, evenly graded stretch of meter-gauge rail in any other location in Europe built on the consistent routine of a timetable. From the angle of a comfortable interior, the act of traveling ceases to exist as an experience of specificities on the ground.[23] The old ways of movement are replaced by mobile parlors at an elevated distance.

Ahead, the train swings left then right in the last turns before the pass opens onto the upper Argolid plain. Between the Z-class steam locomotive, with its tender, and the passenger coaches, a small freight car can be seen out of the right windows as the passengers scan the scene.[24] The enormous differences that locomotives make count for more than how they are experienced by those passengers along for a ride. Reliable, on-time movement in two directions would make the train ideal for postal shipping; a new feature witnessed by Bell on the morning of April 18, after an adventure over the Langada Pass, when she would find her films waiting in Kalamata, having been shipped by rail post. This guarantee would also prove to be of importance for the movement of bulk, mainly agricultural, goods, which begin to travel by land in larger quantities rather than exclusively by sea.[25] The boxcar initiates a competition with the boat, which would have profound consequences for the increasing development of specialized areas of production, a process which would continue over the next century and more with the death of that sustained balance of polyculture: grains on bottomlands, olives on slopes, vines around the edges. Most Greeks who live off the land would rightly welcome this as a relief from old burdens, one that freed them from an existence attended by scarcity. The open fields of the upper plain of Argos, now fully visible on the left of the car, would not remain open for long. Such a sight will be of increasing rarity in most areas of the plain. Indeed, by the end of the coming century the primary output across these flatlands will be oranges—fruits once confined to the enclosed house gardens, areas of comfort and respite, in villages like Argos.[26]

Hugh Bell checks his watch again—five minutes to the station. Black smoke continues to billow from the engine as it enters a long straightaway. The tender

---

23 On traveling by land in ancient Greece, see Casson (1994), Pikoulas (2007a).

24 The trans-Peloponnese line incorporated the Z-class engines, built by Société Alsacienne de Constructions Mécaniques (SACM), from 1890, and by 1899 they had eleven in operation, making them the most common engine (Organ 2006, 38). In 1937, it had become standard practice to enroll two engines for each train on this mountainous line (Naval Intelligence Division 1944 II, 364).

25 The first railroad lines in Greece were employed for the movement of agricultural produce and in mining (Organ 2006).

26 See Segment 11.

is eight-tenths full of coal and six-tenths full of water.[27] For thousands of years land transport had been based on caloric consumption, on biological energy. Now with the train, movement by land draws on an energy base of fossil fuels (as with steamships several decades earlier). Solar energy and animal physiology would no longer define the limits of movement across these old lands as they had done for all previous times.[28] Black smoke, a thing of pride in the late nineteenth century, would contribute its part to rising CO_2 emissions and radical transformations in the water and in the air.[29] With the new mobility comes a new metabolic regime.

While the Bells and Marshall peer out the left windows for hints of Mycenae, Constantine Icomenides makes ready the baggage. A dragoman with deep contempt for professors and fleas, and a profound love of soft-boiled eggs and good Turkish coffee, Icomenides was hired in Athens. For a daily fee of around 50 fr.,[30] he will conduct them to Mycenae, Tiryns, Nauplion, Epidauros, Argos, Tripoli, Sparta, Tegea, Messene, Bassae, Olympia, Delphi, Chaeronea, Thebes, Plataea, and back to Athens. He will arrange for all the travel: the hotels, trains, and the cavalcades of mules, and horses, with Greek saddles (off which Gertrude will take a spill, losing all the skin off her knee in the process). Along the way he will provide four-course meals (in Tripolis, Constantine will bring on a professional cook named Themistocles), a steady supply of hot coffee and tea, and the comforts of home on the road: bedsteads, mattresses, which Gertrude will find to be most luxurious, as well as sheets, covers, and pillows, and more. It is a strange etymological quirk that the term "dragoman" should arise from the mispronunciation of the Arabic term *torgoman*, from the word *targama* or *tarjama*, to interpret or translate. As a dragoman, Constantine Icomenides is more than an interpreter, more than a translator; he is a diplomat, host, courier, facilitator, guide, entertainer, and protector. His purpose was to lessen the dangers of old paths and to make unfamiliar villages familiar; to mollify the drudgeries of travel and to soften hardships. Bell would

27 This estimate assumes a full tender when the train left Athens. Greek railways mainly used imported coal and briquettes (pressed brown coal) (NIH 1944 II, 365–66). By the 1930s some locally derived lignite was incorporated, but this would not have been possible in 1899. For twenty-four years, from 1873, a lignite mine had been in operation on Evia. However, a flood destroyed the mines, both surface and underground, two years before the Bells' journey (see the Public Power Corporation (DEH) website: www.dei.gr/Default.aspx?id=896&nt=18&lang=1). Major lignite production did not resume till after World War I. A general measure of water evaporation according to the Pennsylvania Railroad Company in 1910 was "34.5 pounds of water per hour for each boiler horse-power" (Pennsylvania Railroad 1910, 10).
28 See Chronon (1991, 79–80).
29 See Segments 19 and 27.
30 Based upon the higher recommended rates for the time (see Baedeker 1894, xiv).

keep esteemed company throughout her journey: Sir Edwin and Lady Egerton, the Italian minister at Athens, the Grand Duke of Hesse.[31] She would meet and converse with the leading archaeologists of the day: with D.G. Hogarth, her mentor, in Athens; with Wilhelm Dörpfeld, whom she found to be both agreeable and good-looking, in Athens, Nauplion, Argos, Tripolis, Olympia, and Delphi;[32] and with Paul Perdrizet, the excavator of Delphi. Icomenides, at least during her tour of the Peloponnese, Phocis, and Boeotia, will make sure Gertrude did so in comfort and with style.

Icomenides inspects the lunch basket that he had prepared in Athens. He feels the train even out in another straight segment before the last curves. What he feels was a major step toward an accessible Peloponnese, one laid open to routine crossings with ever-increasing speed, where the only danger is being late.[33] As Icomenides stands ready near the doors, he experiences a smooth and punctual mode of loco-conveyance in comfortable rooms; rooms that extend one city, Athens, into others—Corinth, Argos, and Nauplion. Railway traffic, which could guarantee consistency in both directions, initiates an erosive or, more precisely, *calming* process. This process will eventually undermine the long tradition, the livelihood, of the dragoman, who once smoothed interactions and soothed the woes of travel along difficult old paths. It will undermine other habits as well.

On the other side of the coach from where Icomenides now stands, the low saddle between a conical hill just off Panagorrachi and Mt Trikorpha passes from sight. Through this hollow ran a second old way through the Tretos, a route long forgotten by most. Not fit for carts, Pausanias recommends this way as an *epitomos*, or shortcut, for the vigorous.[34] Fittingly, it once began in the defile near Nemea Station, below the church of Ayios Sostis, which gives its name to the pass. Steep and rugged, it evens out in a vale, before it gradually steepens toward the gap. Here, a series of parallel holloways mark the line traced by countless sandals, boots, and hooves. Compacting the soil, loosening the stones, these provided a depression in which water flowed, creating deep channels. A path now maintained largely by goats amid the accumulations of wayward cobbles in search of a flat stop, this high route constituted a quicker and more direct path for travelers from the north to the plain. But perhaps this emphasis on speed is shortsighted, perhaps travelers chose this route not because of a more expedient traverse, but because of the beauty of the walk or the magnificent view of the plain afforded at the crest of the path or for herbs

31 Diary 21/4/1899: http://gertrudebell.ncl.ac.uk/diary_details.php?diary_id=1890.
32 Bell met up with Dörpfeld in the course of his archaeological tours, or *Peloponnesos-Reisen*.
33 Sloterdijk (2013).
34 Also see Marchand (2009, 155–56), Wiseman (1978, 115–16).

or goats or for the clandestine aversion of the *derveni*, in order to pass unmolested and free of a fee of a piastre or two.[35] Whatever the traveler's rationale, something of the importance of this old way is suggested by the remnants of a stone tower at the apex of the conical hill.[36] In any case, Bell and her party are free of having to make such a decision between routes in the train. And so too is every subsequent traveler. The high road passes into obscurity for everyone save droves and flocks, shepherds and their dogs, archaeologists, and ecological enthusiasts. This route will recede into a forgotten world around walking and riding the bridle paths, which Icomenides knew so well.[37]

Excess steam is released from the blast pipe. A double burst of the steam whistle, one short, one long, follows. The squeal of the brakes permeates the cabin. The train slows as it nears Mykenes Station. Passengers who attempt to catch a glimpse of the citadel from the train window fail to see stone remnants of a tower adjacent to the rail line on the other side of the carriage to the west; vestiges of another kind of geography, one where hardened walls staggered at a distance allowed for controls to be extended across physiologically regulated distances.[38] However, within their field of vision the slowing of the train can be measured in the frequency of passing wooden poles in the foreground. While Bell's letters to her mother would travel back to Athens along this very railroad, the telegraph would reduce far greater distances.[39]

It was not until the advent of the telegraph, as it will later be suggested, "that messages could travel faster than messenger."[40] Marshall McLuhan's point will be that, with the telegraph, information detached itself from such solid commodities as stone and papyrus and introduced a new speed to communication. But McLuhan will neglect his Aeschylus. Troy's fall was signaled in a chain of beacons from Trojan Ida to Agamemnon's Palace.[41] A point connects to a point, which connects to another; never mind what lies between. It is noon. After unloading the baggage on the platform, Constantine Icomenides produces a fine basket lunch.

---

35 Gell (1810, 26).

36 Pikoulas 1995, 175; also see Lord (1939, 80–3), Marchand (2009, 156), Wiseman (1978, 116).

37 Solnit (2001, 12). It should be noted, that after significant overhaul of the entire Peloponnese Railway between 2003 and 2009, it was closed down on January 1, 2011. For more discussion, see http://traino-sos.blogspot.com/.

38 Lord (1941); also see Morris and Papadopoulos (2005).

39 The Argos and Nauplion telegraph stations were established in 1862 as an extension from Corinth line, which was completed in 1861 (see www.ote.gr/en/web/guest/corporate/company/museum/timeline; also Naval Intelligence Division 1944 II, 399–402.

40 McLuhan (1994[1964], 89).

41 Aeschylus's *Agamemnon* begins with the bale-fire blaze of the signal indicating the fall of Troy (also see Prologue).

Bibliography

Alcock, S.E., J.F. Cherry, and J. Davis. 1994. Intensive survey, agricultural practice and the classical landscape of Greece. In I. Morris (ed.), *Classical Greece.* Cambridge: Cambridge University Press. 137–70.

Baedeker, K. 1894. *Greece: A handbook for travellers.* Leipzig: Karl Baedeker.

Baedeker, K. 1909. *Greece: A handbook for travellers.* Leipzig: Karl Baedeker.

Bartky, I.R. 1989. The adoption of standard time. *Technology and Culture* 30(1), 25–56.

Casson, L. 1994. *Travel in the ancient world.* Baltimore, MD: Johns Hopkins University Press.

Chronon, W. 1991. *Nature's metropolis: Chicago and the Great West.* New York, NY: W.W. Norton & Co.

Frazer, J.G. 1898. *Pausanias's Description of Greece.* 6 vols. London: Macmillan & Co.

Gell, W. 1810. *The itinerary of Greece.* London: Payne.

Gell, W. 1817. *Itinerary of the Morea: Being a description of the routes of that peninsula.* London: Rodwell and Martin.

Lambros, S. 1886. Notes from Athens. *The Athenaeum* 3048, 429.

Leake, W.M. 1830. *Travels in the Morea.* London: John Murray.

Lord, L.E. 1939. Watchtowers and fortresses in Argolis. *American Journal of Archaeology* 43(1), 78–84.

Lord, L.E. 1941. *Blockhouses in the Argolid.* Hesperia 10(2), 93–112.

Marchand, J. 2009. Kleonai, the Corinth–Argos Road, and the "axis of history". *Hesperia* 78, 107–63.

McLuhan, M. 1994 [1964]. *Understanding media: The extensions of man.* Cambridge, MA: MIT Press.

Morris, S.P., and J.K. Papadopoulos. 2005. Greek towers and slaves: An archaeology of exploitation. *American Journal of Archaeology* 109, 155–225.

Naval Intelligence Division. 1944. *Greece, Volume I: Physical geography, history, administration and peoples.* Norwich: Jarrold and Sons.

Organ, J. 2006. *Greece narrow gauge.* Midhurst: Middleton Press.

Pennsylvania Railroad. 1910. *Pennsylvania Railroad Company Test Department. Locomotive testing plant at Altoona, Pa. Tests of an E2A locomotive, 1910.* Pennsylvania Railroad Company.

Pikoulas, Y.A. 1995. *Odikó Díktyo kai Amuna. Apó tin Kórintho sto Argos kai tin Arkadía.* Athens: Horos.

Pikoulas, Y.A. 2007a. Travelling by land in ancient Greece. In C.E.P. Adams and J. Roy (eds.), *Travel, geography and culture in Ancient Greece, Egypt, and the near East.* Oxford: Oxbow Books. 78–87.

Sanders, G.D.R., and I.K. Whitbread. 1990. Central places and major roads in the Peloponnese. *Annual of the British School at Athens* 85, 333–61.

Sloterdijk, P. 2011a. *Bubbles: Spheres I.* South Pasadena, CA: Semiotext(e).

Sloterdijk, P. 2013. *In the world interior of capital: For a philosophical theory of globalization.* Cambridge: Polity Press.

Sloterdijk, P. 2014. *Globes: Spheres II.* South Pasadena, CA: Semiotext(e).

Sloterdijk, P. 2016. *Foams: Spheres III.* South Pasadena, CA: Semiotext(e).

Smith, D.E. 1901 [1893]. Standard Time. *The Moderator.* University of Michigan. 83–85.

Solnit, R. 2001. *Wanderlust: A history of walking.* New York, NY: Penguin.

Wiseman, J. 1978. *The land of the ancient Corinthians.* SIMA50. Göteborg: Åström.

9

ABOUT MYCENAE, HISTORY AND ARCHAEOLOGY

A visitor, this happened here, Schliemann's dream, in Schliemann's wake, history and archaeology, blasted out of time, the archaeological paradox, a museum, alienation and hope

Her trip from the crossroads near Phichtia to the Treasury of Atreus and the citadel of the Atreidae takes five minutes.[1] From the main parking area, Angelica skirts the edge of the road, passing along the metal fence above Grave Circle B, and approaches the ticket booth.[2] With the payment of a fee, she passes. Off to her left, a painted metal stele announces Mycenae as a World Heritage site. Before her, a concrete path follows a direct line

---

1 For late-nineteenth-century travelers, like Gertrude Bell, the ride took three-quarters of an hour. A standard itinerary began with the Treasury of Atreus, then the tomb of Clytemnestra, before turning an angle below the strong walls to enter the gate. After a pause at the agora circle, one scrambled up to the palace amid "tinkling flocks" on bare slopes below. Thus is the sequence and something of the description given by Bell herself on April 12, 1899.

2 Angelica is one of the hundreds of thousands of people who visit, and will visit, Mycenae each year.

to the northwest corner of the walls, where it turns abruptly to approach the Lion Gate. From this turn, Angelica walks along an exposure of bedrock, which supports and orients Cyclopean walls, illuminated at night by subsurface lights. Soon, on the left, she pauses at the first in a sequence of seventeen concrete-and-metal, table-like signs along the citadel path. This one is labeled "Lion Gate." After more than a fleeting glance, she continues. Eyeing the headless lions pawing up a platform to stand on both sides of a column, she soon crosses over the great threshold, beneath the giant lintel, and enters strong-walled Mycenae. Here, Agamemnon, honored by Athena and Hera, reigned. Here, in the grave circle, short of directly to the right, Heinrich Schliemann, the dreamer turned archaeologist, found all the gold.

Easing her way through a throng transfixed in the aftermath of the gate, Angelica crosses a long, paved courtyard, foregoing one information sign to stand by another labeled "Grave Circle A." Enclosed by a double ring of standing slabs, the interior of the grave circle is dominated by a large, oval-like crater, containing several stone-lined pits, and an elevated terrace, partially consisting of exposed bedrock, partially cut through by two more rectangular pits. Each sandstone slab of the double ring is carved so as to meet its neighbor along tight seams now worn. Those slabs raised on the stone embankment by the citadel wall are broken. Those closer to the path are set on bedrock, and exist nearly whole. In slabs close to where Angelica stands, sockets are carved into the upper end on the interior face. A minority of broken pieces lay amid yellowing grass on the terrace. And one slab, placed in the wake of excavation, spans the double ring—a solitary indication that the entire structure was formerly capped with such blocks.

How deep was the well of the past contained in the lower slope turned agora circle turned royal sepulchers turned shaft graves? This was not Heinrich Schliemann's question.

As a tour group shuffles by, Angelica brings up a copy of Schliemann's *Mycenæ* on her tablet.[3] Before his dedication to the Emperor of Brazil, His Majesty Dom Pedro II, before his dedication to the Right Honourable William Ewart Gladstone, Schliemann engraved selections from three ancient texts, in their original Greek, as a tripartite epitaph to the book. From Homer he chose Book 11 of the *Iliad*, lines 45 and 46, which make mention of Mycenae as *polychrúsos*, "rich in gold." From Aeschylus he chose lines 1552–54 of the *Agamemnon*, where Clytemnestra proclaims to the Chorus, "By our hands, down he fell, down to death, and down below

---

3 Schliemann (1878, John Murray edition).

shall we bury him—but not with wailings from his household."[4] From Sophocles he chose lines 1–10 from the Electra:

> Son of him who once commanded our forces at Troy, son of Agamemnon!—now you may survey all that your heart has desired for so long. There is the ancient Argos of your yearning, that consecrated land from which the gad-fly drove the daughter of Inachus; there, Orestes, is the Lycian market place, named from the wolf-slaying god; there on the left is Hera's famous temple; and in this place to which we have come, know that you see Mycenae, rich in gold, and here the house of Pelops' heirs, so often stained with bloodshed.[5]

Mycenae, where Agamemnon reigned; Mycenae, where Aegisthus and/or Clytemnestra slayed him upon his return from Troy; Mycenae, abounding with gold and strife; insofar as Schliemann was concerned, these lines serve as a fitting beginning, but not only for all that follows in his book.[6] For here, within these walls, just as Pausanias described, Schliemann found, or so he later believed, the graves of those who, along with Agamemnon, fell down to death.[7] What was lost, what Schliemann alone believed could be found, was returned to history.

Another group crowds around the information sign. A wooden walkway, which descends to enter the circle between the two slab-box projections that frame the opening, is cordoned off. As with a museum, there is a space where viewers gather and a space where things are exhibited. Set on the edge of the delimited viewing area, the sign compels Angelica to stand, read, and observe. On the left, an overall site map, with the footpath highlighted to include points of interest, marks out what to observe along a specified route. To the right of this numbered itinerary is a reconstruction of Grave Circle A.[8] Below, a paragraph informs viewers that the

---

4 Smyth translation. Aeschylus, with an English translation by Herbert Weir Smyth, in two volumes. 2. *Agamemnon*. Cambridge, MA. Harvard University Press. 1926.

5 Jebb translation (1894). *Sophocles. The Electra of Sophocles*. Edited with introduction and notes by Sir Richard Jebb. Cambridge. Cambridge University Press.

6 After a preface by Gladstone, an account of a tomb at Spata, the Fall of Mycenae as described by Diodorus Siculus, and a chapter on Tiryns, Schliemann situates Mycenae topographically, with close reference to Pausanias, Strabo, and other ancient authors. He then sets out the history of Mycenae and the family of Pelops, followed again by Pausanias, who places the royal Sepulchers inside the ruins of Mycenae (1878, 59).

7 Despite acknowledging in his unpublished diaries that the tombs could not possibly be the same as those observed by Pausanias (see Deuel 1977, 229–30).

8 This image is based upon a sketch made by Piet de Jong in 1922. De Jong was the architect and illustrator at Mycenae under Alan Wace from 1920 till 1923, when he became architect for the British School at Athens (see Papadopoulos 2007).

area, once part of an extensive cemetery, was reserved for royal tombs in the sixteenth century BCE. Containing six shaft graves, the enclosure was unearthed by Heinrich Schliemann and Panaiotis Stamatakis in 1876 and 1877. The double circle of sandstone slabs was constructed when the area was incorporated into the citadel around 1250 BCE.

Angelica takes a photo of the map and, in the wake of a large guided party, walks toward the great ramp. At the bottom, their guide, an older woman, parts the crowd for a man in a wheelchair. She recalls fourteen steps that were removed many years ago to make way for a smooth surface.[9] Amid this brouhaha Angelica ascends.

At the top, she pauses by another sign, the fourth in the sequence, to take in the grave circle from a different vantage point. In ignoring the line drawn between history and myth by the scholarly community of his time,[10] Heinrich Schliemann sought to put what he regarded as historical truth to the marvelous ruins of Mycenae. In this he repeated the familiar shift from the contemplation of ancient texts to the acquisition of evidence in support of them. And yet, the written traditions, which captivated Schliemann, were only part of the story. What remained of Mycenae, the presence of strong walls, of the monumental gate surmounted by carved lions, quelled any disbelief as to "the reality of the power that built it."[11] Marvelous ruins survived as proof of that power's existence, for Schliemann, for Pausanias, and for so many others. Against the weight of scholarly consensus as it existed in the early 1870s, Schliemann stood alone in knowing a secret. This secret exemplified how the idea of happiness was bound up with that of redemption, but not in the way that Walter Benjamin would have it.[12] Staunch in his "firm faith," Schliemann appropriated the graves over to the "traditions" as echoed by Pausanias.[13] That is to say, he attempted

---

9 These steps were removed as part of a new site management plan, which began in July of 1998 (Greek Ministry of Culture 1998).

10 The general scholarly attitude, as stated by Wace, "to Homeric descriptions of life and its surroundings was that they were mainly poetic" (1962, 325). Mycenae was regarded as a setting for romantic embellishment and "practically no one believed that the world of Homer had any real basis of fact" (Ibid.).

11 Sloterdijk (2014, 270).

12 Benjamin, Eiland, and Jennings (2006, 389).

13 1878, 335; while faithful to what he regarded as written history, Schliemann knew where to look. In February 1874, he had thirty-four trial trenches dug throughout the acropolis. Two within 100 yards of the Lion Gate were of particular interest, as "he" struck "two Cyclopean house walls" and "found an unsculptured slab resembling a tombstone" along with "a number of female idols and small cows of terra-cotta" (61). While Schliemann's legacy as a father of archaeology is not without controversy (e.g. Calder and Traill 1986; Easton 1984), the use of trial trenches, stratigraphic observation, combined with the innovative use of photography, and, unlike others who followed, rapid publication has sealed his place in disciplinary history (see, for example, Daniel 1967).

to apply a truth, *his* truth, to the face of history, by claiming that "twelve men, three women, and perhaps two or three children" were burned on a pyre and buried below simultaneously. He would claim to have found the remains of Agamemnon and his companions. Little did Schliemann's fidelities waiver in satisfying redemptive ambitions favorable to the self; little was this truth faithful to that expectation owed by the future to the past.[14]

In Schliemann's wake, others would follow; others who would see through the confusion of recorded traditions with the things he found here. While Schliemann was basking in his limelight, Stamatakis cleared the circle further, partially restored the double ring of slabs, and excavated a sixth grave.[15] In the German tradition of *Altertumwissenschaft*, Georg Karo will, after the turn of the century, undertake the comprehensive and detailed analysis the grave circle, shaft graves, and particularly the finds.[16] In aftermath of Christos Tsountas, it was Antonios Keramopoullos, Alan Wace, and others also who scraped through the hollows, under stones formerly unturned, and between walls in an attempt to make sense of what was left. Through the tedious work of typology, ceramics were organized on the basis of similarities in shape, fabric, and decoration.[17] With the stratigraphic verification of these materials, archaeologists built developmental sequences along which ran the stylistic evolution of pottery.[18] As these sequences were further refined, they used imports found throughout Mycenae and elsewhere to establish correlations with Egypt, where dates were more secure.[19] Giving contours to the continuum, relative chronologies follow, and the development of a grave circle, originally part of a larger prehistoric cemetery, is mapped out across the Middle and Late Helladic periods. Its last burial enters the earth nearly four centuries before the great king of Homeric renown.

Over the course of 250 years, some ten generations, tumulary ground is transformed.[20] An area for graves is delimited within a larger cemetery. The

---

14 For Benjamin, there is a weak messianic power upon which the past has claim, such that our coming is expected and a truth is owed to what Schliemann found (Benjamin, Eiland, and Jennings 2006, 390).

15 Prag et al. (2009); also Demakopoulou (1990, 101), Tsountas and Manatt (1897, 83–114).

16 Karo (1915, 1930). *Altertumwissenschaft*: the science of antiquity in which all finds are accorded equal interest. Karo would be seen as bringing the standards of professional scholarship to Schliemann's excavations. Indeed, Karo's efforts are celebrated: see Matz (1964, 639), Mylonas (1957, 103, n.1); also see Davis (2010).

17 Furumark (1941a, 1941b).

18 Schliemann, it should be noted, was among the first to understand the practical utility of stratigraphy in Greece; Wace (1949, 10).

19 Standing stones, carved smooth, in a nearly perfect double circle; do we remember how archaeologists in an era prior to radiocarbon dating would connect the workmanship of Stonehenge to Mycenae in hopes of establishing a relative chronology? See Piggott (1966), Renfrew (1968).

20 Burns (2010, 73–100), Gates (1985), Wace (1949, 59–63); on the larger cemetery, see Alden (2002).

unburned dead are laid in collective shafts, within the earth. These graves are closed and marked by stelae, and, in one case, an altar, perhaps. A double slab circle is raised high on a new terrace. The area of the interior, along with the old stelae, is buried under new fill. New stelae are raised over the old, and the whole structure is enclosed within the walls of the newly expanded citadel, in a prominent position by its main gate.[21]

Free of Schliemann's illuminated delusions, prehistory will prevail in pulling back the veil on a Mycenae forgotten by echoed traditions, but only in its earliest vestiges.[22] Belief that the traditions sustained images faithful to the realities of the society that occupied Mycenae, in the waning days of the Atreidae, proves to be tenacious.[23] This hold is loosened in large part by philology, which would tease out the contours of the Homeric textual tradition.[24] Eventually, scholars come to see the grounds for the heroic society described by Homer as playing out in the Early Iron Age, where, looking to the vestiges of a Mycenaean past as a locus for these stories, a different type of society gave shape to the Homeric world.[25] In revealing a Mycenae before, and at the beginnings of written text on the Greek mainland, prehistory would give priority to material culture, but as the material past it would continue to operate as a form of history.[26]

Next to Angelica, a couple reads the sign aloud. The descriptions put to the stones beyond the grave circle are simple. Objects are named: the Great Ramp and the Hellenistic Chambers, the Ramp House and the House of the Warrior Vase. Functions are suggested: the chambers may have been used for the processing and dyeing of textiles. Objects named are framed as of episodes completed: confined to the temporal box of Late Helladic III or the Hellenistic period. With its homogeneous metrics, chronology gauges the depth between the episodes to which these structures are consigned: 2,100 years, more or less, separate Schliemann from the Hellenistic Chambers; a millennium separates the

21 Gates (1985) argues that the knowledge of the six shaft graves was lost to memory by the thirteenth century BCE. For Gates, the notion of "memory" is exclusively about grey-matter recall, rather than that which is held in objects that persist from these earlier burials.
22 Also see Lucas (2004).
23 Tsountas and Manatt (1897, 347–66).
24 See the section on the "Transmission and History of Interpretation" in Morris and Powell (1997, 3–189).
25 Compare Wace and Stubbings (1962) to Morris and Powell (1997); in particular, see the Editors' Introduction to the latter; also see Davies (1984), Morris (1986). For a contrast to the historic approach, see Nagy (2010).
26 The first example of what would be recognized as Linear B was published a year before Schliemann's demise; see Tsountas and Manatt (1897, 268). Here I am drawing on an argument made by Gavin Lucas (2004, 111). With respect to prehistory as an object of deep-history (something that in another time was derided by David Clarke (1968, 12)), see Shryock and Smail (2011).

Hellenistic Chambers from what lay here in Late Helladic III.[27] Mapping out the past, the minutiae of structures, features, and finds are classified, intensely detailed, and fixed within a temporal framework.[28] Yet again, time capsules are strung like beads of a rosary.[29]

Angelica turns and makes her way along a cable barrier and across a paved viewing platform. A do-not-pass sign and cordon prevent her from accessing a path to the area below. Thus, she turns and continues up the concrete route. Pausing at the corner of an elevated catwalk, she peers downslope. Along the interior of what is called, unknown to Angelica in the moment, the "Hellenistic Tower," and adjacent to an area under a protective roof, are a number of terraces and walls. Though missing the fifth sign in the sequence, she is nonetheless aware that this area, recently trimmed of its weeds, is called the "Cult Centre." The map she now carries as a photo specifies this much. Without a site guide, she does not know that archaeologists working under Lord William Taylour in the 1960s excavated an assortment of various walls and rooms, or that they found terracotta figurines and coiled snakes, tripod tables and faience beads, sundry items of ivory and bronze within one of these structures, "the Temple." Without being guided and governed by the page she does not see what happened here.

Angelica searches for information on her tablet. She learns about the "ritual paraphernalia" found sealed away in a small storage room. From this she sees that archaeologists regarded what they found here as a moment arrested, items left which indicate what occurred here.[30] She understands that what remained was judged largely in terms of function; that is, the role these things played prior to the time of their deposition. While subsequent archaeologists would see through Schliemann's delusion in the ascription of the past event to the wrong remains, they continued to regard material remains as derivative of specific things done in the past—*res gestae*—and these *res gestae* would be set within a causal relation to other events, themselves ordered

27 This is not entirely fair to chronology. The phases of the Late Helladic rest upon subtle changes in ceramic typology (technology and form) and not the sequential ordering of homogeneous time. On some level typologies respond to changes in form, which are specific to ceramic bowls, amphorae, or other objects. Forms are created through negotiations with what exists, which relates less to a matter of date than a practice of dating (see Olivier 2011, 149–77).

28 A tradition that continues here today with the recent publication of the *Archaeological Atlas of Mycenae* (Iakovidis et al. 2003).

29 A connection to Walter Benjamin's metaphor for historicism (also see Segment 2).

30 An "adequate explanation of events," as Colin Renfrew (1980, 290) stated, was seen as flowing rather naturally from their "full description." While his point, in making this assertion, was that such explanations fell short of understanding past experience, such descriptions implicitly portray a frozen instant of time.

sequentially into a homogeneous and universal time.[31] Akin to silhouettes sky-lined along the peaks of earlier generations, the *res gestae* are fixed against a dimly lit background, and, tethered to their location, they continue to sink deeper into the abyss of time.

To avoid being hemmed in by another group, Angelica continues along the path, which from the catwalk takes a dogleg north. A blank space on her photo-graph of the map, through where does she pass? As she walks she overhears a guide describing the work of Christos Tsountas. She seeks and finds out that from May 1886, Tsountas excavated Mycenae on behalf of the Archaeological Society of Athens. Over the course of a decade he laid bare most of the citadel. Tsountas kept few finds. He rarely mentioned stratigraphy or deposits. In docu-menting his excavations, apart from brief annual excavation reports, he wrote few words—only two of possibly four notebooks survive.[32] Faithful to an image of Mycenae under the Pelopid line, he cut through taken-for-granted overbur-den to those enduring features of the Achaean capital. Indeed, it would not be unfair to state that Tsountas was true to the recommendation, voiced by Fustel de Coulanges and evoked by Benjamin, that the "historian who wishes to relive an era" should "blot out everything he knows about the later course of history."[33] Unknowingly, Tsountas's commitment to the remarkable brought about the desolation of what he deemed unremarkable.

Angelica cuts back to the right, just shy of the sixth sign, and takes a zigzagging path up to the "palace." She soon bypasses the seventh, and walks along the paved surface within the portico to the palace. Here, she encounters the trade-off that every archaeologist must accept. Something of one past is left to be experienced, felt, and engaged in its presence, while others, those that came after, are relegated to oblivion. When documented properly something of these things is visualized, circulated, and read, but this trade-off, nonetheless, has been conditioned largely by the concerns of a given time. Who chooses? Perhaps Tsountas anticipated the coming of strangers like Angelica, but not in

---

31 See Olivier's discussion of "history as a void" (2011, 92–96). Here, I have also benefited from Gordon Teskey's discussion of history and archaeology with respect to Milton, Shakespeare and Spenser (2015).

32 Shelton (2006, 159–160). In this article, Kim Shelton wisely passes on weighing Tsountas's field-work practices against present standards. Still, to regard Tsountas as capricious in his excavation methods at the citadel is to be kind. When measured against standards of good practice in archaeology at Mycenae, and elsewhere, in the late nineteenth century, much of Tsountas's work falls short of the mark. Indeed, the absence of consistent collection, which would relegate ceram-ics, never mind deposits (something to which very few would pay serious attention until well into the next century), to spoil tips, was a practice criticized by Stamatakis in his reports to the council of the Archaeological Society regarding Schliemann's excavations (Traill 2012, 81; on the question of good practice at the turn of the century, see Petrie 1904).

33 Benjamin, Eiland, and Jennings (2006, 391).

terms of what this future visitor would demand. Guided by an elevated image of the past, Tsountas went with the grain of history, which demanded the removal of subsequent impurities; that is, the destruction of other things, which hold memories of other pasts. Something of the Bronze Age advances at the expense of what came after. Had Tsountas anticipated Angelica's coming, would he have recognized the dregs of everyday banality as the core objects of archaeological concern?[34]

How much neglect, masked through the celebration of elevated achievement, had to be endured before archaeologists could ask: who lived here under the long shadow of Agamemnon? Who worked here under the skylined silhouettes of the archaeologists? Who cared for these walls now conserved? From where she stands, Angelica can find no answers to these questions, which are behind the trust of Benjamin's evocation of Fustel de Coulanges. Fittingly, Schliemann recognized, more than most, that "the rulers at any time are the heirs of all those who have been victorious throughout history."[35]

Angelica takes a brief pause behind another guided tour.

> Sporadic burning and destructions bring an end to the palatial culture of Late Helladic Mycenae around 1200 BCE, after a period of reoccupation another destruction occurs around 1100 BCE. There is evidence of use through the Early Iron Age, through the Archaic and into the Classical, when Argos destroyed another Mycenae in 468 BCE.

Against this narrative of the whole, everything here now depends; against it everything here is now decided. Historians and archaeologists have long questioned any notion that the past is closed and finalized and therefore stands apart from the conditions through which it comes to be defined in the present. And yet, here, the continuum is presented as given, rather than something that was achieved.

At the top, she leaves the concrete path and stands before another information sign, the eighth in the series. Under an isometric reconstruction of the palace,[36] she reads:

> The palace complex of Mycenae was built on the summit of the hill. Most of the ruins visible today date to the 13th century BC, but there is evidence that the use of the site began in the Early Helladic period

---

34 While it is rare in the history of archaeology that the future, not the present, directs how one deals with what has become of the past, it is not unknown; see, for example, Dawdy (2009), Harrison (2016), Witmore (2009).

35 Benjamin, Eiland, and Jennings (2006, 406).

36 The reconstruction is by Charles K. Williams II; see French (2002, 60).

(3000–2000 BC). The principal part of the palace complex comprises a large court and the megaron, consisting of the entrance portico, the prodromos (antechamber) and the domos of the main hall which had a large circular hearth at the centre. The throne stood half way along the south wall of the domos, which had collapsed down the hillside, together with the southeast part of the room and was reconstructed recently. The megaron was the political, administrative, military and economic hub of Mycenae.[37]

The corridor to the courtyard of the palace is blocked off. And on the other side of the cordon, the palace complex stands frozen, as if to make a leap into the past for the unimaginative observer.

Angelica protests aloud, but no one listens. Around the citadel, concrete pavements, metal walkways, cordons, cable barriers, and information signs accumulate. Smooth walking surfaces, cut weeds, and consolidated walls seem to sanitize the partial, sterilize the broken, stabilize the formerly ruined. With a new corner and supporting foundation for the domos, with consolidated northern walls for the court, with new concrete floors throughout, the palace appears as a composition, an achievement that did and did not exist. She turns to look downhill, toward Grave Circle A. Grave pits, formerly at home deep in the earth, not seen by the Ancients, are now synoptically juxtaposed to the slab circle; a visual connection never made prior to Schliemann is now here. What have archaeologists bequeathed to Angelica?

Was the historical imagination better served *here* by the ruin?[38] Would the archaeological imagination have been better served *here* by the deferral of history?

Angelica protests because she sees the past for what it is—a perpetually accumulating wreckage, masked by an image of the past as a chain of successive and circumscribed events, which, tethered to their temporal grounds, are constantly left behind. Yet, archaeologists here have been implicated in constituting new things, which continue to pile up in the present, irrespective of that perspective that would consign these things to a yonder realm, closed off as what was, as what has passed.[39] In seeking out what happened here *in* the past, archaeologists seem to have missed what happened here *to* the past.[40]

---

37 The textual descriptions on the signs were written by Elisabeth Spathari, former director of the IV Ephoreia of Prehistoric and Classical Antiquities, and Alcestis Papadimitriou, and further edited by Spyridon Iakovidis.
38 Here see Peter N. Miller's excellent discussion of Johann Wolfgang von Goethe (2013, 74–75).
39 See Lucas (2004, 2012) on archaeology as a materializing process.
40 Olivier (2011, 2013), Olsen, Shanks, Webmoor, and Witmore (2012), Shanks (1992).

Angelica looks across the low walls and paved surfaces to the slopes of Sarra and imagines a structure turned ruin, turned quarry, turned foundation for subsequent structures, turned slope known to shepherds with tinkling flocks, turned area of excavation. She looks back down at the exhibition, and at that instant she is fully aware that this ordering remains firmly within the continuum of history. Across that moment flashes a new secret: the grounds for any archaeological debt to the future must begin as if they were blasted out of time altogether.

Angelica walks up the long corridor north of the courtyard. At the end she steps off the concrete path and stands on the gravel, out of the flow of foot traffic. Two men pause nearby. Facing away from Angelica, one unfurls a large, nanoparticle display and holds it aloft, across his field of vision. With two fingers on the transparent screen, the other manipulates an elaborate virtual reconstruction of the Hellenistic temple. Over the scanty remnants of a foundation, they align the idealized form. From Angelica's point of view, they appear to be standing within the floor of the *cella*, buried up to their torsos in stone.[41] Everyone around Angelica—tour groups, guides, the two men with their transparent window, strangers all—seems to weigh what remains here against the expectation that it speaks to an ideal form, to a genuine historical image. Words, plan, image, sign stand in front of the stones. They guide her in situating the past at the anterior to what lies here, in beginning with the past as history. Yet, Angelica questions whether she encounters the flawed manifestations of such a past. The archaeological past, on the contrary, must follow at the posterior—its creative adventure ends where history begins. And yet, here, these positions were confused. Here, Angelica weighs what has become of that confusion.

Do these walls, cleared by Tsountas, consolidated by others, actually tell her "what happened here?" Do the contents of the overburden, again cleared by Tsountas, studied by others actualize the *res gestae*? Without the sign, without the image, without a guide, without the word—which is so easy for Angelica to call up on demand—what is here conveys little in the way of textual or virtual specificity as to what was. To seek out what happened is to ascribe meaning, not so much to the meaningless, but to that which resists the ascription of meaning altogether.[42] If to "read what was never written" is the mark of a true

---

41 On the Hellenistic temple, see Klein (1997).

42 Here I would like to underline a contrast to Cathy Gere (2006), who presents a story where a citadel without heroes is a citadel without wonder, rooted within the epic imagination. Gere plays to an opposition between the literary imagination and the reality of archaeology, the driest dust that blows. However, Angelica finds wonder in the seemingly banal things around her.

historian, then to work through what could not be written is an apt description of an archaeologist.[43] Historians study this? Archaeologists study that? No, the difference is not taxonomic.

Angelica places her hand on a portion of wall. History confidently asserts that hands set these stones. Archaeology trusted in the possibility that these stones were vehicles to the hands behind them. But how can this be, she asks? The memories are held in stone, in walls, in edges, in rapports with surfaces. The memories belong not to human hands long gone but to the things present.[44] Parallel walls, round flat stones set at the corners of a square, encasing a half circle, charred mudbrick, and bits of plaster encased in soil: all these things, without the outward reference, call to themselves. All they can make are silent suggestions as to why they are.[45] Here is the archaeological paradox: in order to adequately address the historical question of what happened here, an archaeologist has to suspend altogether the historical imperative that something actually happened here. For the archaeologist, the past is not here in a causal relation to what is present; rather, the things present are what make the past possible.[46] Holding this paradox close is the only way for the archaeologist to fulfill that debt to the past.

Angelica breaks with the itinerary and, against a steady flow of tourists, walks back the way she came. Mycenae is now a museum—a place holy to the Muses, once again. Here, estrangement and exclusion are aftereffects of curatorial responsibility. Here, distance is maintained by timeline, exhibition, and dubbed overlay. Here, nothing more can occur, or so it would seem. The megaron, the Hellenistic temple and the exhibition space of a museum: all stage, separate, and divide off. All three uphold hierarchies: a space of concentrating observers over here and a space concentrating power over there. Over the hearth sits the lord on the throne. Over the *cella* is shielded the statue of the goddess. Over the page is fixed a past that was.

Severed from the experience of participating in its history, Angelica nonetheless recognizes how what is actually extant within and beyond the strong walls of Mycenae resists submission to historical and museological narratives of

---

43 Benjamin citing Hugo von Hofmannsthal (Benjamin, Eiland, and Jennings 2006, 405).
44 Olivier (2011), Olsen, Shanks, Webmoor, and Witmore (2012), Witmore (2014a).
45 Olsen and Witmore (2015, 194).
46 If, as Laurent Olivier has stated, history deals with what happens to people, then memory deals with what happens to things or places (2011; also, 2013). Of course, this is not memory as a recollective faculty held to be a byproduct of human-centered groups enacting their conscious and willful powers of selection; rather, it is the propensity of a wall to hold an orientation, of a pot to uphold its form. This memory relates to suggestions or expressive statements which are held by the object itself.

continuity and closure. A jumble of gates, walls, and terraces dictate the course taken by visitors like Angelica Nova. Here, something of what was has survived in its redundancy. Here, things silently object to the historicist trope of the past momentary and gone.[47] Here, they refuse to submit to a linear trajectory.[48] Through their material stubbornness, gates, walls, terraces, both partial and strong, are directed ahead of themselves; they are committed to the future, and thus somehow wait to shape what is yet to come.

47 Olsen (2010), Olsen and Pétursdóttir (2015).
48 See Segment 2.

Bibliography

Alden, M.J. 2002. *Well built Mycenae 7: Prehistoric Cemetery – Pre-Mycenaean and Early Mycenaean Graves.* Oxford: Oxbow Books.

Benjamin, W., H. Eiland, and M.W. Jennings. 2006. *Selected writings, Volume 4: 1938–1940.* Cambridge, MA: Belknap Press.

Burns, B.E. 2012. *Mycenaean Greece, Mediterranean commerce, and the formation of identity.* Cambridge: Cambridge University Press.

Calder, W.M., and D.A. Traill. 1986. *Myth, scandal, and history: the Heinrich Schliemann controversy and a first edition of the Mycenaean diary.* Detroit, MI: Wayne State University Press.

Clarke, D.L. 1968. *Analytical archaeology.* London: Methuen & Co.

Daniel, G. 1967. *The origins and growth of archaeology.* Harmondsworth: Penguin.

Davies, J.K. 1984. The reliability of the oral tradition. In L. Foxhall and J.K. Davies (eds.), *The Trojan War: Its historicity and context.* Bristol: Bristol Classical Press. 87–110.

Davis, J.L. 2010. "That special atmosphere outside of national boundaries": Three Jewish directors and the American School of Classical Studies at Athens. *Annuario della Scuola Archeologica Italiana di Atene* 87, 119–31.

Dawdy, S.L. 2009. Millennial archaeology: Locating the discipline in the age of insecurity. *Archaeological Dialogues* 16(2), 131–42.

Demakopoulou, K. (ed.). 1990. *Troy, Mycenae, Tiryns, Orchomenos: Heinrich Schliemann, the 100th anniversary of his death.* Athens: Ministry of Culture of Greece.

Deuel, L. 1977. *Memoirs of Heinrich Schliemann: A documentary portrait drawn from his autobiographical writings, letters, and excavation reports.* New York, NY: Harper & Row.

Easton, D.F. 1984. Schliemann's mendacity: A false trail? *Antiquity* 58, 197–204.

French, E. 2002. *Mycenae: Agamemnon's capital.* Stroud: Tempus.

Furumark, A. 1941a. *The Mycenaean Pottery: Analysis and classification.* Stockholm: K. Vitterhets Historie och Antikvitets Akademien.

Furumark, A. 1941b. *The Mycenaean Pottery: The chronology.* Stockholm: K. Vitterhets Historie och Antikvitets Akademien.

Gates, C. 1985. Rethinking the building history of Grave Circle A at Mycenae. *American Journal of Archaeology* 89(2), 263–74.

Gere, C. 2006. *The Tomb of Agamemnon.* Cambridge, MA: Harvard University Press.

Greek Ministry of Culture. 1998. Nomination of ancient Mycenae for inclusion on the world heritage list. Athens/Nafplion. Unpublished.

Harrison, R. 2016. Archaeologies of emergent presents and futures. *Historical Archaeology* 50(3), 165–80.

Iakovidis, S., E.B. French, K. Shelton, J. Lavery, A.G. Jansen, and C. Ioannides. 2003. *The archaeological atlas of Mycenae.* Athens: Archaeological Society of Athens.

Karo, G. 1915. Die Schachtgräber von Mykenai. *Mitteilungen des Deutschen Archäologischen Instituts, Athenische Abteilung* 40, 113–230.

Karo, G. 1930. *Die Schachtgräber von Mykenai.* Munich: F. Bruckmann.

Klein, N.L. 1997. Excavation of the Greek temples at Mycenae by the British School at Athens. *Annual of the British School at Athens* 92, 247–322.

Lucas, G. 2004. Modern disturbances: On the ambiguities of archaeology. *Modernism/Modernity* 11(2), 109–20.

Lucas, G. 2012. *Understanding the archaeological record.* Cambridge: Cambridge University Press.

Matz, F. 1964. Georg Karo. *Gnomon* 36(6), 637–40.

Miller, P.N. 2013. A tentative morphology of European antiquarianism, 1500–2000. In A. Schnapp, with L. Von Falkenhausen, P.N. Miller, and T. Murray (eds.), *World antiquarianism: Comparative perspectives*. Los Angeles, CA: Getty Publications. 67–87.

Morris, I. 1986. The use and abuse of Homer. *Classical Antiquity* 5(1), 81–138.

Morris, I. 1988. Tomb cult and the "Greek Renaissance": The past in the present in the 8th century BC. *Antiquity* 62, 750–61.

Morris, I., and B.B. Powell. 1997. *A new companion to Homer*. Leiden: Brill.

Mylonas, G.E. 1957. *Ancient Mycenae: The capital city of Agamemnon*. Princeton, NJ: Princeton University Press.

Nagy, G. 2010. *Homer the preclassic*. Berkeley, CA: University of California Press.

Olivier, L. 2011. *The dark abyss of time: Archaeology and memory* (trans. A. Greenspan). Lanham, MD: AltaMira Press.

Olivier, L. 2013. The business of archaeology is the present. In A. González-Ruibal (ed.), *Reclaiming archaeology: Beyond the tropes of modernity*. Abingdon: Routledge. 117–29.

Olsen, B. 2010. *In defense of things: Archaeology and the ontology of objects*. Lanham, MD: AltaMira Press.

Olsen, B., and Þ. Petursdottir (eds.). 2015. *Ruin memories: Materiality, aesthetics and the archaeology of the recent past*. New York, NY: Routledge.

Olsen, B., and C. Witmore. 2015. Archaeology, symmetry and the ontology of things: A response to critics. *Archaeological Dialogues* 22(2), 187–97.

Olsen, B., M. Shanks T. Webmoor, and C. Witmore. 2012. *Archaeology: The discipline of things*. Berkeley, CA: University of California Press.

Papadopoulos, J.K. 2007. *The art of antiquity: Piet de Jong and the Athenian agora*. Princeton, NJ: American School of Classical Studies at Athens.

Petrie, W.M.F. 1904. *Methods and aims in archaeology*. London: MacMillan.

Piggott, S. 1966. Mycenae and barbarian Europe. *Sbornik Narodniho Muzea v Praza* XX, 117.

Prag, A.J.N.W., L. Papazoglou-Manioudaki, R.A.H. Neave, D. Smith, J.H. Musgrave, and A. Nafplioti. 2009. Mycenae revisited Part 1: The human remains from Grave Circle A – Stamatakis, Schliemann and two new faces from Shaft Grave VI. *Annual of the British School at Athens* 104, 233–77.

Renfrew, C. 1968. Wessex without Mycenae. *Annual of the British School of at Athens* 63, 277–85.

Renfrew, C. 1980. The Great Tradition versus the Great Divide: Archaeology versus anthropology? *American Journal of Archaeology* 84, 287–98.

Schliemann, H. 1878. *Mycenae*. London: John Murray.

Shanks, M. 1992. *Experiencing the past: On the character of archaeology*. London: Routledge.

Shelton, K. 2006. The long lasting effect of Tsountas on the study of Mycenae. In P. Darcque (ed.), *Mythos: La préhistoire égéenne du XIXe au XXIe siècle après J.-C. Bulletin de Correspondance Hellenique* Supplement 46, 159–64.

Shryock, A., and D.L. Smail. 2011. *Deep history: The architecture of past and present*. Berkeley, CA: University of California Press.

Sloterdijk, P. 2014. *Globes: Spheres II*. South Pasadena, CA: Semiotext(e).

Teskey, G. 2015. The thinking of history in Spenserian romance. *Cambridge Studies in Medieval Literature* 92, 214–27.

Traill, D.A. 2012. Schliemann's Mycenae excavations through the eyes of Stamatakis. In G. Korres, N. Karadimas and G. Flouda (eds.), *Archaeology and Heinrich Schliemann*. Athens: Detorakis. 79–84.

Tsountas, C., and J.I. Manatt. 1897. *The Mycenaean Age: A study of the monuments and culture of pre-Homeric Greece.* London: Macmillan & Co.

Wace, A.J.B. 1949. *Mycenae, an archaeological history and guide.* Princeton, NJ: Princeton University Press.

Wace, A.J.B. 1962. The history of Homeric archaeology. In A.J.B. Wace and F. H. Stubbings (eds.), *A Companion to Homer.* London: MacMillan & Co. 325–30.

Wace, A.J.B., and F.H. Stubbings (eds.). 1962. *A companion to Homer.* London: MacMillan & Co LTD.

Witmore, C. 2009. Prolegomena to open pasts: On archaeological memory practices. *Archaeologies* 5(3), 511–45.

Witmore, C. 2014a. Archaeology and the new materialisms. *Journal of Contemporary Archaeology* 1(2), 203–24.

10

A PATH TO THE HERAION

Respect for an adopted ancestor, a "shrine," searching for a Bronze Age road, ter-races, agrarian memory, tombs, inherited burdens, illegal garbage and appropri-ation, polis territory, locality, another "shrine," Hero versus tomb cult, a dominion emptied of its dead, another species of appropriation

10:42 a.m., August 16, 2007. We leave the car by the front gates to Agios Geor-gios. The small, whitewashed church is set within the enclosed grounds of a cemetery on the south end of the Panagia ridge, near Mycenae. We cross the concrete surface of the forecourt, into the shade along its northern wall. To our left we pass the first of twenty graves in this section of the cemetery. Raised plat-forms of grey and white marble, some graves are covered by large slabs, and some form stone boxes containing earth, capped with gravel. Surmounted by a cross, the heads of the graves face east, and are turned away from us. We veer into a cluster just past the apse of the church. Tucked in the rear corner, formed by the concrete retaining wall, is the grave of an archaeologist, Humfry Payne.

At odds with its surroundings, the gravestone of white marble is carved as an aedicule;[1] two pillars support an entablature, pediment, and acroteria, which serve to frame the inscription: "HUMFRY PAYNE. SCHOLAR, ARTIST, PHIL-HELLENE. BORN IN ENGLAND February 19, 1902. DIED IN GREECE May 9, 1936." And below, in quotes: "MOURN NOT FOR ADONAIS." In the moment, I fail to recognize these as the words of Shelley.[2] Before the gravestone, an alabaster urn holds dried stems of olive. About its base lie flowers, wilted-red anemones and yellowed-plastic, white roses. A low rectangle of stone, raised scarcely higher than the ground surface, encloses a pebble-strewn covering over the grave plot. The adjacent marble sepulcher of the house of V.I. K. usurps the small enclosure and presses against the edge of Payne's gravestone. Over the revetment wall by the stump of a cypress tree, which once stood here, soil and earth, cobbles and debris spill down the slope.[3] These, too, usurp the enclosure. We pay our respects to the former director of the British School at Athens and excavator of the Heraion at Perachora by placing a round, red cobble atop his gravestone.

We take the path through the center of the cemetery. Leading from the rear of the church to a back gate, this thoroughfare is marked by raised concrete edges, whitewashed to further define its limits. Such heightened delimitations are repeated in the grave plots, around the paved surfaces enveloping the church, around the planting areas reserved for trees or shrubs, and with the stone terrace and concrete revetment wall surrounding the whole cemetery. Ground to be worked and walked, clearly cut off from ground to be reserved and revered.

At the gate we pause to scan the outcrops of Mt Sarra. These grey limestone heights transition into smooth lower slopes, the silhouettes of which are carried aloft on the green canopies of phrygana turned olive. Above these gradients rise the peaks of Mt Euboea (Profitis Elias) beyond. Broken by a series of dry stream channels, our path lies along these olive-covered slopes in the direction of the small, tabletop spur of Euboea, Panagou Rachi, to the south. Beyond lies our destination, another former sanctuary of Hera at Prosymna, a place that will come to be associated with Argos in the Classical period. Our walk will follow the general route of the ancient road that connected Mycenae with the Heraion, and earlier, Mycenae with Prosymna.

1   Aedicule is the diminutive of the Roman *aedes*, which means a temple or house.
2   From "Adonais: An Elegy on the Death of John Keats" by Percy Bysshe Shelley.
3   Indeed, five Mycenaean chamber tombs, excavated by Tsountas in 1895, lay between 50 and 100 meters upslope from Payne's grave, and many more have been identified in the area (see Iakovidis et al. 2003, 47; also Shelton 1993, 208–09).

Slopes off of Mt Sarra towards Profitis Elias and Panagou Rachi.

We scramble down the road cut to the edge of the Tarmac as a large coach loaded with tourists passes on the way to the citadel.[4] We cross the main road and drop into the dry bed of the Chavos on a hairpin track paved over in concrete. My traveling companion points out the Agios Georgios "causeway."[5] An object of some controversy as to its original purpose, this stubborn buttress of Cyclopean masonry holds memories of its former relationship to the ancient surface at the top of the bank by partially extending level ground into the dry channel.[6] My companion also registers the stone terrace about 30 meters north of the Agios Georgios causeway as the remains of a "stout rubble wall" excavated by J.M. Cook in 1950. Cook, who as a young student at the British School worked on material from Perachora and who would later follow in Payne's footsteps as the director of the British School at Athens, was asked to investigate a plot where Geometric pottery had been turned up by plow, here, in an area called Agios Ioannis. Cook focused his excavations along the length of this terrace wall, which, he suggested, had been part of an enclosure connected with sacred activities in the Archaic period. After the abandonment of the site in step with the Argive destruction of Mycenae, it was reconstituted some two centuries later as a shrine of the Argive state—one that Cook associated with Agamemnon on the basis of inscribed pottery bearing his name. For Cook, here on the banks of the Chavos lay the remains of a hero cult, one that in

4 Last year 582,078 recorded site visitors would pass along this road to the citadel (2006 archaeological site visitation numbers from the 4th Ephorate of Prehistoric and Classical Antiquities in the Argolis).
5 I am grateful to Brad Sekedat, at that time a PhD candidate at Brown University, for walking this segment with me.
6 For a discussion of the "causeway," see: Knauss (1997).

The Agios Georgos "causeway" with Mycenae in the background.

its earliest phases responded to a new interest in epic heroes, coinciding with the arrival of the *Iliad*.[7] This shrine he named the "Agamemnoneion."

As we walk along the road, we scan the brush half-heartedly for memories of Cook's excavation in the form of eroded trenches. We continue on and soon pause at a point in line with the causeway. From here, we search for vestiges of the ancient road, presumed to have run south from the causeway and traced by Bernard Steffen in the winter of 1881–82. This he dubbed *Vierte Hochstraße* (the fourth high road).[8] A low terrace comprised of large conglomerate stones, associated since Steffen with the Bronze Age road, heads south through an area of newly planted olive trees, supplied with freshly laid irrigation lines. We shortly move into a fallow plot, no more than 1.5 *stremmata* (50 by 30 meters), where the terrace is obscured under sage, thistle, and volunteer grain. Here, the terrace doubles as a field boundary, delimiting the fallow plot from a higher grove of olive trees. Following the form of a contour beneath the overgrowth, we eventually trudge over a section without stone facing by a pomegranate tree, and continue on a surface so thick with cobbles that few plants break through the margins. On this uneasy ground, we ponder attempts to put dates to terraces.[9]

7 Cook (1953a, 33; 1953b); that the location of the terrace is near the monumental bridge was probably not without significance (Snodgrass 1982, 112).

8 Steffen (1884, 9–10) also see Hope Simpson and Hagel (2006, 148–56), Jansen (1997, 2002, 47–52; 2003, 29–30), Lavery (1990).

9 The literature on terraces and dating them is ever-expanding: see, for example, Frederick and Krahtopoulou (2000), Rackham and Moody (1996, 143–45), Whitelaw (1991).

Construction and overall morphology, orientation and context provide clues from which archaeologists have attempted to build temporal taxonomies of terraces in the area of Mycenae. Alan Wace, the excavator of Mycenae, had considered the stout wall of Cook's "Agamemnoneion" to be Archaic in date (700–480 BCE) due to its "stylistic resemblance" to the temple terrace in the citadel.[10] Cook, in his report, places more emphasis on this physiognomic association in dating the wall than on any stratigraphical relation to the fill behind it.[11] The Mycenae Survey, 1991–93, identified "Mycenaean" terraces on the basis of Cyclopean masonry within their walls and made suggestions regarding those of subsequent eras. And yet, assigning times to terraces is no trivial matter. If found beneath the base stones, charcoal, with its datable carbon molecules, may be associated with land clearing prior to construction, or may relate to episodes a thousand years earlier. Association with pollen or organic residues in accumulated sediments combined with soil micromorphology, or with crystalline minerals, which may disclose when they were last exposed to sunlight, within the raised surfaces retained behind extant walls may date subsequent use but not construction.[12] A best-case scenario for archaeologists would be to find terraces in clear correlation with other datable features, but this, too, is not without its idiosyncratic challenges.

After 130 meters, a terrace line is no longer discernible. Rough, rocky ground gives over to rich, red soils. A small grove of older olives abruptly transitions into an untilled area of maquis. We continue by following another terrace line. Along here, this terrace, like the previous one, divides plots, some better tilled than others. This terrace forms edges where stones, removed from plowed soil, accumulate in a linear cairn. Attempts to associate terraces with a particular period fail to appreciate how they are iterative. Stones are reset and added by those who subsequently work these lands. Agrarians maintain *terracing*. Built through the collective achievements of others before and after, their contrived stasis is that of anonymous accretions, which give contour to the land.

---

10 Cook (1953a, 32).

11 Cook, like Payne, endorsed a largely artifact-centered approach to excavation. Cook's publication of the shrine contained five pages, two of which are plans and photographs, dedicated to the excavation, features, and stratigraphy. The remaining forty-two pages were dedicated to the finds—pottery, terracotta figurines, tiles, metal objects. Deposits, cuts, features, the relations between them, and their relations to these finds, remained woefully under-described. Indeed, the lines delimiting the phases in the stratigraphic profile of the report do not meet with the interior edge of the wall. Did these phases accumulate against the wall's interior edge or were they attenuated by a cut in a construction trench? The report leaves this question unanswered. Importantly, the wall has two faces, whereas most agricultural terraces have one exterior face and are backed with cobbles transitioning to soil.

12 For recent attempts to date the fill behind terraces using Optically Stimulated Luminescence (OSL), see Avni, Avni, and Porat (2009), Davidovich et al. (2012).

Accommodating wayward stones, retaining earth in soil-rich plots with optimal slopes, farmers would rarely choose to release terraces "from the drudgery of being useful."[13]

My companion pulls a scanned copy of the *Archaeological Atlas of Mycenae* from his knapsack. We attempt to find the terrace wall labeled G4:01 where the Mycenae Survey noted "three or four large Cyclopean blocks."[14] Because this terrace is in a direct line with the causeway, they regarded it as remains of the Mycenaean road, Steffen's *Vierte Hochstraße*. Along here, in 1995, Heleni Palaiologou excavated a group of Archaic cist graves in association with the road terrace.[15] Despite our efforts, the ground surface holds neither blocks nor indications of this cemetery. Indeed, from here, an area known as *Tserania*, few memories of the *Vierte Hochstraße* are to be found.

Evenly, our path descends towards an upper channel of the Vathyrema. It is overgrown with scrub and cypress, and we cannot cross here. We walk uphill along a field track running parallel to the ravine in an area where the Mycenae Survey identified a series of at least fifteen weirs. We cross atop of a high cairn pile of fieldstone and scan the channel for large boulders indicative of revetments.

Once across, I pick up a cobble from the plowed earth before me, and cast it back onto the cairn. Eighty meters further on, across well-tilled ground, in a well-tended grove, we come to another upper channel of the Vathyrema. At this point, the gully carves a gash 4 meters deep and thus conveys the reality of its name: "deep channel." A linear lacuna in the midst of agricultural land, this channel accommodates what is relegated to uncultivated areas—maquis, cypress, and illegal garbage. Again, we walk uphill, along an agricultural road and take a field path through an open section of the ravine where farmers have ventured to plant olives.

Here, terracing across the drainage channels softens gradients, traps sediments, and claims new ground. We pass below a terrace, partially shielded by overgrowth, whose composition is a motley patchwork of cobbles and boulders, set at an angle to a massive chunk of bedrock. Of what period is this terrace? Ascribing a time is part of our obligations, our duties as archaeologists to those who came before us, to those among us, and those yet to come, but enclosing such terraces within a particular epoch fails to recognize how it is still here, holding moisture-rich soil for roots, providing flat ground for agricultural labor. For the farmer, utility is revealed at their etymological root as *terra*, earth.[16]

---

13 Benjamin and Jennings (2002, 39).

14 Iakovidis et al. (2003, 60).

15 These were found in the course of digging irrigation ditches (Palaiologou personal communication).

16 Throughout I am mindful of the fact that *terrace* shares the root *terra* with *territory*, from the Latin *territorium*.

Cairn pile of fieldstone.

As we walk out of the upper channels, we find ourselves at the edge between olive and maquis. We follow this ecotone along ground mellowed by tractor and plow. Behind us, terracing holds memories of labor, stones set in relation to one another, each meeting to form a receptacle for subsequent stone, which together hold back soils that accumulate behind them. Before us, the ground also retains the imprint of work—furrows from a disc harrow, the absence of overgrowth. The maintenance of well-kept plots not only becomes visible when it is lacking, everywhere registers the workmanship of the farmer. This is a species of memory that is involuntary.[17] This is a capacity for retention that

17 Olsen (2010, 117–19).

belongs not to human recollection, but to the set stone, to the ripples left in the wake of the disc harrow, to the ridge turned up by the plowshare,[18] competence that belongs to graves, delimited plots, terraces, badly tilled fields, pollarded olives—all things that uphold the myriad pasts of this area. This is the memory that we, here in the midst of an olive grove, confront as archaeologists. This is the memory that those who walked and worked these grounds before us confronted as well.

We head in the direction of Agia Paraskevi on a truck path, which begins, along with power lines, at a water pump. After 150 meters the shallow wheel ruts of our path spill into even deeper grooves of an agricultural road and we follow this left. Like the upper channels of the ravines, which gouge these slopes, several field tracks converge into a single road, one swept bare across both rut and berm from greater use. This leaf-vein pattern is repeated over and between every tongue-like ridge. But no sooner than we meet this road do we take leave of it by way of another into a wide gully of well-kept olives. Bifurcations, and hence detours from the pattern, occur around these ravines, along the main road stems. Here in the bottom, we take note of the soil; the clay enrolled as building material at Mycenae has been sourced to this area.[19] Before long we ascend behind the monastery of Agia Paraskevi.

A high wall of brick and mortar encircles the monastery, which contains two adjacent churches, one dedicated to Agia Paraskevi and the other to the Holy Trinity. Here, two nuns, Pachomia and Triada, worked this land, tended its olives, and maintained its churches. Here, by the apse of Agia Paraskevi, in a position of reverence, they are buried in adjacent sepulchers. Now a single nun lives behind these high walls. She has assumed the obligations of those who came before her, fulfilling her duty to them, to the land, and to God.

To the cadence of cicadas,[20] we continue along the paved road, which originates at the closed metal gate of the monastery. In 150 meters the road turns southwest and runs along the edge of a ravine, a dry branch of the channel called Plesia. We unfold Map 11 of the Mycenae Survey as we walk downhill. The area to our left, bracketed by two upper channels of the Plesia, bears the same toponym, Plesia. Steffen noted ruins here, and here the Mycenae Survey documented several structures around the area of a rock bluff, and more just to

18 Here I am referring to contemporary mechanized agriculture. Three to four generations ago, harrowing would have been accomplished with bundled branches, plowing with oxen or mules; smaller plots would have been hoed by hand.
19 Shelton (2003, 37).
20 An evocation of the myth of the cicadas in the Phaedrus 259a–d.

the east in an area called Sklaveika.[21] Plesia was a village, which, according to Bory de Saint Vincent, had forty inhabitants in the 1829 census. It was later abandoned in the mid-nineteenth century, when its residents moved to the villages of Monastiraki and Inahos.[22] Upholding the stability of the holy here, the modern chapel of Agia Paraskevi takes up the mantle of the earlier church by the same name, which was once associated with this village.[23]

After another 200 meters we come to a crossroads. A wayside shrine (*proskinitario*), a gift of Panagioti Tsppaniti in 1975, stands across from a concrete water trough covered in bees. Under the shade of eucalyptus trees, we pause on two concrete benches. This is where Steffen sited the crossing for the *Vierte Hochstraße*, the road to the Heraion.[24] The cutting associated with this is now obscured by dense overgrowth of fig.

Through a dogleg trench carved in the conglomerate bedrock, we descend into the Plesia on a steep gradient capped with a rippled slab of concrete. Here, at the confluence of two ravines, opens a wide, flat channel. To the right of the road, which cuts directly across this ground, a farmer has ventured to plant citrus. Civil engineering is a vocation not unknown among past generations of farmers here. And yet, since the tractor, since the bulldozer, agrarian rapports with terraces, ravines, roads, and the underground, where graves lay buried, have changed. Within this widened drainage, the surface was leveled and graded from wall to wall with a metal blade.[25] When this new ground was claimed, ostensibly for widening the crossing, the Plesia bridge, according to an unnamed farmer, was buried.[26]

21 *Sklavos* is "slave" in Modern Greek. These words, both Greek and English, share a common etymology, which is connected to "Slav." *Sklavinos*, is the Byzantine word for "Slav," while the medieval Latin is "*sclavus*." On the Muslim slave trade and Slavs in the mid-ninth century, see Gordon (1998, 106–107).
22 Bory de Saint-Vincent (1834, 84), Sarantákis (2007, 55).
23 Sarantákis (2007, 55); the Mycenae Survey assumes the earlier church stood on the same spot of the modern chapel in the monastery. They do not directly correlate the structures J5:04–06, J5:08–11, H6:01–03, H6 05–07, and J6:01 with the abandoned village of Plesia.
24 "Die antiken Wegereste und die Trümmer einer kyklopischen Brücke am Plesia-Bach bei Punkt 128 haben einer von Süden kommenden Strafse angehört" (The ancient remains of the road and the ruins of a Cyclopean bridge on the Plesia stream at point 128 belong to an extension from the south; 1884, 9).
25 Here, few place stones into terraces anymore. A tractor does not feel the jolt of a large cobble or small boulder the in the way of the withers. A tractor does not complain about the added burden of cutting a furrow upslope.
26 As reported by John Lavery in 1990 (165). In the same article Lavery established a new nomenclature for Mycenaean roads. While they would retain the numbering scheme of established by Steffen, they would now be dubbed M-ways. The grading of this area occurred on several occasions; the most recent occurrence was in 1994 (Iakovidis et al. 2003, 62).

Crossing through the Plesia.

My companion points to the bedrock above the road—in the stone around these channels graves have been carved. To the east, into rock bluff below the abandoned village, six Mycenaean chamber tombs were cut. To the north, just off this line, another cluster of thirteen is located. Near the eucalyptus trees, by Steffen's *Vierte Hochstraße*, the memory of chamber tombs may be preserved in cuttings and a well-worked ceiling.[27] And just a hundred meters farther still, to the north, lies a cluster of post-Mycenaean cist graves. The union of people with a particular patch of ground is made visible through tombs. Into the sacred earth, inhabitants, who take up the mantle of descendants, and who cultivate its ground, bury their dead, as did their ancestors, whether hereditary or adopted, before them. In so doing, as Fustel de Coulanges recognized, these inhabitants appropriate a patch of soil, enclosed for themselves within a family line, to the exclusion of others.[28] Our trail is marked with such tombs. Their position near the ancient road intimates an outward expression of this association for all who pass. Their position along our route suggests proximity to a particular portion of land—quarries, clay beds, plots of land—this ground.

Trees, terraces, paths, and cleared fields, the houses, churches, and structures to which generations committed themselves also mark our trail.[29] We walk through the cut uphill and continue along a rough portion of road, bracketed between the

27 These tombs were labeled J5:03 by the Mycenae Survey (Iakovidis et al. 2003, 62). The other chamber tombs are located along the slopes of Gouves above the road—H5:09 and J5:07 (ibid., 61–62).

28 2006, 65; Serres (2011, 14).

29 Olives have become far more pervasive here in the last century. Compare the olive groves (Olivenbäume) marked on the map of the area by Steffen (1884) with those (Ölbaumkulturen) marked on that of the plain by Lehmann (1937).

upper Plesia and olive groves. Working the land is tied to an obligation to predecessors, both hereditary and adopted ancestors, who as parent sparks ignite a fire that continues to burn in those who follow their paths by bearing their abandoned burdens. And yet these things are involved in upholding those very obligations. We mourn not for Adonais, because though biological death has occurred, something yet endures through the things abandoned, recognized by those who work the same land as achievements; as both added encumbrance and helpful support. Just as the oblivion faced by others has not undone the realities of their labors—seen in furrows around fields, plots free of stones, clods, and weeds, terraces sustained, or, indeed, pottery studied, pages written, and corpses laid into graves, these things may yet kindle subsequent fires for those intimately familiar with this land and their toils. Mourn not for those whose life's labors, languages, and lands are sustained by subsequent inheritors.[30]

We take a fork to the right and continue uphill between olive groves. Property lines and the frequency of plots, slope, and drainage impact the pattern of the road network. No one walks from the villages to here and we have encountered no one. The hour is late. The day is hot. Our path follows a steep contour of the hill. Before long, the plain of Argos comes into full view. As the road drops down to a lower terrace we pass a young chaste tree—under the *Vitex agnus-castus* Hera was born. I will later find that Puillon de Boblaye believed the Heraion lay somewhere in this area, between Plesia and Vraserka.[31] Again, stone memories are known to those who work this land or tend their flocks here; yet history would credit another military man, General Gordon of Cairness, with the discovery of the old sanctuary to the cow-eyed goddess in 1831, which occurred by accident while out shooting; at what, I am uncertain.[32]

We soon meet the higher maquis, where the road traces a line between spaces worked and spaces spared, the margin between the cultivated and uncultivated zone of the slope. Located on the threshold of the territory of Argos, the sanctuary of Hera, according to François de Polignac, mediated this difference between land tilled and untilled. Linked into the spatial organization of the polis, the location of the Heraion was positioned, like other extra-urban sanctuaries, "on the edge of [an] area, now humanized, ploughed, and organized" marking "the outer limit of the advance of agrarian civilization and drew attention to its takeover by setting it in opposition to the neighboring domain of mountains and forests."[33] It has been routinely observed, and with greater frequency since de Polignac's study, that the establishment of the Heraion was

30 See Shelley, lines XLV and XLVI.
31 1836, 42–43.
32 Frazer (1898 Vol. III, 165).
33 De Polignac (1995, 34).

foremost an investment in community. As with tombs at the level of family, rooting the gods in place had geo- and psycho-political resonance for the polis as another mode of appropriating land.

We pause in the shade of the last olive tree before bare slope and look across the plain made green by the orange canopies in the direction of the Larissa above Argos. Within what would become the Heraion, a massive terrace was constructed at an elevated position, with stones so large that all would behold them in wonder; together they formed a mark so abrupt as to be seen from the other side of the plain. Though Cyclopean in execution, this terrace and its large rectilinear pavement, most agree, were constructed several centuries after the fall of strong-walled Mycenae, at some point in the eighth century BCE.[34] For de Polignac, and others, this clear delimitation of the sacred through a built intervention into the land was associated with Argos, perhaps in the wake of the destruction of Asini.[35] Investment in the development of the Heraion underwrote the definition of the polis as an integrated whole and allowed for the cultivation of a communal sense of belonging tied to a defined tract of land—Argive territory.

We return to a dusty path, along a maquis-covered slope. We soon encounter rubbish. Along the edges of the dirt road, illicit garbage dumps lays claim to space. On the margins, disused irrigation pipes are stacked, wooden pallets lie jumbled amid piles of plastic, an old kitchen cabinet, and agricultural clippings. At the turn of the road, trash lies in large piles, which spill over into the ravine —heaps of concrete, broken chairs, shattered doors, plastic bags, bottles and jugs, surplus oranges, broken roof tiles, shoes, tattered clothing, and household

Illicit garbage dumps.

34 Wright (1982); also see Antonaccio (1992, 91–98).
35 De Polignac (1995, 20).

waste. Odors emanate from this trash. This garbage reeks. And soon, the smell of death usurps all. Somewhere amid the rubbish lies a rotting animal carcass, perhaps more than one. For an uncomfortable distance, the stench hangs in the air, permeates our nostrils, and clings to our clothing. What garbage shares with the dead, buried and unburied, terraces, shrines, or extra-urban sanctuaries is to be found in the way that all lay claim to space.[36]

The way terminates into a main road at the point where it crosses the gully. Here, a rusted sign states that it is forbidden to dump garbage and debris in the ravine. And here, to the left and right of the road, set against a backdrop of fig and cypress, garbage mounds. Heat, sun, and still air, combined with the lack of water, weigh on us as we walk up the asphalt across another tongue-like ridge. On the right, a high, enclosed grove of oranges followed by a large, concrete cistern serves to announce our arrival at Vraserka, a Slavic toponym meaning "the place with waters." The 1829 census recorded it as a hamlet with twenty inhabitants.[37] At the bottom of a steep slope sits the chapel of Zoodochos Pigi (life-giving source). Overall, this chapel—built the year before the hamlet was abandoned in 1843—along with a separate building for quarters (*kelia*) built in 1956, is associated with the small monastery of the Virgin of Vraserka.[38]

We take respite in the unbroken shade of the lime trees (*Tilia cordata*) by the road below the spring. Nearby sits a water-basin, enclosed by blocks of whitewashed marble and covered by a metal grate. It was here that Frazer, following Steffen, situated the Water of Freedom, used by priestesses of Hera in their purification rituals.[39] Pausanias described this water as flowing by the road to Mycenae, which, as suggested by Jonathan Hall, constituted a sacred way, one that linked the polis of Mycenae with the Heraion.[40]

Following longstanding logic,[41] de Polignac, in linking the Heraion with Argos, suggested that as populations rose in the eighth century BCE, agriculture advanced from the plain into the foothills.[42] Argos staked its claim against that of Mycenae by investing heavily in the Heraion. At its agrarian periphery, the extra-urban sanctuary was linked to the polis by a sacred way, one that bisected

---

36 A triple association recognized by Serres (2011), Sloterdijk (2014, 331–33), and earlier, in Vico (1948[1744], 8–10).
37 Bory de Saint-Vincent (1834, 84).
38 The inscription above the door states: "Donors D. Kanoutsos 1843—cells 1956—olive grove 1958." Also see Sarantákis (2007, 54–55).
39 Frazer (1898 III, 179–81).
40 1995.
41 see Segment 11.
42 De Polignac (1995, 34–35).

The spring at Vraserka.

the plain.[43] Contrary to de Polignac, Hall argued that Argive dominance over
the sanctuary only came in the fifth century, when it assumed the abandoned

43 De Polignac (1995, 34); an association that is reinforced by the famous story of Cleobis and
Biton. The twins, taking up the burden of their labor's companions, yoked oxen, sacred to cow-
eyed Hera, trace the line, which, through repetition, connects Argos, plain, and sanctuary.
Argive participants who through piety and respect to their mother, to Hera, and Hera's rights,
Cleobis and Biton give their very lives within the temple at the Heraion. What can be interpreted as a coping mechanism for irreplaceable loss through the image of beautiful death can
also be read as a story of how a deep association between Argos, labor, plain, and Hera is
reinforced by the demise of its young sons. With Cleobis and Biton the Argive investment in the
sanctuary rises above the level of shrines, temples, festivals, *agalmata*, and animal sacrifices to
that of the death of its strong youths in the prime of life—a death sanctioned by the mother of
gods, at the request of the mother of mortals, encouraged by a reverent community of fellow
Argives. A basic aspect of humans who must anticipate and endure the separation from those
closest to them is to soften such a blow with an image of comfort, for upon these "high-hearted
heroes" is bestowed the greatest of honors. The story is also unique in the sense that the twins

sacred burdens of Mycenae after the citadel's destruction in 468 BCE.[44] Distinctive traditions, as suggested by Hall, could be found on either side of the plain in the Archaic period, and it was the eastern side, centered on Mycenae, and Tiryns, that was more closely associated with Hera.

Under the limes, by the spring, the asphalt ends. From here, a rough field track consisting of two rocky ruts and a high, scrub-laden berm runs up the bank above the citrus groves behind the church. Both de Polignac and Hall agree that investment in the sanctuary is sanctioned by community and that this venture is generally geopolitical in character. Again, for both, the initiative comes from aristocrats seeking to legitimate their present circumstances; their designs and ideologies are often assumed to precede any formal and material expression. And yet, ruins, springs, graves, and abandoned labors lie waiting for those willing to shoulder such burdens.[45] De Polignac, in suggesting that agriculture spread from the plain into the foothills, misses the contribution of idiosyncratic locality, which does not follow. It leads.

As we walk the ruts, we gain an elevated view of oranges concentrated within the thin strip of the catchment basin below the spring. Locals refer to the water here as a *thauma*, something that is both a miracle and a marvel. Rightly so, perennial water is a thing most necessary to life.[46] With dry-agriculture, agrarians in this plain have historically given preference to a diversified regime where soil and moisture determine the best-suited crops.[47] This spring would have proved valuable to any agrarian in contrast with the drier areas of the plain, or along these ridges. Indeed, between here and the Heraion, farmers in the last century cultivated barley

die not individually, but together. A shared death often endured by community on behalf the polis in times of war. Statues and stories, both within the polis, at Delphi and in the words of Solon as told by Herodotus, re-inscribe this moral basis for loss within the community.

44 Hall (1995); also see Strøm (1988, 1995); compare Whitelaw (1991).

45 A point also made by Alcock (1993, 24) and Antonaccio (1994), among others.

46 An ever-so-slight deviation from Vico (1948[1744], 8).

47 I do not wish to imply that this was the pattern in the eighth century BCE—settlement locations, communities, and the rapports between them would have played major roles in agrarian development. My point is that the agricultural regime of the plain is far more diverse than these models have allowed. Jonathan Hall's (1995, 590) assertion that Argive territory only extended as far as the Inachos River fails to recognize how different soils and their moisture content are necessary for a nuanced regime of non-irrigation agriculture (Lehmann 1937, 50–58; also see discussion in Hanson 1999, 76–77). Loams and floodplain deposits have built up significantly since the Classical Period due to inundations of the Inachos (Zangger 1993, 39). The combination of riverine deposition, higher water tables, and moisture retention would suggest favorable agricultural land throughout the Inachos flood zone. Establishing claims to the most favorable soil and moisture regimes would have been a major consideration in the context of significant agrarian development. That pollen cores reveal an upswing in olive in the eighth century BCE suggests a situation where such development was well underway (see Jahns 1993).

or broad beans.[48] Just after a turn, at the apex of the road, a ruined structure is visible on the right. At other times, ruins, remains associated with a particular past, have played a role in the process of appropriation.[49]

After crossing lower ground, framed by high rubble terracing on the left, collapsing in places, and fields under olive on the right, seized by stubble, the rough track meets with a better agricultural road. This continues uphill in the direction of a fenced estate. Near where the road meets the high metal-mesh fence, loose rounded pebbles and cobbles in reddish soil change over to flaky bits of limestone on pale soil. From this white-colored earth, the area gains its name—Asprochromia.

Enclosed within the estate boundaries, groves of citrus encircle a small house raised on a large concrete terrace. Just below this terrace lies another, excavated in the late 1920s by Carl Blegen, the former director of the American School of Classical Studies at Athens.[50] On Blegen's terrace was raised a platform, 12.5 by 8.5 meters. On this platform, at its center, he uncovered "a deposit of burnt débris, black earth and carbonized matter, occupying an irregular area ca. 1.20 m in diameter."[51] Across this platform, and especially in the deeper deposits off the northeastern and southwestern sides, Blegen unearthed bronzes, both fragments and whole objects, including mesophalic phialae, pins, mirrors, discs, and rings, "badly shattered" ceramics of various period and shape, and terracotta figurines.[52] Religious bonds turned obligations are made material as built architectures and as offerings, *agalmata*—a term that is commonly taken to mean "things to take delight in."[53] Blegen suggested that the platform supported a small shrine, one founded in the eighth century BCE, if not earlier.[54] But not all was delightful. Could blood have been spilled here? Was ground soiled in the course of sacrifice? Could this be where flesh was burned? Were vessels broken and discarded in the wake of feasting? Did blood and refuse mark the place of the gods?[55]

At the boundary of a grove, beyond the fenced estate, we pass a track heading downhill to the right. This track leads to other plots of olive and the remains of a large tholos tomb. Excavated by Panagiotis Stamatakis in 1878, a wide circular chamber (9.5 meters in diameter), constructed of stacked limestone slabs set within yellow

48 Blegen (1937, 5).
49 Antonaccio (1994, 1995), Whitley (1988, 1995).
50 For more on the life and work of Blegen, see Vogeikoff-Brogan et al. (2015).
51 Blegen (1939, 410).
52 As with Cook, Blegen's work was heavily artifact centered lacking detailed discussions of deposits, cuts, and micro-stratigraphy.
53 Parker (1991, 317); *agalmata* also denote things that lure one in with feeling; "things which generate delight."
54 1939, 411.
55 See Serres (2011, 15–17).

Tholos tomb excavated by Panagiotis Stamatakis in 1878.

clay, sits at the end of a 3 by 18 meter dromos.[56] A corbeled dome, achieved through the constriction of the circle with each superimposed course, once rose some 10 meters from floor to apex within the chamber. On this dome, a large mound was raised. Encircled by a wall of stone, and crowned perhaps, according to Stamatakis, by a rectangular stele, this mound seems to have stood well into the Classical period.[57] By this time, the three grave pits cut into the floor of the tomb had been evacuated of their contents. This tholos lay some 75 meters southeast of the terrace. Another group of Late Helladic chamber tombs lay roughly the same distance away to the east; another pair (XVII and XVI) lay closer still.[58] Established here near tombs, many have speculated that a cult was instituted to the Helladic dead.[59]

56 Wace (1923, 330–33); this yellow clay was connected by Wace to that used in the construction of the tomb of Aegisthus. This clay has been connected to the sources at Plesia (French 2002, 41).
57 Wace (1923, 333–34).
58 Tomb XVI once contained the burials of five children in three distinct phases (Blegen 1937, 52). Tomb XVII contained at least thirteen interments over the course of some ten generations; LHI, II, and III (Blegen 1937, 55). There was nothing to suggest any material engagement after they go into disuse.
59 De Polignac (1995, 141).

We enter the turn of a ravine, and walk up the slope of West Yerogalaro (old man's sheepfold). Following the line of the old footpath from the Heraion to Mycenae used by nineteenth- and twentieth-century archaeologists,[60] the road rounds the slope to pass between the eroded shafts of two erstwhile chamber tombs, labeled "Tomb WI" and "Tomb I" by Blegen. Along the top edge of an outcrop of heavy conglomerate, it passes over the earth-filled cavities of fourteen chambers, which once benefited from its advantageous geomorphology. Here, the dead formerly lay in carved chambers, some with subchambers or niches, at the end of a descending shaft engraved into the scarp. A zone where no plow can penetrate—a zone on which our road now finds sure foundation—rests but a short distance from the Bronze Age settlement and its associated lands. Within carved stone, Late Helladic inhabitants buried their dead in repeated acts, the sequence of which only bones can tell. In subsequent, perhaps even successive, generations, stones were removed from the doorway. Ground was prepared by moving the skeletons and grave goods of others. The body was laid in the grave. Once again, the doorway was sealed.

The path of the ancient road ran less than 100 meters below this group of tombs to pass just above Blegen's terrace. Once again, we encounter a memory quite apart from the firmamental supports of textual media, one held in rock, in a cut passage, a constructed doorway, in a chamber carved in stone, and a honeycombed outcrop looming over the ancient road. These objects persist. Collapsed roofs over this chthonic realm broadcast the presence of a sepulchral underworld. Here, the domain of the dead offered its qualities to, and was translated into, a usable past—one that, as Ian Morris puts it, was mythologized as stories, later given coherent expression by Hesiod, that related to those sequential races of gold, silver, bronze, heroes, and iron.[61] Heroes rose above a race of iron, whose ruins were everywhere treated as allegories of disruption and loss.[62] Such stories, drawn, as it is often argued, into the legitimization of a new elite, no doubt, displayed local variety, which has fallen away through the selective sieve of talkative history. An illustrious lineage finds a material home in the tombs of anonymous

60 Among those who walked this path were George Alexopoulos and Pantelis Christopoulos of Kharváti (Mycenae). Foremen for Blegen's excavations, these men knew the soil and how to detect the tombs (Blegen 1937, 6–7; see also Hood 1998, 94–97). They would also act as foremen and/or excavators on numerous other excavations carried out under the British and American Schools (see Blegen et al. 1930, vii).

61 Morris (1988, 2000, 195–256); Hesiod myth was by no means an image of protracted decline and fall (Vernant 2006, 25–51).

62 The possibility that inhumations were recognized as of an earlier race, prior to the time of warrior-heroes of the Trojan war who cremated their dead, has been voiced by Ian Morris. For Morris (1988, 754–55) a material difference was translated into a taxonomic distinction given meaning by Homer and Hesiod, whose achievements may have obfuscated other associations with the dead among those whom visited these graves (also see Morris 2000, 270–71).

progenitors. The dead are unable to refute such claims. Again, many have seen this new elite as Argive, arguing that making offerings to the dead was foremost a political act, as was raising a terrace here.[63] Thus, a hero cult, with its shrine and terrace at Mycenae arose as a response to Argive aggression.[64] Legitimating claims in favor of the community shields a ruse where power and prestige for aristocrats, those who find exemplars in the Homeric cycle, are the primary drivers.

From the top of the outcrop my companion gestures towards the conspicuous exposure of the acropolis, where the Old Terrace of the Heraion was constructed near vestiges of an Early to Late Helladic settlement.[65] Hera is the female equivalent of "hero."[66] If "hero," or "of the line of heroes," is the eventual image applied to the nameless dead—an image that belongs to non-consanguine inheritors of this land—one may envision an obligation not immediately connected with the cultivation of the communal self, or the appropriation of community lands. Inheritors attend to dead others out of an almost primordial sense of care, and guilt, that is part of the responsibility one feels towards the dead buried here.[67] The ceded labors of the dead are now shared by those who come next, those who recognize the need for others to do the same for them; others, whether descendants or strangers, yet to come who likewise recognize their memories in close proximity within sacred earth. These compacts ground a renewed interest in the domain of the dead.

Hero cults, to be sure, exist in a way that tomb cults do not, as argued by Carla Antonaccio, among others.[68] The dead, though less ordinary, buried in the sacred earth come to be regarded as ancestors, who are not so much created, as cared for—an adopted dead who demand periodic appeasement from those who assume their relinquished burdens.[69] Innovation, presumed to originate at the top, is grounded in mundane relations with the land, where the immortal dead have long hounded the living. Non-consanguine ancestors are adopted as part of this compact, *foedera generis humani*.[70] Whether common knowledge of these tombs was awash in

---

63 See discussion in De Polignac (1995, 140), Snodgrass (1977, 1980, 33f, 1982, 1987, 30f); Antonaccio (1992, 1994); also Hägg (1987).

64 Whitley (1988, 181).

65 Wright (1982).

66 As matron, queen, legal spouse, mother of the legitimate child, Hera also carries the role of a positive exemplar; see McInerney (2010, 119–20).

67 To resolve our mortality, as argued by Robert Pogue Harrison, "means to first and foremost to acknowledge that its fate belongs as much to others as theirs belongs to" us (Harrison 2003, 155). This is tied to a "world-engendering generosity that flows from the sources of primordial guilt" (Harrison 2003, 157). But this attitude need not be driven by guilt, but also driven by care.

68 1995.

69 Notwithstanding lofty associations of fertility or rebirth (Morris 1988, 758), an iron sickle, which is fundamentally about cutting stalks of grain, undertaking agricultural labor, was found in Tomb IX (Blegen 1937, 378).

70 Vico (1948[1744], 87).

Mnemosyne or doused in Lethe is of no more and no less importance than other obligations, or indeed the presence of rock-cut voids in themselves. It is the tombs that tell these tales. Things, treated as vestiges of a past, as passive recipients of stories told and sung around the common hearth, are participants in the coarticulation of these very stories, which could only be at home here and there, where object memories grounded tales in the sacred earth.[71] The most persuasive narratives were those rooted deeply in land, sustained by the things of this soil. Local idiosyncrasies serve as reminders that coherence is itself an achievement, where stories are not so much concocted as worked out. This labor reached a frenetic pitch in times of contestation, when it bore fruit as increased formal and material expression when the dead who lay here were delimited in a zone set between two monumental terraces under the protection of Hera.[72]

We leave the outcrop and drop down into the Yeragalaro ravine. Just beyond the turn, the road breaks a high terrace of conglomerate and runs along bare scarp. Olive trees hold memories of the old terrace, which would have bracketed the footpath known to Blegen. At the top, our way continues through olive groves across Devilli (East Yeragalaro). Here, Blegen excavated dozens of cist tombs and chamber tombs from the Middle and Late Helladic periods. Many of these tomb groups were found in proximity to Neolithic remains, including graves. We encounter along this path only a very small fraction of those abodes set aside for many undone by death. But here, this abode where the Eternal formerly lay lies empty. In an ascension to the haloed word, new caretakers have cleaned the tombs of all their contents. Itself a form of de-territorialization, unearthing tombs, removing nameless corpses and grave goods, is its own species of appropriation.[73] By sanctioning and transferring these remains to the National Museum in Athens, archaeology falls in with previous claims here, to take part in a national annexation of soil, of locality.[74]

At the bend of the road to the church of I.N. Taxiarches, we take the footpath through Revma tou Kastrou and pause at the rear gate to the archaeological site. A metal gate and a chain-link fence exclude us from entry. In place of the *temenos*, which once surrounded the sacred precinct of Hera, we

---

71 Of course, this requires tombs to be recognized as such. It is the case that rock cut voids offered themselves as kilns and garbage dumps at other times (Antonaccio 1995, 53–65).

72 Marking a grave with a *sema*, a term that is interchangeable with the tomb (Nagy 1983), signals to those unfamiliar with the tomb wider community interest and engagement (De Polignac 1995, 137). Memory, for the traveler Pausanias, will become synonymous with the tomb, *mnema*.

73 On archaeology and appropriation, see Scarre and Coningham (2012).

74 Compare Hamilakis (2007). A recent study failed to locate the human remains from Prosymna in the storerooms of the National Museum (Voutsaki, Ingvarsson-Sundstöm, and Richards 2007, 144).

now encounter a new precinct. From the Greek *temno*, meaning "to cut," "to cut off," or "divide," the word *temenos* indicates the enclosure of place.[75] It is taboo to enter here, so we look down the path towards ground worked over by successive generations of archaeologists. As archaeologists, our access to what has been removed from these grounds requires the voluntary, even reverent, subjugation of our labors to our forebears, those upon which we place the mantle of adopted ancestors.[76]

Two Austrian tourists walk among the exposed trenches of the so-called "Roman Building." My companion reminds me that these are the first people we have seen since setting out from Adonais's grave.

---

75 *Temno* resonates well with those things encountered along our path; of trees pruned, of roads cut, of stone hewed, of animals sacrificed, of land divided.

76 Carl Blegen followed in the footsteps of an earlier Director of the American School, Charles Waldstein; the Mycenae Survey followed in the footsteps of Bernard Steffen; J.M. Cook in the footsteps of Humfry Payne—taking up the labors of others, investing in archaeological sites reinforces their renown and that of the institutions they build.

Bibliography

Alcock, S.E. 1993. *Graecia Capta: The landscapes of Roman Greece.* Cambridge: Cambridge University Press.

Antonaccio, C. 1992. Terraces, tombs, and the Early Argive Heraion. *Hesperia* 61(1), 85–105.

Antonaccio, C. 1994. Contesting the past: Hero cult, tomb cult, and epic in early Greece. *American Journal of Archaeology* 98(3), 389–410.

Antonaccio, C. 1995. *An archaeology of ancestors: Tomb cult and hero cult in early Greece.* London: Rowman & Littlefield.

Avni, G., Y. Avni, and N. Porat. 2009. A new look at ancient agriculture in the Negev. *Cathedra* 133, 13–44.

Benjamin, W., and M.W. Jennings. 2002. *Selected writings, Volume 3: 1935–1938,* Cambridge, MA: Belknap Press.

Blegen, C. 1937. *Prosymna: The Helladic settlement preceding the Argive Heraeum.* Cambridge: Cambridge University Press.

Blegen, C. 1939. Prosymna: Remains of post-Mycenaean date. *American Journal of Archaeology* 43(3), 410–44.

Blegen, C.W., O.T. Broneer, R. Stillwell, and A.R. Bellinger. 1930. *Acrocorinth: Excavations in 1926.* Cambridge, MA: Harvard University Press.

Bory de Saint-Vincent, M. 1834. *Expédition scientifique de Morée: Section des sciences physiques. Tome II – Partie 1. Géographie.* Paris: F.G. Levrault.

Cook, J.M., 1953a. The Agamemneion. *Annual of the British School at Athens* 48, 30–68.

Cook, J.M. 1953b. The Cult of Agamemnon at Mycenae. In A.D. Keramopoullos (ed.), *ΓΕΡΑΣ Αντωνίου Κεραμοπούλλου.* Athens: Typographeion Myrtidi. 112–18.

Davidovich, U., N. Porat, Y. Gadot, Y. Avni, and O. Lipschits. 2012. Archaeological investigations and OSL dating of terraces at Ramat Rahel, Israel. *Journal of Field Archaeology* 37(3), 192–208.

De Polignac, F. 1995. *Cults, territory, and the origins of the Greek city-state* (trans. J. Lloyd). Chicago, IL: Chicago University Press.

Frazer, J.G. 1898. *Pausanias's Description of Greece.* 6 vols. London: Macmillan & Co.

Frederick, C., and A. Krahtopoulou. 2000. Deconstructing agricultural terraces: Examining the influence of construction method on stratigraphy, dating and archaeological visibility. In P. Halstead and C. Frederick (eds.), *Landscape and land use in postglacial Greece.* Sheffield: Sheffield Academic Press. 79–94.

French, E. 2002. *Mycenae: Agamemnon's capital.* Stroud: Tempus.

Fustel de Coulanges, N.D. 2006. *The ancient city: A study of the religion, laws, and institutions of Greece and Rome.* Mineola, NY: Dover Publications.

Gordon, M. 1998. *Slavery in the Arab world.* New York, NY: New Amsterdam Books.

Hägg, R. 1987. Gifts to the heroes in Geometric and Archaic Greece. In T. Linders and G. Nordqvist (eds.), *Gifts to the gods,* Vol. 15. Uppsala: Boreas. 93–99.

Hall, J.M. 1995. How Argive was the "Argive" Heraion? The political and cultic geography of the Argive plain, 900–400 B.C. *American Journal of Archaeology* 99(4), 577–613.

Hamilakis, Y. 2007. *The nation and its ruins: Antiquity, archaeology, and national imagination in Greece.* Oxford: Oxford University Press.

Hanson, V.D. 1999. *The other Greeks: The family farm and the agrarian roots of Western civilization.* Berkeley, CA: University of California Press.

Harrison, R.P. 2003. *The dominion of the dead.* Chicago, IL: University of Chicago Press.

Hood, R. 1998. *Faces of archaeology in Greece: Caricatures by Piet De Jong.* Oxford: Leopard's Head Press.

Hope Simpson, R., and D.K. Hagel. 2006. *Mycenaean fortifications, highways, dams, and canals.* Sävedalen: Paul Åströms Förlag.

Iakovidis, S., E.B. French, K. Shelton, J. Lavery, A.G. Jansen, and C. Ioannides. 2003. *The archaeological atlas of Mycenae.* Athens: Archaeological Society of Athens.

Jahns, S. 1993. On the Holocene vegetation history of the Argive plain. *Vegetation History and Archaeobotany* 2(4),187–203.

Jansen, A. 1997. Bronze Age highways at Mycenae. *Echos du monde classique / Classical Views* 41, 1–16.

Jansen, A. 2002. *A study of the remains of Mycenaean roads and stations of Bronze-Age Greece.* Lewiston, NY: Edwin Mellen Press.

Jansen, A. 2003. The Mycenaean roads in the survey area. In S. Iakovidis, E.B. French, K. Shelton, J. Lavery, A.G. Jansen, and C. Ioannides (eds.), *The archaeological atlas of Mycenae.* Athens: Archaeological Society of Athens. 28–30.

Knauss, J. 1997. Agamemnóneion phréar: Der Stausee der Mykener. *Antike Welt* 5, 381–95.

Lavery, J. 1990. Some aspects of Mycenaean topography. *Bulletin of the Institute of Classical Studies* 37, 165–71.

Lehmann, H. 1937. *Argolis: Landeskunde der Ebene von Argos und ihrer Randgebiete.* Athens: Deutsches Archäologisches Institut.

McInerney, J. 2010. *The cattle of the sun: Cows and culture in the world of the ancient Greeks.* Princeton, NJ: Princeton University Press.

Morgan, C., and T. Whitelaw. 1991. Pots and politics: Ceramic evidence for the rise of the Argive state. *American Journal of Archaeology* 95(1),79–108.

Morris, I. 1988. Tomb cult and the "Greek renaissance": The past in the present in the 8th century BC. *Antiquity* 62, 750–61.

Morris, I. 2000. *Archaeology as culture history.* Oxford: Blackwell.

Nagy, G. 1983. S ma and nó sis: Some illustrations. *Arethusa* 16, 35–55.

Olsen, B. 2010. *In defense of things: Archaeology and the ontology of objects.* Lanham, MD: AltaMira Press.

Parker, R. 1991. Greek religion. In J. Boardman (ed.), *The Oxford history of Greece and the Hellenistic world.* Oxford: Oxford University Press. 306–29.

Puillon de Boblaye, M.E. 1836. *Expédition scientifique de Morée: Recherches géographiques sur les ruines de la Morée.* Paris: F.G. Levrault.

Rackham, O., and J.A. Moody. 1996. *The making of the Cretan landscape.* Manchester: Manchester University Press.

Sarantákis, P. 2007. *Argolída / Oi Ekklisíes kai ta Monastíria tis.* Athens: Ekdóseis OIATIS.

Scarre, C., and R. Coningham (eds.). 2012. *Appropriating the past: Philosophical perspectives on the practice of archaeology.* Cambridge: Cambridge University Press.

Serres, M. 2011. *Malfeasance: Appropriation through pollution?* Stanford, CA: Stanford University Press.

Shelton, K. 1993. Tsountas' chamber tombs at Mycenae. *Archaiologikie ephermeris* 132, 187–210.

Shelton, K. 2003. The cemeteries. In S. Iakovidis, E.B. French, K. Shelton, J. Lavery, A.G. Jansen, and C. Ioannides (eds.), *The archaeological atlas of Mycenae.* Athens: Archaeological Society of Athens. 35–8.

Sloterdijk, P. 2014. *Globes: Spheres II.* South Pasadena, CA: Semiotext(e).

Snodgrass, A.M. 1977. *Archaeology and the rise of the Greek State*. Cambridge: Cambridge University Press.

Snodgrass, A.M. 1980. *Archaic Greece: The age of experiment*. London: J.M. Dent.

Snodgrass, A.M. 1982. Les origines du culte des héros en Grèce antique. In G. Gnoli and J.-P. Vernant (eds.), *La mort, les morts, dons les sociétés ancienne*. Cambridge: Cambridge University Press. 107–19.

Snodgrass, A.M. 1987. *An archaeology of Greece*. Berkeley, CA: University of California Press.

Steffen, B. 1884. *Karten von Mykenai*. Berlin: Dietrich Reimer.

Strøm, I. 1988. The early sanctuary of the Argive Heraion and its external relations (8th-early 6th century B.C.): The monumental architecture. *Acta Archaeologica* 59, 173–203.

Strøm, I. 1995. The early sanctuary of the Argive Heraion and its external relations (8th-early 6th century B.C.): The Greek geometric bronzes. *Proceedings of the Danish Institute at Athens* 1, 37–128.

Vernant, J.-P. 2006. *Myth and thought among the Greeks*. New York, NY: Zone Books.

Vico, G. 1948[1744]. *The new science* (trans. T.G. Bergin and M.H. Fisch). Ithaca, NY: Cornell University Press.

Vogeikoff-Brogan, N., J.L. Davis, and V. Florou (eds.). 2015. *Carl W. Blegen: Personal and archaeological narratives*. Atlanta, GA: Lockwood Press.

Voutsaki, S., A. Ingvarsson-Sundstöm, and M. Richards. 2007. Project on the middle Helladic Argolid: A report on the 2007 season. *Pharos* XV, 137–52.

Wace, A.J.B. 1923. Mycenae: Report of the excavations of the British School at Athens, 1921–1923. *Annual of the British School at Athens* 25, 1–434.

Whitelaw, T. 1991. The ethnoarchaeology of recent rural settlement and land use in Nortwest Keos. In J.F. Cherry, J.L. Davis, and E. Mantzourani (eds.), *Landscape archaeology as long-term history*. Los Angeles, CA: University of California. 403–54.

Whitley, J. 1988. Early states and hero cults: A re-appraisal. *Journal of Hellenic Studies* 108, 173–82.

Whitley, J. 1995. Tomb cult and hero cult: The uses of the past in Archaic Greece. In N. Spencer (ed.). *Time, tradition and society in Greek archaeology: Bridging the "great divide."* London: Routledge. 43–63.

Wright, J.C. 1982. The old temple terrace at the Argive Heraeum and the early cult of Hera in the Argolid. *Journal of Hellenic Studies* 102, 186–201.

Zangger, E. 1993. *The geoarchaeology of the Argolid*. Berlin: Mann.

11

THROUGH GROVES OF CITRUS TO ARGOS

The thousand-year road, of herdsmen and farmers, different commitments to land, long-term fluctuations in land use, transformation of the plain, monoculture, profit-driven agriculture, comfort tree, scarcity to overabundance, water usage, the loss of farmers, passing from the helm, risk and fragility, the return of Poseidon, the return of the herdsman?

May 28, 2012. The gravel path down from the middle terrace clings to the southern edge of the spur upon which are the remnants of the Heraion. The angle of the path varies here and there. And here, as I move down the section below the terrace, I lose my footing and skate atop the gravel in worn running shoes. My caution eases with the slope at the bottom. I pass under cicada-filled pines, by the guard shack, and exit the blue, metal gates of the archaeo-logical site. From the center of the parking lot, I turn to scan the slopes above the Heraion. I wonder why Harold Koster made no mention of the erstwhile sanctuary to the "cow-eyed" goddess when he passed over the ridge, just a week plus forty years ago, with families and their herds.[1]

Koster, in his essay entitled "The Thousand-Year Road," describes a six-day journey along the drove road from the winter pastures in the Southern Argolid to the summer pastures in the western Corinthia.[2] With a flock of over six hundred sheep and goats, Koster, a guest in the company of Nikos,[3] along with his wife Eleni, sons Kostas and Panos, pack mules and donkeys, and their mountain dog Tsopana, had pitched their camp on a steep ridge above the plain. I assume this camp was somewhere on this very ridge, Profitis Elias (Mt Euboea), which is now a wildlife refuge. Having arrived at mid-day, they would spend an anxiety-ridden afternoon stealing sleep in the meager shade of shrubs amid bleached limestone slope. I turn and walk across the empty lot and down the paved road to the southwest.

Framed on either side by olive groves, the surface of the road is riddled with deep, gravel-filled grooves and potholes. A few lonely pines stand on the left. Their mid-morning shade, welcome on an otherwise windless day, quickly passes with increasing distance from the ruined sanctuary. Nikos, his family, and Koster waited for the cover of darkness to descend the slopes somewhere north of here. Crossing the plain in late hours of night afforded the transhumant party a diminished sense of unease in their movement because of an increased likelihood of avoiding landowners or lorry drivers. In the past, families had pooled their flocks and droves into a temporary cooperative called a *tselingaton* during such journeys. On the May 20, 1972 such cooperation was soon to become a memory; the large land holdings had broken up, along with the parcels to which other families who once shared the road would journey. In 1972, Nikos formed a *tselingaton* with Spyros Kalivas, who would travel with his wife Marina, son Giorgos, and daughter Dimitra. Like these herders, I too aim to cross the plain, albeit by a different path.

Amid groves of olives, the paved road before me winds its way in slight turns down slope. In 1972, many groves were fenced off, a practice that shepherds and goatherds encountered with increasing frequency as they moved through areas under cultivation. Fences barred Nikos and his companions from many of the groves of the plain. So, despite the dangers, they stuck to the roads south of Mycenae. By dawn, on the feast day of Agios Konstantinos, they would find respite and celebration in the valley north of Phichtia. The crossing of the plain by these herdsmen was more than an anxiety-ridden event; in

---

1 Koster (1976).

2 This route was recorded ethnographically on May 20 and 21, 1972.

3 Koster does not provide a family surname. Elsewhere he describes them on the basis of ethnicity as a Sarakatsan group (Koster 1977, 9).

a practical sense it brought to the fore two very different modes of existence. Whereas a pastoral mode moves with animals as their desire leads them and thus refuses to root the self to a single plot, an agrarian mode of existence is tied to a delimited patch of earth. Given such discrepancies, Aristotle regarded the herdsman and the farmer as completely different social entities with radically different styles of life, sensibilities, and accumulated wisdoms.[4]

As a herdsman, Nikos was willing to live out his life, and the life of his family, around the wandering flock. His lot revolved around animals, paths of transhumance, seasonal movements between pastures through temporary camps. Unlike the farmers whose plots frame the road before me, Nikos was not fixed to a delimited patch of land. The herdsman, robust in body, knew how to both sustain and consume the herds by maintaining the right combination of breeding and feeder stock. He watched and learned from sheep and goat and knew when to defer to the leadership of the wethers, the lead goat, in moving the droves. The herdsman, however, did not know how to make the best use of land in the way of the farmer.[5] Unlike the herdsman, an agrarian notion of self revolves around an enclosed area of terra firma. And about this, the farmer's commitment has revolved for millennia with the protection of plants, both those that are the fruits of his labors, those of his neighbor, and those of his labor's companion, yoked oxen. The value of land grows through the hard work of breaking earth and raising a crop. Over the millennia, agrarian economy has repeatedly usurped nomadic ecology through the expansion and efficient use of farmland, the value of which grows through their investment.

After a few hundred meters the road swings right and a portion of the valley comes into view. A broad flat plain hemmed in on three sides by foothills with the fourth bordered by the sea. Directly ahead, across an unencumbered expanse of green rises the conical peak of the Larissa above Argos, at a distance of some seven kilometers. A grove of young fruit trees, within a newly fenced tract on the right, will obscure this sight in the coming decades. Behind me, the sound of a sputtering engine meets the road and soon an old farmer passes in his truck. Koster witnessed firsthand this reorganization of land and changing relations with transhumance, which took form as new fences around plots and in new areas drawn into cultivation. With dismay, Nikos encountered new vines planted in the midst of a key grazing area in the valley north of Phichtia. Despite crossing agricultural ground only in a few sections near Trachia and Ligourio, the plains of Argos and Nemea, and the Stymphalia basin, Koster's

---

4 For Koster (1976) the old opposition between the herdsman and the farmer, exemplified by the Christian tradition of Cain, the farmer, and Abel, the shepherd, is too rigid.

5 Also see Sloterdijk (2012b).

journey with Nikos and family was among the last recorded uses of the old way.[6]

Beginning on the slopes of Ortholithi (Megalovouni), the well-worn drove road rounded the Asklepion of Epidaurus, clung to the high ground of Arachneo, followed a line to Moni Vrachou in Nemea, where it pivoted to eventually meet with the pastures high on the slopes of Ziria, otherwise known as Kyllini, the birthplace of Hermes. Like the long-forgotten god of transitions, boundaries, and border crossings, the patron god of shepherds and travelers, anxiety-ridden confrontations between herdsmen and farmers would become a thing of the past along the drove road. Today, if the numbers are faithful then the populations of flocks and droves continue to dwindle.[7] Any that now cross the plain do so in lorries over tarmac where for generations, a thousand years according to Koster, there was but track, sole, hoof, and paw. Goats and sheep have transitioned to mobile enclosures under a new metabolic regime.

After 300 meters I pause under the eucalyptus trees near the crossroad to Agia Kyriaki where I had parked my car earlier in the morning. On the right, adjacent to the road that has been my footpath sits an abandoned farmhouse. On its margins, oleander and pomegranates are in bloom. At its periphery, figs trees are weighed with green fruit. Cypresses line its northern edge. These arboreal boundaries were reinforced with metal fences, now broken down. Inside this well-delineated enclosure is a field, which now lies fallow. There, milk thistle grows green from the graves of its grain.[8] Measured plots of land are the norm in the more productive bottomland of the plain. But this is not a composition a thousand years in the making. It is one that was reestablished in the wake of Greece's new independence and further transformed by subsequent immigration, government land redistribution, and agricultural development.[9]

---

6 Koster accompanied the group again in 1975 (see Koster 1977, 9).

7 In 1911 there were 99,000 goats and 117,000 sheep in the districts of Argos and Nauplia alone (Lehmann 1937, 134). The 2009 livestock census put the number of goats at just under 87,000 and sheep at 94,700 for the whole Argolid (numbers are available through the Hellenic Statistical Authority).

8 An evocation of Swinburne's poem, entitled "A Forsaken Garden":

> A girtle of brushwood and thorn encloses
> The steep square slope of the blossomless bed
> Where the weeds that grew green from the graves of its roses
> Now lie dead.

9 See McGrew (1985), Lawrence (2007). On the history of dual holdings among the Sarakatsani of the southern Argolid, see Koster (1977, 76–8).

Behind me, ahead of me, all around me, lay evidence that the farmer has won out over the herdsman in the last two to three generations. Yet, in the midst of developed plots, I struggle to find memories of deeper times. For over the millennia this plain has witnessed its fair share of demographic swings, of different forms of governance, and of shifts in land holding. In step with these fluctuations, agrarian and pastoral modes, one rooted, one speculative, have ebbed and flowed.[10] The mobility of Nikos's forebears arose, it has been argued, as "a response both to the needs of their animals and to the dangers of a settled way of life."[11] Similar shifts plausibly occurred with those changing land holdings under the yoke of the Venetians, under the Frankish overlords before them, in the devastating aftermath of the mid-sixth-century plague,[12] and with the demographic shifts and reorganization of agricultural lands into large estates under Rome.[13] Valuable farmland was developed for intensive agriculture in the wake of a demographic tide and the development of the ancient Greek city-state.[14] Before the ensuing agrarian crisis, which underlay the expansion of Argive territorial control over the whole of the plain, pastoralism is often argued to have prevailed in the Early Iron Age when land was ample in the shadows of the destructions that put an end to the great palaces as they were known in the Late Bronze Age.[15] Optimal use of land will favor agriculture, but what is optimal is not always favored by agriculturalists.

I wheel the car into the crossroads and continue west. Here, on both sides of the road, groves of olive transition into orange. After 200 meters, I pass an enclosure for sheep. Breezeblock sheds line the edge of a compound whose makeshift fences are constructed from disused wooden pallets. Recently sheared, sheep feed on silage, perhaps from artichoke stalks, at a breezeblock trough. Mounds of manure are piled high in an adjacent plot. Fodder in the bunk and a standing reserve of fertilizer awaiting transport to the fields speak to a rapport between herdsmen and farmers that is of mutual benefit to both parties. Yet, for this to occur here, sheep, which are of greater value than goats, are enclosed and feed is brought to them.

---

10 That cultivation waned and animal husbandry waxed under the Ottomans (McGrew 1985, 13–14; also Gibb and Bowen 1950 1.1, 236) allowing for animal exploitation, which was exaggerated further by the Greek War of Independence, has been called into question (see Davies and Davis 2007).
11 McGrew (1985, 13).
12 On the plague, see Durliat (1989).
13 Alcock (1993, 80–91; 2002, 49); also Bintliff (2012, 353–60).
14 Snodgrass (1977, 1980, 37–42), Hanson (1999, 111–12). Also see McInerney (2010, 168).
15 See discussion in McInerney (2010, 68–73), De Polignac (1995, 33–45). This is not to suggest that a mixed agrarian economy disappeared completely (cf., for example, Wallace 2014).

Here again the rapports of herdsmen and agrarians lie behind longstanding debates among scholars interested in long-term changes in land use and tenure. Models for ancient agriculture vary between, on the one hand, cereal-to-bare fallow rotation, which would imply a separation between arable farming and pastoralism, and on the other, a closer admixture where animals would consume fodder in fields and leave manure on the hoof.[16] With the former, transhumance patterns, like those observed by Koster, predominate. With the latter, one would expect a more integrated regime not unlike what I observe here along the road. And yet these scenarios, as it is often recognized, abstract from contingencies on the ground.[17] A century ago both patterns existed simultaneously within and around the plain.

In 1911, Herbert Lehmann observed, on the one hand, transhumance with droves and flocks in the limestone uplands, where goats were in larger proportions, and, on the other, more integrated grazing in the plain. Here, where sheep were kept in larger numbers, flocks and droves were turned out on annual fallow or recently harvested land, which would have been at the end of May, as it is now.[18] Even at that time, Lehmann noted how the increasing intensification of agriculture was depriving livestock of more and more pasture. Less land was left fallow. Formerly vacant patches were tilled. Marshlands were drained. Church lands were redistributed. In the interval between 1911 and 1930, herd numbers on the plain had dwindled by one fifth. Today, the path ahead, across the flat expanse of the plain, is bereft of the herdsman and his herds.[19]

I stop at the Nafplion/Korinthos road and wait for a lorry, with a refrigerated trailer, and several cars to pass.[20] The road ahead, and the road behind, is framed by orange groves. There are few patches of open ground. There are few locations in this once celebrated horse-bearing plain to bear horses. Oranges, however, have only been a familiar feature out on the plain for less than three generations. Prior to 1950 citrus crops—mandarins, oranges, and lemons—were charming supplements within domestic gardens. Marginal crops, they covered just 0.3% of the total cultivated area in an

---

16 See Margaritis and Jones (2008, 160–61); see Alcock, Cherry, and Davis (1994, 148).

17 See Halstead (2014) for a recent discussion. For a contrast where parcels (voles) held under systems of dual tenure discouraged such integrated regimes, see Cherry, Davis, and Mantzourani (1991, 468).

18 Lehmann (1937, 134).

19 In the decade before 1972, former pastoral families of the mountains had followed incentives to relocate to the foothills around the plain. (See Green and Lemon 1996; Van der Leeuw 1998, 283.) The increasing worth of lands was tied to irrigation agriculture. Those pastoralists who settled on the uncultivated edges now have to bore deep to obtain water.

20 In March 2001, during the construction of this so-called "archaeological road," archaeologists with the fourth Ephorate uncovered a pebbled surface less than 800 meters to the north. This they associated with the main processional road that linked the sanctuary to the city of Argos (Palaiologou 2013; see Segment 10).

The upper portion of the Argive plain and its western mountains, seen from Mycenae. Plate I.I from Lehmann 1937.

otherwise open plain.[21] By 1990 oranges accounted for over 40% of an even larger cultivated area.[22] Still, these numbers say little with respect to the plots on either side of the road.

As I drive on towards Neo Ireo (New Heraion), formerly Chonika, I note a few open fields. Many have recently planted in new trees. Prior to the increased use of surface wells, the moisture content of soils determined the best areas for particular crops. At the dawn of the nineteenth century the drier parts were covered in cereals, areas with more moisture in cotton and vines, and the marshy areas near the sea in rice and *kalambokki* (maize).[23] At the

---

21 Lehmann (1937, 130).
22 Van der Leeuw (1998, 286).
23 Leake (1830 II, 348). Documents mentioning exports from Nafplion shed light on those cash crops grown in the plain for a foreign market. Corn, cotton, wool, oil, and rice were the principal exports when Dodwell was in Nauplia (1819 II, 247). Looking upon what he described as a bare plain in the immediate wake of the revolution, Thomas Alcock spoke of ravages by both Turks and rival chiefs which stripped the plain of its covering in vines, mulberry and olives.

The canopied plain in 2014.

beginning of the twentieth century each village specialized in the crop deemed most profitable given the nature of the soil. A century ago, villagers grew tobacco and cereals in these fields. Around Chonika, over the ensuing decades—up to 1928—they would increasingly turn cultivation towards melons and tomatoes.[24] While the area was self-sufficient, by which I mean that it maintained a diversified production, it also targeted an export market with specialized cultivation. Here, in 1928, one would have encountered melon fields extending for 10 hectares and more.[25]

Plots along the road are broken into thin linear strips that run perpendicular to its edge. I slow down upon passing houses just outside of Neo Ireo. Fronted by low walls, these concrete forms, squares and rectangles, are painted in pastels, and pinks; or, more often, they are simply whitewashed. To my left is a lone strip of

"Tobacco is celebrated, and cotton thrives well: the cultivation of indigo has also been tried with success" (1831, 182). Alcock also states that the plain was almost entirely government property.

24 Herbert Lehmann (1937, 132) calculates the area under cultivation for tobacco, melons, and tomatoes in 1911 at 50.0, 3.0, and 0.4 hectares, respectively. By 1928 the area under tobacco would fall to 40.8 hectares, while melon and tomato cultivation would grow to encompass 65.7 and 7.3 hectares, respectively.

25 Lehmann (1937, 129).

cereals. At the southern corner of this field sits a single-story long house. Another long house lies across the road. These village houses are constructed of the same clay-rich earth once tilled by their occupants. Now they are all the more obvious despite being hemmed between newer concrete structures. I pass the town cemetery on the left. Marble-veneer boxes crowd the yard around the concrete church, whose cross-in-square design recalls the Church of the Dormition of the Virgin Mary at the center of town. The presence of the latter church, as Lehmann also surmised, hints at the importance of this area in the twelfth and thirteenth centuries.[26] Now a village of 493 souls, according to the most recent census, I see few residents out in the mid-day heat.

Squeezed down to half its width by encroaching gables and garden walls, the road courses right into the main road from Prosymna to Argos. Where some of the old houses have gardens still, most south-facing, the newer buildings have concrete patios, driveways, and parking spaces. Concrete house design follows on a repeatable pattern of load-bearing concrete columns.[27] Rooms are defined by brick walls covered in lime plaster. Ahead, some buildings, suspended mid-construction, reveal their reinforced-concrete skeleton as they await partitions. The road passes an Aegean petrol station, the municipal offices for the village, and a few houses before the edge of Neo Ireo.

Abrupt is the transition from village to grove. Here, low, round canopies are closely spaced—little room is left to move between. Here, good clay soils contribute to the most productive trees—each tree can generate from 60 to as much as 200 kilograms of fruit.[28] A shared commitment to caring for trees—locals often speak of them as their children—involves maintaining a low berm for holding water, setting irrigation spouts at the base of the truck, fertilizing, plowing, keeping weeds at bay, and pruning low limbs and superfluous branches for better light penetration, or to remove suckers. I do not know these farmers. I only see their achievements. And to my right piles of recent trimmings in the lanes between boughs suggest that now is best to prune, after harvest.

Fifteen hundred meters after the village I pass the municipality boundary. At the crossroads nearby, on the left, sits a breezeblock shed adjacent to a segment of breezeblock wall. Connecting an electric motor with a centrifugal pump, a drive belt extends out of a makeshift orifice at the base of the northern shed wall. An irrigation pipe stretches from the pump into the nearby orchard. Such borehole irrigation was introduced in step with the proliferation of orange groves in the 1950s and 1960s.

26 While this church is usually assigned to the first half of the twelfth century (Krautheimer and Ćurčić 1992), Sanders (2015b) has recently suggested a thirteenth-century date.

27 For a subtle discussion of concrete as a modern material, see Forty (2012).

28 The estimates for peak production vary widely. Lemon and Blatsou (1999b, 97) put the figure at 120 kilos. Christopher Lawrence (2007, 38), however, puts peak production per tree at 200.

Encouraged at the level of individual farmers,[29] boreholes were drilled in large numbers and in close proximity. Farmers gained in self-sufficiency—labor would no longer be siphoned into digging irrigation channels from community wells to the common edge of the fields; effort would no longer be required to harness the mule to the long arm of the water lift. Farmers gained in consistency—interannual variability in rainfall would not translate into volatility in yields. And yet, with the exponential increase in boreholes and their use came a concomitant decrease in water-table levels. Falling water tables opened the way for seawater intrusion into the upper aquifer. Saline waters were distributed through irrigation. Evapotranspiration on the surface led to the salinization of the soils.[30] Agrarians lost. Farmers responded by drilling deeper, and deeper. Whereas the average water-table depth in this area had been 11 meters before 1950,[31] it would eventually fall to around 100 meters. On the periphery of the plain it would recede to far greater depths, as much as 420 meters.[32] With waters untapped by those living here prior to the mid-twentieth century, the aquifers were drained to support the orange crop.

I pass another pump house on the left, visible over an open field. Farmers who choose to invest in oranges lay claim to more water than the neighbor who cultivates cereals in rotation with melons. Indeed, boundaries between plots fail to keep farmers from appropriating the waters below the fields of their neighbor. Thus, an age-old contract, inscribed into the land as lines of division, held by paths and berms between plots, ceases to maintain peaceful relations between those on either side. What is more, the cumulative effects of salination and pollution, from fertilizers and pesticides, appropriate waters from all—residents on the plain can no longer drink the water from below their feet. By 1999, nitrate concentrations had increased to 172 milligrams/liter, well over three times the accepted limit for adults, nearly nine times the limit for children.[33] Is there a link between these high carcinogenic-nitrate levels and the

---

29 Capital was provided by the Agricultural Bank of Greece; Lemon and Blatsou (1999c, 122); also see Hector (1973).

30 Balabanis (1999, 68).

31 Lehmann (1937, 126) calculates an average depth of 11 meters for the ninety-six wells in and around Chonika. Elsewhere Lehmann states: "In der Feldmark Dalamanara liegt der Grundwasserspiegel durchschnittlich in nur 3 m Tiefe, in der Umgebung von Pirghela muss man 4–5 m bohren, bei Anifi wird eine Tiefe von 8–9 m und nördlich von Chonika eine solche von durchschnittlich 10 m erreicht" (ibid., 57). (In the area of Dalamanara, the average depth of the water table is only 3 meters, in the vicinity of Pirghela one must drill 4–5 meters, at Anifi to a depth of 8–9 meters, and north of Chonika it is 10 meters on average.)

32 The issue reached a critical juncture in the early 1990s; Lemon and Blatsou (1999a); also see Balabanis (1999).

33 See Galanis and Nikitas (2000). The Rural Development Programme of Greece 2007–2013 prioritized reduction of the nitrate levels in the plain (2011, 25–26). http://faolex.fao.org/docs/pdf/gre110023.pdf.

Borehole irrigation pump amid orange trees just west of Neo Ireo (Chronika)

high rates of cancer in the area? Other toxins enter the soil and cling to the fruit through pesticide use. Last year a testing program under the European Food and Safety Authority, coordinated by the Ministry of Rural Development and Food, found Dimethomorph on oranges from Spiliotakis and Thiabendazole on mandarins from Lefkakia.[34] A thirsty plain, indeed—Strabo, had he seen this, would have agreed.[35]

Statistics, even among a population wary of relinquishing such information, are more revealing than the piezometry of receding aquifers or breaches in tacit agrarian contracts between neighbors. Between 1945 and 2007 the number of hectares irrigated in the Argolid rose by well over fourfold, from 5,500 to 25,430. Between 1964 and 2004 the number of water pumps more than tripled, from 2,953 to 10,044, and the number of sprinklers surged from three to 10,635.[36] In 1990, citrus trees accounted for over 63 per cent of the area under

34 Georgios (2014).
35 Strabo (8.6.7) disputes Homer's use of the adjectives "waterless" (*ánhydron*) and "thirsty" (*polydípsion*).
36 These numbers are derived from the Greek National Statistics Service and are also published in Green and Lemon (1996, 191). Numbers specific to the Argive plain were supplied by the Agricultural University of Athens as part of the Archaeomedes Project.

irrigation on the plain.[37] While estimates vary widely, more than 150 million cubic meters of water are used in irrigated agriculture on and around the plain each year.[38] This is nearly enough water to submerge every irrigated hectare of the plain under a meter-deep lake.[39]

From the air-conditioned interior of an automobile, property lines are shielded by arboreal monotony. Beyond a blur of unbroken canopies, the main concrete canal in the Anavalos canal system cuts a line something less than parallel to my own a few hundred meters to the south. Tapping a natural spring that emerges in the sea just south of Kiveri, the ancient *Dinê*,[40] the irrigation system, a massive infrastructure of primary and secondary canals built under the Greek Junta, weaves a route north then east then south across the plain to supply Argive fields and orchards.[41] But the waters, which well up from below the seabed, prove at times to be too salty. Thus, in recent years the system was expanded to include the waters of the Kephalari, the ancient source of the Erasinos, in order to check the depletion of the aquifers and enable their recharge. While fewer boreholes are now drilled, recharge has brought its own series of unanticipated consequences. During the heavy rains of 1996 and 1997, large areas of the plain near Dalamanara and Neo Kios were inundated. Berms between plots cannot hold back the waters.

Anavalos canal pump station just south of Kiveri, the ancient *Dinê*.

37 Van der Leeuw (1998, 286).
38 While Lemon, Seaton, and Park (1994) estimated 95–125 million cubic meters around 1990, Lemon and Blatsou (1999a, 35) up that estimate to 145 million cubic meters in 1990.
39 According to the Archaeomedes Project (Van der Leeuw 1998, 286) 17,680 hectares (of which 11,200 were under oranges) where irrigated for the main crops in the Argolid Valley in 1990— that is 176,800,000 square meters under 150,000,000 cubic meters of water.
40 See Pritchett (1965, 104–05).
41 See Lemon and Blatsou (1999c, 126–29, 130); on the hydrogeology of the Anavalos spring, see Morfis and Zojer (1986). Of relevance here is the work of James C. Scott (1998).

Aqueducts, an ancient strategy for supplying waters not only to cities and towns with baths and fountains but also to agricultural fields, has here crossed a threshold of necessity unknown to farmers in the past.[42] The Ancients knew the area at the source of the Anavalos as *Genethlium*, a natal place, a place of birth connected with the epithet associated with Poseidion *Genesius*. Here, to appease the horse-tamer Poseidon, the Argives once cast horses adorned with bridles into the emerging waters of the *Dinê*.[43] *Dinê* denoted the vortex, something that existed out of equilibrium; something that was independent of human influence.[44] Drowning equine sacrifices was a way of dealing with the irremediable.

Now captured and pumped upwards, waters are subservient—their control depends on technical achievement. Note this inversion. The mastery of waters, against the force of gravity, is in the hands of humans with the aid of concrete enclosures, high-volume water pumps, aqueducts, and control panels with on–off switches. Relief from drought, reversing the downward flow of entire streams, such things eluded the influence of pious worshipers of Poseidon. Since the introduction of bore pumps, now reinforced by the Anavalos system, powers formerly associated with those often callous, always capricious gods who animated the world of the Ancients now rest in human hands operating switches and control valves.[45] Precarious salvation with use, certain catastrophe with end: note this apotheosis, at least insofar as the central plain is concerned—politicians dangle this golden carrot in front of voters and full-time farmers on the periphery who seek to access the system. They await Poseidon still.

I pass a blue sign for the Agricultural Cooperative of Iras. Hundreds of plastic crates are stacked high behind a wire fence. Air mixers rise above the groves adjacent to the co-op. Dense canopies raise the humidity at the ground surface, thereby increasing the likelihood of frost in the winter. Resembling wind pumps, air mixers are used to draw warmer air from above the trees

---

42 Indeed, the Anavalos system expands upon long-standing agrarian pragmatics once witnessed in this portion of plain when the movement of wheeled traffic took a backseat to the movement of waters through raised dikes and galvanized steel pipes across the roads (Lehmann 1937, 129). The farmers who believed in the system feel vindicated, it staved off a total disaster, but for how long? On the expansion of the Anavalos system, see Segment 18.

43 Pausanias 8.7.2.

44 For Democritus, according to Diogenes Laertius, the vortex (*dinê*) was the cause of all things (tís dínis aitías oúsis tís genéseos pánton, 9.7.45). All things happen by virtue of necessity (Pánta te kat anánkin gínesthai); it is worth underlining this curious though unconventional connection between the *dinê* and necessity; here see Cartledge (1998, 18–19). Also see Serres with Latour (1995, 169–70).

45 One can carry this association only so far, of course. There are fundamental differences between the powers of the ancient gods and human-made monstrosity (Sloterdijk 2012a). However, here locality forces a connection that is otherwise lost, given these differences.

down to the surface, thus regulating temperature during times of frost. Given their expense, they are often obtained and distributed by the co-ops.[46] Because they provide variable coverage, their use is not without contention related to charges of political favoritism. Many farmers rely on sprinklers to manage winter temperatures, which extends the growing season. Exerting influence over climate and seasonality, farming has encroached even more into the realm of the formerly independent. Indeed, it would seem that the whole plain has become a contrived bubble of conditioned air to the benefit of one crop.

Citrus trees could not grow into such a dense canopy without a new infra-structure based upon the metabolic regime of fossil fuels: electricity, whether for the borehole pumps or the Anavalos system (also for juice production, refrigeration and storage), is partially supplied by the coal- and lignite-burning power plant in Megalopolis; fertilizers and pesticides; tractors, transportation (for labor and shipping), and packaging. And the fantastic bounty of this plain does not even feed the majority of those who live here. Where does it go? Merlin oranges, exported to the former Soviet Union until 1991, are now des-tined for markets throughout the European Union (EU). Food-miles, the dis-tance from here to where the oranges are consumed, add more fossil fuels.[47] This long reach is based upon a logic of division and specialization. Cold storage in concentrate and shipping favors a single species, rather than "small plots of different species so that the harvest dates do not coincide."[48] This new regime both follows and breaks with a deep agrarian logic.

I enter the village once known as Ano Buti and Kato Buti. When it carried that name, this village sat at the heart of the flat and open plain. From here, everyone once saw the agrarian from Koutsi who ventured to break with the standard pattern. Soon, encouraged by enlightened priests, the agricultural ser-vice of the Argolid, and new outlets, others joined in.[49] They, in turn, encour-age others to do as they have done. Oranges spread across the Argive plain, just as vines overtake the Nemea Valley, artichokes fill in almost every plot around Kandia, lemons spread north from Poros to Troizen; this is not all that far from past logics of rivalry and return. The agrarian rapport with a patch of the plain always has followed a course dictated by what experience deems profitable, by what one's neighbor does, or does not. Amid such change, only the most stubborn, only those who regard oranges as a luxury, hold out. An exception, which is obvious in the midst of green groves, their open fields are still

46 Lemon and Blatsou (1999c, 136).
47 David Pimentel (2006, 14) estimates 1 kcal in orange energy is generated for every 1 kcal of fossil fuel energy invested in Florida orange production.
48 Hanson (1999, 64–65).
49 See Psariotis (2012).

dedicated to those cereals that once provided maximum returns. I pass one such field on the left by the village center.

This village reclaimed the name of *Hera*, Ira. Since 1981 its population has fallen from 455 to 374 (the latter as of 2011).[50] Over the first decade of 2000, the population of Neo Ireo also fell from 585 to 493.[51] The meaning that such numbers once carried for a largely agrarian society has all but disappeared along this road. When Lehmann wrote about demographic trends in Cronika, Upper and Lower Buti, he could trust that those numbers reflected an agrarian impact. When hardened roads and automobility connect the residents of these villages to Argos and Nafplion with ease, a home on the plain no longer translates into work on the plain. Village demography, admittedly, gives us an indirect sense of a problem better understood with broad statistics. Last year, the 2011 census revealed that the rural population of Greece had fallen to 23.4 per cent.[52] The loss of agriculturalists between 1900 and 2000 is indeed a counter-revolution of comparable scope to that at the dawn of the Neolithic. Some even claim this marks a true end to the Neolithic.[53] *Agrarian, agrotes, peasant*—within their etymology these terms have preserved the rapport with tilled plots of land, cultivated soil, earth: *ager, pagus*. The Greek *georgoi* holds on to both "earth," *ge, gaia,* and "work," *ergon*. Here, most of the registered orange producers are elderly, above 65.[54] It is not always difficult to identify their passing—their progeny have severed the agrarian commitment altogether, choosing to sell the land for new houses or harvest sun with solar farms. Under such conditions these old terms, often terms of disdain, are poised to flip into a new meaning.

Orange trees do not demand a full-time commitment on the part of those who tend them. These lands, for the majority of those farmers who cultivate them, provide supplemental income. Café owners, civil servants, lorry drivers, most are either part-time agrarians or retirees. Two generations ago, differences in soil, elevation, proximity to water, and, thus, agricultural potential—in other words, differences in geography—contributed to disparities of wealth between

---

50 In 1981 455, 1991 446.
51 In 1991, the population of Neo Ireo was 547 (NSSG 1994; compare NSSG 2001; NSSG 2011 (revised)).
52 This percentage is based on revised calculations by the Hellenic Statistical Authority using a methodology compatible with other EU countries. Out of a resident population of 10,815,197, 8,284,210 lived in urban areas and 2,530,987 in rural areas according to the 2011 census (ELSTAT 2013, 12). The revised numbers differ from earlier census calculations of 61.4 per cent urban and 38.6 per cent rural. Also see Sutton (1983).
53 Harrison (2003, 31, 34), Serres (2014, 3), Witmore (2018a).
54 National numbers are available through the National Statistics Service of Greece; also see Lawrence (2007, 34–57). Importantly, this is also tied to inheritance, which is the main avenue to the acquisition of land.

plain and mountain dwellers.[55] At harvest time, in those days, supplemental agricultural labor descended onto the plain from the surrounding villages. EU investment in step with new infrastructures flattened disparities among lowlanders and uplanders to the degree that old geo-capital differences were annulled, more or less. Harvests are now undertaken by immigrant labor, landless workers, particularly from Eastern Europe, which is often supplied by orange merchants.[56]

Merlin oranges are generally harvested from December through mid-March. Here and there, some trees bear fruit still—these are a different variety, Valencia. Groves pass on either side in a peripheral cascade of green blurs. A diversity of crops has always been the desirable pattern on most Greek farms, ancient and modern. Diversity minimizes risks from drought, hail, frost, unseasonable rain, gusting winds, and fungal, viral, and bacterial pathogens. The fragility of any one crop is known to everyone here—apricots were lost to *Sharka*, vines to *Aleurotrixus floccosus* and *Phyllozera*, lemons to *Coryphoxera*, oranges to the *Alevrodes* virus.[57] While the EU subsidies soften losses, salination, frost, flooding, all have taken their toll in areas of the plain. Yet here, in the area south of Ira, monoculture seems the rule. Entire plots have been transformed into groves without margins, not even a patch for vegetables. To be sure, some fields remain for other crops, a few olives or pomegranates find purchase in narrow strips by the road, but almost every plot has its exclusive occupant, its sole concern.

The car suspension fails to register the crossing of the Panitza, the ancient Inachos. What in all times past must have been a key transition, a notable break in the monotony of the flat plain, the dry riverbed is spanned now by a smooth asphalt surface over a pier-and-beam bridge. On the other side I pull off to the right and park the car on a paved shoulder. Just north beehives sit along a dirt road above the riverbed. Nearby lies a concrete check-dam. Garbage piles along the banks. Beyond, in the midst of the bed, a horse is tethered to a line. Among the myth tellers in the time of Pausanias was shared a story that the river, born on the high slopes that separate the Argolid from Arcadia, once ran rich with waters. Now this linear patch of dry is an uncultivated lacuna along which bees are kept for honey and pollination, and a lone horse is put to pasture. Water passes under its bed in a concrete siphon associated with the Anavalos system. From here, I will walk the rest of the way to Argos.

55 See Lawrence (2007).
56 Ibid., 40.
57 Van der Leeuw 1998, 286. Uprooting the majority of the apricot crop on the plain occurred as a response to the *Sharka* virus in the early 1990s. *Coryphoxera*, in combination with extreme frosts, decimated the lemon crop in the 1960s (Green and Lemon 1996, 198, n. 30).

This road has no margins, no footpaths. A chain-link fence confines me to the asphalt surface. Overgrowth forces me farther from the shoulder. Yet, out of the air-conditioned interior, under the sun at noon on this windless day, I have a clearer vantage upon a rather subtle, though no less strange inversion; one that is more psychological than economic, more idiosyncratic than common. In this heat I understand how a will to comfort is of tremendous consequence for those tied to the land. It is therefore fitting that the orange tree has been exported from the confines of the enclosed south-facing gardens of local houses and moved wholesale into a land of scarcity and struggle, formerly without shade.

Along with fig, almond, lemon, and other fruit trees, oranges were once associated with a space of reprieve, often enclosed behind high walls of mud-brick or a band of cypress in immediate proximity to houses, free of the hardships of the plain.[58] Within these enclosed gardens, common since Ottoman times, walls shielded trees from north winds, slender cypresses added a distinctive flavor to the fruit, fountains gurgled gently, and the semi-darkness under a canopy of closely spaced trees provided an atmosphere of quiet seclusion from the dusty, parched fields.[59] And in contrast to the open plain, where everyone sees, these garden spaces were often free from the wayward eyes of others. Thus, oranges, like lemons, were once associated with safe and restful interiors. The unprecedented degree to which these comfort trees have proliferated speaks to a subtle inversion of space. Where an open plain once insured everyone knew of everyone else's lot amid a shared drudgery, a green canopy of well-watered trees now shields the farmer's labors.

Nearby I hear a diesel engine sputter into action. The numbers of tractors, headless oxen, multiplied exponentially in step with the proliferation of the comfort tree.[60] Their presence is tied to yet another inversion, one more fundamental to agrarian morals, one far more pervasive in nature. Agricultural production operated with consistent values that had well-defined limits. Everyone knew of them. Even in the best of years, the best land was circumscribed in that it could only produce so much. The productive capacity of a plot of ground had well-understood limits defined by soil and moisture, weather and

---

58 The predominate crop of Merlin oranges was introduced later. While the difference in variety is of great consequence (consider Seremetakis 1994), it does not take away from the argument here, which is more phenomenological in its emphasis. Comfort is a matter of appearance for those people who grew up with these now-forgotten gardens.

59 See Lehmann (1937, 129).

60 Between 1964 and 2004 the number of tractors in the Argolid had risen from 691 to 4136 (1964 figures are provided in Green and Lemon (1996, 191), while 2004 numbers come from the National Statistical Service of Greece).

the divine. Agrarian conservatism works with an understanding of the best and worst of years. For the frugal farmer, waste was all the more potent when it was present.[61] Thus a ban on wastefulness contributed to a culture of scarcity (exemplified in ancient discussions of food reuse where new grain was added to old). Enabled by waters on demand, lignite and oil, fertilizers, and subsidies for overproduction where one is paid to destroy surplus, the agrarian plain has passed from this time of scarcity. A deviation from what experience in working with, and waiting on, cereals and legumes, trees and labor companions had taught generations to expect. Where vengeful, violent gods once intervened, the whole of the plain now follows a pervasive monoculture, which has usurped the expectations once imposed by plain, weather, crop and farmer. Into a sense of excess and overabundance this orange-bearing plain has flipped.[62]

A rusted fence set slightly off the shoulder provides a thin escape as a lorry passes spewing exhaust. Here, I find a lone open field. Here, in this space of exception, other forms of cultivation can take place. Everywhere else, the long-term agrarian logic of return on yield has expanded above a threshold where these returns weigh upon everything. Subsistence on the plain has overturned by several degrees, monoculture is enabled by a metabolic regime of oil and the mastery of waters. Toxic, both soil and water are now rendered as suspect. From arduous work to motorized farming, from scarcity to overproduction, a new sense of wastefulness has descended onto the plain. Do agrarian pragmatics break down once they achieve a certain weight and robustness? Fortunately, the logic of overproduction is undergoing reevaluation. Along the heights where the Inachos is born rise new wind turbines. In scattered plots, farmers promised good terms by a government program have installed solar panels (thus severing their responsibility in sustaining family plots in the way of their forebears).[63]

I look ahead to Argos, a line of white concrete buildings, clustered around the base of the Larissa. The Ancients believed Hera to have won the plain in a contest with Poseidon. After the contest, judged by the rivers themselves, the vengeful sea god took back their life-giving waters.[64] He then inundated the parched plain with seawater. The ancient recognition of the shared lot of plain and sea, sided with the plain as the matrix, which gives birth to all. Hera

---

61 See Gallant (1991), Garnsey (1999), Halstead (1990, 2014).

62 *Miden agan*, "nothing in excess"—maxims inscribed on temples are to no avail here. On overproduction, price supports, and dumping see Lemon and Blatsou (1999b, 115); also Lawrence (2007, 29); on this inversion of value, see Sloterdijk (2013, 227–28).

63 Also see Segment 18.

64 Pausanias 2.15.5; but compare to Paus. 2.22.4, here he discusses a sanctuary of Poseidon Prosclystius (Flooder). After Hera won the contest, Poseidon inundated the land, only to be induced by Hera to take back the waters. The sanctuary set at the point where the tide ebbed.

induced Poseidon to remove his waters. The son of the river Inachos, Phoroneus, became its first inhabitant, and gathered all together.[65] What are we to
make of this close approximation of ancient myth to this current situation?
Waters withdrawn in the ancient past now return with new gods.[66] The saline
waters of Posedion will be held in check not with temples,[67] but by capturing
more of his waters. What returns with them?

This plain did not depend on Argives of the past; Argives depended on it.
Sapping its groundwater will not remove the plain as the major agent of its
own history. With a causality centered in human interactions, human choices
regarding intensification, what role does the plain play? Indeed, it too plays
a role in myth. It too is deciding. Who is listening? A flat plain formed by
a receding sea. Can Hera persuade Poseidon to remove his waters before catastrophe brings about the return of her herds?

The road descends into the dry bed of the Xerias. It was here, in the ancient
Charadrus, that generals, upon their return from military expeditions, were sub-
jected to the scrutiny of demos before being allowed to reenter the city. On the
other side I pause below the raised concrete platform of a football pitch. Here,
what was once a recognized line of pacification for the ancient community is
the edge of the city, whose name literally means "plain." Argos.

---

65 See Segment 12.

66 Cores taken in the plain reveal that the sea once covered large portions of the plain and has
    retreated since c.4000 BCE; see Kraft, Aschenbrenner, and Rapp (1977, 944–45), Zangger
    (1993, 62–65).

67 A temple to Poseidon marked the high water mark of the waters. This served as a reminder of
    the threat of inundation; the ground of the plain was always under the threat of divine reclam-
    ation (Pausanias 2.22.4).

Bibliography

Alcock, T. 1831. *Travels in Russia, Persia, Turkey, and Greece, in 1828–9*. London: Printed by E. Clarke and Son.

Alcock, S.E. 1993. *Graecia Capta: The landscapes of Roman Greece*. Cambridge: Cambridge University Press.

Alcock, S.E. 2002. *Archaeologies of the Greek past: Landscape, monuments, and memories*. Cambridge: Cambridge University Press.

Alcock, S.E., J.F. Cherry, and J. Davis. 1994. Intensive survey, agricultural practice and the classical landscape of Greece. In I. Morris (ed.), *Classical Greece*. Cambridge: Cambridge University Press. 137–70.

Balabanis, P. 1999. Water in Europe: Research achievements and future perspectives within the framework of European research activities in the field of environment. *Revista CIDOB d'Afers Internacionals* 45/46, 59–78.

Bintliff, J.L. 2012. *The complete archaeology of Greece: From hunter-gatherers to the 20th century AD*. Chichester: Wiley-Blackwell.

Cartledge, P. 1998. *Democritus*. New York, NY: Routledge.

Cherry, J.F., J.L. Davis, and E. Mantzourani. 1991. *Landscape archaeology as long-term history: Northern Keos in the Cycladic Islands*. Los Angeles, CA: Cotsen Institute of Archaeology, University of California.

Davies, S., and J.L. Davis. (eds.). 2007. *Between Venice and Istanbul: Colonial landscapes in early modern Greece*. Princeton, NJ: American School of Classical Studies at Athens.

De Polignac, F.1995. *Cults, territory, and the origins of the Greek city-state* (trans. J. Lloyd). Chicago, IL: Chicago University Press.

Dodwell, E. 1819. *A Classical and topographical tour through Greece*. 2 vols. London: Rodwell and Martin.

Durliat, J. 1989. "La peste du VIe siècle." In C. Morrisson and J. Lefort (eds.), *Hommes et richesses dans l'empire byzantin*, vol. 1, *IV–VIIe siècle*. Paris: Éditions P. Lethielleux. 106–19.

ELSTAT. 2013. *Synthíkes diavíosis stin Elláda* [Living conditions in Greece]. Athens: Hellenic Statistical Authority.

Forty, A. 2012. *Concrete and culture: A material history*. London: Reaktion Books.

Galanis, D., and K. Nikitas. 2000. How the Argolid was filled with nitrates (Pós i Argolída gémise nitriká). *TO BHMA*, 01/ 23/2000, www.tovima.gr/relatedarticles/article/?aid=118482 (Accessed: 19 August 2016).

Gallant, T.W. 1991. *Risk and survival in Ancient Greece: Reconstructing the rural domestic economy*. Cambridge: Polity Press.

Garnsey, P. 1999. *Food and society in Classical antiquity*. Cambridge: Cambridge University Press.

Georgios, C. 2014. Checks for pesticide residues in agricultural products (Élenchoi gia ypoleímmata fytofarmákon sta georgiká proïónta). Blog post 3 May, 2012 available at: http://tro-ma-ktiko.blogspot.com/2012/05/blog-post_4105.html (Accessed: 7 March 2016).

Gibb, H.A.R., and H. Bowen. 1950. *Islamic society and the West: A study of the impact of Western civilization on Moslem culture in the Near East. Volume One, Islamic society in the eighteenth century, Part I*. Oxford: Oxford University Press.

Green, S., and M. Lemon. 1996. Perceptual landscapes in agrarian systems: Degradation processes in North-Western Epirus and the Argolid Valley, Greece. *Cultural Geographies* 3(2), 181–99.

Halstead, P. 1990. Waste not, want not: Traditional responses to crop failure in Greece. *Rural History* 1, 147–63.

Halstead, P. 2014. *Two oxen ahead: Pre-mechanized farming in the Mediterranean.* Chichester: Wiley-Blackwell.

Hanson, V.D. 1999. *The other Greeks: The family farm and the agrarian roots of Western civilization.* Berkeley, CA: University of California Press.

Harrison, R.P. 2003. *The dominion of the dead.* Chicago, IL: University of Chicago Press.

Hector, J. 1973. La plaine d'Argos, répercussions socio-économiques d'une spécialisation agricole. *Méditerranée*, deuxième série 13(2), 1–17.

Koster, H. 1976. The thousand-year road. *Expedition* 19(1), 19–28.

Koster, H. 1977. *The ecology of pastoralism in relation to changing patterns of land use in the Northeast Peloponnese.* Doctorial dissertation, Department of Anthropology, University of Pennsylvania.

Koster, H.A., and J.B. Koster. 1976. Competition or symbiosis? Pastoral adaptive strategies in the Southern Argolid, Greece. *Annals of the New York Academy of Sciences* 268(1), 275–85.

Kraft, J.C., S.E. Aschenbrenner, and G. Rapp. 1977. Paleogeographic reconstructions of coastal Aegean archaeological sites. *Science* 195(4282), 941–47.

Krautheimer, R., and S. Ćurčić. 1992. *Early Christian and Byzantine architecture.* New Haven, CT: Yale University Press.

Lawrence, C.M. 2007. *Blood and oranges: European markets and immigrant labor in rural Greece.* New York, NY: Berghahn Books.

Leake, W.M. 1830. *Travels in the Morea.* London: John Murray.

Lehmann, H. 1937. *Argolis: Landeskunde der Ebene von Argos und ihrer Randgebiete.* Athens: Deutsches Archaologisches Institut.

Lemon, M., and N. Blatsou. 1999a. Background to agriculture and degradation in the Argolid Valley. In M. Lemon (ed.), *Exploring environmental change using an integrative method.* Amsterdam: Gordon and Breach Science Publishers. 27–38.

Lemon, M., and N. Blatsou. 1999b. Agricultural production and change. In M. Lemon (ed.), *Exploring environmental change using an integrative method.* Amsterdam: Gordon and Breach Science Publishers. 83–117.

Lemon, M., and N. Blatsou. 1999c. Technology and agricultural production in the Argolid. In M. Lemon (ed.), *Exploring environmental change using an integrative method.* Amsterdam: Gordon and Breach Science Publishers. 119–60.

Lemon, M., R. Seaton, and J. Park. 1994. Social enquiry and the measurement of natural phenomena: The degradation of irrigation water in the Argolid Plain, Greece. *International Journal of Sustainable Development & World Ecology* 1(3), 206–20.

Margaritis, E., and M.K. Jones. 2008. Greek and Roman agriculture. In J.P. Oleson (ed.), *The Oxford handbook of engineering and technology in the Classical world.* Oxford: Oxford University Press. 217–41.

McGrew, W.W. 1985. *Land and revolution in modern Greece, 1800–1881: The transition in the tenure and exploitation of land from Ottoman rule to independence.* Kent, OH: Kent State University Press.

McInerney, J. 2010. *The cattle of the sun: Cows and culture in the world of the ancient Greeks.* Princeton, NJ: Princeton University Press.

Morfis, A., and H. Zojer. 1986. *Karst hydrogeology of the Central and Eastern Peloponnesus.* Venice: Springer Verlag.

National Statistical Service of Greece. 1994. Actual population of Greece by the Census of 17 March 1991 (Pragmatikós plithysmós tis elládos katá tin apografí tis 17is martíou 1991).

National Statistical Service of Greece. 2001. Greece population and housing census 2001.

National Statistical Service of Greece. 2011. De facto population census 2011 (revised).

Palaiologou, E. 2013. Enas dromos pros to Hraio tou Argous. In D. Mulliez (ed.), *Sta Bimata tou Wilhelm Vollgraff: Ekato chronia archaiologikis drastiriotitas sto Argos*. Athènes: Ecole Française d'Athènes. 393–403.

Pimentel, D. 2006. *Impacts of organic farming on the efficiency of energy use in agriculture.* Washington, DC: Organic Center.

Pritchett, W.K. 1965. *Studies in Ancient Greek topography, Pt. 3, Roads.* Berkeley, CA: University of California Press.

Psariotis, T.I. 2012. Kavvathás Sp. Michaíl (1895–1972) - O protergátis tis diádosis tis kalliérgeias tou portokalioú stin Argolída. Available at: http://argolikivivliothiki.gr/2012/01/04/kavathas/

Sanders, G.D.R. 2015b. William of Moerbeke's church at Merbaka: The use of ancient spolia to make personal and political statements. *Hesperia* 84(3), 583–626.

Scott, J.C. 1998. *Seeing like a state: How certain schemes to improve the human condition have failed.* New Haven, CT: Yale University Press.

Serematakis, C.N. 1994. *The senses still: Perception and memory as material culture in modernity.* Chicago, IL: University of Chicago Press.

Serres, M. 2014. *Times of crisis: What the financial crisis revealed and how to reinvent our lives and future.* New York, NY: Bloomsbury Academic.

Serres, M., and B. Latour. 1995. *Conversations on science, culture, and time.* Ann Arbor, MI: University of Michigan Press.

Sloterdijk, P. 2012a. The time of the crime of the monstrous: On the philosophical justification of the artificial. In S. Elden (ed.), *Sloterdijk Now.* Cambridge: Polity Press. 165–81.

Sloterdijk, P. 2012b. Voices for animals: A fantasy on animal representation. In G. R. Smulewicz-Zucker (ed.), *Strangers to nature: Animal lives and humans ethics.* Lanham, MD: Lexington Books. 263–69.

Sloterdijk, P. 2013. *In the world interior of capital: For a philosophical theory of globalization.* Cambridge: Polity Press.

Snodgrass, A.M. 1977. *Archaeology and the rise of the Greek state.* Cambridge: Cambridge University Press.

Snodgrass, A.M. 1980. *Archaic Greece: The age of experiment.* London: J.M. Dent.

Sutton, S.B. 1983. Rural–urban migration in Greece. In M. Kenny and D.I. Kertzer (eds.), *Urban life in Mediterranean Europe: Anthropological perspectives.* Urbana, IL: University of Illinois Press. 225–49.

Van der Leeuw, S.E. 1998. *The Archaeomedes Project: Understanding the natural and anthropogenic causes of land degradation and desertification in the Mediterranean basin.* Luxembourg: Office for Official Publications of the European Communities.

Wallace, S. 2014. *Ancient Crete: From successful collapse to democracy's alternatives, twelfth to fifth centuries BC.* Cambridge: Cambridge University Press.

Witmore, C. 2018a. The end of the Neolithic? At the emergence of the Anthropocene. In S.E. Pilaar Birch (ed.), *Multispecies archaeology.* London: Routledge. 26–46.

Zangger, E. 1993. *The geoarchaeology of the Argolid.* Berlin: Mann.

12

ARGOS, A DEMOCRATIC POLIS, AND PLUTARCH'S PYRRHUS, A *SYNKRISIS* (COMPARISON)

*Plutarch's Pyrrhus, from gates to agora, patient and impatient modes of govern-
ment, risk-taking, omens, democratic poleis, effective communication and building
good citizens, the death of a king in three acts, monuments, Argive storytelling*

272 BCE, as described around 100 CE. Pyrrhus, king of Epirus, waits. Before
the walls of Argos, in the dead of night, he waits for word of the Gauls he has
sent into the city. Not far from the Kylarabis gymnasium, he waits for his war
elephants to move through the gate known as the Diamperes. Too tall for the
passage thrown open by Aristeas,[1] a passage never designed to accommodate
such alien invaders, he waits for the riders to remove the high towers from
pachyderm backs. And again, he waits for them to reposition the animal-

---

1 Contestant in a feud with Aristippus, by whose invitation Pyrrhus had come to Argos.

mounted redoubts in darkness, in confusion, on the other side. He waits until he can wait no more. The Argive defenders' alarm has sounded. With roars, with cries, the famed Molossian king enters Argos.

The Gauls are uneasy in the marketplace. Having positioned themselves in the agora, within earshot of the Sanctuary of Aphrodite, their response to the shouts of Pyrrhus is muffled. The Gauls lack vigor. Under the watchful eyes of far-sighted Athena, they barricade streets and porticos with what is at hand. Perhaps they upturn the wooden stalls of *mageiroi*, Plutarch does not say. Perhaps they pry open doors to the rooms of public buildings and perhaps they form barriers with their movable contents. Whether in these ways or others, the Gauls transform an open space for gathering crowds of flesh and stone, for facilitating interactions, for fertile chance encounters, into a troubled bastion. Below the old, straight-tiered theatre, around the hypostyle hall, not far from the new theatre cut into the bedrock of Larisa, the spaces of assembly are closed off.[2] An open commons, five hundred years and more in the making, is converted into an enclosure barring all Argives.

In the midst of these surroundings, quite alien to illiterate foreigners, unpunished plunderers of the tombs of Macedonian kings at Aegae, the Gauls are apprehensive; so Plutarch says. Argives and their relief forces press upon them in the dark. Worried for the Gauls, Pyrrhus, with his horsemen, makes his way along the narrow street between the Diamperes and the agora. Deep gullies, unseen in the dark, impede their way.[3] Narrow linear spaces between walled rooms for accommodating citizens and others constrain their movements in the dead of night. In the city, without light, effective movement and clear communication are lacking. Pyrrhus, a general of great effect in a sun-enveloped plain, is unsettled amid the physical achievements of Argives past; obstacles cloaked in darkness. Pyrrhus is troubled in Argos, the city whose name, ironically for the king, is synonymous with "plain." All he can do is hold out till first light.

Here, in the dark, there is no strange irony that the Fire of Phoroneus, son of the first legendary king of Argos, a contender with Prometheus for the

2 My description of Argos is not an attempt to grasp Plutarch's Argos with the spade (compare Edwards 2011) as the city actually was, stone for stone, in 272 BCE; for discussions of the topography of Argos, see Piérart (1982), Piérart and Touchais (1996), Tomlinson (1972), Vollgraff (1907). The fidelity of this segment is related to the purposes for which Plutarch wrote the life of Pyrrhus. Whether or not his description was faithful to Argos as it existed at the time of Pyrrhus's death is incidental to the elements of biographical storytelling (see also Larmour 1992). Yet, neither is Argos treated as anecdotic nor dramatic ground; when possible, empirical details are used to further the comparison. On Plutarch's historical methods, see Stadter (1965).

3 Plutarch uses the word *ochetoís*, which can be translated as *water conduits* or *drains*. Following Piérart and Touchais (1996, 44), I use the term *les profonds caniveaux* or *deep gullies*.

bringer of fire to humans, cannot provide light for assailants in the city.[4] Even if Phoroneus carried within himself a sense of kingship as primordial, as born of the very land through which coursed his father, the river Inachus, his fire could provide no comfort to the king and his motley company. In the figure of Phoroneus, the Argives recognized the close relationship between the taming of fire and the founding of the commons.[5] Phoroneus was first to bring the Argives together in a *koinon*, together as a community in cohabitation, for prior to that time they lived apart in isolation.[6] Around this fire, which the Argives keep burning, the community was collectively bound. Somewhere within the vicinity of Phoroneus's fire, Pyrrhus must again wait.

What Pyrrhus now does recalls an important condition for any democratic polis. This condition is an effect of "waiting power"—the facility to wait and to facilitate others in waiting.[7] A democratic polis needs specific areas of assembly and gathering, dates and times for meetings, a guarantee that key matters of concern will be raised, and all these features are tied to the condition of waiting. Areas for hesitation and prolonged consideration, protracted controversy and debate, dedicated space for a diverse assembly, a public assembly (the *aliaia*), where common concerns, given importance in a council of chosen peers (the *bola*),[8] are aired for those present to hear; these are necessary spatial conditions for any democratic polis. Indeed, democratic poleis work hard to preserve the right that an issue is raised, and decisions of the polis transpire, in a free and male public forum. Democratic poleis fight, as the Argives now do, to maintain these spaces against external threats. While every Argive citizen must endure a stay in key decisions of state till a meeting of the assembly, the Molossian king finds himself in his present situation precisely because he is more able to take calculated risks at a distance from country. Quite unlike the restored democratic polis he now faces, Pyrrhus need not wait for an assembly of vested citizens to make a decision; he need not delay in hallowed meeting halls reserved for matters of statecraft. He need not put such matters off for they revolve around him whether he is in Macedonia, Sicily, or the Peloponnese. He need not wait. Indeed, Pyrrhus is impatient.

---

4 Pausanias 2.19.5; on the location of the Fire of Phoroneus with respect to the Agora, also see Piérart (1993).

5 Following Vitruvius, Sloterdijk (2014, 217–28) picks up on this important association.

6 Pausanias 2.15.5

7 Here, in this comparison of impatient and patent modes of governance, I am borrowing the notion of "waiting power" from Sloterdijk (2005b, 944).

8 On Argive democracy in the late fourth, early third century, see Piérart (2000). Not everyone agrees with a *probouleutic* sequence where issues were weighed by the *bola* before they were aired in the *aliaia*; see, for example, Leppin (1999), as discussed by Robinson (2011b, 15–8).

From Italy and Sicily to Thessaly and Macedonia to Sparta and Argos, Pyrrhus had indulged what Plutarch describes as one vain hope after another. And now, in Argos, pursued by Areus, king of Sparta, he fights on behalf of Aristeas in a feud with Aristippus, friend to his rival Antigonus Gonatas, king of Macedon. Pyrrhus's ability to pursue one futile venture after another through sustained aggressiveness was rooted in an entrepreneurial freedom, which no democratic polis would possibility uphold. Widely divergent campaigns carried out over several years at great distances from the decision-making bodies could only occur with maniacally wayward generals acting on behalf of a polis as tyrants, as pseudo-kings. A speculator in hopes never fully realized, Pyrrhus was self-empowered to take calculated risks at a faster rate than slow poleis awaiting messengers from distant lands. Like a far more successful Alexander before him, Pyrrhus anticipates an era of risk ethos when the urge to generate profits will underlie an investment culture that will eventually put kings out of a job.[9]

Yes, decisions that affect the whole of one's country revolve around kings. Pyrrhus carries within himself the center of power for the fatherland. The close approximation of the king-self and *patris* is well understood by everyone around him, especially the king. Before Sparta, according to Plutarch, Pyrrhus declared:

One omen is best: to fight in defense of Pyrrhus.[10]

Such is a reference to the Homeric inducement to fight for *patris*, the fatherland. Still Pyrrhus's forces are of diverse composition—Gauls and Macedonians in addition to Epirotes—Molossians and Chaonians, among others. Putting to one side the latter, foreign loyalties rest not so much on the connection between king and country as on the likelihood of a return on their labor commitment. Pyrrhus's generosity and fairness gained the admiration of his troops, whose allegiances followed on the potential for yields made good through the economic engine of war in the form of its spoils. Such risks demand a poetics of manhood centered upon the warrior ideal embodied in Pyrrhus himself, of the line of Achilles, progeny of Zeus. What Plutarch characterizes as vain hopes can be recast as calculated risks associated with economic prospection. And, if anything, Pyrrhus is a wandering speculator, one who seeks out ventures that can provide returns, fame, and spoils, ventures that match the military investment. In this game of chance, Tyche—Fortune—plays her role. Increasingly of late, she has been seen wearing the mural crown, a walled circle of battlements and towers that signals her protection of the city.[11] Does

---

9 See Sloterdijk (2013, 50–53).

10 Plutarch *Pyrrhus* 29.2.

11 On representations of Tyche in the guise of protectress of the city with the mural crown, see Broucke (1994).

Tyche, from her ancient shrine somewhere within a javelin throw of Pyrrhus's current position, continue to favor the king?[12] Tyche is fickle. Spoils come to both kings and poleis, as anyone who now wanders among the venerated exhibitions in the agora can see by torchlight.

Pragmatically, Pyrrhus must embrace opportunities when they present themselves; otherwise foreign mercenaries could easily find employment with rivals. The speed with which he ventures from one opportunity to the next is in inverse relation to his lifetime tenure. Such excesses of sustained authority, the polis seeks to curtail. In order to permanently delay would-be tyrants, Argos limits representative officials to six-month terms.[13] This rapid turnover in magistracies results in the continual reproduction of expertise where carefully defined tasks are distributed into various offices.[14]

The gods, and their veiled prompts, factor greatly in matters of democratic statecraft. Within Argos, others will always be present to offer a different interpretation, to keep in check major decisions of the polis, to respect what they hold to be messages from the gods. Wise kings are restrained by advisors and rhetoric, oracles and prophesy, gods and their emissaries to a major degree. Yet Pyrrhus finds himself in this present situation because he ignores one grim portent after another, just as man-killing Hector ignored the flights of birds in defending his country.[15] To his favor, Pyrrhus failed to interpret the severed heads of sacrificed cattle licking up their own gore. Within Argos, around the time of Pyrrhus's gory omen, a priestess of Apollo Lykeios, having been possessed of a vision, ran forth from the temple: she beheld the city full of corpses and slaughter and that the eagle "which visited the scene of combat presently vanished away."[16] This vision foreshadowed peril for readers of Plutarch, for Pyrrhus carried a surname, Aetós, "Eagle," as bequeathed to him by the Epirotes.[17] Possessed of executive powers, Pyrrhus may ultimately choose to fail in heeding the messages of the gods, against the sound judgment of his advisors.

---

12 Any suggestion that the shrine of Tyche was present in the early half of the third century BCE runs the risk of anachronism from a historical perspective. Here, again, it is worth emphasizing how this syncretic exercise is written from the perspective of Plutarch around 100 CE, and in his biography of Pyrrhus, *tyche* plays a significant role (see Titchener 2013). On the supposed antiquity of the Argive temple of Tyche as described by Pausanias, see Hutton (2005, 315).

13 New inscriptions confirm this; see Kritzas (2003/04, 58); also Robinson (2011b, 14–15); Aristotle *Politics* 1308a 15–24. Indeed, it is this slowness that would-be oligarchs seek to purge from the city.

14 These offices included the Council (*bola*), the *Damiogoi*, the Generals (*stratagoi*), the *Polemarchs*, the "Eighty" (*ogdoekonta*), and the "Six-Hundred" (*hexakosioi*). Only witnesses from the tribes and treaty negotiators were exempt from abbreviated tenures (see Kritzas 2003/04, 58).

15 Iliad 12.243.

16 Plutarch 31.3.

17 Plutarch 10.1.

And now the great king, with his contingent, is held in by check by walls and gullies, statues and shrines, by armed Argives and the relief forces of Antigonus and Areus, by darkness and confusion, near the centers of polis decision-making in the agora. Does Pyrrhus embrace these dark moments of hesitation to contemplate his precarious situation? Perhaps he should have waited. Too late; fate cannot be avoided. Palamedes's dice have been cast.[18]

Dawn. First light brings portents too bleak for Pyrrhus to ignore. The sight of the Aspis overflowing in armed enemies greatly disturbs the king. Behind new ramparts Argives[19] and their relief troops have mustered in strength during the night. Bearing esteem-inducing effects for the polis, these well-fit walls of polygonal masonry signal the power of what he confronts from within. Bearing a strange inconsistency between surface and joints, whereby roughened limestone faces are broken by seamless lines running at promiscuous angles between stones, every block is poised to its neighbor with utmost complementary precision. Each is unique. This carefully executed dressing reinforces civic pride for those who live behind shares walls, for those who live with shared laws. An enclosure within a larger enclosure, this definitive line incorporates Cyclopean walls,[20] more than a thousand years old, and carries the double dimension of community and protection. A lure for the feeling, they are as much about psychology as containment. Argive walls carry the practical and symbolic weight of group solidarity.

And closer still, another omen. Among the votive offerings in the agora, a wolf and a bull stand before Pyrrhus. An ill-fated sight that as foretold by an ancient oracle would precede his death. This memorial, in the sanctuary of Apollo Lykeios, serves to remind Plutarch's readers of Pyrrhus's mistake in failing to heed the omens as a king, whether the Molossian is himself aware of it or not. Succinctly, this monument portrays an event where a wolf attacked a bull outside of Argos at a time when Danaus sought refuge. Having interpreted the event as an omen correctly, Danaus paid his vows to Apollo Lykeios and won the kingdom of Argos by force. In Plutarch's version, Danaus was a king whose fortunes in taking the city followed on heeding the messages of the gods.[21]

---

18 Palamedes was the son of Nauplion in myth. He was also a sailor, warrior, and inventor of dice, which he dedicated to Tyche in Argos, or so the Argives claimed according to Pausanias (2.20.3).

19 Touchais et al. (2010), Fachard and Bessac, forthcoming.

20 See Touchais et al. (2010, 555–59).

21 Plutarch records a version where Danaus chooses the path of force over supplication. Pausanias, however, offers a version where Danaus, as contender to the throne, was permitted into the city by a vote of the Argives, against the will of their king Gelanor (2.19.3). Plutarch leaves the association between Pyrrhus and the bull to his readers (compare 6.2–5). The association of the wolf was fundamental to Apollo, protector of the city, and thus to Argos. Any reader familiar with

It is here, before the most venerated memorials of Argos; it is here, in the midst of open spaces created through the common act of draining low, marshy ground; here, in an area avoided by all other community structures up to that time; here, in a place far removed from the high ground associated with security and former forms of power, is where living kings do not belong. Here, in the marketplace they belong to founding myths. They belong to stories told about relics on display in the exhibition center of the polis. Kings belong to loci elsewhere, past, Spartan, or foreign. Indeed, who would fail to question the fates, that the return of democracy to Argos was affected by a king, Demetrius Poliorcetes, on the heels of the expulsion of Pleistarchus, brother to Cassander, not thirty years earlier?[22] The same Demetrius Poliorcetes, husband to Pyrrhus's sister, Deidamia, who he wedded here, in Argos. Indeed, many Argives now believe the nocturnal expulsion of Pleistarchus to have been effected by none other than Apollo, protector of the city. This event is inscribed in stone and displayed in the sanctuary to Apollo Pythaeus, below the Aspis, where the demos and others now gather in defense of the city. For a generation, on the seventeenth day of every month, Argives have dutifully commemorated the return to democratic autonomy in a festival.[23] Living kings do not belong in Argos. And yet, three kings, two of them mobile speculators, now vie with each other at Argos: one in the agora; one directing his troops, Cretan and Spartan, in an assault upon Pyrrhus; one outside the city walls. Witness the return of the excluded.

Desperate hopes turn to abandoned ones; amid the turbulence Pyrrhus sounds the retreat. He sends a message-bearer into a chaotic river of armored bodies, with instructions to his son Helenus: "Tear down the walls. Succor those who flow forth through the breach."[24] But this command fails to reach the young prince. Instead, across the waters of flesh and steel, a garbled message affords decisive action—Helenus leads the rest of the elephants and the best of the troops into Argos.

The importance of effective communication was, as Plutarch shows, decisive in conveying the infant Pyrrhus to the Macedonian town of Megara. For, when they were just shy of their hoped-for destination, a swollen river cut off the babe and his guardians from their escape. Drowned out amid turbulence, amid

---

Argive coinage of the time would have been privy to the relationship of Argos, Apollo, and the wolf, encapsulated in the Wolf A coinage of the polis (see Gershenson 1991, 8; Kraay 1976, 96).

22 Plutarch, *Demetrius* 25.1. I leave to one side debates concerning the state of Argive democracy in the early half of the third century CE. Whatever the historical situation, the polis was itself comprised of buildings, institutions of many times, which persist in upholding the community.

23 Vollgraff (1956, 79–84), Piérart and Touchais (1996, 64); also see Platt (2011, 146).

24 Plutarch Pyrrhus 33.1–2.

noise, shouts of supplication to those on the other side were of no avail. To transmit otherwise-inaudible words, they were inscribed on a piece of bark tethered to a projectile. Across the torrent, specific words—of needs and fortunes—were extended through their material presence and the infant Pyrrhus was saved from his pursuers. Now the enveloping ring in Plutarch's biographical narrative comes round. Before a river of a different kind, Pyrrhus trusts in spoken words over the inscribed object. Shouts fail to cross the commotion and turbulence in the street. Communication breaks down.

Here, again, we meet another key facet of Argive "waiting power;" otherwise fleeing words must be captured if they are to be effectively projected into the political domain and beyond.[25] To be a good citizen one must engage with those aspects of polis culture inscribed for posterity. In Argos, spoken words were given a prolonged presence as inscribed bronze plaques. Affixed by iron nails to the temple of Apollo Lykeios, these plaques existed within a milieu, both public and sacred, within the agora that Pyrrhus now risks so much in vacating.[26] The proliferation of these plaques over the decades has led to a situation where they cover large portions of their temple installation. Plaques, many sized to fit within the space of two open hands,[27] cover architraves, triglyphs, metopes, and even portions of the drip edge in the cornice. While nearly every inscribed enactment of the Argive state in the previous two centuries would usually begin or end *aliaiai edoxe*, "decreed by the assembly," a stamp that would become synonymous with the people—*edoxe toi damoi*[28]—the presence of these inscriptions outside of the realm of legible engagement places literate observers in the position of spectator rather than participant.[29] This observation does not foreclose on the legibility of displays at lower levels of the

---

25 Sloterdijk (2005b, 949). Incidentally, the phonetic alphabet makes a difference for a democratic society, as McLuhan argues, in contrast to pictographic or hieroglyphic writing which, with hundreds of signs, require specialists to master. The alphabet, McLuhan presses, can be learned in a short amount of time, and thus by many more people (1994[1964], 87). One, however, should be careful with such a contrast. Though there were more hieroglyphs to be mastered, these signs were also more innate to the Egyptian world, not unlike emoticons today. Moreover, the use of ancient scripts was circumscribed by priests, institutions, modes of living, power dynamics, etc., all of which make a difference.

26 According to Thucydides (5.47.11) the temple of Apollo was used as a repository for official archives of Argos. Here, I am taking some liberties with respect to the specificity of the blocks for the sake of the narrative. In lieu of the actual temple location, which has yet to be excavated, Courtils (1981, 610) rightly leaves open the question as to what kind of building these blocks may have belonged: "*portique ou temple.*"

27 Architectural blocks found in the French excavations of the agora contain impressions, nails, and nail holes, which suggest that the size of the plaques ranged between a height of 5 to 10 centimeters and width between 10 and 25 centimeters (see Courtils 1981; Roux 1953).

28 Robinson (2011b, 10).

29 See Courtils (1981, 609).

temple (to the extent that the possibility for perusal can occur on a passing whim). Still, by shifting some plaques towards the eaves they are moved out of a setting that affords opportunity-to-be-read-in-passing and into a state-of-being-present-under-the-watchful-eyes-of-the-ever-vigilant-Apollo, in the city's most venerated sanctuary.[30] It is also of consequence that a surfeit of bronzen messages extending up and over the whole of the entablature would seem to overwhelm observers, literate or otherwise.[31]

A successful democratic polis contains old messages that are coextensive with citizens now, and which will be there for those yet to come. The importance with which Argos regarded the mnemonic reservoirs of the polis is manifest in its use of stone chests (*petroi*) covered by heavy slabs (weighing as much as 1.5 tons) for the safe deposits of inscribed bronze straps. Left in a storehouse of a treasury under the protection of the goddess of organization, Pallas (Athena), these *chalkeons telamonas* (the latter term carries connotations of bearing or supporting) hold records of land leases, money loans, and deposits. Pierced and held together by bronze wires in some cases, many are organized in groups within chests that are themselves numbered.[32] Acts necessary for maintaining the polis, whose revenues were drawn principally from public and sacred lands,[33] require archival repositories where financial transactions may be known. Notwithstanding their value as surrogates for what has been loaned, such archival consistency is not so much an issue of transparency now,[34] but for transparency not-now, should financial records become an issue at a later date. So effective are these bronze straps within their persistent capsules that they will stubbornly bear their one-hundred-year-old messages for another 2272 years before strangers-yet-to-come will sort through them. For

---

30 Whether or not the memory practices of display involved shifting old decrees up so that new ones could be displayed below, readers of McLuhan will note the importance here of medium over content with respect to bronze plaques nailed to the entablature. On the importance of the sanctuary, see Thucydides 5.47.11; Pausanias 2.19.3.

31 Whether an engagement with the text is direct or vicarious (i.e. read to illiterate citizens by literate ones) is no more and no less important than this relationship with the exhibition space. Still, the implications of such an installation for building citizens are tremendous. Unlike stone reading walls in Athens, Argos seems to ascribe more to a beholder than to a participant citizen with respect to media; while matters of content are left to interested historians, confidence in the polis may be built among passing citizens through the raw presence of these media.

32 Kritzas (2006).

33 Kritzas (1992; 2003/04).

34 Here I am establishing a contrast to Kritzas's argument that the archive was meant to provide absolute transparency (Kritzas 2003/04, 55); a point echoed by Robinson (2011b, 15). If transparency were indeed the objective, the straps would be better displayed in public areas, such as the agora, rather than placed in stone, bronze, or terracotta containers and sealed under massive stone lids.

now, they are safely under the protection of Pallas, who safeguards the city in the midst of this strife, even against claimants to the line of Aeacidae.

Failing to receive clear orders, Helenus charges down the street. A deluge of soldiers, elephants, and horses meets with a surge of retreating forces. Maelstrom. Quite unlike the normal kinetics of a polis which must provide for repetitive movements and means of association between open spaces, rooms for dwelling, places for labor, areas for commerce, and tracts for deriving food, water, clothing, shade, and well-being. Routines are interrupted and normal conditions are inverted. Linear spaces for facilitating movement now constrain the great king and his forces. In tight spaces, war elephants, decisive biotechnologies in former battles, now become liabilities.[35] Seasoned cavalry, quick to turn the tides of battle in the field, are immobilized in the narrows. Pyrrhus urges everyone to turn back, but a fallen colossus blocks the gate. And Nicon, a war elephant overcome with despair for his rider, frantically searches. He finds the body, lifts it upon his tusks and, distraught, turns upon the throng, trampling all in his way.[36] Swordsmanship is of no avail in the mob. Ready steel is pressed through friends under the weight of armored bodies in confined spaces.

About the famed Molossian king heaves this stormy sea. Authority manifest through royal guidance has no outlet. Thus Pyrrhus relieves himself of his coronal, marker of the kingly self, broadcaster of his regal presence. Possessed of the glory of Achilles by blood in claims and by valor in deeds, he takes recourse to action. For a third time in his life Pyrrhus plunges into the tempest.[37] For the last, the king faces his enemy with the charisma and courage that had gained him, on so many occasions, the admiration of his troops:

πολλὰς μὲν ἀύπνους νύκτας ἴαυεν,
ἤματα δ᾽ αἱματόεντα διέπρησσεν πολεμίζων[38]
Many a night did he spend without sleeping,
Many a blood-stained day did he pass amid combats unceasing.[39]

35 Aristotle (Politics 1330b, 21–32) suggested that in times of peace the street plan should work according to Hippodamus, who introduced the regular grid; yet in times of war, the older, more haphazard, form is more appropriate for security.

36 Plutarch 33.4–5.

37 Plutarch arranges these three watershed moments into a biographical ring: first, being carried away as an infant to the north; second, at sea off Italy; and now here in Argos. On ring composition, see Douglas (2007).

38 Plutarch De Alex. 1.1; adapted from Homer, Il. ix. 325–326; Plutarch's life of Pyrrhus, a life of contrasts between epic deeds and tragic hopes, echoes that of Alexander (Mossman 1992), and both find a common model in Achilles.

39 Frank Cole Babbitt's translation of Plutarch. Moralia. Cambridge, MA. Harvard University Press. London. William Heinemann Ltd. 1936.

The first act in a shared murder comes at the end of a spear. Through the breastplate a spike nicks Pyrrhus, struck by an Argive of no illustrious birth. He pivots to stand off against this representative of the armed demos—Plutarch here maintains the anonymity of his assailant in all things but citizenship, for among the shared responsibilities of citizens was to bear arms. For this, good citizens of a polis must be disarmed with respect to each other. Security rests upon an inclusive community, undivided among men of proper birth.[40] In Argos, membership is reinforced by an imagined commonality: the three old Dorian tribes (phylai)—the Dymanes, Hylleis, and Pamphylai—joined later by a fourth—the Hyrnathioi.[41] These phylai served as commons for groups of phratries, twelve to each phylai, and to these were applied names related to the heroes of local traditions.[42] The memory of these tribal forms is both a source of legitimacy and an acknowledgment of the common effort to come together.

The second act comes from above. In the city of Telesilla, it begins with an old woman with a banal roof tile, pried from the top of an Argive structure, perhaps from a dwelling, who stuns the great king. A murderer of countless sons, many of them great warriors, Pyrrhus is forestalled by a mother before he can take yet another son: hers. The vertebrae exposed at the base of his neck are crushed. Pyrrhus slumps down and falls from his horse. Within a city psychologically disposed to women as protectors, the actions of a poor, old mother would come to rank among the great deeds executed by women in protection of their city. Perhaps more than rituals of switching clothes,[43] this would serve to draw Argives even closer in solidarity. This act would come to be reinforced as divine intervention. Future Argives will later maintain that the old woman was none other than Demeter herself.[44]

The third act is a poorly executed death. By the tomb of Licymnius,[45] illegitimate son of Electryon, son of Perseus; by the tomb of a man killed by the son of his nephew Herakles, the great king lies unrecognized by most, save Zopyrus.[46] For the king, who as an infant was reared by the Illyrian ruler

40 Here, I am placing to one side the radical inequalities that exist between citizens and others, foreign, female, worker, slave.
41 For epigraphic evidence, see: Kritzas (1979).
42 Piérart and Touchais (1996, 42, 62).
43 Plutarch, in the Moralia (245.E), describes the "Festival of Impudence," which can be seen as festival of communal solidarity through the exchange of garments, whereby the chiton is worn by women and the peplos by men.
44 Pausanias 1.13.8; on the importance of Demeter in the protection and renewal of the civic body, see De Polignac (1995, 72–73).
45 Pausanias 2.22.8.
46 Zo-pyron is a spark or ember used to kindle a fire; this name underlines the implicit connection between the flame and the polis.

Glaucias and his wife, death comes at the edge of an Illyrian blade. With trembling hands, the soldier serving under Antigonus severs the king's head, along the mouth, with difficulty. Alcyoneus, son of Antigonus, acquires the head, according to Plutarch, and rides forth with the prize to where his father waits.[47]

It is perhaps late in the summer or early in the autumn.[48] A funeral pyre was set up in the middle of the marketplace.[49] Here, the community converges in a ritual of shared cleansing. Death is purged through fire—a cathartic contribution to Argive psycho-political solidarity. Here, the body of a tragic king of Achillean aspiration would persist still in revealing divine virtue. The great toe of his right foot, possessed of healing powers in life, is untouched by the flames in death.[50] The fire-cleansed bones of Pyrrhus would be interred in a sanctuary of Demeter, which, as directed by an oracle, is built on the very spot where he died.[51] A monument of white granite, carved with elephants and instruments of war, would be erected on the spot of the pyre, in the middle of the marketplace.

Details surrounding Pyrrhus's demise will be confused and, among the Argives, the second act will later gain primacy in the story of his death, at the hands of Demeter.[52] Argives would hold on to the sense of divine justice, thus repeating the feat of replacing the deeds of Macedonian kings with the exploits of gods and goddesses.[53] Inwardly, such justificatory stories further strengthen the Argive community's sense of integrity. Outwardly, the polis appears to be upheld through divine sanction, protection, and sustenance. The ongoing maintenance of the polis would memorialize Pyrrhus's failed hopes as another common trial of the Argives. Yet another shared struggle would now be translated into the monumental and displayed in its archive of shared achievements; in this, exhibition culture has much to offer.

Buried within the walls, the bones of Pyrrhus would be interred on the spot where he fell, in the sanctuary of Demeter. His shield would be placed above the doorway of this sanctuary. The monument of white marble, erected where

---

47 Even here, in Alcyoneas's treatment of Pyrrhus's severed head and Antigonus's rebuke and revelation at his own family fortunes, opportunity is taken by Plutarch to reflect on kingly fate and virtue.

48 Pyrrhus's proposition to winter in Sparta (Plutarch 30.1) suggests that they attacked the city in late summer or early fall.

49 Pausanias 2.21.4.

50 Plutarch Pyrrhus 3.5; yet another divine association, Pyrrhus's miraculous big toe was as much in service to Argive exhibition as it was to the figure of Pyrrhus, who used it to heal his subjects.

51 Pausanias 1.13.8.

52 Pausanias 1.13.8–9.

53 Also see Platt (2011, 146), Vollgraff (1908, 240; 1956, 81–82).

the body of Pyrrhus was burned, would lie adjacent to a mound containing the severed head of the Gorgon, Medusa. These objects add to the archival stores of community achievement, along with the shield of Diomedes and the Palladian from Troy stolen by none other than Odysseus and Diomedes, or so the Argives claimed.[54] Such objects are indifferent to the myths of shared association and common origin that will be iteratively connected to them.

Pyrrhus becomes a victim in the repetition of divinely executed deaths in service to the state.[55] A sacrificial victim now subsumed to that familiar schema where common membership is founded, where community solidarity is renewed, through the shared murder.[56] An enemy at first, turned scapegoat at last. And around the scapegoat Argos converges. Through a collective expulsion with cathartic results its sense of community is maintained. Interred in Argive ground, the dead king, speared by an anonymous citizen, stunned by a caring mother, pulled back into the circle of his own remarkable life, is now transformed, drawn into the Argive self-narration of common struggle and self-maintenance of solidarity in communal existence outwardly manifest in shared, beautifully wrought walls and monuments to past achievements.

54 Against rival claims by Athens, Sparta, and Rome, among others (see Nilsson 1992, 435–36).

55 After Achilles and his son Pyrrhus, as Pausanias points out (1.13.9), Pyrrhus is himself the third victim of divine-execution in the line of Aeacidae, to which he laid claim. Plutarch's richly controlled composition is saturated by such subtleties, which his readership would have recognized. Such propositions need not be explicitly unpacked since they are well known to one's audience who look to these biographies for moral guidance and self-crafting; see Larmour (2004).

56 René Girard's thesis of the scapegoat (1986) resonates with Pyrrhus's death. Even if Pyrrhus is not the object of shared violence in Girard's sense, the outcome is in service to community (also see Sloterdijk 2014, 176–79).

Bibliography

Broucke, P.B. 1994. Tyche and the fortune of cities in the Greek and Roman world. *Yale University Art Gallery Bulletin*, 34–49. https://www.jstor.org/stable/i40022585.

Courtils, J. 1981. Note de topographie argienne. *Bulletin de correspondance hellénique* 105 (2), 607–10.

De Polignac, F. 1995. *Cults, territory, and the origins of the Greek city-state* (trans. J. Lloyd). Chicago, IL: Chicago University Press.

Douglas, M. 2007. *Thinking in circles: An essay on ring composition*. New Haven, NJ: Yale University Press.

Edwards, J. 2011. Plutarch and the death of Pyrrhus: Disambiguating the conflicting accounts. *Scholia: Studies in Classical Antiquity* 20, 112–31.

Fachard, S., and J.C. Bessac. Forthcoming. *L'Aspis aux époques Classique et Hellénistique, 1. Les constructions A. Les remparts de l'Aspis.* des fouilles de l'Aspis.

Gershenson, D.E. 1991. *Apollo the wolf god.* Journal of Indo-European Monograph Series, No 8. Mclean, VA: Institute for the Study of Man.

Girard, R. 1986. *The scapegoat* (trans. Y. Freccero). Baltimore, MD: Johns Hopkins University Press.

Hutton, W. 2005. *Describing Greece: Landscape and literature in the Periegesis of Pausanias.* Cambridge: Cambridge University Press.

Kraay, C.M. 1976. *Archaic and Classical Greek coins.* Berkeley, CA: University of California Press.

Kritzas, C. 1979. Katálogos pesónton apó to Árgos», STILI, Tómos eis mnímin N. Kontoléontos, 497–510.

Kritzas, C. 1992. Aspects de la vie politique et economique d'Argos au Ve siècle avant J.-C. In M. Piérart (ed.), *Polydipsion Argos: Argos de la fin des palais mycéniens à la constitution de l'état classique.* Athens: École française d'Athènes. 231–40.

Kritzas, C. 2003/04. Literacy and society: The case of Argos. *Kodai* 13/14, 53–60.

Kritzas, C. 2006. Nouvelles Inscriptions D'Argos: Les Archives des Compes du Trésor Sacré. *Comptes rendus des séances de l'Académie des Inscriptions et Belles-Lettres* 150(1), 397–434.

Larmour, D.H. 1992. Making parallels: *Synkrisis* and Plutarch's "Themistocles and Camillus." *ANRW* 2(6), 4154–200.

Larmour, D.H.J. 2004. Statesman and self in the parallel lives. In L. de Blois (ed.), *The statesman in Plutarch's works.* Leiden: Brill. 43–52.

Leppin, H. 1999. Argos: Eine griechische Demokratie des fünften Jahrhunderts v. Chr. *Ktema* 24, 297–312.

McLuhan, M. 1994[1964]. *Understanding media: The extensions of man.* Cambridge, MA: MIT Press.

Mossman, J.M. 1992. Plutarch, Pyrrhus, and Alexander. In P.A. Stadter (ed.), *Plutarch and the historical tradition.* London: Routledge. 98–116.

Nilsson, M.P. 1992. *Geschichte der griechischen Religion Bd. 1.* Munchen: C.H. Beck.

Piérart, M. 1982. Deux notes sur l'itinéraire argien de Pausanias. *Bulletin de Correspondance Hellénique* 106(1), 139–52.

Piérart, M. 1993. De l'endroit ou l'on abritait quelques statues d'Argos et de la vraie nature du feu de Phoroneus: Une note critique. *Bulletin de correspondance hellénique* 117 (2), 609–13.

Piérart, M. 2000. Argos: Un autre democratie. In P. Flensted-Jensen, T.H. Nielsen, and L. Rubinstein (eds.), *Polis & politics: Studies in ancient Greek history.* Copenhagen: Museum Tusculanum Press. 297–314.

Piérart, M., and G. Touchais. 1996. *Argos: Une ville grecque de 6000 ans.* Paris: CNRS Editions.

Platt, V.J. 2011. *Facing the gods: Epiphany and representation in Graeco-Roman art, literature and religion.* Cambridge: Cambridge University Press.

Robinson, E.W. 2011b. *Democracy beyond Athens: Popular government in the Greek Classical age.* Cambridge: Cambridge University Press.

Roux, G. 1953. Deux études d'archéologie péloponnésienne. *Bulletin de correspondance hellénique* 77, 116–38.

Sloterdijk, P. 2005b. Atmospheric politics. In B. Latour and P. Weibel (eds.), *Making things public: Atmospheres of democracy.* Cambridge, MA: MIT Press. 944–51.

Sloterdijk, P. 2013. *In the world interior of capital: For a philosophical theory of globalization.* Cambridge: Polity Press.

Sloterdijk, P. 2014. *Globes: Spheres II.* South Pasadena, CA: Semiotext(e).

Stadter, P.A. 1965. *Plutarch's historical methods: An analysis of the mulierum virtutes.* Cambridge, MA: Harvard University Press.

Titchener, F.B. 2013. Fate and fortune. In M. Beck (ed.), *A companion to Plutarch.* Oxford: Wiley-Blackwell. 479–87.

Tomlinson, R.A. 1972. *Argos and the Argolis: From the end of the Bronze Age to the Roman occupation.* London: Routledge.

Touchais, G., A. Philippa-Touchais, S. Fachard, K. Nikolopoulou, and A. Gardeisen. 2010. L'Aspis. *Bulletin de correspondance hellénique* 134(2), 551–66.

Vollgraff, W. 1907. Fouilles d'Argos. *Bulletin de Correspondance Hellénique* 31(1), 139–84.

Vollgraff, W. 1908. Praxitèle le jeune. *Bulletin de Correspondance Hellénique* 32(1), 236–58.

Vollgraff, W. 1956. *Le sanctuaire d'Apollon Pythéen à Argos.* Paris: J. Vrin.

13

MODERN SPECTACLE THROUGH AN ANCIENT THEATRE

A national assembly, a theatre, sad relics and a past idealized, modern ambivalence, city planning and a new Argos, common container and common language, Babel

I sit in the Hellenistic theatre of Argos viewing an empty orchestra. I have been here, reclining against a worn and fractured limestone seat, for the last half hour. As I look down from near the top, I do not imagine the dramatic and musical spectacles of the Nemean games, or those that honored Hera. Even further from my thoughts are misplaced images of Classical Theatre. No, I have been contemplating a different performance, that of the Fourth National Assembly (*Ethnosynélefsi D*). It was here, 183 years ago, that this celebrated moment in the formation of the nascent nation-state of modern Greece was staged.

Over the assembly presided the Church. With rite and religion, the proceedings were blessed in the Holy Church of the Assumption, only a five-minute walk from this theatre. In the names of the Holy Trinity and *patrida* (the fatherland) delegates from the Peloponnese, Northern and Central Greece, the

The theatre at Argos.

islands, and Evia swore to ignore regional self-interests and submit to the larger
loyalty of the nation. From the church a procession followed on the road to the
theatre where an initial assembly took place on July 11, 1829. Twenty more
sessions were convened over the next four weeks.[1]

Into this common space they gathered. Onto rows, along tiers, the 236 regional
delegates joined the newly appointed *Kyvernetes* or Governor, Ioannis Kapodistrias,
and other proxies; the crowd was oriented in radiating arcs around what had
become of the circular orchestra. Here, the constitution was further shaped and the
shape of government was approved. Agendas and speeches, shouts and disagreements, the collective murmur and face-to-face discussions in the margins, all were
choreographed within this reclaimed space of concentrations where the seated spec-
tators surrounded an open area for the standing spokesperson.[2]

It is no strange circumstance of history that such an event should occur here. No
purpose-built assembly for struggling Greece as still existed. National assemblies,
formed to make decisions on the form of a government still to be formed, borrowed
their venues from a variety of existing architectures and locales. After a cottage in
(Nea) Epidaurus, a garden in Astros, and a lemon grove in Trizina, this was the first

1 The ensuing sessions ran from July 12 to August 5. On the Fourth National Assembly, see Hellas
(1829); also Koumadorakes (2007).
2 For a comparison of the space of the agora with that of the theatre, see Sennett (1994, 60).

ancient setting to accommodate a national assembly.[3] A ruined theatre carved directly out of the limestone of the Larissa afforded a peculiar locus for this patriotic throng. Here spoken words were carried by the vertical rows of the rock-hewn cavea. The concentric form of the theatre divided the crowd: active voice(s) standing and passive listeners seated within a raw-rock auricle.[4] At the center of this circular crucible of assembly was the stage, the speaker, the spectacle, semi-enveloped by the crowd, beneficiaries of the affordances of ancient design manifest as an acoustically amplified assembly.

The theatre is a place for seeing. Such is the meaning of the Ancient Greek word *theatron*, a locus for viewing. Within the circle, the speaker is exposed: all gestures, expressions, and movements are visible before the congregation. Ultimately, members of the National Assembly bore mutual witness to their own spectacle and, from the circle and tiers below where I sit, they debated Northern European ideals and embraced plans for Northern European institutions. Northern Europeans, in turn, were confident in an image of Greece as the heir to a greatness that spawns all subsequent forms of greatness. To achieve such greatness those delegates of an aspiring state had to simultaneously look both inward and outward.

To the north and west, the incredible power of books, periodicals, and newspapers was witnessed in the extraordinary spread of a revolutionary consciousness.[5] At the turn of the nineteenth century, sentiments of Greek emancipation found accelerated expression for Northern European travelers and poets among whom descriptions of abject and humiliating conditions of local populations were repeatedly framed as an artifact of Ottoman despotism. Yet, the terrible suffering of the Greek people was only part of this story, for the lot of contemporary Greeks was rarely illuminated outside the long shadows of Classical antiquity. The Greeks, for the Englishman Edward Dodwell,

> are replete with intellect and talent, and possess many excellent qualities which might elevate them nearer to a level with their glorious progenitors, if they were liberated from the yoke of bondage, which is such an inveterate foe to all mental energy and all moral worth, which paralyses the more noble sentiments, and freezes 'the genial current of the soul.'[6]

3 See Demakopoúlou (1980, 90–91).
4 Remains suggest that dykes were constructed on either side of the central bedrock section to support additional tiers framed by ashlar walls (see Moretti and Diez 1993).
5 The message of Northern European Enlightenment had fallen neither on unfamiliar ears nor been free of the contribution of Greek thinkers. A vibrant culture of Greek intellectuals in Venice, Vienna, and Paris, including Evgenios Voulgaris (1716–1806), Adamantios Korais (1748–1833) and Rhigas Velentinlis, or Feraios (1757–98), cultivated principles of "freedom of thought, rationalism, faith in modern science," and the natural "rights of man" (see Kitromilides 2013).
6 1819 II, 275; a quote from Thomas Gray's *Elegy Written in a Country Churchyard*.

If the hearts of Northern Europeans were pregnant with the celestial fire of emancipation that no rod of empire could sway then it had more to do with a collective consciousness cultivated among the intelligentsia.[7] This mindset involved "the idealization of ancient Greece as the birthplace of a uniquely European spirit."[8] Through this distorted optic, contemporary deeds were elevated to exemplary, to epic levels, and no Philhellene could stand by, in the words of Chateaubriand, *témoin passif d'une lutte héroique* (passive witness to a heroic struggle).[9]

For those delegates who gathered within this theatre, the self-liberation of *patrida* from within was manifest as the liberation of the hallowed ground of European origins from without. That the dreamlands, colored by Athenian ideals and Arcadian images, which Northern Europeans had experienced through reading books in libraries, salons, and studies, was imagined to be right under the feet of the Greek people was not lost upon those who chose what had become of an ancient theatre as the locus for the National Assembly. This message, that of an idealized Hellas whose revival was entangled with the plight of its contemporary inheritors and the imperative of their freedom, was so well crafted that all other European nations would come to see modern Greece through the lens of that ideal, but not always to their satisfaction.[10]

The fact that the remnants of Greek antiquity were as often met with feelings of melancholy and disappointment is captured by Byron's oft-repeated line "sad relic of departed worth" (a line that is followed by an expressed hope of emancipation).[11] So perplexed was Dodwell by the "entire disappearance" of the "ancient edifices, with which Argos was copiously furnished and splendidly adorned," that he, through the contrived distance of the generic traveler, was inclined to ask: "where are the thirty temples, the costly sepulchers, the gymnasium, the stadium, and the numerous monuments and statues that Pausanias has described?"[12] Such attitudes of loss, turned to mourning what Greece had become, proved to

---

7 An evocation of Gray's *Elegy*.

8 Morris 2000, 37; also 1994, 11–12. What Morris refers to as *Hellenism* should be defined as *Western Hellenism*, which is distinct from its other self-articulated forms among Modern Greeks—*Dynastic Hellenism* and *Eastern Hellenism* (see Constantinidis 2001, 61–80; also Hamilakis 2008, 2009; on the ambiguities of *Western Hellenism*, see Porter 2009).

9 1827, 3.

10 See Hanink (2017, 104–47).

11 "Who shall lead thy scatter'd children forth, And long accustom'd bondage uncreate?" From *Childe Harold's Pilgrimage*, 1812.

12 1819 II, 216.

be tenacious. Even Oscar Wilde later looked upon this very theatre with disappointment.[13] It is a threadbare message.[14]

When Nietzsche declared that he wanted "to sit in the theatre not as an ancient but as a modern" the philologist-philosopher affirmed the conscious freedom to make that choice.[15] Comprehending the success with which modern culture, specifically within the context of philology, had imposed its own unhistorical values on what had become of the past, he recognized Greek antiquity to be fashioned in the moderns' own image, unbeknownst to the moderns.[16] From the theatre seat of the modern, Nietzsche could look upon the spectacle of antiquity's fragments with wonder, foregrounding questions of method with the critical recognition that the production of Greek antiquity was always about the production of the modern world.[17]

In the midst of removing their Ottoman masters, the entrepreneurial ideologues of the fledgling Greek state saw the outward need to cultivate a Greek antiquity so cherished by their European patrons.[18] Yet, unlike their patrons, as Michael Herzfeld has stated, "the Greeks were not seeking a return to a Classical *past*; they were instead seeking inclusion in the European *present*."[19] Any attempt at inclusion was motivated by concerns as much pragmatic as ideological; for any nation-state to form it must strive to create a group bound by common identity. Requisite therefore was the delicate work of translation by

---

13 Nettles and poppy mar each rock-hewn seat:

> No poet crowned with olive deathlessly
> Chants his glad song, nor clamorous Tragedy
> Startles the air; green corn is waving sweet
> Where once the Chorus danced to measures fleet;
> Far to the East a purple stretch of sea,
> The cliffs of gold that prisoned Danae;
> And desecrated Argos at my feet.

From *The Theatre of Argos*, 1877.

14 See Calotychos (2003), Leontis (1995); also Leontis (1997).

15 Nietzsche et al. (1993, 34–35), Porter (2014, 2000, 167–224).

16 Also see Porter (2009, 12–13).

17 Ibid., 42–45.

18 The opportunism of revolutionary Greece was enveloped by the semantics of obligation, as Johanna Hanink has shown (2017). The fledgling government was indebted to their liberators from externalized masters as those liberators were indebted to Ancient Greece. With the Fourth National Assembly, this debt was manifest in the legislation of antiquities. While the delegates voted to prohibit the export of antiquities from Greek soil, they left open the possibility of relinquishing select fragments to foreign academic institutions, allowing the French Expedition some leeway with their excavations at Olympia (Voudouri 2010, 548).

19 Herzfeld (1987, 50); also see Hamilakis (2007); Kotsakis (1991, 2003b); Morris (1994, 23).

politicians caught in a double bind between diverse views from within and with-out, which demanded some degree of betrayal in both directions. As the invol-untary inheritors of an idealized past, their compromises were to be repeatedly judged in brilliant light of an imagined history that never transpired.[20]

I sit within a theatre returned to a state that, for both the ancients and moderns, did not exist in the way that it does.[21] One can only speculate as to what the theatre had become during the summer of 1829. A generation before the National Assembly, the excavated portion contained sixty-seven rows: nine-teen in the upper tier, sixteen in the middle, and thirty-two in the lower.[22] Another sixteen rows were buried. Partially covered by the ruins of the Roman scene house, the circular orchestra was concealed under soil, rubble, and the detritus of centuries. No contrived veneer, however pageant or austere, could hide the fact that the spectacle of the National Assembly was given spatial form within a theatre partially buried.[23] Though here an ancient object contained, amplified, sorted, and contributed to the creation of the state, this dream of Greece was built upon ruins reclaimed from the soil, which could not live up to the dream.[24]

A definitive break with the past is by no means established by revolution and the formation of Hellas as a nation.[25] Even though Ancient Argos was attacked by Pyrrhus of Epirus, even though it transformed under the Romans and over the course of subsequent eras, Hellenistic infrastructure continued to assert itself in 1829, pressing into the future, far beyond the desires of ancient design-ers, affecting others irrespective of the aspirations of its ancient architects. Walls, terraces, ruins mixed and folded into the fabric of the city testified to the fact that the wreckage of the Argive past continued to pile up among the

20 The pathos-enthralled "we" of Northern Europeans rapt with fervor for the common goal of expelling Ottoman overlords was, as Herzfeld argues, really a crypto-colonialism, where the state remained inadequate vis-à-vis Northern Europe; Herzfeld (2002); also Plantzos (2014, 153–54). On nationalism and colonialism, see Chatterjee (1993).

21 In the wake of the extractive endeavors of the *École française d'Athènes* (Vollgraff 1951), which displaced the Roman edifices, ceramics, accumulation, roots, and plants that had laid claim to this space in the shadows of late antiquity, the ancient theatre lies exposed and persists as eighty-three limestone rows.

22 Leake described the state of the theatre in 1806 (1830 II, 396). By Clark's count there were two more seats in the lower division and one less in the upper (1858, 91–92).

23 It is an odd artifact of history that within the rock-carved theatre built within a city losing its democracy a new democracy would be born so close to where the ancient assembly lay buried. Naively given, latent, unbeknownst to anyone at that time, such a future past was yet to be revealed (Ginouvès 1972; McDonald 1943, 80).

24 On the aesthetics of landscape and ancient ruins in the context of nation-building, see Athanas-sopoulos (2002); also Lambropoulos (1984).

25 For more on this non-modern understanding of time, see Latour (1993), Olsen et al. (2012), Witmore (2006).

living in latent, naively given ways. Yet, repeatedly, the banal fashion in which this polychronic agglomeration was operative in the lives of the living would be ignored. Over the course of the 1820s, Argos had been sacked three times, yet ramparts Ancient, Byzantine, Frankish, Venetian, Ottoman, once again offered their propensities as encompassing shells of security for residents to take refuge.[26] This latent past is not only a matter of material, but also of form. Throughout Argos, Classical, Hellenistic, and Roman roads and walls buried under meters of accumulation, nonetheless persist in form at the surface through the orientation of streets, now largely clothed in concrete.[27] Tiers over here and a stage over there, something of the Greek theatre is found in every city worthy of the name, including the Parliament of the Hellenes in Athens.

Ancient areas of assembly, infrastructural forms, and fortifications like the Larissa were hardly sufficient to meet the spatial demands of the fledgling state. Under Kapodistrias, an European vision of urban form underwrote the radical redesign of Greek cities.[28] Iterations of a plan drawn up by the German engineer Rudolph de Borroczün, under the influence of the Parisian-trained urban planner Stamatis Voulgaris, pictured a New Argos.[29] Encircled with a wide moat fringed by a grand esplanade, a sphere of protection was envisioned as encompassing the whole city. A broad tree-lined boulevard led from the causewayed Nafplion Gate to an expansive promenade bordering the Kapodistrias Barracks and the central *plateia* (square). While a regular grid of blocks replaced the irregular layout of the southeastern neighborhoods devastated by the army of Ibrahim Pasha (1825), large European-style gardens, public squares, and widened avenues were added to the urban organizational form. Argos was to be laid open, outfitted with administrative buildings, courts, hospitals, and schools, exhibited for the pedestrian. The plan foregrounded visibility for both observation and security, fortified against assailants from abroad and at home, for the "strategic embellishments" of wide thoroughfares provided the shortest route between the barracks and gates or neighborhoods.[30] It is more than incidental that the shaded promenade met with a primary boulevard at one end of a widened version of the street now known as Theatrou, which terminates below this theatre. Here, the exhibition of ancient relics would separate them out as isolated components that testify to the symbolic weight of Ancient Greece and showcase Argos as a city unlike others.

26 Finlay (1877, 289–91), Olsen et al. (2012, 144).
27 Marchetti (2000, 2013).
28 See Hastaoglou-Martinidis (1995), Hastaoglou-Martinidis et al. (1993).
29 Dorovinis (1980, 520); on Stamatis Voulgaris, see Segment 15.
30 Such design anticipates Haussmann's interventions in Paris; see Benjamin (1999, 12).

New Argos, Borroczün 1831 (redrawn by Caleb Lightfoot).

This modern format for Ancient Argos, later proposed as the capital of Greece,[31] never left the planning table and remained in the paper phases. The new sense of space manifest by a Hellenic ethnos required an even greater escalation

31 See Zenkini (1996).

than Argos or any of the other planned cities could provide. When the Fourth National Assembly adopted a resolution to purchase ships and establish a national fleet, they highlighted the importance of extending a circle of protection around all Greek-speaking peoples.[32] Before a sense of territory encompassing a house for all Hellenes could be developed, a wider definition of the common container had to be articulated with plainly delimited borders, both maritime and terrestrial.[33] The border would be first grasped on paper with clearly defined lines, marked features, and enumerated landmarks. A special commission of the Great Powers was established in 1832 to oversee the survey and mapping of the frontier.[34] A map manifesting the line of demarcation from the plain of Arta to the Gulf of Volos was published in Argos, and London, in 1834.[35]

Geography, old group cohesions, and petty rivalries conspired against a common political-ethnic identity, for those who lived on the land continued to derive their sense of belonging from district, town, village, clan, mountain, valley, from a patch of worked ground.[36] Indeed, the patriotic zeal of those reared on plain of Argos, the islands of Hydra or Psara, centered upon their *chôra*.[37] The influx into mainland Greece of Hellenic peoples from Ottoman lands had already sparked tensions between those who could claim to have a place, the *autochthons*, born of the soil, and those who were without an abode on revolutionary ground, the indigent, the *heterochthons*.[38] Efforts by the enlightened minority to weaken the link between the self and the soil among the agrarian majority—something the delegates at the Fourth National Assembly took a vow to disregard—once again focused on the ancient world as a source for imagined precedents. A larger sense of "agrarian patriotism" was required to habituate the Hellenes to the *ethnos* of the territorial state.

Adamantios Korais had long advocated for national boundaries that would embrace the full extent of the Mediterranean covered by Ancient Greece.[39] Rhigas Velentinlis, or Feraios, had published his *Charta tis Ellados* in 1797, which pictured a wider Greece incorporating ancestral homelands from the Danube to Crete, from the Ionian Sea to Bithynia, centered upon the former capital of the Byzantine

---

32 Hellas (1829, 133–38).

33 See Prologue. On the importance of maps to the Greek national imagination, see Livieratos (2009), Peckham (2000, 2001); on "territory," a concept that, as Stuart Elden has argued, has been insufficiently interrogated, see Elden (2005, 2010, 2013).

34 Baker (1837).

35 Tolias (1992, 26).

36 Petropulos (2015[1968], 20); also see Leontis (1995).

37 Village (*chorió*) and country (*chôra*) were rendered in the same terms (see Finlay 1836, 33–34).

38 As if to repeat how Athenian and Theban myth championed the autochthonous origins of its citizens to specify both equality and to set them apart from other poleis, claims to being truer "sons of the soil" flared up among revolutionaries (Petropulos 2015[1968], 22).

39 Peckham (2000, 24), Hanink (2017, 123).

Empire and hub of the Orthodox Church, Constantinople.[40] These thinkers provided prototypes for what will later constitute yet another dream, a political-ethic aspiration to "recover" these ancestral homelands, the "Great Idea." Although the pull of liberating distant horizons overshadowed the simultaneous need to maintain proximate borders, the new loyalty need not break with a deep orientation to rootedness; it simply had to appeal to a grander vision of *patrida*.[41] Such irredentist fantasies were themselves tied to a Christian image of "casting out evil from the inside and securing the borders," which proved critical to mass appeal.[42]

While the psycho-political work necessary for creating the nation-state required the dream of an idealized past linked to the cultivation of a common spirit, as well as the sense of dwelling within a giant protective enclosure, to achieve unity and solidarity among the Hellenic masses required the formulation of a common language. Where linguistic diversity was regarded as a corrupted artifact of Ottoman rule, prominent Greek thinkers like Korais dreamed of hearing the ring of familiar speech free of distortion. Doused in a bath of ancient, specifically Athenian, Greek these corruptions would be cleansed from spoken language.[43] That this ideal of political-ethnic solidarity for a monolingual nation of Greeks would repeatedly smash against a stubborn reality of local identity, ethnicity, and language norms was perhaps most fittingly imagined within the theatre.[44]

A large school group enters the theatre and children begin climbing the tiers of the lower cavea. I rise to leave. As I descend towards the circular orchestra, I imagine a very different staged performance. *Babel* (*Babylonia*, 1836), the five-act comedy written by Dimitrios Hatziaslanis, testifies to the difficulty associated with smoothing out differences that emanated from locality and mutual isolation.[45] Set in Nafplion, the walled capital of the revolution, in 1827, the dramaturgy for *Babel* is centered upon an inn and a prison. These loci, for Hatziaslanis, were two key topoi for the new nation—the inn to host all those sympathetic strangers to a Greece free of a foreign yoke; the prison to contain the former revolutionaries once their restless energies had secured the expulsion of Ottoman overlords, once freedom had rendered their necessity superfluous.

Following news of the destruction of the Ottoman and Egyptian fleet by the combined navies of the Great Powers—Britain, France, and Russia—the

---

40 Calotychos (2003, 23–30).
41 Compared to the German notion of *heimat*, the concept of home, the Greek notion of *patrida* carries connotations of both fatherland and homeland.
42 Sloterdijk (2014, 177); also (2013, 57).
43 This purified Greek was known as *Katharevousa* (see Mackridge 2009; also Herzfeld 1982, 17–18; 1987, 49–53; Morris 1994, 23).
44 Finlay (1877 VI, 231).
45 Vyzantios (1990); Hatziaslanis wrote under the pseudonym Vyzantios, "the Byzantine."

parochialism that developed over generations under Ottoman overlords is simultaneously released among five customers in a den of excitement and confusion within the small, family-owned inn.[46] With food, drink, and song, four Greeks of different regional and ethnic backgrounds and a scholar revel in the victory, a turning point that will lead to their liberation. After a long celebration, a word with two drastically different meanings is uttered, prompting a Greek-Albanian to shoot a Greek-Cretan.

Misunderstandings are exaggerated with the second act when communication blunders with a police inspector during the investigation lead to the farcical arrest and imprisonment of each witness in turn. Whether or not the perceived insult or the further miscommunication with the inspector or with the scholar, which takes a variety of forms over the following acts, is an artifact of *"the distortion of the Hellenic Language,"* the alternative title of the play, ultimately is left to the audience. *Babel* speaks not only to the difficulty of dissolving the link between the self and locality in favor of a wider *patrida*, but also the simultaneous possibility of diversity maintained from within.

Written against the backdrop of the new constitutional monarchy of Otto, under which the idealized image of antiquity was refashioned according to the post-democratic ideals of the Hellenistic period, the text of the play holds to the polyphony of regional dialects. For Hatziaslanis, who wrote his preface to the 1836 edition in the modern Greek purist vernacular, the Greek language required an injection of ancient vocabulary and grammar.[47] Yet he would soon soften these sentiments by publishing a rewritten play and preface in 1840 that omitted his views on Dynastic Hellenism along with the linguistic programs endorsed by Otto's administration.[48] Whereas the final act of the 1836 edition ends with everyone released from prison amid wine-infused celebration at the inn, the 1840 edition ends with them in jail, forced to make peace over wine while awaiting their freedom. Did the staged illusion of the young Greek state place new yokes of bondage upon its formerly scatter'd children?

I walk around the audience of young students who listen attentively to stories of ancient drama, and head for the gate.

---

46 News of the battle of Navarino arrived with the morning newspaper. In print McLuhan (1994-[1964], 170–798) saw the typographic extension of man as the architect of nationalism, a primary catalyst for what he saw as an end to "parochialism and tribalism." Not only did newspapers serve to elevate their own print languages above other varieties of Greek (Anderson 1983, 44), they also shaped the sentiments of a whole readership with rhetoric, persuasion, selection, and the character of reportage towards a particular agenda—what Karl Kraus (1922) dubbed their *schwarze magie* (black magic). On the politics of early Greek newspapers, see Petropulos (2015[1968], 328, 576–78.

47 Mackridge (2009, 162).

48 See Constantinidis (2001, 76).

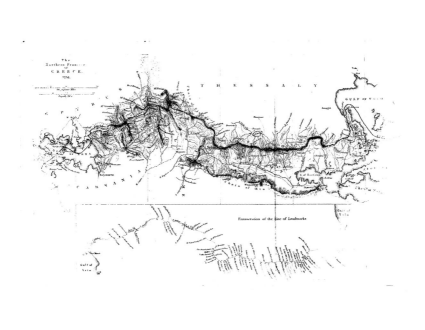

Bibliography

Anderson, B. 1983. *Imagined communities: Reflections on the origin and spread of nationalism.* London: Verso.

Athanassopoulos, E.F. 2002. An "ancient" landscape: European ideals, archaeology, and nation building in early modern Greece. *Journal of Modern Greek Studies* 20(2), 273–305.

Baker, L.-C. 1837. Memoir on the northern frontier of Greece. *Journal of the Royal Geographical Society of London* 7, 81–84.

Benjamin, W. 1999. *The Arcades Project.* Cambridge, MA: Belknap Press.

Calotychos, V. 2003. *Modern Greece: A cultural poetics.* Oxford: Berg.

Chateaubriand, F.-R. 1827. *Itinéraire de Paris à Jérusalem.* Paris: Furne, Jouvet.

Chatterjee, P. 1993. *Nationalist thought and the colonial world: A derivative discourse.* Minneapolis, MN: University of Minnesota Press.

Clark, W.G. 1858. *Peloponnesus: Notes of study and travel.* London: John W. Parker and Son.

Constantinidis, S.E. 2001. *Modern Greek theatre.* London: McFarland & Company.

Demakopoúlou, Ch. 1980. Oi istorikoí tópoi ton Ethnikón Syneléfseon, *Deltíon tis Istorikís kai Ethnologikís Etaireías tis Elládos.* 23.

Dodwell, E. 1819. *A Classical and topographical tour through Greece.* London: Rodwell and Martin.

Dorovinis, V. 1980. Capodistrias et la planification d'Argos (1828–1832). *Bulletin de correspondance hellénique.* Supplément 6, 501–45.

Elden, S. 2005. Missing the point: Globalization, deterritorialization and the space of the world. *Transactions of the Institute of British Geographers* 30(1), 8–19.

Elden, S. 2010. Land, terrain, territory. *Progress in Human Geography* 34(6), 799–817.

Elden, S. 2013. *The birth of territory.* Chicago, IL: University of Chicago Press.

Finlay, G. 1836. *The Hellenic kingdom and the Greek nation.* London: J. Murray.

Finlay, G. 1877. *A history of Greece from its conquest by the Roman to the present time.* Oxford: Clarendon Press.

Ginouvès, R. 1972. *Le théâtron à gradins droits et l'odéon d'Argos.* Paris: J. Vrin.

Hamilakis, Y. 2007. *The nation and its ruins: Antiquity, archaeology, and national imagination in Greece.* Oxford: Oxford University Press.

Hamilakis, Y. 2008. Decolonizing Greek archaeology: Indigenous archaeologies, modernist archaeology and the post-colonial critique. Μουσείο Μπενάκη. 273–84.

Hamilakis, Y. 2009. Indigenous Hellenisms/indigenous modernities: Classical antiquity, materiality, and modern Greek Society. In G. Boys-Stones, B. Graziosi, and P. Vasuni (eds.), *Oxford handbook of Hellenic studies.* Oxford: Oxford University Press. 19–31.

Hanink, J. 2017. *The Classical debt: Greek antiquity in an era of austerity.* Cambridge, MA: Belknap Press.

Hastaoglou-Martinidis, V. 1995. City form and national identity: Urban designs in nineteenth-century Greece. *Journal of Modern Greek Studies* 13(1), 99–123.

Hastaoglou-Martinidis, V., K. Kafkoula, and N. Papamichos. 1993. Urban modernization and national renaissance: Town planning in 19th century Greece. *Planning Perspectives* 8 (4), 427–69.

Hellas. 1829. *Práktika tis en Argeí Ethnikis tetártis ton Ellinon syneléseos.* En Aigini: Ek tis Ethnikis Typografías Dieuthynómenes.

Herzfeld, M. 1982. *Ours once more: Folklore, ideology, and the making of modern Greece.* Austin: University of Texas Press.

Herzfeld, M. 1987. *Anthropology through the looking glass: Critical ethnography in the margins of Europe.* Cambridge: Cambridge University Press.

Herzfeld, M. 2002. The absence presence: Discourses of crypto-colonialism. *South Atlantic Quarterly* 101(4), 899–926.

Kitromilides, P. 2013. *Enlightenment and revolution: The making of modern Greece.* Cambridge, MA: Harvard University Press.

Kotsakis, K. 1991. The powerful past. In I. Hodder (ed.), *Archaeological theory in Europe: The last three decades.* London: Routledge. 65–90.

Kotsakis, K. 2003b. Ideological aspects of contemporary archaeology in Greece. In M. Haagsma, P. Den Boer, and E.M. Moorma (eds.), *The impact of Classical Greece on European and national identities: Proceedings of an international colloquium, held at the Netherlands Institute at Athens, 2–4 October 2000.* Amsterdam: Gieben.

Koumadorakes, O. 2007. *Argos: to polydipsion.* Argos: Ekdoseis Ek Prooimiou.

Kraus, K. 1922. *Untergang der Welt durch schwarze Magie.* Wien-Leipzig: Verlag "Die Frackel".

Lambropoulos, V. 1984. The aesthetic ideology of the Greek quest of identity. *Journal of Modern Hellenism* 4, 19–24.

Latour, B. 1993. *We have never been modern* (trans. C. Porter). Cambridge, MA: Harvard University Press.

Leake, W.M. 1830. *Travels in the Morea.* London: John Murray.

Leontis, A. 1995. *Topographies of Hellenism: Mapping the homeland.* Ithaca, NY: Cornell University Press.

Leontis, A. 1997. Ambivalent Greece. *Journal of Modern Greek Studies* 15(1), 125–36.

Livieratos, E. 2009. *Chartografikés peripéteies tis Elládas, 1821–1919.* Athens: MIET-ELIA. (Cartographic adventures of Greece, 1821–1919).

Mackridge, P. 2009. *Language and national identity in Greece, 1766–1976.* Oxford: Oxford University Press.

Marchetti, P. 2000. Recherches sur les mythes et la topographie d'Argos, V. Quelques mises au point sur les rues d'Argos. À propos de deux ouvrages recents. *Bulletin de Correspondence Hellénique* 124(1), 273–89.

Marchetti, P. 2013. Argos: la ville en ses remparts. In D. Mulliez (ed.), *Sta vímata tou Wilhelm Vollgraff: Ekató chrónia archaiologikís drastiriótitas sto Árgos / Sur les pas de Wilhelm Vollgraff: Cent ans d'activités archéologiques à Argos.* Recherches franco-helléniques, 4. Athènes: École française d'Athènes. 317–34.

McDonald, W.A. 1943. *The political meeting places of the Greeks.* Baltimore, MD: Johns Hopkins Press.

McLuhan, M. 1994[1964]. *Understanding media: The extensions of man.* Cambridge, MA: MIT Press.

Moretti, J.-C., and S. Diez. 1993. *Théâtres d'Argos.* Sites et monuments 10. Athens: École Française d'Athènes.

Morris, I. 1994. Archaeologies of Greece. In I. Morris (ed.), *Classical Greece: Ancient histories and modern archaeologies.* Cambridge: Cambridge University Press. 8–48.

Morris, I. 2000. *Archaeology as culture history.* Oxford: Blackwell.

Nietzsche, F., G. Colli, M. Montinari, F. Bornmann, and M. Carpitella. 1993. *Nietzsche Werke: Kritische Gesamtausgabe.* II.2. Berlin: Walter de Gruyter.

Olsen, B., M. Shanks, T. Webmoor, and C. Witmore. 2012. *Archaeology: The discipline of things.* Berkeley, CA: University of California Press.

Peckham, R.S. 2000. Map mania: Nationalism and the politics of place in Greece, 1870—1922. *Political Geography* 19, 77–95.

Peckham, R.S. 2001. *National histories, natural states: Nationalism and the politics of place in Greece.* London: I.B. Tauris.

Petropulos, J.A. 2015[1968]. *Politics and statecraft in the Kingdom of Greece, 1833–1843.* Princeton, NJ: Princeton University Press.

Plantzos, D. 2014. Dead archaeologists, buried gods: Archaeology as an agent of modernity in Greece. In D. Tziovas (ed.), *Re-imagining the past: Antiquity and modern Greek culture.* Oxford: Oxford University Press. 147–64.

Porter, J.I. 2000. *Nietzsche and the philology of the future.* Stanford, CA: Stanford University Press.

Porter, J.I. 2009. Hellenism and modernity. In G. Boys-Stones, B. Graziosi, and P. Vasuni (eds.), *Oxford handbook of Hellenic studies.* Oxford: Oxford University Press. 7–18.

Porter, J.I. 2014. Nietzsche's radical philology. In A.K. Jensen and H. Heit (eds.), *Nietzsche as a scholar of antiquity.* London: Bloomsbury Academic. 27–52.

Sennett, R. 1994. *Flesh and stone: The body and the city in Western civilization.* New York, NY: W.W. Norton & Company.

Sloterdijk, P. 2013. *In the world interior of capital: For a philosophical theory of globalization.* Cambridge: Polity Press.

Sloterdijk, P. 2014. *Globes: Spheres II.* South Pasadena, CA: Semiotext(e).

Tolias, Y. 1992. 1830–1930: The people and the territory. In *Ekató chrónia chartografías tou ellinismoú: 1830–1930.* Athens: Elliniki etaireía chartografías.

Vollgraff, W. 1951. Le Théatre D'Argos. *Mnemosyne* 4(1), 193–203.

Voudouri, D. 2010. Law and the politics of the past: Legal protection of cultural heritage in Greece. *International Journal of Cultural Property* 17, 547–68.

Vyzantios, D.K. 1990. *Vavylonia* (A and B versions edited by S.A. Eyaggelatos). Athens: Hermes.

Witmore, C. 2006. Vision, media, noise and the percolation of time: Symmetrical approaches to the mediation of the material world. *Journal of Material Culture* 11(3), 267–92.

Zenkini, I.E. 1996. *To Árgos dia mésou ton aiónon.* Athens: Ékdosis Tríti.

14

ARGOS TO ANAPLI ON THE HOOF,
WITH A STOP AT TIRYNS

William Martin Leake, notebooks and note-taking, two maps by Leake, Edward
Dodwell and a camera obscura, one map and three ichnographies

The Ides of March, 1806. Captain William Martin Leake, a British artilleryman, descriptive geographer, and spy mounts his horse outside the house of Kyr Vlasópoulo.[1] Situated in the middle of Argos, the Vlasópoulo residence, which had doubled as Captain Leake's lodgings for the past two nights, is said to be quite unlike most other houses in town. Whereas Argive houses are generally one story and of modest size, the Vlasópoulo residence rises to a conspicuous height; indeed, it is said to be of "palatial" proportion.[2] Originally from Mistra, the local archon derived his fortune from agriculture, including, among other

---

1 Leake will come to be considered a father of Classical topography; see Eliot (1996), Wagstaff (1992); also refer to Stoneman (1987).

2 Sir William Gell had lodged with the Vlasópoulo family two years before Leake; the Elgins, two years before Gell (Smith 1916, 213). This adjectival accolade, however, is owed to Gell, who refers to the residence as a "palace." Gell, as Byron argues in 1811 (see Byron 1833), was not always the most discriminating of critics. Yet, at the house of Vlasópoulo, Lady Elgin did not

things, currants, which he still grows on an estate near Corinth. The fact that Vlasópoulo enjoyed both the protection of the English government and high esteem among foreigners and locals alike would seem to be at variance with his other pursuits, including, when necessary, grain smuggling.[3]

Captain Leake checks his pocket watch—1:51 p.m. Accompanied by his English valet and a *Serrugee*, or postilion,[4] the captain leaves Argos by an unpaved street heading southwest. They pass a number of rectilinear cottages.[5] Standing far apart, many houses frame the line of the streets; most are interspersed with gardens containing fruit trees, orange, lemon, and others; many are enclosed with walls. Cypresses rise here and there. And, here, they pass a line of these spires at a right angle to their path. By Captain Leake's estimate, Argos consists of 1,200 families, mostly "Greek" or Christian, but sixty to eighty are "Turkish" or Muslim. As they progress through Argos, Leake scans the road and its edge for vestiges of the ancient city walls. None are to be seen.

En route from Argos to Anapli (Nafplion, Greece), Leake notes passing the last houses at the edge of town at 2:03. Here, the road splits. To the right, it runs straight across the marshy portion of the plain to meet the shore where, as an elevated *kalderim* with a rugged, stone pavement, it follows a wide arc around the bay.[6] To the left, the cart road proceeds in a direct line towards Tiryns. They take the left path.

Along this stretch of cart road, there are few trees. Fields—some left fallow, some recently plowed, and some sown that morning—crowd the edge of the ditches on either side.[7] From his mount Leake surveys the flat expanse of plain. Soil determines choice of crop. Grains cover the drier portions of the plain.

---

want for accommodation. The description of the town and plain is cobbled together from numerous nineteenth-century authors, including Chateaubriand, Dodwell, Gell, Leake, and Pouqueville.

3 See Gell (1823, 396–97); the Elgins paid Vlasópoulo 655 piastres for excavating at the Treasury of Atreus in 1802 (Smith 1916, 261).

4 Leake neither mentions his valet nor acknowledges the support of the Ottoman post system directly. Nonetheless, his access to *menzil* geldings and mares requires this support. According to Gell, travelers of great importance can request this kind of support from the Ottoman Porte by adding it as a stipulation to their *firmáhn* (a royal mandate). Gell's mistake, however, was to refer to the postilion as a *Menzilgi*. As pointed out by Byron: "*Serrugees* are postilions; *Menzilgis* are postmasters" (1833, 509).

5 Leake neglected to describe the houses of Argos, as would François-René de Chateaubriand, who passed through Argos with a nasty head wound he had received at the edge of a branch while riding his horse from Laconia four months later (1814, 113). A neglect of such contemporary detail was pervasive. William George Clarke, in 1850, would describe them as "built in a rough-and-ready fashion, with neither dressed stones, nor rough-cast, nor stucco—for use and not for show" (1858, 90).

6 Gell (1810, 88), Leake (1830 II, 363). *Kalderim* is a Turkish term for a metaled road for hoofed traffic.

7 A generation later, Francis Hervé mentions the ditches along this stretch of road (1837 I, 256).

Cotton and vines are grown in the parcels adjacent to the road; this portion of the plain is known for its greater moisture. To the right, in the marshy wetland closer to the sea, are lots of *kalambokki*.[8] Of late, these fields had been losing ground to rice. Cultivation of the latter, however, had recently been restricted because the *voyvoda* (district governor) judged the sodden parcels in which rice was grown to be injurious to one's health. Overall, there are few gaps, few neglected margins. The weather, quite free of the frosts and snow Leake had encountered in the plains of Tripolitzá a few days earlier, is, for him, reminiscent of an English summer.

They descend a bank. Precisely eight minutes after leaving the last houses of Argos, Leake and party cross the river Bánitza (the ancient Inachus). Here, the broad, gravelly bed is covered in a thin flow of water fed by recent rains. With no pause for their mounts, they continue across and up the far bank, which is covered in low brush and decked out in spring flowers. At the top, they meet with the smells of freshly plowed soil drawn out by the afternoon sun. Such descriptive detail, however, is of no concern to Leake. Nor should it be.

Fearing French military designs on the Grecian frontier of the Turkish Empire, the British Foreign Office had dispatched Leake, an officer in the Royal Artillery, on a mission to gain more accurate and credible geographical knowledge of Greece. Captain Leake's orders were unequivocal. He was to make himself "acquainted with the Western coast of Albania and the Morea" and, above all, those areas proximate to the Italian coast, especially ports, landing facilities, and fortifications.[9] Moreover, Captain Leake was to suggest to the Turkish commanders "any improvements for the defense."[10] Along with his valet, he was to "take surveys, and lay down plans of the same places."[11] Once these coastal areas were sufficiently documented, Leake and his valet were to proceed to the interior

> for the purpose of acquiring that general knowledge of the face of the country ... and, in particular, to take notice of the roads and passes leading towards Constantinople on the one side and the Morea on the other.[12]

Areas, features, and things of note also included any defensive facilities (especially "fortresses of Venetian construction"), potential obstacles (including the depths of river crossings or difficult passes), points of vulnerability, and every

---

8 While this term can refer to either maize or Egyptian dhurra—sorghum—in this case, it probably refers to the former.

9 Marsden (1864, 16).

10 Ibid.

11 Ibid.

12 Ibid., 17.

kind of resource. Under this heading of "resources" fell everything from Vlasópoulo's currants to olives, goats, bovids, and the associated revenues, from muni-
tions and saltpeter (useful in making gunpowder) to sources of freshwater, and,
at a time when they were generating significant returns for those who undertook the risks of investment, antiquities. Leake was also to "report the political
and military dispositions of the inhabitants," including potential troop numbers,
and to liaise with important officials.[13] These concerns, military concerns, were
to be his primary guide as to what to observe, what to describe, on the
ground.[14] Classical topography was their by-product.

Throughout his travels in Greece, Leake maintained two sets of notebooks:
a series of stationers' notebooks for the narrative of his daily journeys and
a number of smaller survey logbooks. Bound with hard card, marked *N° 12*, his
current stationer's notebook measures 14.6 by 21 centimeters. Its paper is plain,
without rules; its texture is grainy with low ribs. On these pages, between February 16 and March 15, Leake will write the daily narratives of his journeys from
Patra to Anapli, sketch maps of sites, and draw inscriptions seen along the way.[15]
Writing in cursive with pencil on-site, Leake will inscribe the day-by-day narrative
horizontally across the page, beginning from the front of the notebook. From the
back, he will include illustrations of inscriptions, and maps, along with sundry
reflections related to these things. Blending topography, politics, economics,
archaeology, Classical literature, horticultural yields, and so forth, these notes
altogether will amount to no less than a descriptive geography.

While framed by the occasional line of bushes, along here the road is free of trees.
Yet again, cultivated tracts of land crowd the path taken by Leake and party. Ahead,
across the flats, at a distance of just under a mile, looms the tree-spiked silhouette of
Delamanára. Until they enter this village, Leake will refrain from taking notes.

In his pocket, Leake carries a brown, leather-bound survey logbook, which
he purchased from the London bookseller John Booth on Duke Street, Portland
Place. More specifically, the logbook is one of "Hall & Co's much approved
velvet paper memorandum books." Of flip-top design, it is pocket-sized, 10.8 by
14.6 centimeters. Such a compact form allows Leake to hold his survey logbooks
in his palm whether on foot or in the saddle. Working from the ends to the
middle, notes begin, for the most part, at the top of each leaf and progress to
the bottom of the next page. From the front, Leake compiles lists of compass
bearings and maps; from the back, the logbooks contain drawings and sketches

---

13 Ibid., 18. Regarding Leake's orders, also refer to Curtius (1876, 242–43), Wagstaff (2001a,
    191).
14 Also refer to Wagstaff (2001b), Witmore (2004).
15 Bound in brown English leather, No. 13 begins on March 16. Leake's notebooks are now stored
    in the Faculty of Classics Library at Cambridge University.

of inscriptions. These notation practices are as much an artifact of the hand as they are a project of the systematic organization of information. An artifact of tactile preference, Leake finds the weight of the pages better distributed by hanging to the bottom rather than flipped over the top of his hand. Subtle variations in the length and character of his lettering in sections of the logbooks suggest variations in his writing surface—a steady hand on a stable foundation versus a moving steed across variable ground. All timed movements appear to have been written from his mount. Narrative sections are sometimes present within the logbooks, suggesting that Leake did not always carry his large stationer's notebooks during his peregrinations on foot.

Leake's notation practices also rely on other special techniques and tools.[16] Instructions for pencil use are pasted in the front flap of the logbooks:

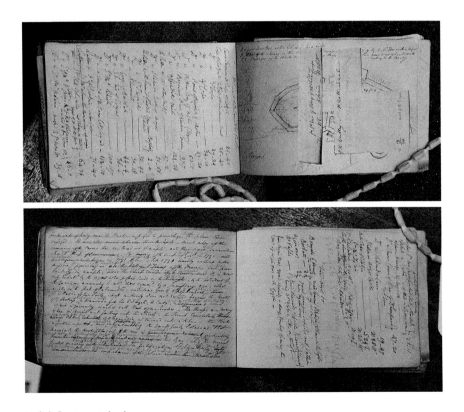

Leake's flip-top notebook.

---

16 On note-taking practices in general, see Te Heesen (2005).

Please keep the point of the pencil smoothly scraped flat; then it may be held in the same direction as a pen, will always be in order, and the Metal, being about two inches in length, it will last a long time.

Leake prefers a length of one inch for note-taking and drawing.[17] In the midst of unstable conditions in the saddle, Leake developed a skill for holding a one-inch pencil firmly between thumb and forefinger. He later compiles and further augments the narrative of his travels with other details back in London—pencil will be carefully traced in pen and emendations will be handwritten in the margins between lines of text. Delayed by other military and scholarly commitments, Leake's notebooks will be published eventually as travelogues: *Travels in the Morea* (1830) and *Travels in Northern Greece* (1835).[18]

Leake notes entering Delamanára at 2:31 p.m. While passing through the village, he observes several remnants of antiquity—mostly squared blocks—in a ruined church. Adjacent to a well nearby lies a former column shaft turned cattle trough. Hereabouts, Leake situates a pyramidal monument to a battle between Proetus and Acrisius mentioned in Pausanias 2.25.7. It commemorates a first—the use of shields in battle. Otherwise, Leake says nothing concerning the local residents whose labors are inscribed in the fields of plain. Why does he neglect what is obvious to others? Here, across the visually unencumbered plain, everyone sees everyone else at work. Here, everyone sees the fruits of everyone else's labor. And everyone knows if anyone deviates from the common agrarian pattern, as with the lone farmer who ventures to plant currants—the soil is too moist, the plant requires years of investment. Leake, the northern European traveler, also wants others to see, but to do so he must operate within a very different systematic and descriptive dimension from those whom he surely passes now in the village.

Marking features worthy of note with temporal coordinates was facilitated with the aid of a good pocket watch.[19] The to-the-minute precision, which characterized Leake's movement from Argos to Anapli, would prove useful for subsequent travelers but in a very different way from the navigational time logs of the period. As with Gell's roadbook, *The Itinerary of the Morea* (1817), Leake noted objects of concern along traversed space. However, this endeavor was

17 On the front flap of Survey Notebook No. 1. Leake crosses out in the recommended length and writes in "one inch."
18 The travelogue was a mixed genre at the turn of the nineteenth century. While the day-by-day account of adventure, hardship, and intrigue in potentially dangerous lands had a wide appeal for a more general audience, the travelogue was also suited to laying out both criteria associated with what was deemed worthy of observation and evidence for argumentation. For the specifics related to the lag time in publication, see Wagstaff (2004b).
19 It is unlikely that Leake carried a chronometer.

itself a by-product of the planimetric acquisition of knowledge, which is ultimately of greater utility to both military officers and scholars of Classical topography wherever they may be.[20] The steady movement of cogs and gears translates into a measure—clockwork—and the repetitive act of temporally referencing one's location regulates one's activities on the ground. The temporal registration of recognizable features along the path, if procedural, if ruthlessly consistent, becomes the measurement of physical distance. And a system of measurement of any kind is a key element in standardization; Leake's system will go a long way towards the production of a reliable map of the Peloponnesian interior, the first of its kind. What constitutes "recognizable features" worthy of registration by watch? This question would ultimately be determined by the scale.

Ahead, the table hill of Paleo-Anapli, as Tiryns is now known, rises like an island above the flat plain. Leake will not reach the ruins until exactly 3:01. Still, he does not change the gait, which is a jog. Since Tripolitzá, Leake's rate of travel has been that of a *menzil*. *Menzil* refers to a post-station, a series of which make up the Ottoman postal infrastructure. And while at his disposal Leake has a post-horse, a constant companion who knows the roads and bridle paths far better than the captain, this subtle notation as to the type of mount is central to his metrology. While speed, of course, varied depending on the mount, a post-horse over an unencumbered plain could cover roughly six miles an hour;[21] a slow trot would suffice. On the basis of the length and pace of an ambling gait, Leake established a system of measurement.[22] Thus, enrolling this ten-minute-mile pace, with deductions for mountainous areas, he could calculate the length of lines, a necessary endeavor in flattening three-dimensional space into two dimensions.

To the right, the fortress of the Palamidhi crowns the steep summit, of the same name, above Anapli. From this angle, the silhouette of summit and town resembles a long, prostrate Sphinx of giant proportion.[23] Leake will enter the fortress on the following afternoon. Even with the aid of both a *buyurdí* (a written order) from the Pashá of the Morea and a general *firmáhn* (a royal mandate) of the Porte (the Ottoman court in Constantinople), Leake's efforts at gaining

---

20 On the seeming irony of a military officer becoming the "father of Classical topography," see Witmore and Buttrey (2008).
21 Leake (1835 IV, 496).
22 January 4, 1810. While traveling in Thessaly, Leake states that "with menzíl geldings [post horses] over the plain, our pace to-day is about six miles an hour"; Leake (1835 IV, 496).
23 This image is borrowed from Herbert Lehmann, who said of Nafplion, "*das wie eine lang hingestreckte Riesensphinx*" (1937, 1).

access to the Palamidhi are not without difficulty.[24] After being obliged to wait
the whole morning, Leake will eventually establish a survey station at the
summit of Palamidhi Castle. With a theodolite[25] he will take bearings and list
them in his logbook under this heading: "Cavo Séraca w Cape of Spetzia,
21–40; Cape of Spetzia w second cape of the Laconian Coast, 25–40; second
cape of the Laconian Coast w third cape of the Laconian Coast, 29–24." From
the station on Argos to the village of Kharvati to the southeast end of Tiryns,
in all, twenty-four points are registered in this way. Subsequently, Leake also
records angles relative to cardinal directions: N28W for the station on Argos
Castle; S24E for the outer Cape of Spetzia and so on. In all, five points would
be taken by compass. Tied to the cardinal directions, these local angles are
secured to the squared world. With this radial coding Leake takes a key step
towards transporting a point of view, a line of sight, and therefore, the landscape features lined up, back to London.

Thirty minutes after passing through Delamanára, Leake's party reaches
Paleo-Anapli. Such clockwork was the basis of calculating distance, and this distance, when combined with the measurement of degrees, provided a basis for
triangulation, which is a necessary step in the translation of the Greek countryside onto a two-dimensional surface while maintaining something of its reality
as seen through linear perspective. Here, time measurement frames a way of
looking; it frames a *mode of engagement*. Chronometry translates into chorometry. And this chorometry is inscribed from the saddle on the hoof.

With his stationer's notebook and survey logbook in hand, Leake dismounts
and enters the great citadel of Tiryns on foot. With unbroken focus aimed at
its mighty walls, Leake begins his description as others would begin, by observing what Pausanias had observed—*argoi lithoi*; the finest examples of Cyclopean
masonry are to be found near the remains of the eastern gate. Here, Leake, like
Edward Dodwell, another Englishman who visited the citadel only three months
earlier, measured the largest of stones—10.6 by 3.9 by 3.6 feet. Leake's block is
a little over a foot longer than the one measured by Dodwell. The measuring
grasp of both Northern Europeans would access the whole of the citadel in
a different way from all who had worked these lands.

24 Leake would later be denied entry to Acrocorinth.
25 Leake mentions use of a sextant or theodolite in his Preface to *Travels in Northern Greece* (1835,
   vii). A sextant of 4 inches radius made by Berge is mentioned in a correspondence with John
   Hawkins referenced as "Tripolitsa March 9, 1805" (Wagstaff personal communication). Matthew
   Berge, the former foreman for the renowned London-based instrument maker Jesse Ramsden
   (1735–1800), inherited the business after Ramsden's death and continued to make instruments
   till his own death in 1819 (refer to Stimson 1985).

Leake, during the one hour and forty-six minutes he passes at Paleo-Anapli, sketches a map of the citadel. Lengthwise on a page in his logbook, he pencils in the inner and outer faces of the walls. Starting from the interior apex of the north wall of the lower enclosure, he strides south. One hundred and fifteen paces, each pace equated to the English yard, is the length of his direct march across the level field to the corner of what is marked as a wall extending off the western gate. He indicates his path across this long axis of the citadel with dashed lines. Twenty-seven paces trace the east face of this wall. Thirty-four paces mark out the distance between the turn of this wall and the exposed edge of a retaining wall at the edge of the upper level. Here, below Leake's feet, successive fills and foundations extend to a depth of 6 meters in the earth. This terrace and the lower field would, in later generations, be sown in caraway. Twenty-five and forty paces mark distances across the summit of the upper terrace to the edge of the galleries.[26] Leake says nothing about the walls exposed on the upper terrace; no yoked team of oxen, no plow could break through this surface. He pencils in five different lines for the north end of the citadel (back in London he will later settle on a version traced in pen). Leake says nothing of whether there is a threshing floor at the south end.[27] Background noise, the immediate state of the citadel eludes observation. Instead, in the left-hand margin of his survey logbook, Leake tallies a vertical list of numbers—115, 27, 34, 25, 40. Totaled to 240, followed by "about 250," the captain figures the length of Tiryns at about 250 yards, the breadth from 40 to 80 yards, and the height from 20 to 50 feet.

Dodwell would also pace out the citadel, which is 244 yards by his measure. He would also take bearings by compass—from the hill behind Tiryns to the extremity of the promontory of Nauplia, S20W; to Prison Island (the Bourtzi), S28W; to the Larissa of Argos, N58W. As with Leake, he would follow the likes of Pausanias and Strabo in deciding what to observe. Unlike Leake, Dodwell would take in a view of the eastern gate with his camera obscura,[28] and this would dictate how to observe it. A wooden box with a pinhole aperture and a slide to adjust scale closes off the outside, with the help of a canopy, to

---

26 An entry, near the middle of his survey logbook No. 3, which he currently carries, will soon contain a map of Tiryns (reproduced as plate 3 in *Travels in the Morea II*, 1830). Three portions are carefully cut from center of the map. Two of these sections, which frame two inscriptions drawn on the opposite page of the Tiryns map, will later be found affixed with red wax in Survey Notebook No. 13. Cutting and gluing allows Leake to manipulate and reshuffle two-dimensional space at a later point from the comfort of the study. Regrettably, the third, remaining, cut-out portion of the Tiryns map could not be found.

27 Here, some three and more generations later, Schliemann and party would take meals and rest in the course of their excavations.

28 Dodwell (1834) would later publish his view.

cast an inverted image onto a sheet of paper.[29] With this "infallible medium of truth and accuracy,"[30] Dodwell simply traced out the two-dimensional image of the three-dimensional world as he saw it. Engagements with the camera obscura will produce landscape panoramas, town scenes, and images of monuments such as Tiryns and redefine what it is to visualize Greece.

Both Dodwell and Leake aim to gather knowledge with empirical fidelity, faithful images of what they regarded as having been lost to obscurity. Thus, their descriptions will say little of local relations with the citadel; for them, local farmers do not see what they, along with other enlightened Europeans, see.[31] Of course, the strange practices and recording procedures of both Dodwell and Leake did not escape the notice, or indeed the understanding, of locals. Nor did they elude counter-observation. Aware of how his experiences with the device highlighted discrepancies in the way the world was understood by locals, Dodwell would bear self-witness to the alarm expressed by two passing *aghas*,[32] and their horses, at the sight of him drawing inside his machine on

GENERAL VIEW OF TIRYNS and the PLAIN OF ARGOS.

General View of Tiryns and the Plain of Argos, Dodwell 1834.

Gennadius Library, ASCSA (photo by Don Lavigne)

---

29 It is possible that Dodwell makes use of two different camera obscuras during his travels in Greece; see Sloan (2013, 39).

30 1819 I, 389.

31 This zeal for discovery was shared by many who lived in the area at the time; see Anderson (2015).

32 *Agha* is an honorific title for officers in the Ottoman Empire, roughly equivalent to "master" or "lord."

an elevated spot to the east of the citadel. Despite being misled by Dodwell's guide, the *aghas* quickly discerned what the Englishman was doing and, understanding the gravity of the recording technique, warned him not to repeat his practices in the vicinity of the Palamidhi fortress.[33]

Whereas local farmers would look for a return on yield in immediate cultivated space, these Northern Europeans would look for returns at a distance of several thousand miles. While Dodwell would flatten the view as seen through an aperture on the ground, Leake would flatten the view as seen from above. Here, the rocky plateau of Tiryns, which resembled a high island above the plain, would on paper attain the shape of the flat expanse surrounding it. Argos, Delamanára, Tiryns, and Nauplia, the course of the Kelalari (Erasinus), the Rema of Argos or Xerias (Charadus), and the Bánitza (Inachus), the shape of the rocky mass of Mount Chaon, and the expanse of the Argive plain would be locationally secured at a scale commensurate with the whole of the measured Peloponnese. Unlike Dodwell, Leake would fix his discoveries with the compilation of a map of the whole Morea, where measures of the interior were faithful to actual points of triangulation.[34] The fruits of these labors will not ripen for some twenty-four years, as his map has to await the publication of his *Travels of Morea* in 1830. In the interval between his travels and their publication, the competition between the British and the French will continue with an emphasis on ever-increasing precision.

It is therefore not without due irony that, here, from this very citadel paced out by both Leake and Dodwell, measurement by both boot and hoof will succumb to measurement by chain. In March of 1829, while Leake is corresponding with John Murray on the *Travels in the Morea*, French officers of staff associated with the *Expédition scientifique de Morée* will put the competition to rest once and for all. A 3,500-meter-long baseline will be staked out from the walls of Tiryns to the southeast, between the two hills, each bearing the name Profitis Elias. This baseline, further refined through calibration of the measuring chain against a meter of copper at various temperatures, will form the line of departure for the survey triangulation associated with the French expedition.[35]

---

33 1819 II, 252.

34 On the differences to Dodwell's map, which is derived exclusively from Admiralty surveys, see Witmore (2013a).

35 Bory de Saint-Vincent (1834, 19–24), Peytier, Puillion de Boblaye, and Servier (1833); also Lepetit (1998, 105); and Prologue. The temperature calibration of the chain would occur in November and December of 1830 when measurements of the chain were taken at different temperatures and compared: Bory de Saint-Vincent (1834, 22–24), Peytier, Puillion de Boblay, and Servier (1833, 93–95).

Though they were unaware of the connection, the French surveyors chose a fitting starting point for their baseline. Maps like this will become the most powerful expression of power possible in the early nineteenth century.[36] One and a half meters below the boots of the surveyors who explored the summit were remnants of rooms and corridors associated with other forms of Bronze Age power (a power whose ichnographies led to tabulation, record-keeping, tracing the area under cultivation). Immediately eclipsing the fruits of Leake's labors, the French map denotes the ultimate submission of land to geometry, the outcome of which would now stand at the beginning with subsequent engagements with these old lands, whether in the vicinity of Tiryns or Pylos.[37] The French map would also stand at the beginning of a cascade of subsequent maps of the region.[38] It will provide the base for the work of both Bernhard Steffen at Mycenae and the railroad engineers through the Tretos.[39] This act of capturing such detail at a distance will go a long way towards underwriting a new geography seen in routine traffic across vast distances: Schliemann will provide Chicago corned beef for lunch during his excavations at Tiryns in 1884, two years before the metal rails of an ever-more-connected Europe will end in Nafplion.

4:47 p.m. Captain Leake and party leave Tiryns for Anapli. To the right of the road the cultivated plain extends for a distance of 200 to 300 yards, where it transforms into a marsh that extends another mile to the sea. To the left, the fields stretch to meet "a thick and extensive grove of olives" at the base of the rocky hills, which dominate the middle ground to the east.[40] Leake notes the largest and loftiest of these insulated masses; its pointed summit is surmounted by a small church. He says nothing of whether these fields are being worked by residents, nothing of these olives. A generation later, this extensive grove will be burned to the ground—60,000 olive trees were estimated to have been destroyed on the plain in the course of the coming revolution.[41] A harsh and violent end to generations of investment in arboreal coexistence, these acts are not so much reminders to local communities as destructive horrors, which exclude everyone from living with former groves. Still, what is a loss to most would prove to be a gain for French surveyors, who will have 3,500 meters of unencumbered plain across which to repeatedly stretch their metal chain for their cartographical baseline.

36 Latour (1986).
37 This is not without its irony given the roots of geometry as *geo-metreo, land measurement* (see Segment 7).
38 See Prologue; also Witmore (2013a).
39 See Segments 8 and 10.
40 Dodwell (1819, 245).
41 See McGrew (1985, 4); this grove is also captured in Dodwell's *General View of Tiryns and the Plain of Argos* (1834).

After fifteen minutes, the road veers on a slight angle to the right. As Leake holds his post-horse to an even gait, his experience speaks to the trials and tribulations cloaked in the final scenography. Maps are black boxes, where a trust in the phantom powers of scenography arise through anonymity. For a view from nowhere to arise, it must be severed from the localized circumstances of its own making. And yet, the true powers of scenography are to be found in its ichnography. *Ichnos* is the word for the trace of the step, the track, the footprint. *Ichnos*, as we learn from the Homeric hymn to Hermes, can also refer to the hoof print.[42] Leake's journey to Tiryns and on to Anapli will link together three different ichnographies. That of his horse across the Morea, that of his pace across Tiryns, and that of his labors in transforming observations amid the Greek pagus into pages in his *Travels in the Morea*. Whereas scenography may on some level be understood as the representation, the ichnography is the pile-up, the cascade that traces the path from the local circumstances of March 15 and 16, 1806 to the global, in the sense of wherever Leake's descriptive geography and map of the Morea find themselves. For the Classical topographer or antiquarian subsequent to Leake it is routine to interact with Leake's map in terms of scenography by, say, plotting out a route from Sparta to Argos. The ichnography, by contrast, is the "complete chain of metamorphoses"[43] that links up the first reliable, optically consistent and standardized map of the Peloponnesian interior to the labors of Captain Leake atop the summit of the Palamidhi. This understanding of the ichnography applies equally to the French labors, and to the subsequent cascade of maps, which will fall from them.

Leake and party bypass a khan half a mile shy of the town walls. Here, travelers who pass the night have been known to find torment amid the insects. After Leake's map, after the subsequent French map, both the white space of the Peloponnesian interior and plain of Argos would be opened up to the repeated encounter of those who will build on the achievements of others at a comfortable distance. This critical step, which will underwrite the refinement of geographically secured knowledge and the information collected in return trips, will ensure the triumph of flattened space. It will also leave open the possibility that an image faithful to certain qualities of the land could be confused with the land itself. Suffice it to say that, in the aftermath of such confusion, there arises a need for the concept and practice of ichnography.

The captain, his valet, and the *Serrugee* enter the Land Gate at 5:27 p.m., just before sunset, when the gates are closed.

---

42 See line 76—I am grateful to Don Lavigne for his immediate recollection of this reference.
43 Serres (1995b, 19).

Bibliography

Anderson, B. 2015. "An alternative discourse": Local interpreters of antiquities in the Ottoman Empire. *Journal of Field Archaeology* 40(4), 450–60.

Bory de Saint-Vincent, M. 1834. *Expédition scientifique de Morée: Section des sciences physiques. Tome II – Partie 1. Géographie.* Paris: F.G. Levrault.

Byron, G.G. 1833. Review of Gell's Geography of Ithaca, and Itinerary of Greece. In *The complete works of Lord Byron including his suppressed poems and others never before published.* Paris: Baudry.

Chateaubriand, F-R. 1814. *Travels in Greece, Palestine, Egypt, and Barbary, during the years 1806 and 1807.* New York, NY: Van Winkle and Wiley.

Clark, W.G. 1858. *Peloponnesus: Notes of study and travel.* London: John W. Parker and Son.

Curtius, E. 1876. William Martin Leake und die Wiederentdeckung der klassischen Länder. *Preussische Jahrbücker* 38, 237–52.

Dodwell, E. 1819. *A Classical and topographical tour through Greece.* 2 vols. London: Rodwell and Martin.

Dodwell, E. 1834. *Views and descriptions of Cyclopian, or, Pelasgic remains, in Greece and Italy; with constructions of a later period.* London: A. Richter.

Eliot, C.W.J. 1996. Leake, William Martin (1777–1860). In N.T. de Grummond (ed.), *An encyclopedia of the history of classical archaeology.* Westport, CT: Greenwood Press. 666.

Gell, W. 1810. *The itinerary of Greece.* London: Payne.

Gell, W. 1823. *Narrative of a journey in the Morea.* London: Longman, Hurst, Rees, Orme, and Brown.

Hervé, F. 1837. *A residence in Greece and Turkey with notes of the journey through Bulgaria, Servia, Hungary, and the Balkan.* 2 vols. London: Whittaker.

Latour, B. 1986. Visualization and cognition: Thinking with eyes and hands. *Knowledge and Society* 6(6), 1–40.

Leake, W.M. 1830. *Travels in the Morea.* 3 vols. London: John Murray.

Leake, W.M. 1835. *Travels in Northern Greece.* 4 vols. London: J. Rodwell.

Lehmann, H. 1937. *Argolis: Landeskunde der Ebene von Argos und ihrer Randgebiete.* Athens: Deutsches Archaologisches Institut.

Lepetit, B. 1998. Missions scientifques et expeditions militaries. Remarques sur leurs modalités d'articulation. In M.N. Bourguet (ed.), *L'invention scientifique de la Méditerranée. Égypt, Morée, Algérie.* Paris: Éd. de l'École des Hautes Études en Sciences Sociales. 97–116.

Marsden, J.H. 1864. *A brief memoir of the life and writings of Lieutenant-Colonel William Martin Leake.* London: privately printed.

McGrew, W.W. 1985. *Land and revolution in modern Greece, 1800–1881: The transition in the tenure and exploitation of land from Ottoman rule to independence.* Kent, OH: Kent State University Press.

Peytier, Puillion de Boblaye, and Servier. 1833. Notice sur les opérations géodésiques exécutées en Morée, en 1829 et 1830, par MM. Peytier, Puillon de Boblaye et Servier; suivie d'un catalogue des positions géographiques des principaux points déterminés par ces opérations. *Bulletin de la Société de géographie* 19, 89–106.

Serres, M. 1995b. *Genesis.* Ann Arbor, MI: University of Michigan Press.

Sloan, K. 2013. Seen through a glass darkly: Dodwell and Pomardi's drawings and watercolors of Greece. In J.M. Camp (ed.), *In search of Greece: Catalogue of an exhibit of drawings at the British Museum by Edward Dodwell and Simone Pomardi from the collection of the Packard Humanities Institute.* Los Altos, CA: Packard Humanities Institute. 31–46.

Smith, A.H. 1916. Lord Elgin and his collection. *Journal of Hellenic Studies* 36, 163–372.

Stimson, A.N. 1985. Some Board of Longitude instruments in the nineteenth century. In P.R. de Clercq (ed.), *Nineteenth-century scientific instruments and their makers.* Amsterdam: Rodpi. 93–115.

Stoneman, R. 1987. *Land of lost gods: The search for classical Greece.* Norman, OK: University of Oklahoma Press.

Te Heesen, A. 2005. The notebook: A paper technology. In B. Latour and P. Weibel (eds.), *Making things public: Atmospheres of democracy.* Cambridge, MA: MIT Press. 582–89.

Wagstaff, J.M. 1992. Colonel Leake in Laconia. In J.M. Sanders (ed.), *PHILOLAKON: Lakonian Studies in Honour of Hector Catling.* Athens: British School at Athens. 277–283.

Wagstaff, J.M. 2001a. Pausanias and the topographers: The case of Colonel Leake. In S. E. Alcock, J.F. Cherry, and J. Elsner (eds.), *Pausanias: Travel and memory in Roman Greece.* Oxford: Oxford University Press. 190–206.

Wagstaff, J.M. 2001b. Colonel Leake: Traveller and scholar. In S. Searight and J. M. Wagstaff (eds.), *Tavellers in the Levant: Voyagers and visionaries.* Durham: Astene. 3–15.

Wagstaff, J.M. 2004b. Leake, William Martin (1777–1860). In *Oxford dictionary of national biography.* Oxford: Oxford University Press.

Witmore, C. 2004. On multiple fields: Between the material world and media – Two cases from the Peloponnesus, Greece. *Archaeological Dialogues* 11(2), 133–64.

Witmore, C. 2013a. The world on a flat surface: Maps from the archaeology of Greece and Beyond. In S. Bonde and S. Houston (eds.), *Representing the past: Archaeology through text and image.* Oxford: Oxbow Books. 127–52.

Witmore, C., and T.V. Buttrey. 2008. William Martin Leake: A contemporary of P.O. Brøndsted, in Greece and in London. In B.B. Rasmussen, J.S. Jenson, J. Lund, and M. Märcher (eds.), *P.O. Brøndsted (1780–1842): A Danish classicist in his European Context.* Copenhagen: Royal Danish Academy. 15–34.

15

A STROLL THROUGH NAFPLION

Walls, squares, town planning, the Land Gate, buildings vacated, the scene of a crime, an exodus, abject spaces, photography as a mode of engagement, history and heritage, restoration and care, catering to distance

When the architect's finished, they change, they frown or smile or even grow resentful with those who stayed behind, with those who went away with others who'd come back if they could or others who disappeared, now that the world's become an endless hotel.

George Seferis, *Thrush*, translated by Edmund Keeley

May 30, 2012. Sigi and I have arranged to meet by the Land Gate. I pass the time near the statue of Staikos Staikopoulos (1798–1835), the famed freedom fighter from the Greek War of Independence, who led the night raid that captured the Palamidhi Fortress in 1822. A group of students wait here for the bus; their backs recline against the smooth, marble surface of the base. One of them, a young man, sits on a former cannonball turned decoration, one of several that frame the pedestal of the statue. This, for me, prompts a connection to another young man and cannonball.

Stamatis Voulgaris (1774–1842) was the first urban planner of liberated Greece.[1] A native of Corfu, urban planning came to Voulgaris by way of chance. In 1799, during the Russian–Turkish siege of Corfu, Voulgaris defused a cannonball, which had landed nearby. In so doing, he saved both the San Giacomo theatre (which is now Corfu City Hall) and a French military detachment, which so happened to be present. Voulgaris was honored with a position in the French guard. When the guard returned to France, Voulgaris joined them. There, he advanced to become an officer, and later went on to study urban planning in Paris. Eventually, he returned to Greece during the revolution and became the first planner for a new nation under Kapodistrias, another native of Corfu, an island closer to the beating pulse of Northern Europe.

With outstretched arms, the first administrators of an aspiring nation-state aimed to create a protected solidarity for a monolingual collective of Greek peoples; they planned open spaces for commingling and, eventually, commemoration; and they sought to offer domesticity to the dispossessed with the neighborhood of the Pronaia at the western base of the Palamidhi. Bringing French city design to a young Greece, Voulgaris was shouldered with a responsibility to address the challenge of self-regulation through place-regulation—a challenge with which every sincere political community must grapple.[2] From dealing with the olfactory and hygienic burdens of clogged sewers to expanding and paving streets to providing squares and parks with monuments to removing what had come to be seen as Ottoman embellishment, Voulgaris would take the first radical steps in the redesign of Nafplion in the image of Northern European cities.[3]

I glance back at the Land Gate and scan the line of rough masonry up to the Grimani Bastion. Rusticated ashlar, surmounted by a line of smoothly finished stone—this style dates to the early eighteenth century. In the middle of the smoothed line stands the winged Lion of St Mark. Positioned along the top of the wall, former artillery platforms are softened by weeds. Right and higher is the Castel del Toro, named for its battered, circular tower. My eyes pause on the abandoned Arvanitia Xenia hotel. Situated in the midst of a castle turned decorative gardens turned overgrown thicket, this building embodies what Clement Greenberg once roughly glossed as "functional geometric rigor and the eschewing of decoration or ornament."[4] Simple white lines stand out against a recessed, red-orange ground amplifying the repeating pattern of rectilinear

---

1 Kyriazis (1976).
2 This is what Sloterdijk has described as the "double imperative of self-determination and place-determination" (2013, 150).
3 See Hastaoglou-Martinidis (1995); for the redesign of Argos, see Segment 13.
4 1980.

balconies, trelliswork, and the overall form. The structure of the Xenia, as envisioned by Aris Konstantinidis, the architect of the Xenia hotels under the Hellenic Tourist Organization, "must be in harmony with nature, so that it does not appear like a strange and incongruous creation but as something that has always been part of that particular landscape."[5] Harmonious now, not in form but in ruin, the Xenia, built under the Junta, constitutes a rectilinear concrete exception to the overall physiognomy of Nafplion.[6] Nonetheless, its situation speaks to how old forms dictate the loci for new accretions.

Beyond the Castel del Toro, to the west, high stone walls meet with partly cloudy skies. In a succession of bastions raised upon the limestone outcrops of Acronafplion and, much later, rebuilt upon ancient polygonal walls, Nafplion was defined by its enveloping form, both geologic and contrived.[7] The earliest fortification, known as the Castle of the Greeks, was erected at the western end of Acronafplion, perhaps in the eleventh century. Along the heights of the headland, subsequent enclosures move east—the Castle of the Franks, followed by

The Land Gate in Nafplion.

5 1966.
6 See Witmore (2017).
7 Schaefer (1961). This distinction does not imply a radical divide between stone outcrops and stonewalls, but only a difference in their realization.

Castle del Toro. The sea walls and the land wall were completed by the end of the fifteenth century. The Grimani, Dolfini, and Mocenigo bastions (the latter two were located off the port), as well as the Palamidhi Fortress, followed with the second Venetian occupation (1686–1715). Where walls were not built, they were apparently grown. Supposedly introduced by the Venetians into Greece as a green-barbed barrier,[8] prickly pear continues to flourish along the south and western portion of Acronafplion.

What was effectively another ship in a seafaring empire at home on the water under early Venetian overlords, Nafplion would provide a protective envelope for a succession of Ottoman then Venetian then Ottoman captors. Its insularity is clearly broadcast in Comocio's view of the town from 1571, which is readily available as a print in the many of the town shops. Whether or not this view was based on an earlier version, it manifests the outward expression of unassailable security. One may note how the high walls and imposing towers even rival the surrounding hills in scale. While this view panders to an ideal

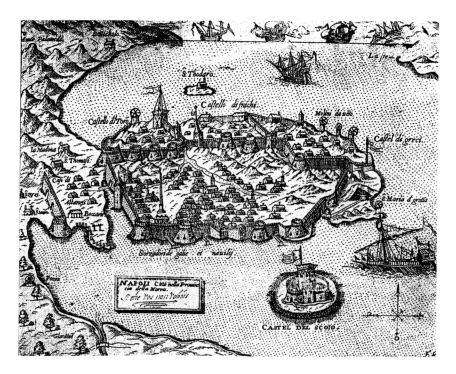

Comocio's view of Nafplion, 1571.

8 Naval Intelligence Division (1944, 110).

aimed at upholding the imperial centers, a circle of security within a sea of increasing turmoil, the psychological impact of these walls and towers should not be underestimated. Indeed, these strong protective walls would prove to be the most important attribute for the first capital. Here, they lend themselves to a paradox in a town which harbors them—protected, cosmopolitan insularity.

Independence and the protracted formation of a nation-state permits the powers over Nafplion to eventually break with the one-upmanship of building better castles. Still, the zones of protection and comfort would not quickly shift from being situated behind stout walls to national borders.[9] Even as it was opening up as a revolutionary center, even as it was foisted zealously into the exhibition space of a capital city, albeit a short-lived situation (from 1829 to 1834), and later in the wake of these unfulfilled grandiose aspirations, so long as the fortifications persisted Nafpliots could keep to them, and to an identity based on the solidarity that comes with living behind shared walls. If anyone doubts this, simply consider the Nafplion uprising against the monarchy in 1862, known as the "Naupliaca." Besieged for nearly two months, the town held out against royalist government forces.

From the western corner of the Grimani Bastion to the edge of the recon-structed wall of the Land Gate runs the weed-ridden profile of the razed ram-part. Four years after the Naupliaca, the town would begin to relinquish these protective walls.[10] What had defined Greek communities on this plain for millennia—a protective envelope of shared walls—at long last would come to an end. Beginning with the northern Venetian seawalls, followed by the Moce-nigo and Dolfini bastions, and finally the Land Gate, more than 2 kilometers of high, thick stone walls, which in offering protection and in controlling move-ment extended its independence and self-determination, were transformed into quarries for fill. Beneath my feet, the moat, which ran from the base of the Grimani Bastion to the port, was filled. The area between here and the old train station was leveled. The land was expanded by the quay and around the neighborhood of Gialos. Today, Amalias, Koletti, and Ypsilanti streets trace the line of the fifteenth-century Venetian seawall, which was demolished between 1866 and 1868.[11] Where defenders were once kept at bay, open park spaces now delimit the Old Town from the new. Where conspicuous security once reined, areas of movement—oeuvres of unobstructed visibility—are prevalent.

Sigi is standing on the bridge, a reconstituted walkway over a reconstituted por-tion of the old moat, by the Land Gate. After a warm exchange of greetings, we

---

9 See Segment 13.

10 The northern sea walls were torn down between 1866 and 1868, the Land Gate in 1897.

11 A portion of this seawall was exposed in 2014 during renovations associated with repaving the streets.

turn and pass over the smooth limestone threshold, under the archway of rusticated ashlar, under the empty recess where once sat an inscription commemorating Morosini's liberation of the city, and under the reset, headless lion.[12] Our meeting here is a gesture to an erstwhile structuring of space and experience. Timed with the opening and closing of the gates, this is where all land traffic formerly entered Nafplion. Just inside the gate, we step over a thin, linear patch of smooth, cobbled road surface with wheel ruts—a memory of the countless boots, hooves, and carts that passed. Lion, threshold, and this patch of cobbles are among the few authentic remains in an otherwise fully reconstructed gateway, within partially reconstructed walls; a new object offering a new past.[13]

We move around puddles of water in the path beyond the gate and weave a course between the parked cars. Looking across the street towards the Armansperg House, I note the juxtaposition of the celebrated Venetian turned Neoclassical building and the grey concrete shell across Plapouta Street. Its windows are papered over with posters for ANTARSYA. An acronym, Sigi interjects, meaning "mutiny," it refers to a new political movement. She gestures towards the line of vacant shops, which continue to bracket the start of Papanikolaou Street.

As we cross Andreas Syggros, a street named after the Greek banker who completed the Corinthian Canal, Sigi recalls a taverna and the tourist police shop. Both buildings are now vacant (the one on the right will later become a car rental agency). We proceed along Papanikolaou, a street barely wide enough for two small cars to pass. Water drips from eaves and splatters from gutters onto the asphalt surface, remnants of the rainstorm that passed over Nafplion for a couple of hours this morning. Clouds gather over the mountains of Achaea and Arcadia and move southeast over the Argive plain—this pattern had been repeated over the last few days.

Sigi has not walked this street in years—she normally follows a direct path from the car park by the port to her shop on Vasileos Konstantinou. Walking along a street now vacated of shops prompts more recollection. A former bakery. A tattoo studio, opened and closed. An old shoe shop turned ice cream parlor. Sigi points to the taverna on Moudzouridou, a favorite among locals (my son Liam took his first bite of food there during a dinner with Sigi and

---

12 See Sturgess (2014, 102–09). Sturgess misinterprets the form of this gate on the basis of the famous watercolor by Karl W. Von Heideck. The second arch seen in the image is as an entrance to the internal vaults of the wall.

13 The gate is demolished in 1897. Its remains are excavated in 1973–74. A new gate is constructed in the 1990s. A modernist hotel is built in the middle of a Venetian castle; a modernist ruin becomes an eyesore and an eyesore becomes heritage. Such fluctuations are common within Nafplion.

Yorgos). Sigi comments on how so many of the buildings are becoming *pensions*. We pass by the Hotel Dias on the right—a commemorative plaque recalling its previous state as the home of Dimitrios Ypsilantis (1794–1832), the revolutionary leader, will later be added to the front of this building. On the left, a nutritionist is followed by law offices. A veterinarian had moved in, but now they have left. Beyond are more waxed windows with signs: *ENOIKIAZETAI*—shops for rent.

Our attention passes over the peeling paint, the crumbling plaster, exposed brick, bare shelves, faded signs, boarded-over windows, and patches of graffiti. Does the Old Town no longer provide a zone of comfort for its residents? Has it been abandoned, as locals will tell you, to tourists and foreigners? When Sigi first arrived in Nafplion, there were two thousand residents in the Old Town. Now there are three hundred to two hundred and fifty permanent residents, and this number continues to fall. Most of the former residents or tenants have moved to the New Town in the Pronoia.

We pass by a man twirling *komboloi*. Otherwise idle mopeds, parked cars, and the occasional cat populate the street. On our right we walk by the roofless shell of what was, it is supposed, the former Venetian Scuole turned quarters for the Ministry of Education turned Hellenic School turned derelict edifice. Amid patches of plaster, an exposed core of rubble masonry, interspersed with hewn blocks of stone, brick, and tile, reveals itself. Set back into this stone wall, square-cut beams of wood, joined by a sloping scarf joint, run the full length of the building. It forms a continuous header for the lower doors and windows; these are boarded over. Midway up the wall, an ornate arm clasping old electrical insulators, ceramic, or perhaps porcelain, marks the path of wiring—a small memory of a time when the town desired nothing more than to be festooned with wires.[14] The upper windows show through to cloud-filled skies—photographs from the 1970s and 1980s capture this L-shaped building with an intact tile roof.

We turn right on Gennadiou. Here the asphalt network that links Nafplion to the rest of Greece in an unbroken surface surrenders to new stone pavements. We pass between a pair of French tourists. They seem transfixed by the silhouette of a second-floor chimney set on stone corbels surmounted by a segmental arch. Well on its way to ruination, two weeks shy of a year from now a section of the upper floors of the old Venetian building will collapse in a thunderous maelstrom of rafters, laths, plaster, mortar, and masonry. A cloud of dust will descend upon a wonderstruck wedding party in Agios Georgios Square—an embarrassment to its owner, the Diocese of the Argolid. This

---

14 Now deemed unsightly, electrical and phone lines are buried under streets.

The former Venetian Scuole.

neglected building interrupts with commotion and dust, thereby interjecting a very different sense of the past.

The street veers left at the square. As we follow its course, Sigi says nothing of the church of Agios Georgios. Instead, she directs my attention to the line of crumbling buildings across the square, the bottom floors of which are now occupied by law offices. Sigi points to the Neoclassical house, the third from the left. Here, between early November 1834 and late March 1835, as Sigi surmises, lived Bettina von Savigny (1805–35), daughter of a well-known German law professor, wife of Constanine Schinas, an official under Otto. Sigi has been reading her collection of letters, drawn from lengthy correspondence with her parents in Berlin.[15] The letters, notable for Savigny's powers of observation, contain a rare wealth of detail relating to the demeanor, dress,

15 Steffen (2002).

Agios Georgios Square.

and physiognomy of residents, to conversations and their settings, to daily routines, the land, travel, and the living conditions of Nafplion during the last months of Otto's residence.

Rainwater from an adjacent roof has peeled back the plaster, revealing the rubble- and mud-filled stick-work of the upper-story walls. Pale blue shutters are closed everywhere but on a door to a second-floor balcony. Sigi mentions how Savigny described events in the square and at the church of Agios Georgios, perhaps observing them from this very balcony, which is more ornate than its first-floor counterpart.

Our attention shifts from these rust-laden balustrades and the crumbling house façade to the square. Even though it is completely devoid of people, Sigi notes how the square is about gathering and seeing. Whether on Sunday or during celebrations, weddings, or funerals, everyone sees everyone else. Every- one sees to being seen by everyone else. The public edifice of Agios Georgios, with its narthex and ornate tower, is more than a backdrop to such events; it takes in each passer-by, and, combined with the open square, it provided a space for the confluence of different overarching powers and religion. The seat for the Bishop of Argos and Nafplion, it was here that Prince Otto was received by bishops, clergy, and dignitaries in 1833—his throne, stripped of all insignia, is still present inside the church. It was here that funerals for key fig- ures in the early state were held—Bishop Germanos of Patras, Kapodistrias, and Ypsilantis. It was here that Morosini was received after his conquest of the city in 1686. Its proximity to the Land Gate ensured church and square as the first expression of this connection to be encountered by those who entered the town. Situated at an angle to the square and surrounding buildings, the church recalls a larger loyalty, not to the orientation of the old town plan, but to the Kaaba in Mecca.[16]

16 From Nafplion, the Kaaba in Mecca bears 132° 44 (see Pantazis and Lambrou 2009). Agios Georgios is oriented at an angle of 133°. Architectural accretions have obscured its original form

We walk by the wide display windows of a vacant concrete building on the corner of Plapouta Street. A household supply and hardware store had occupied this venue ever since Sigi arrived in Nafplion thirty years ago. This area, she remembers, was very alive at that time. We turn left onto Plapouta Street. Sigi shares a litany of former shops—a butcher, a grocer, a barbershop, a coffee roaster's, a tobacco/cigarette emporium, an auto-parts store. With the new crisis everything has been emptied out. Whether or not a cause connects with an economic crisis at the forefront of everyone's consciousness, there are few shops left. Here, new pavements are sprinkled with debris from crumbling façades. Does maintenance only become visible when it is lacking? How long can this old dry-goods store, with its window display containing spindles of green thread, buttons, and zippers, hold out?

We pause at the end of the street. The sound of swifts nesting in the buildings above mixes with music from a bar on the corner of Vasileos Konstantinou. In an effort to stem the exodus of residents, a law passed in 1985 to keep bars separate from houses along certain streets contained a loophole for milk shops. Bars, on the books as milk shops, continued to open along forbidden thoroughfares. Now, residents joke that the Old Town has the highest concentration of *galaktopoleia* in Greece.

We turn left, avoid Staikopoulou with its swirl of tourists, and continue towards Agios Spyridon Square. Enhanced by the pastels of the buildings, the radiance of the morning light dims in the thin space between buildings, made thinner by an extruding upper story, at the end of Anggelou Terzaki. The street gains its name from Angelos Terzakis (1907–79), a novelist, playwright, and journalist, who lived on this street, at No. 20, till the age of nine. On the left, above a side alley hangs a sign for Pension Isabo. A work of historical fiction set in the thirteenth-century Peloponnesus, *Princess Isabeau* is considered one of Terzakis's finest novels.[17] It chronicles, in the words of the author himself, "the amazing adventures of Nikiphóros Sgourós from Anápli, how he was forced to flee his fatherland, how he struggled with his fate on land and sea, and how he raised war against a woman."[18] That woman was Isabeau, none other than Isabelle de Villehardouin, daughter of Guilluame II de Villehardouin. "The Mistress of the Morea!" exclaims Sigi.[19] Published in 1945, themes of

---

as a square with four pillars surmounted by a central dome, attended by four corner domes linked by hypostyle halls. Together, this architectural style combined with its orientation suggest that this seat of the Bishop of Argos and Nafplion was originally built as a mosque in the sixteenth or seventeenth century (see Gregory 1980, 55–56; also Sturgess 2014, 180–85).

17 See Proussis (1966).

18 Terzakis (1945), introductory note. Also see Dova (2014).

19 From the *Chronicle of the Morea*, line 8480.

foreign occupation and estranged "villeins,"[20] of wasteful overlords and depressed peoples, resonated with the recent occupation of Greece by the Italians and Germans. Sigi, herself undertaking research into the fascinating history of the Catalans in Greece, suggests that they resonate still—a subtle repetition of history. Everyone worries over hard times, now and coming.

Anggelou Terzaki ends below a terraced garden and in a hard right. Our path follows a sloped pavement of marble followed by a series of steps, set at a right angle to the square. Packed with cars, Sigi points towards the bronze bust of Terzakis. Obscured by the thick trunk of a cedar and a thicket of potted plants, hemmed in by a Renault wagon and a Citroen C3, Terzakis's bronzen image sits upon a square plinth in a small plot at the center of Aghios Spyridon Square. He looks away from us, to the southwest. Avoiding passing cars, we head in the direction of his gaze.

We are both drawn to the old Ottoman fountain just beyond the edge of the square, beyond the corner of Agios Spyridon, on the left. A recessed niche set in a limestone arch, the fountain consists of three low decorative stone panels, the central one with a hole for a waterspout, two pigeon-holes, and a central plaque with a dedication in raised script placed at eyelevel. A trough below holds memories of a time when the town was shared with horses and mules, donkeys and camels. The Ottoman inscription,[21] illegible to us, records its benefactor, Mahmud Agha, who was associated with the Bektashis dervish order and the ninth detachment of the Janissary forces. He had the horse fountain built in the year 1147 (1734–35), one of several erected along the line of the Turkish aqueduct.[22] A floodlight is affixed to its keystone.

The area of the street before us is marked as the scene of a crime. A glass plate set into the wall by the door to the Church of Agios Spyridon covers the spot where the bullet fired in the assassination of Kapodistrias lodged on October 9, 1831. A marble plaque set above the glass-covered bullet hole records this event in Greek and dates it by the Julian Calendar—September 27, 1831.

Across the street runs a weed-ridden, graffito-covered, ruined wall.[23] Above, set back into the hill, rises a dome. Its wooden door is chained shut. Along the top of the wall runs a projecting curve, remnants of an erstwhile vault. The upper section, behind the dome, forms a patio for the Hotel Byron. A former

20 Here, I am following Dova in translating Terzakis's term *Romiós* as *vilánoi*, villeins (see Dova 2014).
21 This inscription employs mostly Arabic words, as most Ottoman inscriptions do, but it uses Turkish syntax with some Turkish vocabulary.
22 Gregory (1980, 43–46).
23 The scratched ornament plaster is a feature of Ottoman Era buildings.

Ruined Turkish bath on Kapodistriou Street (Yorgos Agathos).

Turkish bath, it was one of two present at the beginning of the nineteenth century.[24] No plaque records the date of its abandonment. No plaque records its post-Ottoman history.

There are significant buildings where one is prodded to situate history, I comment to Sigi. Reinforced in monuments and street names, these are associations to principal residents. Sigi sees this history, but she, like so many others who have lived and worked here, has not participated in it. To posterity passes the exception. To oblivion passes the ordinary.

With this provocation, Sigi points to the house at 19 Kapodistriou. Austen Kark, a journalist who rose to Managing Director of the BBC World Service, and Nina Bawden, author of *Carrie's War* (1973) and *Circles of Deceit* (1987) lived in the upper flat. A plaque states that the house was restored in 1986. The adventure of restoring the house, which included the removal of the entire roof due to the chance discovery of a live grenade, was detailed in Kark's book *Attic in Greece* (1994). Friends of Yorgos and Sigi since the year of the restoration's completion, Kark was killed in the Potters Bar rail crash in England in 2002, and Bawden will pass away less than three months from now.

We turn right and walk down the stairs. At the bottom, bougainvillea falls from a trellis above to the pavement, releasing water onto pedestrians in street. Crossing over Staikopoulou, Sigi points to the tourist shop on the corner. Hidden behind a colonnade of rolling display stands, each fluted by a bewildering array of necklaces and bracelets, draped over regularly spaced hooks, a tourist shop is separated by little more than a green awning from two

24 Gell (1810, 90) describes one of the Turkish baths prior to the Greek War of Independence.

dilapidated and nearly roofless upper stories. The deteriorating upper floors would seem to bear witness, once again, to the pervasive transformation of the town emptying of permanent residents. Sigi mentions that owners only maintain the levels of the buildings where rents are paid. In some cases, different floors have different owners. The leaking roof can be suffered only so long—this building will be renovated in the coming year.

We continue through the cross alley to Vasileos Konstantinou. As we pass former workshops and storage rooms, Sigi looks ahead at the now vacant upper floors of the building on the corner of the main thoroughfare. An old couple lived there till recently. We return, again, to the topic of an exodus. Many long-time residents are moving out. Why? Because, according to Sigi, the buildings of the Old Town are uncomfortable. They require too much effort to renovate; there are too many restrictions; the costs are exorbitant. The streets are loud late into the night. Better living conditions are to be found in the New Town. Better heat in the winter. Better air conditioning in the summer. Less humidity. Less noise. No regulations. Parking.[25]

We turn right on Vasileos Konstantinou. When Sigi first came to Nafplion, this was a normal provincial street with shops, hardware stores, and bakeries providing services to the residents and surrounding population. As the shops vacated the Old Town and the hotels had fewer clients, Sigi and Yorgos relocated their jewelry business here to what had been an electrical shop catering to professional electricians. Their shop is part art studio, part workshop. Inside, display cases, containing elegant and simple necklaces, earrings, and rings, line the front of the shop. A worktable is situated at the rear. Yorgos greets us from the other side of the table. Under a bright lamp he finishes soldering a gold pearl to the apex of a cut through the middle of the fold in a half circle of textured silver sheeting. He hands the piece over to Sigi with instructions on setting it to a chain. He stands, throws his beige photography vest over a blue shirt, and we take to the street.[26]

Neither of us have a destination in mind. We simply begin to wander towards Constitution (Syntagma) Square. Yorgos calls our attention to petals of bougainvillea scattered upon the stone, accumulated in corners, and questions

---

25 Parking is a constant issue with the Old Town, and proximity to automobiles at home is of more importance than proximity during work. For a comparative situation in another port weighed by history, see Herzfeld (1991).

26 From Benjamin to Virilio, all the action for the collective is in the streets, but residing in the Old Town is fundamentally about interiors. Knowledge of interior spaces is a key distinction between tourists and residents. Domestic interiors are off-limits to nonresidents, unless vacated, or renovated as so many are. It is of interest that the pivot of this segment occurs inside when the rest of the segment is focused on exterior spaces, peering through windows into collapsed buildings; the degree to which the outside pierces the inside is a matter of ruination.

the rationale of a shopkeeper as she sweeps them away from a storefront. Lodged in the habitual, does she fail to see beauty? Approaching the edge of the square, he deplores the garlands of kitsch strung across a small kiosk. Its juxtaposition to the Trianon, a mosque turned cinema, elicits even more condemnation.

We avoid the children playing football. We avoid the cafés, which spill out into the shared space of the square. Pointing to a new hotel and taverna called the Xenon, I mention how this is the second hotel to go by such a name in the square. A branch of the old Xenon Hotel was located on the opposite side of the square, above the Kaphaneion Stadion and the old telegraph office, now the Odyssey bookshop. Schliemann and Dörpfeld stayed in the other branch on the quay while excavating Tiryns.

We cut an angle to the southwest across Constitution Square, past the National Bank—a harsh concrete contrast to its surroundings, with its Minoan columns and Mycenaean relieving triangle above the entrance.[27] Taking no notice of the bank or the monument to Kalliope Papalexopoulou (1809–99), a leader in the Naupliaca, or the Lion of St Mark, Yorgos points ahead to the building immediately left of the Archaeological Museum.[28] Oranges, apples, and bananas were once sold here. Now this corner shop caters to tourists.

We turn left towards the Vouleftiko, "Parliament," a former mosque turned venue for the first national assembly in Greece, then right onto Staikopoulou.[29] A generation ago, there were at least ten grocery stores in Nafplion; now there are none. A decade ago, there were five bakeries; the last recently closed. Yorgos recalls a time when there were only ten to fifteen cars in all of Nafplion, a time when there was one-fifth of the tourist shops, a less commercialized time, a more romantic time.

We pass the Old Tavern. Simple wooden tables, covered in a checkerboard cloth, and chairs, covered by seat cushions, line the left side of the street. *Ouzo-mezedes*, *poikilies*, *choirini*, *moscharisia*—items are written in caulk on wooden boards by the doors. Pleasantries are exchanged with the proprietor.

Near the end of the pedestrian section of the street, Yorgos gestures towards a jewelry shop on the corner to the left. This too was once a grocery store

---

27 Carved out under the Venetians at the center of a town, like the morning rains, names wash across this space of peripatetic convergence: Piazza dei Armi (Square of Weapons) under the Venetians; Plateia Platanos (Square of the Plane Trees) under the Ottomans and when Nafplion acted as the first capital; Plateia Loudoviko (Louis Square) in honor of the king of Bavaria, the father of Otto. It gained its current name after the September 3 revolution of 1843.

28 See Segment 16.

29 On the conservation and re-use of the adjacent Koran school as the museum *apotheke*, see Mavroeidi (2011).

owned by an old couple. The wife had learned during World War II to mix herbs into a medicine for the treatment of burns. Over the years she had developed an excellent reputation—her two children even became pharmacists.

We turn left here, pass Spetson, and continue up the stairs. Yorgos takes us to the back streets to escape the crowds—it is against the law to have shops to the south of Staikopoulou. Psaromachalas—this was once the neighborhood of fishermen. Here, the town steps up the northern slope of Acronafplion in a series of terraces. Here, the course of streets is determined more by old-to-ancient walls, erratic protrusions of bedrock, and steep gradients than by a regular grid laid down on a contrived level surface reclaimed with the rubble of the past. Here, the houses are small in stature, simple in form.

Yorgos pauses abruptly by a terracotta flowerpot. With his right boot, he stamps down dozens of wooden skewers turned up in the soil—only last week he had found a tomcat with such a stake through its paw.

We walk up the stairs to Zygomala Street. Yorgos draws my attention to a former house turned pension on the corner, which was completely renovated in 2008. Painted red with green shutters and white trim, he likens the new colors to "Sylvester Stallone's mother," as he puts it. "A 70-year-old woman who plays 19 by wearing too much of the wrong makeup. She once had a warm, orange-yellow patina." He points across the street, to the partial façade of a former house by an ancient polygonal wall at 26 Zygomala Street. Yorgos states his preference for fading patinas, for worn plaster surfaces unmolested by renovation.[30] Though all renovations follow a prescribed palette of colors maintained by the 25th Ephorate of Byzantine Antiquities, acrylic-based paints replace pigments of earth on lime plaster.[31] They are more synthetic than natural, more chemical than ochre, more artificial than warm in tone.

Up Zygomala, past the Hotel Leto, we walk to the confluence of three stairways below the Sagredo Gate. To the right, a great stone staircase, broken by a hard turn into two long flights, leads up the steep slope to a high terrace before a gate cut through the polygonal masonry of ancient walls. Built for the benefit of soldiers, the gate once provided direct access to Acronafplion. A plaque positioned in the pediment above the entrance commemorates its construction in 1713 under Augustino Sagredo. Tagged with graffiti, the ironclad doors of the Sagredo Gate are now permanently shut. Littered with old beer cans, wine bottles, plastic bags, used condoms, and excrement—feline and human—the high terrace is now clandestine space. Reclaimed by weeds, the upper reaches of old staircase have been reduced to a thin footpath.

---

30 For a balanced engagement with the aesthetics of patina, see Dawdy (2016).
31 For a study of the surfaces of the Greek National Bank, see Moropoulou et.al. (2005).

We do not take the old staircase. Instead, we continue to the left. Before another stairway, which leads up Zygomala Street, four pilasters extrude from the walls, forming a square. Two are less than half present. One holds a rusted hook, a component of a door hinge. A gate was once positioned here at the base of the stairs, which we climb.

At the top, a low terrace wall offers an unobstructed, elevated view of the Old Town. On this path, our perspective shifts to a Nafplion of irregular tiled angles and corniced transitions into vertical pastel surfaces, interspersed with windows, broken by new terracotta rooflines. Our attention passes over a skyline studded with antennas, chimneys, water heaters, air conditioners, and heating units. Across this scene dance shadow and sunlight. Distant elements and contrasts are sharp—the air is clear in the wake of the morning rainstorm. "There is a lot of beauty here," Yorgos declares. He speaks of the former head of the Ephorate who fought to maintain the look of the town by bringing the Old Town under the control of the archaeological service. Despite threats to poison her, she championed a style and aesthetic consistent with the town's past. Today Evangelia Protonotariou-Deilaki is celebrated.

The two-stroke engine of a scooter followed by a car horn is met by a salvo of barking dogs. Yorgos beckons me down a stairway to Konstantinoupoleos. A song by Elias Vrettos saturates the space of our descent. He points to the play of shadow over stone and auburn-stained plaster. Variations in light draw out the textures of surfaces, subtle distinctions of tone, differences in patina.

Yorgos stops us on the bottom step. With camera in hand, he wanders these back streets below Acronafplion at least twice a month. In the course of these seemingly nonchalant wanderings, he is repeatedly drawn to this spot.[32] Lured in by the interplay of reticulated surfaces, exposed brickwork, and aged buildings, broken by well-tended plants and fresh, whitewashed surfaces, here he waits with his camera. If the right conditions are present, he will take multiple shots with a wide-angle lens in a sequence from left to right. He collates these images into a panorama—a consistent depth of field is maintained across a wide swath of street and sky. More often than not he returns empty-handed.

"Is it about the engagement?" I query. "It is as much about the documentation as the document," comes his reply.

We wander up a few stairs into a small forecourt of the church of Agia Sophia, perhaps the oldest extant building in the Old Town, and down the narrow side alley on the right. At the apse of the church, Yorgos pauses on a rare cobbled surface. Adjacent is the whitewashed terrace wall of an overgrown garden in a reclaimed

---

32 Though he might embrace the image of the "flaneur," meandering without a destination, this place lures him in with feeling towards a purpose.

Konstantinoupoleos Street (Yorgos Agathos).

ruin (two rubble-sealed doorways reveal another past). He seeks out unrestored surfaces, worn wooden doors, and peeling paint. Ensnared by relationships of figure/
ground, many of his photos reveal an eye for contrasts—plants growing green from
fragile cracks in walls, for distinctions between smooth and mottled surfaces,
between whitewash and mildew, between exposed stone and solid plaster. For
Yorgos, the camera becomes a mode of engagement with marvelous imperfection—
the rot at the base of exposed wooden shutters, the material fatigue that results
from the unrelenting work of aquatic runnels.[33] It would be a mistake to reduce
these engagements to fetish, to a delight in destruction, to so-called "ruin porn." No,
what Yorgos seeks to capture are indications of change. He aims to preserve wear,
to arrest moments of metamorphosis.[34] For Yorgos, the photograph gives one
a sense of time.

As we turn the corner, he calls out the masking of changes and metamorphoses in bright pastels, the covering of aged patinas. Akin to resetting the
clock, this sanitizes change, which is itself a pervasive condition of Nafplion. He
points to the *sahnisi* above. Protruding from upper stories, these wooden
window boxes—effectively enclosed balconies—were a pervasive feature of the
town prior to reconstruction under Kapodistrias. Though they are a feature of
Byzantine architecture, such *sahnisi* came to be seen as Ottoman.[35] Under the

33 Shanks (2012).
34 See Pétursdóttir and Olsen (2014) and comments for critical discussion.
35 This contrast of Nafplion as a "Turkish town" is expressed by Nicholas Dragoumis in 1828:
    according to Dragoumis, "Nauplio was totally a Turkish city with narrow, uneven and muddy
    roads, the houses were made of wood, with many doors, ready to fall apart and with no sym-
    metry ... but the way that people lived, as for the rest of the Greeks, was Asiatic. By the word

Wall near the church of Agia Sophia (Yorgos Agathos).

ruse of hygiene, *sahnisi*, as encouraged by Voulgaris himself, were removed in order to facilitate the circulation of air inside the home.[36]

Striations of white interlace through the purple marble of our steps. At the bottom of the stairs we turn right on Kapodistriou Street. Here, new pavements are being emplaced. Textured squares, of different sizes, and rectilinear blocks with raised ripples, from the quarries of Karnezeika, near Iria,[37] and others in Laconia, replace the smooth purple and tan marbles; the old, worn slabs were slippery in the wake of rainstorms. The entire lower neighborhood of Gialos has had the asphalt surfaces removed to make way for these new pavements. And yet, Yorgos expresses a predilection for the older surfaces. We step over a gap in the pavement, where the concrete foundation

'Asiatic' I don't mean luxurious, because wherever there is no food there cannot be any kind of luxury, but—apart from the *foustanella* [the traditional garment] that looked Greek, everything else seemed to be just like in Turkey. In the workshops the salesmen were seating on the floor with their legs crossed sucking sadly the end of their smoking pipes and waiting in vain for the customers to show. They sold flintstones, needles, thread, Sulphur stones, and things insignificant and low. There were also other workshops, general stores, tailor's stores and kafeneia, valuable and various that contained necessary goods and lots of students" (quoted in Dorovinis 1985; translation provided by Zoe Zgouleta).

36 See Dorovinis (1985, 291, 295), Koumaridis (2006, 217), Tombros (2011).

37 See Segment 20.

awaits its new stone. Here we experience the difference in walking on smooth, flat ground and pock-marked surfaces. This demands our attention. Walkers of these streets, I interject, had not always experienced such luxuries. "Narrow, uneven and muddy" is how Nicholas Dragoumis, a young politician working under Kapodistrias, described the streets of Nafplion in 1828.[38]

As we approach 19 Kapodistriou, Yorgos's demeanor darkens. For him, many transformations have further alienated residents, by severing the connection between those who dwell and the place they dwell. In the wake of such estrangement, he worries that those who work here, rather than dwell here, have forgotten how to care for the place, how to treat the place with respect. But this observation veils a deeper realization: in attempting to capitalize on what is unique about Nafplion, Nafpliots are obscuring it. Pointing ahead to the ruined Turkish bath, he concedes that Nafpliots embrace a heritage aligned more with history and tourism than with life. Elegant architectures whose interiors crumble are regarded as the embodiments of national history, ones peppered with memorialized and, in many cases, monumentalized personalities who give their names to the streets.[39] We walk along Kapodistriou. This heritage, shared by all Greeks, is made to infuse this street with a past prestige. This experience is marketed. We seek to capitalize on what Nafplion has been, which is no doubt important, rather than what it is becoming and what it may yet become, which rest assured is also important.

Paradoxically the narrowed bandwidth of historical interest has inhibited residents from living with what becomes of the past in a different way—that is, as a celebration of new possibilities in light of their own self-definition. Such interests have contributed to the demise of the Old Town as a town in any traditional sense. "Few people," Yorgos says, "live here anymore. Passing in and out, most simply move through. We have to tip the scales so its few residents feel relief rather than burden."[40]

He points out a building restored in 1995 by the same person who undertook the restoration of the Kark/Bawden house. He points to the recently renovated façade of the Church of Agios Spyridon. "Restoration should be about caring for the building, and not 'what is in it for me.'" I wonder whether in some walls he sees the realization of that old dream unique to fables and folktales—income without effort, fortunes unearned through the evasion of work.

---

38 See footnote 30.

39 On the street names of Nafplion, see Chronopoúlou et al. (1994).

40 While it is tempting to situate the current situation as wholly unique—certainly it is in many ways—the movement from a space of burdens to reliefs probably occurred with the shift of residents from the enclosures on Acronafplion to the area of Psaromachalas, and later, the lower portions of the Old Town.

Agios Spyridon Square (Yorgos Agathos).

We step over the grate that marks the end of the new stone pavements. Asphalt in the square of bronzen Terzakis is no longer wet from the morning rains. Yorgos beckons me at a faster pace to the Turkish fountain in the square. An arch of well-carved stone frames a recessed wall with decorative panel, a trefoil pigeon-hole, and an inscription. He puts his hand on a standard water tap. Its presence in the fountain, for Yorgos, denotes disrespect. He gestures to the placement of garbage cans, to the presence of graffiti across stone walls. These things are indicative of negligence. "The past should be kept alive with the highest standards."

We weave our way back to the jewelry shop. Artisans, who have chosen not to live here—their house is in the village of Kiveri—they nonetheless feel the presence of those who lived here in the past and feel privileged to work in the Old Town. Both Sigi and Yorgos are sensitive to change, and seek to make sense of that to which they have borne witness. Sigi forges connections amid interruptions, crafts continuities amid change. She speaks history. Yorgos attempts to gain a sense of time by capturing and caring for metamorphosis and transformation. For those who experience them, these changes are seen as accelerated, excessive, unstable, and devoid of a deeper meaning. Have we learned how to look at this town? How to understand its transformations?

Nafplion, a town whose name is derived from the famed "sailor of ships," was itself once embraced by the sea. Now much of it is kept at bay by a parking lot. A port, Nafplion continues to do as it has always done—open itself towards the outside; only rather than to Venice, Constantinople, Northern Europe, or the rest of a new Greece, it opens itself towards all directions and all distances as a destination for tourists; and when they are found wanting, to

Athens as a weekend retreat.[41] Yet, while it has opened itself up repeatedly to catering to distance, it also cultivated a self-image of solidarity, which it could always fall back on. This cosmopolitan insularity was its paradox, one familiar to many walled ports. Clinging to points of reference outside of itself while holding to a shared self-image. Now, the whole becomes a large series of inns, tourist shops in the midst of an Old Town, which is ceasing to fulfill the basic functions of what constitutes a town, or at least one, which no longer provides a natal space for its decreasing resident population. Pampered space for tourism, west of the reconstituted Land Gate, the superfluous would appear to have won out over the necessary, at least for now.[42]

41 In some sense, modern transportation systems and new media have now rendered all towns as ports.
42 "The subjugation of the necessary by the superfluous" constitutes a general tendency of the "postmodern crystal palace" that is Europe (Sloterdijk 2013, 218). Another way to see this relates increasingly to the preeminence of an imagined future, rather than a cultivated past, as a guide.

Bibliography

Chronopoúlou, N., M. Vougioúka, and V. Megarídis. 1994. *Odonymiká tou Nafplíou: I Simasía ton Onomasión ton Odón kai Plateión tis Póleos tou Nafplíou.* Nafplion: Municipality of Nafplion.

Dawdy, S.L. 2016. *Patina: A profane archaeology.* Chicago, IL: University of Chicago Press.

Dorovinis, V.K. 1985. *O schediasmós tou Nafplíou katá tin Kapodistriakí período (1828 – 33). I eidikí períptosi kai ta genikótera provlímata»,* Anátypo apó ta Praktiká tou Diethnoús Symposíou Istorías NEOELLINIKI POLI. Athens: Society for the Study of Modern Hellenism.

Dova, S. 2014. History, identity, and the hero in Terzakis's princess Ysabeau. In S. Dova (ed.), *Historical poetics in nineteenth and twentieth century Greece: Essays in honor of Lily Macrakis.* Morrisville, NC: Lulu Publishing Services. 131–65.

Gell, W. 1810. *The itinerary of Greece.* London: Payne.

Greenberg, C. 1980. Modern and post-modern. *Quadrant* 24(3), 30–3.

Gregory, T.E. 1980. *Nauplion.* Athens: Lycabettus Press.

Hastaoglou-Martinidis, V. 1995. City form and national identity: Urban designs in nineteenth-century Greece. *Journal of Modern Greek Studies* 13(1), 99–123.

Herzfeld, M. 1991. *A place in history: Social and monumental time in a Cretan town.* Princeton, NJ: Princeton University Press.

Konstantinidis, A. 1966. Architecture of the Xenia hotels. *World Architecture* 3, 144–47.

Koumaridis, Y. 2006. Urban transformation and de-Ottomanization in Greece. *East Central Europe* 33(1–2), 213–41.

Kyriazis, P. 1976. Stamatis Voulgaris. O agonistís, o poleodómos, o ánthropos. In P. Kyriazis and M. Nikolanikos (eds.), *Syllogikó, Prótoi Éllines technikoí epistímones períodou apelefthérosis.* Athens: Technical Office of Greece. 156.

Mavroeidi, V. 2011. Conservation and re-use of an Ottoman monument. In D. Babalis (ed.), *Chronocity: Sensitive interventions in historic environment.* Cities, Design and Sustainability Series, 7. Firenze: Alinea. 46–8.

Moropoulou, A., N.P. Avdelidis, and E.T. Delegou. 2005. NDT and planning on historic buildings and complexes for the protection of cultural heritage. In R. van Grieken and K. Janssens (eds.), *Cultural heritage conservation and environmental impact assessment by non-destructive testing and micro-analysis.* London: A.A. Balkema. 67–76.

Naval Intelligence Division. 1944. *Greece, Volume I: Physical geography, history, administration and peoples.* Norwich: Jarrold and Sons.

Pantazis, G., and E. Lambrou. 2009. Investigating the orientation of eleven mosques in Greece. *Journal of Astronomical History and Heritage* 12(2), 159–66.

Pétursdóttir, Þ., and B. Olsen, 2014. Imaging modern decay: The aesthetics of ruin photography. *Journal of Contemporary Archaeology* 1(1), 7–56.

Proussis, C.M. 1966. The novels of Angelos Terzakis. *Daedalus* 95(4), 1021–45.

Schaefer, W. 1961. Neue Untersuchungen über die Baugeschichte Nauplias im Mittelalter. *Archäologischer Anzeiger* 76, 156–214.

Shanks, M. 2012. *The archaeological imagination.* Walnut Creek, CA: Left Coast.

Sloterdijk, P. 2013. *In the world interior of capital: For a philosophical theory of globalization.* Cambridge: Polity Press.

Steffen, R. (ed.). 2002. *Leben in Griechenland 1834–1835. Bettina Schinas, geb. von Savigny. Briefe und Berichte an ihre Eltern in Berlin.* Münster: Verlag Cay Lienau.

Sturgess, K. 2014. *Wandering in Nafplion: A lover's guide.* Nafplion: Peloponnesian Folklore Foundation.

Terzakis, A. 1945. *Prigkipessa Isabo (Princess Isabeau)*. Athens.

Tombros, N.F. 2011. Sto Metepanastatikó Náfplio tou Kapodístria. Argolid archival library, history and culture. Available at: http://argolikivivliothiki.gr/2011/09/16/στο-μετεπανασ τατικό-ναύπλιο-του-καπο/.

Witmore, C. 2017. Things are the grounds of all archaeology. In J.M. Blaising, J. Driessen, J.P. Legendre, and L. Olivier (eds.), *Clashes of times: The contemporary past as a challenge for archaeology*. Louvain: Louvain University Press.

16

THE ROAD TO EPIDAURUS

Frazer and Pausanias

James George Frazer and Pausanias, two roads taken, Periegesis Hellados *and Frazer's* Pausanias's Description of Greece, *a natal space,* The Golden Bough, *Frazer's fieldwork, the King of the Wood, expulsion and redemption, Christianity and polytheism, truth and falsity, the return*

Modern travelers generally drive to the great Epidaurian sanctuary of Aesculapius by the highroad from Nauplia ... Pausanias, however, went by the more northerly road from Argos.

Frazer *Pausanias's Description of Greece*

No traveler should set out in the footsteps of James George Frazer without some reckoning of the influence Pausanias held over him. For the ancient author's *Periegesis Hellados*, commonly translated as the *Description of Greece*, offered an enchanted portrayal of a polytheistic religion deeply implanted within its locality.[1]

---

1 See Elsner (1992), Hutton (2005, 7).

Frazer was a comparative anthropologist and a Classicist; both pursuits were amply served by every line that purportedly issued from Pausanias. As Frazer suggests, the ten books that comprised the *Periegesis* were written over a period of at least fourteen years, perhaps considerably more, up till 180 CE.[2] Within his time Pausanias is a rare witness to an Ancient Greece in its "mellow autumn," or perhaps its "Indian summer"; and Frazer delighted in its singular glimpses of land, cities, and monuments, and imbibed its vivid descriptions of divinely kindled genealogies, localized myths, and ritual practices.

A Fellow of Trinity College, Cambridge, Frazer is renowned as the author of *The Golden Bough*. Remembered for his contributions to evolutionary theory and comparative method, Frazer sought out the cross-cultural semblance of practices, magical and religious, from all times and all meridians. His juxtapositions of the sacrificial rites of Demeter and patterns of prohibition related to Athena and Virbius with Badaga ceremonies in Southern India, Aztec festivals in Central Mexico, and Catholic customs involving edible effigies of the Madonna slammed the door on the long obsession with elevating Classical cultures above others. His labors of comparison extracted their raw materials from books, reports, and letters. Thriving within the sedentary security of the study at the seat of speculative imagination, Frazer farmed out the nomadic necessities of empirical observation to others. As such, he fell out of favor with anthropology, which would venture vigorously in the direction of intensive fieldwork. Among ensuing generations of anthropologists he is worth contemplating for his egregious errors with the comparative method, for his unequivocal faith in evolution theory culminating in societies guided by objective science, as an object of ridicule for his lack of fieldwork.[3] Otherwise Frazer is rendered as a curiosity of an imperialist era best to be avoided.[4]

With such a reputation it is of no surprise that the disavowed, armchair anthropologist is little known outside Classical circles for his translation and commentary on Pausanias's *Periegesis*. While volumes have been written about the life of Frazer, the same cannot be said for the ancient author of the *Periegesis*. Pausanias is a name that does not appear in his work; rather, the author's name is first associated with the Antonine-era text by Stephanus of Byzantium, some 350 years after the *periegete*'s death.[5] A Roman traveler, a religious pilgrim, an antiquarian, a literary stylist, the story of this author has dropped out of his story, the longest example of ancient travel literature in existence.

---

2 The *Periegesis*, most scholars agree, was an achievement more than a decade in the making (see Frazer 1898 I, xv–xvii; Habicht 1985, 9–11; Hutton 2005, 17–18).
3 Ingold (2008, 82), Leach (1966, 560); for a critical discussion of this attitude, see Willerslev (2011, 505); also see Douglas (1978).
4 Ackerman (1987, 1).
5 Habicht (1985, 1).

Of the *Periegesis Hellados*, "Leading around Greece" more precisely captures its meaning. In the spring of 1890 Frazer joined numerous other scholars and travelers in being led along the high road from Nauplia to the Aesculapion of Epidaurus.[6] Frazer's journey was part of a much larger itinerary, designed to provide new details of archaeology, architecture, art, and scenery to accompany his translation of and commentary on the *Periegesis*.[7] Thus one errs to think of Frazer's career as being totally devoid of fieldwork, even if it is not of an exclusively anthropological variety. Still, in undertaking this journey, Frazer perhaps sought to fulfill an even deeper yearning. For it was in the sanctuary of Aesculapius that Pausanias in passing offers Frazer an important clue to the puzzle of *The Golden Bough*, the first edition of which was published that very June of 1890. There is a deep connection between the Epidaurian sanctuary of healing and the rites performed on the sylvan shores of Nemi, from whence the bough originates. This elevates the journey for Frazer to something approaching a pilgrimage, one worth taking.

Frazer's drive from Nauplia to Epidaurus was subsumed to that of Pausanias, or rather through Pausanias Frazer overwrote his own engagement.[8] Pausanias's mode of description consistently moved from the border of a district along the most direct route to its capital; in this case, Argos. From the marketplace he then progressed street-by-street, then gate-by-gate from the polis along the chief roads, as with radiating spokes, to the border and back.[9] Pausanias left Argos by way of the straight road to Epidaurus, and here, on the last of the principal thoroughfares of Argos, he crossed the border into the Epidauria. In his footsteps followed Frazer with an aim to provide a "faithful and idiomatic rendering" for a market audience of educated travelers.[10] During his travels, Frazer lends descriptive richness to what remained of what Pausanias described

---

6 Only one of Frazer's pocket diaries remains from his 1890 travels in Greece. It does not contain entries for Argos, Nauplia, or Epidaurus. In it he records setting out from Athens for the Peloponnese with a dragoman on April 21. Though he would not leave Greece until June 15, this diary ends at Olympia on May 9. While it is at times difficult to disentangle Frazer's travel notes from those of other accounts that together he collates, something of this journey survives, nonetheless, in his celebrated commentaries to Pausanias's *Periegesis Hellados* (*Description of Greece*). Retrospective remarks in the diary from his 1895 journey state that he visited both Nauplia and Epidaurus in 1890; see the Appendices in Volume V of Frazer's *Pausanias* for more details.

7 Published in six volumes in 1898.

8 See Ackerman (1987, 111–13, 127–29).

9 See Frazer (1898 I, xxiii–xxiv). Also Habicht (1985, 28–63); Hutton (2005, 83–126). As Frazer would himself note, Pausanias would resume and continue the itinerary "across the border when he comes to deal with the next province" (Vol. IV, 91). This, for Frazer, demonstrates careful design and editing on the part of Pausanias. Frazer chose the occasion for making this remark carefully, as Habicht points out, as it was in relation to the exact passage that gave his rival Wilamowitz so much angst in 1873, spurring his hatred for Pausanias.

10 Frazer (1898 I, vii).

and to the aspect of Greek lands in the late nineteenth century. Still, Pausanias was more than Frazer's guide as to where to go and what was worthy of observation, for the very genre of his commentary draws upon the *Periegesis*.

On the straight road from Argos, Pausanias commented on a pyramidal monument marking the first shield-assisted battle between the quarreling brothers Proetus and Acrisius, then Tiryns, the chambers of Proetus's daughters by the sea (at this point passing over Nauplia), and Medeia. He mentions nothing more until he arrives at the village of Lessa, the boundary between Argolis and Epidauria. A participant-observer, Pausanias aimed to sort (*apokrinai*) by discarding what he deemed to be trivial and gather (*legein*) what was worthy of mention (*axiologotata*) into his account (*logos*).[11] Writing as he moved on the ground—by autopsy—Pausanias gathered together the things that were most memorable and remarkable along his routes by land and sea.[12] *Logoi*, both spoken and written words, and *theoremata*, what is to be seen on the ground, are the two core features of his witnessing. A well-blended mixture of direct observation, discussions of inscriptions read, and storytelling on the basis of local reportage characterizes Pausanias's account.[13]

Frazer supplemented the *Periegesis* with assiduous descriptive detail acquired along the route. Routinely drawn by the lure of scenery and landscape setting, he possessed what could be glossed as a competent flair for adjectival embellishment, which had as much to do with the literary framing of the scene within its natural setting, as balancing out Pausanias's account.[14] Frazer was not always kind. The high road from Nauplia "runs through uninteresting scenery between low, barren hills of dull, monotonous aspect."[15] Of the area prior to entering the Kophino Valley, Frazer evidently shared the Classical archaeologist Friedrich Gottlieb Welcker's assessment: "a drearier tract of country is scarcely to be found in Peloponnese."[16]

11 3.11.1.
12 3.2.1.
13 A long litany of Classical scholars and enthusiasts have pondered the supposed selectivity of Pausanias; a nonetheless faithful witness with a predilection for the old and sacred, with what is held as an ambivalence for the countryside and the erstwhile Roman present (Alcock 1993, 27–29; Habicht 1985, 23; Snodgrass 1987, 77–79; for detailed discussion, see Hutton 2005, 81–82, 170). Those who would frame this as an issue of selectivity fail to appreciate what is ordinary and that which is less so. Pausanias's description was bound to the road, which disappears in its naively given status of being there, as it had always been.
14 Ackerman (1987, 111–12).
15 1898 III, 232; Baedeker's *Greece* states that a drive of four hours to Epidaurus, less back, could be secured for 25–35 dr. (1894, 324).
16 See Welcker (1865, 326–27). Perhaps this oft-repeated assessment would lend impetus to the eventual planting of cypresses along this particular stretch of the road.

From the head of the valley, the carriage road cut a path low along the south slopes of barren hills.[17] About midway between Nauplia and the sanctuary, it passed a Cyclopean bridge (among the oldest in Europe, this is unmentioned by Frazer),[18] a waterless torrent bed, and a hill crowned by what he described as "one of the best-preserved fortresses of antiquity in all Peloponnese"— Kazarma. Polygonal walls reaching heights of 18 feet draw Frazer's interest as worthy of careful description.[19] After a mile and more, another fortress appeared on the left, Kastraki. Then, with another mile, the road from Nauplia meets with the route of the straight road from Argos. In Frazer's time the latter was little more than a bridle path connecting the Argive plain with the Soulinari and the village of Katsingri. At these crossroads Frazer's path falls in with that of Pausanias.

Within the *Periegesis* a radically different sense of space had yet to be lost through the coming upheavals of local ontologies. What was observed from the deck of a ship or along roads was, for Pausanias, experienced from within, as emanating out from shared hearths behind city walls separated by surrounding districts and common territorial borders.[20] In the late nineteenth century educated travelers looked upon the world with different eyes. Frazer encountered Argos and Nauplia as two nodes connected by on-time, two-way transportation along paths visualized and known from the angle of 90 degrees, and from these locales a wide world spread out in every direction.[21]

Pausanias need only raise his eyes above Lessa to behold Mt Arachnaeus. It was upon this mountain that he located altars to Zeus and Hera where locals sacrificed in times of drought.[22] Within the *Periegesis*, each god, every goddess, had his or her place, specific topoi where events recorded in myth are terrestrially fastened. Through Pausanias we learn of a natal space saturated with its mytho-historic markers: the earthen mound in the agora of Argos containing the severed head of Medusa; the citadel of Tiryns whose high walls were raised

---

17 Baedeker's *Greece* (1894, 247) mentions two khans, situated close to each other, between Aria and the Cyclopean bridge at Kasarma. One or both of these khans may have been the first dwellings of Pirgiotika, which local history records as having been established by displaced shepherds in the decades after 1870 when their homes in the village of Pirgaki, Arcadia were destroyed by a landslide.

18 The road's course is woven with Bronze Age bridges, towers, and castles consigned to subsequent periods—these stand as suggestions of the enduring importance of this valley as a major east–west corridor.

19 Frazer later visits both Kazarma and Kastraki on December 6, 1895.

20 For more on Pausanias and space, see Segment 22.

21 Frazer includes a map of the Argolis (Map III) with rail lines (completed in 1886) and the route to the Aesculapion from Nauplion in Volume VI. Produced by Stanford's Geographical for Macmillan, the map is derived from the *Carte de la Morée* (see Prologue).

22 On the location of the altars, see Rupp (1976); also see Prologue.

for Proetus by the Cyclopes; the Twisted Olive wrenched into shape by Hercules by the trail up Mt Coryphum.[23] Pausanias speaks of gods who were here, of heroes who walked there, of ancestors who spilled blood, theirs and others, on this plain. Through myth, history, and memory those who worked this ground and buried their dead in this soil were settled into this sacred land.

Beyond olive groves rests the village of Ligourio, which sits prominently on a spur of Mt Arachnaeus.[24] To Frazer's eye, Mt Arachnaeus, and the arid mountains of the Argolic peninsula in general, were in their grey monotony anything but pleasing. Hardy little holly-oak and the infrequent dun-colored shrubs did little to raise his assessment: "Nowhere else in Greece, probably, is the scenery so desolate and forbidding."[25] Clearly, some areas held more allure than others, but Frazer was no materialist. Some stimuli evoked feelings of pain, others of happiness, but for Frazer, who was rather selective in his enthusiasms, the emotions are subordinate to will.[26] Did his wooded-images of picturesque, Classical lands crash against the drab monotony of the mountains before him?

Before reaching the city of Epidaurus, Pausanias arrived at the sanctuary of Aesculapius, which is set within a fine open valley. Known as *to hiero* (the sanctuary), the ruins of the Aesculapion lay toward its upper end. Upon approach, in the presence of verdant fields in spring, Frazer's spirits would seem to lift. "Interspersed with clumps of trees and bushes" the valley is surrounded by "mountains, though grey and barren, with undulating uniform outlines"; these are, for him, "rather still and solemn than stern and sombre in character."[27] While memorable for its literary dramatizations, the key contribution of Frazer's commentary was in how it amplified Pausanias as an ethnographer of ancient religion.

Through the work of Pausanias we learn of how peoples first came to settle this valley. Through information collated by Pausanias we discover that it was here, according to the Epidaurians, that the son of Apollo and Koronis,

---

23 2.16.5.
24 Both Panagiotis Kavvadias and H.G. Lolling identified the area around Kazarma with the Lessa mentioned by Pausanias (see Frazer 1898 III, 233). Frazer throws his weight behind Ligourio, which seems to better agree with Pausanias, who placed it on the straight road (on the association of Ligourio with Lessa, see Mitsos 1935, 16). Today these olive groves are interspersed with solar farms—the Ephorate has had many applications for these in the last few years and wind turbines crown heights of Arachneo. I have elaborated on the significance of Arachneo in the Prologue.
25 Vol. III, 234.
26 See Fraser (1990a, 10), Ackerman (1987, 50).
27 Frazer (1898 III, 236). Frazer later amended his description of the setting. Having obtained a different perspective on the area he heightened the contrast between Arachnaeus and the surrounding mountains; the former had sharp points, while "the hills on the eastern and southern sides of the valley are of softer outline and green with bushes" (1898 V, 580).

daughter of Phlegyas, was abandoned. Exposed upon Myrtle mountain, the babe Aesculapius was suckled by goats, and from this event the mountain acquired a new name: "Nipple." Against this story, Pausanias presents contrasting accounts of the healing god by other communities, highlighting incongruities in how myths were invested in place.[28] Through Pausanias we hear of the restriction on death and birth within the sanctuary bounds. We understand that all sacrifices, "whether offered by a native or a foreigner," are consumed within the *temenos*, the sacred precinct.[29] Through the sacrifices recorded by Pausanias we understand how these localities were sacralized.

Surrounded by boundary stones in every direction, the sacred precinct lends form to Pausanias's description by offering its qualities as an organizational container into which are placed those items deemed most worthy of observation. Beginning with the chryselephantine statue of the god within his temple—Aesculapius is seated upon a throne decorated by myths of Argive heroes (Bellerophon and Perseus), hand on staff, hand over a serpent, dog by his side—Pausanias describes things that call to his attention.[30] God-pleasing works of art and the artists who made them, places with their potent connections to cult, heroes, the gods, and historical events, or objects possessed of the deity (for Pausanias, some statues or images were *entheon*), such are the things he singles out as worthy of mention. Frazer regarded the matter of selection on the part of Pausanias as pertaining to aim—the creation of a guide book—and to interests—both antiquarian and religious, ethnographic and mythic.[31]

Pausanias is a believer in a world where the grounds for a modern, propositional truth are as of yet undisclosed.[32] Thus, things cannot be assumed to reveal themselves to human perception on the same grounds. Open to the presence of the divine, Pausanias was among others who were looked upon by the gods and the objects of the world that they experience.[33] What was deemed worthy of note was also connected to the idiosyncrasies of a literary genre of travel writing and Pausanias's choices are thoroughly conditioned by the articulation of form within a literary tradition.[34] Frazer, who later claims to have

---

28 By his own admission, Pausanias bound himself to record what people said; he was not bound to believe everything he heard (7.152.3; also 2.17.4; 6.3.8; also see Hutton 2005, 307).

29 2.27.1, Frazer's translation (1898 I, 112).

30 For Pausanias, questions of what to observe and describe are conditioned by literary tradition, audience, and intellectual milieu (Hutton 2005, 5). Matters of exhibition—how objects are displayed—and aesthetics also exert their influence.

31 1898 I, xxiv–xxx.

32 Heidegger (2008a).

33 Heidegger (2002, 68).

34 Though Pausanias seems to have written the ten books in the order which they appear (Habicht 1985, 7–8), they are replete with cross-references, both in terms of what came before and in

discarded the "austere form" of a "scientific treatise" in favor of a "more artistic mould," shares this literary aspiration.[35]

The apogee of a pilgrimage comes at the point of reaching one's destination, an object saturated with meaning, with emotion, as a perceived *telos*.[36] After following paths through fields "green with corn, interspersed with clumps of trees and bushes," Frazer paused at the edge of a rather large open trench (upwards of 60 by 100 meters). For how long he stood pondering what had been laid bare by the Greek Archaeological Society under the direction of Panayiotis Kavvadias between 1881 and 1887 one cannot say.[37] Whether he experienced some level of satisfaction, or disappointment, is unknown. Before foundations without labels, Frazer began to form an understanding of what remains of referents central to Pausanias's description—the temple of Aesculapius, the Rotunda, the temple of Artemis, the great colonnade, and tablets of cures.[38]

According to Pausanias, it was here, within the sacred enclosure, that a stone tablet, separated out from others, recorded a dedication by Hippolytus of twenty horses to Aesculapius, who had raised him from the dead. It was here that Pausanias interjected a tale told by the people of Aricia, that Hippolytus, refusing to forgive his father Theseus, a native of nearby Troezen, for the curse which led to his death, left this land for Italy. There, under the name of Virbius, he reigned. There, to Artemis, he consecrated a sanctuary by the sylvan lake where down to the time of Pausanias "the priesthood of the goddess is the prize of victory in a single combat. The competition is not open to free men, but only to slaves who have run away from their masters."[39] Pausanias appears, as Frazer would speculate, to have observed the priest lurking with sword

terms of anticipation as to what will come after. This "interconnectedness beyond the mere juncture of regions and roads on the terrain" in combination with the mytho-historical and mnemonic associations that cluster around landscape features, monuments and other objects of concern is, according to Jas Elsner, indicative of a carefully structured "imaginative geography" in possession of a marked purpose (2001, 7). For Elsner, Pausanias's *Greece* translates the landscape into a rhetorical discourse of the "sublime," whose "structure and choices made in that structure are shared with much more overtly oratorical texts and practices" (2001, 18–20). In placing aside old tendencies to read the *Periegesis* as a direct account of a grand tour through Greece we may understand the text as a refined work of travel literature (Hutton 2005, 20–29).

35 *The Golden Bough*, 3rd ed., I, vii.

36 Also see Augé (1995, 90).

37 Locals would later remember Kavvadias "as an old man who worked all day at his excavations in a frock-coat and hat under a black umbrella" (Levi 1979, 194, note 158). On the excavations of the sanctuary, see Kavvadias (1891, 1900).

38 Aspects of his understanding, such as the location of the hospice and the extent of the sacred precinct, will later be revealed as misapprehensions in the course of his 1895 visit in the company of Koromantsos; see 1898 V, 571.

39 2.27.4. Thus is Frazer's translation, Vol. I, 113.

unsheathed; the ward of the sacred wood and the Golden Bough was unsettled for life.[40]

It was this very custom at Nemi that formed the starting point for *The Golden Bough*. To attain the prize of priesthood, why did the victor have to slay his predecessor? Why must contenders first pluck the Golden Bough before the issuing the challenge? Pausanias presented Frazer with evidence that the custom was more than myth and had survived down to his time. From this sacred ground arose the very conundrum Frazer sought to explain through the arboreal growth of subsequent editions, whose green leaves will branch out to fill an entire shelf.

An anthropological appreciation of Ancient Greece had hitherto been missing from earlier Classical scholars.[41] This appreciation was borne out in the methodology of comparison. A window into this method is to be found in Frazer's commentary on the infant Aesculapius who was suckled by a goat. Providing a litany of examples where persons were nurtured by animals, Frazer mentions Romulus, Remus, and the wolf; wolves and Miletus, Lycastus, and Parrhasius; Telephus and a deer; bears and Atalanta and Paris; the sons of Melanippe and a cow; Hippothous and a mare; Meliteus and bees; Serimamis and doves. From here, his juxtapositions move on stories from Africa and India. Unfettered in his reach, the stipulation that the whole of the sacrificial victim was to be consumed within the *temenos* led from Amphiaraus at Oropus to Arabs who sacrificed to the Morning Star to the Lithuanian festival of first-fruits to North American Indians. No matter how new, how alien, how other, how distant the vignette, Frazer could safely draw it into his encompassing comparatist frame. While the long reach of his speculative analogies seemed to know no bounds,[42] at root such comparisons served to situate the Greeks as a culture among cultures rather than a culture above cultures.[43]

Frazer's emphasis on Nemi will later fall away in favor of an evolutionary thesis on religion and society.[44] His trust in a steady and continuous progression of humanity, which would, as he later clarifies in the second edition of *The Golden Bough*, evolve from magic through religious belief to scientific thought,

---

40 1898 III, xxi–xxii; also see Fraser (1990a, 8–9).

41 Also see Ackerman (1987, 129), Fraser (1994, xxviii).

42 Frazer, as Edmond Leach put it, "used his ethnographic evidence, which he culled from here there and everywhere, to illustrate propositions which he had arrived at in advance by a priori reasoning, but, to a degree which is often quite startling, whenever the evidence did not fit he simply altered the evidence!" Leach (2011, 279).

43 Not that this insight had any substantive bearing on subsequent Classical scholarship over the next century, which largely stuck to their non-Barbarian histories and clung to their Helladic shores (for summary, see Broodbank 2013, 17–23; Shanks 1996, 86–91).

44 1911 III, X and vi.

required an image of a human mind free of the mediating roles of environment, location, and technology.[45] If the right patterns could be discerned in the myths and customs of "primitive" cultures—within which characteristics of the age of magic persisted as what E.B. Tylor called "survivals"—then a genealogy could be articulated which links all beliefs irrespective of local peculiarities to a common origin.[46] Frazer sought to reconcile the relationship between legion cultures separated into their own worlds and one global humanity, and through the evolving pages of *The Golden Bough* he will be borne along the limbs of an arboreal image of human knowledge branching out in every direction.[47] From the solidarity of his Trinity College study, the world must have seemed much smaller.

Into the open trench Frazer climbed. On formerly buried ground, where new shoots sprout from once-dormant seeds, he walks among low walls, blocks of marble, sundry architectural fragments, paved platforms, and a circular foundation freed from the soil by archaeologists. Does he imagine the consumption of sacrifices among these stones? Why did supplicants fear removing sacred food from the sanctuary? To question why the ancients upheld this taboo was to trace out the tendrils of what preceded that knowledge.[48] Thoughts, myths, acts, customs weighed still upon Frazer's contemporaries by giving form to their own beliefs, which are inherited by their progeny.

So why do we believe what we do? To answer this question in *The Golden Bough* Frazer wagered that the text could bring sufficient returns to the study. Back in Cambridge, Frazer had benefited from a sustained accumulation of accounts describing customs and myths among other cultures, no matter how distant, however partial.[49] This library- and text-centered immersion rested upon the assumption that observations were faithful testaments to curious customs among other peoples and thereby provided fodder for the uninhibited labors of comparison.[50] What will be later characterized as the firm separation of eyewitnessing and evaluation[51] was really part of an ancient reader subjectivity, strong within the Classics, which permitted him to stay in one place, and connect through the page, the gateway to the imagination.

---

45 Ackerman (1987, 51–52), Fraser (1990a, 12; 1994, xxx).
46 On Tylor and survivals, see Stocking (1995, 5–6); also Fraser (1990a, 14–15; 1994, xxx).
47 Ackerman (1987, 88–89).
48 Frazer suggests "that the sacred food might be profaned if it were carried outside" (1898 III, 240).
49 As a man of habit, Frazer was loath to leave the comforts of his library. It is said that the ceiling below the library he assembled to write the first edition of *The Golden Bough* buckled like an inflated sail under the immense weight of his books; Ackerman (1987, 144).
50 Frazer (1908, 12 and 17); also see Herzfeld (1987, 72), Stocking (1995, 146).
51 See Ackerman (1987, 87).

To Frazer future generations will not be so kind.[52] At the roots of *The Golden Bough* coming critics will see a self-avowed member of "the enlightened minority" who understood "primitive" systems of meaning in distant corners better than those who lived there. Descending from the educated highlands of the European north, a privileged domain of rational thought freed from the realm of superstition and belief, Frazer provided authoritative answers to questions of motive that lay behind the customs and rituals within what he held to be primitive, belief-centered cultures. On a bookshelf of central prominence in the Library of Globalization, Frazer, so they held, added yet another product of Western Imperialism, one that appeared for all its Eurocentrism irredeemable. Among anthropologists ran another deep misgiving concerning the relationship of the ethnographer to their objects of study.[53] Frazer's complete reliance on textual descriptions took objects out of context. The elevation of a "situation-independent comprehension of meaning"[54] led him to associate stories on the basis of resemblance without analysis.[55] To observe and apprehend others, for future anthropologists, demanded being there, and any understanding of other living cultures generated on the basis of non-*in situ* derived meaning will come to be regarded as anathema.[56]

There is more to what will become the anthropological assessment of Frazer. Ideas common among diverse peoples need not imply common origins. The same ethnological phenomenon, as Franz Boas argued, "may develop in a multitude of ways."[57] To avoid any assumption of the generic formation of diverse customs, the price must be paid for truth which could only be derived through a protracted sojourn in the field. It was Bronisław Malinowski who, despite his own admiration of Frazer, will be bequeathed the title of *Rex Nemeorensis*.[58] After Malinowski, the anthropologist is a participant-observer whose identity is grounded in fieldwork. After Malinowski the "ultimate criterion for anthropological knowledge" was to live among other cultures, to record details of myth, mores, and meaning revealed through direct encounter, and to return with that information.[59] By elevating empirically derived, first-hand information above second-hand witnessing, future anthropologists will acknowledge a new King of the Wood. Frazer's purpose will be emptied of its reality through rivalry. *Le roi est mort; vive le roi!*

---

52 Frazer, as Mary Douglas put it in 1978, "is now attacked as a theorist. He is attacked as a serious thinker. He is even attacked as a stylist" (1978, 152). Compare Leach 2011, Wittgenstein and Rhees 1979; also see Eldridge 1987.
53 Leach (1966, 2011).
54 Sloterdijk (2013, 252).
55 Douglas (1978, 160).
56 See Willerslev (2011).
57 1896, 3.
58 *Rex Nemeorensis* is the King of the Wood.
59 Willerslev (2011, 510).

Strange therefore may seem the issue of context between *The Golden Bough* and *Pausanias's Description*. To realize the former, Frazer held that the material and geographical differences between diverse communities "were insignificant in comparison to the mental elements they shared with all ancient and primitive peoples."[60] Within books these elements could be found. Indeed, apart from Nemi, few are descriptions of the settings in which magic, religion, and science take place in the first two editions of *The Golden Bough*.[61] Yet here, in the course of research with Pausanias close at hand, he walks among foundations exposed and erstwhile walls yet to be laid bare.[62] One may take the epigraph chosen by Frazer for *Pausanias's Description* as an indication of where he stands on the issue of material differences with respect to the present project:

> But all the former are past and gone, have perished in an utterly shameful and pitiable way; and as to the rest, it is no longer possible to form a conception of the pre-eminence and splendor of their deeds and, as well, their sufferings, by looking at the *men* of the present time. Nay, it is rather the stones which reveal the grandeur and the greatness of Hellas, and the ruins of her buildings.[63]

Within books this grandeur and greatness was not to be found. To acquire a sense of "departed worth" one had to travel.

Frazer will revisit the sanctuary for a second time in December 1895. In the company of the superintendent of the excavations, Mr Koromantsos, he paces out the length of walls. With tape in hand he measures the height of columns, the dimensions of blocks, and the diameter of basins. In his diary he describes the layout of former buildings, wall by wall, room by room, feature by feature. Here, with an informant by his side, the anthropologist at home in the armchair once again takes to the field. Where *The Golden Bough* drives away objects that uphold foreign myths and customs, *Pausanias's Description* attempts to draw closer what has become of them.[64] Whether the thing encountered is lost in-between remains an open question.

---

60 Ackerman (1987, 85).

61 While this disinterest in setting or context will change with the third *Golden Bough*, Frazer will rely on scenes concocted more from the imagination than the pages of first-hand accounts (see Ackerman 1987, 237). Frazer does eventually visit Nemi in 1901 (1911 I, 5, note 2).

62 Frazer traces the steps of Pausanias, treads on sacred land, land walked by the pilgrim to whom the study and appreciation of the Classical world owes so much. I have withheld this obvious line of thought, for too many would cast it aside as the elevation of the Classical (see Shanks 1996).

63 Dio Chrysostom *Orationes* 31, section 159–160. English translation, J.W. Cohoon 1932.

64 Frazer was at pains to keep observation separate from comparison (Willerslev 2011, 510). Whereas *Pausanias's Description* demands the former, *The Golden Bough* demands the latter.

What to observe and how to observe it ethnographically will elevate the empirical. Rightly so. But why should such neglect constitute grounds for exclusion? The age-old distinction between the soft and the hard, between working with books and living among cultures should not be confused with a judgment that one direct encounter is more real than the other. What is relegated to the *logos* cannot ever fully account for what sleeps in the earth.[65] And yet objects experienced on the ground and objects of the imagination are equally objects.[66] If *The Golden Bough* stands at the beginning of an anthropological tradition, *Pausanias's Description of Greece* is situated within one already well-defined and therefore subject to its rules.[67] One project cannot be judged in the light of the other for each book demanded different approaches. Each book is utterly specific and can only be weighed in light of its own purposes.

No, Frazer the anthropologist cannot be separated from Frazer the Classicist. *The Golden Bough* more than conditioned Frazer's travels in Greece; Pausanias was intimately tied to making the making of *The Golden Bough*.[68] A student of Herodotus, Pausanias had an eye for odd customs and parallels found elsewhere. His associations were based on resemblance: the wooden image of Athena in the temple at Lessa is exactly like the one on the Larissa, the acropolis of Argos; the same rule prohibiting death or birth within the sacred enclosure of Epidaurus is observed on Delos.[69] A student of the Scottish Enlightenment, Frazer's principles of association drew deeply from the pages of antiquity. Frazer's reliance on the "law of similarity" added the extra step of inferring similar motives to lie behind similar customs.[70] Yet on another level, between Frazer and Pausanias, there is something of a stark, if not sublime, contrast. Frazer, the desk-bound, book-laden generalist-particularist, will never journey farther than Greece and Italy. Pausanias, who is perhaps a Lydian, who is definitely

---

65 See Witmore (2018b).

66 Taking issue with anthropology's "inherent recourse to empirical evidence as the ultimate criterion for anthropological knowledge," Rane Willerslev has defended Frazer on the grounds of "a deliberate speculative interrogation of cross-cultural ethnography—a process whereby abstract thinking gives force and meaning to ethnographic observations" (2011, 510, 504). Ultimately, Willerslev mounts a defense of a virtual totality. Rather than follow this train of thought, here I argue for a grounding in specific objects. Not everything is connected (Harman 2011, Olsen 2010).

67 Ackerman (1987, 131).

68 Robert Ackerman has shown how Frazer's research for his translation and commentary on Pausanias, which included "a considerable quantity of ethnological parallels illustrative of the Greek myths and customs described or referred to by Pausanias," served as a catalyst for a "work on comparative mythology," what will become *The Golden Bough* (1987, 57). Indeed, an advance of £100 on *The Golden Bough* was used to pay for his 1890 trip to Greece (ibid., 58).

69 2.24.9; 2.27.1.

70 Ackerman (1987, 82).

a man of substantial means, seems to have spent much of his life on the move, writing on the basis of first-hand witnessing.[71]

Whatever one makes of *The Golden Bough*, Frazer's work will resist being brushed aside as another example of Victorian prejudice, another justification for imperialism, convinced as he was "of the communality of human consciousness."[72] Given his deep sympathies for other cultures, Frazer's work cannot be paraphrased as racist. While *The Golden Bough* was historicist in its evolutionary framing, it nonetheless offers far more when set "within the purple glow of the imagination."[73] Against all the need to read the book as a definitive anthropological account, why not read it as mythology, a most necessary mythology, which dared to articulate the psychic unity of humanity irrespective of our astounding alterity?

Perhaps the hour is late when the theatre calls to Frazer, which according to Pausanias is especially worth seeing. Taking leave of ruined walls Frazer walks through a ravine and uphill into an anterior background where formerly lay a wood "shewing black and jagged."[74] When Kavvadias arrived at the ancient theatre in 1881 he encountered an area so thick with trees that he was completely unable to penetrate deeper than the auditorium.[75] In order to lay bare what will become one of the best-preserved theatres in all of Greece, Kavvadias had the shady wood removed. Before the theatre he would later utter: "Here I sacrificed and destroyed."[76] Was this an expression of regret at uprooting so many canopy-covered boughs? After the expulsion of the forest, the erstwhile wood can only return through the imagination.

Pausanias passed by the theatre on the cusp of a spatial revolution. Again and again, as Frazer would later state, Pausanias takes notice of depopulated areas, ruins, crumbling facades, collapsed roofs, ivy-clad temples, and here, in the sanctuary, he mentions how only six of the inscriptions remain.[77] Night was falling, but how dark were the skies over the houses of the gods?[78] Pausanias does not say. Whatever Pausanias's motivations, when something comes to be experienced as tenuous, singular, losable it often gains a new status as that

---

71 Habicht (1985, 17).

72 Fraser (1990b); also Fraser (1994, xxxix); charges of imperialism are "nonsense," according to Girard (2014, 22).

73 Frazer quoted in Douglas (1978, 156).

74 Frazer (1911, 12).

75 Petrakos (2007, 25).

76 Ibid.

77 Frazer (1898 I, xiv); on the Epidaurian inscriptions, see LiDonnici (1995).

78 Here I evoke the language of Hölderlin, from his "Bread and Wine."

which is in need of protection, or description through translation onto the page.[79]

After Pausanias, Aesculapius will be evicted from his sanctuary. In the silent background, Christianity, with its sociological power over the underprivileged, the weak, slaves and peasants, those ignored by history, was spreading.[80] Among Christians, statues infused by the gods were already seen in a new light. They have mouths but do not speak; they have eyes but do not see; they have ears but do not hear; they have noses but do not smell; they have hands but do not handle; they have feet but do not walk.[81]

Enormous was the upheaval triggered by the coming of Christianity to Greece. Before its advent this earth was infused by the god Aesculapius. After, these lands were deterritorialized. The old gods were dispossessed of here. At the edge of the *temenos*, near the Propylaia a Christian basilica was constructed just over two centuries after Pausanias.[82] Broken for use as wall fill and a threshold stone in the construction of a medieval house, the remaining stelae would come to lose their former meaning.[83] Upon Mt Arachnaeus a chapel was constructed atop what had become of the altars of Zeus and Hera.[84] Mourning nymphs with tresses torn were banished from their haunted springs;[85] the rich myths and customs once fixed within the *pagus* were fastened firmly to the page.[86]

After the exclusion of many false gods, One True God remains. The empty tomb of Christ serves as a suggestion of how Christianity is not bound to a specific place.[87] A redemptive religion does not provide a home in the here, but in that which is not here, which is at home everywhere.[88] Unlike ancient

79 "Nor were more sudden and violent forces of destruction wanting to quicken the slow decay wrought by time, by neglect, by political servitude, by all the subtle indefinable agencies that sap a nation's strength. In Pausanias's lifetime a horde of northern barbarians, the ominous precursor of many more, carried fire and sword into the heart of Greece, and the Roman world was wasted by that great pestilence which thinned its population, enfeebled its energies, and precipitated the decline of art" (Frazer 1898 I, XV).

80 On early Christianity, see Caraher (2003), Sweetman (2010, 2015); compare Winter (2001).

81 Psalms 115, 2–7.

82 Caraher (2003, 381), Orlandos (1994, 50 and 51).

83 Also see Błaśkiewicz (2014).

84 Rupp (1976).

85 An allusion to Milton's "Ode on the Morning of Christ's Nativity."

86 *Pagan*, she who belongs of the country, comes from the Latin *pagus*, country or district, which is related to the stem, *pangere*, to fit or fasten, which is the Greek *pignynai*, to fasten. The latter term gives rise to the Latin *pagina*, the written page.

87 Harrison (2003, 106–23), Serres (2011, 19).

88 Christianity, like Judaism and Islam, is a religion of the book, which stands in contrast to polytheism, a religion that is deeply rooted in the world. Also see Assmann (2003, 218), Harrison (2003, 111), Serres (2011, 18).

religion which holds onto the particularities of locality, the church "extends its proclamation" into all meridians.[89] Those who worked this soil, those who lived by the precepts of paganism, those who buried their dead in this sacralized ground, were alienated from what had been a natal space. They become but temporary inhabitants. Deterritorialized, the gods no longer dwell here. Desacralized, what is sacred is not here. Pagans were unsettled from the *pagus*, the excluded are now separate from the land, and a new relationship to the terrestrial becomes explicit. Passive and ordinary, the countryside is now that over and above which one holds dominion: *Dominium terrae*. It will become objectifiable as that which is measured, studied, and observed.[90]

Upon this ground literature, science, and religion converge. Between first-hand observation and second-hand speculation, anthropology will distinguish what is true and false by evicting non-truths. Between polytheism and Christianity will run a Mosaic distinction between true and false religion—alongside the one God, all others are false.[91] Between science and myth, the truth of a definitive reality will be asserted against the falsehood of many beliefs. And yet, through both the page and the *pagus* the excluded will return. The gods, customs, and localities will reemerge through the *Periegesis Hellados*. The stones of the god of healing's sanctuary will resurface through science in the form of archaeology. By reading Frazer's commentary, by using it for travel, subsequent travelers will experience something of this formerly sacralized ground.

Pilgrims often return by the road which they came.[92] Neither Pausanias nor Frazer advance to Nauplia by the same road that bore them to Epidaurus.[93]

---

89 Harrison (2003, 111).

90 Serres (2011, 19–20).

91 Hume's thesis of a tolerant polytheism (1757), capable of plurality whatever the differences, and an intolerant monotheism, which clearly stipulates what is incompatible with its truths, no doubt exerted its influence on Frazer (Hume and Beauchamp 2007, 60–2; also see Assmann 2010, 14). If "tolerant" is the wrong word, for it assumes that one endures that which clashes with one's religion (Assmann 2010, 34), Hume was nonetheless a muse, for through *The Golden Bough* Frazer situated Christianity as one religion among others. On Frazer's skepticism towards Christianity, see Girard (2014, 22).

92 On the debate over whether Pausanias should be regarded as a religious pilgrim, see Cherry (2001), Elsner (1992); also see Arafat (1996, 9–11) on implications of the word "pilgrim" versus *pepaideumenos*, a cultured man of education writing in the tradition of Herodotus.

93 Pausanias rounds the southern Argolid, from Troezen to Hermione to Mases, from which he casts off. Passing along the coast by Asine and crossing the bay of Argos to Lerna, and eventually along the coast, by way of Temenion, he reaches Nauplia, which in his time was abandoned. Following in the footsteps of Pausanias, Frazer continued on a path to Old Epidaurus, Troezen, Methana, Poros. Five years later, Frazer journeys to the sanctuary by way of Old Epidaurus. From here, he takes the high road to Nauplia on December 6, 1895.

Bibliography

Ackerman, R. 1987. *J.G. Frazer: His life and work.* Cambridge: Cambridge University Press.

Alcock, S.E. 1993. *Graecia Capta: The landscapes of Roman Greece.* Cambridge: Cambridge University Press.

Arafat, K.W. 1996. *Pausanias' Greece: Ancient artists and Roman rulers.* Cambridge: Cambridge University Press.

Assmann, J. 2003. *The mind of Egypt: History and meaning in the time of the Pharaohs.* Cambridge, MA: Harvard University Press.

Assmann, J. 2010. *The price of monotheism* (trans. R. Savage). Stanford, CA: Stanford University Press.

Augé, M. 1995. *Non-places: Introduction to an anthropology of supermodernity.* London: Verso.

Baedeker, K. 1894. *Greece: A handbook for travellers.* Leipzig: Karl Baedeker.

Błaśkiewicz, M. 2014. Healing dreams at Epidaurus: Analysis and interpretation of the Epidaurian iamata. *Miscellanea Anthropologica Et Sociologica* 15(4), 54–69.

Boas, F. 1896. The limitations of the comparative method of anthropology. *Science* 4(103), 901–08.

Broodbank, C. 2013. *The making of the Middle Sea.* Oxford: Oxford University Press.

Caraher, W.R. 2003. *Church, society, and the sacred in early Christian Greece.* Ann Arbor, MI: UMI Dissertation Services.

Cherry, J.F. 2001. Travel, nostalgia, and Pausanias' Giant. In S.E. Alcock, J.F. Cherry, and J. Elsner (eds.), *Pausanias: Travel and memory in Roman Greece.* Oxford: Oxford University Press. 247–55.

Douglas, M. 1978. Judgements on James Frazer. *Daedalus* 107(4), 151–64.

Eldridge, R. 1987. Hypotheses, criterial claims, and perspicuous representations: Wittgenstein's "Remarks on Frazer's *The Golden Bough.*" *Philosophical Investigations* 10(3) 226–45.

Elsner, J. 1992. Pausanias: A Greek pilgrim in the Roman world. *Past and Present* 135, 3–29.

Elsner, J. 2001. Structuring "Greece": Pausanias's *Periegesis* as a literary construct. In S. E. Alcock, J.F. Cherry, and J. Elsner (eds.), *Pausanias: Travel and memory in Roman Greece.* Oxford: Oxford University Press. 3–20.

Fraser, R. 1990a. *The making of the Golden Bough: The origins and growth of an argument.* New York, NY: St Martin's Press.

Fraser, R. 1990b. When the bough breaks. *London Review of Books* 12(15). Available at: www.lrb.co.uk/v12/n15/letters#letter14.

Fraser, R. 1994. Introduction. In J.G. Frazer, *The Golden Bough: A new abridgement.* Oxford: Oxford University Press.

Frazer, J.G. 1898. *Pausanias's Description of Greece.* 6 vols. London: Macmillan & Co.

Frazer, J.G. 1908. *The scope of social anthropology.* London: Macmillan & Co.

Frazer, J.G. 1911. *The magic art and the evolution of kings, being Part 1 Vol. 1 of The Golden Bough 3rd Edition.* London: Macmillan & Co.

Girard, R. 2014. *The one by whom scandal comes.* East Lansing, MI: Michigan State University Press.

Habicht, C. 1985. *Pausanias' guide to Ancient Greece.* Berkeley, CA: University of California Press.

Harman, G. 2011. *The quadruple object.* Winchester: Zero Books.

Harrison, R.P. 2003. *The dominion of the dead.* Chicago, IL: University of Chicago Press.

Heidegger, M. 2002. The age of the world picture. In J. Young and K. Hayne (eds.), *Off the beaten track*. Cambridge: Cambridge University Press. 57–72.

Heidegger, M. 2008a. On the essence of truth. In D.F. Krell (ed.), *Basic writings*. London: Harper Perennial. 111–38.

Herzfeld, M. 1987. *Anthropology through the looking glass: Critical ethnography in the margins of Europe*. Cambridge: Cambridge University Press.

Hume, D., and T.L. Beauchamp. 2007. *A dissertation on the passions: The natural history of religion – A critical edition*. Oxford: Clarendon Press.

Hutton, W. 2005. *Describing Greece: Landscape and literature in the Periegesis of Pausanias*. Cambridge: Cambridge University Press.

Ingold, T. 2008. Anthropology is not ethnography: Radcliffe-Brown Lecture in social anthropology. *Proceedings of the British Academy* 154, 69–92.

Kavvadias, P. 1891. *Fouilles d'Épidaure*. Athens: S.C. Vlastos.

Kavvadias, P. 1900. *To hieron tou Asklepiou en Epidauroi kai he therapeia ton asthenon*. Athens: Athenesin.

Leach, E.R. 1966. On the "founding fathers." *Current Anthropology* 7, 560–76.

Leach, E.R. 2011. Kingship and divinity: The unpublished Frazer Lecture. *HAU: Journal of Ethnographic Theory* 1(1), 279–98.

Levi, P. (ed.). 1979. *Pausanias' guide to Greece I – Central Greece*. London: Penguin Classics.

LiDonnici, L.R. 1995. *The Epidaurian miracle inscriptions: Text, translation and commentary*. Atlanta, GA: Scholars Press.

Mitsos, M. 1935. *Hellenika* VIII, 16.

Olsen, B. 2010. *In defense of things: Archaeology and the ontology of objects*. Lanham, MD: AltaMira Press.

Orlandos, A.K. 1994. *He Xylostegos Palaiochristianike Basilike tes Mesogeiakes Lekanes*. Athenai: He en Athenais Archaiologike Hetaireia.

Petrakos, V. Ch. 2007. The stages of Greek archaeology. In P. Valavanes and A. Delevorrias (eds.), *Great moments in Greek archaeology*. Los Angeles, CA: J. Paul Getty Museum. 16–35.

Rupp, D.W. 1976. The altars of Zeus and Hera on Mt Arachnaion in the Argeia, Greece. *Journal of Field Archaeology* 3(3), 261–68.

Serres, M. 2011. *Malfeasance: Appropriation through pollution?* Stanford, CA: Stanford University Press.

Shanks, M. 1996. *Classical archaeology of Greece: Experiences of the discipline*. London: Routledge.

Sloterdijk, P. 2013. *In the world interior of capital: For a philosophical theory of globalization*. Cambridge: Polity Press.

Snodgrass, A.M. 1987. *An archaeology of Greece*. Berkeley, CA: University of California Press.

Stocking, G. 1995. *After Tylor: British social anthropology, 1888–1951*. Madison, WI: University of Wisconsin Press.

Sweetman, R.J. 2010. The Christianization of the Peloponnese: The topography and function of Late Antique churches. *Journal of Late Antiquity* 3(2), 203–61.

Sweetman R.J. 2015. Memory, tradition, and Christianization of the Peloponnese. *American Journal of Archaeology* 119(4), 501–531.

Welcker, F.G. 1865. *Tagebuch einer Griechischen Reise*. Vol. 1. Berlin: Verlag von Wilhelm Herss.

Willerslev, R. 2011. Frazer strikes back from the armchair: A new search for the animist soul. *Journal of the Royal Anthropological Institute* 17, 504–26.

Winter, B.W. 2001. *After Paul left Corinth*. Grand Rapids, MI: Eerdmans.

Witmore, C. 2018b. Traces of the past: Classics between history & archaeology, Karen Bassi, 2016. Ann Arbor, MI: University of Michigan Press. *Cambridge Archaeological Journal* 27(3), 515–18.

Wittgenstein, L., and R. Rhees 1979. *Remarks on Frazer's Golden Bough*. Retford: Brynmill.

17

PALEOLITHIC TO BRONZE AGE
AMID VENETIAN

A museum

*Arsenal turned museum, peripatetic narrative, spatializing a history, temporalizing
a region, a grave, care and obligation*

Marked by a strange discrepancy between its overall form and the degenerating
condition of individual stone and mortar, the former Venetian arsenal turned
museum dominates the western end of Constitution Square. Five simple arches
strain under the substantial weight of a plain façade. Set in the unadorned
masonry above the central arch, a small marble Lion of St Mark with its Latin
inscription holds a decorative memory of the building's erstwhile existence.
From the square, the grey, wooden, double doors to the archaeological museum
sit off to the right, at the far end of the portico. One of four archaeological
museums in the Argolid,[1] the Nafplion Museum is the only one that does not

---

1 The other three are Argos, Epidaurus, and Mycenae.

reside in a purpose-built structure. Here, one of Nafplion's longest-lived buildings provides a home to a museum, a house for objects indicative of regional history, and its habitus is to exhibit a path from earliest prehistory to the present.

A blast from an air curtain above the door marks an atmospheric transition as one enters. Two information panels flank a small vestibule. On the left, two maps, town and region. On the right, a floor-by-floor plan of the museum rendered within an axonometric perspective. The color-coding—dark blue, burgundy, pink, red, purple, black and so forth—speaks to the work that such disciplinary architectures do. Museums sort and combine things into their proper compartments. Beyond ordering time with ordered space, the museum also provides an itinerary as to how one may move through the pasts of a region. From here, one must climb a tall flight of stairs to the first floor. Behind a ticket booth stand custodians to this house of the muses. For 6 Euros a visitor may pass.

Situated on two floors, the museum is divided into two rooms more or less corresponding to prehistory and history. The first floor opens through a wide doorway. Venetian walls, a meter thick, are revealed in open windows along both sides. The ceilings have been lowered to provide a controlled atmosphere. An arched support raised upon pillars down the long axis separates the room into two corridors. Display cases line the outer walls and the central pillars,

The Nafplion Archaeological Museum.

The *circus antiquarius* of the exhibition space.

giving the floor the form of a *circus antiquarius*, where observers circumambulate two lanes into end turns around a central *spina*.[2]

To the right, as one enters the room, is a panel entitled "Franchthi Cave, Paleolithic and Mesolithic occupation." To the left, on the center isle sits a low, glass-top display case containing clay hearth structures from "Klisoura Cave, Prosymna, 32,000–21,000 BC." On the western wall sits a large display case with the "Neolithic occupation of Franchthi Cave." Objects are given a thematic treatment and a case-by-case itinerary is structured by the timeline.[3]

Like with like, the objects in the first case are arranged typologically: pottery— pot fragment, cup, ladle, piriform jar, fruitstands, a collared jar; tools—loom weight, spindle whorls, flint tools for bead manufacture, obsidian blades, a flint sickle; ornaments—stone beads, bone trinkets, a shell necklace. Freed from the soil only to be released from dusty shelves in storage rooms (known as *apothekes*), these objects are held to have exhibition value. There is more here than a museal impulse to order, to date, to name, to locate that which is so strange, so very different. Among these objects, a skeleton of a newborn is laid within clean sand, with a miniature marble bowl and a portion of a broken vessel. Among pots, tools, and trinkets, in death does this erstwhile infant find equivalency with these other objects? I will return to this question.

Well-lit display cases are set between windows and under arches amid pillars. Jar, pithos, fruitstand, cooler, objects from a five-hundred-year swath of the third millennium BCE, are raised upon elevated pedestals. A story of

2 The *spina* is the backbone of a Roman *circus*, which forms the dividing barrier between the two avenues.

3 Also see Hamilakis (2007, 46–48), Olsen, Webmoor, and Witmore (2012, 41–7).

surplus enters the scene, with the alluring remains of a circular structure at Tiryns—what is interpreted as a communal building for storage. Franchthi, Tiryns, Asine—key locales for a regional history are exhibited for the viewer. Serpentine seals, a marble mortar and pestle, stone spool-shaped balanced weights, a Cycladic stone pyxis—the museum calls attention to its prized objects, which are ancient and unique. "The third millennium BC, economy, ideology, contacts" periods and themes are defined by cases. Here, a region is staged as an interior itinerary. A synthesis is provided, making sense of what becomes of the past, offering a story framed temporally and thematically. An incalculable antiquity, formerly shrouded in the fogs of ambiguity, has no place here.

Along the corridor, display cases contain a motley inventory of objects. To the right, pottery from the third millennium BCE. A tankard, largely restored from fragments, a decorated cup, various jars, jugs, pyxides, saucers, and *askoi*, a hydra, a ladle, and a lid, from Tiryns, Asine, and Palaia Epidavros, some dated to 2200–2000 BCE, others to 2700–2200 BCE—these alien forms congregate upon pedestals. Here comes a confrontation with the unfamiliar other, well-lit objects, many reconstituted, arranged in rows, anchored by placards for an observer to behold. Here is an alterity made palpable with captions and framing, through organization, display, and thematic treatment. Staged within a structure which sorts, classifies, and, under the weight of relevance that comes with these groupings, scratches and scrapes for some modicum of understanding, holdings are tamed and sanitized. These objects, demarcated within, relegated to, a particular period, are appropriated as regional relics within a state-owned building. The room, its cases, its objects, give form to history's

Pottery of the third millennium BCE.

narrative, which lays claim to its contents. With these secure frames, these hygienic cases, one might suppose that an alien other is made to be recognizable, and thus assimilated. Or, perhaps, there is more at work here than what this threadbare observation supposes.

Time and locus are part of the story of this region, a Greek region, and the museum takes a particular angle—the archaeological.[4] Here, context is king. Displays call back to a place of provenience, to what is elevated as an original and authentic situation—an askos from Room F at Berbati, 2200–2000 BCE. A non-zero sum, archaeology amplifies singular memories—objects found at Birbati or Tiryns—through the circulation of the things framed as of the past, that is, of *this* past, of the third millennium BCE, as here in the present case. The apparatus of exhibition provides the box, ordered within a sequence of other boxes, and thus, as a whole, it spatializes time as itinerary. Within rooms, along corridors, it follows a path that appears to encompass the sum of the changes and continuities. One walks the line of a region here materialized through objects from its exemplary sites, themselves indicative of specific episodes set within a timeline. The museum "interiorizes and spatializes" a very particular temporality of sequence and history, rather than the polychronic mixing indicative of the objects out there.

Lighting, pedestals, elevated displays, and glass bases within glass cases, and textual framing, all these elements of exhibition serve to remind one while walking that the past as such cannot be engaged through the direct, peripatetic encounter. What Benjamin labeled as a "Dream House," a bourgeoisie dream to "absorb everything that is exterior into this interiority" immerses the pedestrian within an exhibition of bygone objects.[5] This dream vision of the past is given authoritative structure through history or, rather, a particular historicism, which would treat these objects as of a separate domain. Yet for objects without their former contexts, the distance is not about time, but about spatial proximities whereby strange things are set out in a staged contact with the alien. Otherworldly objects raised from the earth of the region, extricated from the chthonic oblivion into which they had descended, are encountered in the exhibition and are, despite any traceability to an "original situation," internal to the museum itself.

If the didactic function of this museum is conceived as destroying, through assimilation, the alien other of these objects then one might assume that to ignore or unlearn these habitual frames frees one to recapture the sense of

---

4 Within Greece, the designation of an archaeological museum was based upon historicist reason, as its holdings were distinct from Byzantine, folklore, or modern art (see Venizelos 1998, 123).
5 Sloterdijk and Morse (2009); on the Dream House, see Benjamin (1999, 405–15).

astonishment, of wonderment, that comes through contact with them. Perhaps such an "enlightened condition of foreignness"[6] gives too much weight to the text as generating the fetters of delimitation within the familiar. Though exhibited to exemplify time and locus, these objects nonetheless refuse to comply with our expectations and, in themselves, remain unassimilable.[7]

One need not read labels, which are, in any case, unassuming. Indeed, it is all too commonplace to miss what is fundamental to the museum. Here objects, to use Benjamin's line, "released from the drudgery of being useful" are cared for without saying too much about them.[8] So much work has been achieved here in accommodating a surplus reality that cannot be conveyed through publication. A nondiscursive engagement with things is present before me, and, despite the glass, the possibility of such an engagement is here for anyone to embrace, though not in the way of those responsible for this achievement.[9]

To the left, a display contains a Middle Helladic grave from Berbati (Mastos Hill) at Asine. Laid out in a glass case below a backdrop matted with a view of the site and superimposed plan is an inhumation with grave goods. Arranged in the position that it was found, the skeleton rests upon a bed of sand composed of flakes of brown schist, miniscule and sterile; this is a sanitized caricature of soil, without organics, without microbes, without insects. The display provides context—this is a suggestion of the circumstances under which the objects presented here were found. The display both mimics the burial and offers burial. Masked by a perceived, yet measured, distance (1750–1700 BCE), the display opens a grave to exhibition; the dead lies here in sustained visibility.[10]

Presented before the viewer is a skeleton; a skull, mandible, vertebrae, a clavicle, ribs, humeri, metacarpals, pelvis, femurs, tibiae, fibulae. Here lie broken remains, without a zygomatic arch or maxilla, without complete rib bones or the whole of a pelvis, without entrails or decaying flesh. Long passed from any cadaverous phase, does it matter that what lies here resembles us only in fragmented outline? No longer fouling their environment, these unrotted bits are not without age and patina, but they have been washed and dried, laid not under earth, but exposed to

6 Sloterdijk (2015, 445).
7 Olsen (2010).
8 Benjamin and Jennings (2002, 39); also see Olsen, Webmoor, and Witmore (2012, 205).
9 Archaeologists and curators who study and exhibit these objects are permitted a tactile immediacy open to few. Reopened after renovations in 2009, these new exhibitions were realized under the guidance of the head curator, Evangelia Pappi.
10 On the exhibition of human remains in museums, see Brooks and Rumsey (2007), Nilsson Stutz (2016), Sayer (2010, 95–109), Swain (2016).

air and light under glass.[11] Shorn of microbes or moisture, stripped of the weight of clay, silt, or sand, these skeletal fragments are stabilized, maintained, and exhibited in a display case. Exposed to the lightness of air within a glass box, decomposition is arrested. Dust, grit, residue cannot accumulate, and thus, the earth cannot reclaim the dead. Clean, if not sublime, these bones are well cared for. No, care is not lacking, for the caretakers here are attentive to the wellbeing of all objects, which includes the curation and the hygienic treatment of the dead.

The sign states without ambivalence—this is a grave. A grave, as Robert Pogue Harrison contends, "marks the mortality of its creators" just as much as it "marks the resting place of the dead."[12] Laid among two decorated jars, one with a spout, a jug, a *kantharos*, goods closely related to the deceased are displayed here as they were found—an object lies among other objects within an object. What does this suggest concerning our treatment of the dead? Separated by the measured weight of a linear time, does it matter that death came at a moment seemingly far removed from this present? Does this museum display of a grave alienate us from our obligation to what becomes of another human being? Rendered anonymous through the passing of nearly four millennia, in death does the body move from a dead person to an object, indifferent to any human offence?[13]

Let us not begin by assuming the exception that amplifies a difference between corpse and bowls to the level of that ontological discrepancy between humans and the rest. Let us not confuse the specificity we accord our fellow humans, with taxonomic melodramas. One may speak to the differences of objects, skeletal remains or pots, without recourse to human exceptionalism or privilege.[14] Thus, to ask whether humans find equivalency with objects in death is the wrong question, for it begins with this exception. Instead, let us ask a different question: what specificity do we accord what becomes of our fellow human objects?

Behind the glass case stands a large display with photographs, illustration, and text. The context of the exhumation, with its planimetric relationships to two dozen other burials at Berbati, is exhibited for the viewer. *Sema*, the ancient word for "sign," also denoted the tomb marker, the mound, and the grave.[15] Harrison

---

11 A commonplace objection within museological debates concerning the treatment of the dead relates to how the corpse is rendered as any other museum object. This is striking for being able to single out human remains through an overdramatized contrast to every other museum object despite their profound differences. If the dead silently refuse to be assimilated by the museum, then it has more to do with their rapports with the viewer (see Alberti et al. 2009, 137; Brooks and Rumsey 2006, 2007).

12 Harrison (2003, 20).

13 On this indifference, see Taylor (2012).

14 González-Ruibal (2018, 354); also see discussion in Svestad (2013).

15 See chapters in Henry and Kelp (2016). The meaning of *sema* as grave or tomb is lost in Modern Greek, which holds on to *sema* as a sign, elevated to a trademark.

calls attention to the curious fact that the sign appropriates the ground of signifi-
cation. The primordial sign is tethered always to the place of the dead, yet here it
is subdued. Does the museological exhibition, with its didactic value and modern
spirit, somehow annul our obligations to the human dead?[16] Casting a veil of scientific research over this conserved past gives a false sense of the originary grave,
which lies emptied. Under weight of relevance that comes with the story of the
region, we obscure the appropriation of ground, formerly theirs. Here again we
witness an annexation of the soil in favor of a story of region, of nation, of a state
that disinters the dead interred in the ground.[17] Does this immaculate museum
sever the connection between humanity and humus? Both care and alienation are
present. This display draws the grave within and leaves the humic foundations
without. Notwithstanding the didactic function of the museum, in being cut off
from the earth it sustains that all-too-familiar image of false transcendence, if
only by situating the viewer at the end of, and somehow separate from, all that
came before.[18] Such is far from the case.

Here the dead lies. Thus, that plain human sensitivity to what has become of
another human, one who once lived not far from here, one who drank of this
land's waters, who ate of its fruits, who was buried in its earth and belongs to
the soil, cannot be denied. The simple fact that they were buried; that they
were found in the cut earth, inhumed within soil among dead others, suggests
how to do best by the obligation that we, the living, owe the dead.[19] What
more can the dead give the living that the living cannot give the dead what
they cannot give themselves?

Here the *sema* is separated from the turn post, the pillar. I sweep around past
a square panel with dolphins from a plastered floor at the Palace of Tiryns (thirteenth century BCE) and into the second corridor. Having passed from egalitarian
roots through the rise of surplus, the accumulation of wealth, the story now transitions to the consolidation of elite esteem and the path of the favored few.
Objects in the end display are organized by workshops, central authority based
upon religion, on administration, bureaucracy and relations, interconnections and
trade. The next case addresses funerary ritual and symbolism followed by goods

16 Human remains from prehistory are, for Duncan Sayer, "part of a European past and should be
   displayed, researched and interacted with as a form of commemoration, to remember who they
   were and share the human experience across all of its contexts, both ancient and modern"
   (2010, 96).
17 Of course, there are other rationales for exhuming the dead: see, for example, Crossland and
   Joyce (2015).
18 Harrison (2003, 33–35).
19 As Ewa Domanska (2018) suggests, every human has a right to decomposition.

exhumed from more graves. The journey through regional history generates a common story articulated for objects which may have had nothing in common.

There is not much more to be said here, dear reader. You have to peruse the *circus antiquarius* of this immaculate museum for yourself.

After continuing with the second corridor, pausing for a long while before the four-sided glass display case containing the museum's most prized object, the Dendra panoply, I leave the Dream House to take in photos of archaeological excavations in the hallway. Instead of ascending to the next level, and thus progressing forward with a regional history, I walk downstairs. As I pass along the portico, I glance through the door into ground floor offices of the Fourth Ephorate of Prehistoric and Classical Antiquities.

Bibliography

Alberti, S., P. Bienkowski, and M.J. Chapman. 2009. Should we display the dead? *Museum and Society*. University of Leicester, Department of Museum Studies. 133–49.

Benjamin, W. 1999. *The Arcades Project*. Cambridge, MA: Belknap Press.

Benjamin, W., and M.W. Jennings. 2002. *Selected writings, Volume 3: 1935–1938*. Cambridge, MA: Belknap Press.

Brooks, M.M., and Rumsey, C. 2006. The body in the museum. In V. Cassman, N. Odegaard, and J. Powell (eds.), *Human remains: Guide for museums and academic institutions*. Lanham, MD: Altamira Press. 261–89.

Brooks, M.M., and C. Rumsey. 2007. Who knows the fate of his bones? Rethinking the body on display: Object, art or human remains. In S.J. Knell, S. MacLeod, and S. Watson (eds.), *Museum revolutions: How museums change and are changed*. Abingdon: Routledge. 343–54.

Crossland, Z., and R.A. Joyce. 2015. *Disturbing bodies: Perspectives on forensic anthropology*. Santa Fe, NM: School for Advanced Research Press.

Domanska, E. 2018. *Nekros: Wprowadzenie do ontologii martwego ciała*. Warsaw: Wydawnictwo Naukowe PWN.

González-Ruibal, A. 2018. Archaeology of ethics. *Annual Review of Anthropology* 47, 345–60.

Hamilakis, Y. 2007. *The nation and its ruins: Antiquity, archaeology, and national imagination in Greece*. Oxford: Oxford University Press.

Harrison, R.P. 2003. *The dominion of the dead*. Chicago, IL: University of Chicago Press.

Henry, O., and U. Kelp (eds.). 2016. *Tumulus as sema: Space, politics, culture and religion in the first millennium BC*. Berlin and Boston, MA: De Gruyter.

Nilsson Stutz, L. 2016. To gaze upon the dead: The exhibition of human remains as cultural practice and political process in Scandinavia and the USA. In H. Williams and M. Giles (eds.), *Archaeologists and the dead: Mortuary archaeology in contemporary society*. Oxford: Oxford University Press. 268–92.

Olsen, B. 2010. *In defense of things: Archaeology and the ontology of objects*. Lanham, MD: AltaMira Press.

Olsen, B., M. Shanks, T. Webmoor, and C. Witmore. 2012. *Archaeology: The discipline of things*. Berkeley, CA: University of California Press.

Sayer, D. 2010. *Ethics and burial archaeology*. London: Duckworth.

Sloterdijk, P. 2015. Museum: School of alienation (trans. I.B. Whyte). *Art in Translation* 6 (4), 437–48.

Sloterdijk, P., and E. Morse. 2009. Something in the air. *Frieze Magazine*, 1 Nov. 2009. Available at https://frieze.com/article/something-air.

Svestad, A. 2013. What happened in Neiden? On the question of reburial ethics. *Norwegian Archaeological Review* 46(2), 192–242.

Swain, H. 2016. Museum practice and the display of human remains. In H. Williams and M. Giles (eds.), *Archaeologists and the dead*. Oxford: Oxbow Books. 169–83.

Taylor, J.S. 2012. *Death, posthumous harm, and bioethics*. New York, NY: Routledge.

Venizelos, E. 1998. *Diachronia kai Synergeia. Mia Politiki Politismou*. Athens: Kastaniotis.

18

TO ASINE

Legal objects

An archaeologist, protecting archaeological sites, bureaucratic oversight, two bygone towers, zoning, law and archaeological objects, controversy, Asine and destruction

May 31, 2012. Outside the offices of the Fourth Ephorate of Prehistoric and Classical Antiquities, I meet an archaeologist who oversees cultural heritage in the areas of Epidaurus and Asine. We walk up to the parking lot at Psaromachalas and get into a sweltering car in the early afternoon. We soon wend our way downhill, passing by the last surviving bastion of the old sea wall, below the Amphitryon Hotel, and along Speliadau Street. Our destination is Asine.

Georgia Ivou has worked for the Fourth Ephorate since 2007. That morning she had driven out to Dimena, a village just north of the Asklepion of Epidaurus, to inspect the planned route for an extension to the Anavalos canal system.[1] A new

---

1 See Segment 11.

project of the Ministry of Development, the main canal would tie into the existing system at Tiryns and lead to Dimena. Through sub-canals which tap the main line, water would be supplied to olive groves throughout the Kophino Valley. As a state archaeologist, Georgia is charged with inspecting the proposed route of the canal for objects of archaeological concern and making recommendations as to the best course of action.[2]

We turned right on Andrea Siggrou and left onto 25 Martiou, which curves into the wide thoroughfare of Asklepion Avenue. The Fourth Ephorate is responsible for the Prehistoric and Classical antiquities of the whole of the Argolid prefecture, which had been recently reorganized into four municipalities—Argos-Mykines, Epidaurus, Ermionida, and Nafplio—as part of the Kallikratis government reforms. A separate Ephorate exists for Byzantine and Post-Byzantine antiquities (the 25th) and their remit is significantly larger, encompassing the prefectures of Corinth, Argolis, and Arcadia. Yet another Ephorate covers the nineteenth century to the contemporary. Subsequent restructuring of the Ministry of Culture and Sports will place all cultural heritage in the region under the Ephorate of Antiquities of the Argolis.

We drive past the military engineering training center, under eucalyptus trees unknown to any being here prior to their introduction in the late nineteenth century. We soon pass the former Athos canning plant on the right. Georgia tells me that it is in the final phases of its transformation into the Fougaro, a cultural center with a library of arts and humanities, exhibition space, workshop, concert hall, and café. She then points to Agios Vlasios on the left, a hill half covered in concrete apartment buildings where archaeological excavations in the 1980s unearthed Neolithic and Early and Late Helladic remains. As part of a team of archaeologists, Georgia will work to draw up a proposal concerning the protection of the entire hill, among other archaeological sites, to be submitted to the Central Archaeological Council with the aim of producing a new, or revised, zoning law. The proposal will set out strict guidelines for development in the area—any new houses will require trial trenches. Agios Vlasios will eventually be added as a protected zone. Broader protection zones also will be added at the center of Levkakia, around the remains of a temple, and Agios Ioannis, around what has become of its fourth-century watchtower.

We bypass the roundabout and take the road to Tolo. A patchwork of farm plots interspersed with businesses and villas crowds the straight band of tarmac before us. In the midst of the economic crisis many of the agricultural plots along here are for sale. Georgia oversees the approval of the licenses for

2 For a description of the ecology of Greek archaeology, see Hamilakis (2007, 35–46).

permission to build. Through autopsy she determines whether or not artefacts are present in the area to be developed. If so, the Ephorate will follow up with survey and test trenches. If more substantial remains are found, then rescue excavations are required. Before proceeding with their plans, applicants must wait for the Ephorate to work through their backlog of rescue projects, which can take time. Or, they may opt to pay out of pocket for the archaeological labor. Whatever the path, construction can only occur after the entire structural footprint has been excavated or the building plans have been altered, often substantially.

Much of Georgia's work amounts to such bureaucratic procedure, managing relationships among people, legislation, development, and objects defined (a priori) as cultural heritage.[3] Of late, fewer applications have passed across her desk—applications to the ministry for new construction are down by more than 50 per cent from what they were prior to the economic crisis. Ephorate staff and resources, Georgia hints, have also been reduced and significantly strained.

She gestures ahead to the right. A small solar farm will be built in a field below Agios Ioannis in the coming year. A government program provided incentives to independent farmers who installed solar parks up to 100 kilwatts— lower interest rates were provided by banks and higher prices were guaranteed for selling power to DEI (Public Electricity Service). The program will soon end, and the pledged prices will be reduced. According to Georgia, after peak years in 2010 and 2011, when she reviewed a total of ninety-four applications for solar farms, this year the volume has fallen to but a handful.[4] Most of these applications came from younger inheritors of land who look for alternatives to farming—in place of leaves, solar panels will capture the sun's rays.

Georgia points out the low hill of Agios Ioannis on the far side of groves and fields. Set at its northern edge is a small Orthodox church raised in the midst of a whitewashed, square structure of carefully fitted polygonal masonry. Whereas the vaulted superstructure of the church, which enjoys local renown for its window—a journey through this is held to be miraculous for sick children—is but a few centuries in age, its stone substructure dates to the fourth century

---

3 The word "heritage" designates that which is inherited, a property devolved by right of inheritance, an allotted or reserved portion, that which is transmitted by ancestors, and, only quite recently, features and things of local, national and international interest connected with a will to preserve for future generations (here see Carman 2005). UNESCO defines "heritage" as "our legacy *from the past*, what we live with today, and what we pass on to future generations. Our cultural and natural heritage are both irreplaceable sources of life and inspiration" (http://whc. unesco.org/en/about/; my emphasis).

4 There were eight applications in 2012. It will fall to zero for 2013. After 2012, a new type of application began for solar power installations on the roofs of extant buildings.

BCE.[5] A zone of protection encompasses the area of a circle extending 40 meters from the center of this former tower. Protected land is divided by the Greek government into two zones: A and B. "A" denotes an area where no new construction is permitted; where buildings may be restored but not rebuilt; where agriculture is highly regulated (only shallow agriculture, by hand, is permitted) and any agricultural improvements (irrigation or access roads) require permits. "B" provides permission to build houses, but no commercial properties (hotels, stores, gas stations, etc.).

We enter the village of Asine. Georgia mentions the ruins of another tower south of the Nafplion–Epidaurus road on a low hill known as Kastrakia.[6] It was only recently that these ruins had become an object of concern for the Ephorate—unmentioned as they were in previous accounts of the area—through a dispute with a local farmer over their use. In the 1990s, the farmer allegedly excavated the fill from within the single course of massive stones and constructed a cement cistern inside the 2,400-year-old substructure. A lawsuit was brought against him by the Ephorate for the damage to the monument. By being drawn into the *vinculum juris* of legal action, this ruin was not redefined under the protection of law. Whether explicit or naively given, all ancient monuments are *predefined*; that is, they are legal objects prior to being made public by record.[7]

These bygone towers, as Georgia says, were part of a network of defenses associated with Asine and Argos. Yet, what becomes of the past, through force of law, is strengthened as legally defined objects.[8] Such legal protections amplify the agency of these erstwhile towers; that is, their ability to make a difference with respect to all subsequent change in their midst. As legal objects these ruins resonate through juridical ties. A topology of such protected objects suggests a radically different sense of space—a coextensive ensemble of monuments framed as of many different eras, yet connected to courtrooms, law offices, archives, articles of protection, legal documents, and other such monuments. Through such a legal topology one could never designate these pasts and the contemporary public as two separate domains.

5 Sarantákis (2007), Witmore (2015a, 55).
6 The toponym, Kastrakia ("little castle"), is probably derived from these ruins.
7 According to the archaeological law 3028/2002 "every action that can harm, direct or indirect, monuments is forbidden," irrespective of whether the monument is known or unknown to the authorities. On the history of Greek antiquities law and the state ownership of cultural heritage, see Petrakos (1982, 2007), Voudouri (2010).
8 Indeed, by being drawn into the legal trajectory of a lawsuit the ruined tower turned cistern becomes what Kyle McGee calls a "jurimorph"; that is, an entity fashioned in the course of legal decision (2014; also see Latour 2015; Matthews and Veitch 2016).

Kastrakia, tower turned cistern.

The road weaves a course through the village center with its medley of shops, tavernas, and houses, some concrete, some stone. I mention how Vasileios Petrakos connects the beginnings of archaeology in Greece with the support of laws thereby rendering illicit all activities (plunder, looting, the theft of antiquities, etc.) prior to the assumption of power by Kapodistrias.[9] Protection under the law also guaranteed that the unhistorical reality of objects—erstwhile towers which suggested themselves as containers for subsequent structural forms: a church, a cistern—was derivative to the historical reality of objects—watchtowers dating to the fourth century BCE.[10] Still, with respect to the law, the issue is not whether or not the monument in question is Prehistoric or Classical or Roman or Byzantine—that is

9 Petrakos's addition of law (2007, 19) to the definition of archaeology strikes something of contrast to the defining criteria for the discipline set out by Alain Schnapp (1997). For Schnapp, archaeology emerges through the integration of a trinity of principles—typology, technological evolution, and stratigraphy. In Greece, the first archaeological law, after the resolutions from the National Assemblies (see Segment 13), dates to 1834, thus the beginning of archaeology for Petrakos (for a discussion of archaeology as an ecology of practices, see Olsen et al. 2012, 38; Witmore and Shanks 2013).

10 Though the Kastrakia tower had continued to perform as a cistern by suppling water to the farmer's olive trees as of June 2012, the chains of legislation do not link objects with respect to their own integrities (Olsen 2010).

simply a matter of management by different Ephorates.[11] Rather, if a monument can be established as a pre-1453 monument, or select monuments between the breakpoint years of 1453 and 1830, then it is protected.[12] While the law serves to strengthen stones through its guardianship, so long as they are defined as "cultural heritage" situated within the correct chronological parameters, content counts for very little with respect to legal protections.[13]

I comment on the irony that an archaeologist, someone who is charged with the production of content, information, and specificity, acts as the go-between for legal protections, which take no interest in the depth of those objects. "It is but a means," Georgia replies. "Legal protections provide the necessary conditions for extending these monuments, defined as cultural heritage, into the future. We fill but a link in a chain of obligation tied together by law, but which perpetuates the critical end—*mnimeia*." Her word for the critical end, *mnimeia*, holds on to the dual resonance of both "monument" and "memory," and is part of the terminology used in the protective legislation.

We are halfway through the roundabout when Georgia indicates where two cemeteries, one Hellenistic, another Late Bronze Age, were partially excavated by the Ephorate. The series of buildings that rose in the wake of excavations sit mid-construction, awaiting completions yet to come.

Georgia signals that we have crossed into Zone B, which is defined by a low rise to the right, an extension of Barbouna Hill. The road curves along a cut in the bedrock of the rise, now crowned by a villa. Despite its proximity to sand beaches, and the villages of Asine and Tolo, most of the coastal plain is covered in citrus groves. Georgia and her colleagues have struggled to maintain the agricultural environment around the protected monuments of the area. The only legal frame outside of the protective zones relates to a paragraph in the Archaeological Law of 2002, which mentions "direct and indirect" harm to the monuments. Under the stipulation of "indirect" she has argued that some proposed developments constitute visual harm to the integrity of the monuments. Not everyone agrees with such interpretations.

---

11 In 2014, by order of Presidential Degree 104/2014, FEK 171/A/28-8-2014, the Ephorate of Antiquities of the Argolis became responsible for the protection of all monuments in the region, Prehistoric, Classical and Byzantine. There was another Presidential Degree regarding the Organization of the Ministry in 2018, but it did not affect the arrangement of the Ephorate of the Argolis.

12 1453, the fall of Constantinople to the Ottomans; 1830, the foundation of the Greek state. Refer to articles 2 and 20 of Law No. 3028/2002, On the Protection of Antiquities and Cultural Heritage in General: www.wipo.int/wipolex/en/details.jsp?id=6947.

13 On the absence of content and information in law, see Latour (2010, 244–77); also Harman (2015, 51). On the dangers of attempting to render "heritage" as a matter of common public concern, see Witmore (2013b).

Views to Asine against the Gulf of Argos from the summit of Profitis Elias: upper, from Lehmann 1934 (Plate 3); lower, from 2016.

We park by the taverna under eucalyptus and pine. In the parking lot Georgia pauses to point out how this area of the plain was incorporated as a protected zone in 1995. Georgia describes this as a sensitive area archaeologically, given its proximity to ancient Asine, centered on the promontory known as Kastraki and the Bronze Age cemetery on Barbouna. Such protections are not without controversy.[14] She alludes to a case going back to 1989 of a landowner who purchased a field in the area before the Zone A laws were enacted. The landowner applied to build a house and the Ephorate prevented it.

14 Hamilakis (2007, 38).

In 1995 he applied to build a terrace; he was denied. In 1997 he applied to make a road onto his property; he was turned down. In 2007 he returned to the Ephorate office in Nafplion to air his grievances: "Why," he screamed, "were other buildings being constructed in the area when I was prevented from doing so?"

Rage, frustration, and indignation are understandable responses. State archaeologists are often regarded as heritage police, state agents who tie up dreams with bureaucratic delays and restrictions, or repudiation, which forces those who live with the past into the fetters of alienation and estrangement.[15] While the system is not without its abuses, in this case the landowner's aggression could only be directed at desks, walls, coffee cups, and other links in the chain of law. For when people speak of the past as a burden, when they speak of the excesses of administration, or the elevation of the past above the interests of the living, they err by mistaking the offices of the Ephorate with a tyranny of power that crushes the landowner's dreams. Through law the material past comes to profoundly impact the lives of residents of this plain, yet any prohibitions that occur here result as a matter of speaking on legally justified rather than objective or political grounds.[16] The locus of authority is not within the law; it is preestablished before its work ever begins.[17]

We leave the parking lot and cross a wooden bridge over a trench cut deep by the ancient city walls. As we walk through the archaeological site of the Kastraki, Georgia discusses plans for a new presentation scheme for the site.[18] Walls and surfaces will be cleaned. Open trenches will be filled in. Exhibition spaces and information boards will be linked by pathways, elevated catwalks, and new staircases.[19] As we walk, there is no way to tell among which "ruined lines, edges, points, hollows and curves" the poet lingered.

Three years after George Seferis pondered the weight of stone and ruin, Asine suffered profound devastations under different authorities.[20] Italian troops occupied the Kastraki from April 1941 to September 1943, and transformed

15 Hamilakis (2007, 37–8), Herzfeld (1991, 191–225).

16 Latour (2013, 357–80).

17 Latour (2010), Harman (2015, 51).

18 The project, "Ancient Acropolis of Asine: Reformation of the Kastraki Archaeological Site 2007–2015," is funded by the European National Strategic Reference Framework program and supervised by the Ephorate of Antiquities of Argolis (see Ivou 2016).

19 Protection allows for research and education, conservation and restoration (in appropriate circumstances), and facilitating access. A summary of this work, however brief or extended, is published in *Archaiologikon Deltion* (Archaeological Bulletin). Any more elaborate publication occurs on the basis of interest by the excavator (apropos to the present situation, see Yioutsos 2017).

20 A traumatic episode of the recent past, there were numerous crimes against such protected monuments (MRANE 1946; also see González-Ruibal 2019).

Italian machine-gun nest in acropolis wall, Asine.

the ancient acropolis into yet another fortress in the course of World War II. Little of the Lower Town, a polychonic ensemble of Early, Middle, and Late Helladic, Hellenistic, Roman, and Late Roman walls excavated by archaeologies under the Swedish Institute at Athens, will survive in their wake. The nine-teenth-century church was converted into a dormitory.[21] Venetian battlements were extended and crenellation added to shield bunkhouses from view. Lying exposed, erstwhile walls offered themselves as convenient quarries; ancient city walls gave form to machine-gun nests outfitted with pebble mosaic floors; cis-terns, Hellenistic to Roman in date, lent their cave-like interiors to storerooms and hideouts for Italian soldiers. Trenches were dug, observation posts and pill-boxes were constructed, around the limestone heights of the Kastraki, delimit-ing the promontory, once again enrolling the ancient defenses.[22] Atop the Hellenistic tower, blocks were separated to form embrasures within a parapet for a position above Plaka Beach. The fifth-century CE bath complex was con-verted into storerooms and shelters, and artillery positions were constructed along the southern escarpment of Barbouna Hill.

The destruction was described in a report on the depredations of occupying forces as "final, radical, and complete."[23] Where ruins remain, things reached ahead of themselves, outliving the wished-for expectations of their makers, affording different uses to the occupying latecomers, who, outside of the

21 At least, locals recall such use of the church; see Yioutsos (2017, 173).
22 Nektarios-Peter Yioutsos has laid out admirably all of these transformations to the site (2017).
23 MRANE (1946, 65); cited in Yioutsos (2017, 172).

protections of the law, exploited different qualities in these things that remained. If the law provides means of sustaining what is, which we hold to be suggestive of what was, thereby situating what will be, it can do nothing without the authority established by politics which it presupposes.[24] With our fingers we now touch the Italians' touch upon these stones.[25]

We follow a circuitous path that leads us over stones, and beyond huge fortress walls by Camping Asine. Georgia points to where excavations were undertaken by the Swedish Institute of Archaeology between 1970 and 1974 at the invitation of the Ephorate in the context of rescue and development.[26] Unique in what is known of this era, structural remains found here suggested continuous habitation from the twelfth to the eighth century BCE.[27] This singular ground is now capped by a tennis court.

We turn west and walk along citadel walls in the direction of Tolo.

24 Here, turn a phrase stated by Harman (2015, 57).
25 Here my wordplay draws upon the final line of Seferis's poem, "The King of Asine."
26 Wells (1976, 1983).
27 Morris (2000, 204–05).

Bibliography

Carman, J. 2005. *Against cultural property: Archaeology, heritage and ownership.* London: Duckworth.

González-Ruibal, A. 2019. *An archaeology of the contemporary era.* London: Routledge.

Hamilakis, Y. 2007. *The nation and its ruins: Antiquity, archaeology, and national imagination in Greece.* Oxford: Oxford University Press.

Harman, G. 2015. Politics and law as Latourian modes of existence. In K. McGee (ed.), *Latour and the passage of law.* Edinburgh: Edinburgh University Press. 38–60.

Herzfeld, M. 1991. *A place in history: Social and monumental time in a Cretan town.* Princeton, NJ: Princeton University Press.

Ivou, G. 2016. Archaía Asíni. *Archaiología kai Téchnes,* 120 (April 2016), 120–44.

Latour, B. 2010. *The making of law: An ethnography of the Conseil d'État.* Cambridge: Polity Press.

Latour, B. 2013. *An inquiry into modes of existence: An anthropology of the moderns.* Cambridge, MA: Harvard University Press.

Latour, B. 2015. The strange entanglement of jurimorphs. In K. McGee (ed.), *Latour and the passage of law.* Edinburgh: Edinburgh University Press. 331–53.

Matthews, D., and S. Veitch. 2016. The limits of critique and the forces of law. *Law and Critique* 27(3), 349–361.

McGee, K. 2014. *Bruno Latour: The normativity of networks.* Abingdon: Routledge.

Ministry of Religious Affairs and National Education. 1946. *Zimíai ton Archaiotíton ek tou Polémou kai ton Stratón Katochís.* Athens.

Morris, I. 2000. *Archaeology as culture history.* Oxford: Blackwell.

Olsen, B. 2010. *In defense of things: Archaeology and the ontology of objects.* Lanham, MD: AltaMira Press.

Olsen, B., M. Shanks, T. Webmoor, and C. Witmore. 2012. *Archaeology: The discipline of things.* Berkeley, CA: University of California Press.

Petrakos, V. Ch. 1982. *Dokimio gia tin archaiologikí nomothesía.* Athens: Ypourgeio Politismou–T.A.P.

Petrakos, V. Ch. 2007. The stages of Greek archaeology. In P. Valavanes and A. Delevorrias (eds.), *Great moments in Greek archaeology.* Los Angeles, CA: J. Paul Getty Museum. 16–35.

Sarantákis, P. 2007. *Argolída / Oi Ekklisíes kai ta Monastíria tis.* Athens: Ekdóseis OIATIS.

Schnapp, A. 1997. *The discovery of the past.* New York, NY: Harry N. Abrams.

Voudouri, D. 2010. Law and the politics of the past: Legal protection of cultural heritage in Greece. *International Journal of Cultural Property* 17, 547–68.

Wells, B. 1976. *Asine II: Results of the excavations east of the Acropolis 1970–1974 – Part I.* Stockholm: Svenska Institutet i Athen.

Wells, B. 1983. *Asine II: Results of the excavations east of the Acropolis 1970-1974. Part II.* Stockholm: Svenska Institutet i Athen.

Witmore, C. 2013b. Which archaeology? A question of chronopolitics. In A. González-Ruibal (ed.), *Reclaiming archaeology: Beyond the tropes of modernity.* London: Routledge. 130–44.

Witmore, C. 2015a. Archaeology and the second empiricism. In F. Herschend, C. Hillerdal, and J. Siapkas (eds.), *Debating archaeological empiricism.* London: Routledge. 37–61.

Witmore, C., and M. Shanks. 2013. Archaeology: An ecology of practices. In W.L. Rathje, M. Shanks, and C. Witmore (eds.), *Archaeology in the making: Conversations through a discipline.* Abingdon: Routledge.

Yioutsos, N.-P. 2017. The last occupation of Asine in Argolis. *Opuscula* 10, 164–89.

19

TO VIVARI, BY BOAT

Tolo, from sails to motors, the destruction of caiques, a shipwright, boat design, artisanal fishers, the topography of fish, the death of a blast fisher, a purse seiner, the last Bluefin, overfishing, an aquaculture facility, the "blue revolution," the terrestrial invades the maritime, malfeasance and appropriation, new orientations

June 7, 2012. It is 8:00 a.m. I have arranged to meet Yiannis at the pier by the Romvi Hotel.[1] Somewhat typical of the multi-story hotels that crowd the sandy beach, the Romvi is a regular haunt for coffee, beer, wine, and conversation. This morning, save for a lonely proprietor laying out tablecloths, it is silent. I step off the wet sand, walk up a short ramp, and down a long, wide finger of cracked, sea-scoured concrete jutting out directly from shore. This pier, one of four in Tolo, is the location of Yiannis Gogonas's watersport business. From its end I begin to develop a better sense of this partially sheltered bay.

---

1 This segment could not have been written without the late Yiannis Gogonas. At many turns, I act as his scribe, thus I have maintained his name out of fidelity to his contribution.

Just to the right of opposite the pier, at a distance of 450 meters, rises the north flank of Romvi, the island from which the hotel takes its name. From this angle, the island appears as two limestone hills with a deep pine-covered saddle between them (a third knoll and second saddle are obscured to the south). Plans drawn under Francesco Grimani, *Provveditore Generale dell' Armi in Morea* (1699–1701), situated a church and monastery on the northern prominence (*G. Chiesa e Monastero sun il Scoglio grande*).[2] Ruins are present there. About half a kilometer to the east arises another island, of much smaller size, craggy and enveloped by the greens of pine, cypress, prickly pear, and maquis, crowned by a small church of the Holy Apostles—Koronisi. From the flank of Barbouna Hill to the northeast, a long, thin, sandy beach extends southwest for just under 2 kilometers. It ends at the harbor, which, built in the channel formed between the mainland and Romvi, is protected from the prevailing southeasterly winds. Dozens of caiques and small fiberglass watercraft are moored offshore, at depths of 5 to 10 meters. The Venetian Fleet used this bay as an anchorage in July of 1686. A new nation with its capital in Nafplion would later plan to build the Greek Naval Yard here. Later still, after these plans were abandoned, King Otto would set aside land reclaimed from Ottoman pashas for Cretan refugees.[3] Given the origin of these transplants, the municipality was called "Minoa" and was located along this coast between what would become the villages of Iria and Tolo. The latter formed around the villa of an Ottoman pasha, close to the only water source for the area, a fountain, within a well-watered garden.[4] It is said that the newly settled villagers sold off the farmland, agrarian implements, and oxen given to them by the government and returned to known work, familiar paths, by investing in boats, nets, and the sea.[5]

Local residents recall Tolo as a beautiful fishing village. Small houses with immaculate gardens—this pleasant image is not entirely lost among blocks crammed with crate-like hotels. Most of these whitewashed edifices are stacked so tall as to be at complete odds with their surroundings. As the line of concrete buildings was filled in, they blocked the supply and replenishment of

2 See Andrews (2006[1953], Plate XXIV). A ruined enclosure encircles the heights of the southern promontory. A fortress and church is situated on the island of Daskaleio beyond. Sekeris (N.D. 14) attributes the name to an old Didaskaleio founded in the Byzantine church on the island, which was maintained as a secret school (*kryfó scholeío*) under the Ottomans.

3 Yiannis's family name, Gogonas, is derived from Gogonakis—a surname ending with the diminutive; *akis* is characteristic of Cretan ancestry and harks back to a time when Greeks under Turkish domination were collectively humiliated, or so it is commonly held (for an alternative explanation, see Herzfeld 2003, 303–04).

4 The fountain, set in a square enclosure, is also present on the Grimani Plan (Andrews 2006[1953] Plate XXIV).

5 Sekeris (n.d.).

coastal sediments. Waves carried sands off into the Aegean and the sea encroached upon the hotels and taverns, submitting their concrete foundations to its anarchistic scrutiny. Tolo's renowned wide and sandy beach became not as wide and not as sandy. As a counter to coastal erosion, a series of submerged, concrete groynes, each 40 meters in length, were constructed along the heavily built-up area in 1996.[6] While they have yet to disrupt long shore drift to the point of being fully buried north of the pier, the edge of terra firma has remained firm. Now the best stretch of beach is to be found to the north along the last portion of uninterrupted shore near Barbouna Hill.

I turn back to the sea. Beyond the pier, the water has ripples without crests. The surface between the two islands is smooth—light air—maybe a 1 on the Beaufort Scale. Still, even on this calm morning the sea is anything but monotonous. Differentiated textures suggest a playful dance of winds across the water beyond the islands. It is not uncommon for some swells, pushed along by the southeasterlies, to find their way in past the protective barrier of the islands.[7] In any case, the conditions are excellent for cabotage.

In the company of three companions, Yiannis arrives. A stout man with curly hair, dark sunglasses, and a sober disposition, he greets me with a nod as he walks with unbroken strides to the end of the pier. Without pause, he steps across a plastic boat and into another. His companions follow. Named for Yiannis's wife Jackie, our boat is an open fiberglass hull, 8 meters in length. I wait till everyone is aboard before I clamber in.

To take leave of a solid surface for a pitching deck is to call all your faculties to attention. I am instantly aware of my feet and the need to counter every roll of the boat, intensified by other erratic bodies, with a subtle shift in weight. Before I can find a more stable position at the bow, I exchange introductions with Derrick, Mick, and Liam; all are British holidaymakers who return to Tolo each summer. Yiannis takes his seat at the center console and starts the engine, a four-stroke Suzuki (DF200 V-6) outboard.

Casting off is uneventful. There is no need to appease the earth-upholding sea god whose name is borne upon all Yiannis's business cards.[8] No need to waste thoughts on wind direction or changes in the currents. With a full tank of gas, no need to worry about the return journey. Indeed, it is striking how easy it is to move from standstill to exercise with a motor. It is the motor that takes the winds out of sails, leaving the weather as a constraint rather than

6 Antoniou et al. (2009).
7 Landforms, variations in the wind, and the sea conditions; sedimentation, sea floor, and currents, the capricious circumstances of living by the sea.
8 Yiannis's business is called Poseidon Watersports.

Boats by the dock at Romvi prior to departure.

a necessary companion. As for our three companions and myself, we are not engaged participants, as small sailboats can demand; we are idle passengers.

Throughout the Argolid, the changeover from sail to motor took place during the inter-war years.[9] With or without winds, motors enhanced boats by accelerating their speed and maneuverability. With motors, smaller watercraft, despite being lighter in overall structure, became heavier. This increase in weight affected small villages like Tolo, which were well situated by sandy stretches of beach where boats could be dry-sailed. Hardened ports and stone jetties were built. Boats moored to the pier or in the harbor required improved marine primers and paints. A new environment of select hardened ports transformed the rapport between sea and land. Situated between two wide beaches where watercraft were beached, the rocky exposure of Asine was, on both sides of the turn of the Common Era, the most favorable location. Now the sheltered end of Tolo is preferred.

As we weave a path between moorings, I glance at the line of hotels northeast of the Romvi Hotel. Not a single towel is present on the balconies. Every louver door is shut. Tourism is down, and Yiannis expresses anxieties over the

9 Forbes (1997, 113); also see Lehmann (1937, 137), Naval Intelligence Division (1944 II, 88–89).

coming season. He, like many other villagers, faults the quick transformation of the village into a tourist destination out of balance with its location. After the first hotel, Hotel Tolo, was built in 1954, mimesis took hold.[10] Fishers assumed new vocations in taverns, hotels, tourist shops, or, as in Yiannis's case, water-sports. With Jackie, he opened the first such business in Tolo over thirty years ago. Others followed along similar paths. More concrete foundations proliferated and now there are too many rooms and too few tourists. Having passed the last of the moored boats, we pick up speed. The engine drowns out all lighthearted conversation. We are forced to shout. Yiannis points the prow towards the tip of Asine and steers a straight course a parallel to the shore. Proceeding without ups and downs, in perfect horizontality, we move along the open stretch of beach. All around us, a continuous blue surface is accessible in every direction. Yiannis could steer towards whatever destination he wishes—to be sure, a new sense of control also accompanies engines—but he is not unrestrained in his movement. He takes tourists fishing, and to the islands, hidden beaches, forgot-ten ruins, and shipwrecks—he knows of two in the area. Former fishers, or those descended from fishers, like Yiannis cater to the whims of tourists on banana floats and inflated rings. A sea for vacations and tourism, recreational waters have come to be experienced in a different way. I glance at our three companions and we exchange courteous smiles.

Off port, we pass by an old man in his caique. Two decades ago, traditional wooden caiques dominated the waters of Tolo. These now seem on the verge of becoming a minority. Under the EU Common Fisheries Policy Greek fishers had access to various incentive monies. So-called scrapping subsidies, under which fishers were paid to decommission vessels to reduce pressure on fish stocks, has led to the destruction of an estimated 10,000 such boats.[11] Yiannis mentions how he routinely passes the Tolo boneyard, which sits off the outer road that skirts the northern edge of town near his house. Strewn across an overgrown lot are portions of upturned hull, white plywood cockpits, sections of carvel planking held together by ribs whose tattered and cut edges were determined by the mouth of the backhoe bucket or the line taken with the chainsaw. No one knows the topography of these sad heaps of shredded caiques better than the local shipwright, who, according to Yiannis, picks through the detritus for spare parts.

I shout a query to Yiannis concerning the location of the shipwright. He points back to Tolo. "Past the hotels, studios, and apartments, past the village

---

10 Sekeris (n.d.)
11 These figures are given by the Traditional Boat Association of Greece. The addendum was added to the 1983 EU scrapping subsidy in 1993 that fishermen had to destroy their boats (see Comp-ton 2015, 64).

soccer field, about 800 meters from the sea on the left of the Lefkakia–Tolo Road is his workshop." "A waning craft is the construction of the traditional wooden caique," Yiannis adds. "He is the last."[12]

I will later pay a visit to the shipwright's shop: a plain concrete building that doubles as his house. Before you enter the wide garage door to his first-floor workshop, you are confronted by a pile of pine timbers of every bend and stripped of their bark. The curvature of these timbers, whether innate or contrived (i.e. bent by woodcutters), will lend form to features of similar curve in the boat, if there is one to be made. Inside, only one boat is currently underway, though payment is uncertain. Its curvature in breadth is considerable. Its sheer is pronounced, both fore and aft. Its stem and stern are rounded. Its sternpost is raked. Its slight camber is uniform throughout the deck. Its shape is that of a *trechantiri*. Set against a background of concrete walls embroidered with hanging templates, upon a floor covered in splinters of wood, idle tools, and mounds of sawdust, the caique sits up on blocks. Enveloped by a fresh coat of lead primer, it awaits an engine, currently en route from the UK.

Despite his affinity for a speedboat, Yiannis's knowledge of traditional caiques is detailed. He tells us that the overall form of this ship has changed little since the seventeenth century. Subtle, to be sure, were the transformations in caique design following the shift to motors. Significant curvature in the breath of the sheer line and a deep draught created more stability for boats under sail. However, as sails were phased out, engine-powered caiques became shallower in profile; both sheer and camber were lessened; the form of the hull below the turn

A *trechantiri* in a shipwright's shop.

12 On the diversity of types, see Damianidis (1996, 39–98); also see Compton (2015, 69–70).

of the bilge was augmented; the width of the craft was reduced; the height of the gunwale was lowered; the maximum beam was moved aft to provide proper buoyancy for the engine, which sits in the void left by the mast step.[13] Though added weight came with the engine, the overall wooden structure was lightened. The use of materials also changed. Oak frames were replaced by pine. Oak keels changed over to untapped pine and later iroko, an African hardwood.

It is not difficult to appreciate the differences between an agile plastic speedboat and the old diesel caiques. Agility and speed, ease of maintenance, and lower expenditure win out over sentiment and tradition for all save the most obstinate. In the end, subsidies, convenience, and cost conspire against the old caiques and the independent fishers who made their living with them. Curation, it seems, becomes the last option for those now estranged from former modes of existing with these watercraft.

Off the promontory of Asine, which Yiannis refers to as Kastraki, we turn towards a caique (a *perama*) returning with a gillnet heaped high on the stern deck in front of the pilot's box. Yiannis rounds on the boat with greetings to an old friend—Michaelis. From his position near the rudder arm, Michaelis pulls on a broom handle extending from the wheelhouse. Puffs of black smoke erupt with less frequency and the caique slows. Yiannis inquires about his catch and with a proud smile Michaelis holds up a section of nylon gillnet, so named because its mesh is designed to ensnare fish about the gills. Among other creatures, it contains dozens of *safridhia* or horse mackerel winched in by a belt-driven spool that morning. Our English companions become animated at the sight of the catch, and inquire as to whether he will sell the fish at the Romvi. Meanwhile, I could not help but notice that while Mediterranean horse mackerel grow to between 50 and 60 centimeters, these are barely 20.[14]

Fishermen, Yiannis points out, bring in a diversity of species off Tolo which vary by season. Nutrients drawn from the deep through wind-induced upwelling stimulate plankton in the Gulf of Argos in spring.[15] Mullet of sundry varieties are caught in March. In the shallows of the harbor, Nafpliots of centuries past were recorded as netting large qualities of grey mullet once a year.[16] Many species of fish come to the coast to spawn in April and May.[17] *Safridhia*, other

---

13 See Damianidis (1996, 107).

14 Research suggests that many fish species are shrinking in response to warmer temperatures (Cheung et.al. 2013).

15 Bakun and Agostini (2001).

16 According to Evilya Çelebi (*Seyahatname*, Volume 8, 281a8–10), these "fine plump fish" were drawn by a magical fish charm in front of the Bourtzi. This event, the traveller states, "brings a great wealth of fish to the people of Anapli, and is a wondrous work of the Almighty."

17 Naval Intelligence Division (1944 II, 92).

Gillnet containing horse mackerel.

types of mackerel, and *sardela* (sardines) are now coming into season. Yiannis's descriptions rapidly turn gastronomical—that grilled is the best way to prepare *safridhia*; that sweet is the flavor of *menola* (blotched picarel); that in *kakavia* (soup) *hilou* (wrasse) and *skorpios* (scorpionfish) are excellent; that for him the best tasting are *fagri* (sea bream). I attempt to steer the conversation from taste to topography, but Yiannis bids me to wait with an upraised hand. He thanks Michaelis for the pause and steers us along the coast.

"Fishers, like Michaelis," he says, "are secretive about their favorite haunts." If caught in the act, they can be deceptive, even mendacious, which increasingly seems to be the case. From behind the console, Yiannis waves his right arm over an expanse of sea: "*Gofari* (bluefish), *koutsomoura* (red mullet), *barbouni* (red-striped mullet), and *safridhia* are common throughout the waters of Tolo." These fish routinely fall prey to gillnets stretched out across the even, sandy bottom below us. He points over his right shoulder: "King mullet are found off Cape Rouis. *Hanos* (comber) and *gilos* (rainbow wrasse) are common at Ifalos Tolo." The latter, Tolo Reef, is an underwater promontory that rises to just 3 meters below the surface south of Romvi Island. Yiannis boasts how he once lured a 6 kilogram octopus from one of the reef's crevices and into his boat. In any case, the marine topography discussed by Yiannis suggests that perhaps it is not so much an issue of watching seagulls gather, or looking for surface ripples to reveal the location of fish, as dropping a net at a trusted locale, free of hazards. "Return and check it the next morning."

To the south the silhouette of two islands, Plateia and Psili, fade into the Argolic Gulf. Beyond stretches the open sea. Tolonian fishers have a very different conception of marine space from that of deep-sea fishers and seafarers who call on distant shores.[18] They rarely delve into the realm of pelagic uncertainty, choosing to keep to locales known—smooth shoals, sandy bottoms, or uniform surfaces near rocky outcrops—all within close proximity to land. Their domain is inshore, where the sea is yet to plunge into its wine-dark shades of mysteriousness.

We speed along Plaka Beach. I start to mention how the Italians transformed the archaeological site of Asine into a stronghold during World War II, but to challenge the engine is too much effort. The association continues as a thought. Fearing an Allied landing during World War II, the Italians and Germans covered the beach extensively with landmines. Intrepid and foolish, after the war, some local fishers saw opportunity in retrieving the charges from mines for blast fishing. Improvised explosives were used to rupture the swim bladders of fish in large numbers. With the loss of buoyancy they would either float to the surface or sink to the sea floor. It was an expedient and indiscriminate practice.

Stylianos Perrakis lists one such blast fisherman among his ghosts of Plaka Beach.[19] In the spring of 1945, Pelagotos, a young man from Drepanon, stumbled on a cobble with a rucksack full of mines. The explosion occurred at the sea's edge in front of the estate of the Melissinos family. I fix my gaze on the line of conifers and eucalyptus trees near the middle of the beach.

Abruptly, Yiannis veers towards Plateia Island. Pointing ahead towards the low, maquis-covered rise, he tells us that a German glider wrecked there during World War II. A tuna purse seiner, about 16 meters in length, flying a Greek flag, trailing a small, plastic skiff, cuts through the middle ground of our attention. A *trechantiri*, it has been adapted for modern fishing techniques. Forward is the wheelhouse with a radar mast, crow's nest, and an elevated set of spools; aft is a raised drum winch with a large lifting arm. Between these two positions extends a high shelf holding upwards of a hundred plastic crates. Its eight-man crew will spend all day scouring the sea for schools of tuna, both little tunny and bluefin. Once they are spotted by sonar and lookout, the crew set upon the fast-moving schools and encircle them with a wall of netting drawn by both the *trechantiri* and

18 This is a contrast to Middle Sea-oriented narratives; for example, Broodbank (2013), Horden and Purcell (2000).
19 2006, 49.

motorized skiff. The lines are then winched in. Set on rings, the net is drawn closed, preventing any escape from an ever-constricting purse.[20] The end for bluefin, despite the vulnerability of the species, comes as a starboard slaughter. Yiannis claims that they caught a large bluefin a couple of years ago—700 kilos—adding that the Greek word for tuna is *tonos*, as they can reach 1,000 kilos or a "ton." Adults like this are now rare.

A large predatory fish, a single tuna consumes the equivalent of its own weight every ten days.[21] Moreover, they often prefer to consume other species that are themselves the result of heavy consumption. With few large bluefin, smaller tuna, and the fish they formerly consumed, replace larger ones, often irrespective of whether or not they have spawned.[22] It turned out that tuna could not consume enough to keep up with demand. A recent turn to capture-based tuna aquaculture in the Mediterranean embraces the logic of land-based CAFOs (concentrated animal feeding operations) by exerting control over consumption, and fattening up juveniles tugged to facilities in giant floating cages.[23]

Tuna purse seiner off Plaka Beach.

20 Purse seining is extremely destructive, as by-catch and discard levels are high (Clover 2006, 33).
21 Greenberg (2010).
22 See Clover (2006, 24–40, 198–213).
23 Ottolenghi (2008).

These operations have pushed down global prices and purse seiners are compelled to catch more fish from overexploited stocks.

There are few fish to be caught. Meager catches force more fishers to either take the subsidies or seek out what little remains.[24] Looking for explanations in the immediate, local fishers blame the aquaculture facility for chasing off the fish, but this is not only a matter of locality. Equipped with what is given over in experience, they blame the large trawlers for overfishing, but this is not only a matter of the Aegean.[25] Fisheries all over the Mediterranean have steadily deteriorated, but this is more than a matter of the Middle Sea.[26]

A decade-old analysis "suggests that the global ocean has lost more than 90% of large predatory fishes."[27] But the shock of this insight comes late. Continuously upgraded fishing technologies, oriented towards volume and efficiency, operated under a strained image of the sea as inexhaustible, unchanging, and boundless.[28] Under this classic concept of the insurmountable blue, everyone was slow to realize the more-than-monstrous dimensions of the global fishing industry. Under such an image, wastefulness was overlooked, and sea life was squandered everywhere.[29]

Yiannis stands up as we near the aquaculture facilities off Plateia Island. The large farm consists of dozens of sea cages along the sheltered north of the island. There are also sundry docking areas, storage structures, and clusters of other buildings—including what appears to be a disused hatchery facility—on land. Before us, forty-four large round, floating cages, each nearly 50 meters in circumference, each extending to some indiscernible depth, are moored in parallel lines, in two clusters, 100 meters from shore.[30] Nets, suspended from floating polyethylene pipework, contain both gilthead sea bream (*Sparus auratus*)

---

24 Jellyfish and squid populations are on the rise. Some fishers have turned to spotlighting the latter at night, according to Yiannis.

25 Large trawlers, because of their range, have been less susceptible to the downturn in local fisheries (see Maravelias and Tsitsika 2014).

26 A recent study suggests fish stocks have plummeted since 1990; see Vasilakopoulos et al. (2014); also see Tsikliras, Tsiros, and Stergiou (2013).

27 Myers and Worm (2003, 282).

28 This relationship with the sea is by no means new (see Roberts 2007), but its magnitude is now beyond measure.

29 A 2007 study of 110 independent fishing vessels from the Patraikos Gulf found that on average 10 per cent of fish were discarded due to low commercial value of the species, damage of nets, and destructive handling on board (Tzanatos et al. 2007). In earlier decades, the wastage was probably an order of magnitude higher. Unfortunately, ports only reported landings, not the fish that were actually killed (also see Clover 2006, 13–15).

30 In 2015 the facility included 190 cages (106 round and eighty-four square) in five separate areas. The easternmost area included five larger cages, 30 meters in diameter, with moorings set for three more. The latter suggest an upgrade towards larger containers with more room to swim in an area with greater water circulation due to currents.

and European sea bass (*Dicentrarchus labrax*). The diverse species of fish formerly caught by independent fishers are replaced by select species, largely for an export market. Many see this lack of variety as contributing to a loss of biodiversity.[31]

Yiannis speaks of how they experimented with growing red mullet, but they came out black. He speaks of how bream, striped sea bream, saddled and gilt-head—the latter is known as *gopa*—are readily attracted to the cages, but they stink as a result. He speaks of how the fish farm is a scapegoat for local fishers, who see it as inflicting damage to the sea. With no atmospheric effects above the surface, without taking the plunge, fish caught near the cages are one of the few indicators of what is happening underwater for those without recourse to the so-called hard sciences. Around the cages the waters are murky from the clouds of food waste and excrement. High concentrations of ammonium nitrogen, organic carbon, and phosphorous have been found up and down the water column in and around the cages.[32]

Yiannis pulls alongside one of the bird-net-draped enclosures where a floating platform is laden with a pallet stacked high with nondescript sacks simply stamped *EcoFeed*.[33] From the shade of a parasol, a worker uses a mechanized feeder to launch pellets into the middle of a thrashing throng of thousands. For every 2 kilograms of fishmeal, they will add 1 kilogram of flesh. From fry to marketable fish, aquaculture expedites growth. Whereas here gilt-head sea bream mature in twelve to eighteen months and European sea bass in fifteen to twenty, it can take twice as long in the wild.[34] Through year-round cultivation and accelerated growth these animals are adapted to those pervasive, synchronous routines of supply and demand, where seasonality and locality no longer factor.

We round the southern rim of the cage. Recommended socking densities range between 10 and 50 kilograms per cubic meter.[35] With the concentration of fish, cages can act as incubators for pathogens, running the risk of contaminating wild fish populations with bacteria, viruses, or parasites.[36] Explicit

31 Over 95 per cent of the total production in Greece is comprised of gilthead sea bream and European sea bass (see Food and Agriculture Organization of the United Nations (FAO) 2005–2016a).
32 A study conducted on samples taken between August 2001 and May 2002 found that the concentrations were limited to the area of the farm (Mantzavrakos et al. 2007).
33 EcoFeed S.A. is an animal feed company based in Halandri.
34 The commercial size for both species is 300–400 grams (see Cardia and Lovatelli 2007). In the wild it takes two years to achieve this size for sea bream and thirty-seven months for sea bass.
35 FAO (2005–2016b), Lupatsch et al. (2010).
36 See Austin and Austin (2012); for an example of the transfer of marine myxosporeans in sea bream, see Diamant (1997).

Aquaculture facilities off Plateia Island.

programs of management target a litany of pathogens, recognizable through their effects, and countered either through changes to the environment—improved water flow, decreased stocking density, upgraded cages, lessened stress —or through the synthetic manipulation of endocrinological and immunological systems. Antibiotics are enrolled to minimize the collateral damage from concentration, which can escalate the pace of microbial evolution and antibiotic resistance.[37]

We troll between the shore and the inner line of the westernmost cluster of cages. This facility has been here for twenty-five years. Over that course of time, a single generation, aquaculture has exploded in Greece, with the number of companies farming sea bass and sea bream rocketing from ten in 1986 to 370 in 2008. Farmed fish has become Greece's second largest agricultural export after olive oil.[38] Here, an artificial apparatus expands, this time filling what proprietors of aquaculture see as the market void created by the downturn in wild fish populations worldwide. For better and worse, we are now chained to aquaculture as a necessity that will only continue to expand and upgrade.[39]

We move towards a supply vessel moored off one of the cages, where men wearing fishing bibs are harvesting. In the midst of the worst recession to hit the country since World War II, the sight of non-Greek workers weighs heavily

---

37 Serrano (2005).

38 FAO (2005–2016a).

39 New experiments and research into integrated aquaculture focuses on managing an entire ecosystem where waste from fish cages becomes nutrients for seaweed, mussels, sea urchins, and other invertebrates.

on Yiannis. "While local jobs are lost," he protests, "few are replaced." An industrial assemblage such as this requires corporate control and oversight; it involves absentee decision makers, and the supply of fish moves away from the independent, artisanal fishers who live along these shores. Despite their proximity, there is no direct path from within these cages to the tables of Tolo or Vivari.

A dipnet full of fish is transferred to a large container with a hydraulic loading crane. Abruptly, the operator demands that we stay back, and not film or take photos. We are encouraged to leave. After a short protest, Yiannis yields. As we pull away, I snap another photograph of the supply vessel—a box-like cabin set on a barge-like rectangle rusting about the waterline. Its name is *Kalloni*, "beauty."

Northeast by north, Yiannis steers a course towards Drepanon Bay. The Greek government leases the site to the parent company Selonda Aquaculture, which also has a facility 10 kilometers to the east in Vourlia Bay. Still, no one owns anything below the high water mark.[40] Aquaculture provides a precarious foothold for animal enclosures where none has ever existed. Within an inexorable watery world, contrived containers allow for control, for managed-being. In this, a girded volume of seawater is revealed as a space for cultivating an investment. There are worries that as the terrestrial invades the maritime, that aquaculture will lead to the privatization of the commons. As it is, fishers can no longer drop nets off the north shores of Plateia Island. Does corporate investment in this locality breed territoriality? Does it engender a sense of ownership? Do they think of this patch of sea as their property? From this angle the so-called "blue revolution," as it appears from a boat off Plateia Island, does not stand in such stark contrast to the so-called "agricultural revolution" that swept these shores so long ago.[41]

Yiannis cuts the engine and abruptly wheels around. He leans over the gunwale to fish a 15 liter bucket out of the water. Recent surveys have tried to put quantities to what is adrift in the currents of the sea, but what is one to do with more than "62 million macro-litter items" floating on the surface of the Mediterranean?[42] Only polyethylenes, the plastics that comprise the skeleton of the aquaculture cages, and polypropylenes, which are found in the bucket, float.

40 Nonetheless, the lease includes island and the marine area used by the facility (see FAO 2011–2016).

41 Aquaculture is not radical and new in concept; it is ancient. Managing fish populations, however, was often centered on independent fishers; it was small in scale (see Nash 2011). Also see Segment 20.

42 Suaria and Aliani (2014); another recent study estimated the average density of floating plastic to be one item per 4 square meters (Cozar et al. 2015).

All other plastics, including the nylons of the monofilament lines and nets used by the fishers and aquaculturalists, sink.[43] Within a few moments, Mick hooks a plastic bag. A thin biofilm has begun to form on its surface. With growth, the microorganisms and algae, unless cleaned by scavengers, will cause it to sink. But what is set adrift does not always find its way to shore or seafloor. Derrick mentions how "sea turtles ingest plastic bags, which block up their digestive system, leaving them to starve." "Sea birds," Mick adds, "routinely mistake bits of floating plastic for food."[44] The work of water will unravel plastics into minuscule particles. Diffuse microplastics, present throughout the water column, are ingested by everything, even zooplankton.[45]

With the currents, the collective refuse of billions disperses. As a species born of the humus, we appropriate the aquatic without even noticing. Our garbage is everywhere. Thus, the oceans are revealed as the largest archaeological sites on the planet. Every biologist, every oceanographer, every toxicologist studying the effects of aquacultural effluents, plastics, toxins, not to mention carbon dioxide, in seawater has become an archaeologist. With our malfeasance we billions take possession of the aqueous volumes inhabited by fish, by turtles, by seabirds, by zooplankton. We take possession of their bodies, invading them with our own filth, which, by eating their flesh, returns to ours.[46]

As we round the western end of Drepanon we set our eyes upon the irregular fort, whose battered stone walls closely follow the gnarled limestone contours of the point. A curious material memory of Venetian interest in this well-protected inlet, the unique topography of Drepanon was considered as a suitable dry dock for the fleet.[47] Grimani himself had urged the construction of the fort, plans for which are now part of the collection that bears his name. Once broken only by gun embrasures, this ruined bastion rests uneasily over deep gouges above the waterline on its eastern side. With no groynes to protect its stone and mortar foundations, its form slowly succumbs to the unremitting intrusion of plastic-suffused seas. The outcome of sea versus stone is assured. Perhaps it is best to regard this as a curious material memory of Venetian hubris.

43 Corcoran (2015).
44 A recent study of seabirds (Codina-García et al. 2013) found large amounts of plastic particles in shearwaters.
45 See Cole et al. (2011), Cole et al. (2014). Microplastics particles include fibers, microbeads, and "nurdles," preproduction plastic resin pellets. These plastic particles contain PCBs and other pollutants.
46 This is more than an issue of garbage and effluents in ocean waters. Bottom-trawlers are reworking sediments throughout the world's oceans. For a recent study of this practice in the Mediterranean, see Martín et al. (2014).
47 See Andrews (2006[1953], 239–41).

Cutting deep behind the headland, the inlet, half harbor, half protected lagoon, assumes the shape of a sickle or pruning hook; this is the meaning of "Drepanon." As we move through the middle of the harbor, we overtake a supply scow for the aquaculture facility. The *Phaneromeni III*—the scow's name translates as "revealed" or "manifested." Its name is derived from *phaneros*— clear, visible, conspicuous. We can see fewer independent fishers and caiques, it is clear; we can witness fewer fish being landed, it is visible; we can understand the necessity of aquaculture, it is conspicuous. I can photograph the refuse we pulled from the sea or the occasional white blob in the water, whether plastic or jellyfish. Through measures of ammonium nitrogen, organic carbon, and phosphorous in tables, with quantities of refuse in the ocean in graphs, science counters our experiential blindness to what is not plainly visible by making it so. From within this inlet the sea may appear to be the same, but to embrace this semblance is to invite self-endangerment.

Millennia of naively given relations with the sea have been upended. Here, we face far more than the loss of a long-term culture, which before our eyes is passing from an implicit mode of lived existence. Fragile, losable, in need of care—this is how we now experience the bounty of the formerly fish-filled sea. What was once taken for granted must now be supported through explicit programs of maintenance, or so we are told.[48] Observe here the so-called end of history: the willingness to act is no longer primarily a matter of cultural inheritance. Instead it seems to be more a matter of blanket innovations, constant redesign, and management programs.[49]

When old dependences no longer make sense, what gods do we appease for our crossing? Are they not making themselves known?

We pull up alongside the pier. I bid farewell to Yiannis and his companions, and disembark onto another slab of sea-scoured concrete. Weaving a path around pallets laden with fish pellets and plastic containers of fry, I walk towards the small fishing village of Vivari. At the end of the pier, I find a fish tavern. I sit down at a table. I order a coffee, and I ask the owner, Dimitris, if I can see the fresh catch of the day.

48 This realization does not subdue the perplexity and suspicion one feels when the response to a catastrophe follows the same beacon of growth and profitability that contributed to its creation (see Stengers 2015). It is for all of us—nearly eight billion humans—that the artificial stratagems ensue. But here necessity—we must advert hunger in the midst of catastrophe—becomes a pretense for the satisfaction of those who profit in the name of "for all of us." Against this old ruse, one that in this form is now common knowledge, a sense of higher integrity must always be defended.

49 See Sloterdijk (2009, 44).

Bibliography

Andrews, K. 2006[1953]. *Castles of the Morea*. Princeton, NJ: American School of Classical Studies at Athens.

Antoniou, P.F., H. Kyriakidou, and C. Anagnostou. 2009. Cement filled geo-textile groynes as a means of beach protection against erosion: A critique of applications in Greece. *Journal of Coastal Research, Special Issue* 56, 463–66.

Austin, B., and D.A. Austin. 2012. *Bacterial fish pathogens: Disease of farmed and wild fish*. 5th ed. New York, NY: Springer.

Bakun, A., and V.N. Agostini. 2001. Seasonal patterns of wind-induced upwelling/downwelling in the Mediterranean Sea. *Scientia Marina* 65(3), 243–57.

Broodbank, C. 2013. *The making of the Middle Sea*. Oxford: Oxford University Press.

Cardia, F., and A. Lovatelli. 2007. A review of cage aquaculture: Mediterranean Sea. In M. Halwart, D. Soto, and J.R. Arthur (eds.), *Cage aquaculture: Regional reviews and global overview*. FAO Fisheries Technical Paper. No. 498. Rome: FAO. 156–87.

Cheung, W.W.L., J.L. Sarmiento, J. Dunne, T.L. Frölicher, V.W.Y. Lam, M.L. D. Palomares, R. Watson, and D. Pauly. 2013. Shrinking of fishes exacerbates impacts of global ocean changes on marine ecosystems. *Nature Climate Change* 3(3), 254–58.

Clover, C. 2006. *The end of the line: How overfishing is changing the world and what we eat*. Berkeley, CA: University of California Press.

Codina-García, M., T. Militão, J. Moreno, and J. Gonzáles-Solís. 2013. Plastic debris in Mediterranean seabirds. *Marine Pollution Bulletin* 77, 220–26.

Cole, M.P., P. Lindeque, C. Halsband, and T.S. Galloway. 2011. Microplastics as contaminants in the marine environment: A review. *Marine Pollution Bulletin* 62, 2588–97.

Cole, M.P., H. Webb, P.K. Lindeque, E.S. Fileman, C. Halsband, and T.S. Galloway. 2014. Isolation of microplastics in biota-rich seawater samples and marine organisms. *Nature, Scientific Reports* 4, article 4528, 220–26.

Compton, N. 2015. Traditional boats of Greece: Tenacious survivors of a fading legacy. *WoodenBoat* 247, 64–71.

Corcoran, P.L. 2015. Benthic plastic debris in marine and fresh water environments. *Environmental Science: Processes & Impacts* 17, 1363–69.

Cozar, A., M. Sanz-Martín, E. Martí, J.I. González-Gordillo, B. Ubeda, J.A. Gálvez, X. Irigoien, and C.M. Duarte. 2015. Plastic accumulation in the Mediterranean Sea. *PLoS ONE* 10(4), 1–12.

Damianidis, K. 1996. *Ellinikí Paradosiakí Nafpigikí*. Athens: Cultural Technological Foundation.

Diamant, A. 1997. Fish-to-fish transmission of a marine myxosporean. *Diseases of Aquatic Organisms* 30, 99–105.

FAO. 2005–2016a. National aquaculture sector overview. Greece: National Aquaculture Sector Overview Fact Sheets. Text by Christofilogiannis, P. In *FAO Fisheries and Aquaculture Department* [online]. Rome. Updated November 19, 2010. [Cited January 13, 2016]. www.fao.org/fishery/countrysector/naso_greece/en#tcN700B1.

FAO. 2005–2016b. Cultured aquatic species information programme. *Dicentrarchus labrax*. Cultured Aquatic Species Information Programme. Text by Bagni, M. In *FAO Fisheries and Aquaculture Department* [online]. Rome. Updated February 18, 2005. [Cited January 14, 2016]. www.fao.org/fishery/culturedspecies/Dicentrarchus_labrax/en.

FAO. 2011–2016. National aquaculture legislation overview. Greece. National Aquaculture Legislation Overview (NALO) Fact Sheets. Text by Doffay, B. In *FAO Fisheries and Aquaculture Department* [online]. Rome. Updated January 1, 2011. [Cited January 14, 2016]. www.fao.org/fishery/legalframework/nalo_greece/en#tcNB00FE.

Forbes, H. 1997. Turkish and modern Methana. In C. Mee and H.A. Forbes (eds.), *A rough and rocky place: The landscape and settlement history of the Methana Peninsula, Greece*. Liverpool: Liverpool University Press. 101–17.

Greenberg, P. 2010. Time for a sea change. *National Geographic Magazine*, October. 78–89.

Herzfeld, M. 2003. Localism and the logic of nationalistic folklore: Cretan reflections. *Comparative Studies in Society and History* 45(2), 281–310.

Horden, P., and N. Purcell. 2000. *The corrupting sea: A study of Mediterranean history*. Oxford: Wiley-Blackwell.

Lehmann, H. 1937. *Argolis: Landeskunde der Ebene von Argos und ihrer Randgebiete*. Athens: Deutsches Archaologisches Institut.

Lupatsch, I., G.A. Santos, J.W. Schrama, and J.A.J. Verreth. 2010. Effect of stocking density and feeding level on energy expenditure and stress responsiveness in European sea bass Dicentrarchus labrax. *Aquaculture* 298, 245–50.

Mantzavrakos, E., M. Kornaros, G. Lyberatos, and P. Kaspiris. 2007. Impacts of a marine fish farm in Argolikos Gulf (Greece) on the water column and the sediment. *Desalination* 210, 110–24.

Maravelias, C.D., and E.V. Tsitsika. 2014. Fishers' targeting behavior in Mediterranean: Does vessel size matter? *Fisheries Management and Ecology* 21, 68–74.

Martín, J., P. Puig, P. Masqué, A. Palanques, and Sánchez-Gómez, A. 2014. Impact of bottom trawling on deep-sea sediment properties along the flanks of a submarine canyon. *PLoS ONE* 9(8), e104536. 10.1371/journal.pone.0104536.

Myers, R.A., and B. Worm. 2003. Rapid worldwide depletion of predatory fish communities. *Nature* 423(6937), 280–83.

Nash, C.E. 2011. *The history of aquaculture*. Ames, IA: Wiley-Blackwell.

Naval Intelligence Division. 1944. *Greece, Volume II: Economic geography, ports and communications*. Norwich: Jarrold and Sons.

Ottolenghi, F. 2008. Capture-based aquaculture of bluefin tuna. In A. Lovatelli and P. F. Holthus (eds.), *Capture-based aquaculture: Global overview*. FAO Fisheries Technical Paper 508. Rome: FAO. 169–82.

Perrakis, S. 2006. *The ghosts of Plaka Beach: A true story of murder and retribution in wartime Greece*. Madison, NJ: Fairleigh Dickinson University Press.

Roberts, C. 2007. *The unnatural history of the sea*. Washington, DC: Island Press/Shearwater Books.

Sekeris, P.E. n.d. *Tolon*. No publisher.

Serrano, P.H. 2005. *Responsible use of antibiotics in aquaculture*. FAO Fisheries Technical Paper 469. Rome: FAO.

Sloterdijk, P. 2009. Spheres theory: Talking to myself about the poetics of space. *Harvard Design Magazine* 30, 1–8.

Stengers, I. 2015. *In catastrophic times: Resisting the coming barbarism* (trans. A. Goffey). Ann Arbor, MI: Open Humanities Press.

Suaria, G., and S. Aliani. 2014. Floating debris in the Mediterranean Sea. *Marine Pollution Bulletin* 86(1–2), 494–504.

Tsikliras, A.C., V.Z. Tsiros, and K.I. Stergiou. 2013. Assessing the state of Greek marine fisheries resources. *Fisheries Management and Ecology* 20, 34–41.

Tzanatos, E., S. Somarakis, G. Tserpes, and C. Koutsikopoulos. 2007. Discarding practices in a Mediterranean small-scale fishing fleet (Patraikos Gulf, Greece). *Fisheries Management and Ecology* 14, 277–85.

Vasilakopoulos, P., C.D. Maravelias, and G. Tserpes. 2014. The alarming decline of Mediterranean fish stocks. *Current Biology* 24, 1643–48.

20

INTO THE BEDHENI VALLEY

Foragers and language, farmers and land, proprietary and territorial fallacies,
a path taken by Evliya Çelebi, Ottoman landholding, estranged belonging, monas-
tic lands, pedagogical dispositions and place, a monastery, of kestrels and monks,
an ossuary

It is mid-morning when we pass through Vivari in a van, a white Nissan Primes-
tar. I am among eight students en route to the monastery of Agios Dimitrios
tou Avgou. Set into a high precipice above the lower Bedheni Valley, the monastery and its associated lands have repeatedly lured me back ever since my first
visit just short of a decade earlier. These eight, having tolerated my enthusiasm
concerning the place, must have also felt a lure, for they have all signed on to
accompany me.[1]

---

1 These students are part of a larger contingent of twenty that participated on an itinerant field
   school, City–Country–Borders, which I co-organized with Don Lavigne of Texas Tech University
   in 2010. Most of them are from my home institution; some are from other universities; all, save
   one, are first-time travellers to Greece. We visited the monastery on June 24.

At a point just beyond the center of the village, I direct everyone's attention to the outcrops of limestone behind the houses to the left. It was along these escarpments that a survey led by Curtis Runnels of Boston University sought out overhangs and caves for possible evidence of Mesolithic foragers.[2] There, at the base of the rocky projection just beyond a newly terraced area with houses, they found a rockshelter with an associated scatter of lithics—small flakes, scrapers, and retouched tools. This they labeled "Vivari 1." A little further on, they found a cave, "Vivari 2." Off to the right (I point to Kondili Beach), the survey found two more rock shelters, one at each end of the beach, at the base of the limestone precipice.

I mention in passing how I had attempted to revisit the two sites at Kondili (labeled "Kondili 1" and "2"), with colleagues in 2007.[3] We had walked the length of the limestone crags. Spring-fed ponds and marshes persist there; these made the possibility of seeing anything on the ground, other than wayward plastic bottles and windblown plastic bags, difficult. We did not note any shallow opening that resembled a rockshelter but did find, amid the reverberative invasion of bass from the beach bar, a number of bolted climbing routes along the rock face on the north side of the beach. Handwritten names in red or black ink announced each route's presence at eye level: "stone rider," "powerful stuff," "invincible," "the fly," "beach pillar," "dizzy". Names and bolts specify a route across vertical ground. First-ascenders earn more than naming rights; a linear swath of limestone is now tied to the climbing-self. They are connected to this rock path, which they in turn have opened to others.

Glancing over at Jordin and Ryan, two Classics majors, whose gazes are fixed on the Bay of Drepanon, I return the discussion to the Kandia Mesolithic Survey.

Runnels and his team speculated that Mesolithic hunters, fishers, and gatherers preferred areas of rich diversity. Marshlands fed by rivers and springs would attract deer and boar. Gulfs and bays providing plants and shellfish would draw in seals, turtles, whales, along with myriad coastal fish species.[4] In the article, human–environment relations were, as they often are, couched in terms of the "exploitation" of a variety of "resources."

Will, a sharp-minded student of archaeology, echoes my emphasis on "exploitation" with even greater irony, which invites further reflection.

Notions like "exploitation" and "resource" suggest narrowly defined goals with humans at center, as masters of an environment. Rendering the world as

---

2 Runnels et al. (2005).

3 I revisited the site with Brad Sekedat and Zoe Zgouleta.

4 Despite tremendous changes in sea level, this coastal area, due to uplift, remained relatively stable (Runnels et al. 2005, 263).

a standing reserve, on call *for humans*, not *for other species*, frames this area exclusively in anthropocentric terms. And, within these terms, land is reduced to a mining district, to zones for the extraction of narrowly defined assets, and animals are understood with respect to their use-value.[5]

"Such utilitarian modes of perception," Will interjects, "were alien to hunters, fishers, and gatherers who, as anthropology has consistently shown, carry forth respect and reverence, care and concern, awe and wonder into their worlds."[6] "So," he presses, "it is reductive to attribute a strong form of instrumental rationality—an exclusive regard for things as largely a means to an end—to communities within Mesolithic Greece." And anachronistic, I add. Such reasoning is not given, but has emerged within a particular constellation of entities and relations far removed from the rich life-worlds of those hunter-gatherers who once lived here.

As we move up over the headland of Aniforaki, I glance in the rearview mirror. Anne, a Classics major from UT Austin, and Jenny, an anthropology student from Tech, crane their necks to catch the last views down to the bay. We pass the turn to Kondili Beach, which is framed by a few old stone houses on the right. Krista, a double major in library science and history, comments on seeing a number of plots marked for new construction. Yes, development is transforming this area.

I motion ahead towards the Yannakalis River and the lower Kandia Valley. It was just up the river that the Kandia Mesolithic Survey located a dense concentration of artifacts associated with a rockshelter. Dubbed "Adami 2," there the team noted five to ten times more artifacts than any other survey site. From this they speculated that "Adami 2" was potentially a larger base camp from which Mesolithic hunters/foragers would move out along trails in a seasonal round of strategically located campsites, hunting stands, or quarry sites.[7] "But," Will says, "the sites were defined almost exclusively in terms of procurement."

"What is the alternative," asks Jordin? Rites of passage, respect paid to good spirits or protection against evil ones, obligations to ancestors, the allure of rock outcrops, proper observation of community mores, exchange with other groups—I offer a few suggestions. No doubt, for hunters, the habits of deer and boar, the dispositions of turtles and fishes, were part of these worlds, but there was often a formidable symmetry to rapports between hunters and

---

5 This is, of course, not about a need to acquire the things themselves, but relates to a way of grasping the world, and to how particular modes of perception emerge (see Heidegger 1977). Within archaeology, see Thomas (2008).

6 For an introduction to these issues, see Cummings (2013), Cummings et.al. (2014), Edmonds (1999); also Binford 2001.

7 Runnels et al. (2005, 273).

animals, or the spirit of animals.[8] Although scrapers below a bluff fall short of a maker's expectations; though burins do not hold the beliefs associated with their use, we may nonetheless develop a language that is open to other ways of grasping the world, not only for humans, but also for the plants that sustain them, for the animals that guide them, for the spirits that stare back at them.

"There are," Will interjects, "archaeologists who speak of Mesolithic engagements with land in terms of transitory places and pathways."[9] Yes, and here, I continue, Runnels and his team circumscribed what upholds these former worlds as "sites," but why should discrete patches of ground be taken to delimit those erstwhile life-worlds?

Will signals his affirmation, but the question goes unanswered. Taking my cue from the artichoke plots that we will soon pass in the thin valley bottom, I decide to test their resolve further. Hunter-gatherers, it seems, do not so much construct their sense of belonging and coherence, their sense of solidarity, in relation to a discrete portion of ground that sustains them as much as to other entities and rapports. Commitments that played a role in group definition and maintenance were not explicitly linked to a circumscribed patch of exposed earth, at least in the sense that agriculture compels. For hunter-gatherers, how far enthusiastic allegiances extended beyond one's seasonal shelters mattered less than the locus of dwelling. And even if such an association were made, then it was vaguely defined. The land outside had yet to be sharply expressed in a geometrical sense of delimited space, of spatially determined interiors and exteriors.

I gesture to a sign within a fenced plot marked *poleítai*, "For Sale." Land was far from a parcel invested with the self, even farther from property, a portion that was permanently possessed.[10] Land had not yet come to the fore through agrarian transformation as discrete blocks of terrain, enclosures, or receptacles that undergird a particular person in their self-definition or persons in their coherence together.

As we cross the Yannakalis River, Ryan recalls William Cronon's masterful discussion of how European colonialist understandings of land ownership clashed with Native American perspectives on temporary land tenure in New England.[11] He follows this with a question: "So, how does land come to be defined as property?"

---

8 See, for example, Fausto (2007), Viveiros de Castro (1998), Willerslev (2007).

9 Cf. Bradley (1997, 7), Edmonds (1999), Tilley (1994).

10 For a critical exploration of the fallacy of land understood in terms of ownership in archaeology, see Catapoti and Relaki (2013).

11 2000.

We are drawn out of our discussion by a small tractor on the road, a late-1970s model 548 Steyr. We slow down. An old farmer drives while his companion, who we assume to be his wife, sits on the metal fender above the rear wheel. With oncoming traffic we follow along slowly.

A brown archaeological sign on the roadside prompts Jenny to inquire about Pýrgos Kántias. A fortified residence from the late Ottoman period, Kantias's Tower sits at the crossroads of the village to our left. Locally known as the stronghold of the Turkish Agha prior to the revolution, I explain to everyone that the former tower house has been a matter of mounting controversy over the last couple of years due to its state of preservation. The main entrance, along with the central portion of the roof, has collapsed into a pile of rubble. A local group, Énosis Politón tou Dímou Asínis (the Deme of Asini Citizens' Union), hopes to restore the monument as an exhibition space and community center for local cultural events, including the organization of the annual Feast of the Artichokes in early May.

Artichokes, and our slow progress behind the tractor, prompt a return to Ryan's question. A different sense of land must have come into being in the Neolithic, for to clear ground for an agrarian plot is not the same as managing grasslands or woodlands. A farmer removes obstacles by cutting brush and trees, by moving stone. With hoe and spade, a farmer breaks and turns soil; in so doing a farmer expels all unwanted species at their roots. A farmer stores

Kantias's Tower.

seed, sows when the time is right, waits out the germination of plants, and reaps the benefits of this engagement when the crop deems it so. A farmer weeds, stands guard against other animals, and thus excludes. A farmer further invests in this life-sustaining earth with buildings, monuments, and tombs.[12] Through clearing, tilling, planting, tending, waiting, harvesting, and burying progenitors in the same ground, a different way of apprehending land emerges. In forming and sharing common boundaries with other agrarians, a different sense of space is revealed.[13] Perhaps agriculture caught on in Greece not because it was a better way of life—and few archaeologists buy into this delusion—but because hunter/gatherers did not obsess over the comparison between a patch of ground and the self.

"What do you mean?" Ryan's query comes amid distraction. The tractor slows down long enough for the farmer and his companion to exchange passing greetings with a man checking his irrigation lines. With more traffic from the other direction, I decide to wait a little longer before I attempt to pass.

For mobile foragers, at least initially, circumscribed patches of land had not transformed behind a new frame of reference into that which sustains the self and grounds belonging. One has to work the earth iteratively, to pierce soil repetitively, to form roots, bury the dead, raise walls, and from this arises the connection of those who live here with a terrestrial enclosure. This connection forms the basis for the confusion of land with the self, which is a proprietorial fallacy. At the level of society this agrarian connection may take shape as a collective confusion, what has been called the "territorial fallacy."[14]

"When did farming take hold here," Jordin asks? At some point in the seventh millennium BCE. Whatever the nature of its introduction to the Balkan peninsula,[15] agrarians, by and large, favor the rich valleys of the north. As agriculture develops on more productive lands, hunter-gatherers may choose to seek out other bountiful grounds elsewhere; that is, until none remain due to the presence of agro-pastoralists. In any case, it would be at least another 1,000 years before farmers press south in larger numbers with their proprietorial turned territorial fallacies. The bays and crags of this part of the Peloponnese, it would seem, were initially less attractive to agrarians.[16] Franchthi Cave, about

---

12 See Segments 10 and 11.

13 Archaeologists have long connected these practices with profound changes in how people understand land and identity; see Barker (2010), Robb and Miracle (2007), Thomas (2013); also see Olsen et al. (2012, 163).

14 Sloterdijk (2000); this article originally appeared under the title "Patria y globalización" in Nexos, 1999. It was subsequently adapted as Chapter 30, Die immunologische Transformation: Unterwegs zu den "Gesellschaften" der dünnen Wände, in Sloterdijk (2005a) (English translation, 2013).

15 Compare Perlès (2001) to Kotsakis (2001); see also Bintliff (2012, 47), Kotsakis (2003a).

16 Perlès (2001, 98–120); also Bintliff (2012, 50).

17 kilometers to the southeast, may have been something of an exception.[17] Of course, the differences between the two lifestyles are often overplayed,[18] but a key distinction lies in how the concept of belonging tied to defined areas of land is made explicit.[19]

The farmer and his companion pull off to the right by a field of artichokes just after a gas station at Kandia Beach. Here, for a stretch of about 1 kilometer, the road marks a transition between cultivated plain and uncultivated slope. We speed up.

Fifty generations of living in relative proximity is enough for a way of framing land in relation to the self to mature into being among communities of foragers who understand the implications of "territory," especially when that which traditionally has sustained them recedes.[20] The connection between defined, delimited, discrete space and the self must become a provision of their own being or one comes up short. And once the latecomer foragers are drawn into comparisons with a new agrarianism, they realize that this way of understanding land is best expressed through action.

"In other words," Jordin follows, "they turned to farming." Agrarianism might have provided a practical and mutual basis for living among each other, living among those who are rooted in, those who aim to lay claim to land. Indeed, former hunter-gatherers may well claim legitimacy as being of this land, *autochthous*. Or, it came to violence. Either way, disparities in wealth tied to land and the spark that initiates the long articulation of what emerges as property were perhaps tied to agriculture's revelation.[21] Jordin, Ryan, and Will seem eager to discuss this more, but just as we are about to continue, the crenellated silhouette of Kandia's Castle, a huge resort hotel on the beach front, demands our attention on the right. Jenny quips that whatever the state of Kantias's Tower the resort is empty and gaudy in its mimicry. What stirs me is not so

---

17 Jameson, Runnels, and van Andel (1994, 340–48); remains have also been found at Dendra, which have been identified as early Neolithic (Protonotariou-Deïlaki 1992; on issues of interpretation and dating, see Perlès 2001, 71–72).

18 See discussion in Bailey, Whittle, and Cummings (2005); also Robb and Miracle (2007).

19 One needs to take caution with such an argument, for many hunter-gatherer groups tend to be consistent in a round of seasonal dwellings, hunting grounds, and foraging areas (on niche construction, see Binford 2001, 32–43). Through such iteration a deep fidelity to these loci may translate into a sense of belonging.

20 Iran Malkin has stressed the difference between land, which is tied to the self, and territory, which is tied to the community (1993). Stuart Elden (2010, 2013) has argued for a refined sense of the term "territory," which connects to a particularly politically charged set of conditions for grasping land through technologies of measure and control. The spread of agriculture across Europe involved both cooperation and competitive exclusion (see Shennan 2008).

21 Also see evidence for increasing aridification, which also coincides with the beginning of the Holocene (see discussion and references in Walker et al. 2012, 653).

much the outward impression of pastiche as the reality of a walled-off, inward-oriented, multi-celled space for those who experience an enclosed portion of coastline as a land of vacations.

The road clings to a thin strip between promontory and sea. We soon round the headland, and the plain of Iria comes into view. It is less the form of the whole and more the patchwork of plots that kindle a connection—language preserves several words where land is defined not so much in terms of imposed or inherited boundaries as through work. Work designates the site, the field, and its limits.[22] *Stremma*, the very root of the Greek unit of land measure, denotes "to turn," suggesting an investment in the land by plowing.[23] Another Greek term for a unit of land is the *zeugion* or *zeugarion*. This word combines the noun *zeugos*, "yoke," with *orgo*, from the verb "to plow," and specifies the amount of land that can be plowed with a yoke of oxen in a season.[24] Deeper still, the Ottoman unit of land measurement, the *dunam* or *dönüm*, comes from the Turkish word *dömek*, "to go round," and also indicates the area of land that can be plowed in a day.

Anticipating my next thought, Nathan, a Classics undergrad turned graduate student who will go on to pursue a law degree at Harvard, mentions how "the association, between to plow and the land itself, is ancient—*Aroura*.[25] The word for 'tilled' or 'arable land' is associated with *aroo*, 'to plow,' 'to till.'"

We pass foreign agricultural workers harvesting artichokes in the plots adjacent to the road. I continue. With these words, it is not simply the case, as was a scenario for the early Neolithic, that *I* plow, *I* break soil, *I* prepare ground and invest by marking out an area, and, in leaving what *I* see as my imprint on a place. One may do more than equate tilled ground to *their* labor.[26] These terms are blind to the associations of power, for it could be that *you* plow, *you* break my land, *you* prepare my ground, *you* belong to this land. At times, tenant farmers were characterized as anthropic assets of an estate.[27] A *zeugolation* was a landed estate composed of several *zeugaria*—land was measured in work, but to whom did that land and labor belong?

22 To the following list, one could also add the *zapade*, what could be dug with a *zapa*, or mattock, which was used in the *catastico particolare* as the unit of measure for a vineyard (Jameson, Runnels, and Van Andel 1994, 21).

23 The modern *stremma* is 1,000 square meters. Prior to national regulation, its use and extent varied. Under the Ottomans, during the second occupation, the Morean (Peloponnesian) *stremma* was 1,270 square meters (Forbes 2000b, 323).

24 Also see McGrew (1985, 84).

25 This may be contrasted with geometry, *geometria*—the measurement of land (see Segment 7); see Serres (2017).

26 Also see Malkin (1993).

27 For an example of tenant farmers belonging to particular estates or with the land that passes between proprietors, see Forbes (2000a, 54–55).

I can hear Nathan point out the rectilinear rubble vestiges and disused terraces, flashing by on the left, at the foot of Likalona.[28] In the mirror, everyone else seems absorbed by the patchwork of agricultural plots.

Soon our eastward path cuts north, and begins to follow along the base of the rise at the edge of open, perfectly flat plain—once again, the road draws a tarmac line between cultivated and uncultivated space, but only for a short distance. I mention how this is the very route taken by the Ottoman traveler Evliya Çelebi with his entourage[29] from Nafplion through the Bedheni Valley to the Saronic Gulf in 1669.

Just ahead, on the left, is the church of St Nicholas. Twenty-seven years after Evliya passed through the plain (1696), it was listed as the main church in the village and, by implication, the district.[30] Taking interest in the church, Billy asks about its age. I mention that no one is sure of the precise date of construction, but a year is inscribed above the western entrance, which I promised to later verify: 1381.

We slow down so that everyone can see the church. Again, Nathan calls attention to the nearby ruins. A few stubs of stone and mortar break free of the maquis, to broadcast their persistence. These, I tell him, are what have become of a former tower. He asks whether it could have been a fortified residence like that of Kantias.

When Evliya Çelebi passed here, the plain of Iria was a tenant-farmed estate of Torgüd Paşa.[31] In Evliya's time, land grants, timars, were awarded to cavalrymen, sipahis, who were obliged to military service on behalf of the state.[32] At the center of these estates, it was not uncommon to find a tower surrounded by a small hamlet. Perhaps this was the residence of the pasha, but I am not certain. Of this, the stones are silent. We pick up speed.

Tenants worked the land of Torgüd Paşa. Migrant laborers from the mountains were perhaps also employed at planting and harvest times. In such a quasi-feudal system those who worked the land had no proprietary claims to it.[33]

---

28 Here there is an area of ruined structures and beyond, set upon an outcrop of limestone is a small fort dated to the Hellenistic Period (Kharitonidhis 1966).

29 Evliya mentions travelling with seven horses, six slaves, and several loads of baggage of his own (*Seyahatname* Volume 8, 283a13; MacKay translation, n.d.). In addition, he was likely accompanied by companions of similar rank and status with their own attendants.

30 Sarantakis (2007, 113).

31 *Paşa* is an older form of the title *Pasha*, a rank within the Ottoman political and military system.

32 This system changed in the second Ottoman period, when "rights to collect income from particular lands were sold at auction as tax-farms" (Zarinebaf, Bennet, and Davis 2005, 5).

33 Estrangement would also characterize the lot of those who worked the land under systems of sharecropping or chattel slavery. For a pertinent example from Keos under Turkish overlords, see Cherry, Davis, and Mantzourani (1991, 467–69); in the context of ancient slavery, see Morris and Papadopoulos (2005).

Church of Agios Nicholas, Iria.

Those dispossessed classes that did not live in remote mountains retreats owed their territorial allegiances to an over-demanding, hegemonic elite. To be a tenant is to dwell on the land, but to inhabit is not always to have.[34] The relationship between the Greek, non-Muslim peasantry under the Ottomans and the land they worked within this plain was one of *estranged belonging.*[35] And any estrangement in this sense serves to remind one that the territorial fallacy cannot be fully sustained as a continuous obsession by agriculturalists since the beginnings of the Neolithic.

The lower end of the Bedheni Valley is marked by a finger of Driva, the ridge to the south, which extends into the plain. With the crossing of this land edge come heightened expectations. I mention how it took Evliya and his entourage three hours to travel from the village of Iria to the monastery along steep and difficult roads. This comment meets with a universal sigh.

34 The Latin *habere*, "to have," shares the same root with *habitare*, "to dwell," and *inhabitare*, "to inhabit."
35 Importantly, as suggested here by the comparison of Mesolithic and Neolithic modes of living, proprietary claims to land are not synonymous with claims of belonging (also see Harrison 2003, 24–25).

To the right, the perennial stream of Rados swings in close to the road, at a point where it arcs northeast. To the left and ahead, huge mounds of marble clitter, boulders, and disused debris from the marble quarries of Karnezeika spill over the low limestone hills. From these quarries comes an off-white-to-beige varicose marble. Huge blocks unconcealed along the roads to our left await refinement into countertops, paving stone, tile, or moldings. The marble stands out as white blotches, a contrast heightened against red-and-grey ground.

Jordin suggests that the mounds of debris and large voids created by the quarries are another form of estrangement, for they bar shepherds and sheep, goatherds and goats from these grounds. Recalling our discussion of vocabulary and the Mesolithic, I suggest that those who are locked into the mode of revealing stone blocks, given order by a stone industry, are no less estranged. They are themselves entrapped into a particular way of revealing discrete areas of rock as quarries, as a standing reserve of stone.[36]

As we drive through the small village of Lower Karnezeika, Jordin asks a question about Ottoman landholding and the estranged. Only God had complete sovereignty over property and the Sultan was the sole custodian. However, Ottoman landholding in Greece seemed to deviate from Muslim holy law in practice.[37] After the sixteenth century, all agricultural land not in the possession of a "religious foundation" was *miri*, land ostensibly owned by the Ottoman state.[38]

"What became of the plain after 1685?" Another question follows. The plain was the "chief grazing grounds for cavalry" under the Venetians.[39] The presence of pastures on such prime land suggests both the absence of settled groups and that the land was held as a large estate.[40] Here again, space may have been delimited within different zones of immunity, militarized bottomlands and harsh, yet semi-autonomous, uplands.[41]

---

36 See Heidegger (1977).

37 McGrew (1985, 22–40).

38 These foundations included mosques and other Muslim institutions, such as hospitals, libraries, orphanages, and schools. It extended to Christian monasteries and churches; see McGrew (1985, 25–7).

39 Jameson, Runnels, and van Andel (1994, 123); after Sathas (1880–90).

40 "Pastures required less care and expense than cultivated fields and yielded a more certain income" (McGrew 1985, 14).

41 Over the very long term it was perhaps the case that those of whom we might consider to have been Greek agriculturalists were as much on the move as rooted to one patch of ground. Indeed, archaeological surveys suggest that the long-term agrarian picture is one of ebb and flow where Greek rural life defies such rigid connection to any one plot of land; see, for example, Wright et al. (1990, 602–03). However, the implications of this movement in terms of the generation of different spaces have yet to be fully articulated.

"*Again?*" Nathan's question comes as we pass through Upper Karnezeika. A series of houses are spread out along the road, though mostly to the north. And soon we begin to gain elevation in an increasingly constricted valley.

After a period of relative stability in the early Ottoman period (1460–1685) demographic declines are witnessed across the Morea.[42] The plain of Iria must have been affected. By the time Evliya passed this way in the late seventeenth century, some non-Muslims may have felt compelled to abandon the rich bottomlands for the harsh uplands, and the Muslims, so long as they could find sufficient agrarian labor or leases for their lands, were content to leave it so. In the course of traveling from this plain around the Southern Argolid and back to Nafplion (Anapli), Evliya mentions several areas held by rebellious infidels, which implies a level of autonomy.[43] The presence of areas deemed dangerous by Evliya suggests the presence of very different spaces under the Ottomans, different spheres of belonging and estrangement, of relative comfort and hardship, of safety and risk.

Olive groves press in on either side of the road, which continues to gain in elevation. Krista asks whether all agrarians would have been without private property in the Ottoman-controlled plains. Although contrary to Muslim legal precepts, I tell her that the Ottomans made a concession called *mulk*, which expanded in the second Ottoman period (1715–1821).[44] Within villages, houses and their adjacent gardens were considered *mulk*. Gesturing to the groves to our right, I point out that because olives, fruit trees, or vineyards involved sustained, cross-generational investment, they could also be considered *mulk*, even though the ground from which they grew was not.[45] For agrarians, *mulk* insured that the locus of dwelling was severed from the locus of work. Thus, rather than the worked ground, the *oikos* carried the burdens of association. Indeed, the house will persist as the site of memory and mnemonic referentiality in many areas for ensuing generations of Greek households.[46]

The road veers left at a ravine, but we turn right onto a paved road just before the switchback. After 200 meters the road splits. The paved portion continues down to the marble processing facility for Marmyk Iliopoulos, the company that own the nearby quarries. Our path continues to the left as a dirt

---

42 McGowan (1981), Zarinebaf (2005, 15–17).

43 Examples mentioned by Evliya include the Islands of Poros (195 281b.5–11) and Ydhra (Çamlica; 200 282a.15), the "insurrectionary infidels" of the Monastery of Kastri (Agioi Anargyroi near Ermioni; 204 Folio 282b.9) and of course the Mani (198 Folio 282a.1; 207 Folio 282b.30).

44 McGrew (1985, 27–31).

45 *Phthartai gaiai* and *aphthartai gaiai*, alienable lands and inalienable lands, are the Greek terms for *mulk* and *miri*; ibid., 28.

46 On the *oikos* as the locus of memory, see Forbes (2007, 227–36); this pattern begins to change in the mid-twentieth century (see Segment 5).

road. We soon enter a hard turn in a tight defile. Just below sits one of the warehouses where Marmyk Iliopoulos cut huge blocks of marble into consistent sizes for floor paving, steps, countertops, etc. On the far side of the warehouse, huge rectilinear blocks and pallets of cut stone are arranged in a long yard straddled by a giant, rail-based gantry crane.[47]

Our route clings to the north side of the valley, along slopes of maquis and olive. Two hundred meters and we round a spur of the hill. A view opens along the length of the valley. Bedheni, the name of the valley, comes from the Turkish word for "fort," *beheni*, which has been said to come from a small Classical/Hellenistic fortress at the head of the watershed, near the Saronic Gulf.[48]

"The name," Jordin comments, "fails to do this valley justice." After another couple hundred meters, we enter the wildlife refuge of Stavropodi-Kanapitsa, which was established in 1976. Abandoned terraces can be seen along the slope to our left. I mention how a large portion of this 21 square kilometer refuge was once monastic land. Save for rocks rattling through the undercarriage, the ensuing stretches of graveled road pass in silence, with everyone lost in contemplation.

Half a kilometer and our path swings wide of a lateral tongue projecting into the valley. At the apex of this arc the valley greets us with a picturesque scene. Below, olive groves spill from the foreground into clusters of pink oleander, which, along with lush planes and spires of Italian Cypress, trace the line of the river. On the far side, a clearing in the middleground contains widely spaced olives and a new orchard. Beyond, pines break free of maquis and climb towards crag-studded crests under cloud-speckled skies. These crags extend as serriform lines to the east where the limestone attends in bluffs unbroken.

Directly ahead, perched high amid the red-grey cliff face, a small box is veiled in shadow—the monastery.[49] Ryan slashes through this unspoken realization with a question concerning Evliya Çelebi's visit to the monastery. I respect a few more moments of silence before returning an answer. Evliya only mentions the monastery as "a strange and wonderful inn of hospitality" that

---

47 Soon after this trip, the warehouse will be, if not abandoned, taken off-line for a period, due to economic constraints.

48 Jameson, Runnels, and van Andel (1994, 21).

49 Abel Blouet was also struck by this view to the monastery, framing a picturesque scene: *en regardant derrière soi, on voit les beaux rochers boisés sur lesquels est situé le couvent: au premier plan la rivière, et tout alentour, des montagnes qui, formant comme un encadrement à ce tableau* (Looking out behind you, you can see the beautiful wooded rocks on which the convent is situated: in the foreground the river, and all around it, mountains, which form a frame for this picture; Blouet 1833, 174). For Blouet, this landscape was one of the most remarkable they had met in the course of their travels through the Morea.

distributed charities to travelers and wayfarers.[50] "As religious institutions," Ryan continues, "monasteries were able to acquire and hold property under Ottoman law, right?" Yes, and some acquired vast estates.[51] Indeed, the monastery appears to have grown rich. Thirty-one years after Evliya received hospitality, when the area was once again under Venetian rule, the *catastico ordinario* (1700) mentions that the monastery was comprised of sixteen monks with an equal number of personnel.[52] At that time it possessed 2,210 hectares of pastureland and 1,105 hectares of cultivatable land, one hundred horses, twenty donkeys, twenty-four plow cattle, 180 non-traction cattle, 3,000 sheep, and eight hundred goats.[53] Six hundred and thirty olive trees are also listed. Pelei, a seasonal hamlet about 6 kilometers east of here, was tied to the monastery as a *metochi* (outlying property).[54] The number of animals increases five years later in the *catastico particolare*. These cadasters reveal how the monastery was one the wealthiest economic entities in the whole of the district.[55]

Out the window, the cliffs draw nearer and the monastery takes on a beige hue. "But, the monastery was burned down?" In June of 1825 as a target of the "scorched earth" tactics carried out by the troops of Ibrahim.[56] It did not recover. Only one priest and three attendants were tied to the monastery some eight years later. State monastic archives from 1833 speak of a different monastery from that encountered five generations earlier: cultivated land, 330 *stremmata*;[57] uncultivated land, 1,700 *stremmata*; vineyards, 40 *stremmata*; 5,660 olive trees; one garden; and two *metochia*. In addition, there was only one olive press, 1.5 mills, only three hundred sheep and goats along with forty-three *nomadiká* (nomadics or transhumant herds?), and four animals used for transport and carriage.[58] From its assets, the monastery derived an annual income of 5,000 drachmas.[59]

---

50 *Seyahatname* Volume 8, 281a32; MacKay translation, n.d.

51 McGrew (1985, 25–27).

52 The slightly later *catastico particolare* "lists sixty-six clerical and lay personnel attached to the monastery" (Forbes 2000a, 54).

53 See Forbes (2000a, 48–68). It should be noted that the *catastico particolare* reduced the amount of cultivatable land to 128 hectares; Forbes (2000a, 49). For the dating of the summary cadaster (*catastico ordinario*) and the detailed cadaster (*catastico particolare*) under the Venetians, see Topping (2000, 34).

54 Forbes (2000a, 52).

55 Both the summary cadaster and the detailed cadaster covered the territory of Romania, which comprised the *eparkhia* of Nafplio, in part, and *eparkhia* of Ermionidha, in full.

56 Sarantákis (2007).

57 A *stremma* is one tenth of a hectare. Thus, it seems that the monastery, by this time, had already lost a tremendous portion of its land. Though, it should be noted, that there was more than a nine-fold increase in the number of olives trees.

58 The document even adds that there were two *okades* (an Ottoman unit of measure equivalent to 1.282 kilograms) of copper (*chalkós*).

59 Though it carried a debt of 500 drachmas (see Antonakatou and Mavros 1976, 77–81).

The road ascends to pass through a gap formed between two outcrops of limestone. Here two *proskinitaria*, small shrines, mark this point of transition. Each contains an icon and oil lamp and, normally, each either extends the memory of a loved one who nearby met death or stands as a thank-offering for having eluded it.[60] A dislodged iron cross, a top of the nearby rock suggests an alternative purpose. Beyond, the road transitions to pine forest and begins to plow a boustropic descent into the thalweg.

At the bottom, we pause before the ford to greet the patron plane. Three meters in girth, the hollowed trunk of this tree is fused with boulders and cobbles. Having stood against the perennial deluge of centuries, the concrete causeway has extended the flow of water to the uphill side of the plane, exposing its roots. Yet, still firm it stands, holding its ground. No doubt, I tell everyone, this living specimen was awe-inspiring when the monastery was dissolved; no doubt it arrested attention with its girth when Ibrahim passed here with his troops; no doubt it cast welcome shade when the monks registered by the Venetians lingered by flowing waters nearby …

"… And over a generation earlier when Evliya received hospitality," Jordin adds. "A living extension of time." After a smooth crossing we ascend through twists and turns over a rocky and rill-worn road. Billy scans the understory of pines and road cuts for the remnants of cultivated terraces. In 1833, the inspection of this land was undertaken by specially appointed state commissions and committees. The building, which had twenty rooms, was solid. All 10 *stremmata* of the surrounding gardens (*perivoli*) lay fallow.[61] It was estimated that if the vineyards were well cultivated, they would yield ten times their present amount.[62] Likewise, production from the olives would double.[63] The same document goes on to mention the monies received from the divestment of property and the rental of what it describes as the "dissolved monastery" (*dialyménis Monís*). This document paints a picture of under-productivity and divesture for unspecified gains. From these statements, one may read hints as to their motives: this inventory was tied to the national appropriation of this soil.

The road transitions from pine- to maquis-covered slopes. Soon it turns over an open terrace with three pollarded olive trees. Under the ruse of neglect, waning productivity, and moral degeneration, the young Greek nation-state

---

60 Forbes (2007, 385–86), Murray and Kardulias (2000, 153).

61 The word used in the text is *chérsa*, which also means "wasteland" (Antonakátou and Mávros 1976, 80).

62 "*Oi ampelónes an kalliergithósi, antí 250 bótzais, tas opoías dídoun símeron, boroún na dósoun 2500*". "If the vineyards were well cultivated, instead of the 250 *bótzais* that they give today, they could give up to 2,500" (ibid.).

63 "*… antí 2000 imporeí na dósi 4000*," "… instead of 2,000 they could give 4,000" (Ibid.).

aimed to check the power of the Eastern Church. The monastery was dissolved by royal decree in 1833 and abandoned the following year, though the Orthodox Church would continue to own the land for another century.[64] It would seem, once again, that we return to land as a basis for resources, as a locus for a struggle. It is the young nation-state that realizes the convergence of land and the self to the highest degree through a kind of political-ethnic territorialism, an "agrarian patriotism."[65]

The road continues up the south slope to a clearing just above the monastery. We park by a sign and two piles, one sand, one gravel. Aside from the sign that announces our destination, nothing here is written, and the piles say nothing of the work associated with the restorations.[66] There is no one left here to say where the old monastic lands begin and end, and there are no borders to reference.

A blast of heat enters the air-conditioned interior of the van. The hot sun greets us as we step out. A mid-morning wind rushes up from the valley; it carries the scent of thyme. To here, I have played my part, using knowledge to blanket the arbitrarily exhibited outside in a thin veil of certainty, reinforcing how stories cling to sites that have no say for they do not speak. The disposition to point and speak its story more than denies the things here their due portion; this can facilitate the speaker in laying claim. Have these words been in service to the curiosity of eight students, or to my own sense of self? Can I speak stories without them being tied to me?

Held within a mobile classroom for long enough, everyone embraces the freedom to follow their curiosity. Now we all may be attentive to what is here, to what clashes with descriptions, to what remains vastly unsaid, because the things here resist our attempts, whether to enclose them in self-referentiality, or to articulate something of them through enclosure within the text.

Off the clearing are ruins. Limestone rubble foundations, the remains of erstwhile outbuildings associated with the monastery. I walk down with those who have lingered here. Our path follows a road cut between slope and outcrop. At its base, the *xenónas* or guesthouse sits just off to the right against a stunning background.[67] In our tracks, we hesitate at the bottom in astonishment, attempting to grasp the view down the valley, to the plain, and to the sea beyond.

64 Ioannidou (1992, 100).
65 The expression "agrarian patriotism" is used by Sloterdijk (2000).
66 The Directorate for the Restoration of Byzantine and Post-Byzantine Monuments restored the guesthouse and monastery in the early 1990s.
67 The guesthouse is opened for visitors, especially for those who celebrate the name day of the saint and come here on the first day of Lent.

Agios Dimitrios tou Avgou and the Bedheni Valley.

Soon we all gather on a wide terrace framed by cliff to the left and slope falling off to the right. The edge is partly held by crumbling revetment walls, what have become of subsidiary buildings; these serve to suggest how here other ruins were returned to something of their erstwhile forms.

Agios Dimitrios tou Avgou is set back into the bluff to the south, where the escarpment forms a hollow. *Tou Avgou*, "of the egg"—perhaps it is more than a reference to the bald-topped bluff above.[68] For here both chapel and monastery are *of* this rock and the ground forms the place. Architectures are continuations of limestone outcrops. Precipice suggests design. Sheer cliff renders boundary. Karstic limestone forms shelter. Northern-facing bluffs shade. In times past, those who dwelled here enjoyed a cool atmosphere in the depths of summer. If you position a Mesolithic demeanor atop that of the Neolithic, you may find a sound suggestion of this place.

Before the doorway through the protective wall, we hesitate again. A bronze cross pattée dangles from a wire wrapped around the outer of five juniper boles that form the lintel. And above, set back into the stone and mortar, a niche shelters a painted icon of Agios Dimitrios. Astride a dark horse, the armor-clad soldier turned saint spears the gladiator Lyaeos. Behind him stands the white tower of Thessaloniki. This anachronism serves to reference the city, to which Agios Dimitrios, as its protector, is forever tied. This religious topos reinforces the significance of this protective wall.

A stone ascension, half ramp, half stairway, leads to the low doorway of the monastery. Under the limestone lintel carved with another Greek cross, through a stout wooden door, up stone stairs set between bedrock and wall, we ascend

---

68 According to Maria Veliotis and Dimitris Georgopoulos, "in many local dialects the word 'egg' means naked crest" (*se pollés topikés dialéktous i léxi "avgó" simaínei gymní koryf*; 1990, 9).

to the first story. Along a thin, whitewashed hallway, to the right and at the end of the hall, open doorways lead into cells. Stone pavements here stand out in contrast to simple earthen floors of the plain cells, where the footprints of those who last visited here remain. *Monastery*—the word is derived from the single cell, the circumscribed domain of the monk. Yet, the monastery is also the place where a community of monks choose to live apart in a cenobial manner;[69] a mode of living together that meant to share, in words penned by Giorgio Agamben, "not only a place or a style of dress, but first of all a *habitus* … the mode of 'inhabiting,' according to a rule and a form of life."[70]

Left then right, up a dark stairway, then right again; we emerge in another hallway. Light from the windows falls through more cell doors and penetrates this internal corridor. Immediately to the right, set deep into a limestone cavity, is the chapel. Inside, four arches form together above an ancient Ionic capital, much too large for the lone central column, a reused marble drum brought here from Roman ruins. Over the northwest square, a round cupola admits thin, mote-filled beams of light, which touches lightly upon icons on the wall, drawing out their metallic glint.

We continue to the end of the hallway, up the stairway, and out onto the roof. Out here we join together, around a niche decorated with the painted saint. A squeaking axle echoes off the cliffs. Kestrels are nesting in the limestone above.

The name, *kestrel*, holds on to this rattle-like sound, as in the old French *cresserelle*. However, the Greek word for the bird, *vrachokirkínezo*, does this and more, for it underlines how the kestrel is at home in the *vráchos*, rock or cliff. To accommodate a brood, kestrels will look for a cavity of adequate size; solid ground within a calcareous container of rock-roofed walls. The only bird of prey capable of windhovering, the kestrel will only defend a small domain around its nest. It will remain all year in an area with plentiful prey. Or, if need be, it will move to different winter grounds. It is said that the chapel, built into a cave high in the cliff face, came first and the cells were constructed around it.[71] Did those who lived here follow in the way of the kestrel?

Behind us, at the back of the cupola, is another cave. Three rock steps mark the entrance to a dark passage leading to an ossuary. Buried in individual graves to be later exhumed, the bones of monks were taken there. This place is not at the roots of the monastery, not in the earth below, but like kestrels high in rock cavities above. And there within deep and covered recesses, ribs, scapulae, mandibles, femurs, fibulae, humeri, and skulls mix together.

---

69 From the Greek *koinóbion*, or "common life."

70 Agamben is playing on *habitus* as clothing and *habitus* as mode of living (2013, 16).

71 Sotiriou (1935) dated the church to the eleventh or twelfth century. However, this argument has not gone uncontested; Ioannidou (1992) has argued for a date of the early sixteenth century.

Someone cared enough to place the bones there. In being the last, did the final monk leave because the state deemed it so, or because no one else was left to return the favor?[72] Still, the fact that these bones remain here suggests that the young nation-state never succeeded in the full appropriation of this rock. Later, others returned to light the candles, burn oil for their memory, and leave a coin for the mixed dead. This place may have been built upon bones, but no one is left to recall it. Here history was destroyed with the monastic archives in 1834. Still, the place retains a different story. Without individuation, without names, without defined boundaries between bodies, bones mingle in a pile.

---

72 Whatever the answer, the last monk died far from here, to the south, on the small, isolated island of Parapóla (Velopoula); Antonakátou and Mávros (1976, 81).

Bibliography

Agamben, G. 2013. *The highest poverty*. Stanford, CA: Stanford University Press.

Antonakátou, N., and T. Mávros. 1976. *Elliniká Monastíria/Pelopónnisos*. Vol. 1, Athens.

Bailey, D., A. Whittle, and V. Cummings. 2005. *(Un)settling the Neolithic*. Oxford: Oxbow Books.

Barker, G. 2010. *The agricultural revolution in prehistory: Why did foragers become farmers?* Oxford: Oxford University Press.

Binford, L.R. 2001. *Constructing frames of reference: An analytical method for archaeological theory building using hunter-gatherer and environmental data sets*. Berkeley, CA: University of California Press.

Bintliff, J.L. 2012. *The complete archaeology of Greece: From hunter-gatherers to the 20th century AD*. Chichester: Wiley-Blackwell.

Blouet, G.A. 1831–38. *Expédition scientifique de Morée, Ordonnée par le Gouvernement français: Architecture, Sculptures, Inscriptions et Vues du Péloponèse, des Cyclades et de l'Attique, mesur-ées, dessinées, recueillies et publiées par Abel Blouet*. Vols. I–VI. Paris: Firmin Didot.

Bradley, R. 1997. *Rock art and the prehistory of Atlantic Europe: Signing the land*. New York, NY: Routledge.

Catapoti, D., and M. Relaki. 2013. An archaeology of land ownership: Introducing the debate. In M. Relaki and D. Catapoti (eds.), *An archaeology of land ownership*. London: Routledge. 1–20.

Cherry, J.F., J.L. Davis, and E. Mantzourani. 1991. *Landscape archaeology as long-term history: Northern Keos in the Cycladic Islands*. Los Angeles, CA: Cotsen Institute of Archaeology, University of California.

Cronon, W. 2000. *Changes in the land: Indians, colonists, and the ecology of New England*. New York, NY: Hill and Wang.

Cummings, V. 2013. *The anthropology of hunter-gatherers*. London: Bloomsbury.

Cummings, V., P.D. Jordan, and M. Zvelebil. 2014. *The Oxford handbook of the archaeology and anthropology of hunter-gatherers*. Oxford: Oxford University Press.

Edmonds, M. 1999. *Ancestral geographies of the Neolithic*. London: Routledge.

Elden, S. 2010. Land, terrain, territory. *Progress in Human Geography* 34(6), 799–817.

Elden, S. 2013. *The birth of territory*. Chicago, IL: University of Chicago Press.

Fausto, C. 2007. Feasting on people: Eating animals and humans in Amazonia. *Current Anthropology* 48, 497–530.

Forbes, H. 2000a. The agrarian economy of the Ermionidha around 1700: An ethnohistor-ical reconstruction. In S.B. Sutton (ed.), *Contingent countryside: Settlement, economy, and land use in the Southern Argolid since 1700*. Stanford, CA: Stanford University Press. 41–70.

Forbes, H. 2000b. Land management in the Peloponnesos during the second Venetian occupation. In S.B. Sutton (ed.), *Contingent countryside: Settlement, economy, and land use in the Southern Argolid since 1700*. Stanford, CA: Stanford University Press. 321–24.

Forbes, H. 2007. *Meaning and identity in a Greek landscape: An archaeological ethnography*. Cambridge: Cambridge University Press.

Harrison, R.P. 2003. *The dominion of the dead*. Chicago, IL: University of Chicago Press.

Heidegger, M. 1977. *The question concerning technology, and other essays* (trans. W. Lovitt). New York, NY: Garland Publishing.

Ioannidou, N. 1992. O naós tou Agíou Dimitríou (Avgoú) sta Dídyma tis Ermionídas. *Del-tíon XAE 16 (1991–1992), Períodos D'. In memory of Andre Grabar (1896–1990)*, 97–106.

Jameson, M.H., C.N. Runnels, and T. Van Andel. 1994. *A Greek countryside: The Southern Argolid from prehistory to the present day.* Stanford, CA: Stanford University Press.

Kharitonidhis, S. 1966. Kandia, Iria. *Archaiologikon Deltion* 21(2), 130–31.

Kotsakis, K. 2001. Mesolithic to Neolithic in Greece: Continuity, discontinuity or change of course? *Documenta Praehistorica. Porocilo O Raziskovanju Paleolitika, Neolotika in Eneolitika V Sloveniji. Neolitske Studijes.* 63–73.

Kotsakis, K. 2003a. From the Neolithic side: The Mesolithic/Neolithic interface in Greece. In N. Galanidou and C. Perlès (eds.), *The Greek Mesolithic: Problems and perspectives.* British School at Athens Studies 10. 217–21.

Malkin, I. 1993. Land ownership, territorial possession, hero cults, and scholarly theory. In R.M. Rosen and J. Farrell (eds.), *Nomodeiktes: Greek studies in honor of Martin Ostwald.* Ann Arbor, MI: University of Michigan Press. 225–34.

McGowan, B. 1981. *The economic life in Ottoman Europe: Taxation, trade, and the struggle for land, 1600–1800.* Cambridge: Cambridge University Press.

McGrew, W.W. 1985. *Land and revolution in modern Greece, 1800–1881: The transition in the tenure and exploitation of land from Ottoman rule to independence.* Kent, OH: Kent State University Press.

Morris, S.P., and J.K. Papadopoulos. 2005. Greek towers and slaves: An archaeology of exploitation. *American Journal of Archaeology* 109, 155–225.

Murray, P., and P.N. Kardulias. 2000. The present as past: An ethnoarchaeological study of modern sites in the Pikrodhafni Valley. In S.B. Sutton (ed.), *Contingent countryside: Settlement, economy, and land use in the Southern Argolid since 1700.* Stanford, CA: Stanford University Press. 141–68.

Olsen, B., M. Shanks, T. Webmoor, and C. Witmore. 2012. *Archaeology: The discipline of things.* Berkeley, CA: University of California Press.

Perlès, C. 2001. *The Early Neolithic in Greece.* Cambridge: Cambridge University Press.

Protonotariou-Deïlaki, E. 1992. Paratiriseis stin prokerameiki (apo ti Thessalia ata Dendra tis Argolidos). In *Diethnés Synédrio gia tin Archaía Thessalía sti Mnimi tou Dimitri P. Theochari.* Athènes: Ekdosi Tameiou Archaeiologikon Poron kai Apallotrioseon. 97–119.

Robb, J., and P. Miracle. 2007. Beyond "migration" versus "acculturation": New models for the spread of agriculture. In A. Whittle and V. Cummings (eds.), *Going over: The Mesolithic–Neolithic transition in Western Europe.* Proceedings of the British Academy. London: British Academy. 90–113.

Runnels, C.N., E. Panagopoulou, P. Murray, G. Tsartsidou, S. Allen, K. Mullen, and E. Tourlokis, 2005. A Mesolithic landscape in Greece: Testing a site-location model in the Argolid at Kandia. *Journal of Mediterranean Archaeology* 18(2), 259–85.

Sarantákis, P. 2007. *Argolída/Oi Ekklisíes kai ta Monastíria tis.* Athens: Ekdóseis OIATIS.

Sathas, C.N. 1880–90. *Documents inédits relatifs à l'histoire de la Grèce au moyen âge.* 8 vols. Paris: Maisonneuve.

Serres, M. 2017. *Geometry: The third book of foundations.* London: Bloomsbury Academic.

Shennan, S. 2008. Evolution in archaeology. *Annual Review of Anthropology* 37, 75–91.

Sloterdijk, P. 2000. From agrarian patriotism to the global self (trans. M. Nieto and N. Gardels). *New Perspectives Quarterly* 17(1), 15–18.

Sloterdijk, P. 2005a. *Im Weltinnenraum des Kapitals: Für eine philosophische Theorie der Globalisierung.* Frankfurt am Main: Suhrkamp.

Sloterdijk, P. 2013. *In the world interior of capital: For a philosophical theory of globalization.* Cambridge: Polity Press.

Sotiriou, G.A. 1935. I moni tou Avgou para tous Dhidhimous tis Argolidhos. *Imerologion tis Megalis Ellados*, 457–64.

Thomas, J. 2008. Archaeology, landscape, and dwelling. In B. David and J. Thomas (eds.), *Handbook of landscape archaeology*. Walnut Creek, CA: Left Coast. 300–6.

Thomas, J. 2013. *The birth of Neolithic Britain: An interpretive account*. Oxford: Oxford University Press.

Tilley, C. 1994. *A phenomenology of landscape: Places, paths, and monuments*. Oxford: Berg.

Topping, P.W. 2000. The Southern Argolid from Byzantine to Ottoman times. In S. B. Sutton (ed.), *Contingent countryside: Settlement, economy, and land use in the Southern Argolid since 1700*. Stanford, CA: Stanford University Press. 25–40.

Velióti, M., and D. Georgopoulos. 1990. *Koinotita Didýmon Odoiporiko ston topo kai ton chróno*. Self-published document available at: http://villadidimo.brodimas.gr/κοινότητα-διδύμων-οδοιπορικό-στον-τό/.

Viveiros de Castro, E. 1998. Cosmological deixis and Amerindian perspectivism. *Journal of the Royal Anthropological Institute* (N.S.) 4, 469–88.

Walker, M.J.C., M. Berkelhammer, S. Bjorck, L.C. Cwynar, D.A. Fisher, A.J. Long, J.J. Lowe, R.M. Newnham, S.O. Rasmussen, and H. Weiss. 2012. Formal subdivision of the Holocene series/epoch: A discussion paper by a working group of INTIMATE (Integration of ice-core, marine and terrestrial records) and the Subcommission on Quaternary Stratigraphy (International Commission on Stratigraphy). *Journal of Quaternary Science* 27(7), 649–59.

Willerslev, R. 2007. *Soul hunters: Hunting, animism, and personhood among the Siberian Yukaghirs*. Berkeley, CA: University of California Press.

Wright, J.C., J.F. Cherry, J.L. Davis, E. Mantzourani, S.B. Sutton, and R.F. Sutton, Jr. 1990. The Nemea Valley Archaeological Project: A preliminary report. *Hesperia* 59, 579–659.

Zarinebaf, F. 2005. Soldiers into tax-farmers and reaya into sharecroppers: The Ottoman Morea in the Early Modern period. In F. Zarinebaf, J. Bennet, and J.L. Davis (eds.), *A historical and economic geography of Ottoman Greece: The southwestern Morea in the 18th century*. Hesperia Supplement 34. Princeton, NJ: American School of Classical Studies at Athens. 9–47.

Zarinebaf, F., J. Bennet, and J.L. Davis. 2005. *A historical and economic geography of Ottoman Greece: The southwestern Morea in the 18th century*. Hesperia Supplement 34. Princeton, NJ: American School of Classical Studies at Athens.

21

THROUGH THE SOUTHERN ARGOLID

A road less traveled, an upland valley, the abode of a goatherd, Yorgos, walking with goats, a path abandoned, crawling on all fours, a mandri, *accretion ways, an enclosed basin, into Dhidhima, a well, Agia Marina and Demeter, cairns and boundary stones, the Katafiki Gorge, the Ermioni* kambos, chôra.

June 2014. We left the monastery by way of the upper road. Its gravel surface cuts a line across a small field unencumbered by overgrowth.[1] From here, a view opens to the mountains of Dhidhima to the south. It was a hot day. There was little wind. Turbines, visible along the juniper-covered ridgeline of Tourles, behind Sternovouni, were idle. Our path wound south, then east. Eventually it met with the rim road. Crowded by juniper, this narrow road runs along a thin ledge, skirting the crest of the south cliffs above the upper Bedheni

---

1 This journey was taken in the company of Brandon Baker and Evan Levine.

Valley and below the lower slope of Sternovouni. Water-excavated boulders make for a stone gauntlet. This eased somewhat in the flats between slopes.

After a few hundred meters, we reached the top of a small rise. Before us the road dropped away and the upper Bedheni Valley burst into full view. Asprovouni, the pyramidal profile of Ortholithi, and, directly ahead, in a saddle off Spilies, the broad top of Koni; all stood as silhouettes against haze. After a kilometer, a small field of grain appears in a hollow fringed with olives. From here the road turns south. We descended over a section of road capped with concrete. This strip bears memories of an impatient driver. Grooves reveal the sequence of action across a drying surface. Laid in progression downhill, the deepest tire ruts form at the bottom where the concrete had yet to set. To avoid these hollows, we drove part on, part off, the surface.

Ahead, the mountain opens with limestone slopes of gentle demeanor to cradle an *oropédio* or upland plain known as Malavria. In this basin, an unencumbered expanse of fallow fields is speckled with lonely olives and carobs. On three sides save the west, even gradients of slope are broken by smooth drainages. Each drainage is bisected by terraces. No more and no less than linear stone piles set perpendicular to flow, these catch and hold sediment in long field strips stacked up slope. While the northern portion of the valley is more or less flat, and divided into sizable rectilinear tracts, the eastern margins and the upper end to the south step uphill in broad parcels. A generation ago this valley grew wheat, barley, oats, and fodder crops, including vetch and green barley.[2] These uplands receive different amounts of rainfall from the lower plains.[3] Thus, the amount of labor expended upon this small valley is entirely out of proportion with what remains of human habitation.

We parked just off the road, by a stone cairn, under goat-trimmed kermes oak and juniper, at the plain's northern edge. Stone walls, off to the left, called to Brandon and Evan. Across a rock-strewn field of blooming milk thistle and volunteer grains lay erstwhile rectilinear structures and accretions of rubble enclosures. These retain a fleeting image of herds and droves past, Evan mused. I pointed out our path. A thin road ascended to the saddle at the head of the valley. That is the old land route to Dhidhima, I said. It was taken by Abel Blouet and company in 1829, in the course of the *Expédition scientifique de Morée*.[4] We had come to find and walk what remained of the old way.

---

2 Koster (1977, 159).

3 During the dry season of 1975, the fields of the Malavria Valley produced at a 8:1 harvest-to-seed ration compared to 3:1 for the Dhidhima Plain (Koster 1977, 342).

4 Jameson, Runnels, and Van Andel (1994, 52).

Did Blouet mention any structures here? Brandon asked. Blouet only noted ruins and wall foundations in this *belle vallée*, I said.[5] We packed extra water bottles in our rucksacks, donned sunglasses, and set out on a sweltering earthen road that runs along the western edge of the open valley. A ten-minute walk brought us to a breezeblock *stáni* or sheepfold, situated at the base of the western slope. Abutting the full length of the north wall, a concrete cistern, grey going over to black, held rainwater captured from the block-weighted, corrugated metal roof via plastic pipe. Nearby, behind a makeshift, just shy of derelict, paddock of wire fencing, wooden pallets, and piles of juniper, stands a whitewashed *kalyvi* or cabin. A tall chimney projected skywards at the rear of a metal roof held fast by breezeblocks and brick to stop sheets from taking flight in the wind. Its green door and shutters were shut tight; its gutters drooped low across the front.[6] In passing, we discussed how in 1968 the folds in this valley were burned by an unknown hand out of competition over grazing land.[7]

We avoided a truck path that split on a direct line from the cabin to meet with the straight road through the center of the valley. Our foot pathcut an expedient angle towards the same road. Just beyond a second makeshift enclos- ure beneath two apricot trees, piles of manure laced with rubbish were spread out along the path to dry in the sun. Eventually we came to a grove of maiden olives where we veered off to the left. We walked over recently tilled, deep reddish-brown soil to meet a shepherd. Yorgos had paused from splitting the herd. Halting on top of a large boulder atop a neglected terrace, he leaned on a juniper goatherd's crook.[8] "Good afternoon." We returned the greeting: Good afternoon.

Yorgos wore jeans, long sleeves, thick boots, and a white hat. He appeared to be in his late sixties. His face was less sun-chiseled. His beard less unkempt. He possessed the wiry build of a goatherd. "What is your purpose?" I pointed to the pass and told him that we were hiking a portion of the old way to Dhid- hima. Focusing on our packs, he cautioned us to "take plenty of water." I asked about his work. "I am leading half the goats up to the ridge and my cousin is taking the rest to the other side of the plain." He stared off in the distance and

---

5 1833, 174; here Bouet found *des débris de constructions et des fondations de murailles* (remains of constructions and foundations of walls).

6 In 1979, Claudia Chang documented a fold in the vicinity built in 1968 to replace an older one constructed in 1931 (1981, 243).

7 Koster (1976, 184) states that the burning of the fold occurred in 1969; Chang (1981, 216 and 243) records it as 1968. On conflict in the area, also see Koster (1976).

8 Known as a *mangura*, Yorgos's goatherd's crook is distinct from that of a shepherd, which is known as a *glitsa*.

without provocation, continued: "Given a choice I would not do this work. I would not be here." He looked us over, as if to share another thought, but instead asked if we had a cigarette. No. Out of disappointment, he told us that "this is no place for eclogues, idylls, or pastoral sentiments. Some paths are darkened in the shadow of, as the poet says, the 'deserted direction of will.'"[9] Abruptly, yet amicably, Yorgos bid us "Good day." We did the same and returned to the path.

The truck road meets with the apex of a finger ridge extending out into the plain. Taking leave of the open fields, the rock-littered lane runs in a straight line upslope for half a kilometer and veers east to zigzag uphill towards a low saddle. We passed over rills and runnels, where water had worked deep channels into the bulldozed surface. We passed under, then through, scores of shimmering spider webs. The work of European garden spiders, *Araneus diadematus*, these stout silk threads were strung tightly between juniper boughs. Strands clung to our clothing.

We came upon a rusted, metal cot in the shade of juniper. Branches from seasons past are bunched up against its trunk—a goatherd's haunt. We wonder whether Yorgos once laid a mattress here, to find rest in broken shade, in the company of spiders. This lone indication of the herder was rare among contours kept by goats. Every bush, every clump of dried grass, was attended by their ruminations. Though largely unseen in the juniper, the bells and bleats of goats were ever present. Amid what initially seemed a cacophonic clangor, we began to note distinct clangs. Yorgos must be aware of these differences of tone, Brandon interjected. Herders will select and tune each bell for a particular goat,[10] I replied.

Somewhere in background Yorgos whistled. We noted a chestnut-colored doe with a small bell, then a salt-and-pepper kid with a miniature clapper that resonated with a high-pitched jingle. Ahead, deeper clanks joined in with the ruminant orchestra. The *kesemi* or wethers (lead bucks) were foremost among the others in ascending to the ridge and they carried the largest bells. Though Yorgos was at the rear, urging on strays and stragglers, he was nonetheless aware of the herd's progress and overall distribution, and even the location of specific animals thanks to such caprine carillons.

At the first turn, we stopped for water and took note of our oblique perspective on the upland valley. Juniper green sloped into light green and edged into flat brown. The bottomland was striped with terraces. Goats take no interest in this background; only the ruckus of our company breaks their attention

---

9 I will later find the closest approximation of Yorgos's comment in a line from Nikos Karouzos, translated and quoted in Skiadopoulos and van Gerven Oei (2011).

10 Koster (1977, 203–04); also see Panopoulos (2003).

Goats at Malavria.

on the restless browse. From a measured distance, their heads angle just enough to register our presence, always keeping us within the oblong blacks of their eyes. Each goat was responsive to the slightest motions of others. Forming into distinct groups, individuals avoided allowing gaps to open between ambling bodies. The kinetics of the herd was not unlike that of flowing waters. Even with a herd of several hundred individuals, a goatherd knows each and every animal, which is distinguishable on the basis of color, horns, and bells, I said. Yorgos will likely take a count once they reach the fold.

Between the second and third turn in the road, we encountered a line of large boulders angling uphill. Held in place by dwarf tufts of kermes oak, the eroded terrace marks the line of the old *kalderimi* (the Turkish term for a mule track), the footpath over the pass. We walked along the depression formed in the wake of dislodged paving stones. This path was trodden by so many unnamed others before and after the French, Evan said. Our act of traveling reiterates an experience known to those who formerly took this path, which must have been frequented in the time of the monastery of Agios Dimitrios tou Avgou.[11]

11 Also see Segment 8.

Within a minute of setting out along its line we lost it. The terrace unraveled in a deluge of hoof-trod filaments. Undeterred, we continued route-finding upslope. First over a braided terrain of linear forms held by smoothed or lichen-free stone; then over extruding pillars of grey limestone that bled red earth into rills and pools; then through gaps in thorn and thicket we trudged. The heat was infernal. The need for water was persistent. Pause, drink, and continue. We looked for indications of the *kalderimi* through breaks in the juniper. Growing heavy from the sweat they retained, cotton shirts and denim proved to be the wrong choice. The wind turbines on the ridge were completely still. There was not even the slightest breeze. *Malavria* means *extremely (mala) breezy place* or windy area (*auria*). It fell utterly short of its namesake.

Here and there, we discerned the tenuous form of curb and path. Amid a deluge of ruminant ruts and wayward stones the path receded. Increasingly, it was the ways of goats that we followed.[12] Walking along the old way or in any kind of a direct line became impossible. Juniper, thorny burnet, spiny spurge, kermes oak, plants that had developed a protective armor of barbs against the goats, tore at our trousers. Impenetrable to bipedal locomotion, the juniper branches closed together at thigh height. After doubling back in hopes that a break would give way in the direction of the road, we were compelled to crawl along low corridors passible to shorter quadrupeds. First the dirt road, then the truck path, then old fragmented footpath, then filaments maintained by goats, and at last we crept on all fours. Here, the old route between the Southern Argolid and the Akte has been neglected by all but goats with their grazed passages.[13]

We no longer paused to quench our thirst, but swigged oven-baked water during walks between crawls. With effort, the hollow clanks of copper bells receded down slope and we eventually broke clear of the dense thicket. A short way off, we met the truck path, and tramped through a large clearing in the maquis. We soon came to a galvanized water tank welded to a single-axle trailer in the midst of a dozen metal troughs. All but two were overturned; only one was positioned below the tap of the tank. A large series of stock-pens sat off to the left. This *mandri*, or fold, was divided into three different sections; two cordoned by wire fencing; one fringed by a two-meter-high juniper wall set within a low stone ring. Upon further scrutiny, we discerned two structures built into the juniper section of the *mandri*. A byre covered in faggots of juniper was

---

12 On comparable instances of following animals on the hoof, see Aldred (2018), Lordimer (2006).

13 An inversion of the ever-increasing speed seen in the straightening of roads in other places. Here, the old ways return to the curves abandoned to almost everyone but the goats, or so it would seem.

Mandri in the Malavria Pass.

supported by a beam set upon forked posts and weighted with electric-blue door panels, and an adjacent lean-to, partially covering a bedding of tattered cardboard. Nearby lay the remains of a fire amid three broken breezeblocks, two twisted goat horns, and one cigarette butt.

The juniper portion of the *mandri* is constructed in the same way as those built in the 1970s when Harold Koster undertook dissertation research on shepherding practices in this area, I said.[14] Why, Brandon asked, the need for so many enclosures? Separate pens assist with the sorting of the herd at night, I replied. The roofed pen of juniper is known as the *galaria*, which is where lactating ewes are kept. There is also a *tsarkos* (lamb pen) and the *sterpha*, which is used to contain the remaining portion of the drove.[15] Milk production slackens in July and August. Currently, it seemed, Yorgos is moving the goats up for water and for milking, and down for grazing.

More than a generation ago this *mandri* lay in the heart of a grazing area encompassing the valley and ridge of Malavria. Bounded to the north by the Bedheni Valley, to the west by the heights of Psili Gonias and Profitis Elias, the pastureland skirted the edge of the Dhidhima plain passing just above the Dhidhima cave to the south, and around Gravas to the east, by the heights of Zigos.[16] Conspicuous landmarks and landforms delimited one territory from another and each pasturage stretched over upland areas of maquis and contained cultivated areas for fodder or fallow grazing. In the 1970s and 1980s, two agro-pastoral strategies were present around the Dhidhima basin: smaller flocks of sheep where maintained by farmers at

14 Koster (1977, 176).
15 On the architecture of the fold, see Chang (2000, 129–31).
16 Koster (1977, 186); the adjacent pastures on the slopes of Megalovouni formed the start of Koster's "Thousand Year Road" (see Segment 11). Also see Koster (2000).

the edge of the cultivated plain and herded between areas of maquis and fields of harvested stubble, wastage, and fodder, while larger droves of goats were managed in upland areas.[17]

There are no springs along the coastal area from Salandi to Cape Vourlia to the east, and so those pasturages situated along the Dhidhima mountains had a drovers route for moving herds over its slopes into the Bedheni Valley, an important source of water.[18] The herders of Malavria were well situated to move water up and milk down in the same containers. However, when pressed, they were forced to move the herd down, either to the stream in the Bedheni Valley or to wells in Dhidhima. The cistern constructed below must have afforded some ease. In any case, *transhumance* precisely denotes this routine round: *trans*—across, *humus*—ground, soil. The presence of Yorgos and his cousin suggests that herders have continued to lead the herds over the same patch of upland, yet roads bulldozed to here have altered the longstanding habitus of these engagements.

We follow the truck path out to a paved road just off the ridge. Roads and automobiles allow pastoralists to leave, to return to the village, to their home, their table, their bed. These objects and the differences in movement they afford have altered the shepherd's rapport with his herds, and how those animals move with this land.[19] When the *kalderimi* was in use, the cost of transportation and travel was still high. Browse occurred along the drovers' routes connecting uplands with bottomlands. Shepherds before Yorgos were tethered to their high enclosures or their cabins, for distances maintained their dignity. After roads, the old *kalderimi* was forgotten. After roads, water could be brought here— there was no need to move herds all the way to the stream or wells. After roads, the frequency of these crossings subsided. The habitus of such crossings was upended.

Given the lateness of the day, we turned back. Following the truck road, we returned to our air-conditioned car and drove to our air-conditioned hotel.

⌒

The following morning we return by way of the wide, ridge road built to access the wind turbines. We park near the *mandri*. Neither Yorgos nor his goats are anywhere to be seen. The three of us walk along the ridge road to where

17 Like Lehmann on the Argive plain (see Segment 11), Koster contrasted the two strategies in terms of intensive versus extensive pastoralism (1977, 163–64).
18 See Jameson, Runnels, and Van Andel (1994, 604), Koster (1977, 186).
19 See Forbes (2007, 89–94) on changes brought by roads to Methana; also Jameson, Runnels, and Van Andel (1994).

a shepherd's road branches off to Dhidhima. After 200 meters we find the old *kalderimi*, which breaks with the path of the road and continues downslope into the coomb at the head of a ravine. Although overgrown in places, the *kalderimi* is a well-trodden hollow raised upon a limestone terrace.

I take leave of my companions, who return to the car, and set out on this less trodden path. No sooner do I begin than I pause. A large portion of the Dhidhima Valley can be seen over the hump of an intervening ridge covered in a continuous thicket of juniper. Ringed by ridges, the *oropédio* is dwarfed by the likely source of its namesake, Dhidhima or the "twins," the benign double-peak Megalovouni.[20] Below, the village of Dhidhima sits at the nave of a radial splay of roads and cereal fields encompassing the whole of a flat, round plain. From the oblique angle of the pass, it is not unlike the web of *Araneus diadematus* in its overall outline. Thin threads spray out in every direction, clinging to the encompassing slopes, leading to terraced hollows, meeting with passages into the uplands and between valleys. These road lines are interwoven with delicate agrarian strands formed at margins, along berms, field paths, and by changes in vegetation and labor between plots. This radial pattern is ancient.[21] An artifact of a deep agrarian wisdom, trackways connect dwelling to field and fold along what are held by consensus to be the most direct routes. Their persistence is a matter of accrescence. A rising surface riding upon the accumulation of organic matter, the buildup of manure, the repeated addition of cobble and gravel fills, and the saltatory deposition of earth and mud released by torrential storms into the large receptacle. The continua of roads in this enclosed basin may be extrapolated from the depth of strata built up over untold millennia.[22] These accretion ways were held steady by a potentially unbroken chain of tenure, the inherited obligations that come with cultivated densities, and their own tenacious being, offering a reliable path for generations to follow. Their longevity is as much about form as material.[23] This agrarian geometry has been maintained through its resistance to deviation; that is, a balanced relationship between multitudes unwilling to relinquish precious ground and the road itself which ensures that there is no need.

---

20 The peaks rise to heights of 1,121 and 1,110 meters. Concerning toponyms, see Jameson, Runnels, and Van Andel (1994, 29).

21 Such agrarian forms constitute the objects of *archeogeographie*; see Chouquer (2008); also Watteaux (2017).

22 Due to time constraints, the Dhidhima basin was excluded from any geomorphological sampling as part of a geological survey conducted by the Argolid Exploration Project (AEP). However, the AEP reported hearing of a roughly paved trackway buried under 4 meters of soil near the chapel of Agia Kiriaki 1 kilometer east of the village (Jameson, Runnels, and Van Andel 1994, 52).

23 See Segment 2.

The Dhidhima Valley from the Malavria Pass.

Through this agrarian webform slashes the modern motorway. When it opened in 1953, the motorway followed a circuitous path to the higher pass, the second of two main routes over the ridge from the Bedheni Valley.[24] Breaking with the ancient pattern of paths over the slopes, it followed a smoother gradient until it reached the valley bottom, where it fell in with the old roadway through the village of Dhidhima, only to return to a circuitous route over the ridge to the south. Decades later, this road was widened and in a long arc, northeast to west to southeast, a new bypass was added avoiding the village. Yet again, what had formerly been an obligation for every passer-by came be experienced as an option. Now the newest bypass cuts a direct line across the maquis-covered slopes of Megalovouni, like a deep incision down the full length of a beached whale. Avoiding the Dhidhima Valley altogether, this recently opened motorway severs any connection to the village, the plain, and its ancient pattern of roadways. A break with geography, it jumps from the valley center to the periphery and thereby inverts the foreground and background associated with millennia of movement.

I set out again. The *kalderimi* cuts an angle towards a dry wash then begins to snake along its sides. As an object it gives one some sense of how life was conditioned by hardship. Yet, it is clear that my object is estranged. It is beyond me. I can only experience it from the outside with the sense of aloofness that a night's rest in an air-conditioned room in Nafplion permits. I walk refreshed, well rested, with cold water, and possess very little sense of the proportionality of what it was to walk this path prior to the alleviation of burden with automobile and road. Those who once passed

24 Jameson, Runnels, and Van Andel (1994, 52), Koster (1977, 152).

here had no recourse to such luxury, to such freedom of mobility, to my sense of distance. From the high plain below Malavria to the saddle one gains just over 200 meters in elevation. On this side, the decent to the plain of Dhidhima is over twice that. Just below the first switchback, the foundation terrace of the mule track has fallen away. No need to maintain the way for transport. No need to shore up stones to protect the footing of a labor's companion, donkey or mule. No need to cut back branches in order to protect one's provisions, *touloumia* (goatskins) laden with olive oil or wine and *bedonya* (large tins) filled with goatmilk or water.[25]

Fragments of the *kalderimi* are discernable here and there, as broken terraces or worn sections of angled bedrock. Through a goat-formed breach, the path bypasses the old switchbacks and widens into a long swath covered in unbroken shoals of scree. The descent over the collected fruits of cloven-hooved labors is hard on knees and boots. One might as well attempt to walk on ball bearings. I try to angle down by turning my boots horizontal to the slope, but it makes little difference on shingle-strewn slips. I manage to skate down these surfaces while checking my momentum with juniper limbs. Yorgos was right: this is not a landscape of introspection. Here, dislodging themselves from any ready-to-hand status,[26] the slope, exposures of bedrock, the cut of the dry wash, boulders, juniper, demand your attention and force concentration. I find relief on a severed portion of the *kalderimi* where I pause to clear the accumulation of wayward stones off the path before continuing.

After a few hundred meters, the slope eases and the truck road meets the line of the old *kalderimi*. I walk along the raised bank of the dry streambed. What water passes here in the winter drains through cracks and crevices into the karstic basin of Dhidhima. Little topsoil is present on these slopes.[27] Juniper, sage, and wild olive force roots into fractures and fissures in the bedrock, which slowly cleaves limestone apart. Microbes, lichens, and plants mine nitrogen and carbon and produce organic compounds, which break down rock and form soils.[28] Oxygen and water transform ferrous minerals present in the rock into ferric minerals present in the soil—rust gives the slow soil its red color.[29]

For the next few minutes, the road alternates with changes in gradient between sections of pavement and gravel. Off to the right, a strip of olives propagated on a terrace above the streambed perhaps a generation ago offers the first example of agrarian workmanship. Thin terraces relinquished to overgrowth still

---

25 Skins from billy-goats were tougher, and therefore, preferable for transport (Forbes 2007, 252).

26 See Segment 8, note 8.

27 It does not seem that it was much different two and a half millennia ago; see Jameson, Runnels, and Van Andel (1994, 193–94).

28 Westbroek (1991, 130–31).

29 Raymond and Johnson (2017, 146–48).

capture soils in hollows to the left. Along here olive trees are confined to the low ground up through the last sweep of the valley, where the road enters the dry channel. Beyond, groves increase in frequency and trees increase in thickness. Generations of care are retained in the branchwork and creases of these pollarded olives. Despite their gnarled physiognomy, none of these olives are of great age— the oldest trees have been maintained here for perhaps two centuries.[30] Among these boughs I encounter the handiwork of various geoponists. Pollarded above the reach of goats, some are trimmed back directly above the bough. Some are cut so new shoots spring from a few thick limbs splayed from the trunk. Others are cut in such a way to form a sizable burl. Many trunks are tagged with the owner's initials in spray-paint.

Eventually, concrete and gravel transition to tarmac. From the outlet of the pass the road unfurls as a narrow grey ribbon draped over olive-covered slope and cuts a more or less direct and gentle angle to the valley bottom and into the village at its center. Straight and efficient, what few deviations exist in this line are artifacts of crease and slope. This paved road holds the form of the old, perhaps ancient way. To the left and right, broad terraces, oriented along contours, across drainages, mimic the basin by capturing soils and extending plots upslope. Framed with stone girdles, the geometry of these groves changes as I move closer to the village. Haphazardly planted allotments give over to flawless rows that vary only in the width between them. Along here there are few sentinel trees. Few olives are more than fifty years in age.[31] Where once there were open cereal fields, groves now reign. Within the drier portions of the valley—west, north, east—this pattern finds repetition. Only the moist bottomland south of the village remains open. There plots are sown with other crops. Some places are like vessels, and here this bowl continues to fill up with the gathering of objects, new, old, ancient.

Ahead, the village rises upon an accumulation of ruin heaped with and in the wake of Greco-Roman antiquity.[32] Over the millennia, Dhidhima has retained its ancient name. The toponym suggests an unbroken chain of memory lashed about this valley. I rejoin Brandon and Evan at the edge of the village, just off the old bypass road, by the vacant shell of a building. Half-finished, it stands as graffiti-swathed brick and concrete monument to the expectation of a future that never came and, now that the main road south bypasses the valley altogether, never will.

---

30 The Nani codex (c.1705) listed no olive trees for the Dhidhima plain, which Peter Topping takes to suggest their destruction either through upland skirmishes or a series of exceptionally cold winters (Topping 2000, 35).

31 A 1961 aerial photograph of the Dhidhima basin shows most of the drier portions of the plain under cereals; Jameson, Runnels, and Van Andel (1994, 30).

32 See Blouet (1833, 174); Jameson, Runnels, and Van Andel (1994, 531), Koster (1977, 141).

Our path continues past the vacant building, branches right before a chapel, and follows a line south. We pass houses enclosed behind walls. We pass houses set behind outer courtyards. We pass houses unfinished. We pass bin after bin overflowing in rubbish. We turn left into old Dhidhima, a warren of streets lined with houses, a few shops, and tavernas. Here and there, situated between high, two-story concrete houses, were low, one-story stone houses. The latter were not so much in danger of falling from top to bottom as being swallowed from bottom to top. Around these low abodes everything rose—streets, adjacent buildings, parking areas, rubbish, soil. Some of these stubborn structures have been surrendered to the wreckage of the past below. Some benefit from occupants who keep accrescence at bay. These old houses also stand out for their doors, which open directly onto the street—a subtle suggestion of a past where there was little separation between village and house.[33] Eventually, we arrive at the square by the parish church of Agios Nicholas.

Situated at the confluence of five streets is an ancient well. Now surrounded by a park planted in pine and paved with stone, it marks the point of transition between neighborhoods of Larti (Uptown) and Posta (Downtown).[34] Several plastic chairs are set out before a well. They are for sale. The merchant wears jeans and is shirtless. Taking a break from peddling his goods from village to village over a loudspeaker, he leans on his truck, stacked high with plastic tables and chairs. By the well, a woman sits cross-legged on a blanket, holding an infant swaddled in a white shawl, and slicing peaches into a plastic bowl. A toddler leans on the corner block of the rectilinear puteal. Noting our lack of interest in their goods, they ignore us.

Shaped as a parallelogram, the well is constructed from bottom to lip of squared blocks. At all depths this ashlar revetment is held firm by monolithic beams spanning the central axis. For over two millennia it has withstood pressures from the surrounding earth.[35] Since antiquity, so long as people have dwelt in this plain, a throng, vastly anonymous, little known, has gathered here to draw water from its depths.[36] Dozens of grooves are formed in the inner edge of the low puteal, made lower by rising pavements.[37] Gouged out through

---

33 Koster described how in the 1970s streets hummed with activity and doors were left ajar with neighbors coming and going freely from open house to open house throughout the day (Koster 1977, 143).

34 A generation ago villagers were conditioned from a young age to think in terms of territory. Turf battles fostered both group solidarity and territorial reason with the young maintaining bounded ground (ibid., 139).

35 My description echoes that of Miliarakis (1886, 244), who stood by this well in the late nineteenth century.

36 The well is perhaps Hellenistic or Classical in date; see Jameson, Runnels, and Van Andel (1994, 171).

37 The grooves are concentrated along the shorter ends and around the corners to avoid the stone crossbeams.

Ancient well in old Dhidhima.

the countless efforts of friends, neighbors, kinsmen, competitors, and strangers, these furrows guided legion ropes over the edge. Yet, now the well is suspended in a period of latency. Affixed to the ancient ashlar blocks is a black metal grate. A black pipe capped with a Storz coupling and valve protrudes from the corner—an outlet for water should it ever be required.[38] Closed to most, this past also now persists as an option rather than a necessity. Nearby, other ancient things gather—a *mortarium* from a Roman *trapetum* (oil press), a larger, circular mortar, perhaps Classical in date and holding water and rubbish, and a flat limestone pressbed among other sundry stones. About this well, plenty of room has been maintained should neighbors seek to congregate, should the flocks or droves be brought into the village.[39]

⁓

38 A clash of times, the well has been enrolled in public water systems at several turns. For example, a supplemental gravity-fed catchment system was added around 1970 to provide water for public faucets.

39 An old animal trough carved of stone sits nearby, at the edge of the paved surface.

Chapel of Agia Marina.

Two years later, we will pass the well and take a road heading southeast to the chapel of Agia Marina. Reposed within the hillside by a broad exposure of bedrock, the chapel is located upon the lower slopes of Megalovouni just above the line of cultivation at the southeastern edge of the Dhidhima plain. Upon our approach, its fresh coat of whitewash will stand out against its girdle of maquis. We will come to see a circular stone base or basin built within the corner of the chapel. We will read an inscription borne upon the shaft of this base that records an offering to Demeter by two women, Phanta and Aristomedia.[40] We will enter the nave to view the frescoes, perhaps of a late Byzantine date.[41] We will investigate a low enclosure, probably ancient, that surrounds the chapel. What was perhaps once a shrine sacred to the goddess of grain and harvest is now associated with a saint, a shepherdess disowned by her father, a pagan priest. A topological fold between times, those who worship here honor rites within an enclosure, within which pagan supplicants likely venerated Demeter at her altar.

This plain assembles such objects which give rise to such places. Roads rise upon ancient pathways. Neighborhoods rise around ancient wells, upon the

40 *IG* IV 746; Jameson (1953, 161).
41 The AEP recorded the chapel (D12); Jameson, Runnels, and Van Andel (1994, 478).

wreckage of a Greco-Roman settlement. Chapels rise upon the tutelary grounds of ancient paganism.[42] The ridges and ravines, edges and enclosures about this plain also establish limits, remarkably consistent in their form, which is also held in check by physiology, human and other animals, cultivatable ground, and water.[43] We left by way of a road over the ridge of Vigla to the south.

I remember an earlier journey to this ridge on a late August morning in 2007.[44] We had come to look for what was said to be a series of cairns piled out along its crest. We had come to see what the archaeologist Michael Jameson associated with the outcome of an ancient arbitration (early second century BCE) between Epidaurus and Hermion concerning rights to cropping and pasturage. To observe what Pausanias pointed out as the *boleoi* near Pilanorion, some 20 *stades* from Didymoi. To experience what perhaps had become of the *boleoi-lithoi*, "thrown stones," which upheld an act of arbitration and served to delineate a border, also recorded through inscription upon two stelae, one in ancient Hermion, the other in the Asklepion of Epidaurus.[45]

We hiked along goat paths through juniper thickets to the highest portion of Vigla. At the western exposure of the ridge we found a low mound of stones covering an area roughly 15 meters in diameter. While they had been dispersed through the work of goats, sheep, and herders, they rose well above the exposure of bedrock at a point that afforded a clear view to the Fournoi Valley, the Salandi Valley, and the Dhidhima plain. We found a second pile, also dispersed, at the highest point of Vigla. From there we spread out across the broad expanse of the ridge, moving east between thickets of juniper. A third pile, also spread over a wide area upwards of 15 meters in diameter, soon followed. Jameson identified nine erstwhile cairns in all.[46] Likely, there had been more, which had long since been quarried, perhaps to supply stone for two windmills, now ruined, or any one of the stone enclosures that dot the ridge.

42 Miliarakis suggested that the chapels of Agia Kiriaki and the Assumption of the Virgin Mary lay upon the sites of ancient temples (1886, 244). The AEP investigated the chapel of Agia Kiriaki in 1982 and found indications of Classical or later use.

43 Also see Jameson, Runnels, and Van Andel (1994, 599–600).

44 I visited Vigla with Brad Sekedat.

45 Jameson, Runnels, and Van Andel (1994, 596–603), Witmore (2014b).

46 Jameson, Runnels, and Van Andel (1994, 599).

The arbitration suggests that this was likely disputed ground. Here, judges and witnesses gathered to air grievances and adjudicate. Into stone the decision of the Milesian judges was chiseled. Thus we know that the area of the Sellas, what is now the Salandi Valley, and the Agrioi Limenes (Wild Harbors), likely the bay of Vourlia, up to Strouthous (a bird's name), perhaps the promontory known as Cape Iria, was set aside as common ground.[47] If these cairns were raised here along the middle of this wide ridge, then it was because of the need to define the border of the Philanoreia in an area lacking distinctive geological features. To the west, beyond the last cairn, such measures were unnecessary, as the border ran along the dock-tailed heights, the well-defined ridge of Voskaria, straight down to the sea.

Along this very same ridge runs the border between the two villages as it did in 1700.[48] No, one should not interpret the issue of borders in terms of a continuum. A ridge, an edge, or a precipice, the apex of a saddle, or spur, the form of cairns, objects long known to those who worked this ground, pastured their animals, lend themselves to the definition of borders.[49] Contour and crease offer form; limestone edge and ridge are what make boundaries definable for those who move herds over these heights, for those who cut juniper for a *mandri*, for those who collect herbs and snails on the hillside, or keep terraced plots within drainages.[50]

We left the ridge by way of the main road to Fournoi, the village situated upon ancient Philanorion.[51] We bypassed a severed section of the old road, which in turn bypassed the even older road built in the 1950s, which followed an earlier trackway between Dhidhima and the Fournoi Valley. From here the road angles down to the east and cuts back west, leaving the circuitous tarmacked surface to become a conduit for the illicit dumping of garbage.

47 Ibid., 596–97; for the full text of the arbitration, see Peek (1934: 47–52), Ager (1996: 170–73).

48 Jameson, Runnels, and Van Andel (1994, 599–600).

49 Such boundaries and lands allocated as common created conditions for what is often argued to be an "agro-pastural symbiosis" "with animals providing dung for the fields and the fields providing fodder for the animals" (Alcock 1993, 87; also see Koster 1976, Kron 2009).

50 Stuart Elden (2013) has argued that the concept of "territory" emerges under the unique geo- and techno-political circumstances associated with modernity. That the Greek polis does not operate with the same political technologies of power is clear, for, as Elden suggests, maps, as flat projections of the encompassing lands, were fundamental to manifesting *what* is actually controlled. Still, Elden neglects how boundaries were upheld by specific objects on the ground. The arbitration between Epidaurus and Hermion speaks of the heights of mountains, the crests of ridges, the cairns along a ridge as boundaries, and these features, known to those who lived with the land, defined the *chôra* (see Fachard 2018).

51 See Bintliff (1977, 204, 234), Jameson, Runnels, and Van Andel (1994, 466–67).

I would later return to the Fournoi Valley to walk through the Katafiki Gorge, the more direct route to Ermioni. From the main road I negotiated a braided series of truck roads by following surfaces more worn. My path angled through a notch in a low ridgeline, passed amid olive groves, and swerved around a stand of pine by the church of Agioi Anargyroi. Beyond, the road swings southeast through the area of Papoilias towards the upper end of the gorge. The Katafiki slashes through a ridge that trends from the Franchthi headland between the Fournoi and Loutro valleys along the north side of the Ermioni *kambos* (a small coastal plain) to the edge of the Iliokastro plateau. Shear walls washed in oranges, ochres, and greys, faceted with the textures of limestone, tower over 100 meters. Along its bottom a stream sweeps in a wide arc around a pine-covered spur to meet with the upper Ermioni *kambos*. A direct conduit between the uplands of Dhidhima and the coastal areas of the southeastern Argolid, Paleolithic objects found in the gorge speak to the depth of movement through this pass.[52]

The road ends abruptly in a gravel turnabout by a decorative terrace. Here too, the lush vegetation growing along the streambed drops off. Beyond, the lack of plane trees suggests the underground flow descends into a deeper karstic underworld. A truck path continues across the dry stream bed and follows a cut for 200 meters or so. Blocked by a decision of the Hellenic Council of the State (*Symvoulio tis Epikrateias*) in 1992, efforts to bulldoze a road through the gorge fell short of completion.[53] The turnabout also marks a transition between cultivated plots and the pine forest. *Katafiki* means "refuge." Local lore holds this to be is where local villagers hid from raids by Turks and pirates.

At the end of the roadcut, the well-worn footpath followed the streambed by oleander and under pine. An old iconostasis or icon stand endures off to the left. I remember pausing here a decade earlier. Within its recess a lamp burned, a fragile light for the safe passage of pedestrians amplified by the glimmer of icons—Agios Nikolaos, Agios Antonios, and Agios Georgios. Beyond this waypoint, a sylvan scene against limestone bluffs falls away, as the trail threads round limestone outcrops and under a dense canopy of twisted pines, bristling with cicadas. Along this stretch, pine boughs bear deep scars from resin collection. Brown bark grows thick over rusted cans, which refuse to fall away. Memories of resin extraction carved in boughs suggest many different hands; some

---

52 Van Horn (1976).

53 The court blocked the construction of the road on ecological grounds and due to "the exceptional natural beauty of the gorge" (see decision number 772/1992, www.adjustice.gr/webcenter/portal/).

seasoned, many callow.[54] Consistent were a few of the scars. Seventy-five-centimeter bands of bark, approximately 7 centimeters wide and notched to a V at the bottom, were removed in either strips or stages with a consistent depth of incision.[55]

One might say that these marginal lands were maintained as marginal out of wisdom, yet such insights miss what it is that this gorge contributes to the condition of being marginal. Ground for browsing, trees for resin, stands for wood cutters, perhaps even depressions for charcoal burners, the gorge and its ecology make these activities possible.[56] A locus of transition, crossing through, between, and over are persistent aspects of this area. A rupestral *horos* or boundary marker is carved into the escarpment above this pine-covered spur to the west. A transitional area between communities past, the gorge remains a liminal zone, because it refuses to offer itself to any other relations.

The path drops into the bulldozed cut for a carriage road. At its end stands a bridge. Another indication of the importance of the route and the hazards of the gorge in the rainy season.[57] Here the winds can pick up suddenly in the evenings, funneled between the high limestone walls of the gorge with the changing temperatures. Border areas like this are haunted. Residents of Ermioni claim that the churches of Agioi Anargyroi and Agios Nikolaos were placed at either end to hold the spirits in. Some even transpose the supposed passage to Hades mentioned by Pausanias from the peninsula of ancient Hermion to a cave in the high walls on the right. This rock face is whitewashed with crosses to hold phantoms within. It is said that those who passed through this way fortified themselves against the evil spirits with the sign of the cross and a prayer.

This gorge forms a spectacular repository for lore and myth.[58] Here, fairies, witches, local bandits, once roamed. In the wake of the erosion of superstition this locale holds a sense of re-enchantment which serves as a lure for nonlocals to visit the region to hike and climb the gorge. Climbing routes also line the sheer face. "Heroes," "Villains," and "Saints," "Savage Man," "Sidestep," and "Force War," their names are painted in red at the base of the climb. I remember passing the church

54 Many of these pines are less than 70 centimeters in circumference, suggesting unpermitted extraction. On resin collection in the Fournoi Valley, see Gatsou (2001, 397–413), Gavrielides (1976, 63–64).

55 Used to temper wine, to seal casks, and in the construction of ships, resin was a major cash crop of the region during the nineteenth century (Miliarakis 1886, 230).

56 According to Koster (1977, 102), there were three charcoal burners in Dhidhima. Also see Grove and Rackham (2003, 168–73), Horne (1982), Koster (1976).

57 Jameson, Runnels, and Van Andel (1994, 50).

58 Nakos (2013).

Bridge in the Katafiki Gorge.

of Agios Nikolaos, built in 1740, which marks and protects the transition. I recall oleander, chaste, pistachio, and agave as I walked out through the gates of the gorge and entered the Ermioni *kambos*.

~

I walked this way in July of 2004. I had passed through the gorge in the course of revisiting concentrations of objects located and documented by the Argolid Exploration Project (AEP), a regional archaeological survey.[59] A generation earlier, in August of 1981, this portion of the plain was fieldwalked by AEP survey teams.[60] Within plots on either side of the deeply cut stream channel, surveyors

59 Jameson, Runnels, and Van Andel (1994), Runnels, Pullen, and Langdon (1995), Sutton (2000), Witmore (2005).
60 On fieldwalking, see Segment 6.

encountered concentrated scatters of pottery sherds, roof-tile fragments, and other objects against a continuous background of other bits and pieces. These concentrations were designated as archaeological "sites." To the right, in a terraced field between the ravines, they encountered a clustering of rooftiles and ceramics and defined this as site E58. To the left, in a terraced citrus orchard, they collected sherds and roof-tile fragments, and Early Bronze Age lithics, which they designated as E59. Ahead, on a terraced slope between the road and the channel, they recorded fine- and course-ware fragments, portions of amphora, basins, and *pithoi*, a column base and a mortar amid piles of bull-dozed stone, near an exposed line of blocks. This they labeled E57. Four other scatters where found in the nearby orchards and fields. All these concentrations were interpreted as farmsteads; most were assigned to the Classical or Hellenis-tic period, one was identified as Early Roman, and another as predominantly Late Roman.

Farmstead, it should be emphasized, is a contested concept within the field of Classical archaeology.[61] Farmsteads, for the AEP, were regarded as "dwellings assumed to be inhabited for some part of the year by some members of a household."[62] By comparison to larger settlements, they were dispersed over an area no more than 2 hectares in extent, and offered "a full range of 'domestic' arti-facts (including, in the Classical period, lamps, oil press beds or weights, coins, other metal objects)," accompanied by roof tiles, and, at times, visible structural remains.[63] Controversy surfaces at the disjuncture between what is and what was, between a buried, yet partially visible past of wreckage and ruin encountered in 1981, and again in 2004, and a past imagined as lived and thereby circumscribed in order to be made historically intelligible. For many, this problem of historical iden-tification is annulled by arriving at a dynamic definition of objects understood as foremost as processes, laid out across a continuum inclusive of all their transformations.[64] Less often acknowledged is whether the past outside of history is even historically knowable, or whether a different past might be well realized apart from the expectations of history.[65]

Along here, yes, this concentration of agrarian objects is of multiple times. Here, yes, the presence of these scatters, these terraces, olive trees, are suggestive of manifold agrarian labors situated near a seasonal source of water, now pumped from a station near the church of Agios Nikolaos within the gorge. These things are also suggestive of themselves, and their own stubborn propensity to persist

61 McHugh (2017), Pettegrew (2001).
62 Jameson, Runnels, and Van Andel (1994, 249).
63 Jameson, Runnels, and Van Andel (1994, 249).
64 Bintliff (2004), Pettegrew (2001), Wandsnider (2004a and b).
65 Olivier (2011), Olsen (2010), Pétursdóttir (2012), Shanks (1992), Witmore (2014a).

upholds that which is here.[66] Along this path, each generation of farmers, herders, or seasonal inhabitants receives an increasing share of objects, which proliferate in this plain, as elsewhere along roads taken from Malavria. Likewise, those farmers whose fields were walked by archaeologists in 1981 made their contributions to this polychronic ensemble. As with the fields in the upland plains, olives, a reliable cash-crop planted over the intervening generation, were, in 2004, winning out over cereals on either side of the road. The labors of agrarians and archaeologists suggest how this *chôra* receives their contributions and holds achievements which persist as objects in themselves in their absence.

If Plato's *chôra* is that malleable, enduring substratum, neutral in itself, which takes on the imprint, yet, as both nurse and nurturer, also encompasses and engenders those things that live and accumulate here, then what lay along this broken trail of treaded memories both is, and is not, Plato's *chôra*.[67] *Chôra* to be sure exists along this path as reliable ground, which both holds and gives.[68] Yet, in passing through upland plains, over passes, among goats, within grazing lands, along dry streams, amid memories of woodland rapports, one cannot avoid the fact that this *chôra* no longer constitutes the womb upon which communities depend for their survival in the ways of those before. Though it may still engender a range of possibilities and interests, this *chôra* no longer encompasses the full grounds of production. My path through recollection from Malavria to the Ermioni plain touched upon that which formerly sustained subsistence for those who dwelt along its line, but *chôra* not only receives the impressions of travelers, herders, or agrarians; it takes on characteristics of goats and juniper, microbes and lichens, soil and storm waters, pine trees and buried ruins, limestone uplands and enclosed basins. This is, and is not, Plato's *chôra*. Its being is less that of an invisible and characterless matrix or a medium of intercommunication;[69] this *chôra* is a bewildering assemblage that exceeds the sum of those myriad and heterogeneous objects that comprise it. Unlike the Platonic *chôra* it appears as that which is intelligible, yet it also exceeds every local manifestation. While it nurtures its elements, it cannot exhaust those irreducible surplus realities which belong to sheepfolds, abandoned *kalderimia*, upland plains, pagan sanctuaries, or haunted gorges. We can only hint at the richness of this *chôra* from the path, its margins, and the surrounding plots, that lie along this tarmacked road from the outlet of the gorge across the *kampos* to Ermioni.

66 See Segment 25.
67 *Timaeus* 50b–e.
68 See Segment 1.
69 Whitehead (2010, 134–35).

Bibliography

Ager, S.L. 1996. *Interstate arbitrations in the Greek world, 337–90 B.C.* Berkeley, CA: University of California Press.

Alcock, S.E. 1993. *Graecia Capta: The landscapes of Roman Greece.* Cambridge, MA: Cambridge University Press.

Aldred, O. 2018. Legs, feet, and hooves: The seasonal roundup in Iceland. In S.E. Pilaar Birch (ed.) *Multispecies archaeology.* London: Routledge. 273–94.

Bintliff, J. 2004. Time structure and agency: The annales, emergent complexity, and archaeology. In J. Bintliff (ed.), *A companion to archaeology.* Oxford: Blackwell Publishing. 174–94.

Bintliff, J.L. 1977. *Natural environment and human settlement in prehistoric Greece.* 2 vols. British Archaeological Reports, Supplementary Series 28. Oxford: Archaeopress.

Blouet, G.A. 1831–1838. *Expédition scientifique de Morée, Ordonnée par le Gouvernement français: Architecture, Sculptures, Inscriptions et Vues du Péloponèse, des Cyclades et de l'Attique, mesurées, dessinées, recueillies et publiées par Abel Blouet.* Vols. I–VI. Paris: Firmin Didot.

Chang, C. 1981. *The archaeology of contemporary herding sites in Greece.* Doctoral dissertation, State University of New York at Binghamton.

Chang, C. 2000. The material culture and settlement history of agro-pastoralism in the koinotis of Dhidhima: An ethnoarchaeological perspective. In S.B. Sutton (ed.), *Contingent countryside: Settlement, economy, and land use in the Southern Argolid since 1700.* Stanford, CA: Stanford University Press. 125–40.

Chouquer, G. 2008. *Traité d'archéogéographie: La crise des récits géohistoriques.* Paris: Errance.

Elden, S. 2013. *The birth of territory.* Chicago, IL: University of Chicago Press.

Fachard, S. 2018. Political borders in Pausanias's Greece. In A.R. Knodell and T.P. Leppard (eds.), *Regional approaches to society and complexity studies in honor of John F. Cherry.* London: Equinox. 132–57.

Forbes, H. 2007. *Meaning and identity in a Greek landscape: An archaeological ethnography.* Cambridge, MA: Cambridge University Press.

Forbes, H., and H. Koster 1976. *Fire, axe, plow: Human influence on local plant communities in the Southern Argolid.* New York, NY: New York Academy of Sciences.

Gatsou, V.A. 2001. *The reconstruction of the Ermionida. (I anasynkrótisi tis Ermionídas).* Athens, GA: Archipélagos.

Gavrielides, N. 1976. The impact of olive growing on the landscape in the Fourni Valley. *Annals of the New York Academy of Sciences* 268, 143–57.

Grove, A.T., and O. Rackham. 2003. *The nature of Mediterranean Europe: An ecological history.* New Haven, CT: Yale University Press.

Horne, L. 1982. Fuel for the metal worker: The role of charcoal and charcoal production in ancient metallurgy. *Expedition* 25(1), 6–13.

Jameson, M.H. 1953. Inscriptions of the Peloponessos. *Hesperia* 22(3), 148–71.

Jameson, M.H., C.N. Runnels, and T. Van Andel 1994. *A Greek countryside: The Southern Argolid from prehistory to the present day.* Stanford, CA: Stanford University Press.

Koster, H. 1976. The thousand-year road. *Expedition* 19(1), 19–28.

Koster, H. 1977. *The ecology of pastoralism in relation to changing patterns of land use in the Northeast Peloponnese.* Doctorial dissertation, Department of Anthropology, University of Pennsylvania.

Koster, H. 2000. Neighbors and pastures: Reciprocity and access to pasture. In S.E. Sutton (ed.), *Contingent countryside: Settlement, economy, and land use in the Southern Argolid since 1700*. Stanford, CA: Stanford University Press. 241–61.

Koster, H.A., and J.B. Koster 1976. Competition or symbiosis? Pastoral adaptive strategies in the Southern Argolid, Greece. *Annals of the New York Academy of Sciences* 268(1), 275–85.

Kron, G. 2009. Animal husbandry, hunting, fishing, and fish production. In J.P. Oleson (ed.), *The Oxford handbook of engineering and technology in the Classical world*. Oxford: Oxford University Press. 175–224.

Lordimer, H. 2006. Herding memories of humans and animals. *Environment and Planning D: Society and Space* 24, 497–518.

McHugh, M. 2017. *The ancient Greek farmstead*. Oxford: Oxbow Books.

Miliarakis, A. 1886. *Geographia Politiki, Nea kai Archaia tou Nomou Argolidos kai Korinthos*. Athens.

Nakos, D. 2013. Katafyki Ermionidas Pezoporia sto farangi ton mython. *Epathlo* 92, 36–40.

Olivier, L. 2011. *The dark abyss of time: Archaeology and memory* (trans. A. Greenspan). Lanham, MD: AltaMira Press.

Olsen, B. 2010. *In defense of things: Archaeology and the ontology of objects*. Lanham, MD: AltaMira Press.

Panopoulos, P. 2003. Animal bells as symbols: Sound and hearing in a Greek island village. *Journal of the Royal Anthropological Institute* 9(4), 639–56.

Peek, W. 1934. Griechische Inschriften. *Mitteilungen des Deutschen Archäologischen Instituts, Athenische Abteilung* 59, 35–80.

Pettegrew, D.K. 2001. Chasing the Classical farmstead: Assessing the formation and signature of rural settlement in Greek landscape archaeology. *Journal of Mediterranean Archaeology* 14(2), 189–209.

Pétursdóttir, Þ. 2012. "Small things forgotten now included, or what else do things deserve?" *International Journal of Historical Archaeology* 16(3), 577–603.

Raymond, L.A., and N.E. Johnson 2017. *Crustal earth materials*. Long Grove, IL: Waveland Press.

Runnels, C.N., D.J. Pullen, and S. Langdon (eds.). 1995. *Artifact and assemblage. The finds from a regional survey of the Southern Argolid, Greece*. Stanford, CA: Stanford University Press.

Shanks, M. 1992. *Experiencing the past: On the character of archaeology*. London: Routledge.

Skiadopoulos, N., and V.W.J. van Gerven Oei. 2011. Greek returns: The poetry of Nikos Karouzos. *Continent* 3(1), 201–7.

Sutton, S.B. (ed.). 2000. *Contingent countryside: Settlement, economy, and land use in the Southern Argolid since 1700*. Stanford, CA: Stanford University Press.

Topping, P.W. 2000. The Southern Argolid from Byzantine to Ottoman times. In S. B. Sutton (ed.), *Contingent countryside: Settlement, economy, and land use in the Southern Argolid since 1700*. Stanford, CA: Stanford University Press. 25–40.

Van Horn, D. 1976. The archaeological survey: Chipped stone. *Expedition* 19(1), 50–4.

Wandsnider, L. 2004a. Solving the puzzle of the archaeological labyrinth. In S.E. Alcock and J.F. Cherry (eds.), *Side-by-side survey: Comparative regional studies in the Mediterranean world*. Oxford: Oxbow Books. 49–62.

Wandsnider, L. 2004b. Artifact, landscape, and temporality in eastern Mediterranean archaeological landscape studies. In E.F. Athanassopoulos and L. Wandsnider (eds.),

Mediterranean archaeological landscapes: Current issues. Philadelphia, PA: University of Pennsylvania Museum of Archaeology and Anthropology. 69–79.

Watteaux, M. 2017. What do the forms of the landscapes tell us? Methodological and epistemological aspects of an archeogeographic approach. In J.-M. Blaising, J. Driessen, J.-P. Legendre, and L. Olivier (eds.), *Clashes of Time: The contemporary past as a challenge for archaeology.* Louvain: Presses Universitaries de Louvain. 195–220.

Westbroek, P. 1991. *Life as a geological force: Dynamics of the earth.* New York, NY: W.W. Norton & Company.

Whitehead, A.N. 2010. *Adventures of ideas.* New York, NY: Free Press.

Witmore, C. 2005. *Multiple field approaches in the Mediterranean: Revisiting the Argolid Exploration Project.* Doctoral dissertation, Stanford University.

Witmore, C. 2014a. Archaeology and the new materialisms. *Journal of Contemporary Archaeology* 1(2), 203–24.

Witmore, C. 2014b. (Dis)continuous domains: A case of "multi-sited archaeology" from the Peloponnesus, Greece. In O. Harmansah (ed.), *Drawing on rocks, gathering by the water.* Oxford: Oxbow Books. 213–41.

22

ERMIONI / HERMION / KASTRI

A topology

Scouts and their spaces, quarried temples, measured pavements, of stone-cutters and archaeologists, Pausanias and his spaces, the peribolic, *at home on the sea, the* Periegesis *and space, the flat surface and space, things and space*

Within the pine-covered park, at the head of the Ermionian peninsula, a network of cobble-lined paths and floors coalesce around the pavement of a bygone church built within an ancient temple. Every July, Scout groups visit Ermioni to camp within these grounds. Around the robbed-out remnants of the church/temple, midway along the rise of the park, known as the Bisti, they sweep away straw and debris, set up their canvas tents, clean up rubbish, maintain trails, and, as teams under different totemic animals—Kingfishers, Crocodiles, Gulls, Dolphins, and Penguins—they compete in games—volleyball, wrestling, running, swimming.[1] Wearing red shirts, dark shorts, and hats of various colors, these children shore up the rubble lines that mark their trails, campsites, game fields, courses, and even areas for equipment or shoes with

---

1 Also see McAllister (1969, 174); see https://wiki.3oan.gr/index.php/Ερμιόνη_1991.

stones collected from around the headland. Where they pass, where they compete, where they eat, where they sleep, all their activities are defined by the rock-rimmed zones, which they tend.

⁓

A rectilinear pavement of grey limestone is all that remains of the temple. Set with tight polygonal jointing, these foundations are pocked with gaps around the outer edge marking breaks from which stones were wrenched. A low arc of rubble tracing the curve of an apse at the eastern end of the pavement is the only lingering suggestion of its conversion into a church.[2] Open to marine traffic on three sides, from the ruins on the headland architectural blocks were mined in order to line the organizational spaces of human habitats here, in the village, and on the surrounding islands.[3] Thus, the platform marks the center of a canopied quarry.

⁓

Of the peristyle temple, only the lowest course, the *euthynteria*, remains. What god resided upon this robbed-out platform? What rites of the ancient Hermionians occurred on the ground before the temple now marked out by Scouts who live the map that cordons their activities? Use of these architectural remains as convenient quarries did little to dampen attempts to connect extant ruins with their ancient referents. These large foundations were first associated with the sanctuary of the earth-shaking sea god by Gell (1810). Later, Philadelpheus (1909), followed by Faráklas (1973), identified these remains with the temple of Athena, only to be challenged again by Jameson, who favored Gell's naming.[4] It is not unlikely that the erstwhile temple was dedicated to Poseidon, nor is it less likely that it was associated with Athena.

⁓

This foundation, uncovered in 1909 by Alexandros Philadepheus, suggests a large temple, 16.25 meters by 32.98 meters. Upon measured description archaeological knowledge rests, yet Philadepheus's description is wanting, for when it comes to what has been measured detailed textual accounts are not

2 There are also a series of shallow channels, which Marian Holland McAllister took to be traces allusive of the interior arrangement of the church (1969, 179).
3 Cf. Curtius (1852 II, 457), Leake (1830 II, 461), McAllister (1969, 174–75).
4 Jameson, Runnels, and Van Andel (1994, 590), McAllister (1969).

enough.[5] On this headland, a cascade of texts had already made mention of various pavements, and supplied each with different dimensions.[6] Only a record manifest as a combination of narrative and plan, buttressed with other illustrations, including profiles and photographs, can secure the visual qualities of the pavement in two dimensions and put an stop to the confusion over which remains are being described. This foundation, along with each and every extant block, was measured with tape and drawn in August of 1967, and later inked and published by Marian Holland McAllister.[7]

Tending lines in stone, Scouts maintain the periphery of their grounds, which they dutifully clean. The Greek word for *clean*, *katharízo*, also means *to purify*. In earlier summers they even whitewashed the stones.[8] That these cleansed, rubble-delimited spaces coalesce upon what has become of an erstwhile temple hints at more than the affordances of a foundation for gathering. *Temple*, from the Latin *templum*, shares the Greek root *tem* as in *temenos*, the sacred enclosure, which connects to *temno*, to cut off or sever. Sacralization delimits a space; so it is with childhood memories. Here is where they are held by stones. In order to camp and compete for two weeks, as they have done every summer since 1958, Scouts assume the mantle of tenants within their sacred precincts.

Before the church was raised, the whole of the temple down to the *crepidoma* was removed. Later again, the quarrymen returned to claim the ruined remains of the church. Toppling formed blocks from above, prying finished slabs from foundations, measuring pre-cut masses, the sum of these labors amounts to less than the alternative, which would require the quarrymen to gouge blocks from tenacious rock beds deep in the ground. Quarrymen, stone-cutters, and masons size up volumes. Columns, statue bases, slabs, and stelae were first used as blocks to construct a medieval wall encircling the portion of the headland now held by the park. Later still, these stones were freed for construction, both for buildings and knowledge.[9]

5 Witmore (2006).
6 Bursian (1868–72, 96), Curtius (1852, 457), Frazer (1898 III, 293), Leake (1846, 281), Philade-pheus (1909, 172–81).
7 McAllister (1969, 171).
8 Ibid.
9 Philadelphius (1909, 173–81).

Stone-cutters and masons knew how measure form and calculate proportion. Archaeologists, equipped with tape, grid paper, and pencils, know
how to translate something of what remains onto flat surfaces without distortion. Whether one holds a chisel or a pencil, a common goal is the
transposition of form, yet the difference is in how the object is both *seen*
and *handled*. For the stonemason, armed with line and square, the stone is
measured—length, width, and height—with an aim to generate the maximum number of blocks with the desired proportions—thus, the extracted
form is a matter of economy, which will vary depending on the mason,
and therefore, the point of view. For the archaeologist, armed with *linear*
perspective undergirded by both *geometric stability* and *optical consistency*, the
measured plan removes the idiosyncrasies of an individualistic point of
view and allows for an observer to see things as they are seen by all—
such is the base line of scientific description, which lends itself to
mimesis.[10] For the stonemason, the object is handled from the angle of its
utility where there is no transposition of form without deformation. For
the archaeologist, the object is handled from the angle of its relevance to
the past where manifest in two dimensions its form does not deform
through transposition.

Dated on the basis of architectural comparison to the close of the sixth century BCE, McAllister's actual state plan will allow others to weigh her interpretation for themselves. It is also of consequence that she offers a second view,
a hypothetical image of what might have been—a hexastyle temple with twelve
columns on a side—itself raised upon the preceding state plan.[11] For while the
creation of a *homogeneous space* facilitates the reshuffling of images and the *super-*
imposition of different pictures, by manifesting what is seen from the angle of
a quarter turn, the plan once again determines how to envision what here
might have been.

Rubble lines and flat platforms give rise to spaces divergent from those of
the mapmaker, which here champions the longevity of the page multiplied over
that of singular stone. Yet, through the two-dimensional scenography all such
spaces are judged and in so doing, the many ways in which spaces exist are
subverted. Who comprehends the different spatial realities and senses of space
that formerly pervaded this headland? Another view of this peninsula should be
considered.

≈

10 Latour (1986), Serres (2017); in archaeology, see Witmore (2004, 2006).
11 McAllister (1969, 183).

Pausanias comes ashore with his description of this finger-like promontory, in the vicinity of the temple.[12] Here, within what had become of the old town of the ancient city he places a sanctuary of Poseidon, at the tip of the headland, followed by a temple of Athena, foundations of a stadium where the Dioskouroi allegedly competed. There is also a shrine to Athena, small and in ruin, so he states; there is a temple of Helios, one to Charites, another to Sarapis and Isis, and an unspecified number of megalithic enclosures formed of unhewn stone; within these, secret rites to Demeter are performed. The present town, however, lies 4 *stades* from the promontory of Poseidon. After writing down that which is most worthy of remark in the old city, Pausanias transitions to the new city on the Pron. Here again, he remarks upon that which is most commendable.

To understand how the space Pausanias puts forward is at variance with others, we must consider how he came to be *here*.

Pausanias, the traveler, describes two routes to Hermion: one overland from Troezen and one by sea. From Troezen, the road taken lends its linear qualities to a sequential engagement with those remarkable objects encountered along its route. From Cape Skyllaion, Pausanias, the author, writes in the nautical perspective of a traveler who looks upon land from the vantage point of the ship's deck.[13] From the moment he makes port, the description enters into walls, those of the old and new city, of sanctuaries and temples. The account wanders through open areas for gathering, those of the agora and other spaces of exhibition. In this, stone-rimmed enclosures lend their qualities to how he writes of objects worthy of note.[14] Respecting the spatial integrity of stone walls, Pausanias describes Hermion as two separate spheres harboring concentrations of temples, encompassing sanctuaries, statues, and fountains, with their associated competitions, practices, and festivals. Thus, pride-infused fortifications, common to all who dwell within, lend their morphological qualities as organizational forms.[15]

---

12 For more on the *Periegesis*, see Segment 17.

13 There are reasons to suppose his nautical description draws from another account, for here one encounters a critical mistake on the part of Pausanias. After Cape Skyllaion, which sits off the Saronic Gulf to the east, he describes the route as if travelling from the west—first, Cape Boukephala, then the island of Halioussa (which is actually an island-like peninsula), followed by Pityoussia, Aristera, eventually to Hydrea, which should have been the first island encountered after Cape Skyllaion (2.34.7–10); also see Jameson, Runnels, and Van Andel (1994, 577–79), Hutton (2005, 122–25).

14 Also see Hutton (2005, 142–43).

15 Such is a geometry of the *peribolic*, from the Greek word *peribolos*, the encompassing wall or enclosure that delimits a precinct.

A passing visitor might also envision Ermioni as two encompassing containers: the Bisti, the Albanian word for *tail*, and the Pron, the foreland studded with structures. Anyone who drives by automobile round Ermioni to return along the southern shore is left with an impression of a town encircled by the main road and severed from the shaded promontory. Anyone who visits by boat will, at first sight, verify this dichotomy. By their difference the pine-green forest and the road-edged town of whitewashed walls and terracotta roofs reinforce the impression of duality. Closer observation, however, will reveal other geometries.

Discrepancies are to be found within the residential zone of the interior. The built-up portion of the Bisti largely east of Mialouri Street, along the western shore of the north harbor, and the apex of the Pron (named Miloi after its former windmills) offered themselves to subdivision by grid. Ordinary and homogeneous, measured and reproducible, straight lines intersecting at right angles were imposed on open terrain at the edge of the old village over the latter half of the twentieth century. Yet, the eastern slopes of the Pron are unlike these gridded portions. Here lies an old labyrinth of streets of varying widths and angles, with stairs and small squares; their forms arise out of a polychronic entanglement of objects above and below the surface.

<hr />

At Hermion, the traveler confronted an ancient polis at home on the sea. To live intimately with the sea in all its immensity involved a combination of entrepreneurism and religiosity, unique to maritime communities. Famed throughout the world for its expensive dyes, which bore the polis's name, for centuries the Hermionians had extracted in vast quantities their purple from mollusks, *Murex trunculus*.[16] In order to safeguard the risks that come with maritime industries, additional insurances were sought by courting the divine favor of gods connected with the sea.[17] Foremost from the angle of the seafarer was the temple to Poseidon on the point. Then, first among the temples mentioned in the new town was that of Aphrodite of the Deep Sea and Harbor; her large marble statue was said to be worth seeing for its quality.

16 This industry suggests an awareness of the aquatic world both above and below the shimmering surface. Indeed, of the undersea Bachelard (1994, 205) speaks of "intimate immensity" in the phenomenological sense. Surrounded by subaqueous volumes is arguably the closest one will ever come to the phenomenological ideal of the body as homolog, albeit without an easy recourse to the "six basic and concrete dimensions: above/below or up/down; in front/behind and to the right/to the left" (Tilley 2004, 4). On the production of Hermionian purple, see Jameson, Runnels, and Van Andel (1994, 316–19).

17 See Bachelard (1994, 181–210) on "intimate immensity."

There was also a temple of Dionysos Melanaigis ("of the Black Goatskin"),[18] and to the god of wine and intoxication they held contests in swimming or diving and rowing.[19] Near the hearth of the polis stood a bronze statue of Poseidon with one foot upon a dolphin. Of special significance to the entrepreneur was the sanctuary of Tyche, goddess of fortune. Whether her colossal statue of Parian marble held the cornucopia and rudder, the paired emblems of wealth and risk-taking, Pausanias did not state. Still, it is safe to presume that with the addition of their most recent sanctuary, the Hermionians did not falter in their efforts to extend protections beyond city walls and over the precarious domain of their labors.

⌇

The encirclement of the town by a hardened, concrete girdle, paved over by a road, renews the geometry of protection known to those anonymous inhabitants of Hermion and Kastri, for residents now live behind a shared envelope against the rising waters. While fewer fishers and sailors live with the sea in the ways of their parents and grandparents, one would be ill-advised to limit the town to the shores, for the sea is part of its composition. Such is suggested by Ermioni's two harbors. The northern is simply called Limani, the southern harbor, Mandrakia, after the small enclosures which contain the boats near the shore.

⌇

Pausanias gives the length of the peninsula as about 7 *stades*, the breadth, at the widest, as no more than 3.[20] Never mind what has been lost to the rising sea, the measure given for width is judged as inaccurate: "his maximum width [is] almost twice the 300 m it is today."[21] Upon what does this judgement rest? The assumption is clear enough: the measure is taken to correspond to the length and width of the Hermionian peninsula. Still, we should hesitate. Is there a mutual accordance to what lies here? Let us note with the measure given the geometrical properties of ratio (3:7) and proportion (length = width x 2 + 1).

---

18 This incarnation of the god has been connected with the underworld, and thus, the realm of death (Otto 1965, 169). On the relationship between Dionysus and the sea, see Beaulieu (2016, 167–87). Yet, one should not ignore the association of the goat-skin with that of the wine-skin.

19 On the unique nature of swimming or diving contests, see Larmour (1990); on the connection to leaping into the sea, see Burkert (1983, 210–11).

20 2.34.9; a *stade* was 600 feet. The foot, however, varied, ranging between 0.28 and 0.334 meters; see Boyd and Jameson (1981, 332); also Jameson, Runnels, and Van Andel (1994, 569).

21 Jameson, Runnels, and Van Andel (1994, 584).

Between Pausanias and the peninsula something else intervenes, for here is an altogether different geometry, an idealized form, a balanced proportion.

∽

In Pausanias those scholars interested in the acquisition and explanation of old things could not avoid recognizing a kindred spirit. Yet, in regarding Pausanias as a trustworthy witness to what he encounters, many scholars presume a mutual adherence to the same underlying grounds for truth, one based upon the primacy of empirically derived knowledge with a fidelity to the material world.[22] By assuming a correlation between what is described in the text and what can be found on the ground, such assessments tend to tip Themis's scales more to the side of what, in this case, amounts to similarities rather than differences.[23]

∽

Jorge Luis Borges spoke of an Empire where the craft of cartography attained such a degree of perfection that the map matched the Empire "point for point."[24] In covering all the lands the map became so cumbersome that it, along with cartography, was abandoned. Do lines, whether walls, pavements, roads, or the rubble-rimmed grounds of Scouts, inscribe the projection, as with Borges's famous parable of exactitude? It depends on whether the lines are composed of paper, pixels, or stone.

∽

Nearly every commentator on Pausanias since the late nineteenth century has been compelled to project the *Periegesis* onto a base map. Situating a route, a path, a way through, begins with the situation of the planimetric perspective.[25] This is no less the case with his descriptions of cities than with the longer routes he took through particular territories. In mapping what are assumed to be Pausanias's movements, the projected infrastructure becomes

22 Fachard (2018); also Snodgrass (2001).
23 Scholarly readings, as Stewart has pointed out, "were based on the assumption that Pausanias was an objective and neutral author, somewhat dull and lacking in literary sophistication and not without his flaws, but ultimately a recorder and not an interpreter" (2013, 236).
24 Borges (1972).
25 Compare Elsner (2001) to Habicht (1985) to Hutton (2005).

the beginning for understanding spaces that were never projected.[26] Pausanias's spaces were "to be read" (*ut legitur*) rather than "looked at" (*spectandus*).

⌒

To understand mountains, peninsulas, pavements, or enclosures do you have to put yourself on the ground? One has to plunge into the place, yes, but is that here or there? Thus, writing about Ermioni, Kastri, or Hermion is a question of being where?

As I write, I am able to call up maps of Ermioni. I am able to click through base cartography and satellite photography; click through different scales of the Ermioni peninsula; click from 2D to 3D and shift angles, overlay more layers of information. I may zoom out to a distance of several dozen kilometers or leave the map entirely to observe the blue marble of earth from space. Whereas shuffling between scales was anything but smooth on paper, zooming now pulls off the trick of revealing maps as continuous, unbroken surfaces between the astronautical and the nautical, the extraterrestrial and the terrestrial.[27] Thus, Ermioni is defined from without and above in uninterrupted relation to other lands on a globe. Thus, Greece is experienced as a continuous surface connected to other continuous surfaces round an imperfect sphere.

⌒

A traveler through a world repeatedly defined from within, Pausanias, in moving from one polis to another, confronts one extraordinary locus after another, which was also not without one discrepancy after another. Within the fixed abode of ancient Hermion, the progeny of Phoroneus, first legendary king of Argos, consecrated a temple to Demeter Chthonia.[28] This, the traveler observed, is the most remarkable of Hermion's sanctuaries. Behind it lay a pool (one of three) named after one of these founders, Klymenos. Within the pool is a cave, what the Hermionians held to be a direct conduit to the underworld. Through this, against counter-claims to other locations, Herakles led the hound of Hades. Because of this passage, the Hermionians, it is said, may bypass the river Lethe; they do not require a coin for Charon.[29]

⌒

26 Also see Stewart (2013, 240–43).
27 See Lightfoot and Witmore (2018).
28 On Phoroneus, see Segment 12.
29 Strabo 8.6.12.

Beginning with a monogeotic sense of space, where surfaces spread out evenly in all directions, where all properties are of no more and no less importance— hence isotropic and homogeneous—it is difficult to conceive of the power of a direct conduit to the underworld. Being in the presence of the god, who infests their statue, enhanced by an atmosphere of dancing shadows, wavering lights, and veiling smoke, within his or her house creates a unique spatial connection which no tape can measure. That some places were more potent than others is tied to the fact that they were defined from within.

~

Where does Pausanias write? Whether en route or in a study, one has to envision two different modes of production, one faithful to the continuous movement of the *periegete* on the ground the other to the composition of a book at a desk.

Where is he going? Whether his object is determined by path taken on the ground or the creation of literature, one has to be open to the road and the study.

From where does he come? Whether his path is that of the religious pilgrim or the learned scholar in the tradition of Herodotus, one has to be prepared for both possibilities. Through where does he pass?[30] Pausanias travels through two reputed centers, marked by navel stones, *omphaloi*. Within the walls of Philius, just off the agora, he walked through the center of the Peloponnesus, "if" with their stone "they speak the truth."[31] Later, he will find himself at the navel of the Delphians, which once usurped other contenders in marking the center of the earth.[32] Though Pausanias says nothing about any common house, the broader *oikoumene*, the structure of this text suggests a series of encompassing spheres.[33] In a world whose self-definition emanated out from the common hearth, walled cities, sanctuaries encircled by *temenoi*, temples, and the collecting spaces of agoras asserted themselves as organizational spaces.[34] Beyond radiated another protected enclosure of the shared territorial border, where the

---

30 These four questions draw upon the four key words of space: *Ubi? Quo? Unde? Qua?* (see Serres 2015b, 27).

31 2.13.7. See Pretzler (2005, 159–60).

32 10.16.3. On the place of Greece, and particularly, Delphi in the *oikoumene* of Strabo, see Scott (2013, 150).

33 Notwithstanding the empirical corrections of the Hellenistic and Roman eras, Pausanias is not concerned with formulating any such image; see Pretzler (2005); on space in the ancient world, see Geus (2003), Romm (2010), Scott (2013).

34 Sloterdijk (2014).

extent of the *chôra* was marked by the heights of mountains, a series of cairns, and a sanctuary.[35] Does not the *Periegesis* hint at a geometry of peripheries, of boundaries, of fixed edges arranged concentrically?

Considerations of what merits remark have little claim to what befalls the remarkable. Throughout the duration of stubborn stone, one finds walls, temples, and sanctuaries, along with those objects they once protected, offering the formal qualities of their former portions to other spaces. Upon the Bisti, a medieval castle from which comes the old toponym of the town, Kastri, renewed the protective geometry of the fortified promontory. A solid concrete core of unhewn stone stripped of its revetment is all that remains of the cross wall, which cuts a line across the peninsula at its slimmest extent.

Around the base of two towers one may still inspect how a plinth furnishes a square corner, how a pedestal, laid flat, affords a level foundation, as do rectilinear statue bases, which perhaps once upheld bovine bronzes dedicated to Demeter Chthonia.[36] Archaeologists, epigraphers, historians refer to such blocks as "spolia," a term tinged with condemnation, as in "spoliation," a past ravaged by those considered to be irreverent in their selection. Unknown builders, architects, and masons left a new quarry for Albanian emigrants in the eighteenth and nineteenth centuries who joined others among the ancient ruins on the slopes of the Pron. There, the organization of the groundwork was, in many cases, complete. There, by ancient hands many of the foundations were laid. Thus, the layout was accomplished, the length of the edifice given, as was the width of the walls. There, after foundations of solid bearing, all that remained for new builders, architects, and masons was the height of the superstructure and span of the encompassing roof; the raw material for the former could be quarried from above and below. Thus, Kastri-turned-Ermioni is structured of what forms its roots. Stone lines trace out objects on the ground without the intermediary.

---

35 That Pausanias mentions more boundaries than any other ancient author, to be sure, reflects something of their geopolitical importance (Fachard 2018).

36 Jameson (1953, 148–54).

There is no place without the thing that engenders it. There is no space without the object that upholds it. The enclosure, the foundation, delimits inside from outside and sustains the *peribolic*. The plan, the map, manifests the visual properties of objects from the angle of a quarter turn and upholds the sense of space that follows linear projection. Elsewhere, pressing up from below, ancient things shape spaces within Ermioni. Houses, a former school turned library, property boundaries, steps, streets are all carried on the line of a wall 2,400 years in duration. What was likely a *temenos* now forms portions of other enclosed spaces. Here, where automobiles are ill-served by thin and irregular streets, one encounters space that is anything but ordinary or undifferentiated, space which clashes with the homogeneous, the isomorphic. To park before the church of Agios Taxiarkhis (Archangel Michael) one must pass between the columns. Beyond, other walls, composed of gargantuan blocks, delimit a path within or around the church. What is the difference? Space, long considered primordial, arises from things.

Bibliography

Bachelard, G. 1994. *The poetics of space* (trans. M. Jolas). Boston, MA: Beacon Press.

Beaulieu, M. 2016. *The sea in the Greek imagination*. Philadelphia, PA: University of Pennsylvania Press.

Borges, J.L. 1972. Of exactitude in science. In *A universal history of infamy* (trans. N.T. di Givanni). New York: Dutton. 141.

Boyd, T.D., and M.H. Jameson. 1981. Urban and rural land division in ancient Greece. *Hesperia* 50(4), 327–42.

Burkert, W. 1983. *Homo Necans: The anthropology of ancient Greek sacrificial ritual and myth*. Berkeley, CA: University of California Press.

Bursian, C. 1868–72. *Geographie von Griechenland*. Leipzig: Teubner.

Curtius, E. 1851–52. *Peloponnesos eine historisch-geographiche Bechreibung der Halbinsel*. Gotha: J. Perthes.

Elsner, J. 2001. Structuring "Greece": Pausanias's *Periegesis* as a literary construct. In S. E. Alcock, J.F. Cherry, and J. Elsner (eds.), *Pausanias: Travel and memory in Roman Greece*. Oxford: Oxford University Press. 3–20.

Fachard, S. 2018. Political borders in Pausanias's Greece. In A.R. Knodell and T.P. Leppard (eds.), *Regional approaches to society and complexity studies in honor of John F. Cherry*. London: Equinox. 132–57.

Faráklas, N. 1973. *Ermionis—Alias*. (Archaíes Ellinikés Póleis, tóm 12), ékd. Athinaïkós Technologikós Ómilos – Athinaïkó Kéntro Oikistikís. Athens.

Frazer, J.G. 1898. *Pausanias's Description of Greece*. 6 vols. London: Macmillan & Co.

Gell, W. 1810. The itinerary of Greece. London: Payne.

Geus, K. 2003. Space and geography. In A. Erskine (ed.), *A companion to the Hellenistic world*. Oxford: John Wiley & Sons. 232–46.

Habicht, C. 1985. *Pausanias' guide to ancient Greece*. Berkeley, CA: University of California Press.

Hutton, W. 2005. *Describing Greece: Landscape and literature in the Periegesis of Pausanias*. Cambridge: Cambridge University Press.

Jameson, M.H. 1953. Inscriptions of the Peloponessos. *Hesperia* 22(3), 148–71.

Jameson, M.H., C.N. Runnels, and T. Van Andel. 1994. *A Greek countryside: The Southern Argolid from prehistory to the present day*. Stanford, CA: Stanford University Press.

Larmour, D.H.J. 1990. Boat-races and swimming contests at Hermione. *Aethlon* 7(2), 127–38.

Latour, B. 1986. Visualization and cognition: Thinking with eyes and hands. *Knowledge and Society* 6(6), 1–40.

Leake, W.M. 1830. *Travels in the Morea*. London: John Murray.

Leake, W.M. 1846. *Peloponnesiaca*. London: J. Rodwell.

Lightfoot, C., and C. Witmore. 2018. Describing Hermion/Ermioni. Between Pausanias and digital maps, a topology. In M. Gillings, P. Hacigüzeller, and G. Lock (eds.), *Re-mapping archaeology: Critical perspectives, alternative mappings*. London: Routledge.

McAllister, M.H. 1969. A temple at Hermione. *Hesperia* 38(2), 169–83.

Otto, W.F. 1965. *Dionysus: Myth and cult*. Bloomington, IN: Indiana University Press.

Philadelpheus, A. 1909. Ai en Hermionidi Anaskaphai. *Praktika* 172–84.

Pretzler, M. 2005. Comparing Strabo with Pausanias: Greece in context vs. Greece in depth. In D. Dueck, H. Lindsay, and S. Pothecary (eds.), *Strabo's cultural geography: The making of a Kolossourgia*. Cambridge: Cambridge University Press. 144–60.

Romm, J.S. 2010. Continents, climates, and cultures: Greek theories of global structure. In K. Raaflaub and R. Talbert (eds.), *Geography and ethnography: Perceptions of the world in pre-modern societies*. Chichester: John Wiley & Sons. 215–35.

Scott, M. 2013. *Space and society in the Greek and Roman worlds*. Cambridge: Cambridge University Press.

Serres, M. 2015b. *Statues: The second book of foundations*. London: Bloomsbury.

Serres, M. 2017. *Geometry: The third book of foundations*. London: Bloomsbury Academic.

Sloterdijk, P. 2014. *Globes: Spheres II*. South Pasadena, CA: Semiotext(e).

Snodgrass, A.M. 2001. Pausanias and the chest of Kypselos. In S.E. Alcock, J.F. Cherry, and J. Elsner (eds.), *Pausanias: Travel and memory in Roman Greece*. Oxford: Oxford University Press. 127–41.

Stewart, D.R. 2013. "Most worth remembering": Pausanias, analogy, and Classical archaeology. *Hesperia* 82, 231–61.

Tilley, C. 2004. *The materiality of landscapes: Explorations in landscape phenomenology*. Oxford: Berg.

Witmore, C. 2004. On multiple fields: Between the material world and media – Two cases from the Peloponnesus, Greece. *Archaeological Dialogues* 11(2), 133–64.

Witmore, C. 2006. Vision, media, noise and the percolation of time: Symmetrical approaches to the mediation of the material world. *Journal of Material Culture* 11(3), 267–92.

23

LOOKING SOUTHWEST, TO WHAT
HAS BECOME OF AN ANCIENT *OIKOS*

Looking towards Halieis, at a table with texts and photographs, "House 7", oikos imagined, fecal atmospheres and olfactory burdens, of houses and taverns, the fallacy of expression, things and categories, ruin and abandonment, the dregs of history, alternative pasts

June 2, 2012. From where I sit, at a table on the south harbor of Ermioni, Halieis lies to the southwest, across the shimmering waters of Potokia (Kapari) Bay, over the southern flats of its crescent beach, at Kinetta, beyond the long, dipping edge of the Dhiskouria hills, past Petrothalassa and the eastern flats of the Flambouria plain. Remnants of the short-lived polis, an ancient home to Spartan interests and displaced Tirynthians,[1] are to be found on the southern end of a sheltered bay beset by crenulate shores. There, under the waters of Porto Kheli, and over mild yet steady slopes to the crest of three low hills,

---

1 Boyd and Jameson (1981, 328), Jameson, Runnels, and Van Andel (1994, 373–87).

exposed lines of conglomerate break through ceramic-littered surfaces. Amid former agricultural plots, olive groves, and scattered estates, large, open excavation trenches lay bared, the earth they contained having been displaced by archaeologists over three decades ago.

A dozen manila folders containing photocopied texts, plans, and photographs cover the table. I leaf through them to find a topographical plan of the site. Divided into two zones of *insulae*, Halieis was laid out orthogonally over softly sloping ground, below the heights of its acropolis. Oriented at different angles, each zone consisted of eight parallel streets laid equidistantly, though the western zone occupied roughly half the area of the eastern.[2] These *insulae* were comprised of houses, built in tight proximity. These houses were made up of various rooms, shielded by mudbrick walls. I reach for a photocopy of a Halieis excavation volume and begin to read through a description of one of the houses—"House 7."

Located at the intersection of Avenue C and Street 1, near the Southeast Gate and Tower 9 of the eastern zone, House 7 forms the southwest corner of an *insula* containing other houses.[3] Observed planimetrically, House 7 has a slight rhomboidal shape, with the western and eastern corners constricting at angles of less than 90 degrees. The *prothyron* or porch of the structure opens to the south onto Avenue C, which continues through the city gate only a few meters to the southeast. The door of the *prothyron*, wide enough for a cart, accesses an open courtyard, approximately 64 square meters in area. A private well sits in the northern corner of the courtyard, while just south of its center a pit was cut into the ground. The four walls of this pit are stone-lined; its base is "bedrock or packed stone" (the provision of an alternative material reveals a certain distance between the referent and the author).[4] A tiled drain extended from the pit into Street 1. Overall, the pit measured 2.6 by 1.15 by 1.43 meters, and thus had a capacity of 4.3 square meters. A number of chambers, most with doorways, fringe this court on the northwest and northeast (a location favorable for winter sun and summer shade), while a single alcove is located in the southeast corner. Some of these chambers cluster together to form what may have been an area of private rooms and stores.[5]

Immediately to the left of the main entrance is an antechamber, 3 meters by 4.2 meters. Beyond lies a second room, measuring 4.8 meters by 4.2 meters.

---

2 Boyd and Rudolph (1978), Boyd and Jameson (1981, 328–29).

3 Ault (2005, 13).

4 Working largely with excavation notebooks and photographs, Bradley Ault's description of House 7 (ibid.) was published nearly thirty years after its excavation. Ault's account drew upon his earlier dissertation (1994), which dealt with the architectures of Halieis.

5 Also see the description of House 7 in Nevett (1999, 99).

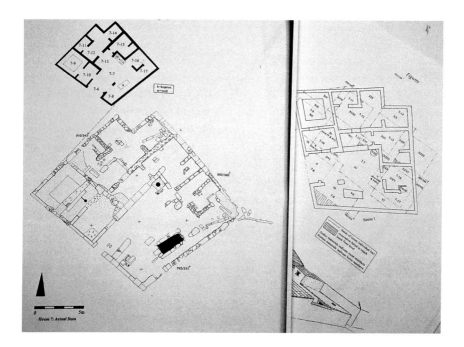

House 7 at Halieis.

The floors of these rooms were plastered. However, the floor of the inner chamber has a raised platform on all sides and was framed by walls accented in red plaster.[6] These raised platforms could have accommodated seven couches or *klinai*. Near the southeast corner of the room, a jar was set into the platform, and from it a channel was cut to the recessed central area. The jar, of plain-ware, was found containing a bowl and cup, both black-glazed. These objects, channel and jar, bowl and cup, suggest some sort of liquid-engagement. The doors in the chamber and antechamber are set off-axis. From the court a viewer could not have seen the segregated events taking place in the inner room. These, taken altogether, are characteristic features of an *andrôn*, or liter-ally the "men's room." The *andrôn* provided a space for relaxed closeness, for the sharing of food and conversation among symposiasts, smoothed by wine and, when possible, music.

Again, it is of a text that I have been speaking.[7] I reach across the table to a folder containing photographs of the site taken nearly a decade earlier. I flick

6 Boyd and Rudolph (1978, 351–53), Ault (2005, 15).
7 Ault (2005).

through them and pause on an image of House 7 or, rather, what has become of it. Behind a chain-linked fence, adjacent to a gravel road, linear arrangements of stone lay exposed, partly overgrown in browning stubble. Conglomerate footings are without walls. Erstwhile floor spaces are without roofs. Former rooms are empty of their contents. Partial, these things endure without their completions. Though the overall form of the erstwhile structure persists as a footprint of former rooms, readily translated into plan, those who venture south seeking out the ancient Greek *oikos* in the open trenches at Halieis must contend themselves with profound feelings of disappointment. When one pursues the ancient *oikos*, when one begins with an image of human dwelling, what has become of it is never enough.

Amid these stones, children laughed, couples loved, cries lingered. Amid these stones, someone slept—the nuptial bed was shielded from wayward eyes—someone cared for a home, kept to a routine, suffered, and knew death. Amid these stones, a hearth radiated its *vital heat*, and drew a household to gather round.[8] The hearth was Hestia, and was situated at the figurative center of the *oikos* where a family shared warmth and meals. Perhaps here fathers introduced newborns to the radiant

Photos of what has become of House 7, 2003.

8 On the concept of "vital heat," see Harrison (2003, 41).

goddess of domestic norms, as a member of the *oikos*, in a ceremony known as the *amphidromia*. Within walls now fallen, they waited out the germination of plants and bided the intervals between holidays. Within, they apportioned the fruits of their labors, and of their labors' companions, for whom shelter was provided within the small courtyard. Here, someone greeted friends, welcomed neighbors, exchanged gifts, and made strangers feel comfortable. In the *andrôn*, men ate, drank, and were entertained. Nearby stood the main entry, with its threshold; here, would not a family have envisaged a comfort-image of "*Puledokos*, the watcher at the gates, of *Nuktos Opopeter*, the watcher by night," of Hermes, *Leister*, the thief who repels thieves?[9] It was not only left to stout walls to keep the thieves and assailants at bay, or to block all the creatures and spirits that lurked outside in the dark of night; manifest as Hermes and Hestia, an additional layer of divine comfort was cast upon the house, the guardian of sleep.

To define the Greek house is to define the household—such is the dual connotation of *oikos*. An enclosure, hearth, within an enclosure, *oikos*, within an enclosure, walled town, within an enclosure, *chôra* (in the sense of "territory"), here a family achieved a fine balance between living apart and living together. Inside shared walls they built upon that which came before and shaped a legacy that would shelter those who come after, born and unborn. Amid these stones, lives were lived, and:

> For them no more blazing hearth shall burn,
> Or busy housewife ply her evening care: No children run to lisp their sire's
> return,
> Or climb his knees the envied kiss to share.[10]

Ultimately, that which is contained within the humus is consummated as that which contained the human.[11]

At the table, as I clumsily recall the lines of Gray's *Elegy*, questions ensue. Do lines of stone hold echoes of those mothers who lived, and died, here? Do these exposed surfaces contain residues of love's embrace? Or, do they speak to segregations of space in a misogynistic, or rather, *gynophobic*, woman-fearing, society?[12] Do we not ask too much of what remains here when we compel these things to comply with such expectations? Do these remains speak *directly* to a world of which they may or may not have formerly been a part?[13] It is

---

9 Vernant (2006, 159).

10 Thomas Gray, *Elegy Written in a Country Churchyard*, 1751.

11 The mortuary associations between the excavated house and tomb should not go unnoted; again, see Harrison (2003, 37–54).

12 Llewellyn-Jones (2011).

13 Olivier (2011).

easy to do, you know, to ask too much, as I do now, sitting here, at this table. For even when they arise from the depths of the classical imagination, images of domestic essence, whether romantic or otherwise, can easily blanket what remains to the southwest, what is captured in the photograph, with comfortable fictions.[14]

I reach for my notebook and begin to thumb through its pages. I pause on some remarks related to Chapter 3 of Sloterdijk's *Sphären II—Globen*.[15] I had noted, in a passage somewhat reminiscent of Sloterdijk in substance and style, how the atmospheric premises of ancient architectures had yet to be considered in the context of ancient Greek *oikos*. "One need not cite," the passage continues, "prohibitions on dumping *kopros* in the sanctuary of Apollo Lykeios at Argos,[16] to build a case that Greek poleis were overflowing with excrement."[17] Bradley Ault's reinterpretation of the pit in the courtyard of House 7 as a "*kopron*" (originally excavated as a "cellar") can be situated as an attempt to pin down the material truth of what everyone suspects with respect to an age before cesspits and sewers; namely, that to live behind the shared walls of an ancient polis was to live within the shared air of community ordure.[18] Yet, the scatological consequences of living without a sewer system must have shaped the Greek house more than most scholars have dared to consider.[19]

If Ault is correct, then to enclose a house around a courtyard was to dwell around a domestic stable, garbage pit, and rudimentary septic tank.[20] Thus, to live in this ancient Greek house was to be at home with shared olfactory burdens, and especially the smell of one's own excrement. Consider how, prior to entering the *andrôn*, symposiasts would pass through the high-walled courtyard where this receptacle was situated.[21] Here, no winds would scatter wayward smells, and even doors propped open would have been to no avail on a street

---

14 Never mind their dubious historicity; on the presence of fixed hearths in Classical houses, see Foxhall (2007, 234). Still, this is the laral value of the house, which is powerful. On the laral value of the house, see Harrison (2003, 50).

15 Sloterdijk (1999).

16 Dillon (1997, 118).

17 See Sloterdijk (2014, 323).

18 Ault (1999); also see Lindenlauf (2000).

19 Is it not in this regard that we may understand the ranking of sewers alongside roads and aqueducts as the greatest of Roman achievements by Dionysios of Halikarnassos?

20 While we are left with speculations, one cannot fault the excavators for undertaking no chemical analyses when these stone-lined pits were excavated in the mid-1970s. Systematic use of phosphates was just beginning to be developed at the time.

21 And by extension, the disposal of waste in fields (here, one has to assume that *kopros* was regarded as valuable compost for fertilizer; see discussion in Alcock, Cherry, and Davis 1994; also Forbes 2013, ND), or in marshes and ravines ensured that visitors encountered the smell of community excrement before they ever entered town walls.

streaming in its own filth. The tang of urine, the smack of rancid grease, rotten provisions uneaten by animals would have lingered within such a container as foul patches of air.[22] The stone cover-slabs of the *kopron* needed to be stout in terms of both stability and smell—no open pits for animals to injure themselves, no open fissures for malodorous vapors to escape. Would any oozing odors in excess be interpreted as a sign of a poorly kept home? Did particularly pungent scent alarms encourage aromatic countermeasures—burning incense, perfumed oils, or the removal of waste? Whatever the answers, proximity to the gate ensured that fewer fellow inhabitants of Halieis would have to endure the unique olfactory emanations of the *oikos* at House 7 as the night-soil cart squeaked towards the fields.

Such ruminations are read from a seat within a deodorized town, and as Sloterdijk points out, those who live under such conditions tend to have different noses for their own stench.[23] While the whiff of *kopros* adds a certain fragrance to conventional airs of "domesticity," others have questioned whether what was called House 7 even relates to a single-family dwelling. I reach across the table for another article. House 7, as Lin Foxhall points out, is peculiar. It lies next to the Southeast Gate. It is the largest house excavated at Halieis. It possessed the most substantial hearth. It also contained an exceptionally large number of cooking-pot fragments, along with high proportions of fine-ware cups and courseware serving vessels. Such differences, among others, led Foxhall to suggest that House 7 may have been a tavern.[24] (Thus, also rendering as somewhat unsavory Ault's interpretation of the pit as a *kopron*.)

I return to the Halieis excavation volume subtitled *The Houses*. Organized by *house* and *room*, the volume discusses the site in terms of occupation or habitation levels, assumed to be relatively synchronous.[25] Objects are regarded as "objective traces of [household] organization, of *oikonomia*."[26] When one reads the descriptions of what was excavated to the southwest, it is framed not only as *of the past*, but *of a very particular moment*, that of human use and interaction.

---

22 I have taken inspiration from Rainer Maria Rilke's description of a demolished house in *The Note-books of Malte Laurids Brigge* (1982, 46–48; also see Harrison 2003, 44–47). It is possible, as Forbes has argued, that feces and food wastes entered separate refuse streams (N.D. 22).

23 Having to endure the occasional sewage truck is not enough for anyone to sensitize themselves to such smells. That the rubric of *miasma* did not expand to cover excrement for the ancients can be taken as a suggestion of as much (see Parker 2010, 2–11). Also see Lindenlauf (2000).

24 2007, 237; also Forbes (2013, 564). Foxhall's intervention reminds us that a room with raised platforms for couches need not always be considered in the restricted context of a domestic symposium. Still, use of such a space for a tavern does not necessary preclude the use of the pit as a *kopron* or the fact that the structure may have been a house at an earlier stage in its life.

25 Ault (2005, 8).

26 Ault (2005, 4); also see Morgan (2010), Nevett (1999).

This is, of course, what archaeologists do. Yet, it is nonetheless strange, if not alchemical, how in both vocabulary and tense, the "house," its "rooms" and "walls," its "contents"—kraters, bowls, roof tiles, etc.—are rendered as conceptual wholes. Through this vocabulary of completions, the partial, fragmentary, broken realities of actual things are suppressed; these wholes, in superseding the banal, are somehow rendered as a concrete and given. The dregs of history are distilled as its liquid—obscured through purification, these dregs have never been allowed to be themselves. Ironically, old things have escaped serious consideration for what they are by beginning with what they might have been.

I pick up the photograph. To look after reading these texts is to behold a material past packaged in such a way that my engagement, however critical, is constrained to its observation. Foxhall's intervention, a welcome reassessment, is likewise circumscribed to operate within the domain of classification and standardization established by the excavation. By neglecting the degree of abstraction necessary for archaeologists to frame actual things insofar as they illustrate particular categories of thought, we fail to register those qualities and competencies of things that exceed such categories. Beginning with actual things and their idiosyncrasies not only has the merit of drawing our realities closer, it allows us to understand how they may be suggestive of alternative pasts.

In the margins of the photocopy I had, at some point, scribbled a line from Serefis: "Houses, you know, grow resentful easily when you strip them bare."[27] How resentful? We cannot know. For the sake of houses, wholes, one must ignore the entire post-history of these stones and surfaces, their former state as ruins, weather-worn, mudbrick and plaster walls returned to the earth, only to be cleared, and once again touched by the light. An engagement with an erstwhile life of an ancient house would seem to drown out other afterlives: nowhere do I find that the excavators of House 7 envisioned their objects in a different light. If one views the archaeological record in the course of excavation through the looking glass of *what was* (wholes), of *what happened here* (habitation), then the result is a devastated excess, formerly holding potential legions of undisclosed things with all their unruly memories. This was *not* the past that was, but what had become of it, which, in reality, derives from *what is*.[28] In the margins of the text the undisclosed riches of Halieis have been consigned to oblivion.[29]

To what degree did the excavators succumb to a fallacy of expression, where the remains were framed in terms of occupation rather than abandonment?[30]

27 Seferis, G. *Thrush*. Translated by E. Keeley.
28 See Lucas (2012), Olivier (2011), Olsen, Shanks, Webmoor, and Witmore (2012).
29 See Segments 2 and 9.
30 Olsen, Shanks, Webmoor, and Witmore (2012, 189). On the abandonment of houses in Classical archaeology, see Morris (2005), Pettegrew (2001).

What can we say regarding the post-history of buildings at Halieis, the memories of their lot as ruins, as potential enclosures, or rubbish heaps? I cannot know from here. Among these texts I find no answers. I do know that archaeologists did not lay bare intimate recesses. I need not find evidence to suggest that the basal interiors turned out through the excavation of soils would have been just alien to those who once knew a home intimately.

How would one now know if what is labeled as House 7 was relinquished prior to the final abandonment and destruction of Halieis? While the solution has obscured our starting points, there are subtle suggestions of such a possible fate. Three large blocks of cut poros were set against the jamb of the Southwest Gate. This could be seen as an indication of duress and preparations for defense, as McAllister suggests, or it may just as readily have been an artifact of partial abandonment in this section of the town. By sealing up the passage and shifting traffic to the nearby East Gate, the waning population of Halieis alleviated the need to manage this area.[31] This may suggest that the house or tavern had already been released to its own trajectories. The motley assortment of ceramic fragments that was found inside the pit, the house, and in the street could be understood in this respect. Here a ruined house may have been a convenient rubbish dump, but such things are not found by seeking out occupation—it has little to do with how homemakers envisioned their house—but rather, beginning with abandonment.[32]

I return to the photographs of the exposed trenches. Year by year, weather has exacted its toil: plaster has cracked and moldered, mud fill has lost its clays, floor surfaces have been cut through by rills or once again been covered in wash. After more than a generation of contact with winds, rain, sun, variations in temperature, and occasional visitors, in the wake of documentation, every exposed stone, every eroded surface has witnessed metamorphosis.[33] But what lies here offers silent suggestions of how it came to be: cracked and moldered plaster speaks to interactions with sun and moisture. Open joints between socle stones suggest interactions with rain as mortars have lost their bonding clays. These are the dregs of history, perceived as incoherent, banal, erratic, shattered,

---

31 McAllister suggests that these stones were cut in haste (2005, 37–8). Such a suggestion would fall under Snodgrass's "positivist fallacy," the act of equating what is archaeologically observable with is what is historically significant; that is, the confusion of what becomes of the past with what was of importance to history (1987).

32 Using Wheeler's box method, lenses of accumulation were not excavated in phase, but as disparate units separated into various loci. For more on contextual interpretation in Classical archaeology, see Haggis and Antonaccio (2015).

33 Archaeologists speak of this in terms of formation processes, but situating processes behind the actual things present merely repeats the pattern of placing other generative agencies behind what lies here; see Witmore (2014a).

always to be understood in terms of what they lack. But the fault is not with these things; they lack nothing in themselves. The fault lies with expectations that they should speak in the way of texts. Walls and surfaces were better kept under soils than left exposed in the wake of the text.

I look back towards the village, now accented by an orange, twilight varnish. Across the harbor road, at the rear corner of an enclosed field wedged between the tavern and a bar, is a ruin. Like ribs of a rotting carcass, roof beams break through a gnarled skin of tiles and planks. Through a gaping hole in its rubble belly, I can see a double-wheel olive press. Around the base of its walls, both inside and out, stone and tile lie in heaps. Wood rots. Rubbish accumulates. The state of the ruin is uncompelled and innate. Its presence amid other buildings, both occupied and abandoned, suggests mixed times and interactions. Exceeding any outcomes of human use or contact, this ruin has been left to its own fate and, thus, transforms according to its own idiosyncratic rapports. To approach this ruin with frames of lived habitation alone would be to direct it to comply with particular expectations that are ultimately foreign to what it is. Should not archaeology begin on these grounds?

I gather up the manila envelopes, stand, and set out to the north.

Bibliography

Alcock, S.E., J.F. Cherry, and J. Davis. 1994. Intensive survey, agricultural practice and the classical landscape of Greece. In I. Morris (ed.), *Classical Greece*. Cambridge, MA: Cambridge University Press. 137–70.

Ault, B.A. 1994. *Classical houses and households: An architectural and artifactual case study from Halieis*. Doctoral dissertation, Indiana University.

Ault, B.A. 1999. Koprones and oil presses at Halieis: Interactions of town and country and the integration of domestic and regional economies. *Hesperia* 68(4), 549–73.

Ault, B.A. 2005. *The excavations at ancient Halieis, Volume 2: The houses – The organization and use of domestic space*. Bloomington, IN: Indiana University Press.

Boyd, T.D., and M.H. Jameson. 1981. Urban and rural land division in ancient Greece. *Hesperia* 50(4), 327–42.

Boyd, T.D., and W.W. Rudolph. 1978. Excavations at Porto Cheli and vicinity, Preliminary Report IV: The lower town of Halieis, 1970–77. *Hesperia* 47(4), 333–55.

Dillon, M.P.J. 1997. The ecology of the Greek sanctuary. *Zeitschrift für Papyrologie und Epigraphik* 118, 113–127.

Forbes, H. 2013. Off-site scatters and the manuring hypothesis in Greek survey archaeology: An ethnographic approach. *Hesperia* 82(4), 551–94.

Forbes, H. n.d. Dumping the trash: How can we understand ancient Greek refuse? Unpublished paper.

Foxhall, L. 2007. House clearance: Unpacking the "kitchen" in Classical Greece. In R. Westgate, N.R.E. Fisher, and J. Whitley (eds.), *Building communities: House, settlement and society in the Aegean and beyond*. London: British School at Athens Studies. 15: 233–42.

Haggis, D.C., and C.M. Antonaccio. 2015. A contextual archaeology of ancient Greece. In D.C. Haggis and C.M. Antonaccio (eds.), *Classical archaeology in context: Theory and practice in excavation in the Greek world*. Berlin: Walter de Gruyter. 1–20.

Harrison, R.P. 2003. *The dominion of the dead*. Chicago, IL: University of Chicago Press.

Jameson, M.H., C.N. Runnels, and T. Van Andel 1994. *A Greek countryside: The Southern Argolid from prehistory to the present day*. Stanford, CA: Stanford University Press.

Lindenlauf, A. 2000. *Waste management in Ancient Greece, from the Homeric to the Classical period: Concepts and practices of waste, dirt, recycling and disposal*. Doctoral dissertation, University of London.

Llewellyn-Jones, L. 2011. Domestic abuse and violence against women in ancient Greece. In S.D. Lambert (ed.), *Sociable man: Essays on ancient Greek social behaviour in honour of Nick Fischer*. Edinburgh: Classical Press of Wales. 231–66.

Lucas, G. 2012. *Understanding the archaeological record*. Cambridge, MA: Cambridge University Press.

McAllister, M.H. 2005. *The excavations at Ancient Halieis, Volume 1: The fortifications and adjacent structures*. Bloomington, IN: Indiana University Press.

Morgan, J. 2010. *The Classical Greek house*. Exeter: Bristol Phoenix Press.

Morris, I. 2005. Archaeology, standards of living, and Greek economic history. In J. G. Manning and I. Morris (eds.), *The ancient economy: Evidence and models*. Stanford, CA: Stanford University Press. 91–126.

Nevett, L.C. 1999. *House and society in the ancient Greek world*. Cambridge, MA: Cambridge University Press.

Olivier, L. 2011. *The dark abyss of time: Archaeology and memory* (trans. A. Greenspan). Lanham, MD: AltaMira Press.

Olsen, B., M. Shanks, T. Webmoor, and C. Witmore 2012. *Archaeology: The discipline of things.* Berkeley, CA: University of California Press.

Parker, R. 2010. *Miasma: Pollution and purification in early Greek religion.* Oxford: Clarendon Press.

Pettegrew, D.K. 2001. Chasing the Classical farmstead: Assessing the formation and signature of rural settlement in Greek landscape archaeology. *Journal of Mediterranean Archaeology* 14(2), 189–209.

Rilke, R.M. 1982. *The notebooks of Malte Laurids Brigge* (trans. S. Mitchell). New York, NY: Random House.

Sloterdijk, P. 1999. *Sphären II – Globen, Makrosphärologie.* Frankfurt am Main: Suhrkamp.

Sloterdijk, P. 2014. *Globes: Spheres II.* South Pasadena, CA: Semiotext(e).

Snodgrass, A.M. 1987. *An archaeology of Greece.* Berkeley, CA: University of California Press.

Vernant, J.-P. 2006. *Myth and thought among the Greeks.* New York, NY: Zone Books.

Witmore, C. 2014a. Archaeology and the new materialisms. *Journal of Contemporary Archaeology* 1(2), 203–24.

24

ACROSS THE ADHERES,
ITERATIONS

A letter, a path taken by Pausanias, in the footsteps of others, toponymic engineering and repatriation, paths to Troizen, old Metallia, Blouet and Gell's path, a monastery, the hospitality of Ioanna

Among other record-storage containers housed in the Metamedia Lab in the Archaeology Center at Stanford University is a white cardboard box marked "Akte." It contains a portion of the research archive of Michael H. Jameson, a Classical archaeologist and epigrapher whose work on the Southern Argolid spans the latter half of the twentieth century.[1] In the company of sundry notebooks, offprints, and correspondence from the 1950s is a letter dated April 14,

---

1 For a conspectus of Jameson's research and scholarship, see Jameson, Stallsmith, and Cartledge (2014).

1959. Addressed from the American School, Souidias, Athens, it begins, "Dear Professor Jameson":

> Just a brief note to tell you that our visit to the Kastro at Thermisia was accomplished successfully. We did the usual walk from Damala to Hermione (getting quite lost several times) arr. Hermione after dark. Next day, being thoroughly conditioned, we were able to ascend the Kastro in 45 minutes from the road.

The letter, on yellowed paper with frayed edges, written in neat cursive and blue ink, proceeds to describe the superb views and the approach to the high redoubt, and confirms the presence of prehistoric remains, which lends support to the notion that W.A. Heurtley, author of *Prehistoric Macedonia* (1939), had indeed located a site on the lower slopes of the Kastro. It expresses hope of return and ends with regrets as to a previous query by Jameson regarding the location of materials from Karpathos. It is signed: "Sincerely, W. McLeod."

Wallace McLeod would later write about the Kastro at Thermisi.[2] Scribbled in pencil in the margins of the letter is a reference to McLeod's article, published in 1962, with the page numbers pertaining to the specific section on the Kastro.[3] The handwriting is Jameson's. He appears to have returned to this letter in the course of reading McLeod's article. Are these marginalia indications of Jameson's preparation for a visit to the erstwhile fortification, which he undertook in August 1965?[4]

Whatever the answer, this letter, which is part of a deeper history of shared correspondence, and its marginalia reveal a backstory seldom discussed in publication, one that speaks to an experiential kinship felt by those who visit forgotten places infrequently visited; those who look for banal objects rarely detailed. McLeod's article and Jameson's subsequent book[5] can also be read as thicker letters between literate friends who not only contribute to an ongoing and open conversation by writing, but also follow in each other's footsteps and share in the delight of being there, experiencing a bygone castle, an object of mutual interest.

---

2 See McLeod (1962).

3 In these pages (1962, 386–89), McLeod argued, on the grounds of architectural style, that the castle remains can be assigned to the first Venetian period (1394–1537) with few alterations and repairs during the following Turkish period (1537–1686).

4 Jameson, Runnels, and Van Andel (1994, 480). An entry in Jameson's notebook (page 27) from August 1965, written in his wife's Virginia's hand, records a visit to the Kastro of Thermisi. This is the last entry before a new series of dates begins in late July 1968.

5 Jameson, Runnels, and Van Andel (1994).

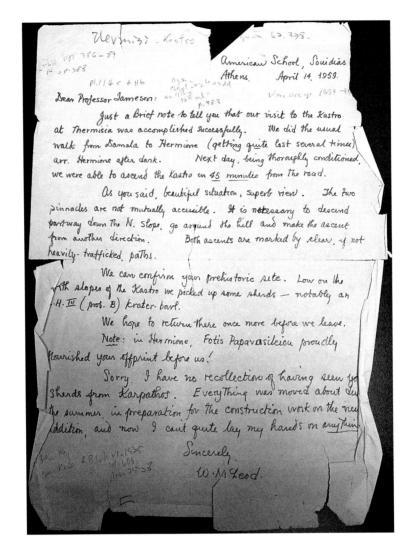

Letter to Professor Jameson.

Indeed, McLeod's visit to the Kastro came at the end of a longer journey, what he refers to simply as the "usual walk," which he took along the old way from Damala (Troizen) to Hermione (Hermion) on the Ides of March, 1959.[6]

6 The letter indicates that McLeod walked to "Hermione" the day before his visit to the Kastro on March 16, 1959 (McLeod 1962, 387, note 39).

427

McLeod hints at retracing a path taken by Jameson, yet both men are part of a literate cultural circle linked by a chain of textual transmission who share in the mutual experience of walking routes taken by Pausanias.

Pausanias took the road from Troizen to Hermion and passed:

> by the rock which was formerly called the altar of Strong Zeus, but which the moderns have named the rock of Theseus ever since Theseus picked up tokens here. Following the mountain road which runs by this rock one passes a temple of Apollo, surnamed Apollo of the Plane-tree Grove; and a place, Eileoi, in which there are sanctuaries of Demeter and her daughter Kore. Towards the sea, on the borders of the Hermionid, there is a sanctuary of Demeter with the surname Thermesia.[7]

In the footsteps of Pausanias, among those who penned their experience, followed William Gell and François Pouqueville with their respective entourages, Abel Blouet with his contingent of troops and savants, the archaeologists Ernst Curtius, Alexander Conze, and Adolf Michaelis.[8]

When Pausanias wrote of the route over the Adheres mountains from Troizen to Hermion he could not have predicted that so many readers would be on the other end to receive his message, much less take up the challenge to share in his path. Irrespective of Pausanias's purposes in writing the *Periegesis*, which are never explicitly given, by releasing this thick letter to its own trajectories it will be read by unanticipated strangers who forge bonds beyond the page along a common path, albeit one less trudged.

⁓

For the first of those long-delayed readers of Pausanias who trailed in the *periegete*'s footsteps from Damala to Kastri, the road, the cities, the towns, the villages, the monuments inscribed into the *Periegesis* had yet to be fully secured.[9] While many ancient appellations had returned to what had become of their locations, many more awaited the eager antiquary or Classical topographer. Pausanias, whose book contains more ancient toponyms than all other ancient

---

7 2.34.6; after Frazer (1898).
8 Gell (1810, 123–26), Pouqueville (1827, 257–258), Blouet 1831–38, 173), Curtius (1851, 451–52), Conze and Michaelis (1861, 6–7); also see Jameson, Runnels, and Van Andel (1994, 575–78), Tausend (2006, 166–69).
9 One of the earliest maps drawn of ancient Greece was drawn by Nikolaos Sophianos and published in Rome in 1540 (see Tolias 2007).

texts combined, not only provided the lexicon, but also, with its geographically ordered nomenclature, gave weight to the taxonomic impulse (and privilege) to name.[10] Against the need to reconnect toponyms with what had become of their ancient referents, contemporary place names proved to be incidental.

Gell believed it was a matter of necessity to use the ancient appellations for a readership ignorant of modern toponyms. What, he asks, "could appear less intelligible to the reader, or less useful to a traveller, than a route from Chione and Zaracca to Kutchukmadi, from thence by Krabata to Schœnochorio, and by the mills of Peali"?[11] "Indiscriminate" was the adjective used by Gell to describe the use of toponyms within Greece for the frequency of their recurrence.[12] The toponym "Kastri," for example, referred to ancient Hermion, Delphi, or any number of ruined fortifications.[13] A disregard for local toponyms is evident in Puillon de Boblaye's introduction to *Recherches géographiques sue les ruines de la Morée* (1836). According to the French military geographer, many of the ancient torrents were now nameless and designated only by the nearby villages.[14] Gell, in speaking of the Xeropotamo, "arid river," suggested that this name was so common "that it is impossible to ascertain whether it be the usual name of a torrent" or one applied by his guides.[15] Both Gell and Puillon de Boblaye neglected the plain utility of such place names, not only in the sense of their benefit to the wayfinding traveler in Greece as Byron had suggested,[16] but more in their austere fidelity to the objects present. *Kastri* broadcast the presence of fortifications. *Xeropotamo* suggested the frequent state of a river.

For those who set out on this long-forgotten path, the impetus related to more than a question of what had become of those stored places Pausanias had described. A general acquisition of knowledge framed their endeavors and, in this, maps played a crucial role as a means of securing ancient places so named.[17] Once committed to paper, ancient toponyms were to be fixed in two dimensions, often alongside their modern counterpart as with Gell's map (at the end of the *Itinerary*) and the *Carte de la Morée*. Akin to a semantic de-distancing of the past, increasingly the modern names, often specified as non-Greek, would drop out.[18]

10 Also see Pikoulas (2007b).
11 1810, xvii.
12 Ibid.
13 1810, 128.
14 Puillon de Boblaye (1836, 4).
15 1810, 71.
16 Byron deplored the use of ancient place names for their lack of utility to the traveler (1832, 360).
17 The map of liberated Greece drawn by Rhegas Velestinlis and published in 1797 (all surviving originals are now considered national monuments) provides a prime example with its use of ancient Greek toponyms (Keramberopoulos 1998); also see Calotychos (2003), Davis (2007), Hanink (2017, 128–31), Peckham (2001).
18 Also see Ploutoglou et al. (2011).

In Greece, this European naming magic was not about christening sites anew; rather, it had to do with simply calling what had become of ancient places by what they were once known, an appellation reclaimed from Lethe. One need not delve into the intricacies of how matters of locality were lost in favor of a national consciousness in order to simply point out that a young Greek nation shared the sentiments of these Northern Europeans in dealing with the Ottoman present with acute discrimination—what Nietzsche described as critical history.[19] With a selective fidelity, a young Greek government embraced a justification concocted by generations of Northern Europeans and educated Greeks who had burnt the midnight oil over texts written by Pausanias, among other ancient authors. What began in texts as juxtapositions circulating among cultures of reading and writing transformed into substitutions, which initiated a process of erasure through the semantics of what can be properly termed repatriation, a return to the nomenclature of the *patridos*. *Toponymic engineering* is an appropriate label for this act.[20]

In the Akte, ancient names would return to give truth to a mono-lingual territory through a process of replacements that has continued into the latter part of the twentieth century.[21] Kastri, by 1845, was officially renamed Ermioni; Karakasi was renamed Iliokastro, after the ancient Eileoi, in 1927;[22] Damala was renamed Trizina after ancient Troizen.[23] Along the path taken by Pausanias, Palaiokastro, or Kastro tou Karakasi would increasingly be known as Eileoi. This was, to some extent, also true of the ravines, the streams and rivers, the plains, harbors, coves, and points where their ancient names could be verified. Tsamliza, for example, was dropped in favor of Idhra for the island of ancient Hydrea. Even the Morea, a Slavic word, was abandoned in favor of the Peloponnese. Sooner or later, virtually every map of Greece since the War of Independence has been found in need of toponymic updating.

Indeed, more legitimacy was given to those places that held on to their ancient toponyms, not from the angle of their resistance to corruption, but as they provided toponymic armatures against which to measure other attributions.

---

19 Davis (2007, 238–39); on Northern European travel in Greece, see Angelomatis-Tsougarakis (1990), Augustinos (1990); also see Segment 13.

20 Such tendencies are, of course, well documented in postcolonial studies (in the context of archaeology, see Lydon and Rizvi (2016).

21 The Ministry of the Interior, as Peckham (2001, 35) points out, established a commission to scrutinize the municipality names in 1897, and another committee to review toponyms in 1909. On toponymic engineering and archaeology, see Alexandri (2002), Bintliff (2003, 138); Hamilakis (2007, 41); also see Herzfeld (1982).

22 Eileoi survived as Ilia, first attested in Venetian documents of 1700 (Topping 2000), and is still used as Sta Ilia (see Jameson, Runnels, and Van Andel 1994, 40).

23 See Jameson, Runnels, and Van Andel 1994, 30–31 and 142; after Khouliarakis (1973; 1975).

Didyma, and the Dhidhima basin, retained the ancient name Didymoi, meaning the "twins."[24] The valley of Salandi, just west of the Dhidhima basin, held its ancient place name in the genitive; Sellantos is derived from Sellas, meaning "seat" or "saddle," a name recorded in an ancient arbitration between the poleis of Hermione and Epidaurus.[25] Thermisi maintained Thermasia, "warmth," the epithet of Demeter whose ancient temple was located in the area.[26] Still, some non-Greek names persist, often where no ancient alternative remained. The Albanian name for the forested half of the peninsula at Ermioni: the Bisti or "tail." The Arvanitic terms for the neighborhoods of Larti (or "Uptown") and Posta (or "Downtown") within Dhidhima. Such toponymic oddities speak to the extraordinary staying power of certain toponyms in relation to the places they designate.

If one defines research in Heideggarian terms "as the working away of concealment"[27] then one could conceive of subsequent research in the vein of Classical topography as that of filling in the white space.[28] Whether they confirmed or disputed previous antiquarian identifications, with Pausanias as their guide later Classical topographers and archaeologists rarely avoided weighing in on the naming of a particular *topos*. Once settled, there are other gaps to be filled. In the Southern Argolid alone, Elieoi, Halieis, Mases, and Philanoreia, the *boleoi*, the sanctuary of Zeus Kokkygion, and the Pron, not to mention specific monuments in Ermioni or Troizen, have been reconnected with their referents, or what remains of them—an object that can never be as it was.[29] This is more than a matter of the "tyranny of the nominal," as Robert Macfarlane puts it, "a taxonomic need to point and name, with the intent of citing and owning."[30] McLeod's letter to Jameson speaks to the experiential kinship that comes with taking to the old path, and here Macfarlane is right to deny any opposition "between precision and mystery," "naming and not knowing."[31] There are aspects of land that will always resist inscription. There is a nondiscursive excess, a surplus reality that can only be glimpsed, heard, felt, smelled, tasted on the path.

<hr />

24 see Jameson, Runnels, and Van Andel (1994, 29); see Sloterdijk (2013, 105).
25 See Witmore (2014b, 228); also see Jameson (1953, 161–67).
26 Pausanias 2.34.12.
27 Sloterdijk (2013, 98); cf. *alêtheia*.
28 See Segment 6.
29 See Witmore (2005, 185–241).
30 Macfarlane (2015, 10); also see "The word-hoard: Robert Macfarlane on rewilding our language of landscape," available at: http://gu.com/p/466pk/sbl
31 Ibid.

For Pausanias, the road was largely, but not always, a taken-for-granted feature of what was there.[32] What need had he for detailing the specific attributes of the exact route, when it was held by the road itself, an object which persisted in connecting towns and cities known to all who dwelled there?[33] Arguably, it is the unnamed, unstated attributes of the trail that serve as an invitation to others. Like McLeod, I have taken the route several times from Ermioni to Troizen, trailing in the footsteps of Jameson, Curtius, Gell, and ultimately Pausanias, except in the opposite direction.

Pausanias's route is now traced by an intricate pattern of interlacing paths. The old ways have migrated from crease to crease. Holloways were abandoned to bulldozed truck roads, which were rilled out by rain, only to be replaced with graveled roads. Those truck roads that linked the villages were widened and not many grew into thoroughfares that were eventually tarmacked. The road along the ridgeline was widened to the width of a double motorway and is now maintained to access the gigantic wind turbines and a solar farm. All together these roads now form braided threads over the Adheres. The untraced segments of the old ways were tended by the lone shepherd, then overgrown, left to fall to Lethe.

It is from the angle of their own fragility that old roads and paths become explicit as objects worthy of the archaeologist's attention. Who can fault others for being insensitive to the pervasive background prior to its inversion into that which is losable and in need of care? Such objects will continue to proliferate, for they now garland the old route of Pausanias. Thus, they provide an impetus for iterations.

From Ermioni there are two general routes to Troizen. One rounds the coast to Thermisi and follows the direct route across the ridge to the Anathema and down. Following bridle paths, both Gell and Pouqueville took this route. In places these were not well maintained. The second route proceeds through Iliokastro. A climb of 200 meters over olive-swathed slopes brings one to the upland plateau. The village of Iliokastro sits near its center, enclosed by vineyards, olive groves, and cereal fields. I have always taken the direct road to the village from whence the road split out into an ancient dendritic pattern of other trails. Even from Iliokastro there are numerous paths to Troizen. I have taken two.

The first road branches right from the *plateia* across the plain to the abandoned mining settlement of old Metallia, a toponym that plainly relates what

---

32 See Segment 17, note 11.
33 On Pausanias and his attentiveness to the route taken, see Alcock (1993, 28–29), Habicht (1985, 104), Snodgrass (1987, 86).

one will find there, "mines." From Metallia, iron-manganese pyrites were extracted for the production of sulfuric acids used in fertilizers from 1905 to 1978.[34] Abandoned workshops, mining facilities, offices, and ruins of extraction lie along the line of a cog railway in a deep ravine. At the road turn, a stone obelisk stands upon a raised terrace—a memorial to the young director of the mines, Andreas Syrigos, who was murdered in 1938. On the ridgeline above, several structures of stacked stone with plaster-lined interiors stand in various states of ruination. The church of Agia Varvara, the protector of mines, survives as the only preserved building at the apex of the settlement. The cog railway connected Metallia with a socialist-style workers' village (a strictly organized series of houses, of consistent size and material) and shipping terminal at Dárdeza, on the coast east of Ermioni. These ruins speak to a familiar story of progress, extraction, and failure.

It was from Metallia that I trailed by foot in the wake of Michael Jameson and Mark Munn, archaeologists who had, on July 28, 1981, taken a direct path, no longer passable by car, following the powerlines, to the top of the ridge in a VW van. They had come to investigate the Soros. A fortified watch post dating back to the Classical period, the contrived mound, crowned with a double-faced enclosure wall, rises above the pass and commands views to the north to the upper Troizen acropolis and to the south to Iliokastro and beyond.[35] Such obstinate objects, seen as landmarks, hold the general course of primary routes.

Old Metallia with the Adheres in the background, 2016.

---

34 See Samara (2018); also Jameson, Runnels, and Van Andel (1994, 145 and 301).
35 Jameson, Runnels, and Van Andel (1994, 521–22).

From the square in Iliokastro, a second route follows the asphalt road through the village and up gentle slopes in places speckled with massive olive bollings, gnarled and torqued with centuries of having endured here. It passes the ancient site of Eileoi, a small village situated at the base of a limestone out-crop and enclosed by Classical walls, visited by a cascade of archaeologists over the years. Philadepheus reported excavating potential Late Helladic graves in the area in 1907.[36] Jameson visited the site in the spring of 1954. Richard Hope Simpson claimed to have found Late Helladic III sherds on the slopes west of the *Kastro* in 1959. Members of the AEP visited the site in 1972 and 1980. Anne Demitrack, Michael Jameson, Mark Munn, and Dan Pullen surveyed it in July of 1981.[37]

From Eileoi, I turned off from the macadam and followed a winding gravel road for more than 2 kilometers to the ridgeline, which is now staked with gigantic wind turbines and, in places, clothed in solar panels. Another 4 kilo-meters will bring one to the old truck road along another ridge crest to Troi-zen. From this point, the path over is easier to work out from the other side.

Curtius crossed in 1840 from the mills above the ancient site of Troizen. He took the path over the Devil's Bridge, a thin stone arch suspended over a deep chasm, past the Hyllikos spring, following old tracks at steep angles up the mountain.[38] Blouet and company crossed in 1829 from Dalmata by way of a steep and winding path to a monastery on a high rock. Beyond, the portion of the pass was so hazardous that one of the pack horses fell into a defile and rolled to a point 60 feet below the trail. It took them six hours and twenty

The Adheres from Eileoi, 2016.

36 Philadelpheus (1909); cf. Jameson, Runnels, and Van Andel (1994, 521).
37 See Witmore 2005, 1–3.
38 1852, 451.

minutes to reach Kastri.[39] Gell had taken the same trail a generation earlier in 1804, when the monastery was occupied by a few priests.[40] From there it followed the valley to a spring near a column, carved out as an animal trough. Curtius, Blouet, and Gell took bridle paths. McLeod and Jameson witnessed these old ways shift from bridle paths to bulldozed shepherd roads. Now the old shepherd roads are less used. The old bridle paths are overgrown. The ridge is now open for routine crossings thanks to service roads for wind turbines.

⌇

I had visited the relinquished bridle path taken by Gell and Blouet on several occasions; first in 2007, then in 2008 with second pair of hands, and again in 2012, with a saw, machete, and blessing from a local nun followed by a warning: beware of snakes. Visitors had passed a Laphiatis (*elaphe quatuorlineata*), a four-lined snake of about 1.5 meters, hanging in a tree along the lower trail.[41] They are harmless.

Leaving from the gate of the monastery on the high rock, the narrow footpath breaks upslope along a straight and steady incline. Each time I followed the obvious ledge over smoothed stones, working against a completely overgrown path. Each time I pressed farther into a gauntlet of scrub oak, tree heath, thorny burnet, and juniper. My aim was to reach Gell's column, which was situated at a spring. The path once provided access to a series of terraces stepping upslope behind an outcrop of limestone and planted in olive. These trees had long been abandoned to overgrowth. On the last occasion, after several hundred meters of toil, slashed clothing, and bleeding wounds the path crossed over boggy ground where the maquis, having obtained an impressive height, locked together to form an impenetrable thicket laced with vertical entanglements of wire-like creepers. I never reached the spring. I never located Gell's column.

When I first visited Agios Dimitrios Damala in 2007, the monastery was in ruin. It consisted of three freestanding blocks, all mortar and rubble, joined around a courtyard. In the middle of the courtyard stood the catholicon. The

---

39 Blouet recorded the distance from Trozien to Kastri as follows: "En parlant de l'église ruinée, on trouve, à 45 minutes, Demala. À 15 m., le lit d'un torrent; la roule tourne au sud pour entrer dans la montagne. A 18 m., monastère et fontaine. A 35 m., sommet du mont. A 40 m., on commence à descendre. A 95 m., torrent au fond d'un ravin. A 10 m., belle vallée. A 45 m., fin de la vallée; bois d'oliviers. A 61 m., citerne, partie de route pavée. A 16 m., Kastri. Distance totale, 6 heures 20 minutes" (1833, 173).

40 Pouqueville (1827 V, 257–58) provides to-the-minute descriptions of the walk, which took him a total of four hours and thirty minutes.

41 For the association of the Laphiatis with the *pareias* of Asklepeius, see Ogden (2013, 374–78).

only fully extant structure at that time, this chapel contained a painted document over its inner doorway, which stated that its icons were executed at the expense of a monk named Nektarios, dated 1694. Two of the blocks are composed of lower-story vaults with upper-story cells; one of them was but a single low vault, long collapsed. Both two-story blocks were without portions of their roofs. One contained a gaping hole torn through the upper ceiling and across the eastern façade. One could see into three of the upper chambers and part of the lower vault. Weeds grew on every surface and out every crack. Still, the place had not been fully left to its own. The area in front of the chapel was well kept. Set with platforms and benches, the terrace walls around the courtyard were whitewashed. The weeds in the courtyard were cut back. All loose stones were neatly stacked within the surrounding cells.

The following year, a few stones had loosened and a few walls remained firm. Weeds continued to grow within the cells, but were trimmed back in the courtyard.

Four years later I returned to a different monastery, one abuzz with activity. Three workmen were busy rebuilding stone walls formerly left to ruin in the southern block. One chipped away at bedrock with a demolition hammer. One set cobblestones in the outer wall of the lower vault. Another ferried fresh mortar and materiel. Upon seeing me waiting outside, the runner paused to ring the bell. He bid me to wait.

Ioanna came out to greet me. A Greek Orthodox nun, she wore a long black robe and an enveloping mantle. Ioanna had been here for the last two years restoring the monastery. She invited me to see the renovations. Work began with Ioanna's kitchen, library, and sleeping quarters in the northern block of the complex. She showed me the kitchen and bid me to sit at the table. She offered peach jelly, fig jam, apricots, and water. Ioanna told me that the church hired an Athenian architect to redesign the monastery. She pointed out the loft, where she sleeps; the old oven turned decorative nook; and the east corner,

Ruined monastery in 2007.

Renovated monastery in 2012.

which is raised upon the limestone outcrop, a portion of which was left exposed without plaster.

I explained how strange this space was for me. All the elements of comfort are now present in a whitewashed room, lit by florescent bulbs, which only four years earlier had been in ruin. The ceiling had collapsed. These walls were unplastered, with portions tumbling down. The floor was covered in a carpet of weeds. Now I encountered the return of form, the return of a cool reprieve, the return of life and hospitality; an eddy in time.

The workmen invited me to sit for a beer by the catholicon. They invited me to share in a giant plate of communal pasta, prepared by Ioanna. We spoke of their work rebuilding the monastery. We spoke of the trail, and my purpose in tracing paths walked by others, and paths lost. After a heaping mound of spaghetti and a glass of beer, I thanked them for their hospitality, left a small donation, and set out for Troizen.

Bibliography

Alcock, S.E. 1993. *Graecia Capta: The landscapes of Roman Greece.* Cambridge: Cambridge University Press.

Alexandri, A. 2002. Names and emblems: Greek archaeology, regional identities, and national narratives at the turn of the 20th century. *Antiquity* 76(291), 191–199.

Angelomatis-Tsougarakis, H. 1990. *The eve of the Greek revival: British travellers' perceptions of early nineteenth-century Greece.* London: Routledge.

Augustinos, O. 1990. *French odysseys: Greece in French travel literature from the Renaissance to the Romantic era.* Baltimore, MD: Johns Hopkins University Press.

Bintliff, J. 2003. The ethnoarchaeology of a "passive" ethnicity: The Arvanites of Central Greece. In Brown, K.S., and Y. Hamilakis (eds.), *The usable past: Greek metahistories.* Lanham, MD: Lexington Books. 129–44.

Blouet, G.A. 1831–38. *Expédition scientifique de Morée, Ordonnée par le Gouvernement français: Architecture, Sculptures, Inscriptions et Vues du Péloponèse, des Cyclades et de l'Attique, mesurées, dessinées, recueillies et publiées par Abel Blouet.* Volumes I–VI. Paris: Firmin Didot.

Byron, G.G. 1832. Review of Gell's Geography of Ithaca, and Itinerary of Greece. In George Noël Gordon Byron (ed.), *The complete works of Lord Byron including his suppressed poems and others never before published.* Paris: Baudry.

Calotychos, V. 2003. *Modern Greece: A cultural poetics.* Oxford: Berg.

Conze, A., and A. Michaelis, 1861. Rapporto d'un viaggio fatto nella Grecian el 1860. *Annali dell'Instituto de Corrispondenza Archaeologica* 33, 5–12.

Curtius, E. 1851–52. *Peloponnesos eine historisch-geographiche Bechreibung der Halbinsel.* Gotha: J. Perthes.

Davis, J.L. 2007. Memory groups and the state: Erasing the past and inscribing the present in the landscapes of the Mediterranean and Near East. In N. Yoffee (ed.), *Negotiating the past in the past: Identity, memory, and landscape in archaeological research.* Tucson, AZ: University of Arizona Press. 227–56.

Frazer, J.G. 1898. *Pausanias's Description of Greece.* 6 vols. London: Macmillan & Co.

Gell, W. 1810. *The itinerary of Greece.* London: Payne.

Habicht, C. 1985. *Pausanias' guide to ancient Greece.* Berkeley, CA: University of California Press.

Hamilakis, Y. 2007. *The nation and its ruins: Antiquity, archaeology, and national imagination in Greece.* Oxford: Oxford University Press.

Hanink, J. 2017. *The Classical debt: Greek antiquity in an era of austerity.* Cambridge, MA: Belknap Press.

Herzfeld, M. 1982. *Ours once more: Folklore, ideology, and the making of modern Greece.* Austin, TX: University of Texas Press.

Jameson, M.H. 1953. Inscriptions of the Peloponessos. *Hesperia* 22(3), 148–71.

Jameson, M.H., C.N. Runnels, and T. Van Andel. 1994. *A Greek countryside: The Southern Argolid from prehistory to the present day.* Stanford, CA: Stanford University Press.

Jameson, M.H., A.B. Stallsmith, and P. Cartledge. 2014. *Cults and rites in ancient Greece: Essays on religion and society.* Cambridge: Cambridge University Press.

Keramberopoulos, D. 1998. *Harta tis Ellados tou Riga Veletinli.* Athens: Epistemoniki Hetaireia Meletes Pheron-Velestinou-Rega.

Khouliarakis, M. 1973. *Geografiki dhioikitiki kai plithismiaki exelexis tis Elladhos, 1821–1971.* Vol. 1.1. Athens: Ethniko Kentro Koinonikon Erevnon.

Khouliarakis, M. 1975. *Geografiki dhioikitiki kai plithismiaki exelexis tis Elladhos, 1821–1971.* Vol. 2. Athens: Ethniko Kentro Koinonikon Erevnon.

Lydon, J., and U.Z. Rizvi (eds.). 2016. *Handbook of postcolonial archaeology.* London: Routledge.

Macfarlane, R. 2015. *Landmarks.* London: Hamish Hamilton.

McLeod, W.E. 1962. Kiveri and Thermisi. *Hesperia* 31(4), 378–92.

Ogden, D. 2013. *Drakon: Dragon myth and serpent cult in the Greek and Roman worlds.* Oxford: Oxford University Press.

Peckham, R.S. 2001. *National histories, natural states: Nationalism and the politics of place in Greece.* London: I.B. Tauris.

Philadelpheus, A. 1909. Ai en Hermionidi Anaskaphai. *Praktika,* 172–84.

Pikoulas, Y.A. 2007b. The settlement pattern. In M. Georgopoulou, C. Guilmet, Y. A. Pikoulas, K. Sp. Staikos, and G. Tolias (eds.), *Following Pausanias: The quest for Greek antiquity.* New Castle, DE: Oak Knoll Press. 224–25.

Ploutoglou, N., M. Pazarli, C. Boutoura, M. Daniil, and E. Livieratos. 2011. Two emblematic French maps of Peloponnese (Morée): Lapie's 1826 vs the 1832 map (Expédition Scientifique). A digital comparison with respect to map geometry and toponymy. *Proceedings, 25th International Cartographic Association Conference,* 3–8 July 2011, Paris. Available at: https://icaci.org/files/documents/ICC_proceedings/ICC2011/.

Pouqueville, F.C.H.L. 1827. *Voyage de la Grèce.* Vol. 5. Paris: Firmin Didot.

Puillon de Boblaye, M.E. 1836. *Expédition scientifique de Morée: Recherches géographiques sur les ruines de la Morée.* Paris: F.G. Levrault.

Samara, M. 2018. Metalleía Ermiónis. *Blomichaniká Deltía Apografís* (Industrial Inventory Bulletin). Available at: https://vida-omada.blogspot.com/2018/01/blog-post_4.html

Sloterdijk, P. 2013. *In the world interior of capital: For a philosophical theory of globalization.* Cambridge: Polity Press.

Snodgrass, A.M. 1987. *An archaeology of Greece.* Berkeley, CA: University of California Press.

Tausend, K. 2006. *Verkehrswege der Argolis: Rekonstruktion und historische Bedeutung.* Stuttgart: F. Steiner.

Tolias, G. 2007. The resonance of the Periegesis during the 16th and 17th centuries. In M. Georgopoulou, C. Guilmet, Y.A. Pikoulas, K. Sp. Staikos, and G. Tolias (eds.), *Following Pausanias: The quest for Greek antiquity.* New Castle, DE: Oak Knoll Press. 96–104.

Topping, P.W. 2000. The Southern Argolid from Byzantine to Ottoman times. In S. B. Sutton (ed.), *Contingent countryside: Settlement, economy, and land use in the Southern Argolid since 1700.* Stanford: Stanford University Press. 25–40.

Witmore, C. 2005. *Multiple field approaches in the Mediterranean: Revisiting the Argolid Exploration Project.* Doctoral dissertation, Stanford University.

Witmore, C. 2014b. (Dis)continuous domains: A case of "multi-sited archaeology" from the Peloponnesus, Greece. In O. Harmansah (ed.), *Drawing on rocks, gathering by the water.* Oxford: Oxbow Books. 213–41.

25

TROIZEN, VERDANT AND IN RUIN

Of signs and stones, into the garden, ruins, allegorical burdens, Philip Ernest Legrand, churches, ruins overtaken by history, preservation, gardens without frames, letting it be

The "Stone of Thiseas" sits at the crossroads to the "Devil's Bridge" and the "Antiquities." Or so the signs say. In a truth, the stone, a grey limestone block, is an erstwhile portion of polygonal masonry from the nearby city wall of ancient Troizen. Set upon a concrete slab, the stone lies not above a sword or sandals, a mythical message between grandfather and grandson, but below an array of signs. Three blue signs proclaim in both Greek and English what we already know. A long brown sign, provided by the Greek Archaeological Service, indicates with a left arrow the way to the "Tower of Diateichisma." Lastly, a small white sign—written in Greek only—points to the right towards the church of Agios Ioannis. Here, at the crossroads, all these signs are clustered in competition above the stone.

Nearby, no more than a dozen meters down the left fork, another blue sign stands before a ruin: "*Iero ton Mouson*." The Greek is translated into English as the "Temple of the Mousses." Whatever may be suggested by the structure's collapsed double-vaults and partial walls of *opus testaceum*, this sign, with its effervescent misspelling of "Muses," situates the ruin as part of a sacred complex mentioned by Pausanias.[1] All these signs fulfill an impulse to name, to frame, and explain what lies here in ruin. Yes, here again we encounter signs before stones, for this is what has become of the muses.[2]

I always park by this structure, near these crossroads, before wandering through the nearby garden world of ruin. Through the kindness and generosity of those who tend this ground, their orchards and groves are left open to the delight of strangers. A dozen and more visits over the years, and yet my path always begins in the same way. From the sign-laden stones it crosses the main road and dips through overgrowth into the agricultural plots to the northeast, in the direction of the chapel of Agios Georgios. Working its way across a grove of fragrant lemon and gnarled olive trees, it veers north before reaching the whitewashed church to traverse an open, concrete channel of rushing water at a chaste tree. Falling in with a field track by an ancient, twisted olive trunk, it continues along a vine-covered stone wall to descend through a hollow carved through the lush drapery of a vine-covered olive tree. Here, a triglyph and metope frieze forms a step in the line of a rubble terrace.

From this spot my wanderings have unfurled along a dozen different paths among giant olives with moss-green boles, along field walls slowly segmented by the restless growth of majestic cypresses. Throughout this garden, bits and pieces of antiquity are lodged in terraces, piled in cairns, or heaped into the stone girdles that enclose individual parcels. Here and there, cuts and cavities open windows to what lies below, and over the years I have witnessed numerous metamorphoses in what ruins here. In this arboreal garden of the living, which embraces the ruins and ruination of Troizen, ancient and modern, there are few predetermined narratives of what will be found. There are few fences barring entry into the adjacent plots. There are no prescribed paths. No signs framing ancient architectural blocks. No placards making demands of observers. No presentations congealing this locus with history.[3] Without narrative frames, old things, by and large, are simply here.[4] Amid the smell of citrus and thyme,

---

1 The association of the barrel-vaulted structure, perhaps part of a former Roman bath complex, with the Mouseion mentioned by Pausanias is to be found in Welter (1941, 18).
2 See Segments 8 and 16.
3 See Segment 8.
4 The counter-image, of course, is the total administration of the past as discussed by Shanks and Tilley (1987, 18).

Terrace below the chapel of Agios Georgios.

a prostrate, unfluted, grey column spilling out of a nearby terrace works as the lure. The pleasure of exploring a stone edifice slowly overtaken by creeping fig, the excitement that comes with the discovery of a partially buried marble pedestal, or the later recognition of its dislodgment in the preparation of a bed for new plantings, such endeavors serve as their own gratification. Even though the things of this garden are frameless, ruins are not without their allegorical burdens.

The notion of ruin proceeds from a sense of incompleteness, damage, and loss. *Ruin*, from the Latin *ruina*, as both noun and verb, conjures the precipitous rush, the downward fall, collapse. The Greek word, *ereipion*, also holds this sense of downwardness: to cast or throw down, to fall down. Splendor shattered, decaying fragments laid low, reduced to comingle with earth are what remain of Greek antiquity.[5] Thus, that antiquity's revival, according to Nietzsche, was marked by "the sentimentality of ruins ... and in excavations this longing [*Sehnsucht*] was satisfied."[6]

Not far from the triglyph and metope block turned step, Philippe-Ernest Legrand "satisfied this longing" in a field owned by Dimitrios Loris.[7] There,

5 Byron, Child Harold's Pilgrimage.
6 From *Encyclopädie der klassischen Philologie*, 349, quoted in Miller (2015, 20); also Miller (2013).
7 Though histories of the professionalization of archaeology would suggest otherwise, its practitioners are not immune to Nietzsche's longing. Even if the former ruins were regarded as sources of information or evidence that did not exhaust the allure that the field abandoned as an artifact of Romantic sentimentality. A member of the French School in Athens, Legrand lived and studied in Greece from 1888–1891. It was during this period that he undertook the excavations of Troizen (Lantier 1953).

beneath a meter of soil he laid bare the foundations of a sizable temple, measuring 26 by 11 meters. Within its interior Legrand found indications of both a *pronaos* and *cella*. Throughout this garden, below the slopes of the ancient acropolis, between the ravine of Agios Athanasius and the Devil's Gorge through which courses the Gephyraion stream, Legrand situated the agora of ancient Troizen.[8] In those waning days of the nineteenth century, Legrand explored these groves with spade and sought to account for this collapse, this loss, by recovering what had fallen away.

For those with lofty ambitions to greater expressions of human possibility, ruins send the wrong message. When seen as belonging to a world that they have outlasted, crumbled walls of brick and mortar elicit feelings of desire, but also melancholy, and even anger.[9] Against a presumed, former totality, a complete form no longer here, the disheveled and deteriorating vault is weighed, and, for some, found wanting. The imagination, as Goethe maintained, compensates for this deficiency.[10] Under the influence of history it leads us to recognize here as where a bath complex stood, within the agora of a once-celebrated polis, as mentioned by an ancient traveler. Still, ruins may also be imagined as vestiges of a future, which never came to exist. For in laying the first stone of any edifice followed projected hopes. Were they ever realized? Even if Theseus were to lift the carved frieze it will not reveal this secret.

Whereas individual death looms before all with the certainty of a finite longevity that will run its course within a human lifetime, in the raw, ruins hold temporal ambiguity. Yet despite such former opacity, their strangeness may have, to some extent, suggested distance.[11] Those agrarians who tended these plots prior to antiquity's revival knew columns and carved blocks to be prior to their labors, prior to those of their ancestors, prior to the vines and the trees. Indeed, there is much to the argument, so well voiced by Robert Pogue Harrison, that the sight of ruins is "a reflexive and in some cases unsettling experience" for they reveal "what human building is ultimately up against"—deep, geological time; or, in the least, the inevitable deterioration that comes to all human societies.[12] Ruins thus evoke a sense of our limitations, our imperfections in the face of oblivion. Just as the idea of our own death arises from the corpse, the idea of our own destruction surfaces from ruins.[13] Ruins, from this

---

8 1905.
9 See Miller (2013, 70).
10 Johann Wolfgang von Goethe to Wilhelm von Humboldt, August 23, 1804, quoted in Goethe and Gearey (1994, 107–08); also Miller (2013, 74).
11 Also see Schnapp (2013, 163).
12 2003, 3.
13 After Harrison (2003, 92).

angle, call forth images of an impending demise and, thus, our collective mortality. Altogether, ruins bind past, present, and future: the knowledge of the absent, what is no longer here; the present as that which we confront; and the future as the fate that awaits each and every one of us.

Persistent figures of our own frailties, of human finitude, such are the images conjured within the eschatological imagination. Perhaps this is why so many churches are to be found here. While churches and chapels have a calming effect, more narrowly, they appropriate and sanitize ruins, precisely because they are raised out of them.[14] Both Agios Georgios and Agios Ioannis, the latter rebuilt in 1899, lay upon the foundations of larger churches, and these were situated among the remnants of ancient structures.[15] Agios Soteira, now in ruin, was also built upon a larger church, and Legrand speculated as to whether this earlier structure was erected on the site of the former temple of Artemis Soteira.

My most recent path, taken in June of 2016 in the company of four students, continued north from the frieze, along the eastern wall of the lemon grove where several more grey, unfluted columns were gathered. It dropped over a break in a terrace and continued through a field sprouting with both newly planted olives and architectural fragments. Meeting with a water-filled channel and pipes, it turned west with these irrigation lines to a square marble pedestal that had been wrestled to the edge of a lemon grove. From there it wove a circuitous route across terraced cells in the direction of Agios Ioannis to the northwest. During this walk we passed over what has become of Loris's field. Now, more than a century after Legrand's excavation, the foundations of the temple are buried below the cultivated earth of another garden plot.

In laying out future prospects for excavation at Troizen, Legrand deemed it unfortunate that this area was so richly cultivated.[16] It is hard to know what more to make of this sentiment aside from the fact that Legrand felt agriculture had brought about the further destruction of its ruins, and the garden shielded antiquity from its revival. This conflict between scholarship and the garden was further exaggerated through Legrand's own archaeological labors.[17] For

---

14 For examples, see Sweetman (2010, 2015); also Caraher (2003, Appendix D).

15 Legrand (1905).

16 For Legrand, "par malheur, cet espace est un des plus richement cultivés" (1905, 287). In light of this statement, it should be pointed out that Legrand's later interest in Greek bucolic poetry showed a deep appreciation of the rustic idyll. Indeed, he would later produce a prize-winning doctoral thesis on Theocritus in 1898 (also see Mollat 1954, 416).

17 Among archaeologists these are common sentiments. In his *Formation Processes in the Archaeological Record*, Michael Schiffer comments on how plants can be "agents of disturbance"— though, it should be noted, he also allows room for them to be agents of stabilization (1987, 210–12).

foundations freed from the humus would seem to come to odds with the ethos of the garden, which is to "give more to the soil than you take away."[18] To be fair, Legrand's garden was not to be found here. In generating a bounty of objects, descriptions, visualizations, and catalogues his extractive labors enriched the loams of scholarship from which history grows elsewhere. Archaeology, to be sure, works in non-zero sums. Yet, fulfilling the obligations that came with antiquity's revival levied its toll against the imagination, and for those who draw nourishment from ruins, as Goethe had suggested, they are better catalysts when left to their own.[19]

Whether or not one agrees with Goethe, any perceived conflict between scholarship and ruins fails to allow for the positive side of ruination, which is enriched by the archaeological imagination—ruination reveals as much as it obscures.[20] Peeling plaster discloses earlier shades. Crumbling walls open vistas into formerly closed interiors. Roots push up stones long buried. Insofar as ruination bares what lies beneath, it brings forth the new, if only for an instant. Within this garden, one may encounter myriad memories that teeter as a flash on the brink of oblivion. If among ruins, to evoke Seferis, is "where we now remain unsubstantial,"[21] then in this garden we may find substantiation.

Our path eventually broke through a thicket by the church of Agios Ioannis, where we took pause on a whitewashed bench set into a terrace and draped in the afternoon shade of an olive. Nearby, marble columns, column bases, and chunks of carved limestone are collected within and without chapel walls. Whether these stones served as constant reminders of prior calamity, whether they were seen as apocalyptic portents of coming catastrophe, or simply appreciated as relics of a deeper past, they do not say. There are no signs here. Lodged into ecclesiastical grounds and whitewashed, they could be readily drawn into the lessons of the church. Yet, exhibited here, these stones are less likely to perturb in unsettling ways.

Just over 600 meters from where we sat, to the northwest, across the Gephyraion stream, in the area of Kokkinia, are the antiquities to which the sign at the crossroads directs travelers. It is there, within a fenced enclosure, that visitors will find what has become of Legrand's redemptive labors at Troizen. There, worn paths lead over fields of stubble and under olive trees to open trenches exposing that which was formerly covered: the remains of the sanctuary of Hippolytus.[22] Tended by trimming overgrowth and keeping plants at bay,

18 From Karel Capek's *The Gardner's Year*, quoted in Harrison (2008, 33).
19 See discussion in Miller (2013, 74).
20 DeSilvey (2006), Pétursdóttir and Olsen (2014); also Shanks (2012).
21 From the *King of Asini*, translated by Edmund Keeley and Philip Sherrard (Seferis 1995).
22 See Welter (1941), Faráklas (1972).

the *temenos* of the sanctuary, the foundations of the temple of Hippolytus, and the remains of the Asklepion among others have been returned to what is familiar to readers of Greek myth. Exposed for everyone to contemplate, those ruins have been overtaken by explanation in light of a particular past. That is, given the emphases of Legrand and Gabriel Welter after him, this place was accommodated to history. Enclosed within its fence, it is severed from an agrarian present. Over there, ruins are now less unsettling, for history has encompassed them.[23]

It is therefore not without some measure of irony that just beyond the Asklepion, upon what Welter identified as the Stadion of Hippolytus, lay the remains of the Church of Palaio-Episkopi.[24] For if one were to look for an example of what Georg Simmel described as the "peaceful unity of belonging" in his essay, *The Ruin*, then at Troizen they would find no better candidate.[25] Within its towering stretches of broken walling, composed of ancient spolia, Simmel's two potencies—"the striving upward and the sinking downward"—work "serenely together."[26] Partial partitions raised upon recessed arches contain surfaces covered by patches of plaster with patinas similar in tone to the surrounding earth. Standing on the edge of a rise, against the backdrop of the fertile plain, the tranquil bay, and the rugged mountains of distant Methana, the old basilica appears to exemplify what Simmel suggests a ruin should be.[27]

But there is a subtle difference here—other signs have been placed before the remains of this basilica. Despite their tattered state, they persist by demanding "attention" by shouting "keep away." The First Ephorate of Byzantine Antiquities rightly raised these signs out of an obligation to care—it is dangerous to enter, both for pedestrians and for high walls. But the signs also reveal that the old three-aisled basilica does not decay through positive indifference. In order to care for the ruin as it is, lime mortars have been capped by cement, and formerly peeling plasters are prevented from furthermore peeling owing to techniques of consolidation. Life-sustaining soil and vegetation, at home among Simmel's ruin, have been removed.[28] To arrest decay through an intervention into entropy is to introduce new materials to the composition of the erstwhile basilica. It is not that such an intervention has exhausted the former basilica of

23 Once could understand this in light of a particular chronopolitics as I have discussed elsewhere (Witmore 2013b).
24 See Welter (1941, 37–38); this church was described by numerous antiquarians, including, Dodwell (1819, 269–70).
25 1959, 263–64.
26 Ibid., 263.
27 Ibid. Also see Pétursdóttir and Olsen (2014).
28 Simmel (1959, 263–64).

The old basilica of Palaio-Episkopi.

its integrity as a ruin. It has not robbed it of its former dynamism, for the intervention is part of this; rather, it affects the atmosphere in which it once persisted in perishing.[29] Do ruins lose their ability to disturb through our attentiveness to their wellbeing?

As if under the gaze of Medusa, the basilica may seem paralyzed. To artificially prop up ruins for exhibition is to veil that truth to which all human constructs will eventually succumb; or in the least it is to make an attempt. No civilization knows the secret to endurance. If from this angle preservation is, paradoxically, the ruination of ruins,[30] then now, in the midst of an economic crisis, it is failing in its deprivations. In the wake of preservationist interventions, such erstwhile buildings come to require a burdensome amount of care. With the Ephorate overstretched in the upkeep of such sites, at Palaio-Episkopi one confronts not only a Byzantine ruin of gathered ancient remnants, but also a ruin of preservation's own failures with the ruination of the preserved form.

---

29 This confusion of the past with history is more pervasive than ever—it underwrites an ideal revealed at other sites, such as Nemea and Epidaurus, where the ruin as it is appears insufficient; for more of an original form is returned to temples as pristine blocks rise once again within their fenced enclosures.

30 Also see DeSilvey (2014, 87); for discussion, see Cooper (2013).

Whether for the archaeologist or gardener, care, as Harrison reminds us, "is constantly being thrown back upon the limitations of its powers of action."[31]

We left the churchyard and crossed the paved road surface towards a large olive with a whitewashed trunk. Beyond, we ascended the bank on a raised agricultural track tucked between a field wall above and a terrace below. Soon the stacked stone wall on the left transitions into a jumbled mass of mortared rubble, mixed with large, hewn blocks of shelly limestone. We passed through a thin break between these blocks and threaded our way into recesses formed by the confluence of field walls, ancient olives, and ruins.

Over two hundred years ago, the beauty of this citrus garden drew the admiration of antiquarians.[32] When Legrand excavated here, plots kept by the families of Golaris, Kanotzis, Kouvardou, Logothetis, Loris, Manetas, Pardalis, and Pappageorgiou, among others, were "verdant with vines, olives, lemon-groves, and fig-trees" according to Frazer, who bestowed accolades upon their well-kept groves in his *Golden Bough*.[33] The gift of humus held in deep beds behind terrace walls, the raised irrigation mounds encircling the base of lemon trees, the pollarded crown of medieval olives; built among these ruins was a well-tended garden and it has continued to patiently reach ahead of itself into the future.[34]

Along these wandering paths, we may choose to see, as Legrand did, faltering façades and agricultural plots in conflict—the forces of destruction verses those of cultivation. But the presence of a garden amid ruins stands as a lesson that life persists and does not fall away, precisely because it continues to grow and develop here. Around us, we might have observed a restless struggle to prepare this soil, to enroll these stones, and build these beds. This struggle involves all life—slow-growing roots and bacteria, oxen and farmers—for all life—lemon and olive, weeds and lichens, archaeologists and gardeners. No, the garden need not be regarded as the antithesis of ruins. It has not fostered the destruction of the past; if anything these plants have contributed to the wreckage of debris that grows towards the sky.[35]

Our path wound its course uphill. Across small orchards, through breaches in terrace walls we were drawn towards two tall sections of mortared stone

---

31 2008, 28.
32 See Gell (1810, 118, 122); compare Dodwell (1819, 267–73).
33 See Frazer (1898 III, 273, 1925, 6–7). The family names come from Legrand (1905); also see Miliarakis (1886, 195).
34 Harrison has made much of this contrast in his book *Gardens: An Essay on the Human Condition* (2008).
35 Olive trees serve to stabilize terraces, as much as dislodge stones. Roots serve to hold soils in place more than disrupt them. On the positive differences made by plants, see Farstadvoll (2019b).

walling encompassing a large cairn comprised of column fragments, bases, other architectural pieces, and rubble. Beyond, the "Tower of Diateichisma" loomed in the distance. A plinth of Hellenistic ashlar surmounted by a broken crown of Frankish rubble masonry, this variegated stone sentinel persists as a lofty vestige of the separation wall from which it gains its name (a combination of *dia*, through, and *teichisma*, fortification or fortress). The "sentimentality of ruins" and the historical imagination, both obscure what has become of the past and, therefore, the other forms that the past may take. Have we forgotten how to look at such places without conceiving of the past exclusively in terms of history?

By holding to a view of ruins as partial expressions of their erstwhile forms, we deny them their integrity as what they are. Pausanias produced his topography at a time when sanctuaries and other monuments had begun to fall into ruin, yet the traveler never set eyes on this field wall draped in vines. For here things do not carry allegorical burdens. Crumbling stone walls hold back sediment and uphold the formerly intimate distribution of rooms in an erstwhile structure. Downward-dragged rubble continues to raise berms and seal once scabbing surfaces deep below. Weathered foundations give form to edges overgrown in green and sustain the cross-section of architectural plans. These things uphold their pasts while offering other qualities, fulfilling other obligations. Within this garden such things resist being completely subsumed to history where a supposedly original, more definitive form is framed within the time of past human interaction, the highest expression of their integrity. These things lack nothing, yet these other propensities readily fall through the sieve of textual prejudice. Just as ruins do not belong solely to the world they outlasted, so too the things of this garden do not exist solely *for us*. There are other ways to revere without preservation, without placing ruins in a framework. We need not treat ruins as lesser fragments of a whole, but as things in themselves that persevere in striving upwards.

We continued uphill. Through a breach formed in a stone terrace, I stepped across a carved block of limestone. It is the archaeologist's duty to give demonstrable form to what lies here. It is their charge to put names to old stones, to generate catalogues of what is found, and to shelve it away in museums and stores far removed from these parcels. Once a common encounter before the middle of the last century, we have made these places rare in our drive to make explicit their pasts. Too few now are those ancient poleis left open and unframed in verdant ruin.

We made our way through low canopies of citrus. Some plots showed evidence of neglect. Here and there, rotting oranges, lemons, and figs covered the ground. Fruit trees had not been trimmed in a few seasons. Weeds and shrubs thrived. Throughout the plain old farmhouses have been abandoned, the nearby watermills have fallen in, and ruination takes hold of this agrarian world. Has this garden been forsaken? While such examples stand out against the backdrop of well-maintained plots, to suggest that we are in danger of losing this place is to advance it to the level of that which is in need of protection. But our care need not take always take the form of a curation seen as a struggle against loss through management and oversight or, indeed, explanation.[36] With this pervasive trope, one longstanding within Classical archaeology, we run the risk of ruining what becomes of the past here.

We crossed numerous pipes and channels fed by waters from the Gephyraion stream, one of the few sources of persistently flowing waters in the Peloponnesus, to emerge on the road. Ruins do not send the wrong message—they resist any one message. They resist narrative assimilation, they outlast the painted signs, for the stones know how to endure, even when only dry winds talk among them.[37] "Released from the burden of being useful" is to shed a burden that, as ruins remind us, has no lasting value.[38]

Rendered as evidence, judged by history, shall we always weigh the collapsed vault from the angle of its limitations and thus fail to appreciate what it is, what is here? Raising this question need not lead us to a position of indifference, but rather to the cultivation of a more open space of engagement. We have much to learn from the gardeners of Troizen.

---

36 Notable here is the work of Caitlin DeSilvey; see her *Curated Decay: Heritage Beyond Saving* (2017).

37 Nothing useful is of lasting value: dry wind only is still talking among the oldest stones. From A. R. Ammons, *Conserving the Magnitude of Uselessness* (1970).

38 We may contrast the will to explanation with simply letting things be. Understanding, for *Sein-lassen*, "precisely lets what is inexplicable stand as such." Indeed, as Þora Pétursdóttir has pointed out in her discussion of Heidegger's *Gelassenheit* or "releasement towards things" (2015, 347), one should be open to releasing ourselves from the ways that we normally approach things, which often eliminates their otherness. Also see Love and Meng (2016).

Bibliography

Caraher, W.R. 2003. *Church, society, and the sacred in early Christian Greece.* Ann Arbor, MI: UMI Dissertation Services.

Cooper, D.E. 2013. Should ruins be preserved? In C. Scarre and R. Coningham (eds.), *Appropriating the past: Philosophical perspectives on the practice of archaeology.* Cambridge, MA: Cambridge University Press. 222–36.

DeSilvey, C. 2006. Observed decay: Telling stories with mutable things. *Journal of Material Culture* 11(3), 318–338.

DeSilvey, C. 2014. Palliative curation. Art and entropy on Orford Ness. In B. Olsen and Þ. Petursdottir (eds.), *Ruin memories: Materiality, aesthetics and the archaeology of the recent past.* New York, NY: Routledge. 79–91.

DeSilvey, C. 2017. *Curated decay: Heritage beyond saving.* Minneapolis, MN: University of Minnesota Press.

Dodwell, E. 1819. *A classical and topographical tour through Greece.* London: Rodwell and Martin.

Faráklas, N. 1972. *Troizinía, Kalávreia, Méthana* (Archaíes Ellinikés Póleis, tóm 10), ékd. Athinaïkós Technologikós Ómilos – Athinaïkó Kéntro Oikistikís: Athens.

Farstadvoll, S. 2019b. Growing concerns: Plants and their roots in the past. *Journal of Contemporary Archaeology* 5(2), 174–93.

Frazer, J.G. 1898. *Pausanias's Description of Greece.* 6 vols. London: Macmillan & Co.

Frazer, J.G. 1925. *The golden bough: A study of magic and religion.* New York, NY: Macmillan.

Gell, W. 1810. *The itinerary of Greece.* London: Payne.

Goethe, J.W., and J. Gearey 1994. *Essays on art and literature: The collected works.* Princeton, NJ: Princeton University Press.

Harrison, R.P. 2003. *The dominion of the dead.* Chicago, IL: University of Chicago Press.

Harrison, R.P. 2008. *Gardens: An essay on the human condition.* Chicago, IL: University of Chicago Press.

Lantier, R. 1953. Eloge funèbre de M. Philippe Legrand, membre libre non résidant. *Comptes rendus des séances de l'Académie des Inscriptions et Belles-Lettres* 97(3), 243–47.

Legrand, P.E. 1905. Antiquités de Trézène, Notes de topographie. *BCH* 29, 269–318.

Love, J., and M. Meng. 2016. Histories of the dead? *Time and Mind* 9(3), 223–44.

Miliarakis, A. 1886. *Geographia Politiki, Nea kai Archaia tou Nomou Argolidos kai Korinthos.* Athens, GA.

Miller, P.N. 2013. A tentative morphology of European antiquarianism, 1500–2000. In A. Schnapp, with L. Von Falkenhausen, P.N. Miller, and T. Murray (eds.), *World antiquarianism: Comparative perspectives.* Los Angeles, CA: Getty Publications. 67–87.

Miller, P.N. 2015. *Peiresc's Mediterranean world.* Cambridge, MA: Harvard University Press.

Mollat, G. 1954. Notice sur la vie et les travaux de M. Philippe Legrand, membre de l'Académie. *Comptes rendus des séances de l'Académie des Inscriptions et Belles-Lettres* 98(4), 413–18.

Pétursdóttir, Þ. 2015. Things out-of-hand: The aesthetics of abandonment. In Olsen, B. and Þ. Pétursdóttir (eds.), *Ruin memories: Materiality, aesthetics and the archaeology of the recent past.* New York, NY: Routledge. 335–64.

Pétursdóttir, Þ., and B. Olsen 2014. Imaging modern decay: The aesthetics of ruin photography. *Journal of Contemporary Archaeology* 1(1), 7–56.

Schiffer, M.B. 1987. *Formation processes in the archaeological record*. Salt Lake City, UT: University of Utah Press.

Schnapp, A. 2013. Conservation of objects and monuments and the sense of the past during the Greco-Roman era. In A. Schnapp, with L. Von Falkenhausen, P.N. Miller, and T. Murray (eds.), *World antiquarianism: Comparative perspectives*. Los Angeles, CA: Getty Publications. 159–175.

Seferis, G. 1995. *Collected poems*. Princeton, NJ: Princeton University Press.

Shanks, M. 2012. *The archaeological imagination*. Walnut Creek, CA: Left Coast Press.

Shanks, M., and C. Tilley. 1987. *Social theory and archaeology*. Cambridge: Polity Press.

Simmel, G. 1959. The ruin. In K.W. Wolff (ed.), *Georg Simmel, 1858–1918: A collection of essays, with translations and a bibliography*. Columbus, OH: Ohio State University Press. 259–66.

Sweetman, R.J. 2010. The Christianization of the Peloponnese: The topography and function of Late Antique churches. *Journal of Late Antiquity* 3(2), 203–61.

Sweetman, R.J. 2015. Memory, tradition, and Christianization of the Peloponnese. *American Journal of Archaeology* 119(4), 501–531.

Welter, G. 1941. *Troizen und Kalaureia*. Berlin: Verlag Bebr. Mann.

Witmore, C. 2013b. Which archaeology? A question of chronopolitics. In A. González-Ruibal (ed.), *Reclaiming archaeology: Beyond the tropes of modernity*. London: Routledge. 130–44.

26

TO METHANA

*A janissary, an Englishman, and an artist, under-cultivated fertility, malaria, effi-
cacious air pockets and marshes, an isthmus, a wall and concrete ruins, evicting
fairies, plots and walls, page and* pagus, *truth and falsity, retracing our steps
through reason, science and history, an ethnographer, mononaturalism and multi-
culturalism, object-oriented politics*

"Pig!" "Dog!" Such were the insults Ibrahim routinely inflicted upon Greek
peasants who crossed his path. Upon leaving Poros, where Ibrahim was sub-
jected to the same species of abject humiliation that he was in the habit of
doling out, his normal indignation had boiled into sheer outrage, which could
only be expelled through violence. As the janissary rode in the company of
Edward Dodwell, the Englishman in whose service he was employed, and the
Italian artist Simone Pomardi, towards "the pointed and lofty promontory of
Methana," he vowed to Mohamed to "vent his spleen on the first Greek" he
encountered. Only with threats of dismissal did Dodwell manage to convince
the janissary to rein in his rage. The requisite patience, for Ibrahim, was the
"hardest morsel" he had ever chewed. The contemptuous jeers, which gave
relief to Ibrahim's petty and despotic attitude, were, according to Dodwell,

indicative of a "common Turk" "accustomed from his infancy to consider [Greeks] as slaves."[1] What Ibrahim experienced on Poros was, for the Englishman, "redistributive justice."

It was December 19, 1805. Two days earlier, Ibrahim, Dodwell, and Pomardi had encountered the plain of Trizina as mixture of cultivation and barrenness; vineyards and deserted cottages, interlocking fields of corn and thistle, areas "luxuriating," areas "relinquished to desolation." The general fertility of the earth was evidenced by the dimensions of the weeds and bushes. In this plain, "the comely agnos, and the elegant rhododaphne ... assume more the character of trees than of shrubs."[2] Despite the potency of its soils, the greater part of the plain was in a state of neglect, which the Englishman attributed to a deficiency of population. Unhealthy air, according to Dodwell, was an after-effect of this shortage. Not only was it "impregnated with the sour smells" of the Mediterranean spurge, *euphorbia characias*, in the summer months the air was productive of fevers.[3] Moreover, the water and wine were heavy and anti-diuretic—their poor quality did not go unnoticed by the ancients.[4]

Ibrahim, Dodwell, and Pomardi broke off from the path to Damala and took the coastal route on the eastern side of the plain. Along this way they bypassed the marshes at its northern end. With their unwholesome vapors, "pestilential effluvia," and rancid miasmas,[5] these waterlogged grounds were to be avoided, especially in a weakened state. "Exposed to fevers and putrid disorders," according Dodwell, the human frame subsisted with difficulty in such areas.[6] *Elonosia*, the Modern Greek word for malaria, translates into *marsh sickness* (*elos-nosia*). *Plaudism*, or the French *plaudisme*, another word for malaria, is derived from the Latin *palus*, marsh. Moisture-laden atmospheres, mists over marshes, low fogs over swamps; an area of waterlogged ground and a pocket of visible or malodorous air were understood from the angle of one's vulnerability—an association found in Hippocratic doctrine.[7] Bad air, *kakos aeras*, hung metaphorically over those with unscrupulous morals, with depraved states of mind.[8] Again, depending on the time of year, depending on one's state of health, it was

---

1 "Turk," for Dodwell, was not a matter of ethnicity but religion (see Dodwell 1819 II, 274–75).

2 1819 II, 273–74.

3 1819 II, 267, 271.

4 Isocrates, *Aegineticus*, 22; in Jones (1809, 40).

5 On Dodwell and marshland, see 1819 I, 213; on the unwholesomeness of the plain, see Frazer (1898 III, 273), Forbes (2007, 80).

6 1819 I, 116.

7 See Hippocrates, *On Airs, Waters, and Places*, part 7; also Lucretius 6.1090–1137.

8 See "malaria, n." in the OED Online 2019, www.oed.com/view/Entry/112765. Accessed April 30, 2019.

deemed wise to give wide berth to the marshes—not even the *Eleionomae*, those ancient marsh naiads, could ensnare these travelers.

Having lost the way from the valley to the headland, Ibrahim, Dodwell, and Pomardi directed their horses with difficulty over a series of rough hills to the summit above Dara. From here Dodwell would survey his surroundings (a scene which Pomardi will illustrate the following day).[9] The heights of Aegina and Hymettos, then the Attic coast to Sounion, lay to the east. To the west, towering Ortholithi is followed by the coast of Epidaurus, and, beyond the Corinthian isthmus, Parnassos gleamed white under snow. Methana extended to the north. Near the base of its western slopes, the travelers could see their destination, the ancient city and, just above it, the contemporary village.

Both during, and in the wake of, the Greek War of Independence, Methana would see its population grow with an influx of refugees.[10] Many descendants of these same families would be forced to develop agricultural holdings in the northern portion of the plain of Troizen, near the marshes.[11] Given the distance and difficulty of moving between these plots and Methana, they would stay a night or two out in the open, and only later in their field-houses (*kalivia*). Roofs and walls would not protect them from malaria. Once contracted, the fever could stay on for more than two years. Some infected women miscarried. Some parents lost loved daughters and sons, too young to fight off the fevers.

Disease-ridden mosquitoes with their protozoans would overturn the relationship to unwholesome marsh vapors. After Laveren and Ross linked malaria to parasites developed within mosquitoes, the efficacy of swamp air and marsh-fogs vanished in all ways but literally—*mal-aria*.[12] Mal-airs and mal-areas would drain away like so many beliefs, so many fetishes deemed false into Lethe. Pathogenic others, revealed by science, would now shoulder the blame. Endemic to the plain, malaria was only evicted with the post-World War II disease control programs.[13]

I fall in with the route taken by Ibrahim, Dodwell, and Pomardi in Taktikoupoli, which they knew as Dara.[14] From the road, Methana is a jagged silhouette set against blue skies. I imagine the December weather, cold; the colors, low;

---

9 See the *Presqu'ile de Methana* in Pomardi (1820, 136).

10 Compare Dodwell (1819 II, 281–82), who mentions only the village of Methana, to Bory de Saint Vincent (1834, 67), who lists five other villages; also see Forbes (1997, 108–10).

11 Forbes (2007, 76, 80); on the contrast between agricultural development on Methana and in the plain, see Miliarakis (1886, 195, 209–10); compare Frazer (1898 III, 286–87).

12 See Gell (1823, 390) on quarantine; Hippocrates, *On Airs, Waters, and Places*, part 7.

13 Forbes (2007, 237).

14 The village was renamed in the twentieth century. The notion of "tactical city" is said to be related to its location, vis-à-vis the nearby castle of Favierou used during the Greek War of Independence (see www.koutouzis.gr/taktikoupolis.htm).

the atmosphere, moist; all in a stark contrast to this bright June day. By now, darkness would have begun to extend its grease-grey grasp—the brevity of daylight is no concern for me, as it would have been for them.

After a few switchbacks the road follows a direct line along the east slope of the isthmus. A hand-painted sign, set up by the Arsinoe Club of Megalochori in 2010, points out the path to the fort of Fabvier (*Kastro Favierou*).[15] On the highest point of the isthmus, the French Philhellene, Charles Nicolas Fabvier, oversaw the construction of a small square fort in 1826. Along its north side it incorporated an elliptical enceinte, perhaps of the Hellenistic period.

I slow down to take the turnoff to Vathy and Megalochori. Off to the left, the hollow skeletons of three concrete silos loom behind what seems to have been the supports for a giant hopper. Abandoned components of a concrete facility left to ruin before completion are now used for storage by the aquaculturalists who raise fishstock in Steno and Thynni Bay, on the east and west of the isthmus. Another sign just inside the turn registers this as the way to the ancient acropolis and the volcano beyond. Below this, suspended on the same chains, hangs another sign, which points again to the fort of Fabvier and the ancient wall. White lettering on brown ground, these hand-painted, rectilinear signs are reminiscent of the official signs set up by the archaeological service—these are nowhere to be seen.

The road veers back to the right in an acute angle. Dodwell noted the wall, which runs directly across the isthmus at this point. Here, at the thinnest and lowest portion of the isthmus a wall of coarse masonry persists at a length of 180 meters. Whether this wall is of ancient or modern construction is, for them, left undecided. Nonetheless, its presence prompts Dodwell to evoke Thucydides and Diodorus Siculus, who inform us that the isthmus was fortified in the seventh year of the Peloponnesian War.

Off to the left, the road passes a small church, *to Genethlion tis Theotokou*, the last roof-covered vestige of the dispersed settlement known as Steno.[16] Beyond, on a wide and level terrace carved from the slope, rise the columns and beams of an unrealized cement factory. Begun by the Heracles cement company in the 1970s, this factory was to exploit the Middle Triassic limestone of Mali Bardi or Asprovouni (White Mountain), which now bears its scars. Abandoned in the wake of the Junta, along with its quarries, the area now accommodates an illicit garbage dump. Here, in recent years, illegal aggregate quarrying apparently has proliferated.[17]

15 The Arsinoe Club takes its name from Arsinoe II, wife of Ptolemy II, who was honored by the polis, Methana, changing its name to Arsinoe; on Arsinoe in the Peloponnese, see Gill (2007).

16 Registered as MC26 by the Methana Survey Project (Koukoulis 1997, 255).

17 Forbes (1997, 102); on the illegal activities, see: www.porosnews.gr/latest-news/σοβαρές-καταγγελίες-για-αυθαιρεσίες/.

After a long straight section, the road descends into a turn cut deep through the limestone. This rock corridor emerges onto Skoubis Bay where aquiculture containers are now moored. Directing their horses to proceed by tracks barely practicable for donkeys and mules, Ibrahim, Dodwell, and Pomardi made their way along the worst paths they had yet to encounter. Barely discernable in places, they lost their way on more than one occasion. Dodwell would later reckon their pace at no more than a mile and a half per hour.

I drive at a crawl around the small cove. Here, the road follows the course of the old *kalderimi*, which given Dodwell's description must have been built in the years after the janissary, the Englishman, and the artist passed somewhere along here. Unkempt trails were an impediment to routine crossings, yet the travelers would encounter a world sealed off by more than once formidable walls and barely discernable paths. Both Dodwell and Pomardi count themselves among the first Northern Europeans to venture to Methana.[18] That Methanites seem to have kept to their own bubble at the time was suggested by the *proto-papas* (archpriest) in the village of Methana, who had never seen people wearing broad hats.[19] Even Dara was considered so remote from Ottoman control that its villagers openly displayed surplus wealth without fear of loss. Despite jutting out into the midst of the familiar maritime space of the Saronic Gulf, Methana in 1805 was, from the angle of terrestrial space, as peripheral as one can get.

The old *kalderimi* breaks upslope just after some disused terraces on the north side of the cove. It follows a line above the Cave of Peristeri, named after pigeon-shaped stalagmites found within. I pause below the cave. Here, two Arsinoe Club signs hang on the rock by the road. Stories that suggest that the cave was once haunted by nereids who troubled travelers after sunset come to conflict with accounts that the cave was discovered in 1973 when blasting associated with the concrete works opened an entrance.[20] The integrity of the former diminishes when one learns that nereids were reputably evicted from their residence after a witch recommended three nails be placed above the entrance, for this solution was transposed here from another cave by that very name, *Tria Karphia*, Three Nails.[21] The impulse to remythologize such locales would seem to follow economic speculation that the cave would bring tourists.[22]

---

18 Only Richard Chandler seems to have preceded them; see Pomardi (1820, 135–36).

19 Broad hats are not unusual in other parts of the Morea; Gell (1823, 159); see Dodwell (1819 II, 281); on the paucity of contact with the Turkish dominated outside world, see Forbes (1997, 107).

20 The story is retold here: http://troizinia.info/το-σπήλαιο-των-μεθανων-περιστέρι/. Also see Petrocheilou (1974).

21 I am grateful to Hamish Forbes for this information.

22 Ibid.

The road soon passes through a low drainage in the area of Skoubia. Here, I leave behind the last of the limestone scarps exposed in the road cut and transition into volcanic alluvium under olive trees. The road cut on the other side of the drainage reveals pyroclastic deposits over limestone followed by more pyroclastic deposits and andesite domes and flows.

Northern European travelers like Dodwell saw themselves as catalysts for opening such places to the outside.[23] Dodwell would connect Palaiokastro to the ancient polis of Methana and the descriptions of Pausanias. He would be the first antiquarian to procure autonomous coins of Methana and identify the pileus-wearing figure on their obverse with the god of fire and forge, Hephaestus, whose Roman name, Vulcan, will lie behind the word "volcano." A speculator who understands this distance from the angle of opportunism, Dodwell recommends the area for scientific research, and particularly the study of volcanoes. Subsequent researchers will answer the call,[24] and through such work, at least to some degree, what had been unspoken will come to the fore as another option for how local peoples understood these lands.

Again the road breaks with the old *kalderimi*, which continues directly over the terraced headland. Near here, the Methana Archaeological Survey identified a rectangular structure as a Late Roman farmstead.[25] The paved road swings around the headland of Pounda and takes a line adjacent to the shore. Ahead, Megalochori—what Ibrahim, Dodwell, and Pomardi knew as Methana—comes into view, as does the plain around the acropolis of the ancient polis, now known as Palaiokastro.

The road hugs the shoreline into Vathy, where I leave the car in the parking area of *To Palaiokastro* fish tavern. An official archaeological sign directs me to follow the raised stone surface of an old *kalderimi* towards the acropolis. The path is no more than a thin line through an otherwise stubble-enveloped road. Ahead, stone terraces are integrated into pockets wedged between the variegated volcanic outcrops. Terraces extend dressed fragments of the ancient wall. Beyond, terraced land rises several hundred meters up the slopes around Megalochori, now obscured behind the rock dome of the acropolis. I pause before a bend to the east.

23 Dodwell's journey can be read as a continuation of the history of the Modern Age, from Sloterdijk's angle of "a spatial revolution into the outside." Importantly, "this history brings about the catastrophe of local ontologies" (2014, 791).
24 M.E. Puillon de Boblaye and M. Virlet were the first to take up the study of the volcanoes as part of the *Expedition scientific de Morée*, followed by Fouqué (1867), Reiss and Stübel (1867), and Washington (1894). For a litany of scholars interested in the archaeology, see Forbes and Mee (1997, 1–4).
25 Mee et al. (1997, 149).

When Ibrahim, Dodwell, and Pomardi came here, the paths were overgrown and the areas under cultivation, near the only village, were open. Now the roads are open and the areas of former cultivation are overgrown. Only the small plot behind the tavern is cultivated. Barren are the surrounding fields. Open plots do not even appear to be used as pasture.

My attention is drawn to an old well, below me, to the left. A rusting wheel and a set of bevel gears are all that remain of a water-lifting device known as a *mangani*. Once turned by donkey, a chain of metal buckets would have rotated around the suspended wheel, drawing up brackish waters.[26] Nearby, set within the junction of the road revetment and another terrace wall, is a container packed with agricultural refuse and overrun with fig and arbutus. Rendered redundant by a piped water supply, this former water-holding tank was associated with the irrigation of the surrounding parcels.

Along brush-covered terraces and through more plots surrendered to unguided germination I make my way around the west side of the acropolis. A series of wide, fallow plots step up the west side towards the scrub-enveloped summit. Walking here, one understands how scholars known and agrarians unknown understood this acropolis so very differently. What Dodwell grasped with Thucydides, Diodorus Siculus, Pausanias, and Strabo, with coins of

Abandoned *mangani* below the Methana acropolis.

26 Forbes (2007, 242).

former poleis, and with other Northern Europeans through reading and in conversation, farmers comprehended with plow, yoked partners in agriculture, hoe, and with others who worked the land. Recognizing walls without that which they once enveloped in security, or spaces once cultivated, or fruit-bearing trees untrimmed as the relinquished burdens of others, named and nameless, what questions did those who labored here ask of these things? What other tales were associated with these walls? What stories did the plowman put to coins turned up in the furrow?[27] Always secure in the knowledge of history, neither the Cambridge-educated antiquarian nor the Italian artist records them.

I walk transfixed below high ashlar walls by two barrel-vaulted chambers. Stacked along the base of these ancient walls runs a terrace of fieldstones cleared from the path of the mule-turned plow. As an archaeologist it is my charge to recognize these walls as indicative of specific styles, assignable to particular periods. I am supposed to know that these walls are isodomic ashlar and therefore possibly Hellenistic in date, probably third century. As an archaeologist my obligation is to refine and maintain such abstractions.

I pull myself up on a cornerstone—its volcanic surface is coarse to the touch —and scramble over the end of walls largely unseen under the cover of *Aristolochia*. Like these vines, our abstractions, our stories, grow. Do they reveal or obscure what lies below? The answer depends on how one renders the very things that we hold in common with those agrarians who worked this land and with Dodwell and Pomardi who marveled at their state of preservation, which they gave form through illustration.[28]

Terraces below the walls of Methana acropolis.

27 Coins, like other scraps of metal, were often collected into hoards, to be transformed into items of utility when enough metal was available (for an example of this practice in Thessaly in 1810, see Leake 1835 IV, 486).

28 See Methana Mount Ortholithi in Dodwell (1819 II, 282).

I continue ambling along the north side of the acropolis. Here, isodomic ashlar walls are boundaries to plots. They lend themselves to the orientation, to the definition of parcels. Ancient fortifications assert themselves as obstacles to movement. Towering above me, these formidable barriers are too stout to be undone by toil to one's advantage. So, the farmer worked with them, enrolling lofty walls to the benefit of his labors. Ahead, these walls support the rough stones of agricultural terraces established high on the summit. From what angle do we approach these walls? From the *page*? Who lived here? How did this place come to be? Or, from the *pagus*? Whose burdens do I assume? How might these labors be enrolled in raising a crop? To be sure, both the questions and the answers varied.

The ground below me is hard; it has yet to be broken this season. Buried under the alluvium of this debris-strewn, scrub-covered plot are the remains of a settlement. Pottery suggests that the site had been occupied more or less consistently for several millennia, up to the beginning of the Turkish period (post-1458 CE) when the settled community moved farther upslope to the area of Panayitsa above Megalochori.[29] In 1805, according to Dodwell and Pomardi, Megalochori, which at that time retained its ancient place name, Methana, was the only settlement on the peninsula. By 1830, it would be one of six villages.[30] Yet, Methanites' own stories seem to run counter to those of archaeologists who have studied the settlement of the peninsula.[31] Their own sense of belonging runs deep, like the roots of the olive trees, like the foundation stones of this wall.

I weave my way through a field unkempt towards an agricultural wall stacked solid with cobbles unhewn. I shuffle up onto the terrace below the junction of Classical and Hellenistic masonry in the acropolis wall. At this temporal pleat, I find a precarious pew among the cobbles. With my pen I begin to plow my own furrows on the white page.

Dodwell and Pomardi counted themselves among the first to visit a previously semi-separate world. While surely this world possessed its own oral traditions, the written page backs the one-sidedness of these travelers. Beginning with their pages, this land will accommodate lost gods once again. Somewhere here was a temple to Isis. From the soil rise coins impressed with the image of the god Hephaestus. Satisfied with fragments, did they see the antiquity of practices that lay before them in what was formerly a settlement, the erstwhile *astu*, returned to countryside, to the *chôra*? If they did, they failed to mention it.

---

29 Forbes (1997, 103).
30 Bory de Saint Vincent (1834, 67); also see Forbes (1997, 107).
31 Forbes (2007, 221).

Dodwell tells us what counts as an object worthy of his curiosity. Falling into that long cascade of Northern Europeans who would bring descriptive relief to what had hitherto been imagined by reading Classical texts at a distance, he presents his readers with a "Classical" tour. Anything that does not gain relief when observed from the angle of ancient history, of poetry, of ageless "genius" becomes, as he plainly states, "irrelevant matter," "superfluous detail."[32] It is telling that Dodwell does not mention the story which struck Pausanias the most—a threat to their budding vines, Methanites dealt with the *Lips*, or south-westerly wind (the *Garbis* or *Libeccio*) by ripping a white cock in two and circling the vines in opposite directions; they would bury the halves in the ground where they met, which is where they started.[33] "Nothing extraneous has been willfully introduced; and everything essential has been studiously retained."[34] Did such discriminating ambivalence contribute to yet another form of deterritorialization, as anticipated with the coming of Christianity, where sacrifices and incantations would lose their potency to turn away hailstorms?[35]

What counted as the "real history" of Palaiokastro had more than a century to settle into the consciousness of those who lived here. After a war for independence, the birth of a nation, the influx of new populations, and several more wars, these hidden recesses would lose many of their imagined associations before folklorists or ethnographers could respond. After being saturated under the trickle of subsequent scholars, we only know these walls in terms of a definitive historical reality supported by ancient history and Classical archaeology. As Dodwell put it, with the accuracy afforded through first-hand observation, "obscurity" should be "dispersed", "misrepresentation" could be "removed," and "inaccuracies" would be "rectified."[36] In this way the *page* wins out over the *pagus*.

I pack up the notebook and return to the overgrown plots. We need to retrace our steps. Along this path we have seen reason and science provide grounds for certainty and irrationality, truth and falsity. Was Ibrahim's intolerance an artifact of his upbringing?[37] Or, did Dodwell bear witness to the identity complex of a soldier who began life as one of the Greek peasants he detested, and, by the grace of Allah, was given a Muslim name? What of those

---

32 Dodwell (1819 II, iii, iv).

33 Pausanias 2.34.3.

34 Dodwell (1819 II, iii-iv).

35 The Roman pilgrim claimed personally to have seen Methanites turn away hail-storms (Pausanias 2.34.3).

36 Dodwell (1819 II, iii).

37 Dodwell is not without his own foibles—he chastises haughty Poriotes in publication (1819 II, 275, 281).

Methanites who contracted malaria when vapors and mists were to blame? Does our confidence in those latent parasitic protozoans passed by mosquitoes relegate these agrarians to perpetual ignorance? Reason values all cultures equally and chastises those who languish without the capacity for rational thought. Science makes explicit the true culprit, a harsh, unforgiving nature, and seen from the angle of the present, the past becomes a locus for delusions stripped of any claims to reality. Reason civilizes according to those who hold a monopoly. Science reveals an indisputable nature by making explicit what was latent for others.

What of history? Does Dodwell judge other pasts against the certainty, which only he can provide with the aid of Pausanias and Strabo? Somewhere through here runs a prejudicial divide between those who merely believe and those who securely know. But let us not rehearse the argument that truth is an artifact of power. We need to remain here among these trees and terraces, plots and walls.

The field is separated from a path by a low wall of lichen-covered stone. I step onto this stone wall, shifting several cobbles under my weight, and jump into the path. Momentum carries me for a few steps and I continue out to the paved road to Megalochori. Here, the ethnographer has sought to understand the ways communities relate to the land they work by documenting their achievements and practices, by listening to and recording the stories that they tell. Hamish Forbes invested over thirty years in grasping how Methanites saturated these lands with life, with meaning. Walking these landscapes and sharing in the labors of those who lived here, Forbes came to know agricultural features like the old *kalderimi* or these field walls, the mechanized water-lifting device (*mangani*) or the water-holding tank as prompts for the performance of knowledge, as stimuli for shared stories. Often, such things were reminders of former hardships—prior to the paved road across the isthmus, a farmer who grew grapes in the plain of Troizen had to hire a boat to bring his harvest to Methana.[38] In a grape-treading floor by the shore he pressed the fruit before transporting the must within goatskins. Hauled uphill on the back of his labor's companion along old mule-paths framed with sharp rocks, transporting valuable must in easily torn containers was not without its anxieties.

I walk downhill along the smooth Tarmac surface. The Methanite past, according to Forbes, is often regarded as a locus for adversity, ignorance, and evil. Images of scarcity, hardship, the shared miseries and simplicities of agricultural life, and fear of pirates and bandits pervade Methanite oral histories.[39]

38 Forbes (2007, 256).
39 Ibid., 222.

Perceived periods of shortage, such as the Turkish Occupation, are familiar loci for association—local residents link the intensive terracing of these high slopes to this period.[40] Conversely, the archaeologist who reads Dodwell, and subsequent scholars who ventured to and described this land, argue that intensive terracing on the steeper slopes, well beyond Megalochori, began after the Greek War of Independence.[41]

Framed by cemented stone walls—one of recent construction on the right, one enveloped by stubble on the left—the divide between road and plot is rigidly defined. Forbes described how another story, related to a raid upon the abandoned village of Panayitsa located above Megalochori, was placed in the time of an elder informant's grandparents. Archaeologists suggest that the site was largely abandoned by 1700. Given the discrepancy in dates, for Forbes, such oral traditions constitute "descending anachronisms." Evoking a notion developed by Jan Vansina, Forbes describes this as a case where "events or situations are made younger."[42] Ultimately, by forgetting, as he puts it, "their disparate pasts, Methanites were able to conceptualise themselves as autochthonous —hence, as always having belonged to their landscapes."[43] The selective erosion of their differences, according to Forbes, provided grounds for a shared sense of belonging, a singular identity as Methanites.

I pause above the church of Agios Nikolaos. Partially buried by over a meter of alluvium, partially constructed with architectural blocks from Palaiokastro, the church, consisting of three apses and a central dome set on a rectilinear core, has been dated to the twelfth or thirteenth century on the basis of architectural form.[44] The discrepancy between oral traditions and official historical documents is a major concern for Forbes, who is careful to give them balanced consideration. Still, what fidelity do we assume when oral traditions are deemed anachronistic? Are they judged against a homogeneous, universal time, as if they were claimants to the same grounds for truth? This is not that image of prisoners released from their bondage and delusion, and compelled to bear witness to a more definitive reality. Do we commit an injustice when the path of certainty and truth is determined in advance? What if their truths exist in accordance with different things? Is not their fidelity to memories of progenitors? Are they not loyal to familial association? Do they not proceed from relations with the

---

40 Ibid., 78–79, 242.
41 Dodwell (1819 II, 281) describes cultivation as prevailing on a small portion of the promontory and particularly within this plain where the ancient acropolis stood (also see Forbes 1997, 103–13).
42 Forbes (2007, 222); on the date of the village abandonment, see Forbes (1997, 105–6).
43 Forbes (2007, 285).
44 Koukoulis (1997, 250–55).

undated plot, from common labors and shared burdens that come with working this land? One might understand this not so much as an *anachronic* domain but as a *polychronic* one where time arises out of rapports unique to Methanite, rather than scholarly, communities.

From my elevated position, I note a marble column drum incorporated into a low platform and bench of cement and rubble. These features are built up around the entrance to protect the interior from winter floods. What was once understood within the domain of the inexplicable, save by the grace of God, revealer of insight, was uncoverable as an "undisguised proclamation" with amplified sight through a microscope.[45] The prosthetic impulse for a precisely delineated optic of Dodwell and Pomardi required their "infallible" camera obscura, which they carried around with them.[46] Truth, for Dodwell, was, among other things, an exact window onto Greek lands, where a "scrupulous fidelity" to the things seen allowed them to return with images of Greece as if they were imprinted on the viewer's eye.[47] Among other things, this mode of visualization continues to underwrite archaeological truth.[48] The achievements of science, history, and archaeology are just as constructed as Methanite oral histories.

Should not reason, science, and history be submitted to the same scrutiny accorded to "beliefs," "fetishes," and "anachronistic oral traditions"? The former truths rely upon books, microscopes, refined knowledges maintained by institutions, camera obscuras, and routines made synthetic, just as archaeologists here linked texts, ceramic typologies, masonry styles, and architectural forms. No one holds a monopoly on reason. True naivety demands that I treat my own beliefs in the same terms as others.

The ground between the church and the shore is low. Reeds grow tall in small stands to the west. Mists form here under the right conditions. While Forbes refuses to relegate Methanite oral tradition to that cemetery of misguided beliefs and irrationalities, he nonetheless situates this tradition against the unity of one material world. For Forbes, "without meanings given to [landscapes] by human groups, they are merely environments."[49] Here, Forbes assumes a default position, which bifurcates nature into two taxonomic domains.[50] A singular world made known by science, undergirded by reason, is what provides an unquestionable backdrop to history, but is, in itself, devoid of

---

45 "Undisguised proclamation" is Sloterdijk's spin on Heidegger's concept of *alêtheia*, unconcealment (2013, 96).
46 See Segment 14.
47 Dodwell (1819 I, x).
48 Witmore (2004, 2006, 2013a).
49 Forbes (2007, 5 and 395).
50 On the bifurcation of nature, see Whitehead (2006, 14–25); also see Latour (2005, 115–20).

that which only humans can bring to it. Assumed to be common to all,[51] nature is depoliticized and placed off-limits to all but the natural sciences,[52] while humans are elevated to a half share in the constitution of any situation. Should not this world and human rift have been a site of negotiation? How can one know in advance what the solid, indisputable, unquestionable reality *really is*? I wish to take nothing away from Forbes's tremendous achievement[53] when I say that one must go farther with respect to the assumed distribution of unity and multiplicity.

Across the road the old *kalderimi* follows a line south of the acropolis back to the taverna. I return to a thin trail trodden through stubble. Forbes resists the lure of serving good historical truths against bad "folk fictions". He does not allow Methanite stories to necessarily run against a bedrock of certainty and shatter into shards of ludicrous belief. Yet, any conflicts between truth and illusion are superficial to a common nature devoid of perspectives or values. Disagreements may be kept to the level of passions, meanings, and representations, and not substance, not reality, not understanding. History follows suit. Local stories are situated against a backdrop of a definitive past. So long as this unity underlies all cultural multiplicities, they may be tolerated. And yet, leaving open the question of what is more real without assuming a ready-made, surpassing existence—that is, on the grounds of our own basic ignorance—is precisely what is at stake in any attempt to work towards what is common to all.[54]

The cobbles of the field wall are blotted with an assortment of sun-warmed lichen—bright orange and white, various shades of grey and green. Things may be facts, they may act as prompts, they may lure different groups in with feeling, but they are a lot of other things in addition. Rage, marshes, vapors, parasitic protozoans, cement corporations, quarries, roads, nereids, volcanoes, ancient fortifications, institutions, terraces, oral histories, and field walls, one has to take all these things seriously as efficacious entities. Preordained taxonomies of what is human and what is environment close down the propensities of these things to surprise, to play a role in other modes of existence.[55] Among these walls, I seek "a way of speaking about historical matters that would be discreet, polyvalent, non-totalizing, and, above all, aware of its own perspectival

---

51 Indeed, Forbes goes to some length to situate Methanites in terms of the common ground of a Western perspective (ibid.).
52 This de-politicization was anticipated with the de-sacralization of the Christian tradition; see Segment 17.
53 At long last, a researcher situates the handiwork and stories of those who live here alongside those favored by history, rather than at their expense, which is a political project.
54 For more see Latour (2002, 2004a, 2004b), Stengers (2008); also Harman (2014, 57–70). In archaeology, see Alberti (2016); also Alberti et al. (2011).
55 Olsen and Witmore (2015).

conditionality."[56] I also seek a different distribution of unity and multiplicity, one that is the outcome of common effort and not an a priori arbiter of disagreement made known by science.

The Hellenistic tower on the acropolis is partially shielded from view by almond and olive trees in the fenced-off plot to my right. What would happen if these green limbs were to wilt; if science were to assert that *Xylella* bacteria have managed to jump here from Puglia; if responsible agricultural practices required every parcel to be plowed and maintained to control the spittlebug population? Conflicting definitions of healthy trees, suspicion of officials, mistrust of scientists, faith in the tenacity of long-lived olive trees, outrage at the loss of history materialized through generations of commitment by progenitors, hereditary and adopted, should leave no doubts about ensuing controversies. One could imagine how other disputes will arise should another cement company seek to destroy Asprovouni with progress as a ruse, or if *Plasmodium vivax* should return to the marshes of Troizen,[57] but one cannot jump to a common solution in advance.

I walk the last few meters of the *kalderimi* to the road. We should beware of the loss of one's ability to identify blatant errors, as in the case of the Cave of Peristeri, to evict phantasms, or root out ill will and self-gain. One should not give up on reason.[58] However, to assume a transcendent and unquestionable arbiter from the start is not only to deny other possible realities, and the dignity of those who hold to them, it is to reenact the power play, however unwittingly, that followed on Northern European indifference. Common ground will not be achieved without due process. An object-oriented politics requires us to aspire to the weakness of excluding nothing.[59]

In the heat of the late afternoon, the shady atmosphere of the reed-covered veranda of the fish-taverna beckons me. I take a seat at an open table, order a drink, strike up a conversation, and put to one side the fact that we have a ferry to catch.

---

56 Sloterdijk (2013, 4).
57 On *Xylella* bacteria and olive trees, see Nadeau (2015). On the resurgence of *Plasmodium vivax* in Greece, see Danis et al. (2013).
58 Latour (2013, 355).
59 I pronounce no judgments on the choices Methanites make (Fotiadis 1995). I do not seek to freeze them as if their worlds varied little. Ambivalent to a prodigious world of knowledge, what agrarian rationalizations, free of the influence of distant pages, were lost before they could have been known? I stand for diversity, for the variegated, for the motley, for variety as such, which includes the afterlives of the acropolis of ancient Methana (see Serres (1995b, 24–5); also see Harman (2014).

Bibliography

Alberti, B. 2016. Archaeologies of ontology. *Annual Review of Anthropology* 45, 163–214.

Alberti, B., S. Fowles, M. Holbraad, Y. Marshall, and C. Witmore. 2011. "Worlds otherwise": Archaeology, anthropology, and ontological difference. *Current Anthropology* 52(6), 896–912.

Bory de Saint-Vincent, M. 1834. *Expédition scientifique de Morée: Section des sciences physiques. Tome II – Partie 1. Géographie.* Paris: F.G. Levrault.

Danis K., A. Lenglet, M. Tseroni, A. Baka, S. Tsiodras, and S. Bonovas. 2013. Malaria in Greece: Historical and current reflections on a re-emerging vector borne disease. *Travel Medicine and Infectious Disease* 11(1), 8–14.

Dodwell, E. 1819. *A Classical and topographical tour through Greece.* London: Rodwell and Martin.

Forbes, H. 1997. Turkish and modern Methana. In C. Mee and H.A. Forbes (eds.), *A rough and rocky place: The landscape and settlement history of the Methana Peninsula, Greece.* Liverpool: Liverpool University Press. 101–17.

Forbes, H. 2007. *Meaning and identity in a Greek landscape: An archaeological ethnography.* Cambridge: Cambridge University Press.

Forbes, H., and C. Mee. 1997. Introduction. In C. Mee and H. Forbes (eds.), *A rough and rocky place: The landscape and settlement history of the Methana Peninsula, Greece.* Liverpool: Liverpool University Press. 1–4.

Fotiadis, M. 1995. Modernity and the past-still-present: Politics of time in the birth of regional archaeological projects in Greece. *American Journal of Archaeology* 99(1), 59–78.

Fouqué, F. 1867. *Les Anciens Volcans de la Grèce. Revue des deux Mondes LVIII.* Paris: J. Claye.

Frazer, J.G. 1898. *Pausanias's Description of Greece.* 6 vols. London: Macmillan & Co.

Gell, W. 1823. *Narrative of a journey in the Morea.* London: Longman, Hurst, Rees, Orme, and Brown.

Gill, D.W.J. 2007. Arsinoe in the Peloponnese: The Ptolemaic base on the Methana Peninsula. *Egyptian stories: A British Egyptological tribute to Alan B. Lloyd, Alter Orient und Alter Testament* 347, 87–110.

Harman, G. 2014. *Bruno Latour: Reassembling the political.* London: Pluto Press.

Jones, W.H.S. 1809. *Malaria and Greek history.* Manchester: Manchester University Press.

Koukoulis, T. 1997. Catalogue of churches. In C. Mee and H.A. Forbes (eds.), *A rough and rocky place: The landscape and settlement history of the Methana Peninsula, Greece.* Liverpool: Liverpool University Press. 211–56.

Latour, B. 2002. *War of the worlds: What about peace?* (trans. C. Brigg). Chicago, IL: Prickly Paradigm Press.

Latour, B. 2004a. *The politics of nature: How to bring the sciences into democracy.* Cambridge, MA: Harvard University Press.

Latour, B. 2004b. Why has critique run out of steam? From matters of fact to matters of concern. *Critical Inquiry* 30(2), 225–48.

Latour, B. 2005. *Reassembling the social: An introduction to actor-network-theory.* Oxford: Oxford University Press.

Latour, B. 2013. *An inquiry into modes of existence: An anthropology of the moderns.* Cambridge, MA: Harvard University Press.

Leake, W.M. 1835. *Travels in northern Greece.* 4 vols. London: J. Rodwell.

Mee, C., H. Bowden, L. Foxhall, D. Gill, T. Koukoulis, and G. Taylor, 1997. Catalogue of sites. In C. Mee and H. Forbes (eds.), *A rough and rocky place: The landscape and settlement history of the Methana Peninsula*. Liverpool: Liverpool University Press. 118–210.

Miliarakis, A. 1886. *Geographia Politiki, Nea kai Archaia tou Nomou Argolidos kai Korinthos*. Athens: Vivliopoleíon Estías, Typografeíon Korínnis.

Olsen, B., and C. Witmore. 2015. Archaeology, symmetry and the ontology of things: A response to critics. *Archaeological Dialogues* 22(2), 187–97.

Petrocheilou, A. 1974. To Spilaion "Peristeri" Megalochorio, Methanon. *Arith. Sp. Mitroou* 4325. Available at: http://geolib.geo.auth.gr/index.php/bssg/article/view/6073.

Pomardi, S. 1820. *Viaggio nella Grecia fatto da Simone Pomardi negli anni 1804, 1805, e 1806*. Vol. II. Rome: Vincenzo Poggioli.

Reiss, W., and A. Stübel. 1867. *Ausflug nach den vulkanischen Gebirgen von Ägina und Methana*. Heidelberg: Verlagsbuchhandlung von FR. Bassermann.

Serres, M. 1995b. *Genesis*. Ann Arbor, MI: University of Michigan Press.

Sloterdijk, P. 2013. *In the world interior of capital: For a philosophical theory of globalization*. Cambridge: Polity Press.

Sloterdijk, P. 2014. *Globes: Spheres II*. South Pasadena, CA: Semiotext(e).

Stengers, I. 2008. Experimenting with refrains: Subjectivity and the challenge of escaping modern dualism. *Subjectivity* 22(1), 38–59.

Washington, H.S. 1894. A petrographical sketch of Aegina and Methana. *Journal of Geology* 2(8), 789–813.

Whitehead, A.N. 2006. *The concept of nature: The Tarner Lectures delivered in Trinity College November 1919*. Teddington: Echo Library.

Witmore, C. 2004. On multiple fields: Between the material world and media – Two cases from the Peloponnesus, Greece. *Archaeological Dialogues* 11(2), 133–64.

Witmore, C. 2006. Vision, media, noise and the percolation of time: Symmetrical approaches to the mediation of the material world. *Journal of Material Culture* 11(3), 267–92.

Witmore, C. 2013a. The world on a flat surface: Maps from the archaeology of Greece and Beyond. In S. Bonde and S. Houston (eds.), *Representing the past: Archaeology through text and image*. Oxford: Oxbow Books. 127–52.

27

INTO THE SARONIC GULF

Disembarking, a view from sea, without sails, the nephos, *pollution and ships, pollution from land, the* Agia Zoni II, *appropriation, volcanoes, growing beyond Leviathan and the proportionality of the human, the new climate regime, into the haze before us*

Calling at Methana, Aegina, and Piraeus, the *Apollon Hellas* departs from Poros at 13:25. An officer waves for me to drive forward and we lurch up the gangplank. Inside, a seaman in grey coveralls directs me to turn around and, with a series of brusque gesticulations, guides me to park midships adjacent to the starboard hull. No sooner than I shut off the engine are we urged to get out. I open the passenger door as another car stops a finger's width from the bumper. Over us washes a cacophony of rubber on steel. Motors are revved by those waiting for us to move out the of way. I grab my two-year-old son and wade through a stream of cars toward the stern portal. The hold is stifling. Exhaust fumes from automobiles and motorcycles packing into the steel interior render the air all but unbreathable. Engine emissions lay claim to the pocket of air in the hold.

Clutching my son, I climb the stairs. My wife and four-year-old son await us in the lounge. Over the next twenty minutes, young travelers and Athenian holidaymakers cram into what seats remain. Backpacks, bags, and boxes pile up around the shared table. Within this air-conditioned pocket of air, the hubbub of the growing crowd makes conversation tedious. We opt to relocate to the upper deck, hoping for fresh air and a view of Poros. We arrive aft to see the last two lorries backed into the hold. Within minutes the stern ramp is raised. We embark.

Black exhaust bellows from the vents and colors the expanding distance between ship and port. From two massive MAN diesel engines, this fossil-fuel-metabolizing monster exudes vibration and noise, nitrogen, and carbon. The trade-off for such pollution is the extension of terrestrial road surfaces; that is, a mobile platform linking asphalt-laced lands across the open sea. Built in the shipyards of Ambelaki, in the very straights of Salamis where Greeks with wooden triremes powered by wind and muscle were victorious over Persians, this steel ferry, at less than 2,000 tons, accommodates up to one hundred automobiles. It is among the smallest of the conventional ferries in the fleet. Yet, there is more to the *Apollon Hellas* than a moving parking lot—bar, salon, theatre, seaside sundeck, all are here.[1]

Diesel exhaust forces us to relocate to the starboard railing. The ferry moves along the northern portion of the passage between the coast of Galatas and Poros, which gives the pine-covered island its name: *Poros* means *passage*. Alongside runs, at a quickening pace, the southern shore of the island: the Naval Yard, the first of a young nation-state to be built in 1830, the neighborhood of Perlia, the villas on Boudouri, the formerly pine-covered slopes of Neorion, scorched bare by fire in June of 2007, and Russian Bay. Within this sandy anchorage, with its ruined warehouses and bakeries, the Russian fleet maintained dockyards in the nineteenth century. Beyond, the promontory is uninhabited. Over the rise above Russian Bay lies the waste treatment facility for the island. Metabolizing excrement, it envelopes the surrounding lands with its smell. Who would go there, much less choose to dwell there? Thus, it annexes the nearby ground with its malodorous vapors.

We turn the headland of Nedha and thread a course through the narrows. Across the open waters to the north a heat haze hangs over Aegina. I recall to my family the yellowish-brown brume that in summer would escape from Athens into the gulf and envelope Aegina.[2] Twenty years ago these pollutants

---

1 Constructed by the Vassiliadis Brothers, the *Apollon Hellas* was launched on the Ides of March, 1990 under the name *Georgios*, and was later renamed *Sun Beach* prior to attaining the appellation of the Greek sun god in 1999.

2 Güsten et al. (1988).

acquired the shape of a cloud—the *nephos*. Emitted by cars, trucks, ships, and power plants crowding Attic shores, plains, and mountains, the smog cloud would form above the Attic basin. There it would remain, enclosed by the heights of Aigaleo, Parnitha, Penteli, and Hymettus. Largely comprised of nitrogen oxides, ozone, and particulate matter, this cloud would with higher temperatures take on darker hues. The *nephos* brought to the fore the matter of breathable air for the whole of Attica and the Saronic Gulf. Its effects were etched in lungs, trees, and marble. Under the cloud of exhaust, asthma rates skyrocketed. Shrouded within ozone mists, pines turned brown with the chlorotic mottling of their needles. Washed by acid rains, the Parthenon lost some of its sparkle.[3] The greater Athens metropolis marked its territory with its own pollution.

Starboard; the abandoned Dána Lighthouse sits upon the point just above the shoreline on a water-carved exposure of rock. A round, glass-enclosed lantern, raised upon a square tower, raised upon a stone rectangle, from 1870 until it was snuffed out by German forces during World War II, a dioptric, kerosene lamp cast a white light 20 kilometers through clear skies into the gulf.[4] A solarized beacon elevated upon a metal tower—a secondary aid to those who navigate through screens and electronics—eventually rendered the old lighthouse obsolete amid increasing opaque skies.

The helmsman takes a wide arc into the sea lane before steering toward the heights of Methana. Part of the great volcanic arc of the Aegean, the peninsula harbors upwards of thirty volcanoes.[5] Ovid spoke of one. In the *Metamorphoses*, he mentions a steep, high hill that was once a level plain.[6] As if positioned upon inflated bellows, a primeval inferno lifted the land, rendering it uninhabitable to plants and animals alike. Thus, the volcano annexed the plain. Strabo, in the *Geography*, states that the heat and smell of sulphur made the area unapproachable by day. By night, the mountain exhibited itself to a great distance. The sea boiled hundreds of meters from shore and was turbid to an even greater distance.[7] Thus, the volcano seized volumes of air and sea. Today, this dome is known as Kaimeno Vouno.

A plastic sack full of rubbish is blown from the upper deck, swerves in a vortex of wind just beyond reach, and is carried off into the boundless blue. Over the next two years a survey of garbage accumulation on the seafloor in this portion of gulf will dredge up the densest concentrations of benthic marine

---

3 See Cohen (1974).
4 It was relit in 1948 and updated in the 1950s; De Wire and Reyes-Perigioudakis (2010, 75).
5 D'Alessandro et al. (2008).
6 XV, 296–306.
7 1.3.18.

litter in Greece, 90 per cent plastic.[8] With our garbage we terrestrials appropriate the sea.

A thousand industrial plants, shipyards, refineries, and military installations from Elefsina Bay in the north to Piraeus in the south dirty the Saronic Gulf with less biodegradable forms of excrement. From Elefsina to Skaramagas to Perama to Keratsini to Piraeus, over 75 kilometers of shipping terminals, berths, piers, and harbor moles trace a hardened bulwark between the terrestrial and aquatic, transgressed singly by the former (but that is changing). Until the mid-1990s, the untreated sewage outfall of Athens, domestic and industrial, flowed at a rate of about 600,000 cubic meters a day into the Saronic Gulf from Karatsini.[9] A nearby fertilizer plant added solid and liquid waste until 1979.[10] Wastewater, urban runoff, and fertilizers release microbes, heavy metals, and other contaminants into the sea. Not all disperses into the gulf and the Aegean beyond; much settles into the sediments of the seabed, only to be stirred up by marine life.[11] The nearshore benthic ecosystem of the northern gulf has been radically transformed.[12] Toxicology studies on mussels in the area have detected carcinogenetic compounds such as polycyclic aromatic hydrocarbons (PAH).[13] Even with the necessary efforts to curb it, such pollution reaches ahead of itself into the future.

My four-year-old son stares into the shimmering waters south of Aegina. I tell him the story told by Pausanias of how the gulf came by its name, Saronic.[14] In relentless pursuit of his object, a doe, Saron, progeny of Poseidon, third king of Troizen, dove into the sea. He swam into the open gulf to the point of exhaustion and his own peril. Unable to relinquish his ambition to slay the doe, the king drowned. Why did he not turn back? Hubris, pride, confidence in excess; Saron was blind to dangers, present and future. In the waters south of the straits soiled by the blood of the fallen dead at Salamis; near Psyttaleia island, site of one of Europe's largest waste treatment facilities, site of a former prison for exiled political dissidents of the last century, and ground

---

8 See Ioakeimidis et al. (2014). These researchers suggest that water circulation in the gulf traps garbage from the metropolitan area of Athens, leading to its eventual deposition in the depths of the west. On plastics in the Mediterranean, see Segment 19. On the archaeology of marine litter, see Arnshav (2014), Pétursdóttir (2017).

9 A massive sewage treatment plant on Psyttaleia island went into operation in 1994. On pollution from the untreated outflow and its afterlife, see Makra et al. (2001), Theodorou, and Perissoratis (1991); also Kapsimalis et al. (2014), Scoullos et al. (2007).

10 Angelidis and Grimanis (1989).

11 Kapsimalis et al. (2014).

12 See Fatta et al. (1997).

13 Valavanidis et al. (2008), Vlahogianni et al. (2007); for the Aegean, see Gatidou, Vassalou, and Thomaidis (2010).

14 2.30.7.

fouled perhaps by the blood of Persians killed by order of Aristides,[15] the *Agia Zoni II* will go down. Five years from now, this single-hulled tanker of 91 meters—the very same length as this ferry—will sink with 2,200 tons of crude oil and 370 tons of marine fuel. From its hull, built in the Lindenau shipyard in Kiel in the 1970s, oil will seep into these waters, emulsify within its volumes, rise to the surface, and coat beaches, headlands, and birdlife far beyond the limits of its steel tanks. Traces of oil sludge will enter into fish, shellfish, and the humans that consume them. Fouled by hydrocarbons, heavy metals, and plastics, even these storied waters lose something of their shimmer.[16]

The *Apollon Hellas* slows as it nears Loutra, the modern spa-town of Methana. On a broad, concrete pier, five cars and perhaps two dozen people with their possessions wait to board. White turbulence is churned by the propellers as the ferry goes through its docking maneuvers. Over a century ago, James Frazer's dragoman claimed the steamers in this bay made the sharks leave in search of calmer waters near Epidaurus.[17] Steam ships took possession of the briny domain of some aquatic life. Now there are no calmer waters to be found.

With their exhaust fumes, cars and their drivers appropriate the hold of this ship; with the fetor of excrement, a treatment facility annexes a promontory; with garbage, sewage, heavy metals, oil, terrestrial entities take possession of aquatic volumes, bodies of marine life, underlying sediments, the blue below the brine formerly held to be *res nullius*, property of no one. Reaching ahead of the associated events by fouling and, thereby, claiming future habitats of those who have yet to be born, these annexations are growing.[18] From car, to ship, to waters near, volcanoes beyond, to Attica and the gulf, to the Mediterranean, to the earth; let us rehearse these and other escalations.

From the beginnings of the Neolithic, these shores had witnessed the evolution of terrain defined in the form of a patch of ground delimited by labor and berm.[19] Here, enclosures delimiting inside from out, self from other, proliferated. These old lands were privy to the definition of waters coursing in its streams and at its springs, through channels and aqueducts.[20] Here, soil and

---

15 On the archaeology of the island, see Petrákos (2005); on the identification of Psyttaleia with Leipsokoutali, see Wallace (1969b).

16 The Aboriginal aesthetic of *bir'yun*, "shimmer," amplifies the brilliant glint of sun on the water to the vibrancy of the world around us, which draws upon one's ability to register, that is, behold and experience, ancestral power. The loss of biodiversity is, for Deborah Bird Rose, akin to a world losing its shimmer (2017).

17 1898 III, 288.

18 Throughout this segment, I have been following an argument developed by Michel Serres (2011), appropriation through pollution.

19 See Segment 20.

water have been fouled by the blood of thousands. There, a plain and its surroundings—air and sea—were annexed by a volcano. *Oikos* and polis were not without their malodorous vapors; the stink of excrement, the stench of tanneries, the fetor of death. (Whether or not these, along with the malarious mists over marshes, gave rise to a miasmatic conception of a defined cloud prior to the twentieth century is open to debate.)[21] A patch of land, a volume of water, and a pocket of air, thus defined, are subject to appropriation by contaminating them with one's own filth. Although the winds blew and the currents shifted, these areas were always relatively containable and defined.

With the *nephos*, the atmospheric milieu for entire basins and gulfs came to be seen as losable and in need of care. The *nephos* claimed the atmosphere within and above the whole bowl of northern Attica; that is, until the rains washed the cloud over the streets and buildings of Athens and into the sea or the winds dispersed it over the Saronic Gulf to be diffused into the beyond. Objects like the *nephos*, or the coming *Agia Zoni II* oil spill, do not obey terrestrial ground rules; they not only sweep away the old borders between Athens and Aegina, Troizen and Epidaurus, but also those of the Greek nation-state. Increasing atmospheric carbon is emitted from here and, even more so, from elsewhere; thus, polluters from here and elsewhere occupy here as everywhere.

We set out from Loutra and begin to round the Methana peninsula. My four-year-old son urges us to climb to the upper deck. We find seats near the portside railing. Agricultural terraces, now abandoned, drape the coastal slopes northeast of Loutra and step up the eastern flank of the Kossona lava dome to so vertiginous an angle as to, from this distance, resemble ladders. The density of terracing suggests the magnitude of human manipulation. Methana terraces are polychronic—in places they may be ancient in form, at others they ebbed and flowed over generations.[22] The ladder-like terraces of the highest elevations seem to have been constructed in a short burst of investment around the beginning of the last century.[23] And yet, the agency required to harden entire coastlines, to change the composition of the earth's atmosphere, to affect the temperature and chemistry of the oceans and seas emerges as something bigger-than-monstrous, something that has grown beyond *oikos*, polis, nation, Leviathan.

---

20 Even if the Romans maintained waters as *res nullus*, they were co-opted for fountains and agriculture (see Segment 7).

21 For Sloterdijk, one can point to a definitive historical moment when a defined sphere of air was decoupled from the surrounding atmosphere by being rendered unbreathable and thus forced a new level of explication "for the climatic and atmospheric premises of human existence" (2016, 97): Ypres, April 22, 1915.

22 James, Mee, and Taylor (1994), Mee and Forbes (1997, 27 and 28).

23 Forbes (2007, 78).

We, nearly eight billion humans entangled with trillions of other things, now rival volcanoes, oceans, tectonic plates with a comparable collective agency.

We gaze at the passing volcanoes before us. Our collective humanity cannot be measured against Ovid or Strabo's rising lava dome on the northwest coast of Methana. The scale is too small. The range is too local. The eruption of Krakatoa in 1883 caused a rise in barometric pressure across Europe, followed by "magnificent sunlight effects, lurid skies, prolonged dawns, and lengthened twilights."[24] The Javan volcano of Mount Tambora killed an estimated 170,000 people, along with an untallied number of other animals, as well as plants, insects, and microbes; it also produced vivid sunsets across Greece in 1815.[25] Claiming 9,000 square kilometers of land, the volcanic fissure of Laki, which erupted in Iceland in 1783, spewed massive amounts of sulphur dioxide and devastated crops across Europe.[26] Who can fail to recognize the equipotency of these catastrophes in Fukushima or Chernobyl? After the nuclear disaster at Fukushima, which displaced 160,000 people, low concentrations of radiative pollution from the lava-producing meltdown were detected in Athens.[27] After the Chernobyl eruption, which seized 2,600 square kilometers of land in what is now appropriately called the exclusion zone, radionuclides were deposited over the whole of Greece and elsewhere.[28] With increasing number, weight, and extent, automobiles and exhaust fumes, industries and pollution, cities and garbage, transform and annex progressively larger areas of land, volumes of water, pockets of air.

In growing beyond locality, beyond Leviathan, those who live around the Saronic Gulf have joined other human populations with their trillions of things. Annexed areas of *terra firma*, seized water columns, and purloined air pockets now encompass continental swaths of land, the whole of the sea, the entirety of the atmosphere. A carbon-fueled capitalism has appropriated all by changing the composition of the global atmosphere. Absorption of this CO_2 by the Mediterranean and the oceans beyond changes the chemistry of all waters.[29] Acidification appropriates aquatic habitats to the exclusion of other species. As the global atmosphere warms, the deep is being emptied of its diversity here, there,

24 Sturdy (1884).
25 It would impact weather for the remainder of the year of Waterloo and for the whole of 1816; Hamilton (2010); also see Krafft (1993).
26 Krafft (1993).
27 Kritidis et al. (2012).
28 Petropoulos et al. (2001).
29 Here we encounter a world object in the sense of Serres (1995a, 15–16) or a hyperobject in the sense of Morton (2013), through the massive distribution of CO_2 to the point of taking on global dimensions.

everywhere.[30] With this new reality, the fate of everyone around this gulf is tied to the fate of everyone around the earth. For our collective humanity to rework geology globally and thus write what becomes of it into the 4.6-billion-year geostory of the world, the proportionality of what it is to be human had to upend. This rupture corresponds with the emergence of the supermonstrous, the hyperteratical, and the coming groundswell will not subside from the low plains or the hardened bulwarks around these shores; neither Hera nor Poseidon can save what has become of us.

As the slopes of northeastern Methana begin to recede into the distance, my wife and I take note of the abandoned agricultural terraces that cover the slopes below Kypseli, the entire extent of the ridge above Agios Georgios, and everywhere in-between.[31] These formerly cultivated slopes were released to ruin in the wake of World War II with a massive exodus to Athens and abroad, fueled by the lure of increasing options that came with expanding urban densities.[32] For those who remained, motorized equipment could not cope with the narrow terraced fields, and there were few viable paths apart from the tourist industry. Isolated villas and holiday homes now dot an estranged world of Arcadian nature, vacations, and tourism. Today, few Methanites live primarily by agriculture,[33] and the operative conditions that underwrote agrarian cultures for 400 generations have ceased to delineate what it is to be human. There, as elsewhere across these shores, the modes of living inaugurated over eight millennia ago have drawn to a close.[34] Against this background of ceded obligation, of agrarian ruin, of nonetheless persistent memories, some of the differences are apparent.

Every human routine, from flying to Greece, driving a car to Poros, taking this ferry to Aegina, or buying bottled water can be linked to the supermonstrous.[35] No one is absolved of responsibility. Looking to the headland, having walked, driven, and read through these old lands, it is clear that the grounds for production are no longer visible in the way that they formerly were. So very few are tethered to the soil by work. Few lifeways are chosen on the basis of agrarian inheritance; we only speak of constant innovation. Lifeways and values are defined less by scarcity than overabundance, less by hardship than comfort, less by seasonality than untimeliness, less by singularity than pervasiveness, less by what is here than what is distant. Alienated from the humus that

---

30 Lacoue-Labarthe et al. (2016).
31 On the abandonment of the agrarian landscape on Methana, see Forbes (1997, 116; 2007, 94).
32 Forbes (2007, 95).
33 Ibid.
34 Witmore (2017).
35 Sloterdijk (2013, 227–28).

begets the human, from our old lands in the ways we formerly lived, we pass here in ease at a comfortable distance.

Into that progressive image of a homogeneous time which feeds into a technocratic accelerated capitalism,[36] there is a need for interruption. And while we all struggle to work out what regime can replace carbon-fueled capitalism, we do not confront a wholly autodidactic situation. Before us is a bewildering repository from which to learn what it is to inhabit and live after carbon-capitalism,[37] for memories of other *modus vivendi*, for better and worse, are gathered and to be engaged throughout these old lands. A harlequin ensemble of upland forests, lowland fields, and pastural margins, that accommodates life and love, death and ruin, including what will become of the super-modern carbon economy that is failing us everywhere. Held by the terraces before us, resilient soils continue to develop by accretion, superposition, symbiosis, even without human care. Such reliable land cannot be appropriated. "One belongs to it," as Bruno Latour rightly points out, "it belongs to no one."[38] From the vantage point of the sea, it becomes clear that we must reform roots, not only into the soil that is here, but into the whole of the world that we all share.

The deck beneath our feet undulates almost imperceptibly at 14 knots, the speed of a brisk canter. Upon this medium-sized ship whose vast weight dulls the ebb and flow of the sea, one is aware less of what Whitman read as the sea's poem. No winds, no currents, no weather. What grounded being and gave proportionality to human modes of life has been dulled through an inappreciable distance that has less to do with whatever height lies between the waterline and this high deck than the rising aquatic temperatures and lowering pH that arise through the carbon cycle. Here we only feel the driving force of the engines churning ever forward. Like Saron, in possession of a hubris that refuses to heed the warnings, will we press ahead to our own unavoidable peril? Will the gales of winter, the high waves, the rising waters assert themselves, so that the sea's poem becomes that of an elegy?

36 Stengers (2015).
37 For an appeal to come down to earth, see Latour (2018).
38 2018, 92.

Bibliography

Angelidis, M., and P.A. Grimanis, 1989. Geochemical partitioning of Co, Cr, Fe, Sc and Zn in polluted and non-polluted marine sediments. *Environmental Pollution* 62, 31–46.

Arnshav, M. 2014. The freedom of the seas: Untapping the archaeological potential of marine debris. *Journal of Maritime Archaeology* 9(1), 1–25.

Cohen, D. 1974. Polluted Parthenon. *New Scientist* 28, 671–72.

D'Alessandro, W., L. Brusca, K. Kyriakopoulos, G. Michas, G. Papadakis. 2008. Methana, the westernmost active volcanic system of the South Aegean Arc (Greece): Insight from fluids geochemistry. *Journal of Volcanology and Geothermal Research* 178, 818–28.

De Wire, E., and D. Reyes-Pergioudakis. 2010. *The lighthouses of Greece.* Sarasota, FL: Pineapple Press.

Fatta, D., K.J. Haralambous, A. Papadopoulos, M. Loizidou, and N. Spyrellis. 1997. An evaluation of the pollution level in Saronic Gulf waters. *Journal of Environmental Science and Health, Part A* 32(8), 2403–14.

Forbes, H. 1997. Turkish and modern Methana. In C. Mee and H.A. Forbes (eds.), *A rough and rocky place: The landscape and settlement history of the Methana Peninsula, Greece.* Liverpool: Liverpool University Press. 101–17.

Forbes, H. 2007. *Meaning and identity in a Greek landscape: An archaeological ethnography.* Cambridge, MA: Cambridge University Press.

Frazer, J.G. 1898. *Pausanias's Description of Greece.* 6 vols. London: Macmillan & Co.

Gatidou, G., E. Vassalou, and N.S. Thomaidis. 2010. Bioconcentration of selected endocrine disrupting compounds in the Mediterranean mussel, *Mytilus galloprovincialis. Marine Pollution Bulletin* 60(11), 2111–16.

Güsten, H., G. Heinrich, T. Cvitas, L. Klasing, B. Rustic, D.P., Lalas, M. Petrakis. 1988. Photochemical formation and transport of ozone in Athens, Greece. *Atmospheric Environment* 22, 1855–61.

Hamilton, J. 2010. The lure of volcanoes. *History Today* 60(7), 34–41.

Ioakeimidis, C., C. Zeri, H. Kaberi, M. Galatchi, K. Antoniadis, N. Streftaris, F. Galgani, E. Papathanassiou, and G. Papatheodorou. 2014. A comparative study of marine litter on the seafloor of coastal areas in the Eastern Mediterranean and Black Seas. *Marine Pollution Bulletin* 89(1–2), 296–304.

James, P.A., C.B. Mee, and G.J. Taylor. 1994. Soil erosion and the archaeological landscape of Methana, Greece. *Journal of Field Archaeology* 21(4), 395–416.

Kapsimalis, V., I.P. Panagiotopoulos, P. Talagani, I. Hatzianestis, H. Kaberi, G. Rousakis, T. D. Kanellopoulos, and G.A. Hatiris. 2014. Organic contamination of surface sediments in the metropolitan coastal zone of Athens, Greece: Sources, degree, and ecological risk. *Marine Pollution Bulletin* 80, 312–24.

Krafft, M. 1993. *Volcanoes: Fire from the earth.* London: Thames & Hudson.

Kritidis, P., H. Florou, K. Eleftheriadis, N. Evangeliou, M. Gini, M. Sotiropoulou, E. Diapouli, and S. Vratolis. 2012. Radioactive pollution in Athens, Greece due to the Fukushima nuclear accident. *Journal of Environmental Radioactivity* 114, 100–4.

Lacoue-Labarthe, T., P.A.L.D. Nunes, P. Ziveri, M. Cinar, F. Gazeau, J.M. Hall-Spencer, N. Hilmi, P. Moschella, A. Safa, and D. Sauzade. 2016. Impacts of ocean acidification in a warming Mediterranean sea: An overview. *Regional Studies in Marine Science* 5, 1–11.

Latour, B. 2018. *Down to earth: Politics in the new climate regime.* Cambridge: Polity Press.

Makra, A., M. Thessalou-Legaki, J. Costelloe, A. Nicolaidou, and B.F. Keegan. 2001. Mapping the pollution gradient of the Saronikos Gulf benthos prior to the operation of the Thens sewage treatment plant, Greece. *Marine Pollution Bulletin* 42, 1417–419.

Mee, C., and H. Forbes (eds.). 1997. *A rough and rocky place: The landscape and settlement history of the Methana Peninsula.* Liverpool: Liverpool University Press.

Morton, T. 2013. *Hyperobjects: Philosophy and ecology after the end of the world.* Minneapolis, MN: University of Minnesota Press.

Petrákos, V.Ch. 2005. I archaiología tis Psyttáleias, *O Méntor* 18(74–75), 33–72.

Petropoulos, N.P., M.J. Anagnostakis, E.P. Hinis, and S.E. Simopoulos. 2001. Geographical mapping and associated fractal analysis of the long-lived Chernobyl fallout radionuclides in Greece. *Journal of Environmental Radioactivity* 53(1), 59–66.

Pétursdóttir, Þ. 2017. Climate change? Archaeology and Anthropocene. *Archaeological Dialogues* 24(2), 175–205.

Rose, D.B. 2017. Shimmer: When all you love is being trashed. In A.L. Tsing, N. Bubandt, E. Gan, and H.A. Swanson (eds.), *Arts of living on a damaged planet: Ghosts and monsters of the Anthropocene.* Minneapolis, MN: University of Minnesota Press. 51–63.

Scoullos, M.J., A. Sakellari, K. Giannopoulou, V. Paraskevopoulou, and M. Dassenakis. 2007. Dissolved and particulate metal levels in the Saronikos Gulf, in 2004: The impact of the primary wastewater treatment plant of Psittalia. *Desalination* 210, 98–109.

Serres, M. 1995a. *The natural contract.* Ann Arbor, MI: University of Michigan Press.

Serres, M. 2011. *Malfeasance: Appropriation through pollution?* Stanford, CA: Stanford University Press.

Sloterdijk, P. 2013. *In the world interior of capital: For a philosophical theory of globalization.* Cambridge: Polity Press.

Sloterdijk, P. 2016. *Foams: Spheres III.* South Pasadena, CA: Semiotext(e).

Stengers, I. 2015. *In catastrophic times: Resisting the coming barbarism* (trans. A. Goffey). Ann Arbor, MI: Open Humanities Press.

Sturdy, E.W. 1884. The volcanic eruption of Krakatau. *Atlantic Monthly* 5, 385–91.

Theodorou, A.J., and C. Perissoratis. 1991. Environmental considerations for design of the Athens sea outfall, Saronikos Gulf, Greece. *Environmental Geology* 17(3), 233–48.

Valavanidis, A., T. Vlachogianni, S. Triantafillaki, M. Dasennakis, F. Androutsos, and M. J. Scoullos. 2008. Polycyclic aromatic hydrocarbons in surface seawater and in indigenous mussels (*Mytilus galloprovincialis*) from coastal areas of the Saronikos Gulf (Greece). *Estuarine, Coastal and Shelf Science* 79, 733–39.

Vlahogianni, T., M. Dassenakis, M.J. Scoullos, and A. Valavanidis. 2007. Integrated use of biomarkers (superoxide dismutase, catalase and lipid peroxidation) in mussels *Mytilus galloprovincialis* for assessing heavy metals' pollution in coastal areas from the Saronikos Gulf of Greece. *Marine Pollution Bulletin* 54, 1361–71.

Wallace, P.W. 1969b. Psyttaleia and the trophies of the Battle of Salamis. *American Journal of Archaeology* 73(3), 293–303.

Witmore, C. 2017. Things are the grounds of all archaeology. In J.M. Blaising, J. Driessen, J.P. Legendre, and L. Olivier (eds.), *Clashes of times: The contemporary past as a challenge for archaeology.* Louvain: Louvain University Press. 231–46.

EPILOGUE

On chorography

When Strabo prioritized the positioning of places and the distances between them above other aspects of chorography, first-hand knowledge of the wider inhabited world was hard to come by.[1] Built upon the texts of others, always valued as trustworthy to greater and lesser degrees, this knowledge could only be improved through direct experience where possible. By stressing distance and position, he might encourage others to observe similar concerns; eventually, some degree of consistency could be established in a world of heterogeneous spaces. Now, at a time when dimensions are known with millimeter precision, when positions are tethered to a homogeneous ground spreading out in every direction, we find ourselves in desperate need of that heterogeneity.[2] If chorography opens a path towards manifold spaces then it is in part because as a literary craft it prefigures that preordained image of ground interpretation where every land is apprehended from the angle of a quarter turn. Ancient descriptions of Greece offer perspectives on these old lands where objects encountered on the ground display themselves from within themselves.[3]

Ancient chorographers are not without their differences. Strabo, who embraced the term "chorography," championed a form of ethnographic historiography that situated Greece as a part of the common world house or *oikoumene*.[4] In so doing, he seems to have derived his knowledge of Greece in large part from texts, rather than *autopsy*, or participant immersion with a locale. Such an engagement with the land in its absence forms a strong

---

1 *Geography* 2.5.1; 10.3.5; 8.3.17.
2 I make these points fully aware of the archaeological emphasis given to these qualities; see, for example, Snodgrass (1987, 67–92); also see Hutton (2005, 81).
3 The alternative, of course, is for objects to show themselves from without, which is how the Modern Age, as Heidegger (2002) indicated, envisions the world as picture (also Sloterdijk 2013, 94–7).
4 Pretzler (2005).

contrast to Pausanias. Drawing upon a periegetic tradition of in-situ-derived description, where architecture, monuments, artworks, inscriptions, histories, borders, and religious practices were encountered along the road, within the *temenos*, or behind high walls, Pausanias, as discussed elsewhere in this book, presented a profusion of grounded detail.[5] Supplied with the ten books of the *Periegesis*, the reader was left to combine its nine regions into a fuller picture of Greece.[6] Faced with the fact that Pausanias described neither his practices nor his modes of articulation, we may well embrace chorography as an apposite characterization.[7]

Offering a model for the strong observation of locality, the *Periegesis* served as a guide book for antiquarian depictions of Greece in the seventeenth, eighteenth, and early nineteenth centuries.[8] Spon and Wheler, Dodwell, Gell, Leake, and Pouqueville, among others, invested in the transcription of the shape and character of a region from the bridle path, with Pausanias and Strabo in hand. Wrapped into their thick descriptions were matters of toponymy, botany, agrarian practice, excerpts from ancient authors, philological source criticism, and digressions into the political state of the country. These antiquarians were not without their differences of opinion, emphasis, and prejudice, already well covered in this book.[9] Yet among their common concerns were questions of empirical detail, authenticity, and faithful witnessing, which are longstanding attributes of chorographical practice. With their eyes for old things, for the lie of the land, they forged connections with history, they pondered questions of loss and ruin, yet this was hardly severed from life or its present grounds, which permeated these texts. Not all of these antiquarians generated what they would call chorography. Gell and Leake were more topographers, concerned with questions of cartographic mapping, calculation and the measurement of distances, in making initial steps that will go towards standardizing how archaeologists and others will approach regions.[10] That chorography should eventually fall out of favor relates to the way in which regions come to be seen.[11]

---

5 Concerning Pausanias and the *Periegesis*, see Segments 16 and 22.

6 Elsner (2001), Hutton (2005).

7 See Diller (1956, 86) with regard to a tenth-century scholium that may describe Pausanias's text as chorography.

8 Pretzler (2013, 130–50).

9 Concerning antiquarian engagements, see Segments 3, 8, 14, 24, and 26.

10 Shanks and Witmore (2010, 101–2).

11 There is, of course, a rich tradition of chorography in modern Greece that did not wane completely with the professionalization of fields like archaeology. Antonios Miliarakis's *Geographia Politiki* (1886) contains what he describes as detailed chorographic descriptions of the thirty-two municipalities of the prefecture of the Argolid and Corinthia. This is literally a work that is about defining space; from what are quite detailed topographical descriptions of the shape and character of the land and coast, agricultural areas, land use, imports and exports. Still, for

After the publication of maps based on triangulation around 1830, every space will come to be preconditioned by the two-dimensional projection. Before the privileged viewer, the measured form of the Peloponnese affords an encompassing view that precludes anyone wayfinding in uncharted uplands, calculating distances with a pocket watch, or gauging angles with a compass for themselves.[12] In standing apart from the map, one is also lured into disregarding their true lot alongside other things on the ground—this compulsion is what Heidegger termed the "forgetfulness of being," which came to predominate visually enhanced human engagements with the world.[13] Yet, to behold the image of the land is not to behold the land itself. Anyone who reads Pausanias or Strabo while withholding the imposition of a view from without should understand the error of only seeing this region as a continuous surface.

By placing to one side any preconceptions of a "homogeneous, arbitrarily divisible representational space" where all points are accorded "equal value," and returning to the ground among actual things, it may be possible to release our imagination towards the heterogeneity of spaces.[14] Still, such a phenomenological feat of non-cartographically-enabled perception only goes so far. Requisite is a different understanding of space, one grounded in and among derelict enclosures and forsaken passes, exhumed foundations and reconstituted gates.[15] If different spaces arise from the propensities of a throne room to separate an audience and their lord, or from the encompassing nature of a tomb or a berm between field plots, or from the linearity of a shore or the subaqueous volumes of the sea, then space can be conceived as a quality within, and a verve between, things—that is, within and between doorways, walls, and occupants of a megaron; within and between tombs, springs, soil, and agrarians; within and between shoreline, wooden fishing boats, fish, and fishers. In this, it would be unwise to ignore the sense of space that arises with a map in hand; the point is to situate any engagement with the projection as one mode of generating space among manifold spaces.

What the ancients do for *chôros*, the antiquarians, and heirs to their tradition, do for *chôra*. Spon was disposed towards what had become of ancient monuments. Both Gell and Leake invested in the panoramic and diagrammatic

Miliarakis chorography has its sharply defined limits, for a different term, "hydrography," was to be used in his discussions of seas or anything worthy of the title "river."

12 Latour (1986, 1987); Witmore (2013a, 142–43).
13 Heidegger termed this *Seinsvergessenheit* (2008b); also see Sloterdijk (2014, 79).
14 Sloterdijk (2013, 27).
15 My views here and throughout on the nature of space and land have been at variance with those expressed by the anthropologist Tim Ingold. I neither share Ingold's attempt to deny the existence of space (2009) nor reduce land to something merely homogeneous and quantifiable, the "lowest common denominator of the phenomenal world" (1993, 153–54).

registration of historically charged ground.[16] To scratch at the surface of the history of human inhabitation, while remaining true to a lived encounter in the present, is to indirectly gauge the depth and longevity of the countryside. It is through the cascade of antiquarian texts that one may glean differences in the description of a ruined temple, whether in the presence of inscriptions turned building blocks or the absence of columns carved into animal troughs. It is through the cascade that one may track mutations in village form or fluctuations in land tenure. By virtue of the juxtaposition of these texts one is afforded some sense of change, which gains relief against those durations and metamorphoses encountered among objects of the land: the fallen architraves that now retain soil washed by primordial waters that continue to course through Troizen groves; the upland valley that receives saltational accretions through centuries of seasonal erosion; the long-buried surfaces that return to the sun and repay the touch of the poet Sefaris at Asine. Such an archive directs us to return to the *chôra*, that inexhaustible, polychronic ensemble where the wreckage of the past piles up, where life is engendered, where we encounter time.[17]

There is something to old words that has an unsettling effect. Chorography as a concept is not near. If one envisages a commitment to both *chôros* (a distinct space or place) and *chôra* (land and countryside, receptacle and procreator), then an author is afforded a measure of freedom with respect to matters of emphasis and coverage. Chorography offers another way from that consistent path to production opened by standardization, consistency of method, and routinized practices. Its fidelity is not to an economy that portions out the undividable to fit predetermined boxes held in place by scholastic divisions of knowledge. Driven by curiosity, the autonomy of movement demanded by following the object to where it might lead generates a space for creative possibility; one that is true to the object encountered without its predefinition through disciplinary circumscription. This freedom also comes from the fact that as an ancient genre, chorography was never fully circumscribed, and therefore it continues to hold productive potential. Likewise, in the seventeenth and eighteenth centuries no divisions of scholarly labor were applied because the genre existed before scholarly labor's divisions applied. Pausanias, Strabo, and the antiquarians, are not relegated to the status of sources for the way things were, but as contemporaries, as examples of how to move, what to observe (whether that follows on what they witnessed or what they failed to see), and how one might

---

16 Shanks and Witmore (2010, 102–3).
17 Unlike space, which is characterized by higher redundancy through the character of surfaces, roads, hallways, paths, forms, time is far less redundant, far more idiosyncratic (see Serres 1995b, 116).

reconceive of spaces. If this is the timely use of an untimely genre, then it is because chorography is a pre-disciplinary genre for a post-disciplinary time.

⤙

I first set foot in the Eastern Peloponnese twenty-five years ago; beckoned by its storied citadels, Mycenae and Tiryns; enticed by its legendary cities, Nafplion and Argos. I would later return to undertake research for a dissertation by revisiting an archaeological survey in the Southern Argolid, seeking to understand changes that had occurred in the land over the previous generation among communities leaving behind agrarianism, herding, and fishing for service industries and tourism. I sought to verify what was encountered, to understand, assess, and expand field practices, and to reimagine the ways archaeologists document and write about regions.[18] Under the influence of phenomenology and science studies I was drawn to questions of engagement, articulation, and manifestation. I was perplexed by how the things encountered on the ground were transformed into material pasts and, in the production of knowledge, packaged for the pages.[19] With Michael Shanks, I was lured to the antiquarian tradition of William Camden in Britain, Ole Worm in Denmark, and, later, William Martin Leake in Greece for other examples of how archaeologists might approach regional description, refusing to separate what has become of the past from the present into which it gathers.[20] With Bjørnar Olsen, I began to wonder whether objects regarded as evidence of the past were accorded their "rightful share," whether in terms of what they are, what they bring to the encounter, or what memories they hold.[21]

This chorography has emerged through repeated and habitual engagements with land through journeys to monuments and ruins, movement along major roads and well-trodden paths. Later, seeking out those ignored expanses in-between, myriad ventures unfolded amid field and grove. Trailing in the footsteps of Pausanias, Evilya Çelebi, the antiquarians, Frazer, and archaeologists such as Michael Jameson, itineraries were formulated, added, and cut. Through repeated crossings I documented field scatters, exposed wall stone, the line of the trail. I detailed these field enquiries in day notebooks. I sought to carefully

18 This work focused on the Argolid Exploration Project (1979–81); Jameson, Runnels, and Van Andel (1994), Runnels, Pullen, and Langdon (1995), Sutton (2001), Van Andel and Runnels (1987), Witmore (2005).

19 Witmore (2004, 2006, 2009); for other work on archaeological knowledge production, see Edgeworth (2006), Lucas (2018, 1–17), Chapman and Wylie (2016).

20 Pearson and Shanks (2001).

21 Olsen (2003, 2010); also Olivier (2008) (English translation, 2011).

describe objects of archaeological concern, and their ground state, particularly their relation to terrace, parcel, trees, signage, and more. I saturated the path with video, photography, illustration, and sound. Later, without these modes of engagement, I returned to contemplate the positive differences made by terraces, open fields, fences raised around archaeological sites. I attempted to revisit areas under different light, at different seasons, to bear witness to the land under variant conditions.[22] Given the demands of an academic schedule, these engagements were relegated largely to summers, an occasional late spring and early fall, a rare winter. Embracing that effective disposition of being there, *in medias res*, I struggled to cultivate the requisite patience to trust that the path and those raw things encountered along its course would come to shape the story; as does the style of writing, which, to borrow the words of Gombrich, establishes a broad horizon of expectation.[23]

What makes objects of experience stand out as worthy of inclusion and therefore objects of contemplation? This question has been asked of the ancients—Pausanias selected only those things that he deemed to be worthy of mention (*axiológótata*), or most worthy of remembering (*málista áxia mnímis*) in the context of history, genealogy, and polytheism rooted in locality.[24] This question has been asked of the antiquarians—Leake was dispatched as a spy for the British military to observe ports, facilities, and fortifications to take surveys and plan such places "to acquire a general knowledge of the face of the country."[25] This chorography opens paths to heterogeneous spaces and times within the Eastern Peloponnese through an engagement with its lands at a time when human relations with *chôra*, environment, the world are undergoing profound and unanticipated changes. Thus, this book was, in addition to the aforementioned considerations, also motivated by a concern for estranged relations with land rising amid massive transformations wrought by the minions of supermodernity. It was written mindful of the supposed compression of distances with new mobilities, which is simply oblivious to the incompressible. It was composed with an awareness of the new climate regime, rising on hopes for learning how to inhabit well, by speaking to the long-term proportionality of existence, human and otherwise, at a time when our sense of it, shaken amid calamity, rests on dubious grounds. It arose out of an understanding that when practical knowledge, no longer sustained by tradition, irreducible to the pages of history, is relegated to Lethe (the river of forgetfulness in Hades), coming down to

---

22 Coming to know a place and creative observation are longstanding attributes of the phenomeno-logical tradition in archaeology; see Tilley (2010); also Bradley (2003).
23 Gombrich (1956, 60).
24 3.11.1.
25 Marsden (1864, 17); concerning Leake, see Segment 14.

shared ground in these old lands allows us to take bearings in our precarious times.

Driving to Corinth from the Canal, walking through the heart of a Roman forum, climbing Acrocorinth, reading descriptions from others, racing along a section of the A7 motorway to destinations south; such experiences are informed by history, theory, practice, and previous engagements, and altogether they nudge one towards particular matters of concern. Academics do not confront these old lands without the literature that stands as a precondition for any experience. However, that literature need not take the place of privilege by always weighing objects with respect to their narrative potential. One must be ready to hesitate in the face of things, to remain open to how an empty tomb might not yield under the weight of relevance that comes with writing. Taking things seriously, as Þora Pétursdóttir has shown, requires one to embrace the risk that follows on sacrificing one's own expectations, by surrendering to the dispositions, the suggestions of things.[26]

I share Alphonso Lingis's aspiration; taking years to be disposed to suggestions, one finds a way through by trusting that a solution will present itself though it may be unknown at the start.[27] Chorography on one level simply directs one to follow the path and to be open to whatever objects suggest themselves within a zone, a theoretical space disposed to suggestions.[28] Thus, the thesis, the idea, the problem is provoked by the thing encountered on the ground, while the zone—agrarian practices, pollution, new mobilities, Lucretian poetics—conditions the angle of approach. Of course, a zone must be grounded in the locale. Central to this chorography is a recursive method, not unlike that articulated by Martin Holbraad,[29] where initial expectations are transformed, even relinquished, in the course of an engagement.[30] At every turn one must be willing to pass on the impulse to mobilize the trellis in support a thesis, the tracks to carry an idea, the abandoned mining village to illustrate a problem.[31] One must cultivate the art of noticing that which is trivial or banal, by drawing out the naively given or un-looked-for textures of land and inhabitation. Under these influences things may declare themselves in ways they may not have otherwise.

There is also something to be said for learning through wayfinding. By following in the footsteps of others or within sites over-saturated with scholarly

26 2012.
27 Lingis (1998).
28 Also see Morton (2013, 140–44).
29 2012.
30 See Pétursdóttir and Olsen (2017).
31 See Edgeworth (2012, 2016).

labor, choices are often laid out before us, though novelty nonetheless abounds. By attempting to find a way along paths long neglected, the orientation to the route taken transforms. Along such a path, obstacles and obstructions, the lay of the land, the bend of hill, the terrace line, "define the choices made."[32] Walking transpires at a different pace, with a slowness that enables an attentiveness to the neglected margins, to seemingly facile details of locality, of flora, of agrarian practice. Without circumscribing both object and approach in advance—an operation characteristic of scientific method—room is left for those chance departures that can occur in the open set aside for the unexpected. Along such segments, the things encountered suggested a purpose, and by walking that route I trusted in that possibility. The route, the pace, and that which calls to the chorographer are more than prompts for discussion or pieces that fit into a particular narrative; here they have been co-participants in the account. Integrated with the movement, at times objects nudge an idea along. At others they disrupt, by demanding digression through simple description. What is worthy of observation ultimately comes with the drawback of uneven details, which can only be judged in light of the purposes for which the description serves.

Such a project eschews mimesis, not method. The word "method" comes from the Greek *meta*, in the sense of after or beyond, and *odos*, the path, the way. Thus, any method involves reflection upon the mode of investigation, and this chorography aspires to remain open to anything one might want to say about a place and anything that a place might suggest about itself.[33] My chorographic methodology is devoted not to application of a theory or consistency of approach, but to an engagement where the solution emerges in being pulled along by the route in direct contact with things. Its disposition was to be as subtle as the situation at hand in hopes that each segment will reveal its unique scenario in a new light. This book asserts that chorography offers an integrated method that tarries by the road, pauses in the field, observes the soil, the trees, the vines, the weeds, that emerges with things, that forms out of land, yet refuses to lose sight of our common lot on Earth.

⁓

These twenty-seven segments are not so much stories of traversed ground as compositions pieced together with the things encountered in the course of traversal. The ins and outs of each segment relate, by and large, to those objects

---

32 Serres (1985, English translation, 2008a, 261).
33 Here, I acknowledge the influence of "Deep Mapping"; see Pearson and Shanks (2001, 162–78); after Heat-Moon (1991).

which determine them—the grave of Humfry Payne or a fence barring entry to the Argive Heraion; the house of Vlasópoulo in Argos or the Land Gate in Anapli. Within each and every segment the argument is carefully interwoven with the journey. A rumination on agrarian patriotism is melded with examples from passing cove, limestone outcrop, terraced slope, or field plot called forth with eight students into the Bedheni Valley. With ideas elicited from *plateia*, coaxed out by ruined fountain, called forth by temple turned quarry turned heritage, the writing of Ancient Corinth weaves a different theory of time into the walk, into the place. Objects also interrupt the movement, break the narrative chain. The bridge, the terrace, the ravine, the grave, the enclosure; all have provoked shifts, connections, and in asserting themselves, one had to contend with them. No chorographer can be attentive to every edifice, every stone, tree, tomb, or agrarian plot they pass. Thus, the shape of the foregoing narrative is also a matter of aesthetics and purpose. As an angle took shape in one segment it came to impact the concerns of others. Chorography must also stay true to the evolution of thought and to learning from the experience.

"What makes a narrative good is not the story itself," asserts Joseph Brodsky, "but what follows what."[34] Field tracks, then weeds, then cairn piles, then cypress boughs, then rubbish, such writing does not avoid those digressions demanded by such objects. As the style of writing has been faithful to things, it is appropriate that what follows, what takes readers into excursus, deviates from what is expected, and does not paper over disjuncture or ambiguity. Though this book unfolds along the road, the path, the dirt track, or rows between trellises, though it encompasses accounts that deal with the succession of moments related to a journey, this chorography is not travelogue. The sequence of the segments taken through these old lands has not been continuous. Though they may seem to coalesce in a two-dimensional sense, some segments are profoundly nonlinear and topological, with ideas crosscutting and interspersing with the pleats and folds of place—where old lines of stone lend their form to subsequent terrace walls, where old plane trees have borne witness to a thousand summers, where an old way is preserved in an agricultural road hemmed in by plots of land and the labors of those who keep them. Segments have been marked by differences of date and tense, with various presents, recollected pasts, and projected futures. Segments have moved back and forth between the ground of the chorographical present and the historical past with earlier travelers. At various turns they have fallen out of time altogether, weaving stories and experiences without the temporal coordinates, broken by discrete memories. Segments shift in and out of different perspectives, but they

34 1992, 38.

are not limited to human interlocutors, for segments have followed with waters, ruination, goats, or the memories of companion animals.

Some readers may be left perplexed when it comes to matters of academic audience: which scholarly readership does this chorography serve? None of the aforementioned concerns are alien to my home field of archaeology; a profession, which, as I stated in the preface, deeply informs this chorography. From another angle, this book might be described as a subtle reworking of Classical Studies, where ancient modes of articulation are every bit as much thoughtful examples for how to proceed in our time, as they are objects of study shut off in their own time. I have also written this chorography with other readers in mind: anthropologists, cultural geographers, philosophers, travelers to Greece, or those who dwell there. I have already stated how, in following alongside objects, I placed my trust in the thing encountered to open thought in its direction. The intensity by which I hold to this obligation prevents me from championing any one field and thereby catering to the interests of any specific readership. Above, I evoked the term "post-disciplinary" in the context of our times. One might well situate this book as "post-disciplinary," if it were not for the fact that this word, with its qualifying prefix, rests uneasily in suggesting the abandonment of what came before while, from it, gaining its meaning.[35] Such words eventually fall to their contraries. There is, to be sure, another question to ask, which helps to frame the issue of readership: for what does this book stand?

This chorography stands in defense of the otherness and integrity of these lands, and the things that comprise them, against approaches that would subject them to compression, oversimplification, sameness. A master of description, the Roman *periegete* was perplexed by the inadequacy of words to capture some objects and practices.[36] Like Pausanias, other chorographers must grapple with their own inevitable shortfalls of expression. The structure and style of the writing is sensitive to the idiosyncrasies of the route. Like the land, there are rough patches, harsh edges, monotonous portions. The shape of the sentence resonates with the textures of the journey and that which exceeds it. Smooth sentences for uniform surfaces; sentences without pause for flowing water. The character of descriptions may quicken or slow with the pace of movement, whether walking, running, riding, driving, within mobile rooms of car, train,

---

35 This gesture would qualify the concept as "modernist," in Latourian (1993) terms; that is, a distinct mode of separating society, culture, or moderns off from things, nature, or the ancients that gains its dynamism from a perpetual repetition of radical breaks with the past where again and again, in ever-overturning forward, it builds upon a successive trajectory of one contradiction after another.

36 Compare 1.38.7 and 5.11.9; also see Elsner (2001, 17–8).

boat, ferry. Still movement is not the only experience of the chorographical present. Some segments are written while sitting at a table or in a theatre. Often demanding clearly demarcated genres—site report, regional history, interpretive expositions that separate theory from application—this chorography has offered an alternative to normal modes of academic writing; something less common among archaeologists.[37] It asks a lot of its readers who must join fully in the journey for the reward of its lessons, which unfold along the path. Still, at every turn points are backed by the anything but "spurious scholarly apparatus of footnotes," which, in continuing with the words of Shanks, "amplify the ebullience of detail with reference to" archaeological, Classical, and historical sources.[38]

Chorography could be considered a style of travel writing. At times, it is not unlike that of Patrick Leigh Fermor or Robert Macfarlane, where through the voice of the first-person one speaks from experience, with honesty, true to the encounter. For what is addressed rests upon my ability to notice and connect. Indeed, one has to reconcile authentic witnessing, what we might understand as empirical fidelity, with a vital and committed authorial voice of our own. Being explicit with your own position is central to the articulation of any chorography. The Eastern Peloponnese has been my "research area" for over a decade, and yet, these are lands through which I have only passed and I have never inhabited; renting rooms, here and there, relying on the hospitality of Greeks and non-Greeks. I follow in the footsteps of others that have lived and died here; others who have loved and fought for this land: ancient geographers, Roman pilgrims, Venetian officials, Ottoman travelers, antiquarians and archaeologists, farmers and fishermen. As an author, a word rooted in Roman law that refers to "the guarantor of authenticity, of loyalty, of an affirmation, of a testimony or an oath," I cannot speak for all.[39]

To claim any representational authority in writing about a region of the Peloponnese invites certain anxieties of authorship. One must own up to the awkward legacy of being an American archaeologist working in Greece, with all the wealth, privilege, and high-handedness that has characterized that tradition and weighed upon all who follow in its wake.[40] For all its excesses, it would be to our impoverishment if one were not also to acknowledge the role of a wider Western, philhellenic heritage in fueling intellectual creativity and opening a path to mutual understanding between students of antiquity (or the past at

---

37 For modes of archaeological writing, see Lucas (2018). For an excellent example of style responsive to subject in historiography, see Miller (2015).
38 2012, 87; also Shanks and Witmore (2010, 98).
39 Serres with Latour (1995, 81).
40 See Dyson (1998), Morris (1994).

large) and those who live among what has become of its objects in their after-lives. While I fully acknowledge the former, I wholly embrace the latter. Faced with an object as nuanced and multifaceted as the Eastern Peloponnese, one cannot help but to pursue a diversity of concerns. That this pursuit might be compounded with a diversity of perspectives also would seem requisite.

This chorography has not always stayed within the frame of prose that is first-person led, or in some cases first-person dominated. Through avatars, other interlocutors, this chorography has entered the historical narrative of the past with the parataxis of Ottoman and Northern European perspectives on Acrocorinth in the late seventeenth century. At other times "I" has taken a back seat to companions who drive, or lead, whether by surrendering to the interests of others in the Nemea Valley, in Nafplion, en route to Asine, or off Tolo. By inviting others to have a say, the path unfolds dialogically, so as to be shaped collectively. One may read into this a refusal to take any one perspective, and that is not unjustified. A chorographer may aspire to go even further in effacing their own authorial perspective. "How would my words let the world without words speak without me?"[41] I share Michel Serres's aspiration, which serves as an inspiration, "to efface myself enough to let" these old lands "ring."

Any sense of completion or closure on the part of a chorography would be at best misguided or dishonest, at worst symptomatic of a pathology of control that aims for a spurious mastery. In the end a collage of twenty-seven segments may be read as one narrative, or many narratives. It is left to the reader to piece together into a prose surface suggestive of the Eastern Peloponnese.

Bibliography

Bradley, R., 2003. Seeing things: perception, experience and the constraints of excavation. *Journal of Social Archaeology* 3(2), 151–68.

Brodsky, J. 1992. *Watermark*. New York, NY: Farrar, Straus and Giroux.

Chapman, R., and A. Wylie. 2016. *Evidential reasoning in archaeology*. London: Bloomsbury.

Diller, A. 1956. Pausanias in the Middle Ages. *Transactions and Proceedings of the American Philological Association* 87, 84–97.

Dyson, S.L. 1998. *Ancient marbles to American shores: Classical archaeology in the United States*. Philadelphia, PA: University of Pennsylvania Press.

Edgeworth, M. (ed.). 2006. *Ethnographies of archaeological practice: Cultural encounters – Material transformations*. Lanham, MD: AltaMira Press.

Edgeworth, M. 2012. Follow the cut, follow the rhythm, follow the material. *Norwegian Archaeological Review* 45(1), 76–92.

Edgeworth, M. 2016. Grounded objects: Archaeology and speculative realism. *Archaeological Dialogues* 23(1), 93–113.

41 Serres (2015a, 118).

Elsner, J. 2001. Structuring "Greece:" Pausanias's *Periegesis* as a literary construct. In S. E. Alcock, J.F. Cherry, and J. Elsner (eds.), *Pausanias: Travel and memory in Roman Greece*. Oxford: Oxford University Press. 3–20.

Gombrich, E.H. 1956. *Art and illusion: A study in the psychology of pictorial representation*. Princeton, NJ: Princeton University Press.

Heat-Moon, W.L. 1991. *PrairyErth*. London: Andre Deutsch.

Heidegger, M. 2002. The age of the world picture. In J. Young and K. Hayne (eds.), *Off the beaten track*. Cambridge: Cambridge University Press. 57–72.

Heidegger, M. 2008b. Letter on humanism. In D.F. Krell (ed.), *Basic writings*. London: Harper Perennial. 217–65.

Holbraad, M. 2012. *Truth in motion: The recursive anthropology of Cuban divination*. Chicago, IL: University of Chicago Press.

Hutton, W. 2005. *Describing Greece: Landscape and literature in the Periegesis of Pausanias*. Cambridge: Cambridge University Press.

Ingold, T. 1993. The temporality of landscape. *World Archaeology* 25(2), 152–74.

Ingold, T. 2009. Against space: Place, movement, knowledge. In P.W. Kirby (ed.), *Boundless worlds: An anthropological approach to movement*. New York, NY: Berghahn Books. 29–43.

Jameson, M.H., C.N. Runnels, and T. Van Andel. 1994. *A Greek countryside: The Southern Argolid from prehistory to the present day*. Stanford, CA: Stanford University Press.

Latour, B. 1986. Visualization and cognition: Thinking with eyes and hands. *Knowledge and Society* 6(6), 1–40.

Latour, B. 1987. *Science in action*. Cambridge, MA: Harvard University Press.

Latour, B. 1993. *We have never been modern* (trans. C. Porter). Cambridge, MA: Harvard University Press.

Lingis, A. 1998. *The imperative*. Bloomington, IN: Indiana University Press.

Lucas, G. 2018. *Writing the past: Knowledge and literary production in archaeology*. London: Routledge.

Marsden, J.H. 1864. *A brief memoir of the life and writings of Lieutenant-Colonel William Martin Leake*. London: Privately printed.

Miliarakis, A. 1886. *Geographia Politiki, Nea kai Archaia tou Nomou Argolidos kai Korinthos*. Athens.

Miller, P.N. 2015. *Peiresc's Mediterranean world*. Cambridge, MA: Harvard University Press.

Morris, I. 1994. Archaeologies of Greece. In I. Morris (ed.), *Classical Greece: Ancient histories and modern archaeologies*. Cambridge: Cambridge University Press. 8–48.

Morton, T. 2013. *Hyperobjects: Philosophy and ecology after the end of the world*. Minneapolis, MN: University of Minnesota Press.

Olivier, L. 2008. *Le Sombre abîme du temps: Mémoire et archéologie*. Seuil: Paris.

Olivier, L. 2011. *The dark abyss of time: Archaeology and memory* (trans. A. Greenspan). Lanham, MD: AltaMira Press.

Olsen, B. 2003. Material culture after text. Re-Membering things. *Norwegian Archaeological Review* 36, 87–104.

Olsen, B. 2010. *In defense of things: Archaeology and the ontology of objects*. Lanham, MD: AltaMira Press.

Pearson, M., and M. Shanks. 2001. *Theatre/archaeology*. London: Routledge.

Pétursdóttir, Þ. 2012. "Small things forgotten now included, or what else do things deserve?" *International Journal of Historical Archaeology* 16(3), 577–603.

Pétursdóttir, Þ., and B. Olsen. 2017. Theory adrift: The matter of archaeological theorizing. *Journal of Social Archaeology* 18(1), 97–117.

Pretzler, M. 2005. Comparing Strabo with Pausanias: Greece in context vs. Greece in depth. In D. Dueck, H. Lindsay, and S. Pothecary (eds), *Strabo's cultural geography: The making of a Kolossourgia*. Cambridge: Cambridge University Press. 144–60.

Pretzler, M. 2013. *Pausanias: Travel writing in Ancient Greece*. London: Bristol Classical Press.

Runnels, C.N., D.J. Pullen, and S. Langdon (eds.). 1995. *Artifact and assemblage: The finds from a regional survey of the Southern Argolid, Greece*. Stanford, CA: Stanford University Press.

Serres, M. 1985. *Les Cinq Sens*. Paris: Grasset.

Serres, M. 1995b. *Genesis*. Ann Arbor, MI: University of Michigan Press.

Serres, M. 2008a. *The five senses: A philosophy of mingled bodies*. London: Continuum.

Serres, M. 2015a. *Biogea*. Minneapolis, MN: University of Minnesota Press.

Serres, M., and B. Latour. 1995. *Conversations on science, culture, and time*. Ann Arbor, MI: University of Michigan Press.

Shanks, M. 2012. *The archaeological imagination*. Walnut Creek, CA: Left Coast Press.

Shanks, M., and C. Witmore. 2010. Echoes across the past: Chorography and topography in antiquarian engagements with place. *Performance Research* 15(4), 97–106.

Sloterdijk, P. 2013. *In the world interior of capital: For a philosophical theory of globalization*. Cambridge: Polity Press.

Sloterdijk, P. 2014. *Globes: Spheres II*. South Pasadena, CA: Semiotext(e).

Snodgrass, A.M. 1987. *An archaeology of Greece*. Berkeley, CA: University of California Press.

Sutton, S.B. (ed.). 2000. *Contingent countryside: Settlement, economy, and land use in the Southern Argolid since 1700*. Stanford, CA: Stanford University Press.

Tilley, C. 2010. *Interpreting landscapes: Geologies, topographies, identities*. Walnut Creek, CA: Left Coast Press.

Van Andel, T.H., and C. Runnels. 1987. *Beyond the acropolis: A rural Greek past*. Stanford, CA: Stanford University Press.

Witmore, C. 2004. On multiple fields: Between the material world and media – Two cases from the Peloponnesus, Greece. *Archaeological Dialogues* 11(2), 133–64.

Witmore, C. 2005. *Multiple field approaches in the Mediterranean: Revisiting the Argolid Exploration Project*. Doctoral dissertation, Stanford University.

Witmore, C. 2006. Vision, media, noise and the percolation of time: Symmetrical approaches to the mediation of the material world. *Journal of Material Culture* 11(3), 267–92.

Witmore, C. 2009. Prolegomena to open pasts: on archaeological memory practices. *Archaeologies* 5(3), 511–45.

Witmore, C. 2013a. The world on a flat surface: Maps from the archaeology of Greece and beyond. In S. Bonde and S. Houston (eds.), *Representing the past: Archaeology through text and image*. Oxford: Oxbow Books. 127–52.

MAPS

By Caleb Lightfoot

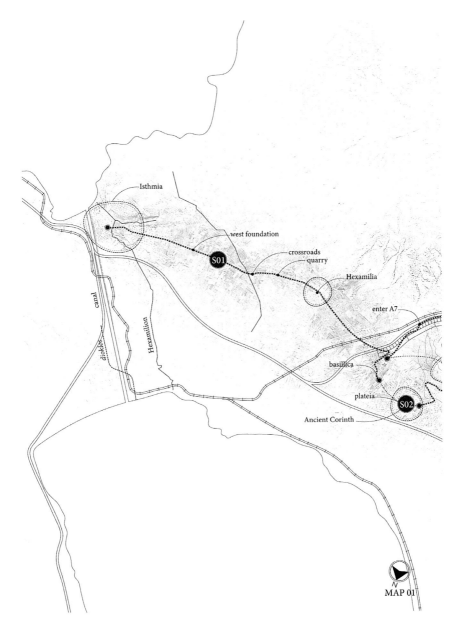

Isthmia

west foundation

crossroads
quarry

Hexamilia

enter A7

basilica

plateia

Ancient Corinth

S01

S02

canal

diolkos

Hexamilion

N
MAP 01

Map 1 Segments 1 and 2.

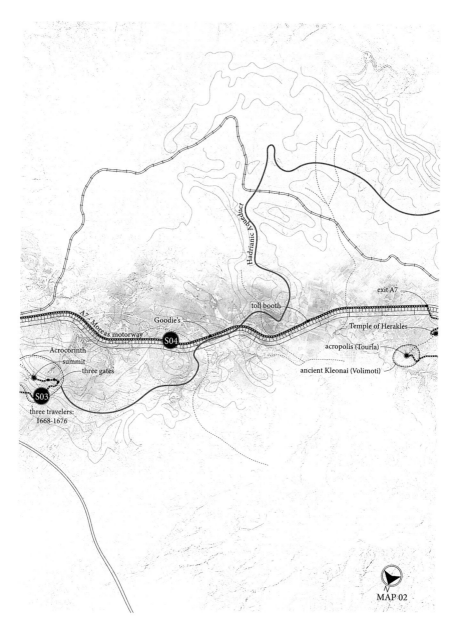

Map 2 Segments 3 and 4.

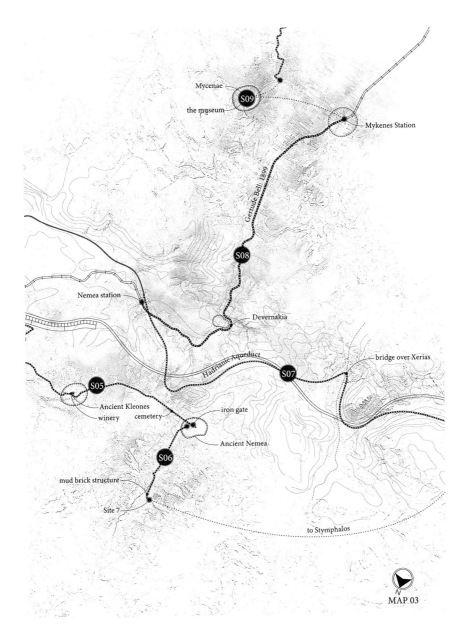

Mycenae

the museum

S09

Mykenes Station

Gertrude Bell: 1899

S08

Nemea station

Devernakia

bridge over Xerias

Hadrianic Aqueduct

S07

S05

Ancient Kleones

winery   cemetery   iron gate

Ancient Nemea

S06

mud brick structure

Site 7

to Stymphalos

N

MAP 03

Map 3 Segments 5 to 9.

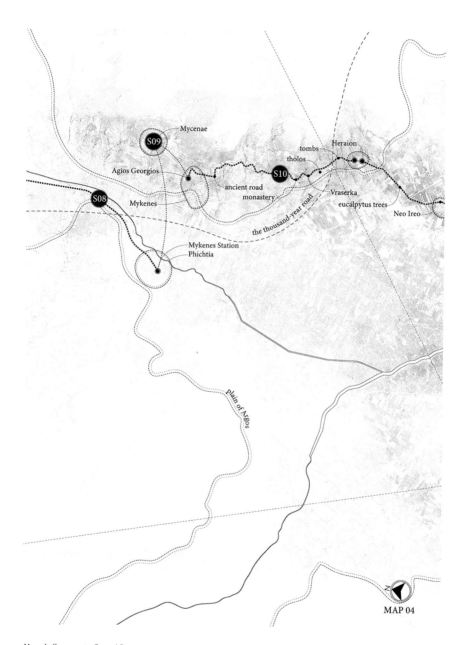

Map 4 Segments 8 to 10.

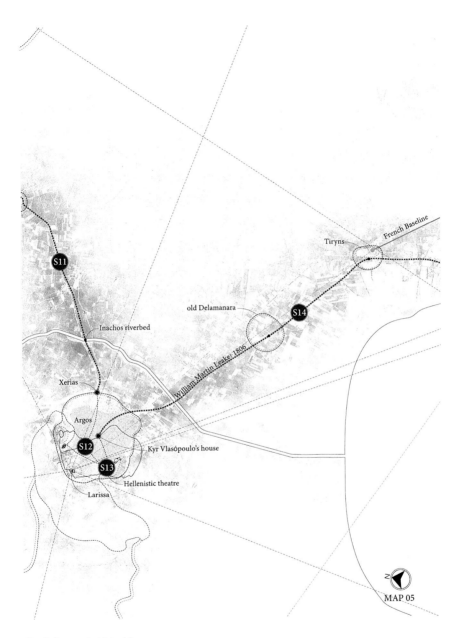

Map 5 Segments 11 to 14.

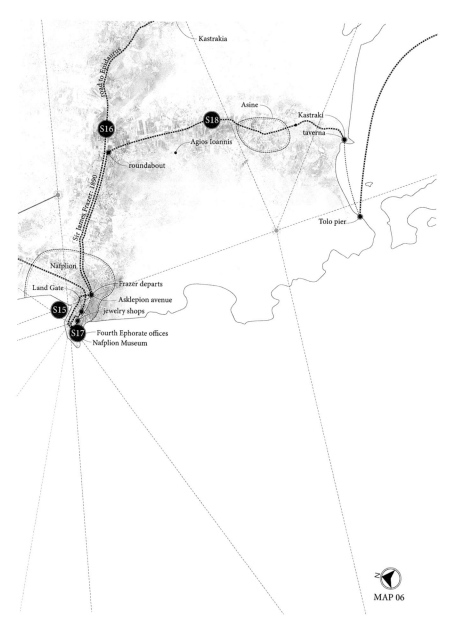

Kastrakia

road to Epidaurus

Asine

S18

Agios Ioannis

Kastraki

taverna

S16

roundabout

Tolo pier

Sir James Frazer 1890

Nafplion

Frazer departs

Land Gate

Asklepion avenue

S15

jewelry shops

S17

Fourth Ephorate offices

Nafplion Museum

N

MAP 06

Map 6 Segments 15 to 18.

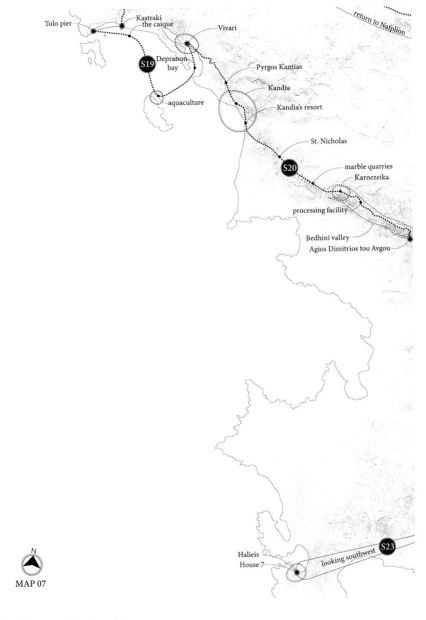

Tolo pier

Kastraki
the caique

Vivari

Depranon
bay

S19

aquaculture

Pyrgos Kantias

Kandja

Kandia's resort

St. Nicholas

marble quarries

Karnezeika

S20

processing facility

Bedhini valley

Agios Dimitrios tou Avgou

Halieis

House 7

looking southwest

S23

N

MAP 07

Map 7 Segments 19, 20, and 23.

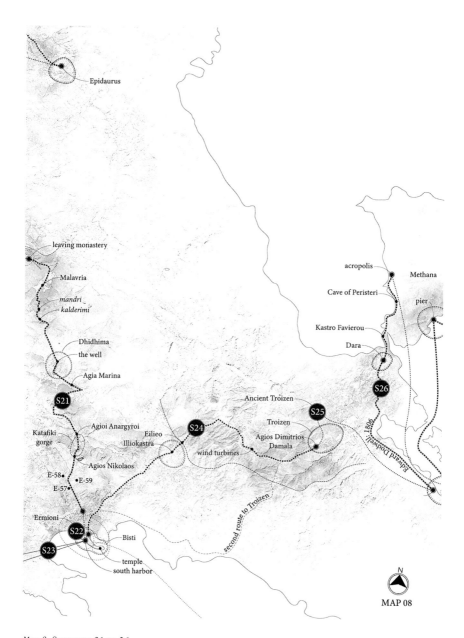

Epidaurus

leaving monastery

Malavria

*mandri
kalderimi*

Dhidhima

the well

Agia Marina

S21

Agioi Anargyroi

Katafiki
gorge

Eilieo

Illiokastra

S24

wind turbines

Ancient Troizen

Troizen

S25

Agios Dimitrios
Damala

acropolis

Methana

Cave of Peristeri

pier

Kastro Favierou

Dara

S26

Agios Nikolaos

E-58

E-59

E-57

Ermioni

S22

Bisti

S23

temple
south harbor

second route to Troizen

Edward Dodwell, 1806

N

MAP 08

Map 8 Segments 21 to 26.

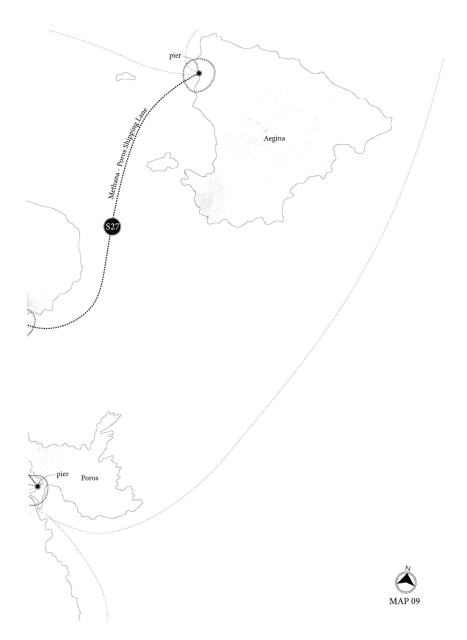

pier

Methana - Poros Shipping Lane

Aegina

S27

pier   Poros

N
MAP 09

Map 9 Segment 27.

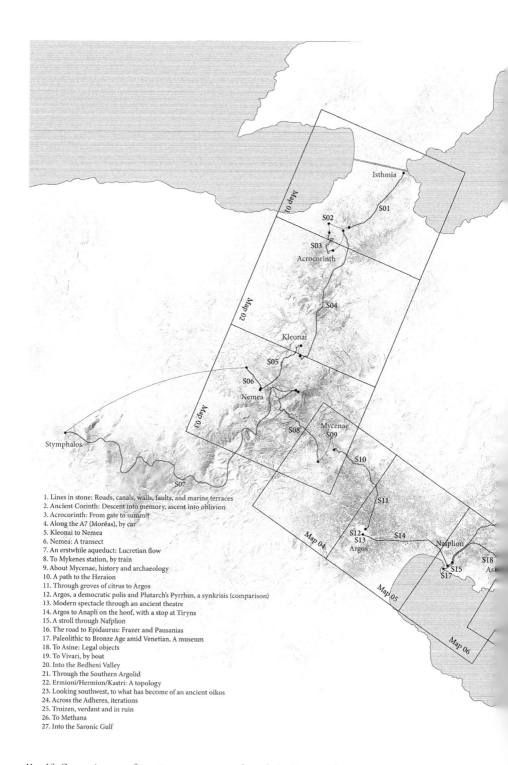

Isthmia

S01

S02

S03
Acrocorinth

Map 01

S04

Map 02

Kleonai

S05

S06

Nemea

S08

Mycenae
S09

Stymphalos

S10

Map 03

S07

S11

1. Lines in stone: Roads, canals, walls, faults, and marine terraces
2. Ancient Corinth: Descent into memory, ascent into oblivion
3. Acrocorinth: From gate to summit
4. Along the A7 (Moréas), by car
5. Kleonai to Nemea
6. Nemea: A transect
7. An erstwhile aqueduct: Lucretian flow
8. To Mykenes station, by train
9. About Mycenae, history and archaeology
10. A path to the Heraion
11. Through groves of citrus to Argos
12. Argos, a democratic polis and Plutarch's Pyrrhus, a synkrisis (comparison)
13. Modern spectacle through an ancient theatre
14. Argos to Anapli on the hoof, with a stop at Tiryns
15. A stroll through Nafplion
16. The road to Epidaurus: Frazer and Pausanias
17. Paleolithic to Bronze Age amid Venetian, A museum
18. To Asine: Legal objects
19. To Vivari, by boat
20. Into the Bedheni Valley
21. Through the Southern Argolid
22. Ermioni/Hermion/Kastri: A topology
23. Looking southwest, to what has become of an ancient oikos
24. Across the Adheres, iterations
25. Troizen, verdant and in ruin
26. To Methana
27. Into the Saronic Gulf

S12
S13
Argos

S14

Naíplion

Map 04

S18
As

S15
S17

Map 05

Map 06

Map 10 Composite map of twenty-seven segments through the Eastern Peloponnesus (two-page spread).

Aegina

S27

Methana

Poros

S26

S25
Troizen

rachneo

Epidaurus

S24

Dhidhima

S21

S20

Ermioni S22

S23

Haliεis

Map 09

Map 08

Map 07

0 1 2 3 4 5   10   15   20
                                              KM

N

MAP 10

COLLATED BIBLIOGRAPHY

Ackerman, R. 1987. *J.G. Frazer: His life and work.* Cambridge: Cambridge University Press.

Agamben, G. 2013. *The highest poverty.* Stanford, CA: Stanford University Press.

Ager, S.L. 1996. *Interstate arbitrations in the Greek World, 337–90 B.C.* Berkeley, CA: University of California Press.

Alberti, B. 2016. Archaeologies of ontology. *Annual Review of Anthropology* 45, 163–214.

Alberti, B., et al. 2011. "Worlds otherwise": Archaeology, anthropology, and ontological difference. *Current Anthropology* 52(6), 896–912.

Alberti, S., P. Bienkowski, and M.J. Chapman. 2009. Should we display the dead? *Museum and Society.* University of Leicester, Department of Museum Studies. 133–49.

Alcock, S.E. 1993. *Graecia Capta: The landscapes of Roman Greece.* Cambridge: Cambridge University Press.

Alcock, S.E. 1997. The heroic past in a Hellenistic present. *Echos du monde classique: Classical Views* 38(2), 221–34.

Alcock, S.E. 2002. *Archaeologies of the Greek past: Landscape, monuments, and memories.* Cambridge: Cambridge University Press.

Alcock, S.E., J. Bodel, and R.J.A. Talbert. 2012. *Highways, byways, and road systems in the pre-modern world.* Chichester: Wiley-Blackwell.

Alcock, S.E., and J.F. Cherry (eds.). 2004. *Side-by-side survey: Comparative regional studies in the Mediterranean world.* Oxford: Oxbow Books.

Alcock, S.E., and J.F. Cherry, with M. Shanks and C. Witmore. 2013. Susan E. Alcock and John F. Cherry. In W.L. Rathje, M. Shanks, and C. Witmore (eds.), *Archaeology in the making: Conversations through a discipline.* London: Routledge. 229–47.

Alcock, S.E., J.F. Cherry, and J. Davis. 1994. Intensive survey, agricultural practice and the classical landscape of Greece. In I. Morris (ed.), *Classical Greece.* Cambridge: Cambridge University Press. 137–70.

Alcock, T. 1831. *Travels in Russia, Persia, Turkey, and Greece, in 1828–9.* London: Printed by E. Clarke and Son.

Alden, M.J. 2002. *Well built Mycenae 7: Prehistoric cemetery – Pre-Mycenaean and Early Mycenaean Graves.* Oxford: Oxbow Books.

Aldred, O. 2018. Legs, feet, and hooves: The seasonal roundup in Iceland. In S.E. Pilaar Birch (ed.), *Multispecies archaeology.* London: Routledge. 273–94.

Aldred, O., and G. Lucas. 2019. The map as assemblage: Landscape archaeology and map-work. In M. Gillings, P. Hacigüzeller, and G. Lock (eds.), *Re-mapping archaeology: Critical perspectives, alternative mappings.* London: Routledge. 29–46.

Alexandri, A. 2002. Names and emblems: Greek archaeology, regional identities, and national narratives at the turn of the 20th century. *Antiquity* 76(291), 191–99.

Amandry, P. 1957. À propos de Polyclète: Statues d'Olympioniques et carrière de sculpteurs. In K. Schauenburg (ed.), *Charites: Studien zur Altertumswissenschaft (Festschrift für E. Langlotz)*. Bonn: Athenaeum Verlag. 63–87.

Ammons, A.R. 1970. Conserving the magnitude of uselessness. *Poetry* 115(5), 299.

Anderson, B. 1983. *Imagined communities: Reflections on the origin and spread of nationalism.* London: Verso.

Anderson, B. 2015. "An alternative discourse": Local interpreters of antiquities in the Ottoman Empire. *Journal of Field Archaeology* 40(4), 450–60.

André, J. 1958. *Notes de Lexicographie Botanique Grecque.* Paris: H. Champion.

Andrews, K. 2006[1953]. *Castles of the Morea.* Princeton, NJ: American School of Classical Studies at Athens.

Andrews, M. 1999. *Landscape and Western art.* Oxford: Oxford University Press.

Angelidis, M., and P.A. Grimanis. 1989. Geochemical partitioning of Co, Cr, Fe, Sc and Zn in polluted and non-polluted marine sediments. *Environmental Pollution* 62, 31–46.

Angelomatis-Tsougarakis, H. 1990. *The eve of the Greek revival: British travellers' perceptions of early nineteenth-century Greece.* London: Routledge.

Antonaccio, C. 1992. Terraces, tombs, and the Early Argive Heraion. *Hesperia* 61(1), 85–105.

Antonaccio, C. 1994. Contesting the past: Hero cult, tomb cult, and epic in early Greece. *American Journal of Archaeology* 98(3), 389–410.

Antonaccio, C. 1995. *An archaeology of ancestors: Tomb cult and hero cult in early Greece.* London: Rowman & Littlefield.

Antonakátou, N., and T. Mávros. 1976. *Elliniká Monastíria/Pelopónnisos.* Vol. 1, Athens.

Antoniou, P.F., H. Kyriakidou, and C. Anagnostou. 2009. Cement filled geo-textile groynes as a means of beach protection against erosion: A critique of applications in Greece. *Journal of Coastal Research, Special Issue* 56, 463–66.

Aquinas, T. 1972 [1256–59]. *Quaestiones disputatae de veritate.* Roma: Editori di San Tommaso. https://www.oldbooks.gr/books/cc/book/24660?catid=120

Arafat, K.W. 1996. *Pausanias' Greece: Ancient artists and Roman rulers.* Cambridge: Cambridge University Press.

Arakawa, T., et al. 2015. A sniffer-camera for imaging of ethanol vaporization from wine: The effect of wine glass shape. *The Analyst* 140(8), 2881–86.

Arnaud, P. 2005. *Les routes de la navigation antique: itinéraires en Méditerranée.* Paris: Editions Errance.

Arnshav, M. 2014. The freedom of the seas: Untapping the archaeological potential of marine debris. *Journal of Maritime Archaeology* 9(1), 1–25.

Assmann, J. 2003. *The mind of Egypt: History and meaning in the time of the Pharaohs.* Cambridge, MA: Harvard University Press.

Assmann, J. 2010. *The price of monotheism* (trans. R. Savage). Stanford, CA: Stanford University Press.

Athanasoulis, D. 2009. *The castle of Acrocorinth and its enhancement project (2006–2009).* Ancient Corinth: 25th Ephorate of Byzantine Antiquities.

Athanassopoulos, E.F. 2002. An "ancient" landscape: European ideals, archaeology, and nation building in early modern Greece. *Journal of Modern Greek Studies* 20(2), 273–305.

Athanassopoulos, E.F. 2016. *Nemea Valley Archaeological Project, Volume II: Landscape archaeology and the Medieval countryside.* Princeton, NJ: American School of Classical Studies.

Augé, M. 1995. *Non-places: Introduction to an anthropology of supermodernity.* London: Verso.

Augustinos, O. 1990. *French odysseys: Greece in French travel literature from the Renaissance to the Romantic era.* Baltimore, MD: Johns Hopkins University Press.

Ault, B.A. 1994. *Classical houses and households: An architectural and artifactual case study from Halieis.* Doctoral dissertation, Indiana University.

Ault, B.A. 1999. Koprones and oil presses at Halieis: Interactions of town and country and the integration of domestic and regional economies. *Hesperia* 68(4), 549–73.

Ault, B.A. 2005. *The excavations at ancient Halieis, Volume 2: The houses — The organization and use of domestic space*. Bloomington, IN: Indiana University Press.

Austin, B., and D.A. Austin. 2012. *Bacterial fish pathogens: Disease of farmed and wild fish*. 5th ed. New York, NY: Springer.

Avni, G., Y. Avni, and N. Porat. 2009. A new look at ancient agriculture in the Negev. *Cathedra* 133, 13–44.

Bachelard, G. 1994. *The poetics of space* (trans. M. Jolas). Boston, MA: Beacon Press.

Baedeker, K. 1894. *Greece: A handbook for travellers*. Leipzig: Karl Baedeker.

Baedeker, K. 1909. *Greece: A handbook for travellers*. Leipzig: Karl Baedeker.

Bailey, D., A. Whittle, and V. Cummings. 2005. *(Un)settling the Neolithic*. Oxford: Oxbow Books.

Bakasietas, K. 2011. The Agiorgitiko Vine variety. In S. Kourakou-Dragona (ed.), *Nemea: Beloved land of Zeus and Dionysos*. Athens: Foinikas Publications. 185–90.

Baker, L.-C. 1837. Memoir on the Northern Frontier of Greece. *Journal of the Royal Geographical Society of London* 7, 81–84.

Bakun, A., and V.N. Agostini. 2001. Seasonal patterns of wind-induced upwelling/downwelling in the Mediterranean Sea. *Scientia Marina* 65(3), 243–57.

Balabanis, P. 1999. Water in Europe: Research achievements and future perspectives within the framework of European research activities in the field of environment. *Revista CIDOB d'Afers Internacionals* 45/46, 59–78.

Baleriaux, J. 2016. Diving underground: Giving meaning to subterranean rivers. In J. McInerney, I. Sluiter, and B. Corthals (eds.), *Valuing landscape in Classical antiquity: Natural environment and cultural imagination*. Leiden: Brill. 103–21.

Bandinelli, R.B. 1976. *Introduzione all'archeologia classica come storia dell'arte antica* (Vol. 334). Roma: Laterza.

Banilas, G., et al. 2009. Olive and grapevine biodiversity in Greece and Cyprus: A review. In E. Lichtfouse (ed.), *Climate change, intercropping, pest control and beneficial microorganisms*. Dordrecht: Springer, 401–28.

Barfoed, S. 2009. *An archaic votive deposit from Nemea: Ritual behavior in a sacred landscape*. MA thesis, University of Cincinnati.

Barker, G. 1995. *A Mediterranean valley: Landscape archaeology and Annales history in the Biferno Valley*. London: Leicester University Press.

Barker, G. 2010. *The agricultural revolution in prehistory: Why did foragers become farmers?* Oxford: Oxford University Press.

Barker, G., and D. Mattingly (eds.). 1999–2000. *The archaeology of Mediterranean landscapes*. Vols. 1–5. Oxford: Oxbow Books.

Barthes, R. 1981. *Camera lucida: Reflections on photography* (trans. R. Howard). New York, NY: Hill and Wang.

Bartky, I.R. 1989. The adoption of standard time. *Technology and Culture* 30(1), 25–56.

Baumann, H., 1993. *The Greek plant world in myth, art, and literature* (trans. W.T. Stearn and E.R. Stearn). Portland, OR: Timber Press.

Beaulieu, M. 2016. *The sea in the Greek imagination*. Philadelphia, PA: University of Pennsylvania Press.

Benjamin, W. 1999. *The Arcades Project*. Cambridge, MA: Belknap Press.

Benjamin, W., H. Eiland, and M.W. Jennings. 2006. *Selected writings, Volume 4: 1938–1940*. Cambridge, MA: Belknap Press.

Benjamin, W., and M.W. Jennings. 2002. *Selected writings, Volume 3: 1935–1938*, Cambridge, MA: Belknap Press.

Beresford, J. 2013. *The ancient sailing season*. Leiden: Brill.

Bergson, H. 1859. *Extraits de Lucrèce, avec un commentaire, des notes et une étude sur la poésie, la philosophie, la physique, le texte et la langue de Lucrèce*. Paris: C. Delagrave.

Bergson, H. 1998. *Creative Evolution*. Mineola, NY: Dover.

Bergson, H., and W. Baskin. 1959. *The philosophy of poetry: The genius of Lucretius.* New York, NY: Philosophical Library.

Bewley, J.D. 1997. Seed germination and dormancy. *Plant Cell* 9, 1055–66.

Biers, W.R. 1978. Water from Stymphalos? *Hesperia* 2, 171–84.

Binford, L.R. 2001. *Constructing frames of reference: An analytical method for archaeological theory building using hunter-gatherer and environmental data sets.* Berkeley, CA: University of California Press.

Bintliff, J. 2003. The ethnoarchaeology of a "passive" ethnicity: The Arvanites of Central Greece. In K.S. Brown and Y. Hamilakis (eds.), *The usable past: Greek metahistories.* Lanham, MD: Lexington Books. 129–44.

Bintliff, J. 2004. Time structure and agency: The Annales, emergent complexity, and archaeology. In J. Bintliff (ed.), *A companion to archaeology.* Oxford: Blackwell Publishing. 174–94.

Bintliff, J.L. 1977. *Natural environment and human settlement in prehistoric Greece.* 2 vols. *British Archaeological Reports*, Supplementary Series 28. Oxford: Archaeopress.

Bintliff, J.L. 1991. *The Annales school and archaeology.* Leicester: Leicester University Press.

Bintliff, J.L. 2012. *The complete archaeology of Greece: From hunter-gatherers to the 20th century AD.* Chichester: Wiley-Blackwell.

Bjerck, H.B., et al. 2016. *Marine Ventures: Archaeological perspectives on human-sea relations.* Bristol, CT: Equinox Publishing.

Błaśkiewicz, M. 2014. Healing dreams at Epidaurus: Analysis and interpretation of the Epidaurian iamata. *Miscellanea Anthropologica Et Sociologica* 15(4), 54–69.

Blegen, C. 1937. *Prosymna: The Helladic settlement preceding the Argive Heraeum.* Cambridge: Cambridge University Press.

Blegen, C. 1939. Prosymna: Remains of post-Mycenaean date. *American Journal of Archaeology* 43(3), 410–44.

Blegen, C.W. 1930. Excavations at the summit. In C.W. Blegen, O.T. Broneer, R. Stillwell, and A.R. Bellinger (eds.), *Acrocorinth: Excavations in 1926.* Cambridge, MA: Harvard University Press. 3–28.

Blegen, C.W., O.T. Broneer, R. Stilwell, and A.R. Bellinger et al. (eds.). 1930. *Acrocorinth: Excavations in 1926.* Cambridge, MA: Harvard University Press.

Bloch, M. 1962. *Feudal society.* Chicago, IL: University of Chicago Press.

Bloch, M. 1967. *Land and Work in Medieval Europe.* Berkeley, CA: University of California Press.

Blouet, G.A. 1831–38. *Expédition scientifique de Morée, Ordonnée par le Gouvernement français: Architecture, Sculptures, Inscriptions et Vues du Péloponèse, des Cyclades et de l'Attique, mesurées, dessinées, recueillies et publiées par Abel Blouet.* Vols. I–VI. Paris: Firmin Didot.

Boas, F. 1896. The limitations of the comparative method of anthropology. *Science* 4(103), 901–08.

Bon, A. 1936. The Medieval fortifications of Acrocorinth and vicinity. In R. Carpenter and A. Bon (eds.), *Corinth III ii: The defenses of Acrocorinth and the lower town.* Cambridge, MA: Harvard University Press. 128–281.

Bookidis, N. 2003. The sanctuaries of Corinth. In C.K. Williams and N. Bookidis (eds.), *Corinth, the centenary: 1896–1996.* Princeton, NJ: American School of Classical Studies at Athens. 247–59.

Bookidis, N., and R.S. Stroud. 2004. Apollo and the Archaic Temple at Corinth. *Hesperia* 73(3), 401–26.

Borges, J.L. 1972. Of exactitude in science. In J.L. Borges (ed.), *A Universal history of infamy* (trans. N.T. di Givanni). New York, NY: Dutton. 141.

Bory de Saint-Vincent, M. 1834. *Expédition scientifique de Morée: Section des sciences physiques. Tome II – Partie 1. Géographie.* Paris: F.G. Levrault.

Bourguet, M.N. (ed.). 1998. *L'invention scientifique de la Méditerranée. Égypte, Morée, Algérie.* Paris: École des Hautes Études en Sciences Sociales.

Boyd, T.D., and M.H. Jameson. 1981. Urban and rural land division in ancient Greece. *Hesperia* 50(4), 327–42.

Boyd, T.D., and W.W. Rudolph. 1978. Excavations at Porto Cheli and vicinity, Preliminary Report IV: The lower town of Halieis, 1970–77. *Hesperia* 47(4), 333–55.

Bracken, C.P. 1975. *Antiquities Acquired: The spoliation of Greece.* Newton Abbot: David & Charles.

Bradley, R. 1997. *Rock art and the prehistory of Atlantic Europe: Signing the land.* New York, NY: Routledge.

Bradley, R. 2003. Seeing things: Perception, experience and the constraints of excavation. *Journal of Social Archaeology* 3(2), 151–68.

Braudel, F. 1972. *The Mediterranean and the Mediterranean world in the age of Philip II.* New York, NY: Harper and Row.

Brodsky, J. 1992. *Watermark.* New York, NY: Farrar, Straus & Giroux.

Broneer, O. 1937. Studies in the topography of Corinth in the time of St. Paul. *Archaiologikí efimerís* 76, 125–33.

Broneer, O. 1962. Excavations at Isthmia 1959–1961. *Hesperia* 31(1), 1–25.

Broodbank, C. 2013. *The making of the Middle Sea.* Oxford: Oxford University Press.

Brooks, M.M., and C. Rumsey. 2006. The body in the museum. In V. Cassman, N. Odegaard, and J. Powell (eds.), *Human remains: Guide for museums and academic institutions.* Lanham, MD: Altamira Press. 261–89.

Brooks, M.M., and C. Rumsey. 2007. Who knows the fate of his bones? Rethinking the body on display: Object, art or human remains. In S.J. Knell, S. MacLeod, and S. Watson (eds.), *Museum revolutions: How museums change and are changed.* Abingdon: Routledge. 343–54.

Broucke, P.B. 1994. Tyche and the fortune of cities in the Greek and Roman world. *Yale University Art Gallery Bulletin,* 34–49.

Brück, J. 2005. Experiencing the past? The development of a phenomenological archaeology in British prehistory. *Archaeological Dialogues* 12(1), 45–72.

Bryant, L. 2011. *The democracy of objects.* Ann Arbor, MI: Open Humanities Press.

Bryant, L. 2014. *Onto-cartography: An ontology of machines and media.* Edinburgh: Edinburgh University Press.

Burkert, W. 1983. *Homo Necans: The anthropology of ancient Greek sacrificial ritual and myth.* Berkeley, CA: University of California Press.

Burns, B.E. 2012. *Mycenaean Greece, Mediterranean commerce, and the formation of identity.* Cambridge: Cambridge University Press.

Bursian, C. 1868–72. *Geographie von Griechenland.* Leipzig: Teubner.

Byron, G.G. 1833. Review of Gell's Geography of Ithaca, and Itinerary Of Greece. In G.G. Byron (ed.), *The complete works of Lord Byron including his suppressed poems and others never before published.* Paris: Baudry.

Byron, R. 1937. *The road to Oxiana.* London: Macmillan & Co.

Calder, W.M., and D.A. Traill. 1986. *Myth, scandal, and history: The Heinrich Schliemann controversy and a first edition of the Mycenaean diary.* Detroit, MI: Wayne State University Press.

Calotychos, V. 2003. *Modern Greece: A cultural poetics.* Oxford: Berg.

Caraher, W., D. Nakassis, and D.K. Pettegrew. 2006. Siteless survey and intensive data collection in an artifact-rich environment: Case studies from the eastern Corinthia, Greece. *Journal of Mediterranean Archaeology* 19(1), 7–43.

Caraher, W.R. 2003. *Church, society, and the sacred in early Christian Greece.* Ann Arbor, MI: UMI Dissertation Services.

Cardia, F., and A. Lovatelli. 2007. A review of cage aquaculture: Mediterranean Sea. In M. Halwart, D. Soto, and J.R. Arthur (eds.), *Cage aquaculture: Regional reviews and global overview.* FAO Fisheries Technical Paper. No. 498. Rome, FAO. 156–87.

Carman, J. 2005. *Against cultural property: Archaeology, heritage and ownership*. London: Duckworth.

Carpenter, R. 1929. Researches in the topography of ancient Corinth. *American Journal of Archaeology* 33(3), 345–60.

Carpenter, R. 1936. The Classical fortifications of Acrocorinth. In R. Carpenter and A. Bon *Corinth III.ii: The defenses of Acrocorinth and the lower town*. Cambridge, MA: Harvard University Press. 1–43.

Cartledge, P. 1998. *Democritus*. New York, NY: Routledge.

Casson, L. 1994. *Travel in the ancient world*. Baltimore, MD: Johns Hopkins University Press.

Catapoti, D., and M. Relaki. 2013. An archaeology of land ownership: Introducing the debate. In M. Relaki and D. Catapoti (eds.), *An archaeology of land ownership*. London: Routledge. 1–20.

Chang, C. 1981. *The archaeology of contemporary herding sites in Greece*. Doctoral dissertation, State University of New York at Binghamton.

Chang, C. 2000. The material culture and settlement history of agro-pastoralism in the koinotis of Dhidhima: An ethnoarchaeological perspective. In S.B. Sutton (ed.), *Contingent countryside: Settlement, economy, and land use in the Southern Argolid since 1700*. Stanford, CA: Stanford University Press. 125–40.

Chapman, R., and A. Wylie. 2016. *Evidential reasoning in archaeology*. London: Bloomsbury.

Charitos, K.B. 1968. *Kleonai*. Athens.

Chateaubriand, F.-R. 1814. *Travels in Greece, Palestine, Egypt, and Barbary, during the Years 1806 and 1807*. New York, NY: Van Winkle and Wiley.

Chateaubriand, F.-R. 1827. *Itinéraire de Paris à Jérusalem*. Paris: Furne, Jouvet.

Chatterjee, P. 1993. *Nationalist thought and the colonial world: A derivative discourse*. Minneapolis, MN: University of Minnesota Press.

Chatwin, B. 1987. *The songlines*. New York, NY: Viking.

Cherry, J.F. 1983. Frogs around the pond: Perspectives on current archaeological survey projects in the Mediterranean region. In R. Keller and D.W. Rupp (eds.), *Archaeological survey in the Mediterranean area*, BAR 155. Oxford, UK: British Archaeological Reports (BAR). 375–416.

Cherry, J.F. 2001. Travel, nostalgia, and Pausanias' Giant. In S.E. Alcock, J.F. Cherry, and J. Elsner (eds.) *Pausanias: Travel and memory in Roman Greece*. Oxford: Oxford University Press. 247–55.

Cherry, J.F. 2003. Regional survey and its future. In J.K. Papadopoulos and R.M. Leventhal (eds.), *Theory and practice in Mediterranean archaeology: Old World and New World perspectives*. Los Angeles, CA: Cotsen Institute of Archaeology, University of California. 137–59.

Cherry, J.F. 2005. Survey. In C. Renfrew and P. Bahn (eds.), *Archaeology: The key concepts*. London: Routledge. 186–89.

Cherry, J.F. 2011. Still not digging, much. *Archaeological Dialogues* 18, 10–17.

Cherry, J.F., et al. 1988. Archaeological survey in an artifact-rich landscape: A Middle Neolithic example from Nemea, Greece. *American Journal of Archaeology* 92, 159–76.

Cherry, J.F., J.L. Davis, and E. Mantzourani. 1986. *A report to the Ephoreia of Antiquities, Nauplion, on sites within the survey which require protection*. Unpublished.

Cherry, J.F., J.L. Davis, and E. Mantzourani. 1991. *Landscape archaeology as long-term history: Northern Keos in the Cycladic Islands*. Los Angeles, CA: Cotsen Institute of Archaeology, University of California.

Cheung, W.W.L., et al. 2013. Shrinking of fishes exacerbates impacts of global ocean changes on marine ecosystems. *Nature Climate Change* 3(3), 254–58.

Chouquer, G. 2007. Les centuriations: Topographie et morphologie, reconstitution et mémoire des formes. *Archeologia Aerea. Studi di aerotopografia archeologia* II, 65–82.

Chouquer, G. 2008. *Traité d'archéogéographie: La crise des récits géohistoriques*. Paris: Errance.

Chow, T.J. 1970. Lead accumulation in roadside soil and grass. *Nature* 225(5229), 295–96.

Christoforidis, A., and N. Stamatis. 2009. Heavy metal contamination in street dust and roadside soil along the major national road in Kavala's region, Greece. *Geoderma* 151, 257–63.

Chronon, W. 1991. *Nature's metropolis: Chicago and the Great West*. New York, NY: W.W. Norton & Co.

Chronopoúlou, N., M. Vougioúka, and V. Megarídis. 1994. *Odonymiká tou Nafplíou: I Simasía ton Onomasión ton Odón kai Plateión tis Póleos tou Nafplíou*. Nafplion: Municipality of Nafplion.

Clark, W.G. 1858. *Peloponnesus: Notes of study and travel*. London: John W. Parker and Son.

Clarke, D.L. 1968. *Analytical archaeology*. London: Methuen & Co.

Clarke, E.D. 1818. *Travels in various countries of Europe, Asia and Africa* Section 2, Vol. 6. London: T. Cadell and W. Davies.

Clendenon, C. 2009. Karst hydrology in ancient myths from Arcadia and Argolis, Greece. *Acta Carsologica* 38(1), 145–54.

Cloke, C.F. 2016. *The landscape of the lion: Economies of religion and politics in the Nemean countryside (800 B.C. to A.D. 700)*. Doctoral dissertation, University of Cincinnati.

Clover, C. 2006. *The end of the line: How overfishing is changing the world and what we eat*. Berkeley, CA: University of California Press.

Codina-García, M., et al. 2013. Plastic debris in Mediterranean seabirds. *Marine Pollution Bulletin* 77, 220–26.

Cohen, D. 1974. Polluted Parthenon. *New Scientist* 28, 671–72.

Cole, M.P., et al. 2011. Microplastics as contaminants in the marine environment: A review. *Marine Pollution Bulletin* 62, 2588–97.

Cole, M.P., et al. 2014. Isolation of microplastics in biota-rich seawater samples and marine organisms. *Nature, Scientific Reports* 4, article 4528, 220–26.

Collier, R.E.L. 1990. Eustatic and tectonic controls upon quaternary coastal sedimentation in the Corinth Basin, Greece. *Journal of the Geological Society, London*, 147, 301–14.

Compton, N. 2015. Traditional boats of Greece: Tenacious survivors of a fading legacy. *WoodenBoat* 247, 64–71.

Constantine, D. 2011. *In the footsteps of the gods: Travellers to Greece and the quest for the Hellenic ideal*. London: I.B. Tauris.

Constantinidis, S.E. 2001. *Modern Greek theatre*. London: McFarland & Company.

Conze, A., and A. Michaelis. 1861. Rapporto d'un viaggio fatto nella Grecian el 1860. *Annali dell'Instituto de Corrispondenza Archaeologica* 33, 5–12.

Cook, J.M. 1953a. The Agamemneion. *Annual of the British School at Athens* 48, 30–68.

Cook, J.M. 1953b. The cult of Agamemnon at Mycenae. In A.D. Keramopoullos (ed.), *GÉRAS Antoníou Keramopoúllou*. Athens: Typographeion Myrtidi. 112–18.

Cooper, D.E. 2012. Should ruins be preserved? In C. Scarre and R. Coningham (eds.), *Appropriating the past: Philosophical perspectives on the practice of archaeology*. Cambridge: Cambridge University Press. 222–36.

Corcoran, P.L. 2015. Benthic plastic debris in marine and fresh water environments. *Environ. Sci. Processes Impacts* 17, 1363–69.

Cosgrove, D. 2004. Landscape and landschaft. *German Historical Institute Bulletin*, 35(Fall), 57–71.

Cosgrove, D., and S. Daniels (eds.). 1988. *The iconography of landscape: Essays on the symbolic representation, design and use of past environments*. Vol. 9. Cambridge: Cambridge University Press.

Courtils, J. 1981. Note de topographie argienne. *Bulletin de correspondance hellénique* 105(2), 607–10.

Cozar, A., et al. 2015. Plastic accumulation in the Mediterranean Sea. *PLoS ONE* 10(4), 1–12.

Cronon, W. 2000. *Changes in the land: Indians, colonists, and the ecology of New England.* New York, NY: Hill and Wang.

Crossland, Z., and R.A. Joyce. 2015. *Disturbing bodies: Perspectives on forensic anthropology.* Santa FE, NM: School for Advanced Research Press.

Crouch, D.P. 2004. *Geology and settlement: Greco-Roman patterns.* Oxford: Oxford University Press.

Cummings, V. 2013. *The anthropology of hunter-gatherers.* London: Bloomsbury.

Cummings, V., P.D. Jordan, and M. Zvelebil. 2014. *The Oxford handbook of the archaeology and anthropology of hunter-gatherers.* Oxford: Oxford University Press.

Curtius, E. 1851–52. *Peloponnesos eine historisch-geographiche Bechreibung der Halbinsel.* Gotha: J. Perthes.

Curtius, E. 1876. William Martin Leake und die Wiederentdeckung der klassischen Länder. *Preussische Jahrbücker* 38, 237–52.

Curtius, G. 1879. *Grundzüge der griechischen Etymologie.* Leipzig: Teubner.

D'Alessandro, W., et al. 2008. Methana, the westernmost active volcanic system of the South Aegean Arc (Greece): Insight from fluids geochemistry. *Journal of Volcanology and Geothermal Research* 178, 818–28.

Dalakoglou, D. 2010. The road: An ethnography of the Albanian–Greek cross-border motorway. *American Ethnologist* 37(1), 132–49.

Dalakoglou, D., and P. Harvey. 2012. Roads and anthropology: Ethnographic perspectives on space, time and (im)mobility. *Mobilities* 7(4), 459–65.

Damianidis, K. 1996. *Ellinikí Paradosiakí Nafpigikí.* Athens: Cultural Technological Foundation.

Danforth, L.M., and A. Tsiaras. 1982. *The death rituals of rural Greece.* Princeton, NJ: Princeton University Press.

Daniel, G. 1967. *The origins and growth of archaeology.* Harmondsworth: Penguin.

Danis, K., et al. 2013. Malaria in Greece: Historical and current reflections on a re-emerging vector borne disease. *Travel Medicine and Infectious Disease* 11(1), 8–14.

Dankoff, R., and S. Kim (eds.). 2010. *An Ottoman traveller: Selections from the book of travels of Evilya Çelebi.* London: Eland.

Davidovich, U., et al. 2012. Archaeological investigations and OSL dating of terraces at Ramat Rahel, Israel. *Journal of Field Archaeology* 37(3), 192–208.

Davies, J.K. 1984. The reliability of the oral tradition. In L. Foxhall and J.K. Davies (eds.), *The Trojan War: Its historicity and context.* Bristol: Bristol Classical Press. 87–110.

Davies, S., and J.L. Davis (eds.). 2007. *Between Venice and Istanbul: Colonial landscapes in early modern Greece.* Princeton, NJ: American School of Classical Studies at Athens.

Davis, J.L. 2007. Memory groups and the state: Erasing the past and inscribing the present in the landscapes of the Mediterranean and Near East. In N. Yoffee (ed.), *Negotiating the past in the past: Identity, memory, and landscape in archaeological research.* Tucson, AZ: University of Arizona Press. 227–56.

Davis, J.L. (ed.). 2008. *Sandy Pylos: An archaeological history from Nestor to Navarino.* 2nd ed. Princeton, NJ: American School of Classical Studies at Athens.

Davis, J.L. 2010. "That special atmosphere outside of national boundaries": Three Jewish directors and the American School of Classical Studies at Athens. *Annuario della Scuola Archeologica Italiana di Atene* 87, 119–31.

Dawdy, S.L. 2009. Millennial archaeology: Locating the discipline in the age of insecurity. *Archaeological Dialogues* 16(2), 131–42.

Dawdy, S.L. 2016. *Patina: A profane archaeology.* Chicago, IL: University of Chicago Press.

De Certeau, M. 1988. *The practice of everyday life.* Berkeley, CA: University of California Press.

De Polignac, F. 1995. *Cults, territory, and the origins of the Greek city-state* (trans. J. Lloyd). Chicago, IL: Chicago University Press.

De Waele, F.D. 1930. The Roman market north of the temple at Corinth. *American Journal of Archaeology* 34(4), 432–54.

De Wire, E., and D. Reyes-Pergioudakis. 2010. *The lighthouses of Greece.* Sarasota, FL: Pineapple Press.

Demakopoúlou, C. 1980. Oi istorikoí tópoi ton Ethnikón Syneléfseon, *Deltíon tis Istorikís kai Ethnologikís Etaireías tis Elládos* 23.

Demakopoulou, I. 2005. Pýrgoi: Oi ochyrés katoikíes tis proepanastatikís Peloponnísou. In I. Demakopoulou (ed.) Scripta Minora. Érevnes stin architektonikí kai érga gia tin syntírisi ton mnimeíon. *Archaiologikoú Deltíou* 88, 217–328.

Demakopoulou, K. (ed.). 1990. *Troy, Mycenae, Tiryns, Orchomenos: Heinrich Schliemann, the 100th anniversary of his death.* Athens: Ministry of Culture of Greece.

DeSilvey, C. 2006. Observed decay: Telling stories with mutable things. *Journal of Material Culture* 11(3), 318–38.

DeSilvey, C. 2014. Palliative curation. Art and entropy on Orford Ness. In B. Olsen and Þ. Petursdottir (eds.), *Ruin memories: Materiality, aesthetics and the archaeology of the recent past.* New York, NY: Routledge. 79–91.

DeSilvey, C. 2017. *Curated decay: Heritage beyond saving.* Minneapolis, MN: University of Minnesota Press.

Deuel, L. 1977. *Memoirs of Heinrich Schliemann: A documentary portrait drawn from his autobiographical writings, letters, and excavation reports.* New York, NY: Harper & Row.

Diamant, A. 1997. Fish-to-fish transmission of a marine myxosporean. *Diseases of Aquatic Organisms* 30, 99–105.

Diller, A. 1956. Pausanias in the Middle Ages. *Transactions and Proceedings of the American Philological Association* 87, 84–97.

Dillon, M.P.J. 1997. The ecology of the Greek sanctuary. *Zeitschrift für Papyrologie und Epigraphik* 118, 113–27.

Division, N.I. 1944. *Greece Volume I: Physical geography, history, administration and peoples.* Norwich: Jarrold and Sons.

Dodwell, E. 1819. *A Classical and topographical tour through Greece.* 2 vols. London: Rodwell and Martin.

Dodwell, E. 1834. *Views and descriptions of Cyclopian, or, Pelasgic remains, in Greece and Italy; with constructions of a later period.* London: A. Richter.

Domanska, E. 2018. *Nekros: Wprowadzenie do ontologii martwego ciała.* Wydawnictwo Naukowe PWN.

Dorovinis, V. 1980. Capodistrias et la planification d'Argos (1828–1832). *Bulletin de correspondance hellénique.* Supplément 6, 501–45.

Dorovinis, V.K. 1985. O schediasmós tou Nafplíou katá tin Kapodistriakí período (1828 – 33). I eidikí períptosi kai ta genikótera provlímata», *Anátypo apó ta Praktiká tou Diethnoús Symposíou Istorías NEOELLINIKI POLI.* Athens: The Society for the Study of Modern Hellenism.

Douglas, M. 1978. Judgements on James Frazer. *Daedalus* 107(4), 151–64.

Douglas, M. 2007. *Thinking in circles: An essay on ring composition.* New Haven, CT: Yale University Press.

Doukellis, P.N. 1994. Le territoire de la colonie romaine de Corinthe. In P.N. Doukellis and L.G. Mendoni (eds.), *Structures rurales et sociétés antiques: Actes du colloque de Corfou, 14–16 mai 1992.* Paris: Les belles lettres. 359–90.

Dova, S. 2014. History, identity, and the hero in Terzakis's Princess Ysabeau. In S. Dova (ed.), *Historical poetics in nineteenth and twentieth century Greece: Essays in honor of Lily Macrakis.* Morrisville, NC: Lulu Publishing Services. 131–65.

Driver, F. 2001. *Geography militant: Cultures of exploration and empire.* Oxford: Wiley-Blackwell.

Durliat, J. 1989. "La peste du VIe siècle." In C. Morrisson and J. Lefort (eds.), *Hommes et richesses dans l'empire byzantin, vol. 1, IV–VIIe siècle.* Paris: Éditions P. Lethielleux. 106–19.

Dyson, S.L. 1998. *Ancient marbles to American shores: Classical archaeology in the United States.* Philadelphia, PA: University of Pennsylvania Press.

Easton, D.F. 1984. Schliemann's mendacity: A false trail? *Antiquity* 58, 197–204.

Edgeworth, M. (ed.). 2006. *Ethnographies of archaeological practice: Cultural encounters – Material transformations.* Lanham, MD: AltaMira Press.

Edgeworth, M. 2011. *Fluid pasts: Archaeology of flow.* London: Bloomsbury.

Edgeworth, M. 2012. Follow the cut, follow the rhythm, follow the material. *Norwegian Archaeological Review* 45(1), 76–92.

Edgeworth, M. 2016. Grounded objects: Archaeology and speculative realism. *Archaeological Dialogues* 23(1), 93–113.

Edmonds, M. 1999. *Ancestral geographies of the Neolithic.* London: Routledge.

Edwards, C.M. 1994. The arch over the Lechaion Road at Corinth and its sculpture. *Hesperia* 63(3), 263–308.

Edwards, J. 2011. Plutarch and the death of Pyrrhus: Disambiguating the conflicting accounts. *Scholia: Studies in Classical Antiquity* 20, 112–31.

Elden, S. 2005. Missing the point: Globalization, deterritorialization and the space of the world. *Transactions of the Institute of British Geographers* 30(1), 8–19.

Elden, S. 2010. Land, terrain, territory. *Progress in Human Geography* 34(6), 799–817.

Elden, S. 2013. *The birth of territory.* Chicago, IL: University of Chicago Press.

Elden, S., and E. Mendieta. 2009. Being-with as making worlds: The "second coming" of Peter Sloterdijk. *Environment and Planning D: Society and Space* 27, 1–11.

Elderkin, G.W. 1910. The fountain of Glauce at Corinth. *American Journal of Archaeology.* 14(1), 19–50.

Eldridge, R. 1987. Hypotheses, criterial claims, and perspicuous representations: Wittgenstein's "Remarks on Frazer's *The Golden Bough.*" *Philosophical Investigations* 10(3) 226–45.

Elias, X., and Z. Elias. 2003. *The former municipality of Kleonon 19th–20th century.* Vol. 1. Athens: Dim. Kleidas & Co.

Eliot, C.W.J. 1996. Leake, William Martin (1777–1860). In N.T. de Grummond (ed.), *An encyclopedia of the history of classical archaeology.* Westport, CT: Greenwood Press. 666.

Elsner, J. 1992. Pausanias: A Greek pilgrim in the Roman world. *Past and Present* 135, 3–29.

Elsner, J. 2001. Structuring "Greece": Pausanias's *Periegesis* as a literary construct. In S.E. Alcock, J.F. Cherry, and J. Elsner (eds.), *Pausanias: Travel and memory in Roman Greece.* Oxford: Oxford University Press. 3–20.

ELSTAT. 2013. *Synthíkes diavíosis stin Elláda [Living conditions in Greece].* Athens: Hellenic Statistical Authority.

Etienne, R., and F. Etienne. 1992. *The search for ancient Greece.* London: Thames & Hudson.

Fachard, S. 2018. Political borders in Pausanias's Greece. In A.R. Knodell and T.P. Leppard (eds.), *Regional approaches to society and complexity studies in honor of John F. Cherry.* London: Equinox. 132–57.

Fachard, S., and J.C. Bessac. Forthcoming. *L'Aspis aux époques Classique et Hellénistique, 1. Les constructions A. Les remparts de l'Aspis.* des fouilles de l'Aspis.

Fachard, S., A.R. Knodell, and E. Banou. 2015. The 2014 Mazi Archaeological Project (Attica). *Antike Kunst* 58, 178–86.

FAO. 2005–16a. National aquaculture sector overview. Greece. National aquaculture sector overview fact sheets. Text by Christofilogiannis, P. In *FAO Fisheries and Aquaculture Department* [online]. Rome. Updated 19 November 2010. [Cited 13 January 2016]. www.fao.org/fishery/countrysector/naso_greece/en#tcN700B1.

FAO. 2005–16b. Cultured aquatic species information programme. *Dicentrarchus labrax.* Cultured aquatic species information programme. Text by Bagni, M. In *FAO Fisheries and Aquaculture Department* [online]. Rome. Updated 18 February 2005. [Cited 14 January 2016]. www.fao.org/fishery/culturedspecies/Dicentrarchus_labrax/en.

FAO. 2011–16. National Aquaculture Legislation Overview. Greece. National Aquaculture Legislation Overview (NALO) Fact Sheets. Text by Doffay, B. In *FAO Fisheries and Aquaculture Department* [online]. Rome. Updated 1 January 2011. [Cited 14 January 2016]. www.fao.org/fishery/legalframework/nalo_greece/en#tcNB00FE.

Faráklas, N. 1972. *Troizinía, Kalávreia, Méthana* (Archaíes Ellinikés Póleis, tóm 10), ékd. Athinaïkós Technologikós Ómilos – Athinaïkó Kéntro Oikistikís: Athens.

Faráklas, N. 1973. *Ermionis—Alias*. (Archaíes Ellinikés Póleis, tóm 12), ékd. Athinaïkós Technologikós Ómilos – Athinaïkó Kéntro Oikistikís: Athens: Athinaïkó Kéntro Oikistikís.

Farstadvoll, S. 2019a. *A speculative archaeology of excess: Exploring the afterlife of a derelict landscape garden*. Doctoral dissertation, UiT The Arctic University of Norway.

Farstadvoll, S. 2019b. Growing concerns: Plants and their roots in the past. *Journal of Contemporary Archaeology* 5(2), 174–93.

Fatta, D., et al. 1997. An evaluation of the pollution level in Saronic Gulf waters. *Journal of Environmental Science and Health, Part A* 32(8), 2403–14.

Fausto, C. 2007. Feasting on people: Eating animals and humans in Amazonia. *Current Anthropology* 48, 497–530.

Finkel, O.M., et al. 2017. Understanding and exploiting plant beneficial microbes. *Current Opinion in Plant Biology* 38, 155–63.

Finlay, G. 1836. *The Hellenic kingdom and the Greek nation*. London: J. Murray.

Finlay, G. 1877. *A history of Greece from its conquest by the Roman to the present time*. Oxford: Clarendon Press.

Fish, S.K., and S.A. Kowalewski. 1990. *The archaeology of regions: A case for full-coverage survey*. Washington, DC: Smithsonian Institution Press.

Flannery, D.V. (ed.). 1976. *The early Mesoamerican village*. London: Academic Press.

Forbes, H. 1997. Turkish and modern Methana. In C. Mee and H.A. Forbes (eds.), *A rough and rocky place: The landscape and settlement history of the Methana Peninsula, Greece*. Liverpool: Liverpool University Press. 101–17.

Forbes, H. 2000a. The agrarian economy of the Ermionidha around 1700: An ethnohistorical reconstruction. In S.B. Sutton (ed.), *Contingent countryside: Settlement, economy, and land use in the Southern Argolid since 1700*. Stanford, CA: Stanford University Press. 41–70.

Forbes, H. 2000b. Land management in the Peloponnesos during the second Venetian occupation. In S.B. Sutton (ed.), *Contingent countryside: Settlement, economy, and land use in the southern Argolid since 1700*. Stanford, CA: Stanford University Press. 321–24.

Forbes, H. 2007. *Meaning and identity in a Greek landscape: An archaeological ethnography*. Cambridge: Cambridge University Press.

Forbes, H. 2013. Off-site scatters and the manuring hypothesis in Greek survey archaeology: An ethnographic approach. *Hesperia* 82(4), 551–94.

Forbes, H. n.d. Dumping the trash: How can we understand ancient Greek refuse? Unpublished paper.

Forbes, H., and H. Koster. 1976. *Fire, axe, plow: Human influence on local plant communities in the Southern Argolid*. New York, NY: New York Academy of Sciences.

Forbes, H., and C. Mee. 1997. Introduction. In C. Mee and H. Forbes (eds.), *A rough and rocky place: The landscape and settlement history of the Methana Peninsula*. Liverpool: Liverpool University Press. 1–4.

Forbes, R.J. 1964. *Studies in ancient technology*. Vol. 4. Leiden: E.J. Brill.

Forty, A. 2012. *Concrete and culture: A material history*. London: Reaktion Books.

Fotiadis, M. 1995. Modernity and the past-still-present: Politics of time in the birth of regional archaeological projects in Greece. *American Journal of Archaeology* 99(1), 59–78.

Fouqué, F. 1867. *Les Anciens Volcans de la Grèce*. *Revue des deux Mondes LVIII*. Paris: J. Claye.

Fowler, H.N. 1932. Corinth and the Corinthia. In H.N. Fowler and R. Stillwell (eds.), *Corinth I.i: Introduction, topography, architecture*. Cambridge, MA: Harvard University Press. 18–114.

Foxhall, L. 2007. House clearance: Unpacking the "kitchen" in Classical Greece. In R. Westgate, N.R.E. Fisher, and J. Whitley (eds.), *Building communities: House, settlement and society in the Aegean and beyond*. London: British School at Athens Studies. 15, 233–42.

Fraser, R. 1990a. *The making of the Golden Bough: The origins and growth of an argument*. New York, NY: St Martin's Press.

Fraser, R. 1990b. When the bough breaks. *London Review of Books* 12(15). Available at: www.lrb.co.uk/v12/n15/letters#letter14.

Fraser, R. 1994. Introduction. In J.G. Frazer, *The Golden Bough: A new abridgement*. Oxford: Oxford University Press. ix–xxxix.

Frazer, J.G. 1898. *Pausanias's Description of Greece*. 6 vols. London: Macmillan & Co.

Frazer, J.G. 1908. *The scope of social anthropology*. London: MacMillan and Co.

Frazer, J.G. 1911. *The magic art and the evolution of kings, being Part 1 Vol. 1 of The Golden Bough 3rd Edition*. London: Macmillan & Co.

Frazer, J.G. 1925. *The golden bough: A study of magic and religion*. New York, NY: Macmillan.

Frederick, C., and A. Krahtopoulou. 2000. Deconstructing agricultural terraces: Examining the influence of construction method on stratigraphy, dating and archaeological visibility. In P. Halstead and C. Frederick (eds.), *Landscape and land use in postglacial Greece*. Sheffield: Sheffield Academic Press. 79–94.

French, E. 2002. *Mycenae: Agamemnon's capital*. Stroud: Tempus Publishing.

Frey, J.M. 2016. *"Spolia" in fortifications and the role of the common builder in late antiquity*. Leiden: Brill.

Furumark, A. 1941a. *The Mycenaean Pottery: Analysis and classification*. Stockholm: K. Vitterhets Historie och Antikvitets Akademien.

Furumark, A. 1941b. *The Mycenaean Pottery: The chronology*. Stockholm: K. Vitterhets Historie och Antikvitets Akademien.

Fustel de Coulanges, N.D. 2006. *The ancient city: A study of the religion, laws, and institutions of Greece and Rome*. Mineola, NY: Dover Publications.

Galanis, D., and K. Nikitas. 2000. How the Argolid was filled with nitrates (Pós i Argolída gémise nitriká). *TO BHMA*, 01/ 23/2000, www.tovima.gr/relatedarticles/article/?aid=118482 (Accessed: 19 August 2016).

Gallant, T.W. 1991. *Risk and survival in Ancient Greece: Reconstructing the rural domestic economy*. Cambridge: Polity Press.

Garnsey, P. 1999. *Food and society in Classical antiquity*. Cambridge: Cambridge University Press.

Gates, C. 1985. Rethinking the building history of Grave Circle A at Mycenae. *American Journal of Archaeology* 89(2), 263–74.

Gatidou, G., E. Vassalou, and N.S. Thomaidis. 2010. Bioconcentration of selected endocrine disrupting compounds in the Mediterranean mussel, *Mytilus galloprovincialis*. *Marine Pollution Bulletin* 60(11), 2111–16.

Gatsou, V.A. 2001. *The reconstruction of the Ermionida. (I anasynkrótisi tis Ermionídas)*. Athens: Archipélagos.

Gauderman, W.J., et al. 2005. Childhood asthma and exposure to traffic and nitrogen dioxide. *Epidemiology* 16(6), 737–43.

Gavrielides, N. 1976. The impact of olive growing on the landscape in the Fourni Valley. *Annals of the New York Academy of Sciences* 268, 143–57.

Gebhard, E.R. 1993. The Isthmian games and the sanctuary of Poseidon in the early empire. In T.E. Gregory (ed.), *The Corinthia in the Roman period*. Ann Arbor, MI: University of Michigan. 78–94.

Gebhard, E.R. 2005. Rites for Melikertes-Palaimon in the early Roman Corinthia. In D.N. Schowalter and S.J. Friesen (eds.), *Urban religion in Roman Corinth: Interdisciplinary approaches.* Cambridge, MA: Harvard University Press. 165–203.

Gell, W. 1810. *The itinerary of Greece.* London: Payne.

Gell, W. 1817. *Itinerary of the Morea: Being a description of the routes of that peninsula.* London: Rodwell and Martin.

Gell, W. 1823. *Narrative of a journey in the Morea.* London: Longman, Hurst, Rees, Orme, and Brown.

Georgios, C. 2014. Checks for pesticide residues in agricultural products (Élenchoi gia ypoleímmata fytofarmákon sta georgiká proïónta). Blog post 3 May, 2012. Available at: http://tro-ma-ktiko.blogspot.com/2012/05/blog-post_4105.html (Accessed 7 March, 2016).

Gere, C. 2006. *The Tomb of Agamemnon.* Cambridge, MA: Harvard University Press.

Gershenson, D.E. 1991. *Apollo the wolf god.* Journal of Indo-European Monograph Series, No. 8. Mclean, VA: Institute for the Study of Man.

Gerstel, S.E.J. (ed.). 2013. *Viewing the Morea: Land and people in the Late Medieval Peloponnese.* Washington, DC: Dumbarton Oaks.

Geus, K. 2003. Space and geography. In A. Erskine (ed.), *A companion to the Hellenistic world.* Oxford: John Wiley & Sons. 232–46.

Gibb, H.A.R., and H. Bowen. 1950. *Islamic society and the West: A study of the impact of Western civilization on Moslem culture in the Near East. Volume One, Islamic society in the eighteenth century, Part I.* Oxford: Oxford University Press.

Gill, D.W.J. 2007. Arsinoe in the Peloponnese: the Ptolemaic base on the Methana Peninsula. *Egyptian stories: A British Egyptological tribute to Alan B. Lloyd, Alter Orient und Alter Testament* 347, 87–110.

Gillings, M. 2011. Chorography, phenomenology and the antiquarian tradition. *Cambridge Archaeological Journal* 21(1), 53–64.

Gillings, M., P. Hacıgüzeller, and G.R. Lock. 2019. *Re-Mapping archaeology: Critical perspectives, alternative mappings.* New York, NY: Routledge.

Ginouvès, R. 1972. *Le théâtron à gradins droits et l'odéon d'Argos.* Paris: J. Vrin.

Girard, R. 1986. *The scapegoat* (trans. Y. Freccero). Baltimore, MD: Johns Hopkins University Press.

Girard, R. 2014. *The one by whom scandal comes.* East Lansing, MI: Michigan State University Press.

Godlewska, A.M.C. 1999. *Geography unbound. French geographical science from Cassini to Humboldt.* Chicago, IL: Chicago University Press.

Goethe, J.W., and J. Gearey. 1994. *Essays on art and literature: The collected works.* Princeton, NJ: Princeton University Press.

Gombrich, E.H. 1956. *Art and illusion: A study in the psychology of pictorial representation.* Princeton, NJ: Princeton University Press.

González-Ruibal, A. 2008. Time to destroy: An archaeology of supermodernity. *Current Anthropology* 49(2), 247–79.

González-Ruibal, A. 2018. Archaeology of ethics. *Annual Review of Anthropology* 47, 345–60.

González-Ruibal, A. 2019. *An archaeology of the contemporary era.* London: Routledge.

Gordon, M. 1998. *Slavery in the Arab World.* New York, NY: New Amsterdam Books.

Greek Ministry of Culture. 1998. Nomination of Ancient Mycenae for inclusion on the world heritage list. Athens/Nafplion. Unpublished.

Green, S., and M. Lemon. 1996. Perceptual landscapes in Agrarian Systems: Degradation processes in North-Western Epirus and the Argolid Valley, Greece. *Cultural Geographies* 3(2), 181–99.

Greenberg, C. 1980. Modern and post-modern. *Quadrant* 24(3), 30–33.

Greenberg, P. 2010. Time for a sea change. *National Geographic Magazine*, October. 78–89.

Greenblatt, S. 2011. *The swerve: How the world became modern.* New York, NY: W.W. Norton.

Gregory, T.E. 1980. *Nauplion.* Athens: Lycabettus Press.

Gregory, T.E. 1993. *Isthmia: Volume V. The Hexamilion and the Fortress.* Princeton, NJ: The American School of Classical Studies at Athens.

Gregory, T.E. 2007. Contrasting impressions of land use in Early Modern Greece: The Eastern Corinthia and Kythera. In S. Davies and J.L. Davis (eds.), *Between Venice and Istanbul: Colonial landscapes in Early Modern Greece.* Princeton, NJ: American School of Classical Studies at Athens. 173–98.

Grove, A.T., and O. Rackham. 2003. *The nature of Mediterranean Europe: An ecological history.* New Haven, CT: Yale University Press.

Güsten, H., et al. 1988. Photochemical formation and transport of ozone in Athens, Greece. *Atmospheric Environment* 22, 1855–61.

Habicht, C. 1985. *Pausanias' guide to Ancient Greece.* Berkeley, CA: University of California Press.

Hägg, R. 1987. Gifts to the heroes in Geometric and Archaic Greece, In T. Linders & G. Nordqvist (eds.), *Gifts to the gods.* Vol. 15. Uppsala: Boreas. 93–99.

Haggis, D.C., and C.M. Antonaccio, 2015. A contextual archaeology of Ancient Greece, In D.C. Haggis and C.M. Antonaccio (eds.), *Classical archaeology in context: Theory and practice in excavation in the Greek world.* Berlin: Walter de Gruyter. 1–20.

Hall, J.M. 1995. How Argive was the "Argive" Heraion? The political and cultic geography of the Argive Plain, 900–400 B.C. *American Journal of Archaeology* 99(4), 577–613.

Halstead, P. 1990. Waste not, want not: Traditional responses to crop failure in Greece. *Rural History* 1, 147–63.

Halstead, P. 2014. *Two oxen ahead: Pre-mechanized farming in the Mediterranean.* Chichester: Wiley-Blackwell.

Hamilakis, Y. 2007. *The nation and its ruins: Antiquity, archaeology, and national imagination in Greece.* Oxford: Oxford University Press.

Hamilakis, Y. 2008. Decolonizing Greek archaeology: Indigenous archaeologies, modernist archaeology and the post-colonial critique. Μουσείο Μπενάκη. 273–84.

Hamilakis, Y. 2009. Indigenous Hellenisms/Indigenous modernities: Classical antiquity, materiality, and modern Greek society. In G. Boys-Stones, B. Graziosi, and P. Vasuni (eds.), *The Oxford handbook of Hellenic studies.* Oxford: Oxford University Press.

Hamilakis, Y. 2013. *Archaeology and the senses: Human experience, memory, and affect.* Cambridge: Cambridge University Press.

Hamilton, J. 2010. The lure of volcanoes. *History Today* 60(7), 34–41.

Hanink, J. 2017. *The Classical debt: Greek antiquity in an era of austerity.* Cambridge, MA: Belknap Press.

Hanson, V.D. 1999. *The other Greeks: The family farm and the agrarian roots of Western civilization.* Berkeley, CA: University of California Press.

Harley, J.B., 2002. *The new nature of maps: Essays in the history of cartography.* Baltimore, MD: Johns Hopkins University Press.

Harman, G. 2011. *The quadruple object.* Winchester: Zero Books.

Harman, G. 2013. *Bells and whistles: More speculative realism.* Washington, DC: Zero Books.

Harman, G. 2014. *Bruno Latour: Reassembling the political.* London: Pluto Press.

Harman, G. 2015. Politics and law as Latourian modes of existence. In K. McGee (ed.), *Latour and the passage of law.* Edinburgh: Edinburgh University Press. 38–60.

Harman, G. 2016a. *Immaterialism: Objects and social theory.* Cambridge: Polity Press.

Harman, G. 2016b. On behalf of form. In M. Bille and T.F. Sørensen (eds.), *Elements of architecture: Assembling archaeology, atmosphere and the performance of building Spaces.* New York, NY: Routledge. 30–46.

Harrison, R. 2016. Archaeologies of emergent presents and futures. *Historical Archaeology* 50(3), 165–80.

Harrison, R.P. 2003. *The dominion of the dead*. Chicago, IL: University of Chicago Press.

Harrison, R.P. 2008. *Gardens: An essay on the human condition*. Chicago, IL: University of Chicago Press.

Hastaoglou-Martinidis, V. 1995. City form and national identity: Urban designs in nineteenth-century Greece. *Journal of Modern Greek Studies* 13(1), 99–123.

Hastaoglou-Martinidis, V., K. Kafkoula, and N. Papamichos. 1993. Urban modernization and national renaissance: Town planning in 19th century Greece. *Planning Perspectives* 8 (4), 427–69.

Hayward, C. 2003. The geology of Corinth: The study of a basic resource. In C. K. Williams and N. Bookidis (eds.), *Corinth, the centenary: 1896–1996*. Princeton, NJ: American School of Classical Studies at Athens. 15–42.

Hayward, C. 2004. A reconstruction of the pre-8th Century BC palaeotopography of central Corinth, Greece. *Geoarchaeology* 19(5), 383–405.

Heat-Moon, W.L. 1991. *PrairyErth*. London: Andre Deutsch.

Hector, J. 1973. La plaine d'Argos, répercussions socio-économiques d'une spécialisation agricole. *Méditerranée*, deuxième série 13(2), 1–17.

Heidegger, M. 1977. *The question concerning technology, and other essays* (trans. W. Lovitt). New York, NY: Garland Publishing.

Heidegger, M. 2002. The age of the world picture. In J. Young and K. Hayne (eds.), *Off the beaten track*. Cambridge: Cambridge University Press. 57–72.

Heidegger, M. 2003. Overcoming metaphysics. In J. Stambaugh (ed.), *The end of philosophy* (trans. J. Stambaugh). Chicago, IL: University of Chicago Press. 84–110.

Heidegger, M. 2008a. On the essence of truth. In D.F. Krell (ed.), *Basic writings*. London: Harper Perennial. 111–38.

Heidegger, M. 2008b. Letter on humanism. In D.F. Krell (ed.), *Basic writings*. London: Harper Perennial. 217–65.

Heikell, R. 2010. *West Aegean: The Attic coast, Eastern Peloponnese and Western Cyclades*. 2nd ed. St Ives: Imray Laurie Norie & Wilson.

Hellas. 1829. *Práktika tis en Argeí Ethnikis tetártis ton Ellinon syneleúseos*. En Aigini: Ek tis Ethnikis Typografías Dieuthynómenes.

Hellenic Republic, Ministry of Rural Development and Foodstuff. 2011. *Prógramma agrotikís anáptyxis tis Elládas (2007–2013) (Rural Development Program of Greece (2007–2013))*. Athens: Greek Ministry of Rural Development and Foodstuff.

Hellenic Statistical Authority. 2013. Greece in numbers.

Henry O., and U. Kelp (eds.). 2016. *Tumulus as sema: Space, politics, culture and religion in the first millennium BC*. Berlin and Boston, MA: De Gruyter.

Hervé, F. 1837. *A residence in Greece and Turkey with notes of the journey through Bulgaria, Servia, Hungary, and the Balkan*. 2 vols. London: Whittaker.

Herzfeld, M. 1982. *Ours once more: Folklore, ideology, and the making of modern Greece*. Austin, TX: University of Texas Press.

Herzfeld, M. 1987. *Anthropology through the looking glass: Critical ethnography in the margins of Europe*. Cambridge: Cambridge University Press.

Herzfeld, M. 1991. *A place in history: Social and monumental time in a Cretan town*. Princeton, NJ: Princeton University Press.

Herzfeld, M. 2002. The absence presence: Discourses of crypto-colonialism. *South Atlantic Quarterly* 101(4), 899–926.

Herzfeld, M. 2003. Localism and the logic of nationalistic folklore: Cretan reflections. *Comparative Studies in Society and History* 45(2), 281–310.

Higgins, M.D., and R.A. Higgins. 1996. *A geological companion to Greece and the Aegean*. London: Duckworth.

Holbraad, M. 2012. *Truth in motion: The recursive anthropology of Cuban divination*. Chicago, IL: University of Chicago Press.

Hood, R. 1998. *Faces of archaeology in Greece: Caricatures by Piet De Jong.* Oxford: Leopard's Head Press.

Hope Simpson, R., and D.K. Hagel. 2006. *Mycenaean fortifications, highways, dams, and canals.* Sävedalen: Paul Åströms Förlag.

Horden, P., and N. Purcell. 2000. *The corrupting sea: A study of Mediterranean history.* Oxford: Wiley-Blackwell.

Horne, L. 1982. Fuel for the metal worker: The role of charcoal and charcoal production in ancient metallurgy. *Expedition* 25(1), 6–13.

Hume, D., and T.L. Beauchamp. 2007. *A dissertation on the passions: The natural history of religion – A critical edition.* Oxford: Clarendon Press.

Hutton, W. 2005. *Describing Greece: Landscape and literature in the Periegesis of Pausanias.* Cambridge: Cambridge University Press.

Iakovidis, S., et al. 2003. *The archaeological atlas of Mycenae.* Athens: Archaeological Society of Athens.

Ingold, T. 1993. The temporality of landscape. *World Archaeology* 25(2), 152–74.

Ingold, T. 2007a. *Lines.* London: Routledge.

Ingold, T. 2007b. Materials against materiality. *Archaeological Dialogues* 14(1), 1–16.

Ingold, T. 2008. Anthropology is not ethnography: Radcliffe-Brown Lecture in social anthropology. *Proceedings of the British Academy* 154, 69–92.

Ingold, T. 2009. Against space: Place, movement, knowledge. In P.W. Kirby (ed.), *Boundless worlds: An anthropological approach to movement.* New York, NY: Berghahn Books. 29–43.

Ingold, T. 2011. *Being alive: Essays on movement, knowledge and description.* London: Routledge.

Ioakeimidis, C., et al. 2014. A comparative study of marine litter on the seafloor of coastal areas in the Eastern Mediterranean and Black Seas. *Marine Pollution Bulletin* 89(1–2), 296–304.

Ioannidou, N. 1992. O naós tou Agíou Dimitríou (Avgoú) sta Dídyma tis Ermionídas. *Deltíon XAE 16 (1991-1992), Períodos D'. In memory of Andre Grabar (1896–1990),* 97–106.

Ivou, G. 2016. Archaía Asíni. *Archaiología kai Téchnes,* 120 (April 2016), 120–44.

Jackson, A.H. 2015. Arms from the age of Philip and Alexander at Broneer's West Foundation near Isthmia. In E. Gebhard and T.E. Gregory (eds.), *Bridge of the untiring sea: The Corinthian Isthmus from prehistory to Late Antiquity.* Princeton, NJ: American School of Classical Studies at Athens. 133–57.

Jahns, S. 1993. On the Holocene vegetation history of the Argive Plain. *Vegetation History and Archaeobotany* 2(4), 187–203.

James, P.A., C.B. Mee, and G.J. Taylor. 1994. Soil erosion and the archaeological landscape of Methana, Greece. *Journal of Field Archaeology* 21(4), 395–416.

James, S. 2019. The South Stoa at Corinth: New evidence and interpretations. *Hesperia* 88(1), 155–214.

Jameson, M.H. 1953. Inscriptions of the Peloponessos. *Hesperia* 22(3), 148–71.

Jameson, M.H., C.N. Runnels, and T. Van Andel. 1994. *A Greek countryside: The Southern Argolid from prehistory to the present day.* Stanford, CA: Stanford University Press.

Jameson, M.H., A.B. Stallsmith, and P. Cartledge. 2014. *Cults and rites in Ancient Greece: Essays on religion and society.* Cambridge: Cambridge University Press.

Jansen, A. 1997. Bronze Age highways at Mycenae. *Echos du monde classique/Classical Views* 41, 1–16.

Jansen, A. 2002. *A study of the remains of Mycenaean roads and stations of Bronze-Age Greece.* Lewiston, NY: Edwin Mellen Press.

Jansen, A. 2003. The Mycenaean Roads in the Survey Area. In S. Iakovidis, E.B. French, K. Shelton, J. Lavery, A.G. Jansen, and C. Ioannides (eds.) *The archaeological atlas of Mycenae.* Athens: Archaeological Society of Athens. 28–30.

Jarvis, K.E., S.J. Parry, and J.M. Piper. 2001. Temporal and spatial studies of autocatalyst-derived platinum, rhodium, and palladium and selected vehicle-derived trace elements in the environment. *Environmental Science & Technology* 35, 1031–36.

Jones, W.H.S. 1809. *Malaria and Greek history.* Manchester: Manchester University Press.

Kalivas, D., and K. Bakasietas. 2011. Soil and climate conditions of the vine-growing district of Nemea. In S. Kourakou-Dragona (ed.), *Nemea: Beloved land of Zeus and Dionysos.* Athens: Foinikas Publications. 191–99.

Kaplan, L.G. 2001. Modern Corinth, 1676–1923. Corinth Computer Project. Available at: http://corinth.sas.upenn.edu/moderncorinth.html.

Kaplan, L.G. 2010. "Writing down the country": Travelers and the emergence of the archaeological gaze. In A. Stroulia and S.B. Sutton (eds.), *Archaeology in situ: Sites, archaeology, and communities in Greece.* Lanham, MD: Lexington Books. 75–108.

Kapsimalis, V., et al. 2014. Organic contamination of surface sediments in the metropolitan coastal zone of Athens, Greece: Sources, degree, and ecological risk. *Marine Pollution Bulletin* 80, 312–24.

Kardulias, P.N. 1995. Architecture, energy, and social evolution at Isthmia, Greece: Some thoughts about Late Antiquity in the Korinthia. *Journal of Mediterranean Archaeology* 8(2), 33–59.

Kardulias, P.N. 2005. *From Classical to Byzantine: Social evolution in Late Antiquity and the Fortress at Isthmia, Greece.* Oxford: British Archaeological Reports.

Karo, G. 1913. Archäologische Funde in Yahre 1912. *Archäologischer Anzeiger* 28, 95–121.

Karo, G. 1915. Die Schachtgräber von Mykenai. *Mitteilungen des Deutschen Archäologischen Instituts, Athenische Abteilung* 40, 113–230.

Karo, G. 1930. *Die Schachtgräber von Mykenai.* Munich: F. Bruckmann.

Katzef, M.L. 1972. The Kyrenia ship. In G.F. Bass (ed.), *A history of seafaring.* London: Thames & Hudson. 50–52.

Kavvadias, P. 1891. *Fouilles d'Épidaure.* Athens: S.C. Vlastos.

Kavvadias, P. 1900. *To hieron tou Asklepiou en Epidauroi kai he therapeia ton asthenon.* Athens: Athenesin.

Kelepertzis, E., et al. 2016. Copper accumulation in vineyard soils from Nemea, Greece. *Bulletin of the Geological Society of Greece* 50(4), 2192–99.

Keramberopoulos, D. 1998. *Harta tis Ellados tou Riga Veletinli.* Athens: Epistemoniki Hetaireia Meletes Pheron-Velestinou-Rega.

Keraudren, D., and D. Sorel. 1987. The terraces of Corinth (Greece): A detailed record of eustatic sea-level variations during the last 500,000 years. *Marine Geology* 77, 99–107.

Kharitonidhis, S. 1966. Kandia, Iria. *Archaiologikon Deltion* 21(2), 130–31.

Khouliarakis, M. 1973. *Geografiki dhioikitiki kai plithismiaki exelexis tis Elladhos, 1821–1971.* Vol. 1.1. Athens: Ethniko Kentro Koinonikon Erevnón.

Khouliarakis, M. 1975. *Geografiki dhioikitiki kai plithismiaki exelexis tis Elladhos, 1821–1971.* Vol. 2. Athens: Ethniko Kentro Koinonikon Erevnón.

Kilian-Dirlmeier, I. 1985. Fremde Weihungen in Griechischen Heiligtumern vom. 8. Bis zum Beginn des 7. Jahrhunderts v. Chr. *JRGZM* 32, 215–54.

Kitromilides, P. 2013. *Enlightenment and revolution: The making of modern Greece.* Cambridge, MA: Harvard University Press.

Klein, N.L. 1997. Excavation of the Greek temples at Mycenae by the British School at Athens. *Annual of the British School at Athens* 92, 247–322.

Knappett, C. (ed.). 2013. *Network analysis in archaeology.* Oxford: Oxford University Press.

Knauss, J. 1997. Agamemnóneion phréar: Der Stausee der Mykener. *Antike Welt* 5, 381–95.

Knodell, A.R., S. Fachard, and K. Papangeli. 2016. The 2015 Mazi Archaeological Project: Regional survey in Northwest Attica (Greece). *Antike Kunst* 59, 132–52.

Knodell, A.R., S. Fachard, and K. Papangeli. 2017. The 2016 Mazi Archaeological Project: Survey and settlement investigations in Northwest Attica (Greece). *Antike Kunst* 60, 146–63.

Knodell, A.R., and T. Leppard (eds.). 2017. *Regional approaches to society and complexity studies in honor of John F. Cherry*. London: Equinox.

Konstantinidis, A. 1966. Architecture of the Xenia hotels. *World Architecture* 3, 144–47.

Koster, H. 1976. The thousand-year road. *Expedition* 19(1), 19–28.

Koster, H. 1977. *The ecology of pastoralism in relation to changing patterns of land use in the Northeast Peloponnese*. Doctorial dissertation, Department of Anthropology, University of Pennsylvania.

Koster, H. 2000. Neighbors and pastures: Reciprocity and access to pasture. In S.E. Sutton (ed.), *Contingent countryside: Settlement, economy, and,land use in the Southern Argolid since 1700*. Stanford, CA: Stanford University Press. 241–61.

Koster, H.A., and J.B. Koster. 1976. Competition or symbiosis? Pastoral adaptive strategies in the Southern Argolid, Greece. *Annals of the New York Academy of Sciences* 268(1), 275–85.

Kotínis, C. 1985. *Ellinikós Ampelografikós Átlas*. Athens.

Kotsakis, K. 1991. The powerful past. In I. Hodder (ed.), *Archaeological theory in Europe: The last three decades*. London: Routledge. 65–90.

Kotsakis, K. 2001. Mesolithic to Neolithic in Greece: Continuity, discontinuity or change of course? *Documenta Praehistorica. Porocilo O Raziskovanju Paleolitika, Neolotika in Eneolitika V Sloveniji. Neolitske Studijes*. 63–73.

Kotsakis, K. 2003a. From the Neolithic side: The Mesolithic/Neolithic interface in Greece. In N. Galanidou and C. Perlès (eds.), *The Greek Mesolithic: Problems and perspectives*. British School at Athens Studies 10. London: British School at Athens. 217–21.

Kotsakis, K. 2003b. Ideological aspects of contemporary archaeology in Greece. In M. Haagsma, P. Den Boer, and E.M. Moorma (eds.), *The impact of Classical Greece on European and national identities: Proceedings of an international colloquium, held at the Netherlands Institute at Athens, 2–4 October 2000*. Amsterdam: Gieben. 55–70.

Koukoulis, T. 1997. Catalogue of churches. In C. Mee and H.A. Forbes (eds.), *A rough and rocky place: The landscape and settlement history of the Methana Peninsula, Greece*. Liverpool: Liverpool University Press. 211–56.

Koumadorakes, O. 2007. *Argos: to polydipsion*. Argos: Ekdoseis Ek Prooimiou.

Koumaridis, Y. 2006. Urban transformation and de-Ottomanization in Greece. *East Central Europe* 33(1–2), 213–41.

Kourakou-Dragona, S. 2011. From Agiogitiko wine to Nemea's appellation of origin wines. In S. Kourakou-Dragona (ed.), *Nemea: Beloved land of Zeus and Dionysos*. Athens: Foinikas Publications. 151–66.

Kourelis, K. 2017. Flights of archaeology: Peschke's Acrocorinth. *Hesperia* 86(4), 723–82.

Koutsoumba, D., and Y. Nakas. 2013. Díolkos. ena simantikó techniko ergo Tis archaiotitas. In K. Kissas and W.D. Niemeier (eds.), *The Corinthia and the Northeast Peloponnese: Topography and history from prehistoric times until the end of antiquity*. München: Hirmer. 191–206.

Kraay, C.M. 1976. *Archaic and Classical Greek Coins*. Berkeley, CA: University of California Press.

Krafft, M. 1993. *Volcanoes: Fire from the earth*. London: Thames & Hudson.

Kraft, J.C., S.E. Aschenbrenner, and G. Rapp. 1977. Paleogeographic reconstructions of coastal Aegean archaeological sites. *Science* 195(4282), 941–47.

Kraus, K. 1922. *Untergang der Welt durch schwarze Magie*. Wien-Leipzig: Verlag "Die Frackel."

Krautheimer, R., and S. Ćurčić. 1992. *Early Christian and Byzantine architecture*. New Haven, CT: Yale University Press.

Kritidis, P., et al. 2012. Radioactive pollution in Athens, Greece due to the Fukushima nuclear accident. *Journal of Environmental Radioactivity* 114, 100–04.

Kritzas, C. 1979. Katálogos pesónton apó to Árgos, *STILI, Tómos eis mnímin N. Kontoléontos*, 497–510.

Kritzas, C. 1992. Aspects de la vie politique et economique d'Argos au Ve siècle avant J.-C. In M. Piérart (ed.), *Polydipsion Argos: Argos de la fin des palais mycéniens à la constitution de l'état classique*. Athens: École française d'Athènes. 231–40.

Kritzas, C. 2003–04. Literacy and society: The case of Argos. *Kodai* 13/14, 53–60.

Kritzas, C. 2006. Nouvelles Inscriptions D'Argos: Les Archives des Compes du Trésor Sacré. *Comptes rendus des séances de l'Académie des Inscriptions et Belles-Lettres* 150(1), 397–434.

Kron, G. 2009. Animal husbandry, hunting, fishing, and fish production. In J.P. Oleson (ed.), *The Oxford handbook of engineering and technology in the Classical world*. Oxford: Oxford University Press. 175–224.

Kuntz, E., and H.D. Kuntz. 2008. *Hepatology: Textbook and atlas*. 3rd ed. Heidelberg: Springer.

Kyriazis, P. 1976. Stamatis Voulgaris. O agonistís, o poleodómos, o ánthropos. In P. Kyriazis and M. Nikolanikos (eds.), *Syllogikó, Prótoi Éllines technikoí epistímones periódou apelefthérosis*. Athens: Technical Office of Greece. 156.

Lacoue-Labarthe, T., et al. 2016. Impacts of ocean acidification in a warming Mediterranean Sea: An overview. *Regional Studies in Marine Science* 5, 1–11.

Lambropoulos, V. 1984. The aesthetic ideology of the Greek quest of identity. *Journal of Modern Hellenism* 4, 19–24.

Lambros, S. 1886. Notes from Athens. *The Athenaeum* 3048, 429.

Lantier, R. 1953. Eloge funèbre de M. Philippe Legrand, membre libre non résidant. *Comptes rendus des séances de l'Académie des Inscriptions et Belles-Lettres* 97(3), 243–47.

Larmour, D.H. 1992. Making parallels: Synkrisis and Plutarch's "Themistocles and Camillus." *ANRW* 2(6), 4154–200.

Larmour, D.H.J. 1990. Boat-races and swimming contests at Hermione. *Aethlon* 7(2), 127–38.

Larmour, D.H.J. 2004. Statesman and self in the parallel lives. In L. de Blois (ed.), *The statesman in Plutarch's works*. Leiden: Brill. 43–52.

Latimer, J. 2013. Being alongside: Rethinking relations amongst different kinds. *Theory, Culture & Society* 30(7–8), 77–104.

Latour, B. 1986. Visualization and cognition: Thinking with eyes and hands. *Knowledge and Society* 6(6), 1–40.

Latour, B. 1987. *Science in action*. Cambridge, MA: Harvard University Press.

Latour, B. 1993. *We have never been modern* (trans. C. Porter). Cambridge, MA: Harvard University Press.

Latour, B. 2002. *War of the worlds: What about peace?* (trans. C. Brigg). Chicago, IL: Prickly Paradigm Press.

Latour, B. 2004a. *The politics of nature: How to bring the sciences into democracy*. Cambridge, MA: Harvard University Press.

Latour, B. 2004b. Why has critique run out of steam? From matters of fact to matters of concern. *Critical Inquiry* 30(2), 225–48.

Latour, B. 2005. *Reassembing the social: An introduction to actor-network-theory*. Oxford: Oxford University Press.

Latour, B. 2010. *The making of law: An ethnography of the Conseil d'État*. Cambridge: Polity Press.

Latour, B. 2015. The strange entanglement of jurimorphs. In K. McGee (ed.), *Latour and the passage of law*. Edinburgh: Edinburgh University Press. 331–53.

Latour, B. 2013. *An inquiry into modes of existence: An anthropology of the moderns*. Cambridge, MA: Harvard University Press.

Latour, B. 2018. *Down to earth: Politics in the new climate regime*. Cambridge: Polity Press.

Laurent, P.E. 1821. *Recollections of a Classical tour*. London: G. and W.B. Whittaker.

Lavery, J. 1990. Some aspects of Mycenaean topography. *Bulletin of the Institute of Classical Studies* 37, 165–71.

Lavezzi, J.C. 1978. Prehistoric investigations at Corinth. *Hesperia* 47(4), 402–51.

Lawrence, C.M. 2007. *Blood and oranges: European markets and immigrant labor in rural Greece*. New York, NY: Berghahn Books.

Lazarakis, K. 2006. *The wines of Greece*. London: Mitchell Beazley.

Leach, E.R. 1966. On the "founding fathers." *Current Anthropology* 7, 560–76.

Leach, E.R. 2011. Kingship and divinity: The unpublished Frazer Lecture. *HAU: Journal of Ethnographic Theory* 1(1), 279–98.

Leake, W.M. 1830. *Travels in the Morea*. 3 vols. London: John Murray.

Leake, W.M. 1835. *Travels in Northern Greece*. 4 vols. London: J. Rodwell.

Leake, W.M. 1846. *Peloponnesiaca*. London: J. Rodwell.

Leck, M.A., V.T. Parker, and R.L. Simpson. 1989. *Ecology of soil seed banks*. New York, NY: Academic Press.

Legrand, P.E. 1905. Antiquités de Trézène, Notes de topographie. *BCH* 29, 269–318.

Lehmann, H. 1937. *Argolis: Landeskunde der Ebene von Argos und ihrer Randgebiete*. Athens: Deutsches Archaologisches Institut.

Lemon, M., and N. Blatsou. 1999a. Background to agriculture and degradation in the Argolid Valley. In M. Lemon (ed.), *Exploring environmental change using an integrative method*. Amsterdam: Gordon and Breach Science Publishers. 27–38.

Lemon, M., and N. Blatsou. 1999b. Agricultural production and change. In M. Lemon (ed.), *Exploring environmental change using an integrative method*. Amsterdam: Gordon and Breach Science Publishers. 83–117.

Lemon, M., and N. Blatsou. 1999c. Technology and agricultural production in the Argolid. In M. Lemon (ed.), *Exploring environmental change using an integrative method*. Amsterdam: Gordon and Breach Science Publishers. 119–60.

Lemon, M., R. Seaton, and J. Park. 1994. Social enquiry and the measurement of natural phenomena: The degradation of irrigation water in the Argolid Plain, Greece. *International Journal of Sustainable Development & World Ecology* 1(3), 206–20.

Leontis, A. 1995. *Topographies of Hellenism: Mapping the homeland*. Ithaca, NY: Cornell University Press.

Leontis, A. 1997. Ambivalent Greece. *Journal of Modern Greek Studies* 15(1), 125–36.

Leontsinis, G. 2010. The wreck of the *Mentor* on the coast of the island of Kythera and the operation to retrieve, salvage, and transport the Parthenon sculptures to London (1802–1805). In A.M. Tamis, C. Mackie, and S. Byrne (eds.), *Philathenaios: Studies in honour of Michael J Osborne, Greek Epigraphic Society*. Athens: Arts Books. 249–73.

Lepetit, B. 1998. Missions scientifques et expeditions militaries. Remarques sur leurs modalités d'articulation. In M.N. Bourguet (ed.), *L'invention scientifique de la Méditerranée. Égypt, Morée, Algérie*. Paris: Éd. de l'École des Hautes Études en Sciences Sociales. 97–116.

Leppin, H. 1999. Argos: Eine griechische Demokratie des fünften Jahrhunderts v. Chr. *Ktema* 24, 297–312.

Levi, P. (ed.). 1979. *Pausanias' guide to Greece I: Central Greece*. London: Penguin Classics.

LiDonnici, L.R. 1995. *The Epidaurian miracle inscriptions: Text, translation and commentary*. Atlanta, GA: Scholars Press.

Lightfoot, C., and C. Witmore. 2018. Describing Hermion/Ermioni. Between Pausanias and digital maps, a topology. In M. Gillings, P. Hacigüzeller, and G. Lock (eds.), *Remapping archaeology: Critical perspectives, alternative mappings*. London: Routledge.

Lindenlauf, A. 2000. *Waste management in Ancient Greece, from the Homeric to the Classical period: Concepts and practices of waste, dirt, recycling and disposal.* Doctoral dissertation, University of London.

Lindenlauf, A. 2003. The sea as a place of no return in Ancient Greece. *World Archaeology* 35(3), 416–33.

Lingis, A. 1998. *The imperative.* Bloomington, IN: Indiana University Press.

Livieratos, E. 2009. *Chartografikés peripéteies tis Elládas, 1821–1919.* Athens: MIET-ELIA. (Cartographic adventures of Greece, 1821–1919).

Llewellyn-Jones, L. 2011. Domestic abuse and violence against women in Ancient Greece. In S.D. Lambert (ed.), *Sociable man: Essays on Ancient Greek social behaviour in honour of Nick Fischer.* Edinburgh: Classical Press of Wales. 231–66.

Lohmann, H. 2013. Der Diolkos von Korinth–eine antike Schiffsschleppe? In K. Kissas and W.D. Niemeier (eds.), *The Corinthia and the Northeast Peloponnese: Topography and history from prehistoric times until the end of antiquity.* München: Hirmer. 207–30.

Lolos, Y.A. 1997. The Hadrianic Aqueduct of Corinth (with an appendix on the Roman aqueducts in Greece). *Hesperia: The Journal of the American School of Classical Studies at Athens* 66 (2), 271–314.

Lopez, B. 1986. *Arctic Dreams.* New York, NY: Scribner.

Lopez, B. 1998. *Apologia.* Athens, GA: University of Georgia Press.

Lord, L.E. 1939. Watchtowers and fortresses in Argolis. *American Journal of Archaeology* 43(1), 78–84.

Lord, L.E. 1941. *Blockhouses in the Argolid.* Hesperia 10(2), 93–112.

Lordimer, H. 2006. Herding memories of humans and animals. *Environment and Planning D: Society and Space* 24, 497–518.

Love, J., and M. Meng. 2016. Histories of the dead? *Time and Mind* 9(3), 223–44.

Lucas, G. 2004. Modern disturbances: On the ambiguities of archaeology *Modernism/Modernity* 11(2), 109–20.

Lucas, G. 2012. *Understanding the archaeological record.* Cambridge: Cambridge University Press.

Lucas, G. 2015. Archaeology and contemporaneity. *Archaeological Dialogues* 22(1), 1–15.

Lucas, G. 2018. *Writing the past: Knowledge and literary production in archaeology.* London: Routledge.

Lucas, S.C. 2005. Liquid history: Serres and Lucretius. In Abbas, N.B. (ed.), *Mapping Michel Serres.* Ann Arbor, MI: University of Michigan Press. 72–83.

Lupatsch, I., et al. 2010. Effect of stocking density and feeding level on energy expenditure and stress responsiveness in European sea bass Dicentrarchus labrax. *Aquaculture* 298, 245–50.

Lydon, J., and U.Z. Rizvi (eds.). 2016. *Handbook of postcolonial archaeology.* London: Routledge.

Macfarlane, R. 2012. *The old ways.* New York, NY: Viking.

Macfarlane, R. 2015. *Landmarks.* London: Hamish Hamilton.

Macfarlane, R. 2019. *Underland: A deep time journey.* New York, NY: W.W. Norton & Company.

MacKay, P. 1968. Acrocorinth in 1668, a Turkish account. *Hesperia* 37(4), 386–97.

Mackridge, P. 2009. *Language and national identity in Greece, 1766–1976.* Oxford: Oxford University Press.

Makra, A., et al. 2001. Mapping the pollution gradient of the Saronikos Gulf benthos prior to the operation of the Thens sewage treatment plant, Greece. *Marine Pollution Bulletin* 42, 1417–19.

Malkin, I. 1993. Land ownership, territorial possession, hero cults, and scholarly theory. In R.M. Rosen and J. Farrell (eds.), *Nomodeiktes: Greek studies in honor of Martin Ostwald.* Ann Arbor, MI: University of Michigan Press. 225–34.

Malkin, I. 2003. Networks and the emergence of Greek identity. *Mediterranean Historical Review* 18(2), 56–74.

Manning, R. 1891. On the flow of water in open channels and pipes. *Transactions of the Institution of Civil Engineers of Ireland* 20, 161–207.

Mantzavrakos, E., et al. 2007. Impacts of a marine fish farm in Argolikos Gulf (Greece) on the water column and the sediment. *Desalination* 210, 110–24.

Maravelias, C.D., and E.V. Tsitsika. 2014. Fishers' targeting behavior in Mediterranean: Does vessel size matter? *Fisheries Management and Ecology* 21, 68–74.

Marchand, J. 2009. Kleonai, the Corinth–Argos Road, and the "axis of history." *Hesperia* 78, 107–63.

Marchand, J.C. 2002. *Well-built Kleonai: A history of the Peloponnesian city based on a survey of the visible remains and a study of the literary and epigraphic sources.* Doctoral dissertation, University of California, Berkeley.

Marchetti, P. 2000. Recherches sur les mythes et la topographie d'Argos, V. Quelques mises au point sur les rues d'Argos. A propos de deux ouvrages recents. *Bulletin de correspondance hellénique* 124(1), 273–89.

Marchetti, P. 2013. Argos: la ville en ses remparts. In D. Mulliez (ed.), *Sta vímata tou Wilhelm Vollgraff: Ekató chrónia archaiologikís drastiriótitas sto Árgos / Sur les pas de Wilhelm Vollgraff: Cent ans d'activités archéologiques à Argos.* Recherches franco-helléniques, 4. Athènes: École française d'Athènes. 317–34.

Margaritis, E., and M.K. Jones. 2008. Greek and Roman agriculture. In J.P. Oleson (ed.), *The Oxford handbook of engineering and technology in the Classical world.* Oxford: Oxford University Press. 217–41.

Marsden, J.H. 1864. *A brief memoir of the life and writings of Lieutenant-Colonel William Martin Leake.* London: Privately printed.

Martín, J., et al. 2014. Impact of bottom trawling on deep-sea sediment properties along the flanks of a submarine canyon. *PLoS ONE* 9(8), e104536.

Mattern, T., 2012. Das «wohlgebaute Kleonai» Neue Ausgrabungen in einer Stadt des «Dritten Griechenlands». *Antike Welt*, 46–54.

Mattern, T. 2013. Kleonai. Neue Forschungen in einer Stadt des «Dritten Griechenlands». In K. Kissas and W.D. Niemeier (eds.), *The Corinthia and the Northeast Peloponnesus: Topography and history from prehistory until end of the antiquity.* München: Hirmer. 323–32.

Matthews, D., and S. Veitch. 2016. The limits of critique and the forces of law. *Law and Critique* 27(3), 349–61.

Matz, F. 1964. Georg Karo. *Gnomon* 36(6), 637–40.

Mavroeidi, V. 2011. Conservation and re-use of an Ottoman monument. In D. Babalis (ed.), *Chronocity: Sensitive interventions in historic environment.* Cities, Design & Sustainability Series, 7. Firenze: Alinea. 46–48.

McAllister, M.H. 1969. A temple at Hermione. *Hesperia* 38(2), 169–83.

McAllister, M.H. 2005. *The excavations at Ancient Halieis, Volume 1: The fortifications and adjacent structures.* Bloomington, IN: Indiana University Press.

McDonald, W.A. 1943. *The political meeting places of the Greeks.* Baltimore, MD: Johns Hopkins Press.

McDonald, W.A., and G.R. Rapp (eds.). 1972. *The Minnesota Messenia Expedition: Reconstructing a Bronze Age regional environment.* Minneapolis, MN: University of Minnesota Press.

McGee, K. 2014. *Bruno Latour: The normativity of networks.* Abingdon: Routledge.

McGovern, P.E., and G.R. Hall. 2016. Charting a future course for organic residue analysis in archaeology. *Journal of Archaeological Method and Theory* 23(2), 592–622.

McGowan, B. 1981. *The economic life in Ottoman Europe: Taxation, trade, and the struggle for land, 1600–1800.* Cambridge: Cambridge University Press.

McGrew, W.W. 1985. *Land and revolution in modern Greece, 1800–1881: The transition in the tenure and exploitation of land from Ottoman rule to independence.* Kent, OH: Kent State University Press.

McHugh, M. 2017. *The Ancient Greek farmstead.* Oxford: Oxbow Books.

McInerney, J. 2010. *The cattle of the sun: Cows and culture in the world of the ancient Greeks.* Princeton, NJ: Princeton University Press.

McInerney, J., and I. Sluiter. 2016. General introduction. In J. McInerney, I. Sluiter, and B. Corthals (eds.). *Valuing landscape in Classical antiquity: Natural environment and cultural imagination.* Leiden: Brill, pp. 1–21.

McLeod, W.E. 1962. Kiveri and Thermisi. *Hesperia* 31(4), 378–92.

McLuhan, M. 1994[1964]. *Understanding media: The extensions of man.* Cambridge, MA: MIT Press.

Mee, C. et al. 1997. Catalogue of sites. In C. Mee, and H. Forbes (eds.), *A rough and rocky place: The landscape and settlement history of the Methana Peninsula.* Liverpool: Liverpool University Press. 118–210.

Mee, C., and H. Forbes (eds.). 1997. *A rough and rocky place: The landscape and settlement history of the Methana Peninsula.* Liverpool: Liverpool University Press.

Megaloudi, F. 2005. Burnt sacrificial plant offerings in Hellenistic times: An archaeological case study from Messene, Peloponnese, Greece. *Vegetation History and Archaeobotany* 14, 329–40.

Melville, R. 1997. *Lucretius on the nature of the universe.* Oxford: Clarendon Press.

Meritt, B.D. 1947. Honors to Faustina at Corinth. *Classical Philology* 42(3), 181–82.

Meskell, L. (ed.). 2005. *Archaeologies of materiality.* Oxford: Blackwell.

Miliarakis, A. 1886. *Geographia Politiki, Nea kai Archaia tou Nomou Argolidos kai Korinthos.* Athens: Vivliopoleíon Estías, Typografeíon Korínnis.

Miller, P.N. 2013. A tentative morphology of European antiquarianism, 1500–2000. In A. Schnapp, with L. Von Falkenhausen, P.N. Miller, and T. Murray (eds.), *World antiquarianism: Comparative perspectives.* Los Angeles, CA: Getty Publications. 67–87.

Miller, P.N. 2015. *Peiresc's Mediterranean world.* Cambridge, MA: Harvard University Press.

Miller, P.N. 2017. Coda: Not for lumpers only. In B. Anderson, and F. Rojas (eds.), *Antiquarianisms: Contact, conflict, comparison.* Oxford: Oxbow. 210–19.

Miller, S. 1990. *Nemea: A guide to the site and the museum.* Berkeley, CA: University of California Press.

Ministry of Environment, Energy & Climate Change. 2014. *National Biodiversity Strategy & Action Plan.* Athens: MEECC. Available at: www.cbd.int/doc/world/gr/gr-nbsap-01-en.pdf (Accessed: 17 March 2016).

Ministry of Religious Affairs and National Education. 1946. *Zimíai ton Archaiotíton ek tou Polémou kai ton Stratón Katochís.* Athens.

Mitsos, M. 1935. *Hellenika* VIII, 16.

Mollat, G. 1954. Notice sur la vie et les travaux de M. Philippe Legrand, membre de l'Académie. *Comptes rendus des séances de l'Académie des Inscriptions et Belles-Lettres* 98(4), 413–18.

Morel, P.-M. 2002. Les ambiguïtés de la conception épicurienne du temps. *Revue philosophique de la France et de l'étranger* 127(2), 195–211.

Moretti, J.-C., and S. Diez. 1993. *Théâtres d'Argos.* Sites et monuments 10. Athens: École Française d'Athènes.

Morfis, A., and H. Zojer. 1986. *Karst hydrogeology of the Central and Eastern Peloponnesus.* Venice: Springer Verlag.

Morgan, C., and T. Whitelaw. 1991. Pots and politics: Ceramic evidence for the rise of the Argive state. *American Journal of Archaeology* 95(1), 79–108.

Morgan, D.H. 1936. Excavations at Corinth, 1935–1936. *AJA* 40(6), 466–84.

Morgan, J. 2010. *The Classical Greek house.* Exeter: Bristol Phoenix Press.

Moropoulou, A., N.P. Avdelidis, and E.T. Delegou. 2005. NDT and planning on historic buildings and complexes for the protection of cultural heritage. In R. van Grieken and K. Janssens (eds.), *Cultural heritage conservation and environmental impact assessment by non-destructive testing and micro-analysis*. London: A.A. Balkema. 67–76.

Morris, I. 1986. The use and abuse of Homer. *Classical Antiquity* 5(1), 81–138.

Morris, I. 1988. Tomb cult and the "Greek renaissance": The past in the present in the 8th century BC. *Antiquity* 62, 750–61.

Morris, I. 1994. Archaeologies of Greece. In I. Morris (ed.), *Classical Greece: Ancient histories and modern archaeologies*. Cambridge: Cambridge University Press. 8–48.

Morris, I. 2000. *Archaeology as culture history*. Oxford: Blackwell.

Morris, I. 2003. Mediterraneanization. *Mediterranean Historical Review* 18(2), 30–55.

Morris, I. 2005. Archaeology, standards of living, and Greek economic history. In J.G. Manning and I. Morris (eds.), *The ancient economy: Evidence and models*. Stanford, CA: Stanford University Press. 91–126.

Morris, I., and B.B. Powell. 1997. *A new companion to Homer*. Leiden: Brill.

Morris, S.P., and J.K. Papadopoulos. 2005. Greek towers and slaves: An archaeology of exploitation. *American Journal of Archaeology* 109, 155–225.

Morton, J. 2001. *The role of the physical environment in Ancient Greek seafaring*. Leiden: Brill.

Morton, T. 2013. *Hyperobjects: Philosophy and ecology after the end of the world*. Minneapolis, MN: University of Minnesota Press.

Mossman, J.M. 1992. Plutarch, Pyrrhus, and Alexander. In P.A. Stadter (ed.), *Plutarch and the historical tradition*. London: Routledge. 98–116.

Murray, P., and P.N. Kardulias. 2000. The present as past: An ethnoarchaeological study of modern sites in the Pikrodhafni Valley. In S.B. Sutton (ed.), *Contingent countryside: Settlement, economy, and land use in the Southern Argolid since 1700*. Stanford, CA: Stanford University Press. 141–68.

Myers, R.A., and B. Worm. 2003. Rapid worldwide depletion of predatory fish communities. *Nature* 423(6937), 280–83.

Mylonas, G.E. 1957. *Ancient Mycenae: The capital city of Agamemnon*. Princeton, NJ: Princeton University Press.

Nadeau, B. 2015. The Battle of Olives. *Scientific American* 313(5), 52–59.

Nagy, G. 1983. Sēma and nóēsis: Some illustrations. *Arethusa* 16, 35–55.

Nagy, G. 2010. *Homer the Preclassic*. Berkeley, CA: University of California Press.

Nakos, D. 2013. Katafyki Ermionidas Pezoporia sto farangi ton mython. *Epathlo* 92, 36–40.

Nash, C.E. 2011. *The history of aquaculture*. Ames, IA: Wiley-Blackwell.

National Statistical Service of Greece. 1994. Actual population of Greece by the census of 17 March 1991 (Pragmatikós plithysmós tis elládos katá tin apografí tis 17is martíou 1991).

National Statistical Service of Greece. 2001. Greece population and housing census 2001.

National Statistical Service of Greece. 2011. De facto population census 2011 (revised).

Nativ, A. 2018. On the object of archaeology. *Archaeological Dialogues* 25(1), 1–47.

Naval Intelligence Division. 1944. *Greece, Volume I: Physical geography, history, administration and peoples*. Norwich: Jarrold and Sons.

Naval Intelligence Division. 1944. *Greece, Volume II: Economic geography, ports and communications*. Norwich: Jarrold and Sons.

Netz, R. 2000. Why did Greek mathematicians publish their analyses? In P. Suppes, J.M. E. Moravcsik, H. Mendell, and W.R. Knorr (eds.), *Ancient & Medieval traditions in the exact sciences: Essays in memory of Wilbur Knorr*. Stanford, CA: CSLI Publications, Center for the Study of Language and Information. 139–57.

Netz, R. 2004. *The transformation of mathematics in the early Mediterranean world: From problems to equations*. Cambridge: Cambridge University Press.

Netz, R. 2016. Mathematics. In G.L. Irby (ed.), *A companion to science, technology, and medicine in Ancient Greece and Rome*. Vol. 1. Chichester: John Wiley & Sons. 77–95.

Neugebauer, O. 1949. The early history of the astrolabe. *Studies in Ancient Astronomy IX*. *Isis*. 40(3), 240–56.

Nevett, L.C. 1999. *House and society in the Ancient Greek world*. Cambridge: Cambridge University Press.

Nietzsche, F. 1993. Encyclopädie der klassischen Philologie. In F. Bornmann and M. Carpitella (eds.), *Nietzsche Werke* pt. 2. Vol. 3. Berlin: Walter de Gruyter. 341–437.

Nietzsche, F., et al. 1993. *Nietzsche Werke: Kritische Gesamtausgabe*. II.2. Berlin: Walter de Gruyter.

Nightingale, A.W. 2004. *Spectacles of truth in Classical Greek philosophy: Theoria in its cultural context*. Cambridge: Cambridge University Press.

Nikitidis, N., and V. Papiomitoglou 2011. *Green plants and herbs of Greece* (trans. J. Pittinger). Rethymno: Mediterraneo Editions.

Nilsson, M.P. 1992. *Geschichte der griechischen Religion Bd. 1*. München: C.H. Beck.

Nilsson Stutz, L. 2016. To gaze upon the dead: The exhibition of human remains as cultural practice and political process in Scandinavia and the USA. In H. Williams and M. Giles (eds.), *Archaeologists and the dead: Mortuary archaeology in contemporary society*. Oxford: Oxford University Press. 268–92.

Ogden, D. 2013. *Drakon: Dragon myth and serpent cult in the Greek and Roman worlds*. Oxford: Oxford University Press.

Oliver, G.J. 2001. Regions and micro-regions: Grain for Rhamnous. In Z. Archibald, J. Davies, V. Gabrielsen, and G.J. Olivier (eds.), *Hellenistic economies*. London: Routledge. 137–73.

Olivier, L. 2008. *Le Sombre abîme du temps: Mémoire et archéologie*. Seuil: Paris.

Olivier, L. 2011. *The dark abyss of time: Archaeology and memory* (trans. A. Greenspan). Lanham, MD: AltaMira Press.

Olivier, L. 2013. The business of archaeology is the present. In A. González-Ruibal (ed.), *Reclaiming archaeology: Beyond the tropes of modernity*. Abingdon: Routledge. 117–29.

Olsen, B. 2003. Material culture after text. Re-Membering things, *Norwegian Archaeological Review* 36, 87–104.

Olsen, B. 2010. *In defense of things: Archaeology and the ontology of objects*. Lanham, MD: AltaMira Press.

Olsen, B. 2012. Symmetrical archaeology. In I. Hodder (ed.), *Archaeological theory today*. Cambridge: Polity Press. 208–28.

Olsen, B., and Þ. Pétursdóttir (eds.). 2015. *Ruin memories: Materiality, aesthetics and the archaeology of the recent past*. New York, NY: Routledge.

Olsen, B., and C. Witmore. 2015. Archaeology, symmetry and the ontology of things: A response to critics. *Archaeological Dialogues* 22(2), 187–97.

Olsen, B., M. Shanks, T. Webmoor, and C. Witmore. 2012. *Archaeology: The discipline of things*. Berkeley, CA: University of California Press.

Organ, J. 2006. *Greece narrow gauge*. Midhurst: Middleton Press.

Orlandos, A.K. 1994. *He Xylostegos Palaiochristianike Basilike tes Mesogeiakes Lekanes*. Athenai: He en Athenais Archaiologike Hetaireia.

Otto, W.F. 1965. *Dionysus: Myth and cult*. Bloomington, IN: Indiana University Press.

Ottolenghi, F. 2008. Capture-based aquaculture of bluefin tuna. In A. Lovatelli and P.F. Holthus (eds.), *Capture-based aquaculture: Global overview*. FAO Fisheries Technical Paper 508. Rome, FAO. 169–82.

Pagnoux, C., et al. 2015. Inferring the agrobiodiversity of *Vitis vinifera L.* (grapevine) in Ancient Greece by comparative shape analysis of archaeological and modern seeds. *Vegetation History and Archaeobotany* 24(1), 75–84.

Palaiologou, E. 2013. Enas dromos pros to Hraio tou Argous. In D. Mulliez (ed.), *Sta Bimata tou Wilhelm Vollgraff: Ekató chrónia archaiologikís drastiriótitas sto Argos*. Athènes: École française d'Athènes. 393–403.ß.

Palinkas, J., and J.A. Herbst. 2011. A Roman road southeast of the forum at Corinth: Technology and urban development. *Hesperia* 80(2), 287–336.

Pallas, D.I. 1970. Anaskafikí erevna eis tin Vasilikín tou Kraneiou en Koríntho. *Praktika*, 98–117.

Panopoulos, P. 2003. Animal bells as symbols: Sound and hearing in a Greek island village. *Journal of the Royal Anthropological Institute* 9(4), 639–56.

Pantazis, G., and E. Lambrou. 2009. Investigating the orientation of eleven mosques in Greece. *Journal of Astronomical History and Heritage* 12(2), 159–66.

Papadopoulos, J.K. 2007. *The art of antiquity: Piet de Jong and the Athenian Agora*. Princeton, NJ: American School of Classical Studies at Athens.

Parker, R. 1991. Greek religion. In J. Boardman (ed.), *The Oxford history of Greece and the Hellenistic world*. Oxford: Oxford University Press. 306–29.

Parker, R. 2010. *Miasma: Pollution and purification in early Greek religion*. Oxford: Clarendon Press.

Pearson, M., and M. Shanks. 2001. *Theatre/archaeology*. London: Routledge.

Peckham, R.S. 2000. Map mania: Nationalism and the politics of place in Greece, 1870–1922. *Political Geography* 19, 77–95.

Peckham, R.S. 2001. *National histories, natural states: Nationalism and the politics of place in Greece*. London: I.B. Tauris.

Peek, W. 1934. Griechische Inschriften. *Mitteilungen des Deutschen Archäologischen Instituts, Athenische Abteilung* 59, 35–80.

Pelet, J.J.G. 1832. *Carte de la Morée, rédigée et gravée au Dépôt général de la guerre*. Paris: Dépôt général de la guerre.

Pennsylvania Railroad. 1910. *Pennsylvania Railroad Company Test Department. Locomotive testing plant at Altoona, Penna. Tests of an E2A locomotive, 1910*. Pennsylvania Railroad Company.

Pereira, J. 1842. *The elements of materia medica and therapeutics*. Vol. II. London: Longman, Brown, Green, and Longmans.

Perlès, C. 2001. *The Early Neolithic in Greece*. Cambridge: Cambridge University Press.

Perrakis, S. 2006. *The ghosts of Plaka Beach: A true story of murder and retribution in wartime Greece*. Madison, WI: Fairleigh Dickinson University Press.

Petrákos, V.Ch. 2005. I archaiología tis Psyttáleias, *O Méntor* 18(74-75), 33–72.

Petrakos, V.Ch. 1982. *Dokimio gia tin archaiologikí nomothesía*. Athens: Ypourgeio Politismou–T.A.P.

Petrakos, V.Ch. 2007. The stages of Greek archaeology. In P. Valavanes and A. Delevorrias (eds.), *Great moments in Greek archaeology*. Los Angeles, CA: J. Paul Getty Museum. 16–35.

Petrie, W.M.F. 1904. *Methods and aims in archaeology*. London: MacMillan.

Petrocheilou, A. 1974. To Spilaion "Peristeri" Megalochorio, Methanon. *Arith. Sp. Mitroou* 4325. Available at: http://geolib.geo.auth.gr/index.php/bssg/article/view/6073.

Petropoulos, N.P., et al. 2001. Geographical mapping and associated fractal analysis of the long-lived Chernobyl fallout radionuclides in Greece. *Journal of Environmental Radioactivity* 53(1), 59–66.

Petropulos, J.A. 2015[1968]. *Politics and statecraft in the Kingdom of Greece, 1833–1843*. Princeton, NJ: Princeton University Press.

Pettegrew, D.K. 2001. Chasing the Classical farmstead: Assessing the formation and signature of rural settlement in Greek landscape archaeology. *Journal of Mediterranean Archaeology* 14 (2), 189–209.

Pettegrew, D.K. 2006. *Corinth on the Isthmus: Studies of the end of an ancient landscape*. Doctoral dissertation, Ohio State University.

Pettegrew, D.K. 2011. The Diolkos of Corinth. *American Journal of Archaeology* 115(4), 549–74.

Pettegrew, D.K. 2015. Corinthian suburbia: Patterns of Roman settlement on the Isthmus. In E. Gebhard and T.E. Gregory (eds.), *Bridge of the untiring sea: The Corinthian Isthmus from prehistory to Late Antiquity.* Princeton, NJ: American School of Classical Studies at Athens. 289–310.

Pettegrew, D.K. 2016. *The Isthmus of Corinth: Crossroads of the Mediterranean world.* Ann Arbor, MI: University of Michigan Press.

Pétursdóttir, Þ. 2012. "Small things forgotten now included, or what else do things deserve?" *International Journal of Historical Archaeology* 16(3), 577–603.

Pétursdóttir, Þ. 2015. Things out-of-hand: the aesthetics of abandonment. In Olsen, B. and Þ. Pétursdóttir (eds.) *Ruin memories: Materiality, aesthetics and the archaeology of the recent past.* New York, NY: Routledge. 335–64.

Pétursdóttir, Þ. 2017. Climate change? Archaeology and Anthropocene. *Archaeological Dialogues* 24(2), 175–205.

Pétursdóttir, Þ., and B. Olsen, 2014. Imaging modern decay: The aesthetics of ruin photography. *Journal of Contemporary Archaeology* 1(1), 7–56.

Pétursdóttir, Þ., and B. Olsen. 2017. Theory adrift: The matter of archaeological theorizing. *Journal of Social Archaeology* 18(1), 97–117.

Peytier, Puillion-Boblaye, and Servier. 1833. Notice sur les opérations géodésiques exécutées en Morée, en 1829 et 1830, par MM. Peytier, Puillon-Boblaye et Servier; suivie d'un catalogue des positions géographiques des principaux points déterminés par ces opérations. *Bulletin de la Société de géographie* 19, 89–106.

Philadelpheus, A. 1909. Ai en Hermionidi Anaskaphai. *Praktika*, 172–84.

Pickett, A.A. 1993. Cereals: seed shedding, dormancy and longevity. *Aspects of Applied Biology* 35, 17–28.

Piérart, M. 1982. Deux notes sur l'itinéraire argien de Pausanias. *Bulletin de correspondance hellénique* 106(1), 139–52.

Piérart, M. 1993. De l'endroit ou l'on abritait quelques statues d'Argos et de la vraie nature du feu de Phoroneus: Une note critique. *Bulletin de correspondance hellénique* 117(2), 609–13.

Piérart, M. 2000. Argos: Un autre democratie. In P. Flensted-Jensen, T.H. Nielsen, and L. Rubinstein (eds.), *Polis & politics: Studies in Ancient Greek history.* Copenhagen: Museum Tusculanum Press. 297–314.

Piérart, M., and G. Touchais. 1996. *Argos: Une ville grecque de 6000 ans.* Paris: CNRS Editions.

Piggott, S. 1966. Mycenae and barbarian Europe. *Sbornik Narodniho Muzea v Praza* XX, 117.

Pikoulas, Y.A. 1995. *Odikó Díktyo kai Amuna. Apó tin Kórintho sto Argos kai tin Arkadía.* Athens: Horos.

Pikoulas, Y.A. 2007a. Travelling by land in Ancient Greece. In C.E.P. Adams and J. Roy (eds.), *Travel, geography and culture in Ancient Greece, Egypt, and the Near East.* Oxford: Oxbow Books. 78–87.

Pikoulas, Y.A. 2007b. The settlement pattern. In M. Georgopoulou, C. Guilmet, Y.A. Pikoulas, K. Sp. Staikos, and G. Tolias (eds.), *Following Pausanias: The quest for Greek antiquity.* New Castle, DE: Oak Knoll Press. 224–25.

Pikoulas, Y.A. 2011. Ancient vineyards at the Temple of Zeus at Nemea. In S. Kourakou-Dragona (ed.), *Nemea: Beloved land of Zeus and Dionysos.* Athens: Foinikas Publications. 73–78.

Pimentel, D. 2006. *Impacts of organic farming on the efficiency of energy use in agriculture.* Washington, DC: Wasghing Organic Center.

Plantzos, D. 2014. Dead archaeologists, buried gods: Archaeology as an agent of modernity in Greece. In D. Tziovas (ed.), *Re-imagining the past: Antiquity and modern Greek culture.* Oxford: Oxford University Press. 147–64.

Platt, V.J. 2011. *Facing the gods: Epiphany and representation in Graeco-Roman art, literature and religion*. Cambridge: Cambridge University Press.

Ploutoglou, N., et al. 2011. Two emblematic French maps of Peloponnese (Morée): Lapie's 1826 vs the 1832 map (Expédition scientifique). A digital comparison with respect to map geometry and toponymy. *Proceedings, 25th International Cartographic Association Conference*, 3–8 July 2011, Paris. Available at: https://icaci.org/files/documents/ICC_proceedings/ICC2011/.

Pomardi, S. 1820. *Viaggio nella Grecia fatto da Simone Pomardi negli anni 1804, 1805, e 1806*. Vol. II. Rome: Vincenzo Poggioli.

Pomey, P., and A. Tchernia. 1978. Le Tonnage maximum des navires de commerce romains. *Archaeonautica* 2, 233–51.

Porter, J.I. 2000. *Nietzsche and the philology of the future*. Stanford, CA: Stanford University Press.

Porter, J.I. 2009. Hellenism and modernity. In G. Boys-Stones, B. Graziosi, and P. Vasuni (eds.), *The Oxford handbook of Hellenic studies*. Oxford: Oxford University Press. 7–18.

Porter, J.I. 2014. Nietzsche's radical philology. In A.K. Jensen and H. Heit (eds.), *Nietzsche as a scholar of antiquity*. London: Bloomsbury Academic. 27–52.

Pouqueville, F.C.H.L. 1827. *Voyage de la Grèce*. Vol. 5. Paris: Firmin Didot.

Powell, B. 1905. The Temple of Apollo at Corinth. *American Journal of Archaeology* 9(1), 44–63.

Prag, A.J.N.W., et al. 2009. Mycenae revisited Part 1: The human remains from Grave Circle A – Stamatakis, Schliemann and two new faces from Shaft Grave VI. *Annual of the British School at Athens* 104, 233–77.

Pretzler, M. 2005. Comparing Strabo with Pausanias: Greece in context vs. Greece in depth. In D. Dueck, H. Lindsay, and S. Pothecary (eds.), *Strabo's cultural geography: The making of a Kolossourgia*. Cambridge: Cambridge University Press. 144–60.

Pretzler, M. 2013. *Pausanias: Travel writing in Ancient Greece*. London: Bristol Classical Press.

Pritchett, W.K. 1965. *Studies in Ancient Greek Topography, Pt. 3, Roads*. Berkeley, CA: University of California Press.

Protonotariou-Deïlaki, E. 1992. Paratiriseis stin prokerameiki (apo ti Thessalia ata Dendra tis Argolidos). In *Diethnés Synédrio gia tin Archaía Thessalía sti Mnimi tou Dimitri P. Theochari*, Athènes: Ekdosi Tameiou Archaeiologikon Poron kai Apallotrioseon. 97–119.

Proussis, C.M. 1966. The novels of Angelos Terzakis. *Daedalus* 95(4), 1021–45.

Psariotis, T.I. 2012. Kavvathás Sp. Michaíl (1895–1972) - O protergátis tis diádosis tis kalliérgeias tou portokalioú stin Argolída. Available at: http://argolikivivliothiki.gr/2012/01/04/kavathas/.

Psychoyos, O., and Y. Karatzikos. 2015. Mycenaean cult on Mount Arachnaion in the Argolid. In I. Tournavitou and A.L. Schallin (eds.), *Mycenaeans up to date: The archaeology of the north-eastern Peloponnese, current concepts and new directions*. Stockholm: Svenska Institutet i Athen. 261–76.

Psychoyos, O., and Y. Karatzikos 2016. The Mycenaean sanctuary at Prophitis Ilias on Mount Arahnaio within the religious context of the 2nd Millennium B.C. In E. Alram-Stern, F. Blakolmer, S. Deger-Jalkotzy, R. Laffineur, and J. Weilhartner (eds.), *Metaphysis: Ritual, myth and symbolism in the Aegean Bronze Age*. Leuven: Peeters. 311–19.

Puillon de Boblaye, M.E. 1836. *Expédition scientifique de Morée: Recherches géographiques sur les ruines de la Morée*. Paris: F.G. Levrault.

Pullen, D.L. 2011. *Nemea Valley Archaeological Project, Volume I: The Early Bronze Age village on Tsoungiza Hill*. Princeton, NJ: American School of Classical Studies.

Rackham, O., and J.A. Moody. 1996. *The making of the Cretan landscape*. Manchester: Manchester University Press.

Ramsey, R.W. 1942. Sir George Wheler and his travels in Greece, 1650–1724. *Essays by Divers Hands, being the Transactions of the Royal Society of Literature of the United Kingdom.* New Series 19, 1–38.

Raymond, L.A., and N.E. Johnson. 2017. *Crustal earth materials.* Long Grove, IL: Waveland Press.

Redding, C. 1833. *A history and description of modern wines.* London: Whittaker, Treacher, & Arnot.

Redman, C. 1974. *Archaeological sampling strategies.* Reading, MA: Addison-Wesley.

Reiss, W., and A. Stübel. 1867. *Ausflug nach den vulkanischen Gebirgen von Ägina und Methana.* Heidelberg: Verlagsbuchhandlung von FR. Bassermann.

Reitze, A.W. 2001. *Air pollution control law: Compliance and enforcement.* Washington, DC: Environmental Law Institute.

Renfrew, C. 1968. Wessex without Mycenae. *Annual of the British School of at Athens* 63, 277–85.

Renfrew, C. 1972. *The emergence of civilization: The Cyclades and the Aegean in the third millennium B.C.* London: Methuen & Co.

Renfrew, C. 1980. The Great Tradition versus the Great Divide: Archaeology versus anthropology? *American Journal of Archaeology* 84, 287–98.

Rhodes, R.F. 2003. The earliest Greek architecture in Corinth and the 7th-century temple on Temple Hill. In C.K. Williams and N. Bookidis (eds.), *Corinth: Results of excavations conducted by the American School of Classical Studies at Athens.* Vol. 20. Princeton, NJ: American School of Classical Studies at Athens. 85–94.

Richardson, R.B. 1897. The excavations at Corinth in 1896. *American Journal of Archaeology* 1(6), 455–80.

Richardson, R.B. 1900. The fountain of Glauce at Corinth. *American Journal of Archaeology.* 4(4), 458–75.

Rife, J. 2008. Leo's Peloponnesian fire-tower and the Byzantine watch-tower on Acrocorinth. In W.R. Caraher, L.J. Hall, and R.S. Moore (eds.), *Archaeology and history in Roman, Medieval and post-Medieval Greece: Studies on method and meaning in honor of Timothy E. Gregory.* Aldershot: Ashgate. 281–306.

Rife, J.L. 2012. *Isthmia IX: The Roman and Byzantine graves and human remains.* Princeton, NJ: American School of Classical Studies at Athens.

Rilke, R.M. 1982. *The notebooks of Malte Laurids Brigge* (trans. S. Mitchell). New York, NY: Random House.

Robb, J., and P. Miracle. 2007. Beyond "migration" versus "acculturation": New models for the spread of agriculture. In A. Whittle and V. Cummings (eds.), *Going over: The Mesolithic–Neolithic transition in Western Europe.* Proceedings of the British Academy. London: British Academy. 90–113.

Roberts, C. 2007. *The unnatural history of the sea.* Washington, DC: Island Press/Shearwater Books.

Robinson, B.A. 2011a. *Histories of Peirene: A Corinthian fountain in three millennia.* Princeton, NJ: American School of Classical Studies at Athens.

Robinson, E.W. 2011b. *Democracy beyond Athens: Popular government in the Greek Classical age.* Cambridge: Cambridge University Press.

Robinson, H. 1976. Excavations at Corinth: Temple Hill, 1968–1972. *Hesperia* 45(3), 203–39.

Rohl, D. 2011. The chorographic tradition and seventeenth-and eighteenth-century Scottish antiquaries. *Journal of Art Historiography* 5(5), 1–18.

Rohl, D. 2012. Chorography: History, theory and potential for archaeological research. In M. Duggan, F. McIntosh, and D.J. Rohl (eds.), *TRAC 2011: Proceedings of the Twenty-First Theoretical Roman Archaeology Conference.* Oxford: Oxbow Books. 19–32.

Romano, D.G. 2003. City planning, centuriation, and land division in Roman Corinth: Colonia Laus Iulia Corinthiensis & Colonia Iulia Flavia Augusta Corinthiensis. *Corinth:*

Results of excavations conducted by the American School of Classical Studies at Athens. 279–301.

Romano, D.G. 2005. Urban and rural planning in Roman Corinth. In D.N. Schowalter (ed.), *Urban religion in Roman Corinth: Interdisciplinary approaches.* Cambridge, MA: Harvard University Press. 25–59.

Romm, J.S. 2010. Continents, climates, and cultures: Greek theories of global structure. In K. Raaflaub and R. Talbert (eds.), *Geography and ethnography: Perceptions of the world in pre-modern societies.* Chichester: John Wiley & Sons. 215–35.

Rose, D.B. 2017. Shimmer: When all you love is being trashed. In A.L. Tsing, N. Bubandt, E. Gan, and H.A. Swanson (eds.), *Arts of living on a damaged planet: Ghosts and monsters of the Anthropocene.* Minnesota, MN: University of Minnesota Press. 51–63.

Roux, G. 1953. Deux études d'archéologie péloponnésienne. *Bulletin de correspondance hellénique* 77, 116–38.

Runnels, C.N. 2009. Mesolithic sites and surveys in Greece: A case study from the Southern Argolid. *Journal of Mediterranean Archaeology* 22(1), 57–73.

Runnels, C.N., et al. 2005. A Mesolithic landscape in Greece: Testing a site-location model in the Argolid at Kandia. *Journal of Mediterranean Archaeology* 18(2), 259–85.

Runnels, C.N., D.J. Pullen, and S. Langdon (eds.). 1995. *Artifact and assemblage: The finds from a regional survey of the Southern Argolid, Greece.* Stanford, CA: Stanford University Press.

Rupp, D.W. 1976. The altars of Zeus and Hera on Mt Arachnaion in the Argeia, Greece. *Journal of Field Archaeology* 3(3), 261–68.

Salmon, J.B. 1984. *Wealthy Corinth: A history of the city to 338 BC.* Oxford: Oxford University Press.

Samara, M. 2018. Metalleía Ermiónis. *BIomichaniká Deltía Apografís* (Industrial Inventory Bulletin). Available at: https://vida-omada.blogspot.com/2018/01/blog-post_4.html.

Sanders, G.D.R. 2005. Urban Corinth: An introduction. In D.N. Schowalter (ed.), *Urban religion in Roman Corinth: Interdisciplinary approaches.* Cambridge, MA: Harvard University Press. 11–24.

Sanders, G.D.R. 2014. Landlords and tenants: Sharecroppers and subsistence farming in Corinthian historical context. In S.J. Friesen, S.A. James, and D.N. Schowalter (eds.), *Corinth in contrast: Studies in inequality.* Leiden: Brill, 101–25.

Sanders, G.D.R. 2015a. Telling the whole story at multi-period sites: Corinth. Paper delivered at Telling the Whole Story at Multi-Period Sites, April 15, 2015, American School of Classical Studies at Athens.

Sanders, G.D.R. 2015b. William of Moerbeke's church at Merbaka: The use of ancient spolia to make personal and political statements. *Hesperia* 84(3), 583–626.

Sanders, G.D.R., et al. 2017. *Ancient Corinth: Site guide.* Princeton, NJ: American School of Classical Studies at Athens.

Sanders, G.D.R., and I.K. Whitbread. 1990. Central places and major roads in the Peloponnese. *Annual of the British School at Athens* 85, 333–61.

Sarantákis, P. 2007. *Argolída/Oi Ekklisíes kai ta Monastíria tis.* Athens: Ekdóseis OIATIS.

Sathas, C.N. 1880–90. *Documents inédits relatifs à l'histoire de la Grèce au moyen âge.* 8 vols. Paris: Maisonneuve.

Sayer, D. 2010. *Ethics and burial archaeology.* London: Duckworth.

Scarre, C., and R. Coningham (eds.). 2012. *Appropriating the past: Philosophical perspectives on the practice of archaeology.* Cambridge: Cambridge University Press.

Schaefer, W. 1961. Neue Untersuchungen über die Baugeschichte Nauplias im Mittelalter. *Archäologischer Anzeiger* 76, 156–214.

Schaldach, K. 2004. The Arachne of the Amphiareion and the origin of Gnomonics in Greece. *Journal for the History of Astronomy* 35(4), 435–45.

Schiffer, M.B. 1987. *Formation processes in the archaeological record*. Salt Lake City, UT: University of Utah Press.

Schliemann, H. 1878. *Mycenae*. London: John Murray.

Schnapp, A. 1997. *The discovery of the past*. New York, NY: Harry N. Abrams.

Schnapp, A. 2013. Conservation of objects and monuments and the sense of the past during the Greco-Roman era. In A. Schnapp, with L. Von Falkenhausen, P.N. Miller, and T. Murray (eds.), *World antiquarianism: Comparative perspectives*. Los Angeles, CA: Getty Publications. 159–75.

Schon, R. 2004. *Seeding the landscape: Experimental contributions to regional survey methodology*. Doctoral dissertation, Bryn Mawr College.

Scott, J.C. 1998. *Seeing like a state: How certain schemes to improve the human condition have failed*. New Haven, CT: Yale University Press.

Scott, M. 2013. *Space and society in the Greek and Roman worlds*. Cambridge: Cambridge University Press.

Scott, W. 1814. *Border antiquities of England and Scotland*. London: Longman, Hurst, Rees, Orme, and Brown, Paternoster-row; J. Murray, Albermarle-street; John Greig, Upper-street, Islington; and Constable and Co. Edinburgh.

Scotton, P.D. 1997. *The Julian Basilica at Corinth: An architectural investigation*. Doctoral dissertation, University of Pennsylvania.

Scoullos, M.J., et al. 2007. Dissolved and particulate metal levels in the Saronikos Gulf, in 2004: The impact of the primary wastewater treatment plant of Psittalia. *Desalination* 210, 98–109.

Scranton, R.L. 1951. *Corinth, I.iii: Monuments in the lower Agora and north of the Archaic temple*. Princeton, NJ: American School of Classical Studies at Athens.

Seferis, G. 1995. *Collected poems*. Princeton, NJ: Princeton University Press.

Sekeris, P.E. n.d. *Tolon*. No publisher.

Sennett, R. 1994. *Flesh and stone: The body and the city in Western civilization*. New York, NY: W.W. Norton & Company.

Serematakis, C.N. 1994. *The senses still: Perception and memory as material culture in modernity*. Chicago, IL: University of Chicago Press.

Serrano, P.H. 2005. *Responsible use of antibiotics in aquaculture*. FAO Fisheries Technical Paper 469. Rome: FAO.

Serres, M. 1977. *La naissance de la physique dans le texte de Lucrèce*. Paris: Les Editions de Minuit.

Serres, M. 1985. *Les Cinq Sens*. Paris: Grasset.

Serres, M. 1987. *Statues. Le second livre des fondations*. Paris: Éditions François Bourin.

Serres, M. 1989. *Detachment* (trans. G. James and R. Federman). Athens: Ohio University Press.

Serres, M. 1993. *La Légende des anges*. Paris: Flammarion.

Serres, M. 1995a. *The natural contract*. Ann Arbor, MI: University of Michigan Press.

Serres, M. 1995b. *Genesis*. Ann Arbor, MI: University of Michigan Press.

Serres, M. 2000. *The birth of physics*. Manchester: Clinamen Press.

Serres, M. 2008a. *The five senses: A philosophy of mingled bodies*. London: Continuum.

Serres, M. 2008b. *Le Mal Propre: Polluer pour s'approprier?* Paris: Éditions Le Pommier.

Serres, M. 2011. *Malfeasance: Appropriation through pollution?* Stanford, CA: Stanford University Press.

Serres, M. 2014. *Times of crisis: What the financial crisis revealed and how to reinvent our lives and future*. New York, NY: Bloomsbury Academic.

Serres, M. 2015a. *Biogea*. Minneapolis, MN: University of Minnesota Press.

Serres, M. 2015b. *Statues: The second book of foundations*. London: Bloomsbury.

Serres, M. 2017. *Geometry: The third book of foundations*. London: Bloomsbury Academic.

Serres, M., and B. Latour. 1995. *Conversations on science, culture, and time*. Ann Arbor, MI: University of Michigan Press.

Sfikas, G. 2001. *Trees and shrubs of Greece*. Athens: Efstathiadis Group S.A.

Shanks, M. 1992. *Experiencing the past: On the character of archaeology*. London: Routledge.

Shanks, M. 1996. *Classical archaeology of Greece: Experiences of the discipline*. London: Routledge.

Shanks, M. 1997. Photography and archaeology. In B.L. Molyneaux (ed.), *The cultural life of images: Visual representation in archaeology*. Routledge: London. 73–107.

Shanks, M. 2007. Symmetrical archaeology. *World Archaeology* 39(4), 589–96.

Shanks, M. 2012. *The archaeological imagination*. Walnut Creek, CA: Left Coast Press.

Shanks, M., and C. Tilley. 1987. *Social theory and archaeology*. Cambridge: Polity Press.

Shanks, M., and C. Tilley. 1992. *Reconstructing archaeology*. London: Routledge.

Shanks, M., and C. Witmore. 2010. Echoes across the past: Chorography and topography in antiquarian engagements with place. *Performance Research* 15(4), 97–106.

Shelton, K. 1993. Tsountas' chamber tombs at Mycenae. *Archaiologikie ephermeris* 132, 187–210.

Shelton, K. 2003. The cemeteries. In S. Iakovidis, E.B. French, K. Shelton, J. Lavery, A. G. Jansen, and C. Ioannides (eds.), *The archaeological atlas of Mycenae*. Athens: Archaeological Society of Athens. 35–38.

Shelton, K. 2006. The long lasting effect of Tsountas on the study of Mycenae. In P. Darcque (ed.), *Mythos: La préhistoire égéenne du XIXe au XXIe siècle après J.-C. Bulletin de correspondance hellénique* Supplement 46, 159–64.

Shennan, S. 2008. Evolution in archaeology. *Annual Review of Anthropology* 37, 75–91.

Shipley, G. 2011. *Pseudo-Skylax's Periplous: The circumnavigation of the inhabited world text, translation and commentary*. Exeter: Bristol Phoenix Press.

Shryock, A., and D.L. Smail. 2011. *Deep history: The architecture of past and present*. Berkeley, CA: University of California Press.

Simmel, G. 1959. The ruin. In K.W. Wolff (ed.), *Georg Simmel, 1858–1918: A collection of essays, with translations and a bibliography*. Columbus, OH: Ohio State University Press. 259–66.

Skiadopoulos, N., and V.W.J. van Gerven Oei. 2011. Greek returns: The poetry of Nikos Karouzos. *Continent* 3(1), 201–07.

Slavitt, D.R. 2008. *De rerum natura: The nature of things – A poetic translation*. Berkeley, CA: University of California Press.

Sloan, K. 2013. Seen through a glass darkly: Dodwell and Pomardi's drawings and watercolors of Greece. In J.M. Camp (ed.), *In search of Greece: Catalogue of an exhibit of drawings at the British Museum by Edward Dodwell and Simone Pomardi from the collection of the Packard Humanities Institute*. Los Altos, CA: Packard Humanities Institute. 31–46.

Sloterdijk, P. 1999. *Sphären II – Globen, Makrosphärologie*. Frankfurt am Main: Suhrkamp.

Sloterdijk, P. 2000. From Agrarian patriotism to the global self (trans. M. Nieto and N. Gardels). *New Perspectives Quarterly* 17(1), 15–18.

Sloterdijk, P. 2005a. *Im Weltinnenraum des Kapitals: Für eine philosophische Theorie der Globalisierung*. Frankfurt am Main: Suhrkamp.

Sloterdijk, P. 2005b. Atmospheric politics. In B. Latour and P. Weibel (eds.), *Making things public: Atmospheres of democracy*. Cambridge, MA: Massachusetts Institute of Technology Press. 944–51.

Sloterdijk, P. 2009. Spheres theory: Talking to myself about the poetics of space. *Harvard Design Magazine* 30, 1–8.

Sloterdijk, P. 2011a. *Bubbles: Spheres I*. South Pasadena, CA: Semiotext(e).

Sloterdijk, P. 2011b. Society of centaurs: Philosophical remarks on automobility (trans. K. Ritson). *Transfers* 1(1), 14–24.

Sloterdijk, P. 2012a. The time of the crime of the monstrous: On the philosophical justification of the artificial. In S. Elden (ed.), *Sloterdijk Now*. Cambridge: Polity Press. 165–81.

Sloterdijk, P. 2012b. Voices for animals: A fantasy on animal representation. In G.R. Smulewicz-Zucker (ed.), *Strangers to nature: Animal lives and humans ethics*. Lanham, MD: Lexington Books. 263–69.

Sloterdijk, P. 2013. *In the world interior of capital: For a philosophical theory of globalization*. Cambridge: Polity Press.

Sloterdijk, P. 2014. *Globes: Spheres II*. South Pasadena, CA: Semiotext(e).

Sloterdijk, P. 2015. Museum: School of alienation (trans. I.B. Whyte). *Art in Translation* 6(4), 437–48.

Sloterdijk, P. 2016. *Foams: Spheres III*. South Pasadena, CA: Semiotext(e).

Sloterdijk, P., and E. Morse. 2009. Something in the air. *Frieze Magazine*, 1 Nov. 2009. Available at https://frieze.com/article/something-air.

Smith, A.H. 1916. Lord Elgin and his collection. *Journal of Hellenic Studies* 36, 163–372.

Smith, D.E. 1901[1893]. Standard Time. *The Moderator*. University of Michigan, 83–85.

Smith, R.A.K., et al. 2017. *Ayia Sotira: A Mycenaean chamber tomb cemetery in the Nemea Valley, Greece*. Philadelphia, PA: INSTAP Academic Press.

Snead, J.E., C.L. Erickson, and J.A. Darling. 2009. *Landscapes of movement: Trails, paths, and roads in anthropological perspective*. Philadelphia, PA: University of Pennsylvania Press.

Snodgrass, A.M. 1977. *Archaeology and the rise of the Greek state*. Cambridge: Cambridge University Press.

Snodgrass, A.M. 1980. *Archaic Greece: The age of experiment*. London: J.M. Dent.

Snodgrass, A.M. 1982. Les origines du culte des héros en Grèce antique. In G. Gnoli and J.-P. Vernant (eds.), *La mort, les morts, dons les sociétés ancienne*. Cambridge: Cambridge University Press. 107–19.

Snodgrass, A.M. 1987. *An archaeology of Greece*. Berkeley, CA: University of California Press.

Snodgrass, A.M. 2001. Pausanias and the chest of Kypselos. In S.E. Alcock, J.F. Cherry, and J. Elsner (eds.), *Pausanias: Travel and memory in Roman Greece*. Oxford: Oxford University Press. 127–41.

Solnit, R. 2001. *Wanderlust: A history of walking*. New York, NY: Penguin.

Solnit, R., B. Pease, and S. Siegel. 2010. *Infinite city: A San Francisco atlas*. Berkeley, CA: University of California Press.

Sorabji, R. 1983. *Time, creation and the continuum*. London: Duckworth.

Sotiriou, G.A. 1935. I moni tou Avgou para tous Dhidhimous tis Argolidhos. *Imerologion tis Megalis Ellados*, 457–64.

Souvatzi, S.G., A. Baysal, and E.L. Baysal. 2019. *Time and history in prehistory*. London: Routledge.

Spon, J. 1673. *Recherche des Antiquités et Curiosités de la ville de Lyon*. Lyons: Imprimerie de Jacques Faeton.

Spon, J. 1678. *Voyage d'Italie, de Dalmatie, de Grèce et du Levant*. 3 vols. Lyon: Cellier.

Spon, J. 1679. *Réponse à la critique publiée par M. Guillet sur le Voyage de Grèce de Jacob Spon*. Lyon: Amanlei.

Stadter, P.A. 1965. *Plutarch's historical methods: An analysis of the mulierum virtutes*. Cambridge, MA: Harvard University Press.

Stavropoulos, N. 1996. *Greece: Country report to the FAO International Technical Conference on Plant Genetic Resources*. Leipzig. Available at: www.fao.org/fileadmin/templates/agphome/documents/PGR/SoW1/Europe/GREECE.PDF (Accessed: 17 March 2016).

Steffen, B. 1884. *Karten von Mykenai*. Berlin: Dietrich Reimer.

Steffen, R. (ed.). 2002. *Leben in Griechenland 1834–1835. Bettina Schinas, geb. von Savigny. Briefe und Berichte an ihre Eltern in Berlin*. Münster: Verlag Cay Lienau.

Stengers, I. 2008. Experimenting with refrains: Subjectivity and the challenge of escaping modern dualism. *Subjectivity* 22(1), 38–59.

Stengers, I. 2015. *In catastrophic times: Resisting the coming barbarism* (trans. A. Goffey). Ann Arbor, MI: Open Humanities Press.

Stewart, D.R. 2013. "Most worth remembering": Pausanias, analogy, and Classical archaeology. *Hesperia* 82, 231–61.

Stillwell, R. 1932. The Temple of Apollo. In H.N. Fowler and R. Stillwell (eds.), *Corinth I. i: Introduction, topography, architecture.* Cambridge, MA: Harvard University Press. 115–34.

Stimson, A.N. 1985. Some Board of Longitude Instruments in the nineteenth century. In P.R. de Clercq (ed.), *Nineteenth-century scientific instruments and their makers.* Amsterdam: Rodpi. 93–115.

Stocking, G. 1995. *After Tylor: British social anthropology, 1888–1951.* Madison, WI: University of Wisconsin Press.

Stoneman, R. 1987. *Land of lost gods: The search for Classical Greece.* Norman, OK: University of Oklahoma Press.

Stoneman, R. 2008. *Alexander the Great: A life in legend.* New Haven, CT: Yale University.

Strasser, T.F. 2010. Stone Age seafaring in the Mediterranean: Evidence from the Plakas region for Lower Palaeolithic and Mesolithic habitation of Crete. *Hesperia* 79, 145–90.

Strøm, I. 1988. The early sanctuary of the Argive Heraion and its external relations (8th–early 6th century B.C.): The monumental architecture. *Acta Archaeologica* 59, 173–203.

Strøm, I. 1995. The early sanctuary of the Argive Heraion and its external relations (8th–early 6th century B.C.): The Greek geometric bronzes. *Proceedings of the Danish Institute at Athens* 1, 37–128.

Stroulia, A., and S.B. Sutton. 2009. Archaeological sites and local places: Connecting the dots. *Public Archaeology: Archaeological Ethnographies* 8(2–3), 124–40.

Sturdy, E.W. 1884. The volcanic eruption of Krakatau. *Atlantic Monthly* 5, 385–91.

Sturgess, K. 2014. *Wandering in Nafplion: A lover's guide.* Nafplion: Peloponnesian Folklore Foundation.

Suaria, G., and S. Aliani. 2014. Floating debris in the Mediterranean Sea. *Marine Pollution Bulletin* 86(1-2), 494–504.

Sürmelihindi, G., et al. 2013. Laminated carbonate deposits in Roman aqueducts: Origin, processes and implications. *Sedimentology* 60(4), 961–82.

Sutton, S.B. 1983. Rural–urban migration in Greece. In M. Kenny and D.I. Kertzer (eds.), *Urban life in Mediterranean Europe: Anthropological perspectives.* Urbana, IL: University of Illinois Press. 225–49.

Sutton, S.B. 1995. The making of an ancient site: Travellers, farmers, and archaeologists in nineteenth century Nemea. *Simeion Anaforas (Point of Reference)* 3, 14–21.

Sutton, S.B. 1997. Disconnected landscapes: Ancient sites, travel guides, and local identity in modem Greece. *Anthropology of Eastern Europe Review* 15, 27–34.

Sutton, S.B. (ed.). 2000. *Contingent countryside: Settlement, economy, and land use in the Southern Argolid since 1700.* Stanford, CA: Stanford University Press.

Sutton, S.B. 2001. A temple worth seeing: Pausanias, travelers, and the narrative landscape at Nemea. In S.E. Alcock, J. Cherry, and J. Elsner (eds.), *Pausanias: Travel and memory in Roman Greece.* Oxford: Oxford University Press. 175–89.

Svestad, A. 2013. What happened in Neiden? On the question of reburial ethics. *Norwegian Archaeological Review* 46(2), 192–242.

Swain, H. 2016. Museum practice and the display of human remains. In H. Williams and M. Giles (eds.), *Archaeologists and the dead.* Oxford: Oxbow Books. 169–83.

Sweetman, R.J. 2010. The Christianization of the Peloponnese: The topography and function of Late Antique churches. *Journal of Late Antiquity* 3(2), 203–61.

Sweetman, R.J. 2015. Memory, tradition, and Christianization of the Peloponnese. *American Journal of Archaeology* 119(4), 501–31.

Tartaron, T.F., et al. 2006. The Eastern Korinthia Archaeological Survey: Integrated methods for a dynamic landscape. *Hesperia* 75(4), 453–523.

Tausend, K. 2006. *Verkehrswege der Argolis: Rekonstruktion und historische Bedeutung.* Stuttgart: F. Steiner.

Taylor, J.S. 2012. *Death, posthumous harm, and bioethics.* New York, NY: Routledge.

Te Heesen, A. 2005. The notebook: A paper technology. In B. Latour and P. Weibel (eds.), *Making things public: Atmospheres of democracy.* Cambridge, MA: MIT Press. 582–89.

Terzakis, A. 1945. *Prigkipessa Isabo (Princess Isabeau).* Athens.

Teskey, G. 2015. The thinking of history in Spenserian romance. *Cambridge Studies in Medieval Literature* 92, 214–27.

Theodorou, A.J., and C. Perissoratis. 1991. Environmental considerations for design of the Athens sea outfall, Saronikos Gulf, Greece. *Environmental Geology* 17(3), 233–48.

Thomas, J. 2008. Archaeology, landscape, and dwelling. In B. David and J. Thomas (eds.), *Handbook of landscape archaeology.* Walnut Creek, CA: Left Coast Press. 300–6.

Thomas, J. 2013. *The birth of Neolithic Britain: An interpretive account.* Oxford: Oxford University Press.

Thrift, N. 2008. *Non-representational theory: Space, politics, affect.* London: Routledge.

Tilley, C. 1994. *A phenomenology of landscape: Places, paths, and monuments.* Oxford: Berg.

Tilley, C. 2004. *The materiality of landscapes: Explorations in landscape phenomenology.* Oxford: Berg.

Tilley, C. 2010. *Interpreting landscapes: Geologies, topographies, identities.* Walnut Creek, CA: Left Coast Press.

Titchener, F.B. 2013. Fate and fortune. In M. Beck (ed.), *A companion to Plutarch.* Oxford: Wiley-Blackwell. 479–87.

Tolias, G. 2007. The resonance of the Periegesis during the 16th and 17th centuries. In M. Georgopoulou, C. Guilmet, Y.A. Pikoulas, K. Sp. Staikos, and G. Tolias (eds.), *Following Pausanias: The quest for Greek antiquity.* New Castle, DE: Oak Knoll Press. 96–104.

Tolias, Y. 1992. 1830–1930: The people and the territory. *Ekató chrónia chartografías tou ellinismoú: 1830–1930.* Athens: Elliniki etaireía chartografías.

Tombros, N.F. 2011. Sto Metepanastatikó Náfplio tou Kapodístria. Argolid archival library, history and culture. Available at: http://argolikivivliothiki.gr/2011/09/16/στο-μετεπαναστατικό-ναύπλιο-του-καπο/.

Tomlinson, R.A. 1972. *Argos and the Argolis: From the end of the Bronze Age to the Roman occupation.* London: Routledge.

Topping, P.W. 2000. The Southern Argolid from Byzantine to Ottoman times. In S. B. Sutton (ed.), *Contingent countryside: Settlement, economy, and land use in the Southern Argolid since 1700.* Stanford, CA: Stanford University Press. 25–40.

Touchais, G., et al. 2010. L'Aspis. *Bulletin de correspondance hellénique* 134(2), 551–66.

Traill, D.A. 2012. Schliemann's Mycenae excavations through the eyes of Stamatakis. In G. Korres, N. Karadimas, and G. Flouda (eds.), *Archaeology and Heinrich Schliemann.* Athens. 79–84.

Tsakos, K., E. Pipera-Marsellou, and D. Tsoukala-Kondidari. 2003. *Corinth Canal: Ancient Corinth, Lechaion, Kenchreai, Isthmia, Loutraki, Heraion: Historical and archaeological guide.* Athens: Hesperos.

Tsikliras, A.C., V.Z. Tsiros, and K.I. Stergiou. 2013. Assessing the state of Greek marine fisheries resources. *Fisheries Management and Ecology* 20, 34–41.

Tsountas, C., and J.I. Manatt. 1897. *The Mycenaean Age: A study of the monuments and culture of pre-Homeric Greece.* London: Macmillan & Co.

Tuan, Y.-F. 1977. *Space and place: The perspective of experience.* London: Arnold.

Turnbull, D. 1994. *Maps are territories: Science is an atlas.* Chicago, IL: University of Chicago Press.

Turnbull, D. 2000. *Masons, tricksters and cartographers: Comparative studies in the sociology of scientific and indigenous knowledge.* Amsterdam: Harwood Academic Publishers.

Tzanatos, E., et al. 2007. Discarding practices in a Mediterranean small-scale fishing fleet (Patraikos Gulf, Greece). *Fisheries Management and Ecology* 14, 277–85.

Valavanidis, A., et al. 2008. Polycyclic aromatic hydrocarbons in surface seawater and in indigenous mussels (*Mytilus galloprovincialis*) from coastal areas of the Saronikos Gulf (Greece). *Estuarine, Coastal and Shelf Science* 79, 733–39.

Vallet, G., and F. Villard. 1964. *Megara Hyblaea 2: La céramique Archaïque*. Paris: Boccard.

Van Andel, T.H., and C. Runnels. 1987. *Beyond the Acropolis: A rural Greek past*. Stanford, CA: Stanford University Press.

Van der Leeuw, S.E. 1998. *The Archaeomedes Project: Understanding the natural and anthropogenic causes of land degradation and desertification in the Mediterranean basin*. Luxembourg: Office for Official Publications of the European Communities.

Van Horn, D. 1976. The archaeological survey: Chipped stone. *Expedition* 19(1), 50–54.

Vasilakopoulos, P., C.D. Maravelias, and G. Tserpes. 2014. The alarming decline of Mediterranean fish stocks. *Current Biology* 24, 1643–48.

Velióti, M., and D. Georgopoulos. 1990. *Koinotita Didýmon Odoiporiko ston topo kai ton chróno*. Self-published document available at: http://villadidimo.brodimas.gr/κοινότητα-διδύμων-οδοιπορικό-στον-τό/.

Venizelos, E. 1998. *Diachronia kai Synergeia. Mia Politiki Politismou*. Athens: Kastaniotis.

Verdelis, N.M. 1958. Die Ausgrabung Des Diolkos Wahrend Der Jahre 1957–1959. *AM* 73, 140–45.

Verdelis, N.M. 1962. Anaskafí tou Díolkou. *Prakt*, 48–50.

Vernant, J.-P. 2006. *Myth and thought among the Greeks*. New York, NY: Zone Books.

Vico, G. 1948[1744]. *The new science* (trans. T.G. Bergin and M.H. Fisch). Ithaca, NY: Cornell University Press.

Virilio, P. 2006. *Speed and politics: An essay on dromology*. Los Angeles, CA: Semiotext(e).

Virilio, P. 2009a. *The aesthetics of disappearance*. Los Angeles, CA: Semiotext(e).

Virilio, P. 2009b. *Grey ecology*. New York, NY: Atropos Press.

Viveiros de Castro, E. 1998. Cosmological deixis and Amerindian perspectivism. *Journal of the Royal Anthropological Institute* (N.S.) 4, 469–88.

Vlahogianni, T., et al. 2007. Integrated use of biomarkers (superoxide dismutase, catalase and lipid peroxidation) in mussels *Mytilus galloprovincialis* for assessing heavy metals' pollution in coastal areas from the Saronikos Gulf of Greece. *Marine Pollution Bulletin* 54, 1361–71.

Vlassopoulos, K. 2007. Beyond and below the polis: Networks, associations, and the writing of Greek history. *Mediterranean Historical Review* 22(1), 11–22.

Vogeikoff-Brogan, N., J.L. Davis, and V. Florou (eds.). 2015. *Carl W. Blegen: Personal and archaeological narratives*. Atlanta, GA: Lockwood Press.

Volk, K. 2010. Lucretius' prayer for peace and the date of "De Rerum Natura". *Classical Quarterly* 60(1), 127–31.

Vollgraff, W. 1907. Fouilles d'Argos. *Bulletin de correspondance hellénique* 31(1), 139–84.

Vollgraff, W. 1908. Praxitèle le jeune. *Bulletin de correspondance hellénique* 32(1), 236–58.

Vollgraff, W. 1951. Le Théatre D'Argos. *Mnemosyne* 4(1), 193–203.

Vollgraff, W. 1956. *Le sanctuaire d'Apollon Pythéen à Argos*. Paris: J. Vrin.

Vorstenbosch, T., et al. 2017. Famine food of vegetal origin consumed in the Netherlands during World War II. *Journal of Ethnobiology and Ethnomedicine*. 13(1), 63.

Voudouri, D. 2010. Law and the politics of the past: Legal protection of cultural heritage in Greece. *International Journal of Cultural Property* 17, 547–68.

Voutsaki, S. 2003. Archaeology and the construction of the past in nineteenth-century Greece. In H. Hokwerda (ed.), *Constructions of Greek past: Identity and historical consciousness from antiquity to the present*. Groningen: Egbert Forsten. 231–55.

Voutsaki, S., A. Ingvarsson-Sundstöm, and M. Richards. 2007. Project on the Middle Helladic Argolid: A report on the 2007 season. *Pharos* XV, 137–52.

Vyzantios, D.K. 1990. *Vavylonia* (A and B versions edited by S.A. Eyaggelatos). Athens: Hermes.

Wace, A.J.B. 1923. Mycenae: Report of the excavations of the British School at Athens, 1921–1923. *Annual of the British School at Athens* 25, 1–434.

Wace, A.J.B. 1949. *Mycenae, an archaeological history and guide*. Princeton, NJ: Princeton University Press.

Wace, A.J.B. 1962. The history of Homeric archaeology. In A.J.B. Wace and F.H. Stubbings (eds.), *A companion to Homer*. London: Macmillan & Co. 325–30.

Wace, A.J.B., and F.H. Stubbings (eds.). 1962. *A companion to Homer*. London: Macmillan & Co.

Wagstaff, J.M. 1992. Colonel Leake in Laconia. In J.M. Sanders (ed.), *PHILOLAKON: Lakonian Studies in Honour of Hector Catling*. Athens: British School at Athens. 277–83.

Wagstaff, J.M. 2001a. Pausanias and the topographers: The case of Colonel Leake. In S.E. Alcock, J.F. Cherry, and J. Elsner (eds.), *Pausanias: Travel and memory in Roman Greece*. Oxford: Oxford University Press. 190–206.

Wagstaff, J.M. 2001b. Colonel Leake: Traveller and scholar. In S. Searight and J.M. Wagstaff (eds.), *Tavellers in the Levant: Voyagers and visionaries*. Durham: Astene. 3–15.

Wagstaff, J.M. 2004a. Surveying the Morea: The French expedition, 1828–1832. In C. Foster (ed.), *Travellers in the Near East*. London: Stacey International. 167–82.

Wagstaff, J.M. 2004b. Leake, William Martin (1777–1860). In *Oxford dictionary of national biography*. Oxford: Oxford University Press.

Walbank, M.E.H. 1989. Pausanias, Octavia and Temple E at Corinth. *Annual of the British School at Athens* 84, 361–94.

Walbank, M.E.H. 2002. What's in a name? Corinth under the Flavians. *Zeitschrift für Papyrologie und Epigraphik* 139, 251–64.

Walker, M.J.C., et al. 2012. Formal subdivision of the Holocene Series/Epoch: A discussion paper by a working group of INTIMATE (Integration of ice-core, marine and terrestrial records) and the Subcommission on Quaternary Stratigraphy (International Commission on Stratigraphy). *Journal of Quaternary Science* 27(7), 649–59.

Wallace, P.W. 1969a. Strabo on Acrocorinth. *Hesperia* 38(4), 495–99.

Wallace, P.W. 1969b. Psyttaleia and the trophies of the Battle of Salamis. *American Journal of Archaeology* 73(3), 293–303.

Wallace, S. 2014. *Ancient Crete: From successful collapse to democracy's alternatives, twelfth to fifth centuries BC*. Cambridge: Cambridge University Press.

Wallis, J. 1769. *The natural history and antiquities of Northumberland*. London: W. and W. Strahan.

Wandsnider, L. 2004a. Solving the puzzle of the archaeological labyrinth. In S.E. Alcock and J.F. Cherry (eds.), *Side-by-side survey: Comparative regional studies in the Mediterranean world*. Oxford: Oxbow Books. 49–62.

Wandsnider, L. 2004b. Artifact, landscape, and temporality in Eastern Mediterranean archaeological landscape studies. In E.F. Athanassopoulos and L. Wandsnider (eds.), *Mediterranean archaeological landscapes: Current issues*. Philadelphia, PA: University of Pennsylvania Museum of Archaeology and Anthropology. 69–79.

Warren, J. 2006. Epicureans and the present past. *Phronesis* 51(4), 362–87.

Washington, H.S. 1894. A petrographical sketch of Aegina and Methana. *Journal of Geology* 2(8), 789–813.

Watteaux, M. 2017. What do the forms of the landscapes tell us? Methodological and epistemological aspects of an archeogeographic approach. In J.-M. Blaising, J. Driessen, J.-P. Legendre, and L. Olivier (eds.), *Clashes of time: The contemporary past as a challenge for archaeology*. Louvain: Presses Universitaries de Louvain. 195–220.

Webb, D. 2006. Michel Serres on Lucretius: Atomism, science, and ethics. *Angelaki* 2(3), 125–36.

Webmoor, T. 2012. STS, symmetry, archaeology. In P. Graves-Brown, R. Harrison, and A. Piccini (eds.), *The Oxford handbook of the archaeology of the contemporary world*. Oxford: Oxford University Press. 105–20.

Weinberg, S.S. 1960. *Corinth I.v: The Southeast Building, the Twin Basilicas, the Mosaic House*. Princeton, NJ: American School of Classical Studies at Athens.

Welcker, F.G. 1865. *Tagebuch einer Griechischen Reise*. Vol. 1. Berlin: Verlag von Wilhelm Herss.

Wells, B. 1976. *Asine II: Results of the excavations east of the Acropolis 1970–1974 – Part I*. Stockholm: Svenska Institutet i Athen.

Wells, B. 1983. *Asine II: Results of the excavations east of the Acropolis 1970–1974. Part II*. Stockholm: Svenska Institutet i Athen.

Welter, G. 1941. *Troizen und Kalaureia*. Verlag Bebr. Mann: Berlin.

West, A.B. 1931. *Corinth VIII.ii: Latin Inscriptions 1896–1926*. Cambridge, MA: Harvard University Press.

Westbroek, P. 1991. *Life as a geological force: Dynamics of the earth*. New York, NY: W.W. Norton & Company.

Wheler, G. 1682. *A journey into Greece*. London: Printed for William Cademan, Robert Kettlewell, and Awnsham Churchill.

Whitehead, A.N. 2006. *The concept of nature: The Tarner Lectures delivered in Trinity College November 1919*. Teddington: Echo Library.

Whitehead, A.N. 2010. *Adventures of ideas*. New York, NY: Free Press.

Whitelaw, T. 1991. The ethnoarchaeology of recent rural settlement and land use in Nortwest Keos. In J.F. Cherry, J.L. Davis, and E. Mantzourani (eds.), *Landscape archaeology as long-term history*. Los Angeles, CA: University of California. 403–54.

Whitley, J. 1988. Early states and hero cults: A re-appraisal. *Journal of Hellenic Studies* 108, 173–82.

Whitley, J. 1995. Tomb cult and hero cult: The uses of the past in Archaic Greece. In N. Spencer (ed.), *Time, tradition and society in Greek archaeology: Bridging the "great divide."* London: Routledge. 43–63.

Willerslev, R. 2007. *Soul hunters: Hunting, animism, and personhood among the Siberian Yukaghirs*. Berkeley, CA: University of California Press.

Willerslev, R. 2011. Frazer strikes back from the armchair: A new search for the animist soul. *Journal of the Royal Anthropological Institute* 17, 504–26.

Williams, C.K. 1978. Corinth 1977, Forum Southwest. *Hesperia* 47(1), 1–39.

Williams, C.K. 1981. The city of Corinth and its domestic religion. *Hesperia* 50(4), 408–21.

Williams, C.K. 1989. A re-evaluation of Temple E and the west end of the Forum of Corinth. In S. Walker and A. Cameron (eds.), *The Greek renaissance in the Roman Empire*. London: University of London, Institute of Classical Studies. 156–62.

Winter, B.W. 2001. *After Paul left Corinth*. Grand Rapids, MI: Eerdmans.

Wiseman, J. 1963. A Trans-Isthmian fortification wall. *Hesperia* 32(3), 248–75.

Wiseman, J. 1978. *The land of the ancient Corinthians*. SIMA50. Göteborg: Åström.

Witmore, C. 2004. On multiple fields: Between the material world and media – Two cases from the Peloponnesus, Greece. *Archaeological Dialogues* 11(2), 133–64.

Witmore, C. 2005. *Multiple field approaches in the Mediterranean: Revisiting the Argolid Exploration Project*. Doctoral dissertation, Stanford University.

Witmore, C. 2006. Vision, media, noise and the percolation of time: Symmetrical approaches to the mediation of the material world. *Journal of Material Culture* 11(3), 267–92.

Witmore, C. 2007a. Symmetrical archaeology: Excerpts of a manifesto. *World Archaeology* 39(4), 546–62.

Witmore, C. 2007b. Landscape, time, topology: An archaeological account of the Southern Argolid, Greece. In D. Hicks, G. Fairclough, and L. McAtackney (eds.), *Envisioning Landscape*. One World Archaeology. Walnut Creek, CA: Left Coast Press. 194–225.

Witmore, C. 2009. Prolegomena to open pasts: On archaeological memory practices. *Archaeologies* 5(3), 511–45.

Witmore, C. 2013a. The world on a flat surface: Maps from the archaeology of Greece and beyond. In S. Bonde and S. Houston (eds.), *Representing the past: Archaeology through text and image*. Oxford: Oxbow Books. 127–52.

Witmore, C. 2013b. Which archaeology? A question of chronopolitics. In A. González-Ruibal (ed.), *Reclaiming archaeology: Beyond the tropes of modernity*. London: Routledge. 130–44.

Witmore, C. 2014a. Archaeology and the new materialisms. *Journal of Contemporary Archaeology* 1(2), 203–24.

Witmore, C. 2014b. (Dis)continuous domains: A case of "multi-sited archaeology" from the Peloponnesus, Greece. In O. Harmansah (ed.), *Drawing on rocks, gathering by the water*. Oxford: Oxbow Books. 213–41.

Witmore, C. 2015a. Archaeology and the second empiricism. In F. Herschend, C. Hillerdal, and J. Siapkas (eds.), *Debating archaeological empiricism*. London: Routledge. 37–61.

Witmore, C. 2015b. No past but within things: A cave and archaeology in the form of a dialogue. In M. Mircan and V.W.J. van Gerven Oei (eds.), *The allegory of the cave painting reader*. New York, NY: Mousse Publishing. 375–94.

Witmore, C. 2017. Things are the grounds of all archaeology. In J.M. Blaising, J. Driessen, J.P. Legendre, and L. Olivier (eds.), *Clashes of times: The contemporary past as a challenge for archaeology*. Louvain: Louvain University Press. 231–46.

Witmore, C. 2018a. The end of the Neolithic? At the emergence of the Anthropocene. In S.E. Pilaar Birch (ed.), *Multispecies archaeology*. London: Routledge. 26–46.

Witmore, C. 2018b. Traces of the past: Classics between history & archaeology, Karen Bassi, 2016. Ann Arbor, MI: University of Michigan Press. *Cambridge Archaeological Journal*. 515–18.

Witmore, C. 2019a. Symmetrical archaeology. In C. Smith (ed.), *The encyclopedia of global archaeology*. New York, NY: Springer.

Witmore, C. 2019b. Hypanthropos: On apprehending and approaching that which is in excess of monstrosity, with special consideration given to the photography of Edward Burtynsky. *Journal of Contemporary Archaeology* 6(1), 136–53.

Witmore, C. 2019c. Chronopolitics and archaeology. In C. Smith (ed.), *The encyclopedia of global archaeology*. New York, NY: Springer.

Witmore, C. 2020. Objecthood. In L. Wilkie and J. Chenoweth (eds.), *A cultural history of objects: Modern period, 1900 to present*. London: Bloomsbury.

Witmore, C., and T.V. Buttrey. 2008. William Martin Leake: A contemporary of P.O. Brøndsted, in Greece and in London. In B.B. Rasmussen, J.S. Jenson, J. Lund, and M. Märcher (eds.), *P.O. Brøndsted (1780–1842) – A Danish Classicist in his European Context*. Copenhagen: Royal Danish Academy. 15–34.

Witmore, C., and M. Shanks. 2013. Archaeology: An ecology of practices. In W.L. Rathje, M. Shanks, and C. Witmore (eds.), *Archaeology in the making: Conversations through a discipline*. Abingdon: Routledge. 380–98.

Wittgenstein, L., and R. Rhees. 1979. *Remarks on Frazer's Golden Bough*. Retford: Brynmill.

Wright, J.C. 1982. The old temple terrace at the Argive Heraeum and the early cult of Hera in the Argolid. *Journal of Hellenic Studies* 102, 186–201.

Wright, J.C. et al. 1990. The Nemea Valley Archaeological Project: A preliminary report. *Hesperia* 59, 579–659.

Wright, J.C., and M.K. Dabney. 2019. *The Mycenaean settlement on Tsoungiza Hill*. Princeton, NJ: American School of Classical Studies at Athens.

Yioutsos, N.-P. 2017. The last occupation of Asine in Argolis. *Opuscula* 10, 164–89.

Zangger, E. 1993. *The geoarchaeology of the Argolid.* Berlin: Mann.

Zarinebaf, F. 2005. Soldiers into tax-farmers and reaya into sharecroppers: The Ottoman Morea in the Early Modern period. In F. Zarinebaf, J. Bennet, and J.L. Davis (eds.), *A historical and economic geography of Ottoman Greece: The southwestern Morea in the 18th century.* Hesperia Supplement 34. Princeton, NJ: American School of Classical Studies at Athens. 9–47.

Zarinebaf, F., J. Bennet, and J.L. Davis. 2005. *A historical and economic geography of Ottoman Greece: The southwestern Morea in the 18th century.* Hesperia Supplement 34. Princeton, NJ: American School of Classical Studies at Athens.

Zenkini, I.E. 1996. *To Árgos dia mésou ton aiónon.* Athens: Ékdosis Tríti.

Zervos, O.H., et al. 2009. An early Ottoman cemetery at ancient Corinth. *Hesperia* 78 (4), 501–615.

Zinn, P. 2016. Lucretius on time and its perception. *Kriterion* 30(2), 125–51.

INDEX